AIA

PAPER 11

FINANCIAL ACCOUNTING 2

STUDY TEXT

In this March 2014 edition

- A **user-friendly format** for easy navigation
- **Exam-centred topic coverage**, directly linked to AIA's syllabus
- **Exam focus points** showing you what the examiner will want you to do
- Regular **fast forward** summaries emphasising the key points in each chapter
- **Questions** and **quick quizzes** to test your understanding
- End of chapter **exam standard questions** with answers
- **Exam question bank** containing further exam standard questions with answers
- **2 Mock exams** for real exam practice using the May 2013 and November 2012 exams
- A full index

FOR EXAMS IN 2014

BPP LEARNING MEDIA

First edition 2007
Seventh edition March 2014

ISBN 9781 4453 7120 7
(previous ISBN 9781 4453 6691 3)

eISBN 9781 4453 7088 0
(previous eISBN 9781 4727 0059 9)

British Library Cataloguing-in-Publication Data
A catalogue record for this book is available from the British
Library

Published by

BPP Learning Media Ltd
BPP House, Aldine Place
142-144 Uxbridge Road
London W12 8AA

www.bpp.com/learningmedia

Printed in the United Kingdom by

Ricoh UK Limited
Unit 2
Wells Place
Merstham
RH1 3LG

Your learning materials, published by BPP Learning
Media Ltd, are printed on paper obtained from traceable
sustainable sources.

We are grateful to the Association of International
Accountants for permission to reproduce past examination
questions. The suggested solutions in the exam answer bank
have been prepared by BPP Learning Media Ltd.

BPP
LEARNING MEDIA

Contents

Introduction

The introduction pages contain lots of valuable advice and information. They include tips on studying for and passing the exam, also the content of the syllabus and what has been examined.

How the BPP Learning Media Study Text can help you pass – Help yourself study for your AIA exams – Syllabus – AIA list of examinable Standards – Command words and learning outcomes – The exam paper

BPP
LEARNING MEDIA

How the BPP Learning Media Study Text can help you pass

> It provides you with the knowledge and understanding, skills and application techniques that you need to be successful in your exams

This Study Text has been targeted at the **Financial Accounting 2** syllabus.

- It is **comprehensive**. It covers the syllabus content. No more, no less.

- It is written at the **right level**. Each chapter is written with AIA's syllabus in mind.

- It is aimed at the **exam**. We have taken account of recent exams, guidance the examiner has given and the assessment methodology.

> It allows you to study in the way that best suits your learning style and the time you have available, by following your personal Study Plan (see page vii)

You may be studying at home on your own or you may be attending a course. You may like to read every word, or you may prefer to do a fast read through and learn through doing practise questions the rest of the time. However you study, you will find the BPP Learning Media Study Text meets your needs in designing and following your personal Study Plan.

BPP Learning Media's ground-breaking **Learning to Learn Accountancy** book is designed to be used both at the outset of your AIA studies and throughout the process of learning accountancy. It challenges you to consider how you study and gives you helpful hints about how to approach the various types of paper which you will encounter. It can help you **focus your studies on the subject and exam**, enabling you to **acquire knowledge, practise and revise efficiently and effectively**.

Help yourself study for your AIA exams

Exams for professional bodies such as AIA are very different from those you have taken at college or university. You will be under **greater time pressure before** the exam – as you may be combining your study with work. Here are some hints and tips.

The right approach

1 **Develop the right attitude**

Believe in yourself	Yes, there is a lot to learn. But thousands have succeeded before and you can too.
Remember why you're doing it	You are studying for a good reason: to advance your career.

2 **Focus on the exam**

Read through the Syllabus	This tells you what you are expected to know and is supplemented by **Exam focus points** in the text.
Study the Exam paper section	Past papers are likely to be good guides to what you should expect in the exam.

3 **The right method**

See the whole picture	Keeping in mind how all the detail you need to know fits into the whole picture will help you understand it better. • The **Introduction** of each chapter puts the material in context. • The **Syllabus content** and **Exam focus points** show you what you need to **grasp**.
Use your own words	To absorb the information (and to practise your written communication skills), you need to **put it into your own words**. • **Take notes**. • Answer the **questions** in each chapter. • Draw **mindmaps**. • Try **'teaching' a subject** to a colleague or friend.
Give yourself cues to jog your memory	The Study Text uses **bold** to **highlight key points**. • Try **colour coding** with a highlighter pen. • Write **key points** on cards.

4 **The right recap**

Review, review, review	Regularly reviewing a topic in summary form can **fix it in your memory**. The Study Text helps you review in many ways. • **Chapter roundups** summarise the 'Fast forward' key points in each chapter. Use them to recap each study session. • The **Quick quiz** actively tests your grasp of the essentials. • Go through the **Examples** in each chapter a second or third time.

Developing your personal Study Plan

BPP Learning Media's **Learning to Learn Accountancy** book emphasises the need to use a study plan. Planning and sticking to the plan are key elements of learning successfully.
There are five steps you should work through.

Step 1   **How do you learn?**

First you need to be aware of your style of learning. BPP Learning Media's **Learning to Learn Accountancy** book commits a chapter to this **self-discovery**. What types of intelligence do you display when learning? You might be advised to brush up on certain study skills before launching into this Study Text.

Our **Learning to Learn Accountancy** book helps you to identify what intelligences you show more strongly and then details how you can tailor your study process to your preferences. It also includes handy hints on how to develop intelligences you exhibit less strongly, but which might be needed as you study accountancy.

Step 2   **What do you prefer to do first?**

If you prefer to get to grips with a theory before seeing how it is applied, we suggest you concentrate first on the explanations we give in each chapter before looking at the examples and case studies. If you prefer to see first how things work in practice, read through the detail in each chapter, and concentrate on the examples and case studies, before supplementing your understanding by reading the detail.

Step 3   **How much time do you have?**

Work out the time you have available per week, given the following.

- The standard you have set yourself
- The other exam(s) you are sitting
- Practical matters such as work, travel, exercise, sleep and social life

                                                                   Hours

Note your time available in box A.   A [   ]

Step 4   **Allocate your time**

- Take the time you have available per week for this Study Text shown in box A, multiply it by the number of weeks available and insert the result in box B.   B [   ]

- Divide the figure in box B by the number of chapters in this text and insert the result in box C.   C [   ]

Remember that this is only a rough guide. Some of the chapters in this book are longer and more complicated than others, and you will find some subjects easier to understand than others.

Step 5   **Implement**

Set about studying each chapter in the time shown in box C, following the key study steps in the order suggested by your particular learning style.

This is your personal **Study Plan**. You should try to combine it with the study sequence outlined below. You may want to modify the sequence to adapt it to your **personal style**.

> BPP Learning Media's **Learning to Learn Accountancy** gives further guidance on developing a study plan, and deciding where and when to study.

Tackling your studies

The best way to approach this Study Text is to tackle the chapters in order. Taking into account your individual learning style, you could follow this sequence for each chapter.

Key study steps	Activity
Step 1 **Topic list**	This topic list helps you navigate each chapter; each numbered topic is a numbered section in the chapter.
Step 2 **Introduction**	This sets your objectives for study by giving you the big picture in terms of the context of the chapter. The content is referenced to the syllabus, and Exam guidance shows how the topic is likely to be examined. The Introduction tells you **why** the topics covered in the chapter need to be studied.
Step 3 **Knowledge brought forward boxes**	These highlight information and techniques that it is assumed you have 'brought forward' with you from your earlier studies. Remember that you may be tested on these areas in the exam. If you are unsure of these areas, you should consider revising your more detailed study material from earlier papers.
Step 4 **Fast forward**	Fast forward boxes give you a quick summary of the content of each of the main chapter sections. They are listed together in the roundup at the end of each chapter to help you review each chapter quickly.
Step 5 **Explanations**	Proceed methodically through each chapter, particularly focusing on areas highlighted as significant in the chapter introduction, or areas that are frequently examined.
Step 6 **Key terms and Exam focus points**	• Key terms can often earn you **easy marks** if you state them clearly and correctly in an exam answer. They are highlighted in the index at the back of this text. • Exam focus points state how the topic has been or may be examined, difficulties that can occur in questions about the topic, and examiner feedback on common weaknesses in answers.
Step 7 **Note taking**	Take brief notes, if you wish. Don't copy out too much. Remember that being able to record something yourself is a sign of being able to understand it. Your notes can be in whatever format you find most helpful; lists, diagrams, mindmaps.
Step 8 **Examples**	Work through the examples very carefully as they illustrate key knowledge and techniques.
Step 9 **Case studies**	Study each one, and try to add flesh to them from your own experience. They are designed to show how the topics you are studying come alive in the real world.
Step 10 **Questions**	Attempt each one, as they will illustrate how well you have understood what you have read.
Step 11 **Answers**	Check yours against ours, and make sure you understand any discrepancies.
Step 12 **Chapter roundup**	Review it carefully, to make sure you have grasped the significance of all the important points in the chapter.
Step 13 **Quick quiz**	Use the Quick quiz to check how much you have remembered of the topics covered and to practise questions in a variety of formats.
Step 14 **Question practice**	Attempt the Question suggested at the very end of the chapter. These are all AIA past exam questions, so provide an excellent indication of the type and standard of question that you can expect in your real exam. Some of these questions cover more than one subject area, which is a common feature of exam questions.

BPP
LEARNING MEDIA

AIA Achieve

AIA provides an interactive course of study AIA Achieve, which offers students the tools, resources and learning environment to study for the exams. The study tools include a course of study e-book, personal study planner, marked practice questions, marked mock exam paper and feedback and technical advice via an e-Tutor. Contact the Study Support team at: study@aiaworldwide.com.

Moving on...

When you are ready to start revising, you should still refer back to this Study Text.

- As a source of **reference** (you should find the index particularly helpful for this)
- As a way to **review** (the Fast forwards, Exam focus points, Chapter roundups and Quick quizzes help you here)

Remember to keep careful hold of this Study Text – you will find it invaluable in your work.

> More advice on Study Skills can be found in BPP Learning Media's **Learning to Learn Accountancy** book. Order online at www.bpp.com/learningmedia

Syllabus

Aims

The objective of the paper is to examine the candidate's understanding of the theoretical framework of accountancy, ability to prepare and interpret accounting statements and to prepare appropriate accounts for specialised transactions.

In addition to addressing more advanced applications of the topics covered in Paper 1 Financial Accounting 1 the syllabus covers the following areas:

Accounting Theory – The regulatory framework and its application; with particular reference to the convergence project and the impact of the IASB and its Framework. Various capital maintenance and income measurements in conditions of changing price levels.

International Accounting Standards.

Proprietorship accounting including; sole traders and partnerships (where appropriate for the demonstration of specialised transactions), limited companies including basic group accounts, covering the preparation of accounts according to statutory requirements, IFRS (where appropriate) and the treatment of taxation in accounts.

Accounting for specialised transactions.

Financial analysis, interpretation and reporting including ratio analysis and statements of cash flows (cash flow statements).

FIG. 11 INTER-RELATIONSHIP OF UNITS

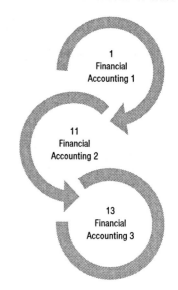

Descriptors

After successfully completing this paper students should be able to:

- Discuss the content and underlying rationale of the IASB Conceptual Framework and of its contribution to a 'regulatory framework'.

- Apply and discuss the appropriateness of specific international accounting standards.

- Prepare financial statements for limited companies and other entities and appropriate financial statements for specialised transactions.

- Interpret financial statements of limited companies and other entities.

- Assess and discuss alternative valuation methods and the problems associated with their application.

Structure of the Paper

A three-hour paper with15 minutes reading time consisting of up to eight compulsory questions.

Candidates must answer all questions.

Allocation of marks to parts of a question will be disclosed.

The questions are of a case study/scenario type which will be mainly computational.

In addition to those areas specified in the syllabus candidates are expected to be familiar with current issues and developments in financial reporting.

Candidates will not be expected to provide in depth answers concerning International Accounting Standards that have been in force for less than 6 months prior to the examination date.

Note: the following International Accounting Standards will not be examined by this paper:

IFRS: 2

IAS: 19, 21, 29

Syllabus

11.1 Accounting Theory

Topic Weighting   20%

- Regulatory framework – discuss the role of international accounting standards in regulating accounting and financial reporting.

- Statutory framework – describe the statutory requirements relating to the preparation, publication and audit of financial statements. Questions on the topic will be based on the UK Companies Act 2006.

- Standard setting bodies – discuss the role of the International Accounting Standards Committee Foundation (IASCF) and other national standard setting bodies.

- Conceptual framework for the preparation and presentation of financial statements – discuss the role and general content of the IASB Conceptual Framework for Financial Reporting and its impact on the convergence project.

- Capital maintenance and income measurement – contrast capital maintenance and income measurement in Historic Cost Accounting (HCA), Constant Purchase Power Accounting (CPP) and Current Cost Accounting (CCA). (Basic calculations may be examined).

- IAS 1 – describe and assess the objective, definitions and requirements of IAS 1 as far as they relate to the presentational impact of accounting policies.

- IAS 8 – discuss the standard's requirements dealing with errors, changes in accounting estimates and changes in policy.

- IAS 18 – describe the standard's requirements in accounting for revenue arising from sale of goods, rendering of services and from interest, royalties and dividends. Demonstrate the standard's implications for the financial statements.

- IAS 24 – discuss the purpose of related party disclosures

- IFRS 1 – discuss the standard's general principles and objectives relating to the first-time adoption of international reporting standards

- IFRS 5 – discuss the purpose and impact of reporting non-current assets held for sale on the financial statements

11.2 International Accounting Standards

Topic Weighting   20%

[This section specifically covers the following Accounting Standards. Note that these and other IFRS may be incorporated into questions in other sections of the syllabus].

- IAS 10 – discuss the accounting and disclosure of events occurring after reporting period.

- IAS 16 – discuss the recognition and measurement of tangible non-current assets; including the impact of borrowing costs under IAS 23. Account for revaluations and depreciation of tangible non-current assets.

- IAS 20 – discuss the general requirements of accounting for government grants.

- IAS 24 – identify 'related parties' and assess the requirements of the standard regarding disclosures of related party transactions.

- IAS 36 – apply and discuss the basic concept of impairment and the procedures involved in undertaking an impairment review.

- IAS 37 – distinguish provisions and contingent liabilities. Discuss the recognition of a provision and the disclosure requirements of the standard relating to provisions, contingent liabilities and contingent assets.

- IAS 38 – describe the initial recognition and measurement of goodwill and intangible assets. Discuss the subsequent treatment of recognised goodwill and intangible assets. Discuss the treatment of internally generated intangible assets at the research and development phase.

- IAS 40 – apply the accounting requirements for investment property and discuss their effect on the measurement of profit or loss.

11.3 Proprietorship Accounting and Entity Accounting

Topic Weighting   20%

- IAS 27, IAS 28, IFRS 3, IFRS 10, IFRS 12 – discuss the purpose, definitions, exemptions, concepts (eg control) and structures of simple groups. Prepare and present financial statements for simple groups including statement of financial position – basic procedures to cover, non controlling interests, dividend flows, goodwill (basic), inter-company trading, associated companies and income statement – inter-company trading and dividends, associated companies.

- Partnerships – accounting for changes in partners. Account for an amalgamation of partnerships and for the conversion of a partnership to a limited liability company.

- IAS 1 – prepare income statements* and statements of financial position (balance sheets) in accordance with the standard. Prepare and evaluate a 'Statement of Changes in Equity' and the movement towards the reporting of all-inclusive comprehensive income.

- Discuss the purpose of disclosures in a director's report and in a Management Commentary (the international equivalent of the UK's operating and financial review). Discuss the general trend towards the reporting of more narrative-style information in corporate reports.

- IAS 12 – apply the basic requirements concerning accounting for current tax and compare and contrast the 'nil provision', 'partial provision' and 'full provision' bases of accounting for deferred tax. Describe the main requirements of IAS 12.

- IAS 34 – discuss the standard's requirements for the content of an interim financial report published by an enterprise.

Note: More complex consolidations and those involving joint ventures, cash flow statements and goodwill (complex ideas eg IFRS3's NCI at fair value) are dealt with in Paper 13 Financial Accounting 3.

11.4 Accounting for Specialised Transactions

Topic Weighting   20%

- Inventories and construction contracts – analyse and apply the IAS 2 and IAS 11 requirements relating to inventories and construction contracts respectively, including disclosure in the income statement* and the statement of financial position (balance sheet).

- Reporting the substance of transactions – Explain the meaning and reasons behind 'Off Balance Sheet Financing' (OBSF) and discuss the application of the 'Substance Over Form' (SOF) concept to prevent such practices. Apply the concept to consignment stock and debt factoring. (Note: This concept can be studied as part of section 11.1)

- IAS 17 – analyse how IAS 17 distinguishes between finance leases and operating leases, and discuss the importance of this distinction to financial reporting. Account for both types of lease in the books of the lessee and in the books of the lessor. Discuss the application of the SOF concept to leases. (Note: Reference to leases also covers simple hire purchase transactions.)

- Financial Instruments – with regard to IFRS 7, distinguish shareholders' funds and liabilities (note: no reference to minority interest is required) and discuss and calculate the allocation of finance on a (simple) discounted bond. (Note: The study of more complex financial instruments is not required).

Note: Discussions should cover the need to design specialised accounting systems to record these transactions.

11.5 Financial Analysis

Topic Weighting   20%

- IAS 7 – prepare statement of cash flows (cash flow statement) for an individual company using the direct and indirect method to disclose operating cash flows. Interpret a statement either one provided or one prepared.

- Financial Analysis – calculate a range of ratios based on historical cost financial statements. Prepare a report interpreting those financial statements, incorporating a discussion on the information revealed by the ratio analysis.

- IAS 33 – prepare calculations of basic and diluted Earnings Per Share (EPS) following the requirements of IAS 33. Calculate the effect of a bonus issue or a rights issue of shares on the reported basic EPS. Calculate the effect of convertible debentures (loans) or convertible preference shares or options on the diluted EPS. (Note: Cumulative changes will not be examined).

- IFRS 8 – analyse and discuss the disclosure requirements of IFRS 8. Prepare a segmental report in line with the standard.

* In an exam the following three titles will be assigned the meanings shown:

- The title 'statement of comprehensive income' (SOCI) will refer to the single statement format by IAS1 as revised in September 2007

- The title 'income statement' will refer to that part of the SOCI which excludes other comprehensive income ie it refers to that part from Revenue (or sales or turnover) down to profit for the year.

- The title 'other comprehensive income' refers to that part of the SOCI which excludes the calculation of profit for the year.

For RPQ (statutory auditor qualification) students (refer to page 5) the relevant UK standards are Financial Reporting Standards (FRS) and Statement of Standard Accounting Practice (SSAP) issued by the FRC. In respect of auditing, the relevant UK standards are all current Auditing Standards (ISAs (UK and Ireland)) issued by the FRC.

Relationship to Overall Syllabus

This paper builds upon the basics of financial accounting and reporting introduced in Financial Accounting 1 and leads the successful student directly on to the final Financial Accounting 3 paper in Professional Level 2 – Module E.

Ethics

Students are advised that the standards outlined in The Code of Ethics for Professional Accountants issued by the International Ethics Standards Board for Accountants (IESBA Code) are implicit in, and examinable throughout, the AIA syllabus. The Code can be accessed via the AIA website at www.aiaworldwide.com

Students following the RPQ (statutory auditor qualification) route will be expected to refer, where appropriate, to the Ethical Standards for Auditors (ESs) published by the FRC. ESs can be accessed via the Financial Reporting Council's website at http://www.frc.org.uk/Our-Work/Codes-Standards.aspx

Essential reading

AIA Journal - International Accountant

ISSN: 1465 – 5144

AIA Text Book

Paper 11   Financial Accounting 2
Publisher: BPP Learning Media
ISBN: 9781 4453 7120 7

The e-Book is available at: recruitment@aiaworldwide.com

You can purchase a hard copy of the text book at: membership@aiaworldwide.com

You can purchase any of the books listed quickly and easily through the publisher's website or link stated below.

Financial Accounting: An International Introduction (5th Edition)
Authors: Alexander D, Nobes C
Publisher: Prentice Hall
ISBN: 9780273773436
Website: http://catalogue.pearsoned.co.uk/educator/product/Financial-Accounting-An-International-Introduction/9780273773436.page

Financial Acccounting and Reporting (with MyAccountinglab) (16th Edition)
Authors: Elliott, B J and Elliott, J
Publisher: Pearson Education Ltd
ISBN: 9780273778172
Website: http://catalogue.pearsoned.co.uk/educator/product/Financial-Accounting-and-Reporting/9780273778172.page

Wiley IFRS Practical Implementation Guide and Workbook (4th edition)
Authors: Mirza, A.A, Orrell, Holt, G.J and Knorr, L
Publisher: John Wiley and Sons Ltd
ISBN: 97811186338590
Website: http://eu.wiley.com/WileyCDA/WileyTitle/productCd-111863859X.html

IFRS in your Pocket 2013 (12th Edition)
Publisher: Deloitte
Website: http://www.iasplus.com/en/publications/global/ifrs-in-your-pocket/ifrs-in-your-pocket-2013

International Financial Reporting Standards IFRS 2013

Authors: The International Accounting Standards Board (IASB)Copies are available from the IFRS Foundation web shop – http://shop.ifrs.org

This RED book is presented in two parts: Part A (the Conceptual Framework and requirements) Part B the accompanying documents.

Free website providing comprehensive information about IFRS:
www.iasplus.com

AIA List of examinable Standards

All extant International Standards on Auditing, International Standards on Quality Control, International Financial Reporting Standards /International Accounting Standards are examinable, subject to the six months rule.

The depth of knowledge of the standards required for the different levels can be defined as:

- Foundation – Students should be aware of the standard and be familiar with the basic concepts involved.

- Professional 1 – Students should be aware of all major requirements of the standard and be able to apply it to straight forward situations. Students should be able to recognise some of the pitfalls and issues associated with the standard.

- Professional 2 – Students must be fully cognisant of the standard and know how to apply it to specialised situations. They must also be fully aware of the important issues, contemporary thinking and criticisms related to the standard.

For RPQ (statutory auditor qualification) students (refer to Exam Scheme & Reading List 2014, page 9) the relevant UK standards are Financial Reporting Standards (FRS) and Statements of Standard Accounting Practice (SSAP) issued by the Accounting Standards Board. In respect of auditing, the relevant UK standards are all current Auditing Standards (ISAs (UK and Ireland)) issued by the Auditing Standards Board.

IASs and IFRSs

In Paper 1 Financial Accounting 1 candidates are required to have studied a limited number of IASs and IFRSs, however in Paper 11 Financial Accounting 2 the bulk of IASs and IFRSs are examinable. There are still some exclusions and these will be covered in Paper 13 Financial Accounting 3. Those studied for in Paper 1 are noted, as are those which are examinable in Papers 5, 7, 11, 13 and 15.

A list of currently examinable IASs and IFRSs is given below.

International Accountings Standards (IASs)		Examinable in Paper						
No	Title	1	3	5	7	11	13	15
1	Presentation of Financial Statements	✓		✓	✓	✓	✓	✓
2	Inventories	✓	✓	✓	✓	✓	✓	✓
7	Statement of Cash Flows	✓		✓	✓	✓	✓	✓
8	Accounting Policies, Changes in Accounting Estimates and Errors					✓	✓	✓
10	Events After the Reporting Period	✓		✓	✓	✓	✓	✓
11	Construction Contracts					✓	✓	✓
12	Income Taxes					✓	✓	✓
16	Property, Plant and Equipment	✓		✓	✓	✓	✓	✓
17	Leases					✓	✓	✓
18	Revenue	✓		✓	✓	✓	✓	✓
19	Employee Benefits						✓	✓
20	Accounting for Government Grants and Disclosure of Government Assistance					✓	✓	✓
21	The Effects of Changes in Foreign Exchange Rates						✓	✓

International Accountings Standards (IASs)		Examinable in Paper						
No	**Title**	**1**	**3**	**5**	**7**	**11**	**13**	**15**
23	Borrowing Costs							✓
24	Related Party Disclosures					✓	✓	✓
27	Separate Financial Statements					✓	✓	✓
28	Investment in Associates and Joint Ventures					✓	✓	✓
29	Financial Reporting in Hyperinflationary Economies						✓	✓
32	Financial Instruments: Presentation						✓	✓
33	Earnings per Share					✓	✓	✓
34	Interim Financial Reporting					✓	✓	✓
36	Impairment of Assets					✓	✓	✓
37	Provisions, Contingent Liabilities and Contingent Assets	✓		✓	✓	✓	✓	✓
38	Intangible Assets	✓		✓	✓	✓	✓	✓
39	Financial Instruments: Recognition and Measurement						✓	✓
40	Investment Property					✓	✓	✓

Note: Free website providing comprehensive information about IFRS: www.iasplus.com

International Financial Reporting Standards (IFRS)		Examinable in Paper			
No	**Title**	**1**	**11**	**13**	**15**
1	First time Adoption of International Financial Reporting Standards		✓	✓	✓
2	Share-based Payment			✓	✓
3	Business Combinations		✓	✓	✓
5	Non-current Assets Held for Sale and Discontinued Operations		✓	✓	✓
7	Financial Instruments: Disclosures		✓	✓	✓
8	Operating Segments		✓	✓	✓
9	Financial Instruments			✓	✓
10	Consolidated Financial Statements		✓	✓	✓
11	Joint Arrangements			✓	✓
12	Disclosure of Interests in Other Entities		✓	✓	✓
13	Fair Value Measurement			✓	✓
IFRS for SMEs	IFRS for Small and Medium-sized Entities			✓	✓

Exposure drafts, discussion papers and IFRIC's are not examinable at Paper 1 and Paper 11. Those still current (ie they have not been superseded by other publications) are examinable in Paper 13 but only an understanding of their basic principles is required.

Command words and learning outcomes

The following list contains active command words and generic learning outcomes appropriate for use at each stage of the AIA qualification. Reference to the learning outcomes and use of the command words is essential to understanding how the assessment is applied in AIA exams.

Foundation Level Command Words

WORD	DEFINITION
ADVISE	To inform as necessary
CALCULATE	Work out a value mathematically
DEFINE	To state and or explain clearly
EXPLAIN	To make clear giving reasons for
EXPRESS	To present thoughts and ideas
DESCRIBE	To give an account of in words or formula including key features
IDENTIFY	Recognise and select
PLAN	Present a method or argument for doing or achieving a task
PREPARE	To make or get ready for use
SELECT	To choose in preference to another
STATE	Express fully and clearly the details/facts
TABULATE	Arrange in a table

BPP LEARNING MEDIA

Professional Level 1 Command Words

WORD	DEFINITION
ADVISE	To inform as necessary
ANALYSE	Examine in detail in order to interpret its meaning or essential features
APPLY	To use information or a technique
CALCULATE	Work out a value mathematically
CATEGORISE	To put into a group things or people with common qualities
COMPARE & CONTRAST	To explain the similarities and differences between things in order to interpret them
DEMONSTRATE	To show or prove by reasoning or evidence
DERIVE	To formulate or decide based on a particular source of information
DEVELOP	To bring to a more advanced stage
DIFFERENTIATE	To show the difference between
DISCUSS	To examine in detail by argument
IMPLEMENT	To carry out
INTERPRET	To explain the meaning of and to work out the significance of
ILLUSTRATE USING THE CASE	To clarify or explain by use of example or comparison
PRIORITISE	Place in order of importance
PRODUCE	To create or bring into existence
RELATE	To have reference or relation to
SOLVE	Find an answer to
VALUE	To assess the worth of something

Professional Level 2 Command Words

WORD	DEFINITION
ADVISE	To inform or notify
APPRAISE	To evaluate and conclude on the basis of arguments for and against, synthesize, argue, develop a view, balance, provide evidence, and identify patterns
ASSESS	Determine the strength, weakness and significance
CRITIQUE/CRITICALLY ANALYSE	Examine in detail using arguments for and against
EVALUATE	Determine the value in light of arguments for and against
EXPLORE	To examine or investigate, in a systematic way
FORMULATE	Plan or describe precisely and clearly
JUSTIFY	Defend an action as being appropriate
RECOMMEND	Advise the appropriate action in terms the recipient will understand
REPORT	Give an account of the results of the investigation

Please note:

1   The word 'Calculate' may be used at all levels of the syllabus

CALCULATE   Select the appropriate method and techniques and apply your knowledge and understanding to work out and show how figures were arrived at.

2   The word 'Advise' may be used at all levels of the syllabus

ADVISE   Notify or inform

3   For the Professional Level 1 exams, examiners may include a command word from the Foundation Level providing it is linked to another command word selected from the Professional 1 list. For example:

"… prepare and discuss a set of accounts…"

4   For the Professional Level 2 exams, examiners may include a command word from the Foundation and Professional Level 1 providing it is linked to another command word from the Professional 2 list. For example:

"…recommend the appropriate action and prepare a memo…"

The exam paper

Analysis of past papers

May 2013

1   IAS 8, IAS 36, Factoring, IFRS 10; ratio analysis
2   CPP accounting
3   IAS 37, IAS 10
4   Partnerships
5   Inventory valuation
6   EPS

November 2012

1   IAS 38, IAS 32, IAS 20, consignment inventory; ratio analysis
2   IAS 1
3   Consolidated statement of financial position
4   IFRS 5, IAS 23
5   IFRS 8
6   IAS 12 (deferred tax)

May 2012

1   Partnership accounts; ratio analysis
2   Changes in accounting policy
3   IAS 37
4   Acquisitions; consolidated statement of financial position
5   Financial instruments
6   Statement of cash flows – preparation and usefulness

November 2011

1   IAS 16, IAS 36, IFRS 5; ratio analysis
2   IAS 18
3   IAS 24
4   Treatment of investments; group statement of financial position
5   Factoring; IAS 2
6   Calculate EPS and P/E ratio; discuss P/E ratio

May 2011

1   Accounting treatment dealing with 'off balance sheet finance', IAS 37, IAS 8, IAS 12; IAS 33
2   Replacement cost income statement; discussion of replacement cost, HCA and CPP
3   IAS 38
4   Consolidated statement of financial position
5   Financial instruments
6   Assess changes in financial position

November 2010

1   Preparation of statement of comprehensive income; *Conceptual Framework*
2   Extraction license; IAS 2
3   IAS11, IAS 37
4   Group statement of income and SOCIE
5   Net cash flow from operating activities; treatment of sale of painting

May 2010

1   Accounting entries dealing with IAS 16, IAS 20, IAS 23, IAS 37, IAS 40, IAS 38
2   Consolidated statement of financial position and income statement
3   Calculation of ratios and comment on results
4   Discussion of 'off balance sheet finance' and *Conceptual Framework*
5   Leases (IAS 17)

November 2009

1   Discussion of IFRS 8, IAS 18, IAS 16
2   Construction contracts
3   IFRS 5, IAS 37
4   IAS 12 *Deferred tax*
5   IAS 40, IAS 16, IAS 2, IAS 11

May 2009

1   Income statement and IAS 18, IAS 37, IAS 16, IAS 38, IFRS 5.
2   Conceptual framework and not-for-profit entities
3   Conversion of partnership to limited company
4   IAS 17 *Leases*
5   Segment reporting

November 2008

1   Statement of cash flows, IAS 16, IAS 36, IAS 38, IAS 37, IAS 12, IAS 17, IAS 32, IAS 10
2   IAS 8 and IAS 11 *Construction contracts*
3   IAS 1 *Presentation of financial statements*
4   IAS 40 *Investment property*
5   Substance over form
6   *Conceptual Framework* and SMEs

May 2008

1   IAS 11, IAS 37, IAS 10 and IFRS 5
2   Accounting regulation, IAS 24 and IAS 34
3   Combined financial statements for a head office and branch (no longer examinable)
4   IAS 33 *Earnings per share*
5   IFRS 5 *Non-current assets held for sale and discontinued operations*

November 2007

1   Profit measurement and capital maintenance concepts
2   IAS 36 *Impairment of assets*
3   IAS 12 *Income taxes*
4   IAS 32 and discounted bonds
5   IAS 7 *Statement of cash flows*
6   Combined financial statements for a head office and branch (no longer examinable)

May 2007

1   IAS 18 *Revenue recognition*
2   IAS 38, IAS 8 and IAS 10
3   IAS 1 *Presentation of financial statements*
4   IAS 11 *Construction contracts*
5   Integration of a manufacturing company's accounts
6   IAS 20 *Accounting for government grants*

November 2006

1   IAS 1 *Presentation of financial statements* and IFRS 5
2   IAS 17 *Leases*
3   IAS 14 *Segment reporting*
4   IAS 16 *Property, plant and equipment*
5   IAS 37 *Provisions, contingent liabilities and contingent assets*
6   IAS 8 *Accounting policies, changes in accounting estimates and errors*

May 2006

1   Preparation of financial statements
2   Basic and diluted earnings per share
3   IAS 16 *Property, plant and equipment*
4   Construction contracts
5   IAS 38 *Intangible assets*
6   IAS 18 *Revenue*

November 2005

1   Statements of cash flows using the indirect method
2   Preparation of income statement and statement of changes in equity
3   Ratio analysis and discussion
4   Financial instruments
5   Function of business within IASCF, IASB, SAC and IFRIC discussion
6   IFRS 5 *Non-current assets held for sale and discontinued operations*

May 2005

1	Ratio analysis and evaluation
2	Partnership accounts
3	IAS 1 *Presentation of financial statements*
4	IAS 37 *Provisions, contingent liabilities and contingent assets*
5	Taxation
6	IAS 24 *Related party disclosures*

November 2004

1	Statement of cash flows and discussion
2	Branch accounts and financial statements (no longer examinable)
3	Recognised gains and losses, discontinued operations
4	Impairment
5	Taxation
6	Partnership accounts

May 2004

1	Earnings per share
2	Ratio analysis
3	Construction contracts and statement of financial position
4	Purchase of own shares
5	Government grants and events after the reporting period
6	Qualitative characteristics of financial statements

Accounting theory

Revision of basic accounts and concepts

Topic list	Syllabus reference
1 Introduction to Paper 11	–
2 The regulatory system of accounting	11.1
3 IAS 1 *Presentation of financial statements*	11.1
4 Revision of basic accounts	11.1

Introduction

Paper 11 *Financial Accounting 2* has a demanding syllabus to cover, but don't let this put you off. As long as you give yourself plenty of time to work through the whole syllabus, you should not find any of the subject areas too complicated.

This chapter acts mainly as revision, so that you are sure of the skills and knowledge you have brought from your earlier studies. If you have any doubts, go back to your earlier study material and revise those aspects which seem unclear.

IAS 1 *Presentation of financial statements* has been revised recently. Only that part of IAS 1 which deals with accounting policies is covered here. The remainder of IAS 1 will be dealt with in Chapter 3.

1 Introduction to Paper 11

> Paper 11 covers a **demanding syllabus**, but if your approach is methodical, and you leave yourself enough time, you will succeed.

1.1 Fundamentals

Paper 11 is obviously a harder paper than Paper 1. Most of that difficulty stems from the **breadth of the syllabus,** which covers the bulk of financial accounting topics. You will find, however, that you are only expected to understand the simpler aspects of complicated areas.

Exam focus point

> Your aim should be to set aside enough time to work through the whole of the BPP Learning Media Study Text for Paper 11 well before the exam.
>
> Go to the introductory pages of this text. Make sure you read the following.
>
> - Syllabus
> - Format of the examination paper

1.2 International Accounting Standards (IASs and IFRSs)

Which IASs and IFRSs are examinable under Paper 11? You studied only a limited number for Paper 1, but in Paper 11 the bulk of IASs and IFRSs are examinable. There are still some exclusions, however, and these will not be covered until you tackle Paper 13 *Financial Accounting 3.*

A list of current IASs and IFRSs is given below. Only those examinable by the AIA are included. Those you have studied for Paper 1 are noted, as are those which are not examinable until you reach Paper 13.

IAS		Examinable in Paper		
No	Title	1	11	13
1	Presentation of financial statements	✓	✓	✓
2	Inventories	✓	✓	✓
7	Statement of cash flows	✓	✓	✓
8	Accounting policies, changes in accounting estimates and errors		✓	✓
10	Events after the reporting period	✓	✓	✓
11	Construction contracts		✓	✓
12	Income taxes		✓	✓
16	Property, plant and equipment	✓	✓	✓
17	Leases		✓	✓
18	Revenue	✓	✓	✓
19	Employee benefits			✓
20	Accounting for government grants and disclosure of government assistance		✓	✓
21	The effects of changes in foreign exchange rates			✓
23	Borrowing costs		✓	✓
24	Related party disclosures		✓	✓
27	Separate financial statements		✓	✓

IAS		Examinable in Paper		
No	Title	1	11	13
28	Investments in associates		✓	✓
29	Financial reporting in hyperinflationary economies			✓
32	Financial instruments: Presentation			✓
33	Earnings per share		✓	✓
34	Interim financial reporting		✓	✓
36	Impairment of assets		✓	✓
37	Provisions, contingent liabilities and contingent assets	✓	✓	✓
38	Intangible assets	✓	✓	✓
39	Financial instruments: recognition and measurement			✓
40	Investment property		✓	✓

IFRS		Examinable in Paper		
No	Title	1	11	13
1	First time adoption of International Financial Reporting Standards		✓	✓
2	Share-based payment			✓
3	Business combinations		✓	✓
5	Non-current assets held for sale and discontinued operations		✓	✓
7	Financial instruments: disclosures		✓	✓
8	Operating segments		✓	✓
9	Financial instruments			✓
10	Consolidated financial statements		✓	✓
11	Joint arrangements			✓
12	Disclosure of interests in other entities		✓	✓
13	Fair value measurement			✓

Exposure drafts, discussion papers and IFRICs are not examinable at Paper 11.

1.3 Keeping up-to-date

In the case of subjects such as financial accounting and auditing you must keep up-to-date. In particular, you should read any further information about the syllabus and examinable standards issued by the AIA.

1.4 Be professional!

Before we go on to some revision topics, which should get you back into the swing of financial accounting, here is an important reminder.

Paper 11 is a Professional level exam.

You must demonstrate a professional approach in the exam. This does not only apply to **what you write**, but **how you write it.** Start cultivating the right approach now!

1.5 Section summary

Your overall approach to Paper 11 should be:

- Spend plenty of time on this paper: it is a big leap from your earlier studies
- Read the introductory pages of this Study Text
- Be professional!

2 The regulatory system of accounting

FAST FORWARD ▶▶ This is just an outline, you will deal with the regulatory system in more detail in Chapter 2.

2.1 Introduction

The purpose of this section is to give a general picture of some of the **factors which have shaped financial accounting**. We will concern ourselves with the accounts of limited liability companies because the limited liability company is the type of organisation whose accounts are most closely regulated by statute or otherwise.

The following **factors** can be identified.

- National/local legislation
- Accounting concepts and individual judgement
- Accounting standards
- Other international influences
- Generally accepted accounting principles (GAAP)
- True and fair view (or fair presentation)

2.2 National/local legislation

Limited liability companies may be **required by law** (eg the UK Companies Act 2006) to prepare and publish accounts annually. The form and content of the accounts may be regulated primarily by national legislation, but must also comply with International Financial Reporting Standards (IFRS).

2.3 Accounting concepts and individual judgement

Financial statements are prepared on the basis of a number of **fundamental accounting assumptions and conventions** as we will see below. Many figures in financial statements are derived from the application of judgement in putting these assumptions into practice.

It is clear that different people exercising their judgement on the same facts can arrive at very **different conclusions**. Suppose, for example, that an accountancy training firm has an excellent reputation amongst students and employers. How would you value this? The firm may have relatively little in the form of assets which you can touch, perhaps a building, desks and chairs. If you simply drew up a statement of financial position showing the cost of the assets owned, then the business would not seem to be worth much, yet its income earning potential might be high. This is true of many service organisations where the people are among the most valuable assets.

Other examples of areas where the judgement of different people may differ are as follows.

- **Valuation of buildings** in times of rising or falling property prices

- **Research and development**: is it right to treat this only as an expense? In a sense it is an investment to generate future revenue

- Accounting for **inflation**

- **Brands** such as 'Mars Bar' or 'iPod'. Are they assets in the same way that a fork lift truck is an asset?

Working from the same data, different groups of people would produce very different financial statements. If the exercise of judgement is completely unfettered, any **comparability** between the accounts of different organisations will disappear. This will be all the more significant in cases where deliberate manipulation occurs in order to present accounts in the most favourable light.

2.4 Accounting standards

In an attempt to deal with some of the subjectivity, and to achieve comparability between different organisations, accounting standards have been developed. These are developed at both a **national level** (in most countries) and an **international level**. In this text we are concerned with International Accounting Standards (IASs) and International Financial Reporting Standards (IFRSs), and a brief summary of the current regime for producing IFRSs is given here. We go into much more depth in Chapter 2.

2.4.1 International Financial Reporting Standards

International Financial Reporting Standards (IFRSs) are produced by the **International Accounting Standards Board (IASB)** The IASB is the standard setting body of the IFRS Foundation (previously known as the International Accounting Standards Committee Foundation (IASCF). The IASB was set up in 1973 (as the International Accounting Standards Committee) to work for the improvement and harmonisation of financial reporting. The IASB develops IFRSs through an international process that involves the world-wide accountancy profession, the preparers and users of financial statements, and national standard setting bodies. Old Standards were called *International Accounting Standards* (IASs). **Throughout this text, any reference to IFRSs includes both IASs and IFRSs.**

2.4.2 Objectives of the IFRS Foundation

The IFRS Foundation oversees two main areas – the standard-setting process and the IFRS Advisory Council (previously known as the Standards Advisory Council). The standard-setting process consists of two bodies, the **IASB** (as discussed above) and the **IFRS Interpretations Committee**. The IASB has the sole responsibility for setting international financial reporting standards.

The formal objectives of the IFRS Foundation are:

(a) To develop a single set of high quality, understandable, enforceable and globally accepted international financial reporting standards (IFRSs) through its standard-setting body, the IASB.

(b) To promote the use and rigorous application of those standards.

(c) To take account of the financial reporting needs of emerging economies and small and medium-sized entities (SMEs); and

(d) To promote and facilitate adoption of IFRS through the convergence of national accounting standards and IFRS.

The IFRS Foundation and the IASB are discussed in detail in Chapter 2.

2.5 Other international influences

There are a few **other international bodies** worth mentioning. You are not required to follow their workings in detail, but knowledge of them will aid your studies and should help your general reading around the subject area.

2.5.1 IASB and the EC/intergovernmental bodies

The European Commission has acknowledged the role of the IASB in harmonising world-wide accounting rules and EC representatives attend IASB Board meetings and have joined Steering Committees involved in setting IFRSs. This should bring to an end the idea of a separate layer of European reporting rules.

The EC has also set up a committee to investigate where there are conflicts between EU norms and International Standards so that compatibility can be achieved. In turn, the IASB has used EC Directives in its work.

All listed entities in member states must use IFRSs in their consolidated financial statements.

The IASB also works closely with the United Nations Working Groups of Experts on International Standards of Accounting and Reporting (UN IASR group), and with the Working Group in Accounting Standards of the Organisation for Economic Co-operation and Development (OECD Working group). These bodies support harmonisation and improvement of financial reporting, but they are not standard-setting bodies and much of their output draws on the work of the IASB (eg using the IASB's *Conceptual Framework* document).

2.5.2 United Nations (UN)

The UN has a Commission and Centre on Transnational Reporting Corporations through which it gathers information concerning the activities and reporting of multinational companies. The UN processes are highly **political** and probably reflect the attitudes of the governments of developing countries to multinationals. For example, there is an inter-governmental working group of 'experts' on international standards of accounting and reporting which is dominated by the non-developed countries.

2.5.3 International Federation of Accountants (IFAC)

The IFAC is a private sector body established in 1977 and which now consists of over 100 professional accounting bodies from around 80 different countries. The IFAC's main objective is to co-ordinate the accounting profession on a global scale by issuing and establishing international standards on auditing, management accounting, ethics, education and training. You are already familiar with the **International Standards on Auditing** produced by the IAASB, an IFAC body. The IFAC has separate committees working on these topics and also organises the World Congress of Accountants, which is held every five years. The IASB is affiliated with IFAC.

2.5.4 Organisation for Economic Co-operation and Development (OECD)

The OECD was established in 1960 by the governments of 21 countries to 'achieve the highest sustainable economic growth and employment and a rising standard of living in member countries while maintaining financial stability and, thus, to contribute to the world economy'. It now has 33 member countries.

The OECD's aim is to bring together the governments of countries committed to democracy and the market economy from around the world to:

- Support sustainable economic growth
- Boost employment
- Raise living standards
- Maintain financial stability
- Assist other countries' economic development
- Contribute to growth in world trade

The OECD supports the work of the IASB but also undertakes its **own research** into accounting standards via *ad hoc* working groups. For example, in 1976 the OECD issued guidelines for multinational companies on financial reporting and non-financial disclosures. The OECD also produces its own corporate governance principles and other publications aimed at improving financial reporting, regulation and removing corruption.

The OECD appears to work on behalf of developed countries to protect them from the extreme proposals of the UN.

2.5.5 Co-ordination with national standard-setters

Close co-ordination between the IASB's due process in setting and updating accounting standards and the due process of national standard-setters is important to the success of the IASB's mandate. The IASB is exploring ways through which it can integrate its due process more closely with national due process. This is discussed in more detail in Chapter 2.

2.6 Generally Accepted Accounting Practice (GAAP)

We also need to consider some important terms which you will meet in your financial accounting studies. GAAP, as a term, has sprung up in recent years and signifies **all the rules, from whatever source, which govern accounting**. The rules may derive from:

(a)   Local (national) company legislation
(b)   National and International Accounting Standards
(c)   Statutory requirements in other countries (particularly the US)
(d)   Stock exchange requirements

GAAP will be considered in more detail in Chapter 2.

2.7 True and fair view (or fair presentation)

It is a requirement of national legislation (in some countries) that the financial statements should give a true and fair view of (or 'present fairly, in all material respects') the financial position of the entity as at the end of the financial year.

The terms 'true and fair view' and 'present fairly, in all material respects' are not defined in accounting or auditing standards. Despite this, a company's managers may depart from any of the provisions of accounting standards if these are inconsistent with the requirement to give a true and fair view. This is commonly referred to as the 'true and fair override'. It has been treated as an important **loophole** in the law in different countries and has been the cause of much argument and dissatisfaction within the accounting profession.

3 IAS 1 *Presentation of financial statements*

FAST FORWARD ▶▶

IAS 1 has been revised recently.

Here we will look at the general requirements of IAS 1 and what it says about **accounting policies**. The rest of the Standard, on the format and content of financial statements, current assets and liabilities and so on, will be covered in Chapter 3.

3.1 Objectives and scope

The main objective of IAS 1 is:

> 'to prescribe the basis for presentation of general purpose financial statements, to ensure comparability both with the entity's financial statements of previous periods and with the financial statements of other entities'.

IAS 1 applies to all **general purpose financial statements** prepared in accordance with IFRSs, ie those intended to meet the needs of users who are not in a position to demand reports tailored to their specific needs.

3.2 Purpose of financial statements

The **objective of financial statements** is to provide information about the financial position, performance and cash flows of an entity that is useful to a wide range of users in making economic decisions. They also show the result of **management stewardship** of the resources of the entity.

In order to fulfil this objective, financial statements must provide information about the following aspects of an entity's results.

- Assets
- Liabilities
- Equity
- Income and expenses (including gains and losses)
- Contributions by and distributions to owners in their capacity as owners
- Cash flows

Along with other information in the notes and related documents, this information will assist users in predicting the entity's **future cash flows**.

3.3 Responsibility for financial statements

Responsibility for the preparation and presentation of an entity's financial statements rests with the **board of directors** (or equivalent).

3.4 Components of financial statements

A complete set of financial statements includes the following components.

- Statement of financial position
- Statement of profit or loss and other comprehensive income
- Statement of changes in equity
- Statement of cash flows
- Accounting policies and explanatory notes
- Comparative information

Some of these terms may not seem familiar from your previous studies. An amendment to IAS 1 was published in June 2011. This amendment changed the name of the full statement from 'statement of comprehensive income' to 'statement of profit or loss and other comprehensive income'. The statement down to 'Profit (loss) for the year', which had previously been referred to as the 'income statement', then became the 'statement of profit or loss'. These terminology and conceptual changes will be covered in more detail in Chapter 3.

Exam focus point

> We have used the revised terminology in this text although the examiner may use the term 'income statement' instead of 'statement of profit or loss' and 'statement of comprehensive income' instead of 'statement of profit or loss and other comprehensive income'.

In addition to the financial statements, IAS 1 recognises that many entities wish to present, outside the financial statements, a **financial review** by management (which is *not* part of the financial statements), explaining the main features of the entity's performance and position, and the principal uncertainties it faces. The report may include a review of the following.

(a) **Factors/influences determining performance**: changes in the environment in which the entity operates, the entity's response to those changes and their effect, and the entity's policy for investment to maintain and enhance performance, including its dividend policy

(b) Entity's **sources of funding**, the policy on **gearing** and its **risk management policies**

(c) **Strengths and resources** of the entity whose value is not reflected in the statement of financial position under IFRSs

IFRSs are only concerned with the financial statements, so IAS 1 has no mandatory rules concerning such a review.

3.5 Fair presentation and compliance with IFRS

Most importantly, financial statements should **present fairly** the financial position, financial performance and cash flows of an entity. **Compliance with IFRS** is presumed to result in financial statements that achieve a fair presentation.

The following points made by IAS 1 expand on this principle.

(a)   **Compliance with IFRS** should be disclosed

(b)   **All relevant IFRS** must be followed if compliance with IFRS is disclosed

(c)   Use of an **inappropriate accounting treatment** cannot be rectified either by disclosure of accounting policies or notes/explanatory material

There may be (very rare) circumstances when management decides that compliance with a requirement of an IFRS would be misleading. **Departure from the IFRS** is therefore required to achieve a fair presentation. The following should be disclosed in such an event.

(a)   Management confirmation that the financial statements fairly present the entity's financial position, performance and cash flows

(b)   Statement that all IFRS have been complied with *except* departure from one IFRS to achieve a fair presentation

(c)   Details of the nature of the departure, why the IFRS treatment would be misleading, and the treatment adopted

(d)   Financial impact of the departure

3.5.1 Extreme case disclosures

In very rare circumstances, management may conclude that compliance with a requirement in a Standard or interpretation may be so **misleading** that it would **conflict with the objective** of Financial Statements set out in the *Conceptual Framework*, but the relevant regulatory framework prohibits departure from the requirements. In such cases the entity needs to reduce the perceived misleading aspects of compliance by **disclosing**:

(a)   The title of the Standard, the nature of the requirement and the reason why management has reached its conclusion

(b)   For each period, the adjustment to each item in the Financial Statements that would be necessary to achieve fair presentation

IAS 1 states what is required for a fair presentation.

(a)   Selection and application of **accounting policies**

(b)   **Presentation of information** in a manner which provides relevant, reliable, comparable and understandable information

(c)   **Additional disclosures** where required

The IAS then goes on to consider certain important assumptions which underpin the preparation and presentation of financial statements, which we might call **fundamental assumptions.**

3.6 Going concern

Key term

> The entity is normally viewed as a **going concern**, that is, as continuing in operation for the foreseeable future. Financial statements are prepared on a going concern basis unless management intends to liquidate the entity or to cease trading.

This assumption is based on the notion that, when preparing a normal set of accounts, it is always expected that the business will **continue to operate** in approximately the same manner for the foreseeable future (at least the next 12 months should be considered). In particular, the entity will not go into liquidation or scale down its operations in a material way.

The main significance of the going concern assumption is that the assets of the business **should not be valued at their 'break-up' value**, which is the amount that they would sell for if they were sold off piecemeal and the business were thus broken up.

If the going concern assumption is not followed, that fact must be disclosed, together with:

- The **basis** on which the financial statements have been prepared
- The **reasons** why the entity is not considered to be a going concern

3.7 Accrual basis of accounting

Key term

> **Accrual basis of accounting.** Items are recognised as assets, liabilities, equity, income and expenses when they satisfy the definition and recognition criteria for those elements in the *Conceptual Framework*.
>
> *(IAS 1)*

Entities should prepare their financial statements on the basis that transactions are recorded in them, not as the cash is paid or received, but as the revenues or expenses are **earned or incurred** in the accounting period to which they relate.

According to the accrual assumption, then, in computing profit revenue earned must be **matched against** the expenditure incurred in earning it.

3.8 Consistency of presentation

To maintain consistency, the presentation and classification of items in the financial statements should **stay the same from one period to the next. There are two exceptions**.

(a)   There is a significant change in the **nature of the operations** or a review of the financial statements presentation indicates a **more appropriate presentation**.

(b)   A change in presentation is **required by an IFRS**.

3.9 Materiality and aggregation

All material items should be presented separately in the financial statements.

Amounts which are **immaterial** can be aggregated with amounts of a similar nature or function and need not be presented separately.

Key term

> **Materiality.** Omissions or misstatement of items are material if they could, individually or collectively, influence the economic decisions that users make on the basis of the financial statements. Materiality depends on the size and nature of the omission or misstatement judged in the surrounding circumstances. The size or nature of the item, or a combination of both, could be the determining factor.   *(IAS 1)*

An error which is too trivial to affect anyone's understanding of the financial statements is referred to as **immaterial**. In preparing accounts it is important to assess what is material and what is not, so that time and money are not wasted in the pursuit of excessive detail.

Determining whether or not an item is material is a very **subjective exercise**. There is no absolute measure of materiality. It is common to apply a convenient rule of thumb (for example, to define material items as those with a value greater than 5% of the net profit disclosed by the accounts). But some items disclosed in accounts are regarded as particularly sensitive and even a very small misstatement of such an item would be regarded as a material error. An example in the accounts of a limited liability company might be the amount of remuneration paid to directors of the company.

The assessment of an item as material or immaterial may **affect its treatment in the accounts**. For example, the statement of profit or loss and other comprehensive income of a business will show the expenses incurred by the business grouped under suitable captions (heating and lighting expenses, rent and property taxes etc); but in the case of very small expenses it may be appropriate to lump them together under a caption such as 'sundry expenses', because a more detailed breakdown would be inappropriate for such immaterial amounts.

In assessing whether or not an item is material, it is not only the amount of the item which needs to be considered. The **context** is also important.

(a) If a statement of financial position shows non-current assets of $2 million and inventories of $30,000, an error of $20,000 in the depreciation calculations might not be regarded as material, whereas an error of $20,000 in the inventory valuation probably would be. In other words, the total of which the erroneous item forms a part must be considered.

(b) If a business has a bank loan of $50,000 and a $55,000 balance on bank deposit account, it might well be regarded as a material misstatement if these two amounts were displayed on the statement of financial position as 'cash at bank $5,000'. In other words, incorrect presentation may amount to material misstatement even if there is no monetary error.

Users are assumed to have a reasonable knowledge of business and economic activities and accounting and a willingness to study the information with reasonable diligence.

3.10 Offsetting

IAS 1 does not allow **assets and liabilities to be offset** against each other unless such a treatment is required or permitted by another IFRS.

Income and expenses can be offset only when:

(a) An IFRS requires/permits it; *or*

(b) Gains, losses and related expenses arising from the same/similar transactions are not material (aggregate).

3.11 Comparative information

IAS 1 requires comparative information to be disclosed for the previous period for all **numerical information**, unless another IFRS permits/requires otherwise. Comparatives should also be given in narrative information where helpful.

Comparatives should be **reclassified** when the presentation or classification of items in the financial statements is amended (see IAS 8: Chapter 5).

3.12 Disclosure of accounting policies

There should be a specific section for accounting policies in the notes to the financial statements and the following should be disclosed there.

(a)   **Measurement bases** used in preparing the financial statements

(b)   Each **specific accounting policy** necessary for a proper understanding of the financial statements

To be clear and understandable it is essential that financial statements should disclose the accounting policies used in their preparation. This is because **policies may vary**, not only from entity to entity, but also from country to country. As an aid to users, all the major accounting policies used should be disclosed in the same place.

There is a wide range of policies available in many accounting areas. Examples where such differing policies exist are as follows, although the list is not exhaustive and it contains some items which you will only meet later on in this text.

- **General**

    - Overall valuation policy (eg historical cost, general purchasing power, replacement value)
    - Events subsequent to the reporting date
    - Leases, hire purchase or instalment transactions and related interest
    - Taxes
    - Construction contracts
    - Franchises

- **Assets**

    - Receivables
    - Inventories and related cost of goods sold
    - Depreciable assets and depreciation
    - Land held for development and related development costs
    - Investments: subsidiary and associate companies and other investments
    - Research and development
    - Patents and trademarks
    - Goodwill

- **Liabilities and provisions**

    - Warranties
    - Commitments and contingencies
    - Severance and redundancy payments

- **Profits and losses**

    - Methods of revenue recognition
    - Maintenance, repairs and improvements
    - Gains and losses on disposals of property
    - Reserve accounting, statutory or otherwise

Try the following questions as revision of IAS 1.

| Question | Quality |

Compare the following two statements of profit or loss prepared for a sole trader who wishes to show them to the bank manager to justify continuation of an overdraft facility. Assume that there is no other comprehensive income.

YEAR ENDED 31 DECEMBER 20X7

	$	$
Sales revenue		25,150
Less: production costs	10,000	
selling and administration	7,000	
		17,000
Gross profit		8,150
Less: interest charges		1,000
Profit after interest		7,150

YEAR ENDED 31 DECEMBER 20X8

	$
Sales revenue less selling costs	22,165
Less: production costs	10,990
Gross profit	11,175
Less: administration and interest	3,175
Net profit	8,000

Which accounting concept is being ignored here? Justify your choice.

How do you think the changes in the format of these financial statements affect the quality of the accounting information presented?

Answer

The accounting assumption breached here is that of **consistency**. This concept holds that accounting information should be presented in a way that facilitates comparisons from period to period.

In the statement of profit or loss for 20X7 sales revenue is shown separately from selling costs. Also interest and administration charges are treated separately.

The new format is poor in itself, as we cannot know whether any future change in 'sales revenue less selling costs' is due to an increase in sales revenue or a decline in selling costs. A similar criticism can be levelled at the lumping together of administration costs and interest charges. It is impossible to divide the two.

It is not possible to 'rewrite' 20X7's accounts in terms of 20X8, because we do not know the breakdown in 20X7 between selling and administration costs.

The business's bank manager will not, therefore, be able to assess the business's performance, and might wonder if the sole trader has 'something to hide'. Thus the value of this accounting information is severely affected.

Question
Valuation

You are in business in a small town, whose main source of economic prosperity is the tourist trade. On 25 March 20X8 the town celebrated the 1,000th anniversary of its existence. The town held a number of festivals to mark this occasion and to bring in more tourists.

Your business has had the good fortune to be involved in the event. You have made 1,000 commemorative mugs. These were all made by 31 December 20X7 to be ready at the beginning of the year. They cost 40 cents each to make and during the anniversary year they were for sale at 75 cents each. At the end of the anniversary year, there are 200 still unsold. You estimate that you are unlikely to sell any more at 75 cents, but you might be able to sell them at 30 cents each.

Required

Which fundamental accounting assumption and other matters will you consider when assessing a value for the mugs in your statements of financial position:

(a)   At the end of 20X7?
(b)   At the end of 20X8?

On the basis of your considerations, note down the value of the mugs you would include in the statement of financial position at 31 December 20X7 and 31 December 20X8.

Answer

The accounting assumption mainly involved is **accruals**.

The accruals assumption states that income and expenditure should be matched in the same period if reasonably possible. It is also generally accepted that revenue should not be anticipated. However, you are reasonably certain of selling the mugs, so you would value them in the statement of financial position at the beginning of the year at *cost*, as an *asset* (rather than treating them as an expense in the statement of profit or loss for that earlier year).

At 31 December 20X8 you have 200 spare, whose selling price is less than the cost of making them. Generally accepted accounting practice (IAS 2) is that inventories are valued in the statement of financial position at the lower of these two amounts (ie sales value if it is lower than cost).

You could argue that valuing them at a lower amount means a conflict with the accruals assumption, because the loss is accounted for before the sale. This is true. However, the loss is certain to occur, and this should be reflected in the accounts.

As a consequence, at 31 December 20X7, the mugs would be valued at 40 cents each. At 31 December 20X8, the remaining mugs would be valued at 30 cents each.

Question   Materiality

You work for a multinational company and you are preparing two accounting documents.

(a)   A statement for a customer, listing invoices and receipts, and detailing the amounts owed

(b)   A report sent to the senior management of a division, who want a brief comparative summary of how well the firm is doing in Thailand and in Malaysia

How would considerations of **materiality** influence your preparation of each document?

Answer

Materiality as a 'fundamental concept' does have strict limitations. It refers primarily to financial *reporting*, but has no bearing at all on detailed procedural matters such as bank reconciliations or statements of account sent to customers.

Consequently, the statement sent to the customer, described in option (a), must be accurate to the last cent, however large it is. After all, if you receive a bill from a company for $147.50, you do not 'round it up' to $150 when you pay. Nor will the company billing you be prepared to 'round it down' to $145. A customer pays an agreed price for an agreed product or service. Paying more is effectively giving money away, and if you are going to do that, there might be worthier beneficiaries of your generosity. Paying less exposes your supplier to an unfair loss.

On the other hand, if you are preparing a performance report comparing how well the company is doing in Thailand and Malaysia, entirely different considerations apply.

There is little point in being accurate to the last cent (and inconsistencies might occur from the choice of currency rate used). This is because senior management are interested in the broad picture, and they are looking to identify comparisons between the overall performance of each division.

Assume that Thailand profits were $1,233,750.57 and profits in Malaysia were $1,373,370.75.

Malaysia	Thailand
$	$
1,373,370.75	1,233,750.57
or	or
$'000	$'000
1,373	1,234

The rounded figures are much easier to understand, and so the relative performance is easier to compare. Considerations of materiality would allow you to ignore the rounding differences, because they are so small and the information is used for comparative purposes only.

3.13 Section summary

Accounting policies are extremely important.

- Accounting policies must be appropriate and applied consistently

- Financial statements complying with IFRSs will normally present fairly the results of the entity

- Important concepts are: going concern, accruals, consistency, materiality, prudence and substance over form

- All accounting policies should be fully disclosed

4 Revision of basic accounts

In the next part of this text we move on to the mechanics of preparing financial statements. It would be useful at this point to refresh your memory of the basic accounting you have already studied and these questions will help you. Make sure that you understand everything before you go on.

Question   Basics

A friend has bought some shares in a company quoted on a local stock exchange and has received the latest accounts. There is one page he is having difficulty in understanding.

Briefly, but clearly, answer his questions.

(a)   What is a statement of financial position?
(b)   What is an asset?
(c)   What is a liability?
(d)   What is share capital?
(e)   What are reserves?
(f)   Why does the statement of financial position balance?
(g)   To what extent does the statement of financial position value my investment?

Answer

(a)   A **statement of financial position** is a statement of the assets, liabilities and capital of a business as at a stated date. It is laid out to show either total assets as equivalent to total liabilities and capital or net assets as equivalent to capital. Other formats are also possible but the top half (or left hand) total will always equal the bottom half (or right hand) total. Some statements of financial position are laid out vertically and others horizontally.

(b)   An **asset** is a resource controlled by a business and is expected to be of some future benefit. Its value is determined as the historical cost of producing or obtaining it (unless an attempt is being made to reflect rising prices in the accounts, in which case a replacement cost might be used). Examples of assets are:

(i)   Plant, machinery, land and other **non-current assets**

(ii)   **Current** assets such as inventories, cash and debts owed to the business with reasonable assurance of recovery: these are assets which are not intended to be held on a continuing basis in the business

(c)   A **liability** is an amount owed by a business, other than the amount owed to its proprietors (capital). Examples of liabilities are:

(i)   Amounts owed to the government (sales or other taxes)
(ii)   Amounts owed to suppliers
(iii)   Bank overdraft
(iv)   Long-term loans from banks or investors

It is usual to differentiate between 'current' and 'long-term' liabilities. The former fall due within a year of the reporting date.

(d)   **Share capital** is the permanent investment in a business by its owners. In the case of a limited company, this takes the form of *shares* for which investors subscribe on formation of the company. Each share has a **nominal** or **par** (ie face) **value** (say $1). In the statement of financial position, total issued share capital is shown at its par value.

(e)   If a company issues shares for more than their par value (at a **premium**) then (usually) by law this premium must be recorded separately from the par value in a 'share premium account'. This is an example of a reserve. It belongs to the shareholders but cannot be distributed to them, because it is a **capital reserve**. Other capital reserves include the revaluation reserve, which shows the surpluses arising on revaluation of assets which are still owned by the company.

Share capital and capital reserves are not distributable except on the winding up of the company, as a guarantee to the company's creditors that the company has enough assets to meet its debts. This is necessary because shareholders in limited liability companies have 'limited liability'; once they have paid the company for their shares they have no further liability to it if it becomes insolvent. The proprietors of other businesses are, by contrast, personally liable for business debts.

Revenue reserves constitute accumulated profits (less losses) made by the company and can be distributed to shareholders as **dividends**. They too belong to the shareholders, and so are a claim on the resources of the company.

(f)   Statements of financial position do not always balance on the first attempt, as all accountants know! However, once errors are corrected, all statements of financial position balance. This is because in **double entry bookkeeping** every transaction recorded has a dual effect. Assets are always equal to liabilities plus capital and so capital is always equal to assets less liabilities. This makes sense as the owners of the business are entitled to the net assets of the business as representing their capital plus accumulated surpluses (or less accumulated deficit).

(g)   The statement of financial position is not intended as a statement of a business's worth at a given point in time. This is because, except where some attempt is made to adjust for the effects of rising prices, assets and liabilities are recorded at **historical cost** and on a prudent basis. For example, if there is any doubt about the recoverability of a debt, then the value in the accounts must be reduced to the likely recoverable amount. In addition, where non-current assets have a finite useful life, their cost is gradually written off to reflect the use being made of them.

Sometimes non-current assets are **revalued** to their market value but this revaluation then goes out of date as few assets are revalued every year.

The statement of financial position figure for capital and reserves therefore bears **no relationship** to the market value of shares. Market values are the product of a large number of factors, including general economic conditions, alternative investment returns (eg interest rates), likely future profits and dividends and, not least, market sentiment.

Question

Company financial statements

The accountant of Fiddles Co, a limited liability company, has begun preparing final accounts but the work is not yet complete. At this stage the items included in the list of account balances are as follows.

	$'000
Land	100
Buildings	120
Plant and machinery	170
Depreciation provision	120
Ordinary shares of $1	100
Reserve balance brought forward	200
Trade accounts receivable	200
Trade accounts payable	110
Inventory	190
Operating profit	80
Loan stock (16%)	180
Allowance for receivables	3
Bank balance (asset)	12
Suspense	1

Notes (i) to (vii) below are to be taken into account.

(i)   The accounts receivable control account figure, which is used in the list of account balances, does not agree with the total of the sales ledger. A contra of $5,000 has been entered correctly in the individual ledger accounts but has been entered on the wrong side of both control accounts.

(ii)   A batch total of sales of $12,345 had been entered in the double entry system as $13,345, although the individual ledger accounts entries for these sales were correct. The balance of $4,000 on the sales returns account has inadvertently been omitted from the trial balance though correctly entered in the ledger records.

(iii) A standing order of receipt from a regular customer for $2,000, and bank charges of $1,000, have been completely omitted from the records.

(iv)   A receivable for $1,000 is to be written off. The allowance for receivables balance is to be adjusted to 1% of receivables.

(v)   The opening inventory figure had been overstated by $1,000 and the closing inventory figure had been understated by $2,000.

(vi)   Any remaining balance on the suspense account should be treated as purchases if a debit balance and as sales if a credit balance.

(vii)   The loan stock was issued three months before the year end. No entries have been made as regards interest.

Required

(a)   Prepare journal entries to cover items in notes (i) to (v) above. You are not to open any new accounts and may use only those accounts included in the list of account balances as given.

(b)   Prepare final accounts for internal use within the limits of the available information. For presentation purposes all the items arising from notes (i) to (vii) above should be regarded as material.

Answer

(a)   JOURNAL ENTRIES FOR ADJUSTMENTS

		Debit $	Credit $
(i)	Trade accounts payable	10,000	
	Trade accounts receivable		10,000
	Operating profit	1,000	
	Trade accounts receivable		1,000
	Operating profit	4,000	
	Suspense		4,000
(ii)	Bank	2,000	
	Trade accounts receivable		2,000
	Operating profit	1,000	
	Bank		1,000
(iii)	Operating profit	1,000	
	Trade accounts receivable		1,000
	Allowance for receivables (W1)	1,140	
	Operating profit		1,140
(iv)	Inventories	2,000	
	Operating profit		2,000
	Reserves brought forward	1,000	
	Operating profit		1,000
(v)	Suspense	3,000	
	Operating profit		3,000

(b)   FIDDLES CO
STATEMENT OF FINANCIAL POSITION

	$	$	$
Assets			
Non-current assets			
Land and buildings		220,000	
Plant and machinery		170,000	
Depreciation		(120,000)	
			270,000
Current assets			
Inventories (190 + 2)		192,000	
Accounts receivable (W1)	186,000		
Less allowance	(1,860)		
		184,140	
Bank (12 + 2 – 1)		13,000	
			389,140
Total assets			659,140

	$	$	$
Equity and liabilities			
Equity			
Share capital		100,000	
Revenue reserves		271,940	
			371,940
Non-current liabilities			
Loan stock			180,000
Current liabilities			
Accounts payable (110 – 10)		100,000	
Loan stock interest payable		7,200	
			107,200
Total equity and liabilities			659,140

FIDDLES CO
STATEMENT OF PROFIT OR LOSS AND OTHER COMPREHENSIVE INCOME

	$
Operating profit (W2)	80,140
Debenture interest ($180,000 × 16% × 3/12)	(7,200)
	72,940
Revenue reserves brought forward ($200,000 – 1,000)	199,000
Revenue reserves carried forward	271,940

No other comprehensive income arose in the period.

Workings

1	*Accounts receivable*	$
	Per opening trial balance	200,000
	Contra	(10,000)
	Miscasting	(1,000)
	Standing order	(2,000)
	Written off	(1,000)
		186,000
	Allowance b/f	3,000
	Allowance required	1,860
	Journal	1,140

2	*Operating profit*	$
	Per question	80,000
	Wrong batch total	(1,000)
	Returns	(4,000)
	Bank charges	(1,000)
	Irrecoverable debt	(1,000)
	Allowance for receivables	1,140
	Inventory (2,000 + 1,000)	3,000
	Suspense (sales)	3,000
		80,140

Chapter roundup

- Paper 11 covers a **demanding syllabus**, but if your approach is methodical and you leave yourself enough time you will succeed.
- This is just an outline, you will deal with the regulatory system in more detail in Chapter 2.
- **IAS 1 has been revised recently (2011).**

Quick quiz

1   Where can you find guidance from the examiner on Paper 11?

2   Which IFRSs are examinable under Paper 11?

3   What are the objectives of the IFRS Foundation?

Answers to quick quiz

1   Syllabus

    Further guidance from the AIA

2   Look back to Section 1.2

3   See Paragraph 2.4.2

End of chapter question

Revision of accounting concepts

Explain the following accounting concepts.

(a)   The business entity concept
(b)   The money measurement concept
(c)   The historical cost convention
(d)   The stable monetary unit
(e)   Objectivity
(f)   The realisation concept
(g)   The duality concept

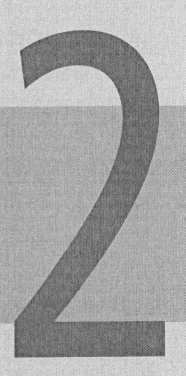

The regulatory framework

Topic list	Syllabus reference
1 The IFRS Foundation and the International Accounting Standards Board (IASB)	11.1
2 International Financial Reporting Standards	11.1
3 Criticisms of the IASB	11.1
4 Statutory framework	11.1
5 Conceptual framework and GAAP	11.1

Introduction

We have already discussed the IFRS Foundation, the IASB and IFRSs to some extent. Here we are concerned with the IASB's relationship with other bodies, and with the way the IASB operates and how IFRSs are produced.

Later in this text we look at some of the theory behind what appears in the accounts. The most important document in this area is the IASB's *Conceptual Framework for Financial Reporting*.

1 The IFRS Foundation and the International Accounting Standards Board (IASB)

FAST FORWARD

> You should be able to describe the **organisation of the IFRS Foundation and the IASB**.

1.1 Introduction

The **IFRS Foundation** is an independent, not-for-profit private sector organisation working in the public interest. It was founded in March 2001 as a not-for-profit corporation called the IASC Foundation. It is incorporated in the United States and is the parent entity of the IASB. In March 2010 it was renamed as the IFRS Foundation in order to reflect more clearly what the Foundation does, being the publication and promotion of IFRS.

The governance and oversight of the IFRS Foundation and its standard-setting bodies rests with the Trustees. The Trustees are appointed for a renewable term of three years and must have an understanding of the issues relevant to the setting and development of IFRSs, but are not involved in a technical capacity. Six of the Trustees must be selected from the Asia/Oceania region, six from Europe, six from North America, one from Africa, one from South America and two from the rest of the world. The Trustees are publicly accountable to a Monitoring Board of public authorities.

The **International Accounting Standards Board** is an independent, privately-funded accounting standard setter based in London. It is a part of the International regulatory framework, reporting to the IFRS Foundation.

From April 2001 the IASB assumed accounting standard setting responsibilities from its predecessor body, the International Accounting Standards Committee (IASC).

The IASB has an important role to play in the regulation of financial information, as it is responsible for issuing accounting standards, which are then adopted for use in many different jurisdictions. Since 2001, almost 120 countries have required or permitted the use of IFRSs in preparing financial information, which makes the IASB the most important accounting body worldwide. The remaining major economies have timelines in place to converge with or adopt IFRSs in the near future.

1.2 How the IASB is made up

The IASB is an independent group of experts with a mix of recent practical experience of standard-setting, or of the user, accounting, academic or preparer communities. Members of the IASB are appointed by the Trustees of the IFRS Foundation

At the time of writing, the 16 full-time members of the IASB come from many different countries and have a diverse range of backgrounds. In order to ensure a broad international basis there will normally be four members from the Asia/Oceania region; four members from Europe; four members from North America; one member from Africa; one member from South America; and two members appointed from any area, subject to maintaining overall geographical balance.

The IASB is publicly accountable to a Monitoring Board of public capital market authorities. The IASB aims to be collaborative in its development of standards by engaging with the worldwide standard setting community, as well as investors, regulators, business leaders and the global accountancy profession.

1.3 Objectives of the IFRS Foundation

The formal objectives of the IFRS Foundation are:

(a)   To develop a single set of high quality, understandable, enforceable and globally accepted international financial reporting standards (IFRSs) through its standard-setting body, the IASB.

(b)   To promote the use and rigorous application of those standards.

(c)   To take account of the financial reporting needs of emerging economies and small and medium-sized entities (SMEs); and

(c)   To promote and facilitate adoption of IFRSs being the standards and interpretations issued by IASB through convergence of national accounting standards and IFRSs.

1.4 Structure of the IFRS Foundation

The structure of the IFRS Foundation has the following main features:

(a)   The IFRS Foundation oversees two main areas – the standard-setting process and the IFRS Advisory Council (previously known as the Standards Advisory Council).

(b)   The standard-setting process consists of two bodies, the **IASB** (as discussed above) and the **IFRS Interpretations Committee**. The IASB has the sole responsibility for setting international financial reporting standards.

(c)   The **IFRS Interpretations Committee** (previously known as the International Financial Reporting Interpretations Committee (IFRIC)) comprises 14 voting members drawn from a variety of countries and professional backgrounds. The IFRS Interpretations Committee provides timely guidance on the application and interpretation of IFRSs. It deals with newly identified financial reporting issues not specifically addressed in IFRSs, or issues where unsatisfactory or conflicting interpretations have developed, or seem likely to develop.

(d)   The **IFRS Advisory Council** (previously the Standards Advisory Council) is the formal advisory body to the IASB and Trustees of the IFRS Foundation. It is comprised of a wide range of representatives from user groups, preparers, financial analysts, academics, auditors, regulators, professional accounting bodies and investor groups that are affected by and interested in the IASB's work. Members of the Advisory Council are appointed by the Trustees. It meets three times a year to advise the IASB on a range of issues including the IASB's agenda and work programme.

The structure of the IFRS Foundation can be illustrated as follows:

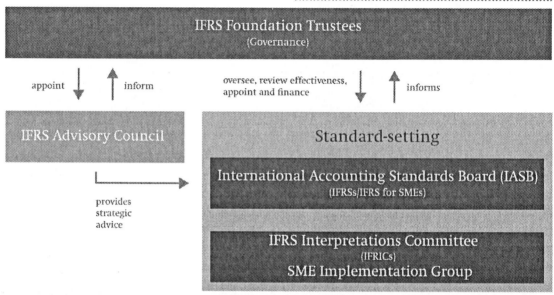

 Question   **Harmonisation**

In accounting terms what do you think are:

(a)   The advantages to international harmonisation?

(b)   The barriers to international harmonisation?

Answer

(a)   **Advantages of international harmonisation**

The advantages of harmonisation will be based on the benefits to users and preparers of accounts, as follows.

(i)   Investors, both individual and corporate, would like to be able to compare the financial results of different companies internationally as well as nationally in making investment decisions.

(ii)   Multinational companies would benefit from harmonisation for many reasons including the following.

(1)   Better access would be gained to foreign investor funds.

(2)   Management control would be improved, because harmonisation would aid internal communication of financial information.

(3)   Appraisal of foreign entities for take-overs and mergers would be more straightforward.

(4)   It would be easier to comply with the reporting requirements of overseas stock exchanges.

(5)   Preparation of group accounts would be easier.

(6)   A reduction in audit costs might be achieved.

(7)   Transfer of accounting staff across national borders would be easier.

(iii)   Governments of developing countries would save time and money if they could adopt International Standards and, if these were used internally, governments of developing countries could attempt to control the activities of foreign multinational companies in their own country. These companies could not 'hide' behind foreign accounting practices which are difficult to understand.

(iv)   Tax authorities. It will be easier to calculate the tax liability of investors, including multinationals who receive income from overseas sources.

(v)   Regional economic groups usually promote trade within a specific geographical region. This would be aided by common accounting practices within the region.

(vi)   Large international accounting firms would benefit as accounting and auditing would be much easier if similar accounting practices existed throughout the world.

(b)   Barriers to harmonisation

(i)   Different purposes of financial reporting. In some countries the purpose is solely for tax assessment, while in others it is for investor decision-making.

(ii)   Different legal systems. These prevent the development of certain accounting practices and restrict the options available.

(iii)   Different user groups. Countries have different ideas about who the relevant user groups are and their respective importance. In the USA investor and creditor groups are given prominence, while in Europe employees enjoy a higher profile.

(iv)   Needs of developing countries. Developing countries are not as advanced in the standard setting process and they need to develop the basic standards and principles already in place in most developed countries.

(v)   Nationalism is demonstrated in an unwillingness to accept another country's standard.

(vi)   Cultural differences result in objectives for accounting systems differing from country to country.

(vii)   Unique circumstances. Some countries may be experiencing unusual circumstances which affect all aspects of everyday life and impinge on the ability of companies to produce proper reports, for example hyperinflation, civil war, currency restriction and so on.

(viii) The lack of strong accountancy bodies. Many countries do not have strong independent accountancy or business bodies which would press for better Standards and greater harmonisation.

1.5 The IASB and current Accounting Standards

The IASB's predecessor body, the IASC, issued 41 International Accounting Standards (IASs). On 1 April 2001 the IASB adopted all of these Standards; it now issues its own International Financial Reporting Standards (IFRSs). So far thirteen new IFRSs have been issued.

1.6 The IASB and IOSCO

The International Organisation of Securities Commissions (IOSCO) is the representative of the world's securities markets regulators. High quality information is vital for the operation of an efficient capital market, and differences in the quality of the accounting policies and their enforcement between countries leads to inefficiencies between markets. IOSCO has been active in encouraging and promoting the improvement and quality of IFRSs over the last ten years. Most recently, this commitment was evidenced by the agreement between IASC and IOSCO to work on a programme of 'core standards' which could be used by publicly listed entities when offering securities in foreign jurisdictions.

The 'core standards' project resulted in 15 new or revised IASs and was completed in 1999 with the issue of IAS 39 *Financial instruments: recognition and measurement.* IOSCO spent a year reviewing the results of the project and released a report in May 2000 which recommended to all its members that they allow multinational issuers to use IASs, as supplemented by reconciliation, disclosure and interpretation where necessary to address outstanding substantive issues at a national or regional level.

IASB staff and IOSCO continue to work together to resolve outstanding issues and to identify areas where new IASB Standards are needed.

1.7 European Commission and IFRSs

The European Commission (EC) has acknowledged the role of the IASB in harmonising world-wide accounting rules and EC representatives attend IASB Board meetings and have joined Steering Committees involved in setting IFRSs.

The EC has also set up a committee to investigate where there are conflicts between European Union norms and International Standards so that compatibility can be achieved. In turn, the IASB has used EC Directives in its work.

From 2005, all listed entities in member states have been required to use IFRSs in their consolidated financial statements.

2 International Financial Reporting Standards

FAST FORWARD

You must understand the **due process** involved in producing IFRSs.

IFRSs are developed through a formal system of due process and broad international consultation involving accountants, financial analysts and other users and regulatory bodies from around the world.

2.1 Setting International Financial Reporting Standards

The due process in developing an accounting standard has six stages as follows:

Step 1 **Setting the agenda.** The IASB evaluates the merits of adding a potential item to its agenda mainly by reference to the needs of investors.

The IASB considers:

- The relevance to users of the information and the reliability of information that could be provided

- Whether existing guidance is available

- The possibility of increasing convergence

- The quality of the standard to be developed

- Resource constraints.

The IFRS Advisory Council and the IFRS Interpretations Committee, other standard-setters and other interested parties may have made comments on accounting issues that could become potential agenda items.

Step 2   **Planning the project.** When adding an item to its work agenda, the IASB considers whether to conduct the project alone or jointly with another standard setter. A working group is usually formed at this stage and the project plan is developed.

Step 3   **Developing and publishing the discussion paper.** It is not mandatory for the IASB to issue a discussion paper in the development of a standard, but it is usual practice where there is a major new topic being developed and the IASB wish to set out their position and invite comments at an early stage in the process. Typically, a discussion paper includes:

- A comprehensive overview of the issue;
- Possible approaches in addressing the issue;
- The preliminary views of its authors or the IASB; and
- An invitation to comment.

Step 4   **Developing and publishing the exposure draft.** This is a mandatory step in the due process. Regardless of whether a discussion paper has been published, the exposure draft is the IASB's main means of consulting the public on the proposed standard. The exposure draft sets out the proposed standard in detail. The development of the exposure draft begins with the IASB considering the following:

- Issues on the basis of staff research and recommendations;

- Comments received on the discussion paper (if one was published)

- Suggestions made by the IFRS Advisory Council, working groups, other standard-setters and public meetings where the proposed standard was discussed.

Once the exposure draft has been published the IASB again invites comments.

Step 5   **Developing and publishing the standard.** Development of a standard occurs at IASB meetings, when the IASB considers comments received on the exposure draft. The IASB must then consider whether a second exposure draft should be published. In doing so, the IASB should:

- Identify substantial issues that emerged during the comment period on the exposure draft that it had not previously considered

- Assess the evidence that has been considered

- Evaluate whether it has sufficiently understood the issues and obtained the views of constituents

- Consider whether the various viewpoints were aired in the exposure draft and adequately discussed and reviewed in the basis for conclusions.

If the IASB decide that the issue should be re-exposed, then the same process should be followed for the second exposure draft as for the first. Once the IASB is satisfied that the issues raised have been dealt with, the IFRS is drafted.

Step 6   **After the standard is issued.** After an IFRS is issued the IASB hold regular meetings with interested parties, including other standard-setting bodies, to help understand unanticipated issues related to the practical implementation and potential impact of its proposals. If there are concerns about the quality of the standard from the IFRS Advisory Council, the IFRS Interpretations Committee, standard-setters and constituents, then the issue may be added to the IASB agenda and the process reverts back to Step 1.

The standard setting process can be illustrated in the diagram below:

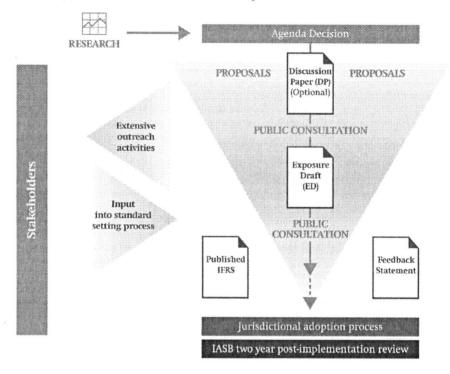

2.2 Co-ordination with national standard-setters

Close co-ordination between IASB due process and the due process of national standard-setters is important to the success of the IASB's mandate.

The IASB is exploring ways in which to integrate its due process more closely with national due process. Such integration may grow as the relationship between IASB and national standard-setters evolves. In particular, the IASB is exploring the following procedure for projects that have international implications.

(a)   IASB and national standard-setters would co-ordinate their work plans so that when the IASB starts a project, national standard-setters would also add it to their own work plans so that they can play a full part in developing international consensus. Similarly, where national standard-setters start projects, the IASB would consider whether it needs to develop a new standard or review its existing standards. Over a reasonable period, the IASB and national standard-setters should aim to review all standards where significant differences currently exist, giving priority to the areas where the differences are greatest.

(b)   National standard-setters would not be required to vote for IASB's preferred solution in their national standards, since each country remains free to adopt IASB standards with amendments or to adopt other standards. However, the existence of an international consensus is clearly one factor that members of national standard-setters would consider when they decide how to vote on national standards.

(c)   The IASB would continue to publish its own Exposure Drafts and other documents for public comment.

(d)   National standard setters would publish their own exposure document at approximately the same time as IASB Exposure Drafts and would seek specific comments on any significant divergences between the two exposure documents. In some instances, national standard-setters may include in their exposure documents specific comments on issues of particular relevance to their country or include more detailed guidance than is included in the corresponding IASB document.

(e)   National standard-setters would follow their own full due process, which they would ideally choose to integrate with the IASB's due process. This integration would avoid unnecessary delays in completing standards and would also minimise the likelihood of unnecessary differences between the standards that result.

2.3 Current IFRSs

The current list is as follows. Compare it with the list in Chapter 1 to see which are examinable.

International Accounting Standards		Date of issue
IAS 1 (revised)	Presentation of financial statements	Jun 2011
IAS 2 (revised)	Inventories	Dec 2003
IAS 7 (revised)	Statement of cash flows	Dec 1992
IAS 8 (revised)	Accounting policies, changes in accounting estimates and errors	Dec 2003
IAS 10 (revised)	Events after the reporting period	Dec 2003
IAS 11 (revised)	Construction contracts	Dec 1993
IAS 12 (revised)	Income taxes	Nov 2000
IAS 16 (revised)	Property, plant and equipment	Dec 2003
IAS 17 (revised)	Leases	Dec 2003
IAS 18 (revised)	Revenue	Dec 1993
IAS 19 (revised)	Employee benefits	Nov 2013
IAS 20	Accounting for government grants and disclosure of government assistance	Jan 1995
IAS 21 (revised)	The effects of changes in foreign exchange rates	Dec 2003
IAS 23 (revised)	Borrowing costs	Mar 2007
IAS 24 (revised)	Related party disclosures	Nov 2009
IAS 26	Accounting and reporting by retirement benefit plans	Jan 1995
IAS 27 (revised)	Separate financial statements	May 2011
IAS 28 (revised)	Investments in associates and joint ventures	May 2011
IAS 29	Financial reporting in hyperinflationary economies	Jan 1995
IAS 32 (revised)	Financial instruments: presentation	Dec 2003
IAS 33 (revised)	Earnings per share	Dec 2003
IAS 34	Interim financial reporting	Feb 1998
IAS 36 (revised)	Impairment of assets	May 2013
IAS 37	Provisions, contingent liabilities and contingent assets	Sept 1998
IAS 38 (revised)	Intangible assets	Mar 2004
IAS 39 (revised)	Financial instruments: recognition and measurement	Dec 2004

International Accounting Standards		Date of issue
IAS 40	Investment property	Dec 2003
IAS 41	Agriculture	Dec 2003
IFRS 1 (revised)	First time adoption of International Financial Reporting Standards	Nov 2008
IFRS 2	Share-based payment	Feb 2004
IFRS 3 (revised)	Business combinations	Jan 2008
IFRS 4	Insurance contracts	Mar 2004
IFRS 5	Non-current assets held for sale and discontinued operations	Mar 2004
IFRS 6	Exploration for and evaluation of mineral resources	Dec 2004
IFRS 7	Financial instruments: disclosures	Aug 2005
IFRS 8	Operating segments	Nov 2006
IFRS 9	Financial instruments	Oct 2010
IFRS 10 (revised)	Consolidated financial statements	Jun 2012
IFRS 11 (revised)	Joint arrangements	Jun 2012
IFRS 12 (revised)	Disclosure of interests in other entities	Jun 2012
IFRS 13	Fair value measurement	May 2011
IFRS 14	Regulatory deferral accounts	Jan 2014
IFRS for SMEs	International Financial Reporting Standard for Small and Medium sized Entities	July 2009

Various exposure drafts and discussion papers are currently at different stages within the IFRS process, but these are not of concern to you at this stage. By the end of your financial accounting studies, however, you will know *all* the Standards, Exposure Drafts and Discussion Papers!

2.4 Benchmark and allowed alternative treatment

Many of the old IASs permitted two accounting treatments for like transactions or events. One treatment is designated as the **benchmark treatment** (effectively the **preferred treatment**) and the other is known as the **alternative treatment**. However, as the Standards are revised, many alternatives are being eliminated.

2.5 Interpretation of IFRSs

The IFRS Interpretations Committee has the responsibility for issuing additional guidance on the application of an accounting standard where unsatisfactory or conflicting interpretations exist. The documents issued are called Interpretations, or IFRICs, and there are currently 17 in issue together with 8 SICs, which were issued by the IFRS Interpretations Committee's predecessor, the Standing Interpretations Committee.

The IFRS Interpretations Committee may also suggest IASB agenda items if there are financial reporting issues that are not specifically covered by an IFRS.

2.6 Scope and application of IFRSs

2.6.1 Scope

Any limitation of the applicability of a specific IFRS is made clear within that Standard. IFRSs are **not intended to be applied to immaterial items, nor are they retrospective**. Each individual IFRS lays out its scope at the beginning of the Standard.

2.6.2 Application

Within each individual country **local regulations** govern, to a greater or lesser degree, the issue of financial statements. These local regulations include accounting standards issued by the national regulatory bodies and/or professional accountancy bodies in the country concerned.

2.7 The importance of IFRSs

Whilst the predecessor organisation of the IFRS Foundation was in existence since the 1970s, the development of International standards has grown in importance only in the last ten years. As business and commerce became more global in nature, many interested parties began to understand the need for a common set of accounting standards. Until that point, many multinational companies prepared financial statements under a variety of GAAPs, which was costly. This also had an impact on the auditors of those financial statements and current and future investors. Companies with stock exchange listings in more than one jurisdiction had to prepare different sets of financial statements for each jurisdiction, which was inefficient.

The starting point for the rapid change of the last few years was the acceptance of international accounting standards for cross border listings by the International Organisation of Securities Commissions (IOSCO). International standards gained more prominence when the European Union decided that from 2005, the group financial statements of companies in its member states would be prepared under IFRS. Since then, many countries have adopted IFRS as their national standards or have a programme in place to adopt standards in the near future.

The USA had initially been reluctant to accept accounts prepared under IFRS, but in 2008, the Securities and Exchange Commission (SEC) proposed its IFRS roadmap proposal for the potential use of IFRS for US entities. This harmonisation project is ongoing (see below). However, some chief financial officers (CFOs) in America are pushing for the IFRS project to be scrapped due to concerns over the cost of new accounting systems and added confusion during the current financial downturn.

A full list of countries adopting IFRS and their progress can be found at http://www.ifrs.org/use-around-the-world/Pages/use-around _the-world.aspx

2.8 Benefits of IFRS for national jurisdictions

Using global accounting standards provide a number of potential benefits:

- Investors are able to compare the financial statements of one entity in one country with those of another entity located in a different country as they are prepared on the same basis

- Financial reporting in multinational entities should become simpler as the financial statements can be prepared using the same standards. This also benefits the auditors of that financial information.

- Many developing nations who do not have the resources to develop and implement their own national standards can adopt IFRS as a full set of standards. This is perhaps more relevant since the issue of the IFRS for Small and Medium-sized entities as previously the level of detail in standards and the amount of disclosure required was a barrier to adoption of IFRS in developing countries.

Many national standard setting bodies are experiencing a change in role as IFRSs have become more important. Many standard setters no longer develop and issue their own accounting standards and instead comment on the work of the IASB the impact of new IFRSs and changing in existing IFRSs on their home jurisdiction.

2.9 IASB and FASB convergence project

IFRS have gained widespread acceptance in Europe and in most other developed countries. However, until recently, the US was one of the few countries in which IFRS financial statements were not accepted. The US Securities and Exchange Commission (SEC) required overseas entities listed on the New York Stock Exchange to present US GAAP information in addition to IFRS financial statements. In practice this meant that entities had to prepare a reconciliation between their IFRS financial statements and their results and financial position as they would be reported under US GAAP.

In September 2002 the US Financial Accounting Standards Board (FASB) and the IASB entered into the 'Norwalk Agreement'. The IASB and the FASB agreed to undertake a short term project to remove a number of differences between IFRS and US GAAP. They also agreed to work together in the longer term to remove other differences between IFRS and US GAAP and to carry out a number of joint projects to develop new accounting standards.

In February 2006 the two boards issued a Memorandum of Understanding: 'A Roadmap for convergence between IFRSs and US GAAP 2006 – 2008'. This set out a joint work programme for the period with the aim of converging the two sets of standards and of removing the need for foreign companies listed in the US to reconcile their IFRS financial statements to US GAAP.

The IASB and the FASB have been working together on a new conceptual framework which is being carried out in phases that will eventually replace the IASB's Framework for the Preparation and Presentation of Financial Statements and its US GAAP equivalent. Whilst some progress has been made the project is yet to be completed and is currently on hold. This is discussed in more detail later in the chapter.

As a result of progress made towards convergence, in November 2007 the SEC announced that it would accept financial statements prepared in accordance with IFRS. At the same time, the FASB recommended that US companies should be allowed to use IFRS, and in November 2008 the SEC issued its IFRS Roadmap in which it was proposed that US listed companies prepare IFRS financial statements on a mandatory basis from 2014. However, this suggestion has proved controversial, as many preparers and users of financial statements still strongly support US GAAP

In June 2010 the convergence strategy documented in the Memorandum of Understanding was modified. The modified work plan retained a target completion date of June 2011 or earlier for the MoU projects for which 'the need for improvement of both IFRSs and U.S. GAAP is the most urgent', however it deferred less important work until after this date.

The Commission formally met again to discuss IFRS in 2010 and issued a statement expressing its strong commitment to the development of a single set of high-quality globally accepted accounting standards. It further clarified that upon completion of the MoU modified workplan by June 2011, the Commission would be in a position to determine whether to incorporate IFRS into the US financial reporting system. A decision regarding the use of IFRS for domestic companies is still pending at the time of writing, but recently the SEC has seemed to move away from allowing IFRSs – see http://blogs.wsj.com/cfo/2014/02/04/secs-new-strategic-plan-backs-away-from-ifrs/ for example.

Exam focus point

> While it will be more important to keep up-to-date with current developments for Paper 13, you will impress the Paper 11 examiner if you show familiarity with some of the above topics.

3 Criticisms of the IASB

You need to be able to understand the problems that can arise.

We will begin by looking at some of the general problems created by **accounting standards**.

3.1 Accounting standards and choice

It is sometimes argued that companies should be given a choice in matters of financial reporting on the grounds that accounting standards are detrimental to the quality of such reporting. There are arguments on both sides.

In favour of accounting standards (both national and international), the following points can be made.

(a)   They **reduce or eliminate confusing variations** in the methods used to prepare accounts.

(b)   They provide a **focal point for debate** and discussions about accounting practice.

(c)   They oblige companies to **disclose the accounting policies** used in the preparation of accounts.

(d)   They are a less rigid alternative to enforcing conformity by means of **legislation**.

(e)   They have obliged companies to **disclose more accounting information** than they would otherwise have done if accounting standards did not exist, for example IAS 33 *Earnings per share*.

Many companies are reluctant to disclose information which is not required by national legislation. However, the following arguments may be put forward **against standardisation** and **in favour of choice**.

(a)   A set of rules which give backing to one method of preparing accounts might be **inappropriate in some circumstances**. For example, IAS 16 on depreciation is inappropriate for investment properties (properties not occupied by the entity but held solely for investment), which are covered by IAS 40 on investment property.

(b)   Standards may be subject to **lobbying or government pressure** (in the case of national standards). For example, in the USA, the Accounting Standard FAS 19 on the accounts of oil and gas companies led to lobbying by powerful oil companies, which persuaded the SEC (Securities and Exchange Commission) to step in. FAS 19 was then suspended.

(c)   Many national standards are not based on a **conceptual framework of accounting**, although IFRSs are (see Chapter 6).

(d)   There may be a **trend towards rigidity**, and away from flexibility in applying the rules.

3.2 Political problems

Any international body, whatever its purpose or activity, faces enormous political difficulties in attempting to gain **international consensus** and the IASB is no exception to this. How can the IASB reconcile the financial reporting situation between economies as diverse as third-world developing countries and sophisticated first-world industrial powers?

Developing countries are suspicious of the IASB, believing it to be dominated by the **USA.** This arises because acceptance by the USA listing authority, the Securities and Exchange Commission (SEC), of IFRSs has been seen as a major hurdle to be overcome. For all practical purposes it is the American market which must be persuaded to accept IFRSs. Developing countries are being catered for to some extent by the issue of a Standard on **agriculture**, which is generally of much more relevance to such countries.

There are also tensions between the **UK/US model** of financial reporting and the **European model**. The UK/US model is based around investor reporting, whereas the European model is mainly concerned with tax rules, so shareholder reporting has a much lower priority.

The break-up of the former USSR and the move in many **Eastern European countries** to free-market economies has also created difficulties. It is likely that these countries will have to 'catch up' to International Standards as their economies stabilise. Progress is being made however with IFRS required for listed companies in Russia from 2012.

You must keep up to date with the IASB's progress and the problems it encounters in the financial press. You should also be able to discuss:

- **Due process** of the IASB
- **Use and application** of IFRSs
- **Future work** of the IASB
- **Criticisms** of the IASB

4 Statutory framework

FAST FORWARD ⟩⟩

The statutory framework refers to the laws surrounding the preparation, presentation and audit of financial information. Regulation is found in company law and stock exchange listing rules.

4.1 Unincorporated businesses

In the UK, unincorporated businesses can usually prepare their financial statements in any form they choose (subject to the constraints of specific legislation, such as the Financial Services Act 1986 for investment businesses, for example).

4.2 Companies

All UK companies must comply with the provisions of the Companies Act 2006 in preparing their financial statements as well as with the requirements of accounting standards.

The regulatory framework over company accounts is based on several sources.

(a) Company law.
(b) Accounting or financial reporting standards and other related pronouncements.
(c) International accounting standards (and the influence of other national standard setting bodies).
(d) The requirements of the Stock Exchange.

4.3 Companies Act 2006

The Companies Act 2006 received the Royal Assent in November 2006 and came into force gradually between 2007 and 2009. The CA 2006 has various key impacts on financial reporting requirements.

4.3.1 Preparation of financial statements

Every UK registered company is required to prepare a set of financial statements each financial year. It is the directors' responsibility to ensure that those financial statements give a true and fair view (fair presentation) of the financial position and performance of the company or group.

The Companies Act allows financial statements to be prepared under UK GAAP or IFRS depending on the type of company:

- For publicly traded companies, IFRS must be used in preparing the group financial statements,

- Unlisted companies may choose whether to prepare their group accounts under UK GAAP or IFRS.

- Individual subsidiaries may choose whether to prepare their group accounts under UK GAAP or IFRS.

- Small and medium sized companies do not need to follow IFRS; they should prepare their financial statements according to the form and content laid out in the CA 2006.

However, in November 2012 the Financial Reporting Council (FRC) issued a new standard, FRS 100 *Application of Financial Reporting Requirements*. This sets out the future of UK GAAP.

From January 2015, UK companies will be required to follow one of four sets of accounting requirements, depending on factors such as their size and whether they are listed:

- Full IFRS

- IFRS together with FRS 101. FRS 101 makes minor amendments to IFRS in order to achieve compliance with the UK Companies Act and reduces IFRS disclosures significantly.

- FRS 102, a new single UK standard based on the *IFRS for Small and Medium-sized Entities*, which will replace existing UK accounting standards.

- FRSSE – the financial reporting standard for small and medium sized entities.

4.3.2 Publication of financial information

For companies not preparing their financial statements under IFRS, the CA 2006 states that individual accounts prepared must include a balance sheet (statement of financial position), a profit and loss account (statement of profit or loss and other comprehensive income) and notes to the accounts. Companies may also be required to prepare a cash flow statement and statement of total recognised gains and losses depending on whether the UK accounting standards require this.

The Companies Act 2006 states that the period allowed for companies to publish their financial information after the financial year end is six months for listed companies and nine months for private companies.

A company has a duty to circulate copies of its annual account and reports for each financial year to:

- Every member of the company
- Every holder of the company's debentures, and
- Every person who is entitled to receive notice of general meetings.

The company can send out summary financial statements to any of the above persons, providing they wish to receive them.

4.3.3 Audit of financial information

In the UK, a company's financial statements are subject to an annual external audit unless the company is exempt, From 1 October 2012 the audit thresholds for small companies have been aligned with accounting thresholds. A small company is entitled to an exemption from statutory audit if it meets two out of three criteria:

(a)   Not more than 50 employees
(b)   Turnover of not more than £6.5 million; and
(c)   Balance sheet total of not more than £3.26 million.

This exemption is only for private companies that are not listed on a stock exchange or required to be regulated by a body such as the Financial Services Authority for banking and insurance companies.

For both public and private companies, an auditor must be appointed for each financial year of the company. The auditor must report to the company's members on the annual accounts and state whether in the auditor's opinion, the accounts:

- Give a true and fair view of the company's affairs,
- Have been properly prepared in accordance with the relevant financial reporting framework, and
- Have been prepared in accordance with the Companies Act.

The auditor must also state whether the information provided in the directors' report is consistent with the rest of the information provided in the financial statements.

In addition, in preparing their opinion on the financial statements, the auditor must form an opinion on whether proper accounting records have been kept and whether the financial statements agree with the accounting records.

4.4 The Stock Exchange

In the UK there are two main markets on which it is possible for a company to have its securities quoted:

(a) The Stock Exchange
(b) The Alternative Investment Market (AIM)

Shares quoted on the main market, the Stock Exchange, are said to be 'listed' or to have obtained a 'listing'. In order to receive a listing for its securities, a company must conform with Stock Exchange regulations contained in the Listing Rules or Yellow Book issued by the Council of The Stock Exchange. The company commits itself to certain procedures and standards, including matters concerning the disclosure of accounting information, which are more extensive than the disclosure requirements of the Companies Acts. The requirements of the AIM are less stringent than the main Stock Exchange. It is aimed at new, higher risk or smaller companies.

Many requirements of the Yellow Book do not have the backing of law, but the ultimate sanction which can be imposed on a listed company which fails to abide by them is the withdrawal of its securities from the Stock Exchange List: the company's shares would no longer be traded on the market.

4.5 Influence of EU directives

Since the United Kingdom became a member of the European Union (EU) it has been obliged to comply with the legal requirements of the EU. It does this by enacting UK laws to implement EU directives. For example, the CA 1989 was enacted in part to implement the provisions of the seventh and eighth EU directives, which deal with consolidated accounts and auditors.

Remember EU directives are only mandatory when enacted into legislation by Parliament. Other EU directives only hold advisory status.

EU directives have influenced the UK financial reporting regime in various key areas.

(a) Implementation of prescribed formats and detailed disclosure requirements for financial statements.

(b) Definition of a subsidiary and permission of various exemptions from Companies Act requirements.

(c) Introduction of various exemptions from Companies Act requirements in respect of small and medium sized companies.

4.6 UK regulatory framework

In the UK, the Financial Reporting Council (FRC) is responsible for issuing financial reporting standards. The structure of the FRC was revised in July 2012.

The FRC enjoys strong governmental support but is not government controlled. **It is a part of the private sector process of self-regulation.**

4.6.1 Financial Reporting Council

The FRC states that its aim is to promote high standards of corporate governance through the UK Corporate Governance Code. It sets standards for corporate reporting and actuarial practice and monitors and enforces accounting and auditing standards. It also oversees the regulatory activities of the actuarial profession and the professional accountancy bodies and operates independent disciplinary arrangements for public interest cases. The members of the FRC board are responsible for ensuring that these aims are achieved. Each year the FRC publishes:

(a)   An annual report describing the activities during the year of its operating bodies including the Accounting Council and the Financial Reporting Review Panel (FRRP)

(b)   Report and financial statements, as required by the Companies Act

(c)   Press releases

(d)   Other relevant information

4.6.2 The Codes and Standards Committee

This is responsible for advising the FRC board on maintaining an effective framework of UK codes and standards. It advises the FRC Board on the Annual Plan for Codes and Standards work and oversees the work of the three councils. These advise the Committee on Accounting, Audit and Assurance and Actuarial work.

4.6.3 The Accounting Council

The Accounting Council replaces the Accounting Standards Board (ASB) in the restructured FRC. The accounting council is responsible for:

(a)   Providing strategic input and thought leadership in accounting and financial reporting

(b)   Considering and advising the FRC Board on draft codes and standards to ensure that a high quality, effective and proportionate approach is taken

(c)   Considering and commenting upon proposed developments in relation to international codes and standards and regulations

(d)   Considering and advising on research proposals

All accounting standards previously issued by the ASB were adopted by the FRC in July 2012.

5 Conceptual framework and GAAP

FAST FORWARD

The IASB's *Conceptual Framework* provides the backbone of the IASB's **conceptual framework**.

5.1 The search for a conceptual framework

Key term

A **conceptual framework**, in the field with which we are concerned, is a statement of generally accepted theoretical principles which form the frame of reference for financial reporting.

These theoretical principles provide the basis for the development of new accounting standards and the evaluation of those already in existence. The financial reporting process is concerned with providing information that is useful in the business and economic decision-making process. Therefore a conceptual framework will form the **theoretical basis** for determining which events should be accounted for, how they should be measured and how they should be communicated to the user. Although it is theoretical in nature, a conceptual framework for financial reporting has highly practical final aims.

5.2 The need for a conceptual framework

A conceptual framework is an important part of the financial reporting system as it underpins the development of accounting standards and sets out the basis of recognition of items in the financial statements such as assets, liabilities, income and expenses.

The **danger of not having a conceptual framework** is demonstrated in the way some countries' standards have developed over recent years; standards tend to be produced in a haphazard and fire-fighting approach. Where an agreed framework exists, the standard-setting body acts as an architect or designer, rather than a fire-fighter, building accounting rules on the foundation of sound, agreed basic principles.

The lack of a conceptual framework also means that fundamental principles are tackled more than once in different standards, thereby producing **contradictions and inconsistencies** in basic concepts, such as those of prudence and matching. This leads to ambiguity, which affects the true and fair concept of financial reporting.

Another problem with the lack of a conceptual framework has become apparent in the USA. The large number of **highly detailed standards** produced by the Financial Accounting Standards Board (FASB) has created a financial reporting environment governed by specific rules rather than general principles. This would be avoided if a cohesive set of principles were in place.

A conceptual framework can also bolster standard setters **against political pressure** from various 'lobby groups' and interested parties. Such pressure would only prevail if it was acceptable under the conceptual framework. As noted earlier the IASB and FASB have been working on a new common conceptual framework.

5.3 Advantages and disadvantages of a conceptual framework

5.3.1 Advantages

(a)   The situation is avoided whereby standards are developed on a patchwork basis, where a particular accounting problem was recognised as having emerged, and resources were then channelled into **standardising accounting practice** in that area, without regard to whether that particular issue was necessarily the most important issue remaining at that time without standardisation.

(b)   As stated above, the development of certain standards (particularly national standards) have been subject to considerable **political interference** from interested parties. Where there is a conflict of interest between user groups on which policies to choose, policies deriving from a conceptual framework will be **less open to criticism** that the standard-setter buckled to external pressure.

(c)   Some standards may concentrate on **profit or loss** whereas some may concentrate on the **valuation of net assets** (statement of financial position).

5.3.2 Disadvantages

(a)   Financial statements are intended for a **variety of users**, and it is not certain that a single conceptual framework can be devised which will suit all users.

(b)   Given the diversity of user requirements, there may be a need for a variety of accounting Standards, each produced for a **different purpose** (and with different concepts as a basis).

(c)   It is not clear that a conceptual framework makes the task of **preparing and then implementing** standards any easier than without a framework.

Before we look at the IASB's attempt to produce a conceptual framework, we need to consider another term of importance to this debate: Generally Accepted Accounting Practices (or principles) or GAAP.

5.4 Generally Accepted Accounting Practices (GAAP)

Key term

> **GAAP** signifies all the rules, from whatever source, which govern accounting.

In individual countries this is seen primarily as a **combination** of:

- National company law
- National accounting standards
- Local stock exchange requirements

Although those sources are the basis for the GAAP of individual countries, the concept also includes the effects of **non-mandatory sources** such as:

- International accounting standards
- Statutory requirements in other countries

In many countries, like the UK, GAAP does not have any statutory or regulatory authority or definition, unlike other countries, such as the USA. The term is mentioned rarely in legislation, and only then in fairly limited terms.

There are different views of GAAP in different countries. The UK position can be explained in the following extracts from *UK GAAP* (Davies, Paterson & Wilson, Ernst & Young, 5th Edition).

> 'Our view is that GAAP is a dynamic concept which requires constant review, adaptation and reaction to changing circumstances. We believe that use of the term "principle" gives GAAP an unjustified and inappropriate degree of permanence. GAAP changes in response to changing business and economic needs and developments. As circumstances alter, accounting practices are modified or developed accordingly... We believe that GAAP goes far beyond mere rules and principles, and encompasses contemporary permissible accounting **practice**.'

> 'It is often argued that the term "generally accepted" implies that there must exist a high degree of practical application of a particular accounting practice. However, this interpretation raises certain practical difficulties. For example, what about new areas of accounting which have not, as yet, been generally applied? What about different accounting treatments for similar items - are they all generally accepted?'

> 'It is our view that "generally accepted" does **not** mean "generally adopted or used". We believe that, in the UK context, GAAP refers to accounting practices which are regarded as permissible by the accounting profession. The extent to which a particular practice has been adopted is, in our opinion, not the overriding consideration. Any accounting practice which is legitimate in the circumstances under which it has been applied should be regarded as GAAP.'

The decision as to whether or not a particular practice is permissible or legitimate would depend on one or more of the following factors:

- Is the practice addressed either in the accounting standards, statute or other official pronouncements?

- If the practice is not addressed in UK accounting standards, is it dealt with in International Accounting Standards, or the standards of other countries such as the US?

- Is the practice consistent with the needs of users and the objectives of financial reporting?

- Does the practice have authoritative support in the accounting literature?

- Is the practice being applied by other companies in similar situations?

- Is the practice consistent with the fundamental concept of 'true and fair'?

This view is not held in all countries, however. In the USA particularly, the equivalent of a 'true and fair view' is 'fair presentation in accordance with GAAP'. Generally Accepted Accounting Practices are defined as those principles which have 'substantial authoritative support'. Therefore, accounts prepared in accordance with accounting principles for which there is not substantial authoritative support are presumed to be misleading or inaccurate.

The effect here is that 'new' or 'different' accounting principles are not acceptable unless they have been adopted by the mainstream accounting profession, usually the standard-setting bodies and/or professional accountancy bodies. This is much more rigid than the UK view expressed above.

A **conceptual framework** for financial reporting can be defined as an attempt to codify existing GAAP in order to reappraise current accounting standards and to produce new standards.

5.5 The IASB's *Conceptual Framework*

In July 1989 the old IASC produced a document, *Framework for the preparation and presentation of financial statements* (*'Framework'*). The *Framework* is, in effect, the **conceptual framework** upon which all IFRSs are based and hence which determines how financial statements are prepared and the information they contain. The Framework is in the process of being revised by the IASB, and some new chapters were issued in September 2010. The revised Framework is called *The Conceptual Framework for Financial Reporting*. The Conceptual Framework is itself in the process of revision, and a Discussion Paper was issued in July 2013. We will look at the IASB's *Conceptual Framework* in more detail in Chapter 6.

Chapter roundup

- You should be able to describe the **organisation of the IFRS Foundation and the IASB.**

- You must understand the **due process** involved in producing IFRSs.

- You need to be able to understand the problems that can arise.

- The statutory framework refers to the laws surrounding the preparation, presentation and audit of financial information. Regulation is found in company law and stock exchange listing rules.

- The IASB's *Conceptual Framework* provides the backbone of the IASB's **conceptual framework**.

Quick quiz

1   One objective of the IFRS Foundation is to promote the preparation of financial statements using the euro.

    True   ☐

    False   ☐

2   How many IASs and IFRSs have been published?

3   A conceptual framework is:

    A   A theoretical expression of accounting standards
    B   A list of key terms used by the IASB
    C   A statement of theoretical principles which form the frame of reference for financial reporting
    D   The proforma financial statements

4   Which body of the IFRS Foundation aids users' interpretation of IFRSs?

5   Which of the following arguments is not in favour of accounting standards, but is in favour of accounting choice?

    A   They reduce variations in methods used to produce accounts
    B   They oblige companies to disclose their accounting policies
    C   They are a less rigid alternative to legislation
    D   They may tend towards rigidity in applying the rules

Answers to quick quiz

1   False

2   41 IASs and 14 IFRSs

3   C

4   The International Financial Reporting Standards Interpretations Committee (IFRSIC).

5   D   The other arguments are all in favour of accounting standards.

End of chapter question

Operating structure (AIA November 2005)

Outline the role of each of the following bodies in the International Accounting Standards operating structure:

(a)   International Financial Reporting Standards Foundation
(b)   International Accounting Standards Board
(c)   International Financial Reporting Standards Advisory Council
(d)   International Financial Reporting Standards Interpretations Committee

(12 marks)

Presentation of published financial statements

3

Topic list	Syllabus reference
1 Limited liability	11.1
2 IAS 1 *Presentation of financial statements*	11.1
3 Statement of financial position	11.1
4 The current/non-current distinction	11.1
5 Statement of profit or loss and other comprehensive income	11.1
6 Statement of changes in equity	11.1
7 Notes to the financial statements	11.1
8 Other information in corporate reports	11.3

Introduction

The bulk of this Study Text looks at the accounts of limited liability companies.

We begin in this chapter by looking at the overall **content and format** of company financial statements. These are governed by IAS 1 (revised) *Presentation of financial statements*.

We looked at what IAS 1 says about **accounting concepts and policies** in Chapter 1. The rest of the Standard is considered here.

1 Limited liability

Limited liability offers various advantages to companies, although there are disadvantages as well.

1.1 Fundamental differences

There are some fundamental differences in the accounts of limited liability companies **compared to sole traders or partnerships**, of which the following are perhaps the most significant.

(a)   The **national legislation** governing the activities of limited liability companies tends to be very extensive. Amongst other things such legislation may define certain minimum accounting records which must be maintained by companies; they may specify that the annual accounts of a company must be filed with a government bureau and so be available for public inspection; and they often contain detailed requirements on the minimum information which must be disclosed in a company's accounts. Businesses which are not limited liability companies (non-incorporated businesses) often enjoy comparative freedom from statutory regulation.

(b)   The **owners of a company** (its members or shareholders) may be very numerous. Their capital is shown differently from that of a sole trader; and similarly the 'appropriation account' of a company is different.

1.2 Advantages of limited liability

You may be able to recognise the relative **advantages and disadvantages** of limited liability. Sole traders and partnerships are, with some significant exceptions, generally fairly small concerns. The amount of capital involved may be modest, and the proprietors of the business usually participate in managing it. Their liability for the debts of the business is unlimited, which means that if the business runs up debts that it is unable to pay, the proprietors will become personally liable for the unpaid debts, and would be required, if necessary, to sell their private possessions in order to repay them. For example, if a sole trader has some capital in his business, but the business now owes $40,000 which it cannot repay, the trader might have to sell his house to raise the money to pay off his business debts.

Limited liability companies offer **limited liability to their owners**. This means that the maximum amount that an owner stands to lose in the event that the company becomes insolvent and cannot pay off its debts, is his share of the capital in the business. Thus, limited liability is a major advantage of turning a business into a limited liability company. However, in practice banks or other lenders will normally seek personal guarantees from shareholders before making loans or granting an overdraft facility and so the advantage of limited liability is lost to a small owner-managed business.

There are also disadvantages to limited liability.

(a)   Compliance with national legislation
(b)   Compliance with national accounting standards and/or IASs/IFRSs
(c)   Any formation and annual registration costs

As a business grows, it needs **more capital** to finance its operations, and significantly more than the people currently managing the business can provide themselves. One way of obtaining more capital is to invite investors from outside the business to invest in the ownership or equity of the business. These new co-owners would not usually be expected to help with managing the business. To such investors, limited liability is very attractive.

Investments are always risky undertakings, but with limited liability the investor knows the maximum amount that he stands to lose when he puts some capital into a company.

1.3 The accounting records of limited liability companies

There is almost always a **national legal requirement** for companies to keep accounting records which are sufficient to show and explain the company's transactions. The records will probably:

(a) Disclose the company's current financial position at any time

(b) Contain:

    (i) Day-to-day entries of money received and spent

    (ii) A record of the company's assets and liabilities

    (iii) Where the company deals in goods:

        (1) A statement of inventories held at the year end, and supporting inventory count records

        (2) With the exception of retail sales, statements of goods bought and sold which identify the sellers and buyers of those goods

(c) Enable the managers of the company to ensure that the **final accounts** of the company give a true and fair view of the company's profit or loss and financial position.

The detailed requirements of accounting records which must be maintained will vary from country to country. See Chapter 2 for the statutory requirements in the UK.

Question   Regulation

How are limited liability companies regulated in your country?

2 IAS 1 *Presentation of financial statements*

FAST FORWARD

IAS 1 covers the **form and content** of financial statements.

As well as covering accounting policies and other general considerations governing financial statements, IAS 1 *Presentation of financial statements* give substantial guidance on the form and content of published financial statements.

As mentioned in Chapter 1 the standard was amended in June 2011, and as a result the 'statement of comprehensive income' was renamed 'statement of profit or loss and other comprehensive income'. The statement down to 'Profit (loss) for the year', which has previously been referred to as the 'income statement', has become the 'statement of profit or loss'. There were also some changes in presentation These changes will be covered in detail later in this chapter.

First of all, some general points are made about financial statements.

2.1 Profit or loss for the period

As we shall see later, a statement of profit or loss and other comprehensive income includes:

- Profit or loss for the period, and
- Other comprehensive income.

The statement of profit or loss and other comprehensive income is the most significant indicator of a company's financial performance, so it is important to ensure that it is not misleading.

Profit or loss will be misleading if costs incurred in the current year are not deducted from the current year income but from the balance of accumulated profits brought forward. This presents the current year's results more favourably.

IAS 1 stipulates that all items of income and expense recognised in a period shall be included in profit or loss unless a **Standard** or an **Interpretation** requires otherwise.

Circumstances where items may be excluded from profit or loss for the current year include the correction of errors and the effect of changes in accounting policies. These are covered in IAS 8.

2.2 How items are disclosed

IAS 1 specifies disclosures of certain items in certain ways.

- Some items must appear on the **face of the statement of financial position or statement of profit or loss and other comprehensive income**
- Other items can appear in a **note to the financial statements** instead
- **Recommended formats** are given which entities may or may not follow, depending on their circumstances

Obviously, disclosures specified by **other standards** must also be made, and we will mention the necessary disclosures when we cover each statement in turn. Disclosures in both IAS 1 and other standards must be made either on the face of the statement or in the notes unless otherwise stated, ie disclosures cannot be made in an accompanying commentary or report.

2.3 Identification of financial statements

As a result of the above point, it is most important that entities **distinguish the financial statements** very clearly from any other information published with them. This is because all IFRSs apply *only* to the financial statements (ie the main statements and related notes), so readers of the annual report must be able to differentiate between the parts of the report which are prepared under IFRS, and other parts which are not.

The entity should **identify each component** of the financial statements very clearly. IAS 1 also requires disclosure of the following information in a prominent position. If necessary it should be repeated wherever it is felt to be of use to the reader in his understanding of the information presented.

- **Name** of the reporting entity (or other means of identification)
- Whether the accounts cover the **single entity** only or a group of entities
- The **reporting date** or the period covered by the financial statements (as appropriate)
- The **presentation currency**
- The **level of rounding** used in presenting the figures in the financial statements

Judgement must be used to determine the best method of presenting this information. In particular, the Standard suggests that the approach to this will be very different when the financial statements are communicated electronically.

The **level of rounding** is important, as presenting figures in thousands or millions of units makes the figures more understandable. The level of rounding must be disclosed, however, and it should not obscure necessary details or make the information less relevant.

2.4 Reporting period

It is normal for entities to present financial statements **annually** and IAS 1 states that they should be prepared at least as often as this. If (unusually) an entity's reporting period is changed, for whatever reason, the period for which the statements are presented will be less or more than one year. In such cases the entity should also disclose:

(a) The **reason(s) why** a period other than one year is used; *and*
(b) The fact that the comparative figures given **are not in fact comparable**

For practical purposes, some entities prefer to use a period which **approximates to a year**, eg 52 weeks, and the IAS allows this approach as it will produce statements not materially different from those produced on an annual basis.

3 Statement of financial position

IAS 1 suggests a **format** for the statement of financial position.

IAS 1 looks at the statement of financial position and statement of profit or loss and other comprehensive income. We will not give all the detailed disclosures as some are outside the scope of your syllabus. Instead we will look at a **'proforma' set of accounts** based on the Standard.

IAS 1 discusses the distinction between current and non-current items in some detail, as we shall see in the next section. First of all we can look at the **suggested format** of the statement of financial position (given in an appendix to the Standard) and then look at further disclosures required.

3.1 Statement of financial position example

The example given by the Standard is as follows.

XYZ GROUP
STATEMENT OF FINANCIAL POSITION AS AT 31 DECEMBER 20X8

	20X8 $'000	20X8 $'000	20X7 $'000	20X7 $'000
Assets				
Non-current assets				
Property, plant and equipment	X		X	
Goodwill	X		X	
Other intangible assets	X		X	
Investments in equity instruments	X̲		X̲	
		X		X
Current assets				
Inventories	X		X	
Trade receivables	X		X	
Other current assets	X		X	
Cash and cash equivalents	X̲		X̲	
		X̲		X̲
Total assets		X̲		X̲

Equity and liabilities

Equity

Share capital	X		X	
Retained earnings	X		X	
Other components of equity*	X̲		X̲	
Total equity		X		X
Non-current liabilities				
Long-term borrowings	X		X	
Deferred tax	X		X	
Long-term provisions	X̲		X̲	
Total non-current liabilities		X		X
Current liabilities				
Trade and other payables	X		X	
Short-term borrowings	X		X	
Current portion of long-term borrowings	X		X	
Current tax payable	X		X	
Short-term provisions	X̲		X̲	
Total current liabilities		X̲		X̲
Total liabilities		X̲		X̲
Total equity and liabilities		X̲̲		X̲̲

*Note: other components of equity includes other reserves

IAS 1 specifies various items which must appear on the **face of the statement of financial position** as a minimum disclosure.

(a)   Property, plant and equipment

(b)   Investment property

(c)   Intangible assets

(d)   Financial assets (excluding amounts shown under (e), (h) and (i))

(e)   Investments accounted for using the equity method

(f)   Biological assets (outside the scope of the Paper 11 syllabus)

(g)   Inventories

(h)   Trade and other receivables

(i)   Cash and cash equivalents

(j)   The total of assets classified as held for sale and assets included in disposal groups classified as held for sale in accordance with IFRS 5

(k)   Trade and other payables

(l)   Provisions

(m)   Financial liabilities (other than (k) and (l))

(n)   Current tax assets and liabilities as in IAS 12

(o)   Deferred tax liabilities and assets as in IAS 12

(p)   Liabilities included in disposal groups classified as held for sale in accordance with IFRS 5

(q)   Non-controlling interests

(r)   Issued capital and reserves

We will look at these items in later chapters.

Any **other line items**, headings or sub-totals should be shown on the face of the statement of financial position when it is necessary for an understanding of the entity's financial position.

The example shown above is for illustration only (although we will follow the format in this Study Text). The IAS, however, does not prescribe the order or format in which the items listed should be presented. It simply states that they **must be presented separately** because they are so different in nature or function from each other.

Whether additional items are presented separately depends on judgements based on the assessment of the following factors.

(a) **Nature and liquidity of assets and their materiality**. Thus goodwill and assets arising from development expenditure will be presented separately, as will monetary/non-monetary assets and current/non-current assets.

(b) **Function within the entity.** Operating and financial assets, inventories, receivables and cash and cash equivalents are therefore shown separately.

(c) **Amounts, nature and timing of liabilities**. Interest-bearing and non-interest-bearing liabilities and provisions will be shown separately, classified as current or non-current as appropriate.

The Standard also requires separate presentation where **different measurement bases** are used for assets and liabilities which differ in nature or function. According to IAS 16, for example, it is permitted to carry certain items of property, plant and equipment at cost or at a revalued amount.

3.2 Information presented either on the face of the statement of financial position or by note

Further **sub-classification** of the line items listed above should be disclosed either on the face of the statement of financial position or in notes to the statement of financial position. The classification will depend upon the nature of the entity's operations. As well as each item being sub-classified by its nature, any amounts payable to or receivable from any **group company or other related party** should also be disclosed separately.

The sub-classification details will in part depend on the requirements of IFRSs. The size, nature and function of the amounts involved will also be important and the factors listed above should be considered. **Disclosures** will vary from item to item and IAS 1 gives the following examples.

(a) **Property, plant and equipment** are classified by class as described in IAS 16 *Property, plant and equipment*

(b) **Receivables** are analysed between amounts receivable from trade customers, other members of the group, receivables from related parties, prepayments and other amounts

(c) **Inventories** are sub-classified, in accordance with IAS 2 *Inventories,* into classifications such as merchandise, production supplies, materials, work in progress and finished goods

(d) **Provisions** are analysed showing separately provisions for employee benefit costs and any other items classified in a manner appropriate to the entity's operations

(e) **Equity capital and reserves** are analysed showing separately the various classes of paid in capital, share premium and reserves

The Standard then lists some **specific disclosures** which must be made, either on the face of the statement of financial position or the related notes.

(a) **Share capital disclosures** (for each class of share capital)

   (i)   Number of shares authorised

   (ii)   Number of shares issued and fully paid, and issued but not fully paid

   (iii)   Par value per share, or that the shares have no par value

   (iv)   Reconciliation of the number of shares outstanding at the beginning and at the end of the year

   (v)   Rights, preferences and restrictions attaching to that class including restrictions on the distribution of dividends and the repayment of capital

   (vi)   Shares in the entity held by the entity itself or by related group companies

   (vii)   Shares reserved for issuance under options and sales contracts, including the terms and amounts

(b) Description of the nature and purpose of **each reserve** within owners' equity

Some types of entity have no share capital, eg partnerships. Such entities should disclose information which is **equivalent** to that listed above. This means disclosing the movement during the period in each category of equity interest and any rights, preferences or restrictions attached to each category of equity interest.

4 The current/non-current distinction

FAST FORWARD

You should appreciate the distinction between **current and non-current** assets and liabilities and their different treatments.

4.1 The current/non-current distinction

An entity must present **current** and **non-current** assets as separate classifications on the face of the statement of financial position. A presentation based on liquidity should only be used where it provides more relevant and reliable information, in which case all assets and liabilities must be presented broadly **in order of liquidity**.

In either case, the entity should disclose any portion of an asset or liability which is expected to be recovered or settled **after more than 12 months**. For example, for an amount receivable which is due in instalments over 18 months, the portion due after more than 12 months must be disclosed.

The IAS emphasises how helpful information on the **operating cycle** is to users of financial statements. Where there is a clearly defined operating cycle within which the entity supplies goods or services, then information disclosing those net assets that are continuously circulating as **working capital** is useful.

This distinguishes them from those net assets used in the long-term operations of the entity. Assets that are expected to be realised and liabilities that are due for settlement within the operating cycle are therefore highlighted.

The liquidity and solvency of an entity is also indicated by information about the **maturity dates** of assets and liabilities. As you will see, IFRS 7 *Financial instruments: disclosure* requires disclosure of maturity dates of both financial assets and financial liabilities. (Financial assets include trade and other receivables; financial liabilities include trade and other payables.) In the case of non-monetary assets, eg inventories, such information is also useful.

4.2 Current assets

Key term

> An asset should be classified as a **current asset** when:
>
> - The entity expects to realise the asset, or intends to sell or consume it, in its normal operating cycle; *or*
> - The asset is held primarily for trading purposes; *or*
> - The asset is expected to be realised within twelve months after the reporting period; or
> - The asset is cash or a cash equivalent which is not restricted in its use.
>
> All other assets must be classified as non-current assets. *(IAS 1)*

Non-current assets includes tangible, intangible, operating and financial assets of a long-term nature. Other terms with the same meaning can be used (eg 'fixed', 'long-term').

The term 'operating cycle' has been used several times above and the Standard defines it as follows.

Key term

> The **operating cycle** of an entity is the time between the acquisition of assets and their realisation in cash or cash equivalents. *(IAS 1)*

Current assets therefore include inventories and trade receivables that are sold, consumed and realised as part of the normal operating cycle. **This is the case even where they are not expected to be realised within 12 months**.

Current assets will also include **marketable securities** if they are expected to be realised within 12 months of the reporting period. If expected to be realised later, they should be included in non-current assets.

4.3 Current liabilities

Key term

> A liability should be classified as a **current liability** when:
>
> - The entity expects to settle the liability in its normal operating cycle; *or*
> - The liability is held primarily for the purpose of trading; *or*
> - The liability is due to be settled within twelve months of the reporting period; *or*
> - The entity does not have an unconditional right to defer settlement of the liability for at least 12 months after the reporting period.
>
> All other liabilities must be classified as non-current liabilities. *(IAS 1)*

The categorisation of current liabilities is very similar to that of current assets. Thus, some current liabilities are part of the **working capital** used in the normal operating cycle of the business (ie trade payables and accruals for employee and other operating costs). Such items will be classed as current liabilities **even where they are due to be settled more than 12 months after the reporting period.**

There are also current liabilities which are not settled as part of the normal operating cycle, but which are due to be settled within 12 months of the reporting period. These include bank overdrafts, income taxes, other non-trade payables and the current portion of interest-bearing liabilities. Any interest-bearing liabilities that are used to finance working capital on a long-term basis, and that are not due for settlement within 12 months, should be classed as **non-current liabilities.**

A **long-term financial liability** due to be **settled within 12 months** of the reporting period should be classified as a **current liability**, even if an agreement to refinance, or to reschedule payments, on a long-term basis is completed after the reporting period and before the financial statements are authorised for issue.

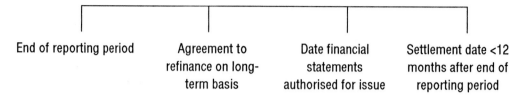

| End of reporting period | Agreement to refinance on long-term basis | Date financial statements authorised for issue | Settlement date <12 months after end of reporting period |

A **non-current financial liability** that is payable on **demand** because the entity **breached** a **condition** of its loan agreement should be classified as **current** at the end of the reporting period even if the **lender** has agreed **after the end of the reporting period**, and **before** the financial statements are **authorised for issue**, **not** to **demand payment** as a consequence of the breach.

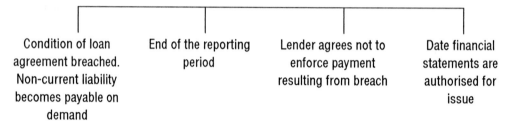

| Condition of loan agreement breached. Non-current liability becomes payable on demand | End of the reporting period | Lender agrees not to enforce payment resulting from breach | Date financial statements are authorised for issue |

However, if the **lender** has **agreed** by the end of the **reporting period** to provide a **period of grace** ending **at least 12 months after the reporting date** within which the entity can rectify the breach and during that time the lender cannot demand immediate repayment, the liability is classified as **non-current**.

5 Statement of profit or loss and other comprehensive income

FAST FORWARD

Once again, IAS 1 suggests formats for the statement of profit or loss and other comprehensive income.

IAS 1 requires a statement of profit or loss and other comprehensive income in which total comprehensive income for a period is presented.

Key terms

Total comprehensive income comprises all components of 'profit or loss' and of 'other comprehensive income'.

Other comprehensive income comprises items of income and expense (including reclassification adjustments) that are not recognised in profit or loss as required or permitted by other IFRSs.

IAS 1 allows income and expense items to be presented in two ways:

1   A single statement of profit or loss and other comprehensive income

2   A statement showing profit or loss (statement of profit or loss) **plus** a second statement beginning with profit or loss showing other comprehensive income (statement of comprehensive income).

Exam focus point

The Paper 11 examiner has indicated that a single statement of profit or loss and comprehensive income will be examinable at this level. Both presentation methods are, however, shown below for completeness.

5.1 Single statement of profit or loss and other comprehensive income

XYZ GROUP
STATEMENT OF PROFIT OR LOSS AND OTHER COMPREHENSIVE INCOME FOR THE YEAR ENDED 31 DECEMBER 20X8

	20X8 $'000	20X7 $'000
Revenue	X	X
Cost of sales	(X)	(X)
Gross profit	X	X
Other income	X	X
Distribution costs	(X)	(X)
Administrative expenses	(X)	(X)
Other expenses	(X)	(X)
Finance costs	(X)	(X)
Profit before tax	X	X
Income tax expense	(X)	(X)
Profit for the year	X	X
Other comprehensive income		
Items that will not be reclassified to profit or loss:		
Gains on property revaluations	X	X
Income tax relating to items that will not be reclassified	(X)	(X)
Items that may be reclassified subsequently to profit or loss:		
Cash flow hedges	(X)	(X)
Income tax relating to items that may be reclassified	(X)	(X)
Other comprehensive income for the year, net of tax	X	X
Total comprehensive income for the year	X	X

Exam focus point

Note that the amendment to IAS 1 now splits items of other comprehensive income into those which can be reclassified to profit or loss and those which cannot be reclassified. In practice none of the items which can be reclassified are examinable at Paper 11 so you will not encounter these in your exam. Examples of statements of profit or loss and other comprehensive income in the remainder of this text do not show this distinction therefore.

5.2 Separate statements

Companies are given the option of presenting this information in two statements as follows:

XYZ GROUP
STATEMENT FOR PROFIT OR LOSS FOR THE YEAR ENDED 31 DECEMBER 20X8

	20X8	20X7
	$'000	$'000
Revenue	X	X
Cost of sales	(X)	(X)
Gross profit	X	X
Other income	X	X
Distribution costs	(X)	(X)
Administrative expenses	(X)	(X)
Other expenses	(X)	(X)
Finance costs	(X)	(X)
Profit before tax	X	X
Income tax expense	(X)	(X)
Profit for the year	X	X

XYZ GROUP
STATEMENT OF PROFIT OR LOSS AND OTHER COMPREHENSIVE INCOME FOR THE YEAR ENDED 31 DECEMBER 20X8 (TWO STATEMENT FORMAT)

Profit for the year	X	X
Other comprehensive income		
Items that will not be reclassified to profit or loss:		
Gains on property revaluations	X	X
Income tax relating to items that will not be reclassified	(X)	(X)
Other comprehensive income for the year, net of tax	X	X
Total comprehensive income for the year	X	X

Note: The Paper 11 examiner has indicated that the following terms will be used in the exam:

- Statement of profit or loss and other comprehensive income to refer to the single statement format

- Statement of profit or loss to refer to the first part of the statement of profit or loss and other comprehensive income i.e. from revenue to profit for the period

- Other comprehensive income to refer to the final part of the statement of profit or loss and other comprehensive income in which other comprehensive income is reported.

This terminology is applied throughout the Study Text. Items of expenditure or income will be referred to as recognised in the statement of profit or loss or in other comprehensive income, to clarify in which part of the statement of profit or loss and other comprehensive income they are shown.

5.2 Statement of profit or loss

IAS 1 offers **two possible formats** for the statement of profit or loss part of the statement of profit or loss and other comprehensive income, the difference between the two being the classification of expenses: by function or by nature.

The above examples both show the classification of expenses by function. Below is an example of a statement of profit or loss where expenses are classified by nature:

XYZ GROUP
STATEMENT OF PROFIT OR LOSS FOR THE YEAR ENDED 31 DECEMBER 20X8

Illustrating the classification of expenses by nature

	20X8 $'000	20X7 $'000
Revenue	X	X
Other operating income	X	X
Changes in inventories of finished goods and work in progress	(X)	X
Work performed by the entity and capitalised	X	X
Raw material and consumables used	(X)	(X)
Employee benefits expense	(X)	(X)
Depreciation and amortisation expense	(X)	(X)
Impairment of property, plant and equipment	(X)	(X)
Other expenses	(X)	(X)
Finance costs	(X)	(X)
Profit before tax	X	X
Income tax expense	(X)	(X)
Profit for the year	X	X

5.3 Information presented in the statement of profit or loss and other comprehensive income

IAS 1 states that in addition to the profit or loss and other comprehensive income sections, the statement of profit and loss and other comprehensive income must show:

(a) Profit or loss

(b) Total other comprehensive income

(c) Comprehensive income for the period (ie the total of profit or loss and other comprehensive income

The Standard also lists the following as the **minimum** to be disclosed in the profit or loss section.

(a) Revenue
(b) Finance costs
(c) Tax expense
(d) a single amount for the total of discontinued operations

In the other comprehensive income section components of other comprehensive income must be classified by nature and must be grouped into those that:

(a) Will not be reclassified subsequently to profit or loss
(b) Will be reclassified subsequently to profit or loss

Income and expense items can only be **offset** when, and only when:

(a) It is permitted or required by an IFRS, *or*

(b) Gains, losses and related expenses arising from the same or similar transactions and events are immaterial, in which case they can be aggregated.

5.4 Information presented either on the face of the statement of profit or loss and other comprehensive income or in the notes

(a)   Where an item of income or expense is material, its nature and amount should be disclosed separately.

(b)   An analysis of expenses must be shown either on the face of the income statement (as above, which is encouraged by the Standard) or by note, using a classification based on *either* the nature of the expenses or their function. This **sub-classification of expenses** indicates a range of components of financial performance; these may differ in terms of stability, potential for gain or loss and predictability. These classifications are discussed in more detail below.

(c)   The amount of income tax relating to each component of other comprehensive income must be disclosed either by:

   (i)   Disclosing each other comprehensive income net of the related income tax, or

   (ii)   Presenting other comprehensive income gross, and disclosing the aggregate tax related to other comprehensive income.

5.4.1 Nature of expense method

Expenses are not reallocated amongst various functions within the entity, but are aggregated in the statement of profit or loss **according to their nature** (eg purchase of materials, depreciation, wages and salaries, transport costs). This is by far the easiest method, especially for smaller entities.

5.4.2 Function of expense/cost of sales method

You are likely to be more familiar with this method. Expenses are classified according to their function as part of cost of sales, distribution or administrative activities. This method often gives **more relevant information** for users, but the allocation of expenses by function requires the use of judgement and can be arbitrary. Consequently, perhaps, when this method is used, entities should disclose **additional information** on the nature of expenses, including staff costs, and depreciation and amortisation expense.

Which of the above methods is chosen by an entity will depend on **historical and industry factors**, and also the **nature of the organisation**. Under each method, there should be given an indication of costs which are likely to vary (directly or indirectly) with the level of sales or production. The choice of method should fairly reflect the main elements of the entity's performance.

5.5 Further points

(a)   An entity must disclose, in the summary of significant accounting policies and/or other notes, the **judgements** made by management in **applying** the **accounting policies** that have the **most significant effect** on the amounts of items recognised in the financial statements.

(b)   An entity must disclose in the notes information regarding **key assumptions** about the **future**, and other sources of **measurement uncertainty**, that have a significant **risk of** causing a **material adjustment** to the carrying amounts of assets and liabilities within the **next financial year**.

6 Statement of changes in equity

FAST FORWARD

IAS 1 requires a statement of changes in equity.

IAS 1 requires a statement of changes in equity. This shows the movement in the equity section of the statement of financial position..

6.1 Format

XYZ GROUP
STATEMENT OF CHANGES IN EQUITY FOR THE YEAR ENDED 31 DECEMBER 20X8

	Share capital $'000	Share premium $'000	Retained earnings $'000	Revaluation surplus $'000	Total $'000
Balance at 31 December 20X7 brought forward	X	X	X	X	X
Changes in accounting policy			X		X
Restated balance	X	X	X	X	X
Changes in equity during 20X8					
Issue of share capital	X	X			X
Dividends			(X)		(X)
Total comprehensive income for the year			X	X	X
Transfer of revaluation surplus on sale of property			X	(X)	–
Balance at 31 December 20X8	X	X	(X)	X	X

A comparative statement for the prior period is also required.

6.2 Dividends

The revised IAS 1 requires that dividends paid are disclosed either in the statement of changes in equity or in the notes to the accounts. They must not be presented as part of the statement of profit or loss and other comprehensive income.

7 Notes to the financial statements

FAST FORWARD
Some items need to be disclosed by way of note.

7.1 Contents of notes

The notes to the financial statements will **amplify** the information given in the statement of financial position, statement of profit or loss and other comprehensive income and statement of changes in equity. We have already noted above the information which the IAS allows to be shown by note rather than on the face of the statements. To some extent, then, the contents of the notes will be determined by the level of detail shown on the **face of the statements**.

7.2 Structure

The notes to the financial statements should perform the following functions.

(a) Provide information about the **basis on which the financial statements were prepared** and which **specific accounting policies** were chosen and applied to significant transactions/events

(b) Disclose any information, not shown elsewhere in the financial statements, which is **required by IFRSs**

(c) Show any additional information that is **relevant to understanding** which is not shown elsewhere in the financial statements

The way the notes are presented is important. They should be given in a **systematic manner** and **cross referenced** back to the related figure(s) in the statement of financial position, statement of profit or loss and other comprehensive income or statement of cash flows.

Notes to the financial statements will amplify the information shown therein by giving the following.

(a)   More **detailed analysis** or breakdowns of figures in the statements

(b)   **Narrative information** explaining figures in the statements

(c)   **Additional information**, eg contingent liabilities and commitments

IAS 1 suggests a **certain order** for notes to the financial statements. This will assist users when comparing the statements of different entities.

(a)   Statement of **compliance** with IFRSs

(b)   Statement of the **measurement basis** (bases) and accounting policies applied

(c)   **Supporting information** for items presented on the face of each financial statement in the same order as each line item and each financial statement is presented

(d)   **Other disclosures**, eg:

(i)   Contingent liabilities, commitments and other financial disclosures

(ii)   Non-financial disclosures

The order of specific items may have to be varied occasionally, but a systematic structure is still required.

7.3 Presentation of accounting policies

The accounting policies section should describe the following.

(a)   The **measurement basis** (or bases) used in preparing the financial statements

(b)   The **other accounting policies** used, as required for a proper understanding of the financial statements

This information may be shown in the notes or sometimes as a **separate component** of the financial statements.

The information on measurement bases used is obviously fundamental to an understanding of the financial statements. Where **more than one basis is used**, it should be stated to which assets or liabilities each basis has been applied.

7.4 Other disclosures

An entity must disclose in the notes:

(a)   The amount of dividends proposed or declared before the financial statements were authorised for issue but not recognised as a distribution to owners during the period, and the amount per share

(b)   The amount of any cumulative preference dividends not recognised

IAS 1 ends by listing some **specific disclosures** which will always be required if they are not shown elsewhere in the financial statements.

(a)   The **domicile and legal form** of the entity, its **country of incorporation** and the **address of the registered office** (or, if different, principal place of business)

(b)   A description of the **nature of the entity's operations** and its **principal activities**

(c)   The name of the **parent entity** and the **ultimate parent entity** of the group

The accountant of Wislon Co has prepared the following list of account balances as at 31 December 20X7.

	$'000
50c ordinary shares (fully paid)	450
10% loan notes (secured)	200
Retained earnings 1.1.X7	235
General reserve 1.1.X7	171
Land and buildings 1.1.X7 (cost)	430
Plant and machinery 1.1.X7 (cost)	830
Accumulated depreciation	
Buildings 1.1.X7	20
Plant and machinery 1.1.X7	222
Inventory 1.1.X7	190
Sales	2,695
Purchases	2,152
Ordinary dividend	8
Loan note interest	10
Wages and salaries	254
Light and heat	31
Sundry expenses	113
Suspense account	135
Trade accounts receivable	179
Trade accounts payable	195
Cash	126

Notes

(a) Sundry expenses include $9,000 paid in respect of insurance for the year ending 1 September 20X8. Light and heat does not include an invoice of $3,000 for electricity for the three months ending 2 January 20X8, which was paid in February 20X8. Light and heat also includes $20,000 relating to salesmen's commission.

(b) The suspense account is in respect of the following items.

	$'000
Proceeds from the issue of 100,000 ordinary shares	120
Proceeds from the sale of plant	300
	420
Less consideration for the acquisition of Mary & Co	285
	135

(c) The net assets of Mary & Co were purchased on 3 March 20X7. Assets were valued as follows.

	$'000
Equity investments	231
Inventory	34
	265

All the inventory acquired was sold during 20X7. The equity investments were still held by Wislon at 31.12.X7. Goodwill has not been impaired in value.

(d) The property was acquired some years ago. The buildings element of the cost was estimated at $100,000 and the estimated useful life of the assets was fifty years at the time of purchase. As at 31 December 20X7 the property is to be revalued at $800,000.

(e) The plant which was sold had cost $350,000 and had a carrying amount of $274,000 as on 1.1.X7. $36,000 depreciation is to be charged on plant and machinery for 20X7.

(f)   The management wish to provide for:

    (i)   Loan note interest due

    (ii)   A transfer to general reserve of $16,000

    (iii)   Audit fees of $4,000

(g)   Inventory as at 31 December 20X7 was valued at $220,000 (cost).

(h)   50% of wages and salaries should be treated as distribution costs.

(i)   Taxation is to be ignored.

Required

Prepare statements of profit or loss and other comprehensive income and financial position for Wislon Co as at 31 December 20X7. You do not need to produce notes to the statements.

Answer

(a)   Normal adjustments are needed for accruals and prepayments (insurance, light and heat, loan note interest and audit fees). The loan note interest accrued is calculated as follows.

	$'000
Charge needed in profit or loss (10% × $200,000)	20
Amount paid so far, as shown in list of account balances	10
Accrual: presumably six months' interest now payable	10

The accrued expenses shown in the statement of financial position comprise:

	$'000
Loan note interest	10
Light and heat	3
Audit fee	4
	17

(b)   The misposting of $20,000 to light and heat is also adjusted, by reducing the light and heat expense, but charging $20,000 to salesmen's commission (distribution costs).

(c)   Depreciation on the building is calculated as $\dfrac{\$100,000}{50} = \$2,000$.

The carrying amount of the property is then $430,000 – $20,000 – $2,000 = $408,000 at the end of the year. When the property is revalued a surplus of $800,000 – $408,000 = $392,000 is recorded as other comprehensive income and credited to the revaluation reserve.

(d)   The profit on disposal of plant is calculated as proceeds $300,000 (per suspense account) less carrying amount $274,000, ie $26,000. The cost of the remaining plant is calculated at $830,000 – $350,000 = $480,000. The depreciation provision at the year end is:

	$'000
Balance 1.1.X7	222
Charge for 20X7	36
Less depreciation on disposals (350 – 274)	(76)
	182

(e)   Goodwill arising on the purchase of Mary & Co is:

	$'000
Consideration (per suspense account)	285
Assets at valuation	265
Goodwill	20

This is shown as an asset on the statement of financial position. The equity investments, being owned by Wislon at the year end, are also shown on the statement of financial position, whereas Mary's inventory, acquired and then sold, is added to the purchases figure for the year.

(f)   The other item in the suspense account is dealt with as follows.

	$'000
Proceeds of issue of 100,000 ordinary shares	120
Less nominal value 100,000 × 50c	50
Excess of consideration over par value (= share premium)	70

(g)   The transfer to general reserve increases it to $171,000 + $16,000 = $187,000.

We can now prepare the financial statements.

WISLON CO
STATEMENT OF PROFIT OR LOSS AND OTHER COMPREHENSIVE INCOME FOR THE YEAR ENDED 31 DECEMBER 20X7

	$'000
Revenue	2,695
Cost of sales (190 + 2,152 + 34 – 220)	(2,156)
Gross profit	539
Other income (profit on disposal of plant)	26
Distribution costs (254 × 50% + 20)	(147)
Administrative expenses (working)	(290)
Finance costs	(20)
Profit for the year	108
Other comprehensive income	
Gain on property revaluation	392
Total comprehensive income for the year	500

Workings

	$'000
Administrative expenses	
Wages, commission and salaries (254 × 50%)	127
Sundry expenses (113 – 6)	107
Light and heat (31 – 20 + 3)	14
Depreciation: buildings	2
plant	36
Audit fees	4
Total	290

WISLON CO
STATEMENT OF FINANCIAL POSITION AS AT 31 DECEMBER 20X7

	$'000	$'000
Assets		
Non-current assets		
Property, plant and equipment		
Property at valuation		800
Plant: cost	480	
accumulated depreciation	182	
		298
Goodwill		20
Equity investments		231
Current assets		
Inventory	220	
Trade receivables	179	
Prepayments	6	
Cash and cash equivalents	126	
		531
Total assets		1,880
Equity and liabilities		
Equity		
50c ordinary shares	400	
Share premium	70	
Revaluation surplus	392	
General reserve	187	
Retained earnings	319	
		1,468
Non-current liabilities		
10% loan stock (secured)		200
Current liabilities		
Trade payables	195	
Accrued expenses	17	
		212
Total equity and liabilities		1,880

WISLON CO
STATEMENT OF CHANGES IN EQUITY
FOR THE YEAR ENDED 31 DECEMBER 20X7

	Share capital $'000	Share premium $'000	Revaluation surplus $'000	General reserve $'000	Retained earnings $'000	Total $'000
At 1 January 20X7	450	–	–	171	235	856
Issue of share capital	50	70				120
Dividends					(8)	(8)
Total comprehensive income			392		108	500
Reserves transfer				16	(16)	–
Balance at 31 December 20X7	500	70	392	187	319	1,468

8 Other information in corporate reports

8.1 Directors' report

The directors' report provides additional information regarding the directors and their holdings in the company, details of share capital transactions and other significant matters of interest to shareholders and others.

Most published corporate reports include a directors' report. In many countries, (for example, the UK) this is a legal requirement. Company legislation normally states specifically what information must be included in the directors' report.

The directors' report is **largely a narrative report**, but certain figures must be included in it. **The purpose of the report is to give the users of accounts a more complete picture of the state of affairs of the company.**

The directors' report is normally **expected to contain a fair review of the development of the business of the company during that year and of its position at the end of it.** It may include details of:

(a)   The company's principal activities during the year and any significant changes compared to the previous year

     (i)   Any significant events after the reporting date

     (ii)   Likely future developments

     (iii)   Research and development activity (if any)

Information may also be included about:

(b)   **Directors** at any time during the financial year – their names and their shareholdings (including those of their families)

(c)   **Employees** (for example, policies in respect of disabled persons and action taken to provide employees with information on matters of concern to them)

(d)   The difference, if significant, between the book value and market value of land held as non-current assets

(e)   Political and charitable contributions

(f)   Purchases (if any) of its own shares

(g)   Dividends declared

8.2 The chairman's report

Most large companies include a **chairman's report** in their published financial statements. This is **purely voluntary** as there is no statutory requirement to do so.

The chairman's report is not governed by any regulations and is often unduly optimistic.

8.3 Management Commentary

The IASB recognises that general purpose financial statements meet the common needs of most users. However financial statements do not provide all of the information that users might need to make economic decisions. This is often due to the fact that the financial statements largely portray the financial effect of past events and also do not necessarily provide non-financial information.

To try to bridge the gap between what financial statements are able to show to users and the needs of these users, the IASB has issued an IFRS Practice Statement *Management Commentary*. This statement is non-mandatory guidance issued to develop the principles and essential content elements necessary to make management commentary reporting useful to users.

In the UK many listed companies now include an Operating and Financial Review (OFR) in their annual report. This is very similar to the IASB's *Management Commentary*. In the UK the ASB (now the FRC) issued a Reporting Statement Operating and Financial Review which sets out the principles regarded as best practice rather than a detailed checklist of disclosures.

The main recommendations of the Reporting Statement are summarised below.

8.3.1 Purpose

An Operating and Financial Review should be a balanced and comprehensive analysis, consistent with the size and complexity of the business, of:

(a)   The **development and performance** of the business of the entity during the financial year

(b)   The **position** of the entity at the end of the year

(c)   The **main trends and factors underlying the development, performance and position** of the business of the entity during the financial year

(d)   The main trends and factors which are likely to affect the entity's **future development**, performance and position, prepared so as to assist members to assess the strategies adopted by the entity and the potential for those strategies to succeed.

8.3.2 Principles

The statement sets out the following principles.

(a)   The OFR should set out the analysis of the business **through the eyes of the directors**.

(b)   The OFR should focus on matters that are of **interest to members**. Other users will be interested in the information, but members' needs must be paramount.

(c)   The OFR should have a **forward-looking orientation**, identifying those trends and factors relevant to the members' assessment of the current and future performance of the business and the progress towards the achievement of long-term business objectives. (The directors may warn readers to treat predictive information with caution.)

(d)   The OFR should **complement as well as supplement the financial statements** in order to enhance the overall corporate disclosure.

(e)   The OFR should be **comprehensive and understandable**. For example, it must consider whether omitting information might influence users of financial statements.

(f)   It should be **balanced and neutral** dealing evenhandedly with good and bad aspects.

(g)   It should be **comparable over time**.

8.3.3 Disclosure framework

The key elements of the disclosure framework are set out below.

(a)   The **nature, objectives and strategies** of the business. This includes a description of the business and the external environment in which it operates, the objectives to generate and preserve value over the longer term, the directors' strategies for achieving the objectives of the business and the inclusion of other performance indicators and evidence.

(b) The **development and performance of the business**, both in the period under review and in the future. This will focus on the business segments that are relevant to an understanding of the development and performance as a whole.

(c) The **resources, risks and uncertainties and relationships** that may affect the entity's long-term value. It will analyse the main trends and factors likely to impact future prospects, and describe the resources available, the principal risks and uncertainties faced by the entity and significant relationships with stakeholders.

(d) **Position of the business** including a description of the capital structure, treasury policies and objectives and liquidity of the entity (particularly cash flow), both in the period under review and the future.

8.3.4 Information required for disclosures

To the extent necessary to meet the requirements set out above, the OFR should include information about:

(a) Environmental matters (including the impact of the business of the entity on the environment)

(b) The entity's employees

(c) Social and community issues

(d) Persons with whom the entity has contractual or other arrangements which are essential to the business of the entity

(e) Receipts from, and returns to, members of the entity in respect of shares held by them

(f) All other matters the directors consider to be relevant

For items (a) to (c) the OFR should include the policies of the entity in relation to those matters and the extent to which they have been successively implemented.

8.3.5 Key performance indicators

An entity should provide information that enables investors to understand each Key Performance Indicator (KPI) disclosed in the OFR.

For each KPI disclosed in the OFR:

(a) The **definition and its calculation method** must be explained.

(b) Its **purpose** must be explained.

(c) The **source of underlying data** must be disclosed and, where relevant, **assumptions** explained.

(d) **Quantification or commentary** on future targets must be provided.

(e) Where information from the financial statements has been **adjusted** for inclusion in the OFR, that fact must be highlighted and a **reconciliation** provided.

(f) Where available, **corresponding amounts** for the financial year immediately preceding the current year must be disclosed.

(g) **Any changes to KPIs** must be disclosed and the calculation method used compared to previous periods, including significant changes in the underlying accounting policies adopted in the financial statements, must be identified and explained.

8.4 The importance of narrative information

Business is becoming **increasingly complex**. This means that **conventional financial statements may not communicate all the information** that a user might need to make an assessment of an entity's performance, position and future prospects.

For example, an entity's **performance may be about more than making a profit**. Shareholders and others may also be interested in the way in which its operations affect the natural environment and the wider community.

Similarly, **many entities depend on assets that are not recognised on the statement of financial position**. These may include research and development, specialised technical knowledge and human resources.

Narrative information such as the OFR is a useful way of helping users to 'put flesh on' the skeleton of details provided by the figures of the accounts themselves. It can also explain aspects of an entity's operations that would not normally be apparent from the financial statements alone. Unlike conventional financial statements, narrative reports can contain information which is forward looking, such as a description of the risks facing the entity and how these risks are managed.

However, narrative information **can present problems**. In practice the directors' report is often a rather dry and uninformative document, perhaps because it must be verified by the company's external auditors. Some companies still treat the OFR as a disclosure checklist or as simply a commentary on the financial statements.

Chapter roundup

- **Limited liability** offers various advantages to companies, although there are disadvantages as well.

- IAS 1 covers the **form and content** of financial statements.

- IAS 1 suggests a **format** for the statement of financial position.

- You should appreciate the distinction between **current and non-current** assets and liabilities and their different treatments.

- Once again, IAS 1 suggests formats for the statement of profit or loss and other comprehensive income.

- IAS 1 requires a statement of changes in equity.

- Some items need to be disclosed by way of note.

- The directors' report provides additional information regarding the directors and their holdings in the company, details of share capital transactions and other significant matters of interest to shareholders and others.

Quick quiz

1   Limited liability means that the shareholders of a company are not legally accountable.

    True   ☐

    False ☐

2   Which of the following are examples of current assets?

    (a)   Property, plant and equipment
    (b)   Prepayments
    (c)   Cash equivalents
    (d)   Manufacturing licences
    (e)   Retained earnings

3   Provisions must be disclosed on the face of the statement of financial position.

    True   ☐

    False ☐

4   Which of the following must be disclosed on the face of the statement of profit or loss and other comprehensive income?

    (a)   Tax expense
    (b)   Analysis of expenses
    (c)   Net profit or loss for the period.

5   *Fill in the blanks.*

    The accounting policies section of the notes describes:

    The ……… used in preparing the financial statements and………………………………… required for a proper understanding of the financial statements.

Answers to quick quiz

1 False. It means that if the company becomes insolvent, the maximum that an owner stands to lose is his share capital in the business.

2 (b) and (c) only

3 True

4 (a) and (c) only. (b) may be shown in the notes.

5 Measurement basis (or bases)
   Specific accounting policies

End of chapter question

Eat² (AIA November 2008)

Joe Salt is the finance director of a food wholesaler Eat² Ltd. The company's statement of profit or loss has always been prepared according to function; which is the traditional format allowed by IAS 1 *Presentation of financial statements*. Joe is now curious to see what the statement of profit or loss would look like if it was prepared according to the alternative method of presentation allowed by IAS 1 which allows information to be presented according to the nature of income and expense. The following shows extracts taken from Joe's accounts working papers for the year ended 31 December 20X7:

TRIAL BALANCE AS AT 31 DECEMBER 20X7	*Dr*	*Cr*
	€m	€m
Equity share capital		19.67
Retained earnings as at 1 January 20X7		2.75
Other reserves		0.80
Plant and equipment at cost	11.00	
Plant and equipment depreciation as at 1 January 20X7		2.45
Trade receivables	16.30	
Cash at bank	3.10	
Inventory at 1 January 20X7	3.30	
Trade payables		3.30
Sales		48.10
Purchases	25.00	
Returns inwards/outwards	1.35	1.25
Carriage inwards	0.45	
Administrative expenses	0.50	
Distribution expenses	0.30	
Warehouse employees' wages	5.05	
Salesmen's salaries	3.20	
Administrative employment costs	3.00	
Hire of delivery lorries	0.95	
Directors' salaries	1.50	
Finance costs	0.17	
Rent receivable		0.35
Dividends paid during the year	3.50	
	78.67	78.67

Notes

(i)   Auditor's fees of €100,000 have yet to be provided for.

(ii)   Inventory at 31 December 20X7 was valued at €4.5m.

(iii) It is estimated income tax of €2.9m will be payable on profits for the year.

(iv)   Plant and equipment is to be depreciated at 20% per annum on a straight-line basis.

(v)   It has been estimated that two-thirds of the plant and equipment is used for distribution with the remainder used for administration purposes.

(vi)   A provision of 2% is to be made for doubtful debts (allowance for receivables).

(vii) During the year the company capitalised €200,000 of wage costs of warehouse employees who were employed on the construction of new equipment.

Required

Prepare Eat² Ltd's statement of profit or loss for the year ended 31 December 20X7 to comply with the alternative method of presentation allowed by IAS 1.   **(15 marks)**

Distributable profits and capital transactions

4

Topic list	Syllabus reference
1 Revenue recognition	11.1
2 Distributable profits	11.1
3 Redemption of shares	11.1

Introduction

The topics in this chapter are relevant to all types of accounting transactions, providing a theoretical framework for the topics already covered and for accounting in general.

A great deal of national legislation governing distributions and capital transactions is concerned with protection of creditors; the aim is to prevent companies favouring shareholders over creditors.

1 Revenue recognition

FAST FORWARD

> **Revenue recognition** is straightforward in most business transactions, but some situations are more complicated.

1.1 Introduction

Accruals accounting is based on the **matching of costs with the revenue they generate**. It is crucially important under this convention that we can establish the point at which revenue may be recognised so that the correct treatment can be applied to the related costs. For example, the costs of producing an item of finished goods should be carried as an asset in the statement of financial position until such time as it is sold; they should then be written off as a charge to profit or loss. Which of these two treatments should be applied cannot be decided until it is clear at what moment the sale of the item takes place.

The decision has a **direct impact on profit** since it would be unacceptable to recognise the profit on sale until a sale had taken place in accordance with the criteria of revenue recognition.

Revenue is generally recognised as **earned at the point of sale**, because at that point four criteria will generally have been met.

(a)   The product or service has been **provided to the buyer**.

(b)   The buyer has **recognised his liability** to pay for the goods or services provided. The converse of this is that the seller has recognised that ownership of goods has passed from himself to the buyer.

(c)   The buyer has indicated his **willingness to hand over cash** or other assets in settlement of his liability.

(d)   The **monetary value** of the goods or services has been established.

At earlier points in the business cycle there will not in general be **firm evidence** that the above criteria will be met. Until work on a product is complete, there is a risk that some flaw in the manufacturing process will necessitate its writing off; even when the product is complete there is no guarantee that it will find a buyer.

At later points in the business cycle, for example when cash is received for the sale, the recognition of revenue may occur in a period later than that in which the related costs were charged. Revenue recognition would then depend on fortuitous circumstances, such as the cash flow of a company's customers, and might fluctuate misleadingly from one period to another.

However, there are times when revenue is **recognised at other times than at the completion of a sale,** for example, in the recognition of profit on long-term construction contracts. Under IAS 11 *Construction contracts* contract revenue and contract costs associated with the construction contract should be recognised as revenue and expenses respectively by reference to the stage of completion of the contract activity at the reporting date.

(a)   Owing to the length of time taken to complete such contracts, to defer taking profit into account until completion may result in the statement of profit or loss reflecting, not so much a fair view of the activity of the company during the year, but rather the results relating to contracts which have been completed by the year end.

(b)   Revenue in this case is recognised when production on, say, a section of the total contract is complete, even though no sale can be made until the whole is complete.

1.2 IAS 18 *Revenue*

IAS 18 governs the recognition of revenue in specific (common) types of transaction. Generally, recognition should be when it is probable that **future economic benefits** will flow to the entity and when these benefits can be **measured reliably**.

Income, as defined by the IASB's *Conceptual Framework* document, includes both revenues and gains. Revenue is income arising in the ordinary course of an entity's activities and it may be called different names, such as sales, fees, interest, dividends or royalties.

1.3 Scope

IAS 18 covers the revenue from specific types of transaction or events.

- **Sale of goods** (manufactured products and items purchased for resale)
- **Rendering of services**
- **Interest, royalties and dividends**

Key terms

> **Interest** is the charge for the use of cash or cash equivalents or amounts due to the entity.
>
> **Royalties** are charges for the use of non-current assets of the entity, eg patents, computer software and trademarks.
>
> **Dividends** are distributions of profit to holders of equity investments, in proportion with their holdings, of each relevant class of capital.

The Standard specifically **excludes** various types of revenue arising from leases, insurance contracts, changes in value of financial instruments or other current assets, natural increases in agricultural assets and mineral ore extraction.

1.4 Definitions

The following definitions are given in the Standard.

Key terms

> **Revenue** is the gross inflow of economic benefits during the period arising in the course of the ordinary activities of an **entity** when those inflows result in increases in equity, other than increases relating to contributions from equity participants.
>
> **Fair value** is the price that would be received to sell an asset or paid to transfer a liability in an orderly transaction between market participants at the measurement date. *(IAS 18 & IFRS 13)*

Revenue **does not include** sales taxes, value added taxes or goods and service taxes which are only collected for third parties, because these do not represent an economic benefit flowing to the entity. The same is true for revenues collected by an agent on behalf of a principal. Revenue for the agent is only the commission received for acting as agent.

1.5 Measurement of revenue

When a transaction takes place, the amount of revenue is usually decided by the **agreement of the buyer and seller**. The revenue is actually measured, however, as the **fair value of the consideration received**, which will take account of any trade discounts and volume rebates.

1.6 Identification of the transaction

Normally, each transaction can be looked at **as a whole**. Sometimes, however, transactions are more complicated, and it is necessary to break a transaction down into its **component parts**. For example, a sale may include the transfer of goods and the provision of future servicing, the revenue for which should be deferred over the period the service is performed.

At the other end of the scale, **seemingly separate transactions must be considered together** if apart they lose their commercial meaning. An example would be to sell an asset with an agreement to buy it back at a later date. The second transaction cancels the first and so both must be considered together.

1.7 Sale of goods

Revenue from the sale of goods should only be recognised when *all* these conditions are satisfied.

(a)   The entity has transferred the **significant risks and rewards** of ownership of the goods to the buyer

(b)   The entity has **no continuing managerial involvement** to the degree usually associated with ownership, and no longer has effective control over the goods sold

(c)   The amount of revenue can be **measured reliably**

(d)   It is probable that the **economic benefits** associated with the transaction will flow to the entity

(e)   The **costs incurred** in respect of the transaction can be measured reliably

The transfer of risks and rewards can only be decided by examining each transaction. Mainly, the transfer occurs at the same time as either the **transfer of legal title**, or the **passing of possession** to the buyer - this is what happens when you buy something in a shop.

If **significant risks and rewards remain with the seller**, then the transaction is *not* a sale and revenue cannot be recognised, for example if the receipt of the revenue from a particular sale depends on the buyer receiving revenue from his own sale of the goods.

It is possible for the seller to retain only an **'insignificant' risk of ownership** and for the sale and revenue to be recognised. The main example here is where the seller retains title only to ensure collection of what is owed on the goods. This is a common commercial situation, and when it arises the revenue should be recognised on the date of sale.

The probability of the entity receiving the revenue arising from a transaction must be assessed. It may only become probable that the economic benefits will be received when an uncertainty is removed, for example government permission for funds to be received from another country. Only when the uncertainty is removed should the revenue be recognised. This is in contrast with the situation where revenue has already been recognised but where the **collectability of the cash** is brought into doubt. Where recovery has ceased to be probable, the amount should be recognised as an expense, *not* an adjustment of the revenue previously recognised. These points also refer to services and interest, royalties and dividends below.

Matching should take place, ie the revenue and expenses relating to the same transaction should be recognised at the same time. It is usually easy to estimate expenses at the date of sale (eg warranty costs, shipment costs, etc). Where they cannot be estimated reliably, then revenue cannot be recognised; any consideration which has already been received is treated as a liability.

1.8 Rendering of services

When the outcome of a transaction involving the rendering of services can be estimated reliably, the associated revenue should be recognised by reference to the **stage of completion of the transaction** at the reporting date. The outcome of a transaction can be estimated reliably when *all* these conditions are satisfied.

(a)   The amount of revenue can be **measured reliably**

(b)   It is probable that the **economic benefits** associated with the transaction will flow to the entity

(c)   The **stage of completion** of the transaction at the reporting date can be measured reliably

(d)   The **costs incurred** for the transaction and the costs to complete the transaction can be measured reliably

The parties to the transaction will normally have to agree the following before an entity can make reliable estimates.

(a)   Each party's **enforceable rights** regarding the service to be provided and received by the parties

(b)   The **consideration** to be exchanged

(c)   The **manner and terms of settlement**

There are various methods of determining the stage of completion of a transaction, but for practical purposes, when services are performed by an indeterminate number of acts over a period of time, revenue should be recognised on a **straight-line basis** over the period, unless there is evidence for the use of a more appropriate method. If one act is of more significance than the others, then the significant act should be carried out *before* revenue is recognised.

In uncertain situations, when the outcome of the transaction involving the rendering of services cannot be estimated reliably, the Standard recommends a **no loss/no gain approach**. Revenue is recognised only to the extent of the expenses recognised that are recoverable.

This is particularly likely during the **early stages of a transaction**, but it is still probable that the entity will recover the costs incurred. So the revenue recognised in such a period will be equal to the expenses incurred, with no profit.

Obviously, if the costs are not likely to be reimbursed, then they must be recognised as an expense immediately. **When the uncertainties cease to exist**, revenue should be recognised as laid out in the first paragraph of this section.

1.9 Interest, royalties and dividends

When others use the entity's assets yielding interest, royalties and dividends, the revenue should be recognised on the bases set out below when:

(a)   It is probable that the **economic benefits** associated with the transaction will flow to the entity; *and*

(b)   The amount of the revenue can be **measured reliably**.

The revenue is recognised on the following bases.

(a)   **Interest** is recognised on a time proportion basis that takes into account the effective yield on the asset

(b)   **Royalties** are recognised on an accruals basis in accordance with the substance of the relevant agreement

(c)   **Dividends** are recognised when the shareholder's right to receive payment is established

The **effective yield** on an asset mentioned above is the rate of interest required to discount the stream of future cash receipts expected over the life of the asset to equate to the initial carrying amount of the asset.

Royalties are usually recognised on the same basis that they accrue **under the relevant agreement**. Sometimes the true substance of the agreement may require some other systematic and rational method of recognition.

Once again, the points made above about **probability and collectability** on sale of goods also apply here.

1.10 Disclosure

The following items should be disclosed.

(a)   The **accounting policies** adopted for the recognition of revenue, including the methods used to determine the stage of completion of transactions involving the rendering of services

(b)   The amount of each **significant category of revenue** recognised during the period including revenue arising from:

    (i)   The sale of goods
    (ii)   The rendering of services
    (iii)   Interest
    (iv)   Royalties
    (v)   Dividends

(c)   The amount of revenue arising from **exchanges of goods or services** included in each significant category of revenue

Any **contingent gains or losses**, such as those relating to warranty costs, claims or penalties should be treated according to IAS 37 *Provisions, contingent liabilities and contingent assets* (covered in your earlier studies and revised in Chapter 11).

Question   Recognition

Discuss under what circumstances, if any, revenue might be recognised at the following stages of a sale.

(a)   Goods are acquired by the business which it confidently expects to resell very quickly.
(b)   A customer places a firm order for goods.
(c)   Goods are delivered to the customer.
(d)   The customer is invoiced for goods.
(e)   The customer pays for the goods.
(f)   The customer's cheque in payment for the goods has been cleared by the bank.

![Answer]

(a) A sale must never be recognised before the goods have even been ordered by a customer. There is no certainty about the value of the sale, nor when it will take place, even if it is virtually certain that goods will be sold.

(b) A sale must never be recognised when the customer places an order. Even though the order will be for a specific quantity of goods at a specific price, it is not yet certain that the sale transaction will go through. The customer may cancel the order, the supplier might be unable to deliver the goods as ordered or it may be decided that the customer is not a good credit risk.

(c) A sale will be recognised when delivery of the goods is made only when:

   (i) The sale is for cash, and so the cash is received at the same time; *or*
   (ii) The sale is on credit and the customer accepts delivery (eg by signing a delivery note).

(d) The critical event for a credit sale is usually the despatch of an invoice to the customer. There is then a legally enforceable debt, payable on specified terms, for a completed sale transaction.

(e) The critical event for a cash sale is when delivery takes place and when cash is received; both take place at the same time.

   It would be over-cautious or 'prudent' to await cash payment for a credit sale transaction before recognising the sale, unless the customer is a high credit risk and there is a serious doubt about ability or intention to pay.

(f) It would again be over-cautious to wait for clearance of the customer's cheques before recognising sales revenue. Such a precaution would only be justified in cases where there is a very high risk of the bank refusing to honour the cheque.

2 Distributable profits

You need to be able to discuss the meaning of distributable and realisable profits.

2.1 Introduction

A **distribution** may be defined by national legislation, but we can state here that it is generally every description of distribution of a company's assets to members (shareholders) of the company, whether in cash or otherwise, with the following **exceptions**.

(a) An issue of **bonus shares**

(b) The **redemption or purchase of the company's own shares** out of capital (including the proceeds of a new issue) or out of unrealised profits

(c) The **reduction of share capital** by:

   (i) reducing the liability on shares in respect of share capital not fully paid up, *or*
   (ii) paying off paid-up share capital

(d) A distribution of assets to shareholders in a **winding up** of the company

In general, in most circumstances, **companies must not make a distribution except out of profits available for the purpose**. These available profits are:

(a) Its **accumulated realised profits**, insofar as these have not already been used for an earlier distribution or for 'capitalisation'

(b)   **Minus its accumulated realised losses**, insofar as these have not already been written off in a reduction or reconstruction scheme

Capital profits and revenue profits (if realised) are taken together and capital losses and revenue losses (if realised) are similarly grouped together. **Unrealised profits** cannot be distributed (for example, profit on the revaluation of non-current assets); nor must a company apply unrealised profits to pay up debentures or any unpaid amounts on issued shares.

Capitalisation of realised profits is the use of profits for one of two purposes.

(a)   To issue bonus shares

(b)   As a transfer to any reserve for the redemption of capital (a **capital redemption reserve**)

Some countries may impose **further restrictions on the distributions of all companies**, or perhaps listed companies or other public interest companies. For example, such a company may not be able to make a distribution if at the time either of these apply.

(a)   The amount of its net assets is less than the combined total of its called-up share capital plus its undistributable reserves.

(b)   The distribution will reduce the amount of its net assets to below the combined total of its called-up share capital plus its undistributable reserves.

'Undistributable reserves' are likely to include the following, although national legislation may dictate otherwise.

(a)   The **share premium account** (capital paid in excess of par)

(b)   Any reserve for the **redemption of capital**

(c)   Any **accumulated surplus** of unrealised profits over unrealised losses

(d)   Any **other reserve** which cannot be distributed, whether by statute, or the company's memorandum or articles of association (ie constitution)

Where such a restriction applies, all **accumulated distributable profits, both realised and unrealised, must exceed the accumulated realised and unrealised losses of the company** before any distribution can be made. The difference between the profits and losses is the maximum possible distribution.

In contrast with the basic definition of distributable profits, this restriction includes consideration of **unrealised** profits and losses, so that if unrealised losses exceed unrealised profits, the amount of distributions which can be made will be reduced by the amount of the 'deficit'.

2.2 Example: Basic distributable profits v special restrictions

Huddle Co is a private company and Publimco is a listed company. Both companies have a financial year ending on 31 December. On 31 December 20X5, the statements of financial position of the companies, by a remarkable coincidence, were identical, as follows.

	Huddle Co		Publimco	
	$'000	$'000	$'000	$'000
Net assets		365		365
Share capital		300		300
Share premium account		60		60
Unrealised losses on asset revaluations		(25)		(25)
Realised profits	50		50	
Realised losses	(20)		(20)	
		30		30
		365		365

What is the maximum distribution that each company can make, if Huddle Co's distributable profits follow the basic definition, but Publimco has special restrictions over its distributable profits as noted above?

Solution

(a)   The distributable profits of Huddle Co are $30,000.

(b)   The distributable profits of Publimco are further restricted to $30,000 – $25,000 = $5,000 (or alternatively, $365,000 – $300,000 – $60,000 = $5,000. This is the surplus of net assets over share capital plus undistributable reserves, which in this example are represented by the share premium account).

2.3 Realised and distributable profits

National legislation may define **realised profits** but in other countries the definition may not be clear. As a general 'rule of thumb' we can state that profits in the **statement of profit or loss** are realised, while amounts in other comprehensive income are **unrealised**.

IAS 1 *Presentation of financial statements* provides a framework for recognising realised profits. If IAS 1 is followed, profits in the statement of profit or loss will be realisable.

2.3.1 Exceptions

In the case of **sale of revalued non-current assets**, the **unrealised profit on revaluation** previously credited to the revaluation surplus may not pass through the statement of profit or loss. It may nevertheless be regarded as **distributable**, unless local legislation states otherwise.

Where an asset has been revalued, the **increase in depreciation charge** can be treated as a realised profit.

Development expenditure is a realised loss in the year in which it is incurred, except when the costs are capitalised within IAS 38 guidelines, in which case the costs are amortised as realised losses over a number of years.

Provisions are generally treated as realised losses.

2.4 The relevant accounts

Which accounts should be used to determine the distributable profits? These are the **most recent audited annual accounts** of the company, prepared in compliance with national standards and legislation, or IFRS. If the auditors have issued a modified opinion, the auditors must state in their report whether they consider that the proposed distribution would contravene any relevant legislation.

Companies may also be permitted to base a distribution on **interim accounts**, which need not be audited. However, in general, such interim accounts must be properly prepared and comply with IFRSs and show a true and fair view.

Question   Implications

Explain the implications of the following items to profits available for distribution in a company, based on the provisions of relevant IFRSs.

(a)   Research and development activities

(b)   Net deficit on a revaluation reserve arising from an overall deficit on the revaluation of non-current assets

(c)   Excess depreciation

(d)   Goodwill arising on consolidation

Answer

(a)   For the purposes of calculating realised profits, development expenditure carried forward in the statement of financial position should be treated as a realised loss. This means that development expenditure may not be regarded as part of net assets.

If, however, there are special circumstances which, in the opinion of the directors, justify the treatment of development expenditure as an asset and not as a loss, then this requirement need not apply. It is generally considered that, if the development expenditure qualifies for treatment as an asset under the provisions of IAS 38, then it may be treated as an asset and not a loss for the purposes of calculating distributable profits.

(b)   A revaluation reserve is a non-distributable reserve because it reflects unrealised profits and losses. An impairment in value causing an overall deficit on the revaluation reserve should be recognised in profit or loss, ie it is a realised loss and therefore reduces distributable profits.

(c)   Excess depreciation is the depreciation on revalued assets in excess of cost. Since excess depreciation is regarded as the realisation (through use) of part of the corresponding revaluation reserve, it is added back to profits available for distribution.

(d)   The normal treatment of such goodwill is to capitalise it but not amortise it. Instead an annual impairment review has to be carried out and any impairment charged to profit or loss.

Where this treatment is adopted, any amount written off for impairment is considered a realised loss and reduces distributable profits.

3 Redemption of shares

FAST FORWARD

You must be able to carry out **simple calculations** showing the amounts to be transferred to the **capital redemption reserve** on purchase or redemption of own shares, how the amount of any **premium** on redemption would be treated, and how much the **permissible capital payment** would be for a company.

3.1 Introduction

Limited liability companies may be permitted to cancel unissued shares and in that way reduce their **authorised** share capital. That change does not alter the financial position of any company.

If a limited liability company wishes to **reduce its issued share capital** (and incidentally its authorised capital of which the issued capital is part) it may do so provided that certain conditions are met (set by national legislation). For example:

(a)   It must have the power to do so in its **articles** of association
(b)   It must pass a **special resolution**
(c)   It must obtain **confirmation** of the reduction **from the court**

Requirement (a) is usually a matter of procedure. Articles usually contain the necessary power. If not, the company in general meeting would first pass a special resolution to alter the articles appropriately and then proceed to pass a special resolution to reduce the capital.

There are various basic methods of reducing share capital, and three of the most common are discussed here.

(a) **Extinguish or reduce liability on partly paid shares**. A company may have issued $1 (par) shares 75c paid up. The outstanding liability of 25c per share may be eliminated altogether by reducing each share to 75c (par) fully paid or some intermediate figure, eg 80c (par) 75c paid. Nothing is returned to the shareholders but the company gives up a claim against them for money which it could call up whenever needed.

(b) **Cancel paid up share capital which has been lost or which is no longer represented by available assets**. Suppose that the issued shares are $1 (par) fully paid but the net assets now represent a value of only 50c per share. The difference is probably matched by a debit balance on the retained reserves. The company could reduce the par value of its $1 shares to 50c (or some intermediate figure) and apply the amount to write off the debit balance wholly or in part. It would then be able to resume payment of dividends out of future profits without being obliged to make good past losses. The resources of the company are not reduced by this procedure of part cancellation of nominal value of shares but it avoids having to rebuild lost capital by retaining profits.

(c) **Pay off part of the paid up share capital out of surplus assets**. The company might repay to shareholders, say, 30c in cash per $1 share by reducing the par value of the share to 70c. This reduces the assets of the company by 30c per share.

3.2 Role of court in reduction of capital

In many countries the sanction of the court (or equivalent) may be required for a redemption of shares or reduction in capital. The purpose here is **creditor protection**. The reduction in capital must not put at risk a company's ability to pay its debts. If it did so, then shareholders would be favoured over creditors for distributions from the company. Creditors may be allowed to petition the court against the proposed transaction, but the company may be able to override this by paying off its creditors. The details will vary from country to country.

3.3 Share premium account

Whenever a company obtains for its shares a consideration in excess of their par value, it must usually transfer the excess to a share premium account (capital in excess of par account). The general rule is that the **share premium account is subject to the same restrictions as share capital**. However, it may be possible to make a bonus issue using the share premium account (reducing share premium in order to increase issued share capital).

Examples of the **other likely permitted uses of share premium** are to pay:

(a) Capital expenses such as preliminary expenses of forming the company
(b) A discount on the issue of shares or debentures
(c) A premium (if any) paid on redemption of debentures

Some companies may also be able to use a share premium account in purchasing or redeeming their own shares out of capital. It must be emphasised that these rules will vary from country to country according to national legislation.

3.4 Redemption or purchase by a company of its own shares

In some countries, there is a **general prohibition** against any voluntary acquisition by a company of its own shares. In other countries, it is possible for a company to voluntarily acquire and keep its own shares, although there may be a limit on the time for which they can be held. For the rest of the chapter, however, we will assume that any of its own shares purchased by a company cannot be held and must be **cancelled immediately**.

Even where purchase of own shares is prohibited, there may be **exceptions**. For example, a company may:

(a)   Purchase its own shares in compliance with an **order of the court**

(b)   Issue **redeemable shares** and then redeem them

(c)   Purchase its own shares under certain **specified procedures**

(d)   **Forfeit** or accept the surrender of its shares

(e)   Accept shares as a **gift**

There may be **conditions** for the issue and redemption of redeemable shares. Again these will vary from country to country, but these are good examples of the likely rules.

(a)   The **articles** must give authority for the issue of redeemable shares. Articles do usually provide for it, but if they do not, the articles must be altered before the shares are issued.

(b)   **Redeemable shares** may only be issued if at the time of issue the company also has issued shares which are not redeemable: a company's capital may not consist entirely of redeemable shares.

(c)   Redeemable shares may only be redeemed if they are **fully paid**.

(d)   The terms of redemption must **provide for payment on redemption**.

(e)   The shares may be redeemed out of **distributable profits**, or the proceeds of a new issue of shares, or capital (this may be restricted for some special companies) in accordance with the relevant rules.

(f)   Any **premium payable** on redemption must be provided out of distributable profits (subject to any exceptions).

One way to preserve reserves for creditor protection is to prevent companies from redeeming shares except by transferring a sum equal to the par value of shares redeemed from distributable profit reserves to a non-distributable reserve, which here we will call the '**capital redemption reserve**'. This reduction in distributable reserves is an example of the **capitalisation of profits**, where previously distributable profits become undistributable.

Such regulations prevent companies from reducing their share capital investment so as to put creditors of the company at risk.

3.5 Example: Capitalisation of profits

Suppose, for example, that Muffin Co had $100,000 of preferred shares, redeemable in the very near future at par. A statement of financial position of the company is currently as follows.

	$	$
Assets		
Cash		100,000
Other assets		300,000
		400,000
Equity and liabilities		
Equity		
Ordinary shares	30,000	
Retained earnings	150,000	
		180,000
Liabilities		
Redeemable preferred shares	100,000	
Trade accounts payable	120,000	
		220,000
		400,000

Now if Muffin were able to redeem the preferred shares without making any transfer from the retained earnings to a capital redemption reserve, the effect of the share redemption on the statement of financial position would be as follows.

	$
Assets	
Non-cash assets	300,000
Equity and liabilities	
Equity	
Ordinary shares	30,000
Retained earnings	150,000
	180,000
Trade accounts payable	120,000
	300,000

In this example, the company would still be able to pay dividends out of profits of up to $150,000. If it did, the creditors of the company would be highly vulnerable, financing $120,000 out of a total of $150,000 assets of the company.

Regulations suggested above will prevent such extreme situations arising. On redemption of the preferred shares, Muffin would have been required to transfer $100,000 from its retained earnings to a non-distributable reserve, called here a capital redemption reserve. The effect of the redemption of shares on the statement of financial position would have been:

	$	$
Assets		
Non-cash assets		300,000
Equity and liabilities		
Equity		
Ordinary shares	30,000	
Reserves		
Distributable (retained earnings)	50,000	
Non-distributable (capital redemption reserve)	100,000	
		180,000
Trade accounts payable		120,000
		300,000

The maximum distributable profits are now $50,000. If Muffin paid all these as a dividend, there would still be $250,000 of assets left in the company, just over half of which would be financed by non-distributable equity capital.

3.6 Further possible rules

When a company redeems some shares, or purchases some of its own shares, they should normally be redeemed:

(a)   **Out of distributable profits**
(b)   **Out of the proceeds** of a new issue of shares

In addition, if there is any premium on redemption, it may be the rule that **the premium must be paid out of distributable profits**, except that if the shares were issued at a premium, then any premium payable on their redemption may be paid out of the proceeds of a new share issue made for the purpose, up to an amount equal to the lesser of:

(a)   The aggregate premiums received on issue of the redeemable shares
(b)   The balance on the share premium account (including premium on issue of the new shares)

This may seem complicated, but it makes logical sense. A numerical example might help.

3.7 Example: Redemption of shares

Suppose that Jingle Co intends to redeem 10,000 shares of $1 each at a premium of 5 cents per share. The redemption must be financed in one of the following ways.

(a)   Out of distributable profits (10,000 × $1.05 = $10,500).

(b)   Out of the proceeds of a new share issue (say, by issuing 10,000 new $1 shares at par). The premium of $500 must be paid out of distributable profits.

(c)   Out of a combination of a new share issue and distributable profits.

(d)   Out of the proceeds of a new share issue where the redeemable shares were issued at a premium. For example, if the redeemable shares had been issued at a premium of 3c per share, then (assuming that the balance on the share premium account after the new share issue was at least $300) $300 of the premium on redemption could be debited to the share premium account and only $200 need be debited to distributable profits.

The following rules may also assist.

(a)   Where a company redeems shares or purchases its own shares wholly out of distributable profits, it must transfer to the capital redemption reserve an amount equal to the par value of the shares redeemed.

In example (a) above the accounting entries would be:

		$	$
DEBIT	Share capital account	10,000	
	Retained earnings (premium on redemption)	500	
CREDIT	Cash		10,500
DEBIT	Retained earnings	10,000	
CREDIT	Capital redemption reserve		10,000

(b)   Where a company redeems shares or purchases its shares wholly or partly out of the proceeds of a new share issue, it must transfer to the capital redemption reserve an amount by which the par value of the shares redeemed exceeds the **aggregate** proceeds from the new issue (ie par value of new shares issued plus share premium).

In example (b) the accounting entries would be:

		$	$
DEBIT	Share capital account (redeemed shares)	10,000	
	Retained earnings (premium)	500	
CREDIT	Cash (redemption of shares)		10,500
DEBIT	Cash (from new issue)	10,000	
CREDIT	Share capital account		10,000

No credit to the capital redemption reserve is necessary because there is no decrease in the creditors' buffer.

(c) If the redemption in the same example as in (b) were made by issuing 5,000 new $1 shares at par, and paying $5,500 out of distributable profits:

		$	$
DEBIT	Share capital account (redeemed shares)	10,000	
	Retained earnings (premium)	500	
CREDIT	Cash (redemption of shares)		10,500
DEBIT	Cash (from new issue)	5,000	
CREDIT	Share capital account		5,000
DEBIT	Retained earnings	5,000	
CREDIT	Capital redemption reserve		5,000

(d) In the example (d) above (assuming a new issue of 10,000 $1 shares at a premium of 8c per share) the accounting entries would be:

		$	$
DEBIT	Cash (from new issue)	10,800	
CREDIT	Share capital account		10,000
	Share premium account		800
DEBIT	Share capital account (redeemed shares)	10,000	
	Share premium account	300	
	Retained earnings	200	
CREDIT	Cash (redemption of shares)		10,500

No capital redemption reserve is required, as in (b) above. The redemption is financed entirely by a new issue of shares.

3.8 Commercial reasons for altering capital structure

These include the following.

- Greater **security of finance**
- Better **image** for third parties
- A **'neater' statement of financial position**
- **Borrowing repaid** sooner
- **Cost of borrowing** reduced

Question	Purchase of own shares

Set out below are the summarised statements of financial position of A Co and B Co at 30 June 20X5.

	A $'000	B $'000
Net assets	520	380
Capital and reserves		
Called up share capital $1 ordinary shares	300	300
Share premium account	60	60
Retained earnings	160	20
	520	380

On 1 July 20X5 A Co and B Co each purchased 50,000 of their own ordinary shares as follows.

A Co purchased its own shares at 150c each. The shares were originally issued at a premium of 20c. The redemption was partly financed by the issue at par of 5,000 10% redeemable preferred shares of $1 each.

B Co purchased its own shares out of capital at a price of 80c each.

A Co can only purchase its own shares using distributable profits.

B Co can purchase its own shares out of capital. All shares must be cancelled on purchase.

Required

Prepare the summarised statements of financial position of A Co and B Co at 1 July 20X5 immediately after the above transactions have been effected.

Answer

Workings for A Co

	$	$
Cost of redemption (50,000 × $1.50)		75,000
Premium on redemption (50,000 × 50c)		25,000
No premium arises on the new issue.		
Distributable profits		
Retained earnings before redemption		160,000
Premium on redemption (must come out of distributable		
profits, no premium on new issue)		(25,000)
		135,000
Remainder of redemption costs	50,000	
Proceeds of new issue 5,000 × $1	(5,000)	
Remainder out of distributable profits		(45,000)
Balance on retained earnings		90,000
Transfer to capital redemption reserve		
Par value of shares redeemed		50,000
Proceeds of new issue		(5,000)
Balance on CRR		45,000

STATEMENT OF FINANCIAL POSITION OF A CO AS AT 1 JULY 20X5

	$'000
Net assets	450
Equity	
Ordinary shares	250
Share premium	60
Capital redemption reserve	45
	355
Retained earnings	90
	445
Liability: preferred shares	5
	450

	$
Workings for B Co	
Cost of redemption (50,000 × 80c)	40,000
Discount on redemption (50,000 × 20c)	10,000
Cost of redemption	40,000
Distributable profits	(20,000)
Permissible capital payment (PCP)	20,000
Transfer to capital redemption reserve	
Par value of shares redeemed	50,000
PCP	20,000
Balance on capital redemption reserve	30,000

STATEMENT OF FINANCIAL POSITION OF B CO AS AT 1 JULY 20X5

	$'000
Net assets	340
Equity	
Ordinary shares	250
Share premium	60
Capital redemption reserve	30
	340

Chapter roundup

- **Revenue recognition** is straightforward in most business transactions, but some situations are more complicated.

- You need to be able to discuss the meaning of distributable and realisable profits.

- You must be able to carry out **simple calculations** showing the amounts to be transferred to the **capital redemption reserve** on purchase or redemption of own shares, how the amount of any **premium** on redemption would be treated, and how much the **permissible capital payment** would be for a company.

Quick quiz

1   To which purposes can a share premium account normally be applied?

(i)   Writing off share/debenture issue expenses
(ii)   Paying a premium on redemption
(iii)   Issuing fully paid bonus shares to members

Which is correct?

A   (i) and (ii)
B   (i) and (iii)
C   (ii) and (iii)
D   All the above

2   Revenue recognition is governed by IAS ....

3   What are the profits generally available for distribution?

4   A company cannot make a distribution if this will reduce its net assets to below the value of its called up share capital plus undistributable reserves.

True   ☐

False   ☐

5   If a company has not got the power to reduce its issued share capital, per the articles of association, then it can never do so.

True   ☐

False   ☐

6   A company can redeem shares out of which sources of funds?

(i)   Distributable profits
(ii)   Proceeds of new shares
(iii)   The share premium account

A   All three
B   (i) and (ii)
C   (ii) and (iii)
D   (i) and (iii)

BPP
LEARNING MEDIA

Answers to quick quiz

1   D (see Section 3.3)

2   18

3   See Section 2.1

4   True

5   False, it can pass a special resolution to change the articles.

6   B   Only if specifically permitted by local statute can a company redeem shares out of capital (share premium account).

End of chapter question

Revenue recognition (AIA May 2007)

Nanotech plc operates in the technology, hardware and equipment sector and has three very distinct business segments:

- Wholesale
- Franchise
- Publications

Recently, the directors of the company have become concerned about increasing criticism of their revenue recognition policies and have asked you to investigate. The company's year end is 31 March 20X7.

The following transactions and agreements have been selected at random; one from each of the company's operating segments:

Wholesale

On 1 January 20X7 the company signed an agreement with Asteroid plc, a retailer, to sell inventory (cost €100,000) for €150,000. This equipment is at the cutting edge of technology and Asteroid wishes to use it mainly for display purposes. For this reason, Nanotech has stipulated in the agreement that it has the option to repurchase the equipment at any time within the next year, if deemed appropriate, for €180,000.

Franchise

Nanotech plc owns the rights to the GigaSpace franchise. This is a collection of retail outlets specialising in the sale of high-tech hardware and equipment to the public. On 1 April 20X6, a Mr Radstone successfully applied to open a new GigaSpace shop in Paris. It was agreed that Nanotech was to be paid a fee of €250,000 for the first year and €27,000 per annum for the remaining 4 years of the franchise's life. Nanotech undertook to provide product related services at a cost of €40,000 per annum throughout the life of the contract. Under normal conditions these services would have a resale value of €48,000.

Publications

On 1 January 20X7, the Company began publication of a new monthly news-report Nannytek. On that day the Company received advance annual subscriptions of €180,000. The intention was that Nannytek would be produced and sold monthly and by the year-end 3 editions had been published. The cost of each edition was approximately €10,000.

Required

Explain how the above three events should be reported in the Nanotech financial statements for the year ended 31 March 20X7; indicating where appropriate the impact of the IASB's *Conceptual Framework*.

(25 marks)

Reporting financial performance

Introduction

IAS 8 deals with accounting policies. It also looks at certain circumstances and transactions which require different treatment to normal profit or loss items.

IFRS 5 on assets held for sale and discontinued operations is an important standard which gives users additional information regarding the sources of the entity's profit and losses.

1 IAS 8 *Accounting policies, changes in accounting estimates and errors*

FAST FORWARD

> IAS 8 deals with the treatment of **changes in accounting estimates, changes in accounting policies and errors**, as defined below.

1.1 Definitions

The following definitions are given in the Standard.

Key terms

> **Accounting policies** are the specific principles, bases, conventions, rules and practices adopted by an entity in preparing and presenting financial statements.
>
> A **change in accounting estimate** is an adjustment of the carrying amount of an asset or a liability or the amount of the periodic consumption of an asset, that results from the assessment of the present status of, and expected future benefits and obligations associated with, assets and liabilities. Changes in accounting estimates result from new information or new developments and, accordingly, are not corrections of errors.
>
> **Material**: as defined in IAS 1 (see Chapter 3)
>
> **Prior period errors** are omissions from, and misstatements in, the entity's financial statements for one or more prior periods arising from a failure to use, or misuse of, reliable information that:
>
> - Was available when financial statements for those periods were authorised for issue, *and*
>
> - Could reasonably be expected to have been obtained and taken into account in the preparation and presentation of those financial statements.
>
> Such errors include the effects of mathematical mistakes, mistakes in applying accounting policies, oversights or misinterpretations of facts, and fraud.
>
> **Retrospective application** is applying a new accounting policy to transactions, other events and conditions as if that policy had always been applied.
>
> **Retrospective restatement** is correcting the recognition, measurement and disclosure of amounts of elements of financial statements as if a prior period error had never occurred.
>
> **Prospective application** of a change in accounting policy and of recognising the effect of a change in an accounting estimate, respectively, are:
>
> - Applying the new accounting policy to transactions, other events and conditions occurring after the date as at which the policy is changed; *and*
>
> - Recognising the effect of the change in the accounting estimate in the current and future periods affected by the change.
>
> **Impracticable**. Applying a requirement is impracticable when the entity cannot apply it after making every reasonable effort to do so. It is impracticable to apply a change in an accounting policy retrospectively or to make a retrospective restatement to correct an error if one of the following apply.
>
> - The effects of the retrospective application or retrospective restatement are not determinable.
>
> - The retrospective application or retrospective restatement requires assumptions about what management's intent would have been in that period.

- The retrospective application or retrospective restatement requires significant estimates of amounts and it is impossible to distinguish objectively information about those estimates that:
  - Provides evidence of circumstances that existed on the date(s) at which those amounts are to be recognised, measured or disclosed; *and*
  - Would have been available when the financial statements for that prior period were authorised for issue, from other information. *(IAS 8)*

2 Accounting policies

FAST FORWARD

Accounting policies must be applied consistently for similar transactions.

Accounting policies are determined by **applying the relevant IFRS or IFRIC** and considering any relevant Implementation Guidance issued by the IASB for that IFRS/IFRIC.

Where there is no applicable IFRS or IFRIC management should use its **judgement** in developing and applying an accounting policy that results in information that is **relevant** and **reliable**. Management should refer to:

(a) The requirements and guidance in IFRSs and IFRICs dealing with **similar** and **related issues**, *and*

(b) The definitions, recognition criteria and measurement concepts for assets, liabilities and expenses in the *Conceptual Framework*

Management may also consider the most recent pronouncements of **other standard setting bodies** that use a similar conceptual framework, other accounting literature and accepted industry practices if these do not conflict with the sources above.

An entity must select and apply its accounting policies for a period **consistently** for similar transactions, other events and conditions, unless an IFRS or an IFRIC specifically requires or permits categorisation of items for which different policies may be appropriate. If an IFRS or an IFRIC requires or permits categorisation of items, an appropriate accounting policy must be selected and applied consistently to each category.

3 Changes in accounting policies

FAST FORWARD

Changes in accounting policies are applied retrospectively.

3.1 Introduction

The same accounting policies are usually adopted from period to period, to allow users to analyse trends over time in profit, cash flows and financial position. **Changes in accounting policy will therefore be rare** and should be made only if:

(a) The change is required by an **IFRS**

(b) If the change will result in a **more appropriate presentation** of events or transactions in the financial statements of the entity, providing more reliable and relevant information

The Standard highlights two types of event **which do not constitute changes in accounting policy**.

(a)   Adopting an accounting policy for a **new type of transaction** or event not dealt with previously by the entity

(b)   Adopting a **new accounting policy** for a transaction or event which has not occurred in the past or which was not material

In the case of tangible non-current assets, if a policy of revaluation is adopted for the first time then this is treated, not as a change of accounting policy under IAS 8, but as a revaluation under IAS 16 *Property, plant and equipment.*

3.2 Adoption of an IAS/IFRS

Where a new IFRS is adopted, IAS 8 requires any transitional provisions in the new IFRS itself to be followed. If none are given in the IFRS which is being adopted, then you should follow the general principles of IAS 8.

3.3 Other changes in accounting policy

IAS 8 requires **retrospective application**, *unless* it is **impracticable** to determine the cumulative amount of change. **Retrospective application** means that the new accounting policy is applied to transactions and events as if it had always been in use. In other words, at the earliest date such transactions or events occurred, the policy is applied from that date. Any resulting adjustment should be reported as an adjustment to the opening balance of retained earnings. Comparative information should be restated unless it is impracticable to do so.

This means that all comparative information must be restated **as if the new policy had always been in force**, with amounts relating to earlier periods reflected in an adjustment to opening reserves of the earliest period presented.

Prospective application is allowed only when it is **impracticable** to determine the cumulative effect of the change (see Key Terms).

3.4 Disclosure

Certain **disclosures** are required when a change in accounting policy has a material effect on the current period or any prior period presented, or when it may have a material effect in subsequent periods.

(a)   Reasons for the change

(b)   Amount of the adjustment for the current period and for each period presented

(c)   Amount of the adjustment relating to periods prior to those included in the comparative information

(d)   The fact that comparative information has been restated or that it is impracticable to do so

An entity should also disclose information relevant to assessing the **impact of new IFRS** on the financial statements where these have **not yet come into force**.

3.5 Presentation of comparatives

IAS 1 revised requires that where an accounting policy is retrospectively applied, a statement of financial position must be presented as at the beginning of the earliest comparative period.

This requirement means that a set of financial statements will include three statements of financial position where there is a change in accounting policy in the period.

4 Changes in accounting estimates

Changes in accounting estimates are not applied retrospectively.

Estimates arise in relation to business activities because of the **uncertainties inherent within them**. Judgements are made based on the most up to date information and the use of such estimates is a necessary part of the preparation of financial statements. It does *not* undermine their reliability. Here are some examples of accounting estimates.

(a) A necessary **doubtful debt provision (allowance for receivables)**
(b) **Useful lives** of depreciable assets
(c) Provision for **obsolescence of inventory**

The rule here is that the **effect of a change in an accounting estimate** should be included in the determination of net profit or loss in one of:

(a) The period of the change, if the change affects that period only
(b) The period of the change *and* future periods, if the change affects both

Changes may occur in the circumstances which were in force at the time the estimate was calculated, or perhaps additional information or subsequent developments have come to light.

An example of a change in accounting estimate which affects only the **current period** is the doubtful debt estimate. However, a revision in the life over which an asset is depreciated would affect both the **current and future periods**, in the amount of the depreciation expense.

Reasonably enough, the effect of a change in an accounting estimate should be included in the **same expense classification** as was used previously for the estimate. This rule helps to ensure **consistency** between the financial statements of different periods.

The **materiality** of the change is also relevant. The nature and amount of a change in an accounting estimate that has a material effect in the current period (or which is expected to have a material effect in subsequent periods) should be disclosed. If it is not possible to quantify the amount, this impracticability should be disclosed.

5 Errors

Material errors relating to a prior period must be corrected retrospectively.

5.1 Introduction

Errors discovered during a current period which **relate to a prior period** may arise through:

(a) Mathematical mistakes
(b) Mistakes in the application of accounting policies
(c) Misinterpretation of facts
(d) Oversights
(e) Fraud

A more formal definition is given in the Key Terms in Section 1.1.

Most of the time these errors can be **corrected through profit or loss for the current period**. Where they are material prior period errors, however, this is not appropriate. The Standard considers two possible treatments.

5.2 Accounting treatment

Retrospective correction

This involves either:

(a) Restating the comparative amounts for the prior period(s) in which the error occurred

(b) When the error occurred before the earliest prior period presented, restating the opening balances of assets, liabilities and equity for that period

so that the financial statements are presented **as if the error had never occurred**.

Where this method of correction is applied, IAS 1 revised requires that a statement of financial position is presented at the start of the earliest comparative period.

Prospective correction

Only where it is **impracticable** to determine the cumulative effect of an error on prior periods can an entity correct an error **prospectively**.

Various **disclosures** are required.

(a) **Nature** of the prior period error

(b) For each prior period, to the extent practicable, the **amount** of the correction

    (i) For each financial statement line item affected
    (ii) If IAS 33 applies, for basic and diluted earnings per share

(c) The amount of the correction at the **beginning of the earliest prior period** presented

(d) If **retrospective restatement is impracticable** for a particular prior period, the **circumstances** that led to the existence of that condition and a description of how and from when the error has been corrected. Subsequent periods need not repeat these disclosures

Question	Error

During 20X7 Global discovered that certain items had been included in inventory at 31 December 20X6, valued at $4.2m, which had in fact been sold before the year end. The following figures for 20X6 (as reported) and 20X7 (draft) are available.

	20X6	20X7 (draft)
	$'000	$'000
Sales	47,400	67,200
Cost of goods sold	(34,570)	(55,800)
Profit before taxation	12,830	11,400
Income taxes	(3,880)	(3,400)
Net profit	8,950	8,000

Retained earnings at 1 January 20X6 were $13m. The cost of goods sold for 20X7 includes the $4.2m error in opening inventory. The income tax rate was 30% for 20X6 and 20X7. No dividends have been declared or paid.

Required

Show the statement of profit or loss for 20X7, with the 20X6 comparative, and retained earnings.

Answer

STATEMENT OF PROFIT OR LOSS

	20X6 $'000	20X7 $'000
Sales	47,400	67,200
Cost of goods sold (W1)	(38,770)	(51,600)
Profit before tax	8,630	15,600
Income tax (W2)	(2,620)	(4,660)
Profit for the year	6,010	10,940

RETAINED EARNINGS

	20X6 $'000	20X7 $'000
Opening retained earnings		
As previously reported	13,000	21,950
Correction of prior period error (4,200 – 1,260)	–	(2,940)
As restated	13,000	19,010
Profit for year	6,010	10,940
Closing retained earnings	19,010	29,950

Workings

1	Cost of goods sold	20X6 $'000	20X7 $'000
	As stated in question	34,570	55,800
	Inventory adjustment	4,200	(4,200)
		38,770	51,600

2	Income tax	20X6 $'000	20X7 $'000
	As stated in question	3,880	3,400
	Inventory adjustment (4,200 × 30%)	(1,260)	1,260
		2,620	4,660

6 IFRS 5 *Non-current assets held for sale and discontinued operations*

FAST FORWARD IFRS 5 requires assets 'held for sale' to be presented separately in the statement of financial position.

6.1 Background

IFRS 5 is the result of a short-term convergence project with the US Financial Accounting Standards Board (FASB).

IFRS 5 requires assets and groups of assets that are 'held for sale' to be **presented separately** in the statement of financial position and the results of discontinued operations to be presented separately in the statement of profit or loss and other comprehensive income . This is required so that users of financial statements will be better able to make **projections** about the financial position, profits and cash flows of the entity.

Key term

> **Disposal group.** A group of assets to be disposed of, by sale or otherwise, together as a group in a single transaction, and liabilities directly associated with those assets that will be transferred in the transaction. (In practice a disposal group could be a subsidiary, a cash-generating unit or a single operation within an entity.)
>
> (*IFRS 5*)

IFRS 5 does not apply to certain assets covered by other accounting standards including:

- Deferred tax assets (IAS 12)
- Financial assets (IAS 39)
- Investment properties accounted for in accordance with the fair value model (IAS 40)

6.2 Classification of assets held for sale

A non-current asset (or disposal group) should be classified as **held for sale** if its carrying amount will be recovered **principally through a sale transaction** rather than **through continuing use**. A number of detailed criteria must be met:

(a)   The asset must be **available for immediate sale** in its present condition

(b)   Its sale must be **highly probable** (ie, significantly more likely than not)

For the sale to be highly probable, the following must apply.

(a)   Management must be **committed** to a plan to sell the asset.

(b)   There must be an active programme to **locate a buyer**.

(c)   The asset must be marketed for sale at a **price that is reasonable** in relation to its current fair value.

(d)   The sale should be expected to take place **within one year** from the date of classification.

(e)   It is unlikely that significant changes to the plan will be made or that the plan will be withdrawn.

An asset (or disposal group) can still be classified as held for sale, even if the sale has not actually taken place within one year. However, the delay must have been **caused by events or circumstances beyond the entity's control** and there must be sufficient evidence that the entity is still committed to sell the asset or disposal group. Otherwise the entity must cease to classify the asset as held for sale.

If an entity acquires a disposal group (eg a subsidiary) exclusively with a view to its subsequent disposal it can classify the asset as held for sale only if the sale is expected to take place within one year and it is highly probable that all the other criteria will be met within a short time (normally three months).

An asset that is to be **abandoned** should not be classified as held for sale. This is because its carrying amount will be recovered principally through continuing use. However, a disposal group to be abandoned may meet the definition of a discontinued operation and therefore separate disclosure may be required (see below).

Question   Held for sale

On 1 December 20X3, a company became committed to a plan to sell a manufacturing facility and has already found a potential buyer. The company does not intend to discontinue the operations currently carried out in the facility. At 31 December 20X3 there is a backlog of uncompleted customer orders. The company will not be able to transfer the facility to the buyer until after it ceases to operate the facility and has eliminated the backlog of uncompleted customer orders. This is not expected to occur until Spring 20X4.

Required

Can the manufacturing facility be classified as 'held for sale' at 31 December 20X3?

Answer

The facility will not be transferred until the backlog of orders is completed; this demonstrates that the facility is not available for immediate sale in its present condition. The facility cannot be classified as 'held for sale' at 31 December 20X3. It must be treated in the same way as other items of property, plant and equipment: it should continue to be depreciated and should not be separately disclosed.

6.3 Measurement of assets held for sale

Key terms

> **Fair value.** The price that would be received to sell an asset or paid to transfer a liability in an orderly transaction between market participants at the measurement date.
>
> **Costs to sell.** The incremental costs directly attributable to the disposal of an asset (or disposal group), excluding finance costs and income tax expense.
>
> **Recoverable amount.** The higher of an asset's fair value less costs of disposal and its value in use.
>
> **Value in use.** The present value of estimated future cash flows expected to arise from the continuing use of an asset and from its disposal at the end of its useful life.

A non-current asset (or disposal group) that is held for sale should be measured at the **lower of** its **carrying amount** and **fair value less costs to sell**. Fair value less costs to sell is equivalent to net realisable value.

IFRS 5 states that **immediately before** the asset (or disposal group) is first classified as 'held for sale' it must be **measured in accordance with applicable IFRSs**. This means that if, for example, an asset is measured using the revaluation model in IAS 16, it must be revalued at the date on which it becomes 'held for sale'. Depreciation must be charged up to the date of classification.

An impairment loss should be recognised where fair value less costs of disposal is lower than carrying amount. Note that this is an exception to the normal rule. IAS 36 *Impairment of assets* requires an entity to recognise an impairment loss only where an asset's recoverable amount is lower than its carrying amount. Recoverable amount is defined as the higher of fair value less costs to sell and value in use.

Exam focus point

> IAS 36 does not apply to assets held for sale.

Non-current assets held for sale **should not be depreciated**, even if they are still being used by the entity.

A non-current asset (or disposal group) that is **no longer classified as held for sale** (for example, because the sale has not taken place within one year) is measured at the **lower of**:

(a) Its **carrying amount** before it was classified as held for sale, adjusted for any depreciation that would have been charged had the asset not been held for sale

(b) Its **recoverable amount** at the date of the decision not to sell

6.4 Presenting discontinued operations

Key terms

> **Discontinued operation:** a component of an entity that has either been disposed of, or is classified as held for sale, *and*:
>
> (a)   Represents a separate major line of business or geographical area of operations
>
> (b)   Is part of a single co-ordinated plan to dispose of a separate major line of business or geographical area of operations, *or*
>
> (c)   Is a subsidiary acquired exclusively with a view to resale.
>
> **Component of an entity:** operations and cash flows that can be clearly distinguished, operationally and for financial reporting purposes, from the rest of the entity.

An entity should **present and disclose information** that enables users of the financial statements to evaluate the financial effects of **discontinued operations** and disposals of non-current assets or disposal groups.

An entity should disclose a **single amount** in the **statement of profit or loss and other comprehensive income** comprising the total of:

(a)   The **post-tax profit or loss** of discontinued operations, *and*

(b)   The post-tax gain or loss recognised on the **measurement to fair value less costs of disposal** or on the disposal of the assets or disposal group(s) constituting the discontinued operation

An entity should also disclose an **analysis** of this single amount into:

(a)   The revenue, expenses and pre-tax profit or loss of discontinued operations

(b)   The related income tax expense

(c)   The gain or loss recognised on the measurement to fair value less costs of disposal or on the disposal of the assets of the discontinued operation

(d)   The related income tax expense

This may be presented either in the statement of profit or loss and other comprehensive income or in the notes. If it is presented in the statement of profit or loss and other comprehensive income it should be presented in a section identified as relating to discontinued operations, ie separately from continuing operations. This analysis is not required where the discontinued operation is a newly acquired subsidiary that has been classified as held for sale.

An entity should disclose the **net cash flows** attributable to the operating, investing and financing activities of discontinued operations. These disclosures may be presented either on the face of the statement of cash flows or in the notes.

Gains and losses on the remeasurement of a disposal group that is not a discontinued operation but is held for sale should be included in profit or loss from continuing operations.

6.5 Illustration

The following illustration is taken from the implementation guidance to IFRS 5. Profit for the period from discontinued operations would be analysed in the notes.

Note: this example assumes no other comprehensive income.

XYZ GROUP
STATEMENT OF PROFIT OR LOSS
FOR THE YEAR ENDED 31 DECEMBER 20X2

	20X2 $'000	20X1 $'000
Continuing operations		
Revenue	X	X
Cost of sales	(X)	(X)
Gross profit	X	X
Other income	X	X
Distribution costs	(X)	(X)
Administrative expenses	(X)	(X)
Other expenses	(X)	(X)
Finance costs	(X)	(X)
Share of profit of associates	X	X
Profit before tax	X	X
Income tax expense	(X)	(X)
Profit for the year from continuing operations	X	X
Discontinued operations		
Profit for the year from discontinued operations	X	X
Profit for the year	X	X
Attributable to:		
Owners of the parent	X	X
Non-controlling interest	X	X
	X	X

An alternative to this presentation would be to analyse the profit from discontinued operations in a separate column in the statement of profit or loss.

Question

Closure

On 20 October 20X3 the directors of a parent company made a public announcement of plans to close a steel works. The closure means that the group will no longer carry out this type of operation, which until recently has represented about 10% of its total revenue. The works will be gradually shut down over a period of several months, with complete closure expected in July 20X4. At 31 December output had been significantly reduced and some redundancies had already taken place. The cash flows, revenues and expenses relating to the steel works can be clearly distinguished from those of the subsidiary's other operations.

Required

How should the closure be treated in the financial statements for the year ended 31 December 20X3?

Answer

Because the steel works is being closed, rather than sold, it cannot be classified as 'held for sale'. In addition, the steel works is not a discontinued operation. Although at 31 December 20X3 the group was firmly committed to the closure, this has not yet taken place and therefore the steel works must be included in continuing operations. Information about the planned closure could be disclosed in the notes to the financial statements.

6.6 Presentation of a non-current asset or disposal group classified as held for sale

Non-current assets and disposal groups classified as held for sale should be **presented separately** from other assets in the statement of financial position. The liabilities of a disposal group should be presented separately from other liabilities in the statement of financial position.

(a)   Assets and liabilities held for sale **should not be offset**.

(b)   The **major classes** of assets and liabilities held for sale should be **separately disclosed** either on the face of the statement of financial position or in the notes.

6.7 Additional disclosures

In the period in which a non-current asset (or disposal group) has been either classified as held for sale or sold the following should be disclosed.

(a)   A **description** of the non-current asset (or disposal group)

(b)   A description of the **facts and circumstances** of the disposal

(c)   Any **gain or loss** recognised when the item was classified as held for sale

(d)   If applicable, the **segment** in which the non-current asset (or disposal group) is presented in accordance with IFRS 8 *Operating segments* (see Chapter 12).

Where an asset previously classified as held for sale is **no longer held for sale**, the entity should disclose a description of the facts and circumstances leading to the decision and its effect on results.

Chapter roundup

- **IAS 8** deals with the treatment of **changes in accounting estimates, changes in accounting policies and errors**, as defined below.

- Accounting policies must be applied consistently for similar transactions.

- Changes in accounting policies are applied retrospectively.

- Changes in accounting estimates are not applied retrospectively.

- Material errors relating to the prior period must be corrected retrospectively.

- **IFRS 5** requires assets 'held for sale' to be presented separately in the statement of financial position.

Quick quiz

1   How should a prior period error be corrected under IAS 8?

2   Give two circumstances when a change in accounting policy might be required.

3   When can a non-current asset be classified as held for sale?

4   How should an asset held for sale be measured?

5   How does IFRS 5 define a discontinued operation?

Answers to quick quiz

1   By adjusting the opening balance of retained earnings.

2   (1)   Required by an IFRS
    (2)   For a more appropriate presentation

3   See Para 6.2

4   See Para 6.3

5   See Para 6.4

End of chapter question

IFRS 5 (AIA November 2005)

IFRS 5 *Non-current assets held for sale and discontinued operations* specifies the accounting treatment of non-current assets classified as 'held for sale' and the presentation of operations classified as discontinued.

Required

(a)   Discuss the need for the disclosure of non-current assets held for sale and explain how they should be presented in a statement of financial position.   **(4 marks)**

(b)   Assess whether or not the following situations meet the definition of discontinued operations in IFRS 5.

   (i)   Goddard had used two factories to manufacture office equipment. A general slump in the economy has resulted in a reduced demand for such equipment and the company has decided to move all the production facilities to one of the factories but keep the now empty factory in the hope that there will be an upturn in demand and require the return to two factory output.   **(3 marks)**

   (ii)   In addition to the manufacture of office equipment, Goddard supplied office stationery to private education establishments. In order to raise much needed cash the office stationery supply business was sold. The office stationery supply business was operated separately from the manufacturing activities.   **(3 marks)**

(Total = 10 marks)

IASB's *Conceptual Framework*

Topic list	Syllabus reference
1 The IASB's *Conceptual Framework*	11.1
2 The objective of general purpose financial reporting	11.1
3 The reporting entity	11.1
4 Qualitative characteristics of useful financial information	11.1
5 The 1989 *Framework*: The remaining text	11.1
6 Future developments	11.1

Introduction

A conceptual framework for financial reporting can be defined as an attempt to codify existing **Generally Accepted Accounting Principles (GAAP)** in order to reappraise current accounting standards and to produce new Standards.

The IASB *Framework for the preparation and presentation of financial statements* was produced in 1989 and is gradually being replaced by the *Conceptual Framework for financial reporting*. In September 2010, the IASB issued two chapters of the *Conceptual Framework for financial reporting* which replaced equivalent chapters in the existing *Framework for the preparation and presentation of financial statements*. The effective *Conceptual Framework* will remain a combination of old and new chapters until the project is completed.

1 The IASB's *Conceptual Framework*

The IASB's *Conceptual Framework* underpins IFRSs.

In July 1989 the IASB (then IASC) produced a document, *Framework for the preparation and presentation of financial statements* (*'Framework'*). This was to be the **conceptual** framework upon which all IFRSs would be based and hence which would determine how financial statements were prepared and the information they would contain.

As part of the IASB's convergence project to harmonise IFRS with US GAAP, the IASB and the US standard setter the FASB have been working on a revised conceptual framework for some time. The aim is to set out the basic principles on which future accounting standards can be set. The project has been taking place in several stages with exposure drafts being issued as each progress stage approaches completion. The first chapters of the new *Framework* were issued on 28 September 2010, and the IASB has decided to make amendments effective on a piecemeal basis, so the revised parts of the *Framework* sit alongside the old *Framework*. The *Framework* has been renamed *The Conceptual Framework for Financial Reporting (Conceptual Framework)*. This chapter will cover both old and new sections. Note that the *Conceptual Framework* is itself in the process of revision, and a Discussion Paper was issued in July 2013. The content of this is not examinable at Paper 11.

The revised *Conceptual Framework* consists of several sections or chapters, following on after a preface and introduction. These chapters are as follows.

(1)   The objective of general purpose financial reporting (issued 28 September 2010)

(2)   The reporting entity (not yet issued)

(3)   Qualitative characteristics of useful financial information (issued 28 September 2010)

(4)   *The 1989 Framework: The Remaining Text*

   –   Underlying assumption
   –   The elements of financial statements
   –   Recognition of the elements of financial statements
   –   Measurement of the elements of financial statements
   –   Concepts of capital and capital maintenance

We will look briefly at the preface and introduction to the *Conceptual Framework* as these will place the document in context with the rest of what you have studied for this paper and in particular the context of the *Conceptual Framework* in the IASB's approach to developing IFRSs.

Exam focus point

As you read through this chapter think about the impact the *Conceptual Framework* has had on IFRSs, particularly the definitions.

1.1 Preface

The preface to the *Conceptual Framework* points out the fundamental reason why financial statements are produced world-wide, ie to **satisfy the requirements of external users**, but that practice varies due to the individual pressures in each country. These pressures may be social, political, economic or legal, but they result in variations in practice from country to country, including the form of statements, the definition of their component parts (assets, liabilities etc), the criteria for recognition of items and both the scope and disclosure of financial statements.

It is these differences which the IASB wishes to narrow by **harmonising** all aspects of financial statements, including the regulations governing their accounting standards and their preparation and presentation.

The preface emphasises the way **financial statements are used to make economic decisions** and thus financial statements should be prepared to this end. The types of economic decisions for which financial statements are likely to be used include the following.

- Decisions to buy, hold or sell equity investments
- Assessment of management stewardship and accountability
- Assessment of the entity's ability to pay employees
- Assessment of the security of amounts lent to the entity
- Determination of taxation policies
- Determination of distributable profits and dividends
- Inclusion in national income statistics
- Regulations of the activities of entities

Any additional requirements imposed by **national governments** for their own purposes should not affect financial statements produced for the benefit of other users.

The *Conceptual Framework* recognises that financial statements can be prepared using a **variety of models**. Although the most common is based on historical cost and a nominal unit of currency (ie pound sterling, US dollar etc), the *Conceptual Framework* can be applied to financial statements prepared under a range of models.

1.2 Introduction

The introduction to the *Conceptual Framework* lays out the purpose, status and scope of the document. It then looks at different users of financial statements and their information needs.

1.2.1 Purpose and status

The introduction gives a list of the purposes of the *Conceptual Framework*.

(a) Assist the Board of the IASB in the **development of future IFRSs** and in its review of existing IFRSs.

(b) Assist the Board of the IASB in **promoting harmonisation** of regulations, accounting standards and procedures relating to the presentation of financial statements by providing a basis for reducing the number of alternative accounting treatments permitted by IFRSs.

(c) Assist **national standard-setting bodies** in developing national standards.

(d) Assist **preparers of financial statements** in applying IFRSs and in dealing with topics that have yet to form the subject of an IFRS.

(e) Assist **auditors** in forming an opinion as to whether financial statements conform with IFRSs.

(f) Assist **users of financial statements** in interpreting the information contained in financial statements prepared in conformity with IFRSs.

(g) Provide those who are interested in the work of IASB with **information** about its approach to the formulation of IFRSs.

The *Conceptual Framework* is not an IFRS and so does not overrule any individual Standard. In the (rare) cases of conflict between an IFRS and the *Conceptual Framework*, the **IFRS will prevail**. These cases will diminish over time as the *Conceptual Framework* will be used as a guide in the production of future IFRSs. The *Conceptual Framework* itself will be revised occasionally depending on the experience of the IASB in using it.

1.2.2 Scope

The *Conceptual Framework* deals with:

(a)   The **objective** of financial reporting

(b)   The **qualitative characteristics** of useful financial information

(c)   The **definition, recognition and measurement** of the elements from which financial statements are constructed

(d)   Concepts of **capital and capital maintenance**

The *Conceptual Framework* is concerned with **'general purpose' financial statements** (ie a normal set of annual statements), but it can be applied to other types of accounts. A complete set of financial statements includes:

(a)   A statement of financial position
(b)   A statement of profit or loss and other comprehensive income
(c)   A statement of changes in equity
(d)   A statement of changes in financial position (ie a statement of cash flows)
(e)   Notes, other statements and explanatory material

Supplementary information may be included, but some items are not included in the financial statements themselves, namely commentaries and reports by the directors, the chairman, management and so on.

All types of financial reporting entities are included (commercial, industrial, business; public or private sector).

1.2.3 Users and their information needs

Users include investors, employees, lenders, suppliers and other trade creditors, customers, government and their agencies and the public.

Question	Users of financial information

What are the information needs of the users of financial information listed above?

Answer

(a)   **Investors** are the providers of risk capital.

   (i)   Information is required to help make a decision about buying or selling shares, taking up a rights issue and voting.

   (ii)   Investors must have information about the level of dividend, past, present and future and any changes in share price.

   (iii)   Investors will also need to know whether the management has been running the company efficiently.

   (iv)   As well as the position indicated by the statement of financial position, statement of profit or loss and other comprehensive income and earnings per share (EPS), investors will want to know about the liquidity position of the company, the company's future prospects, and how the company's shares compare with those of its competitors.

(b)   **Employees** need information about the security of employment and future prospects for jobs in the company, and to help with collective pay bargaining.

(c)   **Lenders** need information to help them decide whether to lend to a company. They will also need to check that the value of any security remains adequate, that the interest repayments are secure,

that the cash is available for redemption at the appropriate time and that any financial restrictions (such as maximum debt/equity ratios) have not been breached.

(d) **Suppliers** need to know whether the company will be a good customer and pay its debts.

(e) **Customers** need to know whether the company will be able to continue producing and supplying goods.

(f) **Government's** interest in a company may be one of creditor or customer, as well as being specifically concerned with compliance with tax and company law, ability to pay tax and the general contribution of the company to the economy.

(g) The **public** at large would wish to have information for all the reasons mentioned above, but it could be suggested that it would be impossible to provide general purpose accounting information which was specifically designed for the needs of the public.

Financial statements cannot meet all these users' needs, but financial statements which meet the **needs of investors** (providers of risk capital) will meet most of the needs of other users.

The *Conceptual Framework* emphasises that the preparation and presentation of financial statements is primarily the **responsibility of an entity's management**. Management also has an interest in the information appearing in financial statements.

1.3 IAS 1 *Presentation of financial statements*

Much of what IAS 1 (revised) states in relation to accounting policies and the formats of financial statements repeats the contents of the *Conceptual Framework* document. IAS 1 (revised) was considered in detail in Chapter 3.

2 The objective of general purpose financial reporting

FAST FORWARD

The *Conceptual Framework* states that the objective of financial reporting is to provide information to users, but clarifies who those users are – existing and potential investors, lenders and other creditors.

This section of the *Conceptual Framework* has been revised as part of the amendments issued on 28 September 2010. The *Conceptual Framework* states that:

> 'The objective of general purpose financial reporting is to provide financial information about the reporting entity that is useful to existing and potential investors, lenders and other creditors in making decisions about providing resources to the entity. Those decisions involve buying, selling or holding equity and debt instruments, and providing or settling loans and other forms of credit.'

The *Conceptual Framework* clarifies that the primary users of the financial statements are existing and potential investors, lenders and other creditors, and that they need information to help them assess the prospects for future net cash inflows to an entity. The type of information needed deals with the resources of the entity, claims against the entity, and how efficiently and effectively the entity's management and governing board have discharged their responsibilities to use the entity's resources.

Despite the information provided in the financial statements, the *Conceptual Framework* states that they cannot provide all of the information that existing and potential investors, lenders and other creditors need. Users need to consider information from other sources such as general economic conditions and expectations, political events and political climate, and industry and company outlooks.

The *Conceptual Framework* also states that other parties such as regulators and members of the public other than investors, lenders and other creditors, may also find general purpose financial reports useful. However, those reports are not primarily directed to these other groups.

2.1 Information about economic resources, claims and changes in resources and claims

General purpose financial reports provide information about the financial position of a reporting entity, which is information about the entity's economic resources and the claims against the reporting entity. Financial reports also provide information about the effects of transactions and other events that change a reporting entity's economic resources and claims. Both types of information provide useful input for decisions about providing resources to an entity.

2.1.1 Economic resources and claims

Information about the nature and amounts of a reporting entity's economic resources and claims can help users to identify the reporting entity's financial strengths and weaknesses. That information can help users to assess the reporting entity's liquidity and solvency, its needs for additional financing and how successful it is likely to be in obtaining that financing. Information about priorities and payment requirements of existing claims helps users to predict how future cash flows will be distributed among those with a claim against the reporting entity.

2.1.2 Changes in economic resources and claims

Changes in a reporting entity's economic resources and claims result from that entity's financial performance, and from other events or transactions such as issuing debt or equity instruments. To properly assess the prospects for future cash flows from the reporting entity, users need to be able to distinguish between both of these changes.

Information about a reporting entity's financial performance helps users to understand the return that the entity has produced on its economic resources, and gives an indication of how well management has discharged its responsibilities to make efficient and effective use of the reporting entity's resources.

2.1.3 Financial performance reflected by accrual accounting

Accrual accounting depicts the effects of transactions on a reporting entity's economic resources and claims in the periods in which those effects occur, even if the resulting cash receipts and payments occur in a different period.

This is important because information about a reporting entity's economic resources and claims and changes in its economic resources and claims during a period provides a better basis for assessing the entity's past and future performance than information solely about cash receipts and payments during that period.

2.1.4 Financial performance reflected by past cash flows

Information about a reporting entity's cash flows during a period also helps users to assess the entity's ability to generate future net cash inflows. It indicates how the reporting entity obtains and spends cash, including information about its borrowing and repayment of debt, cash dividends or other cash distributions to investors, and other factors that may affect the entity's liquidity or solvency.

2.1.5 Changes in economic resources and claims not resulting from financial performance

A reporting entity's economic resources and claims may also change for reasons other than financial performance, such as issuing additional ownership shares. Information about this type of change is necessary to give users a complete understanding of why the reporting entity's economic resources and claims changed and the implications of those changes for its future financial performance.

3 The reporting entity

This section of the *Conceptual Framework* has not yet been issued. In the exposure draft, a reporting entity is defined as:

> 'A circumscribed area of economic activities whose financial information has the potential to be useful to existing and potential equity investors, lenders, and other creditors who cannot directly obtain the information they need in making decisions about providing resources to the entity and in assessing whether the management and the governing board of that entity have made efficient and effective use of the resources provided.'

A reporting entity has three features:

(1)   Economic activities of an entity are being conducted, have been conducted, or will be conducted

(2)   Those economic activities can be objectively distinguished from those of other entities and from the economic environment in which the entity exists

(3)   Financial information about the economic activities of that entity has the potential to be useful in making decisions about providing resources to the entity and in assessing whether the management and the governing board have made efficient and effective use of the resources provided.

These features are necessary but not always sufficient to identify a reporting entity.

4 Qualitative characteristics of useful financial information

FAST FORWARD

For financial information to be useful it should be relevant and faithfully represent what it purports to represent. The usefulness of financial information is enhanced if it is comparable, verifiable, timely and understandable.

This section of the *Conceptual Framework* has been revised as of 28 September 2010. The *Conceptual Framework* states that the qualitative characteristics of useful financial information identify the types of information that are likely to be most useful to the existing and potential investors, lenders and other creditors for making decisions about the reporting entity on the basis of information in its financial report. Additionally, the qualitative characteristics of useful financial information apply to financial information provided in financial statements, as well as to financial information provided in other ways.

4.1 Qualitative characteristics of useful financial information

If financial information is to be useful, it must be relevant and faithfully represents what it purports to represent. The usefulness of financial information is enhanced if it is comparable, verifiable, timely and understandable.

4.2 Fundamental qualitative characteristics

The fundamental qualitative characteristics are relevance and faithful representation.

4.2.1 Relevance

Relevant financial information is capable of making a difference in the decisions made by users. Information may be capable of making a difference in a decision even if some users choose not to take advantage of it or are already aware of it from other sources. Financial information is capable of making a difference in decisions if it has predictive value, confirmatory value or both.

4.2.2 Materiality

Information is material if omitting it or misstating it could influence decisions that users make on the basis of financial information about a specific reporting entity. Materiality is an entity-specific aspect of relevance based on the nature or magnitude, or both, of the items to which the information relates in the context of an individual entity's financial report. It is impossible to specify a quantitative threshold for materiality or predetermine what could be material in a particular situation as it depends on the individual entity.

4.2.3 Faithful representation

To be useful, in addition to being relevant, financial information must also faithfully represent the phenomena that it purports to represent. To be a perfectly faithful representation, a depiction would have three characteristics – it would be complete, neutral and free from error.

Faithful representation does not mean accurate in all respects. Information that is complete means all necessary information is included for the user to understand the item being depicted. Neutral information is prepared without bias in the selection or presentation of the information. Free from error means there are no errors or omissions in the description of the item, and the process used to produce the reported information has been selected and applied with no errors in the process.

4.2.4 Applying the fundamental qualitative characteristics

Information must be both relevant and faithfully represented if it is to be useful. Neither a faithful representation of an irrelevant phenomenon nor an unfaithful representation of a relevant phenomenon helps users make good decisions.

The *Conceptual Framework* suggests that the most efficient and effective process for applying the fundamental qualitative characteristics would be:

- First, identify an economic phenomenon that has the potential to be useful to users of the reporting entity's financial information.

- Second, identify the type of information about that phenomenon that would be most relevant if it is available and can be faithfully represented.

- Third, determine whether that information is available and can be faithfully represented.

4.3 Enhancing qualitative characteristics

Comparability, verifiability, timeliness and understandability are qualitative characteristics that enhance the usefulness of information that is relevant and faithfully represented.

4.3.1 Comparability

Users' decisions involve choosing between alternatives, for example, selling or holding an investment, or investing in one reporting entity or another. Consequently, information about a reporting entity is more useful if it can be compared with similar information about other entities and with similar information about the same entity for another period or another date.

Comparability is the qualitative characteristic that enables users to identify and understand similarities in, and differences among, items. Unlike the other qualitative characteristics, comparability does not relate to a single item. A comparison requires at least two items.

Consistency, although related to comparability, is not the same. Consistency refers to the use of the same methods for the same items, either from period to period within a reporting entity or in a single period across entities. Comparability is the goal; consistency helps to achieve that goal.

4.3.2 Verifiability

Verifiability helps assure users that information faithfully represents the economic phenomena it purports to represent. Verifiability means that different knowledgeable and independent observers could reach consensus, although not necessarily complete agreement, that a particular depiction is a faithful representation.

Verification can be direct or indirect. Direct verification means verifying an amount through direct observation, for example, by counting cash. Indirect verification means checking the inputs to a model, formula or other technique and recalculating the outputs using the same methodology.

4.3.3 Timeliness

Timeliness means having information available to decision-makers in time to be capable of influencing their decisions. Generally, the older the information is, the less useful it is. However, some information may continue to be timely long after the end of a reporting period because, for example, some users may need to identify and assess trends.

4.3.4 Understandability

Classifying, characterising and presenting information clearly and concisely makes it understandable.

Some transactions are inherently complex and cannot be made easy to understand. Whilst excluding information about those transactions from financial reports might make the information in those financial reports easier to understand, this may mean that information would be incomplete and therefore potentially misleading.

The *Conceptual Framework* states that financial reports are prepared for users who have a reasonable knowledge of business and economic activities and who review and analyse the information diligently. At times, even the well-informed, diligent users may need to seek the aid of an adviser to understand information about complex economic phenomena.

4.3.5 Applying the enhancing qualitative characteristics

Enhancing qualitative characteristics should be maximised to the extent possible. However, the enhancing qualitative characteristics, either individually or as a group, cannot make information useful if that information is irrelevant or not faithfully represented.

4.4 The cost constraint on useful financial reporting

Cost is a constraint on the information that can be provided by financial reporting. Reporting financial information imposes costs, and it is important that those costs are justified by the benefits of reporting that information. There are several types of costs and benefits to consider.

Providers of financial information expend most of the effort involved in collecting, processing, verifying and disseminating financial information, but users ultimately bear those costs in the form of reduced returns. Users of financial information also incur costs of analysing and interpreting the information provided. If information needed is not provided, users incur additional costs to obtain that information elsewhere or to estimate it.

Reporting financial information that is relevant and faithfully represents what it purports to represent helps users to make decisions with more confidence.

5 The 1989 *Framework:* The remaining text

The remainder of the *Conceptual Framework* consists of the original *Framework* text. These sections of the existing *Framework* will be replaced in due course as part of the ongoing update.

5.1 Underlying assumption

5.1.1 Going concern

Key term

> **Going concern**. The entity is normally viewed as a going concern, that is, as continuing in operation for the foreseeable future. It is assumed that the entity has neither the intention nor the necessity of liquidation or of curtailing materially the scale of its operations.   *(Conceptual Framework)*

It is assumed that the entity has no intention to liquidate or curtail major operations. If it did, then the financial statements would be prepared on a **different (disclosed) basis**.

5.2 The elements of financial statements

FAST FORWARD

> Transactions and other events are grouped together in broad **classes** and in this way their financial effects are shown in the financial statements. These broad classes are the elements of financial statements.

The *Conceptual Framework* lays out these elements as follows.

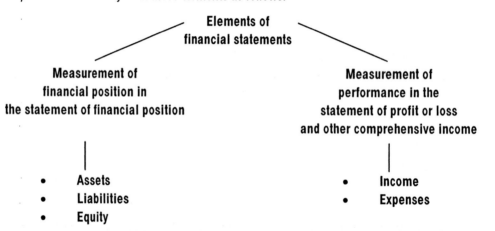

A process of **sub-classification** then takes place for presentation in the financial statements, eg assets are classified by their nature or function in the business to show information in the best way for users to take economic decisions.

5.2.1 Financial position

We need to define the three terms listed under this heading above.

Key terms

> **Asset**. A resource controlled by an entity as a result of past events and from which future economic benefits are expected to flow to the entity.
>
> **Liability**. A present obligation of the entity arising from past events, the settlement of which is expected to result in an outflow from the entity of resources embodying economic benefits.
>
> **Equity**. The residual interest in the assets of the entity after deducting all its liabilities.
>
> *(Conceptual Framework)*

These definitions are important, but they do not cover the **criteria for recognition** of any of these items, which are discussed in the next section of this chapter. This means that the definitions may include items which would not actually be recognised in the statement of financial position because they fail to satisfy recognition criteria, particularly, as we will see below, the **probable flow of any economic benefit** to or from the business.

Whether an item satisfies any of the definitions above will depend on the **substance and economic reality** of the transaction, not merely its legal form. For example, consider finance leases. The business controls the use of the asset and capitalises it in the statement of financial position, but doesn't actually own the asset as legal title remains with the lessor.

5.2.2 Assets

We can look in more detail at the components of the definitions given above.

Key term

> **Future economic benefit**. The potential to contribute, directly or indirectly, to the flow of cash and cash equivalents to the entity. The potential may be a productive one that is part of the operating activities of the entity. It may also take the form of convertibility into cash or cash equivalents or a capability to reduce cash outflows, such as when an alternative manufacturing process lowers the cost of production.
>
> *(Conceptual Framework)*

Assets are usually employed to produce goods or services for customers; customers will then pay for these. **Cash itself** renders a service to the entity due to its command over other resources.

The existence of an asset, particularly in terms of **control**, is not reliant on:

(a) **Physical form** (hence patents and copyrights); *nor*
(b) **Legal rights** (hence leases).

Transactions or events **in the past** give rise to assets; those expected to occur in the future do not in themselves give rise to assets. For example, an intention to purchase a non-current asset does not, in itself, meet the definition of an asset.

5.2.3 Liabilities

Again we can look more closely at some aspects of the definition. An essential characteristic of a liability is that the entity has a **present obligation**.

Key term

> **Obligation**. A duty or responsibility to act or perform in a certain way. Obligations may be legally enforceable as a consequence of a binding contract or statutory requirement. Obligations also arise, however, from normal business practice, custom and a desire to maintain good business relations or act in an equitable manner.
> *(Conceptual Framework)*

It is important to distinguish between a present obligation and a **future commitment**. A management decision to purchase assets in the future does not, in itself, give rise to a present obligation.

Settlement of a present obligation will involve the entity giving up resources embodying economic benefits in order to satisfy the claim of the other party. This may be done in various ways, not just by payment of cash.

Liabilities must arise from **past transactions or events**. In the case of, say, recognition of future rebates to customers based on annual purchases, the sale of goods in the past is the transaction that gives rise to the liability.

5.2.4 Provisions

Is a provision a liability?

Key term

> **Provision.** A present obligation which satisfies the rest of the definition of a liability, even if the amount of the obligation has to be estimated.   *(Conceptual Framework)*

Question   Assets or liabilities?

Consider the following situations. In each case, do we have an asset or liability within the definitions given by the *Conceptual Framework?* Give reasons for your answer.

(a)   Pat Co has purchased a patent for $20,000. The patent gives the company sole use of a particular manufacturing process which will save $3,000 a year for the next five years.

(b)   Baldwin Co paid Don Brennan $10,000 to set up a car repair shop, on condition that priority treatment is given to cars from the company's fleet.

(c)   Deals on Wheels Co provides a warranty with every car sold.

Answer

(a)   This is an asset, albeit an intangible one. There is a past event, control and future economic benefit (through cost savings).

(b)   This cannot be classified as an asset. Baldwin Co has no control over the car repair shop and it is difficult to argue that there are 'future economic benefits'.

(c)   This is a liability; the business has taken on an obligation. It would be recognised when the warranty is issued rather than when a claim is made.

5.2.5 Equity

Equity is defined above as a **residual**, but it may be sub-classified in the statement of financial position. This will indicate legal or other restrictions on the ability of the entity to distribute or otherwise apply its equity. Some reserves are required by statute or other law, eg for the future protection of creditors. The amount shown for equity depends on the **measurement of assets and liabilities.** It has nothing to do with the market value of the entity's shares.

5.2.6 Performance

Total comprehensive income and, in particular, profit is used as a **measure of performance**, or as a basis for other measures (eg EPS). It depends directly on the measurement of income and expenses, which in turn depend (in part) on the concepts of capital and capital maintenance adopted.

The elements of income and expense are therefore defined.

Key terms

> **Income.** Increases in economic benefits during the accounting period in the form of inflows or enhancements of assets or decreases of liabilities that result in increases in equity, other than those relating to contributions from equity participants.
>
> **Expenses.** Decreases in economic benefits during the accounting period in the form of outflows or depletions of assets or incurrences of liabilities that result in decreases in equity, other than those relating to distributions to equity participants.   *(Conceptual Framework)*

Income and expenses can be **presented in different ways** in the statement of profit or loss and other comprehensive income, to provide information relevant for economic decision-making. For example, distinguish between income and expenses which relate to continuing operations and those which do not.

Items of income and expense can be **distinguished** from each other or **combined** with each other.

5.2.7 Income

Both **revenue** and **gains** are included in the definition of income. **Revenue** arises in the course of ordinary activities of an entity.

Key term

> **Gains**. Increases in economic benefits. As such they are no different in nature from revenue.
>
> *(Conceptual Framework)*

Gains include those arising on the disposal of non-current assets.

The definition of income also includes **unrealised gains**, eg on revaluation of property. These gains are recognised in other comprehensive income rather than in profit or loss.

5.2.8 Expenses

As with income, the definition of expenses includes losses as well as those expenses that arise in the course of ordinary activities of an entity.

Key term

> **Losses**. Decreases in economic benefits. As such they are no different in nature from other expenses.
>
> *(Conceptual Framework)*

Losses will include those arising on the disposal of non-current assets.

The definition of expenses will also include **unrealised losses**, eg exchange rate effects on borrowings. These are recognised in other comprehensive income rather than in profit or loss.

5.3 Capital maintenance adjustments

A **revaluation** gives rise to an increase or decrease in equity.

Key term

> **Revaluation**. Restatement of assets and liabilities.　　　　　*(Conceptual Framework)*

These increases and decreases meet the definitions of income and expenses. They are **not included** in the statement of profit or loss under certain concepts of capital maintenance, however, but rather in other comprehensive income (see Section 8).

5.4 Recognition of the elements of financial statements

Key term

> **Recognition**. The process of incorporating in the statement of financial position or statement of profit or loss and other comprehensive income an item that meets the definition of an element and satisfies the following criteria for recognition:
>
> (a)　It is probable that any future economic benefit associated with the item will flow to or from the entity; *and*
>
> (b)　The item has a cost or value that can be measured with reliability.
>
> *(Conceptual Framework)*

Regard must be given to **materiality** (see Section 4 above).

5.4.1 Probability of future economic benefits

Probability here means the **degree of uncertainty** that the future economic benefits associated with an item will flow to or from the entity. This must be judged on the basis of the **characteristics of the entity's environment** and the **evidence available** when the financial statements are prepared.

5.4.2 Reliability of measurement

The cost or value of an item, in many cases, **must be estimated**. The *Conceptual Framework* states, however, that the use of reasonable estimates is an essential part of the preparation of financial statements and does not undermine their reliability. Where no reasonable estimate can be made, the item should not be recognised, although its existence should be disclosed in the notes, or other explanatory material.

Items may still qualify for recognition **at a later date** due to changes in circumstances or subsequent events.

5.4.3 Recognition of items

We can summarise the recognition criteria for assets, liabilities, income and expenses, based on the definition of recognition given above.

Item	Recognised in	When
Asset	The statement of financial position	It is probable that the future economic benefits will flow to the entity and the asset has a cost or value that can be measured reliably.
Liability	The statement of financial position	It is probable that an outflow of resources embodying economic benefits will result from the settlement of a present obligation and the amount at which the settlement will take place can be measured reliably.
Income	The statement of profit or loss and other comprehensive income	An increase in future economic benefits related to an increase in an asset or a decrease of a liability has arisen that can be measured reliably.
Expenses	The statement of profit or loss and other comprehensive income	A decrease in future economic benefits related to a decrease in an asset or an increase of a liability has arisen that can be measured reliably.

5.5 Measurement of the elements of financial statements

Measurement is defined as follows.

Key term

> **Measurement**. The process of determining the monetary amounts at which the elements of the financial statements are to be recognised and carried in the statement of financial position and statement of profit or loss and other comprehensive income.
>
> *(Conceptual Framework)*

This involves the selection of a particular **basis of measurement**. A number of these are used to different degrees and in varying combinations in financial statements. They include the following.

Key terms

> **Historical cost.** Assets are recorded at the amount of cash or cash equivalents paid or the fair value of the consideration given to acquire them at the time of their acquisition. Liabilities are recorded at the amount of proceeds received in exchange for the obligation, or in some circumstances (for example, income taxes), at the amounts of cash or cash equivalents expected to be paid to satisfy the liability in the normal course of business.
>
> **Current cost.** Assets are carried at the amount of cash or cash equivalents that would have to be paid if the same or an equivalent asset was acquired currently.
>
> Liabilities are carried at the undiscounted amount of cash or cash equivalents that would be required to settle the obligation currently.
>
> **Realisable (settlement) value.**
>
> - **Realisable value.** The amount of cash or cash equivalents that could currently be obtained by selling an asset in an orderly disposal.
>
> - **Settlement value.** The undiscounted amounts of cash or cash equivalents expected to be paid to satisfy the liabilities in the normal course of business.
>
> **Present value.** A current estimate of the present discounted value of the future net cash flows in the normal course of business. *(Conceptual Framework)*

Historical cost is the most commonly adopted measurement basis, but this is usually combined with other bases, eg inventory is carried at the lower of cost and net realisable value.

5.6 Concepts of capital and capital maintenance

Most entities use a **financial concept of capital** when preparing their financial statements.

5.6.1 Concepts of capital maintenance and the determination of profit

First of all, we need to define the different concepts of capital. You should be familiar with them from the previous chapter.

Key term

> **Capital.** Under a financial concept of capital, such as invested money or invested purchasing power, capital is the net assets or equity of the entity. The financial concept of capital is adopted by most entities.
>
> Under a physical concept of capital, such as operating capability, capital is the productive capacity of the entity based on, for example, units of output per day. *(Conceptual Framework)*

The definition of profit is also important.

Key term

> **Profit.** The residual amount that remains after expenses (including capital maintenance adjustments, where appropriate) have been deducted from income. Any amount over and above that required to maintain the capital at the beginning of the period is profit. *(Conceptual Framework)*

The main difference between the two concepts of capital maintenance is the treatment of the **effects of changes in the prices of assets and liabilities** of the entity. In general terms, an entity has maintained its capital if it has as much capital at the end of the period as it had at the beginning of the period. Any amount over and above that required to maintain the capital at the beginning of the period is profit.

(a) **Financial capital maintenance**: profit is the increase in nominal money capital over the period.

(b) **Physical capital maintenance**: profit is the increase in the physical productive capacity over the period.

6 Future developments

The IASB issued a Discussion Paper in July 2013. Comments received on this will determine the future direction of the *Conceptual Framework*.

6.1 Revised *Framework*

The IASB has been undertaking a process of convergence of IFRS with US GAAP over the past few years (see Chapter 2). As part of this process a number of accounting standards have been amended or introduced. As the purpose of the *Conceptual Framework* is to provide a basis on which accounting standards can be developed, it follows that as part of the convergence process, the *Conceptual Framework* on which these new and revised converged standards are based may also need to be amended. In October 2004, the IASB and FASB agreed to develop a **common conceptual framework** which would be a significant step towards harmonisation of future standards

The IASB stated that the aim of the project to revise the *Conceptual Framework* was to 'create a sound foundation for future accounting standards that are principles-based, internally consistent and internationally converged.'

As already mentioned, the IASB and FASB planned the project in a number of different stages, focusing on different elements of the *Conceptual Framework* at each stage. The stages are as follows:

A   Objective and qualitative characteristics (completed 28 September 2010)
B   Elements and recognition
C   Measurement
D   Reporting entity
E   Presentation and Disclosure
F   Purpose and status of the *Conceptual Framework*
G   Applicability to not-for profit entities
H   Remaining issues, if any.

6.2 Progress to date

At the time of writing (February 2014) the IASB has issued *The Conceptual Framework for Financial Reporting* which includes the output from Phase A of the project, Objectives and qualitative characteristics. Since 2010 the project has been on hold, however in September 2012 the IASB considered how it could be restarted. A Discussion Paper was issued in July 2013 focussing on elements of financial statements (including recognition and derecognition), measurement, reporting entity and presentation and disclosure. The IASB aims to complete the project by 2015. This will be conducted as an IASB project (not as a joint project with FASB).

Chapter roundup

- The IASB's *Conceptual Framework* underpins IFRSs.

- The *Conceptual Framework* states that the objective of financial reporting is to provide information to users, but clarifies who those users are – existing and potential investors, lenders and other creditors.

- For financial information to be useful it should be relevant and faithfully represent what it purports to represent. The usefulness of financial information is enhanced if it is comparable, verifiable, timely and understandable.

- Transactions and other events are grouped together in broad **classes** and in this way their financial effects are shown in the financial statements. These broad classes are the elements of financial statements.

- The IASB issued a Discussion Paper in July 2013. Comments received on this will determine the future direction of the *Conceptual Framework*.

Quick quiz

1   Define a 'conceptual framework'.

2   What are the advantages and disadvantages of developing a conceptual framework?

3   Who are seen to be the key users of financial information?

4   Define 'relevance'.

5   In which two ways should users be able to compare an entity's financial statements?

6   A provision can be a liability. True or false?

7   Define 'recognition'.

8   The cost or value of items in the financial statements is never estimated. True or false?

9   What is the most common basis of measurement used in financial statements?

Answers to quick quiz

1   This is a statement of generally accepted theoretical principles, which form the frame of reference for financial reporting.

2   *Advantages*

   - Standardised accounting practice
   - Less open to criticism
   - Concentrate on profits or statement of financial position, as appropriate

   Disadvantages

   - Variety of users, so not all will be satisfied
   - Variety of Standards for different purposes
   - Preparing and implementing Standards not necessarily any easier

3   Existing and potential investors, lenders and other creditors

4   Relevant financial information is capable of making a difference in the decisions made by users. Relevant financial information has a predictive value, confirmatory value or both.

5   - Through time to identify trends
   - With other entities' statements

6   True. It satisfies the definition of a liability but the amount may need to be estimated.

7   See Key Term Section 5.4.

8   False. Monetary values are often estimated.

9   Historical cost.

End of chapter question

Framework (AIA May 2009)

Two accountants, Milo and Domna, are discussing the European Financial Reporting Group's (EFRAG) Pro-active Accounting Activities in Europe (PAAinE) initiative to stimulate debate on the IASB/FASB project to converge their existing conceptual frameworks. They have both just read the following extract from EFRAG's October 2006 PAAinE Discussion Paper 'The Conceptual Framework Starting From The Right Place?':

4	ENTITIES WITHIN THE SCOPE OF THE FRAMEWORK
4.1	**Introduction**
4.1.1	The objectives of financial reporting may vary according to the type of entity. It is therefore important to assess whether it is possible to develop concepts and principles in the framework which are common to the financial reporting of all entities, or conversely only applicable to certain types of entity.
4.1.2	An analysis of the needs of users of financial reporting of different types of entity is a key preliminary to assessing whether common reporting concepts and principles are applicable.

The two accountants make the following observations:

Milo: Users have similar needs whatever the type of entity and therefore different entities, such as profit-oriented and non-profit-oriented entities, should be treated in the same way and should use common reporting concepts and principles.

Domna: I don't agree. I accept profit-oriented and non-profit-oriented entities are different but this means they also have different users and different users have different needs. They require different reporting concepts and principles.

Required

To what extent do you agree with Milo and Domna? Should the conceptual framework apply equally to profit-oriented and non profit-oriented entities or just to profit-oriented entities? Explain your choice.

(12 marks)

7

Theoretical aspects of accounting

Topic list	Syllabus reference
1 Comprehensive income	11.1
2 Fair value	11.1
3 Historical cost	11.1
4 Concepts of capital and capital maintenance	11.1
5 Current purchasing power (CPP)	11.1
6 Current cost accounting (CCA)	11.1

Introduction

The topics covered in this chapter fall neatly into two groups.

- Sections 1 and 2 are the first group examining the meaning of profit and capital.

- Sections 3 to 6 are the second group examining the issues with historical cost and alternative methods of adjusting for changing price levels.

1 Comprehensive income

Comprehensive income means **all** transactions for the period, other than those between an entity and its owners. As we have seen in Chapter 3, IAS 1 revised requires the reporting of comprehensive income.

The issue of IAS 1 (revised) in 2007 brought IFRS into line with existing US reporting standards. It was part of a long-term convergence project between the IASB and US FASB, and marked the completion of the first of three phases in a joint *Presentation of financial statements* project.

The next phase is concerned with the presentation and aggregation of items within the statements of financial position, comprehensive income and cash flows. This project is still ongoing.

1.1 Comprehensive income and the FASB

In the US, public companies have been required since 1997 to report comprehensive income. As we have already seen, 'comprehensive income' is defined as *all* gains and losses for the period, ie. all changes in equity, other than those arising from transactions with equity holders. So it does not include transactions such as share issues and dividend payments.

The requirement to report comprehensive income in the US was prompted by the fact that certain items were bypassing the statement of profit or loss and going straight to the statement of changes in equity, specifically foreign currency translation gains and losses, adjustments to the minimum pension liability and unrealised gains or losses on certain financial asset investments. In this way, users were not being given important information.

2 Fair value

The concept of **fair value** has become very important since the issue of IAS 39. Entities are now permitted to remeasure certain financial instruments to fair value. This practice continues under IFRS 9, which will eventually replace IAS 39.

2.1 Background

The fair value concept is relevant to two major areas of accounting.

Following a joint FASB/IASB project on business combinations it was agreed that fair value should be applied to assets and liabilities acquired in a business combination. In many cases this leads to a 'fair value adjustment'.

The EU **Fair Value Directive** required UK and other member states to permit or require companies to account for some of their financial instruments at **fair value**.

The Directive had the declared objective of enabling companies to use more 'transparent' accounting practices.

Exam focus point

IFRS 13 *Fair value measurement* was issued in May 2011 but the detail is not examinable in Paper 11.

2.2 Fair value and IFRS9/IAS 39

IFRS 9, which is in the process of replacing IAS 39, requires that financial instruments are initially measured at the transaction price ie the fair value of the consideration received. Fair value is defined as follows:

Key term

> **Fair value.** The price that would be received to sell an asset or paid to transfer a liability in an orderly transaction between market participants at the measurement date. *(IFRS 9 & IFRS 13)*

IFRS 9 also requires subsequent measurement of certain financial instruments at fair value with changes in fair value normally recognised in profit or loss .

Measurement at fair value is, of course, no problem in the case of financial instruments for which market prices are readily available. Where this is not the case, fair value will have to be estimated using either the transaction price or valuation techniques using observable market data where possible, in accordance with IFRS 13. There is some degree of judgement implied here, which could lead to different valuations of similar assets/liabilities from one company to the next.

The recognition of changes to fair value in profit or loss means that what are essentially unrealised gains and losses are reported in the statement of profit or loss. It will be interesting to see how this one plays out.

3 Historical cost

FAST FORWARD

> There are several advantages and disadvantages to using historical cost accounts. A number of alternatives to historical cost accounting are presently under discussion. Some progress has been made and more can be expected in the future.

3.1 Advantages and disadvantages of historical cost accounting

The **advantage** of historical cost accounting is that cost is known and can be proved (eg by an invoice). There is no subjectivity or bias in the valuation.

There are a number of **disadvantages** and these usually arise in times of rising prices (inflation). When inflation is low, historical cost accounting is usually satisfactory. However, when inflation is high the following problems can occur.

3.1.1 Non-current asset values are unrealistic

The most striking example is property. Although some entities have periodically updated the statement of financial position values, in general there has been a lack of consistency in the approach adopted and a lack of clarity in the way in which the effects of these changes in value have been expressed.

If non-current assets are retained in the books at their historical cost, **unrealised holding gains are not recognised**. This means that the total holding gain, if any, will be brought into account during the year in which the asset is realised, rather than spread over the period during which it was owned. In contrast unrealised holding losses are recognised in the form of impairment of assets.

There are, in essence, two contradictory points to be considered:

(a) Although it has long been accepted that a statement of financial position prepared under the historical cost concept is an historical record and not a statement of current worth, many people now argue that the statement of financial position should at least give an indication of the **current value** of the company's tangible net assets.

(b) Traditionally, generally accepted accounting practice has required that profits should only be recognised when realised in the form of either cash or other assets, the ultimate cash realisation of which can be assessed with reasonable certainty (**prudence**). It may be argued that recognising unrealised holding gains on non-current assets is contrary to this concept.

On balance, the weight of opinion held generally by the IASB is now in favour of restating asset values. It is felt that the criticism based on prudence can be met by ensuring that valuations are made as objectively as possible (e.g. in the case of property, by having independent expert valuations) and by not taking unrealised gains through profit or loss, but instead through other comprehensive income.

3.1.2 Depreciation is inadequate to finance the replacement of non-current assets

The purpose of depreciation is not to enforce retention of profits and therefore ensure that funds are available for asset replacement. It is intended as a measure of the contribution of non-current assets to an entity's activities in the period. However, an incidental effect of providing for depreciation is that not all liquid funds can be paid out to investors and so funds for asset replacement are on hand. What is important is not the replacement of one asset by an identical new one (something that rarely happens) but the replacement of the **operating capability** represented by the old asset.

3.1.3 Holding gains on inventories are included in profit

Another criticism of historical cost accounting is that it does not fully reflect the value of the assets consumed during the accounting year.

During a period of high inflation the monetary value of inventory held may increase significantly while they are being processed. The conventions of historical cost accounting lead to the unrealised part of this holding gain (known as **inventory appreciation**) being included in profit for the year.

The following simple example is given to help your understanding of this difficult concept.

3.1.4 Example: Holding gain

At the beginning of the year a company has 100 units of inventory and no other assets. Its trading account for the year is shown below.

TRADING ACCOUNT

	Units	$		Units	$
Opening inventory	100	200	Sales (made 31 December)	100	500
Purchases (made 31 December)	100	400			
	200	600			
Closing inventory (FIFO basis)	100	(400)			
	100	200			
Gross profit	–	300			
	100	500		100	500

Apparently the company has made a gross profit of $300. But, at the beginning of the year the company owned 100 units of inventory and at the end of the year it owned 100 units of inventory and $100 (sales $500 less purchases $400). From this it would seem that a profit of $100 is more reasonable. The remaining $200 is inventory appreciation arising because the purchase price increased from $2 to $4.

The criticism can be overcome by using a **capital maintenance concept** based on physical units rather than money values.

3.1.5 Profits (or losses) on holdings of net monetary items are not shown

In periods of inflation the purchasing power, and therefore the value, of money falls. It follows that an investment in money will have a lower real value at the end of a period of time than it did at the beginning. A loss has been incurred. Similarly, the real value of a monetary liability will reduce over a period of time and a gain will be made.

3.1.6 The true effect of inflation on capital maintenance is not shown

To a large extent this follows from the points already mentioned. It is a widely held principle that distributable profits should only be recognised after full allowance has been made for any erosion in the capital value of a business. In historical cost accounts, although capital is maintained in **nominal money terms**, it may not be in **real terms**. So, profits may be distributed to the detriment of the long-term viability of the business. This criticism may be made by those who advocate capital maintenance in physical terms.

3.1.7 Comparisons over time are unrealistic

This will tend to an exaggeration of growth. For example, if a company's profit in 1982 was $100 000, and in 2013 $500 000, a shareholder's initial reaction might be that the company had done rather well. If, however, it was then revealed that with $100 000 in 1982 he could buy exactly the same goods as with $500 000 in 2013, the apparent growth would seem less impressive.

The points mentioned above have demonstrated some of the accounting problems which arise in times of severe and prolonged inflation. Of the various possible systems of accounting for price changes most fall into one of three categories as follows:

(a) General price changes bases and in particular, **current purchasing power** (CPP).

(b) **Current value bases**. The basic principles of all these are:

    (i) To show statement of financial position items at some form of current value rather than historical cost.

    (ii) To compute profits by matching the current value of costs at the date of consumption against revenue.

    The current value of an item will normally be based on replacement cost, net realisable value or economic value.

> **Exam focus point**
>
> The May 2011 exam included a question requiring the preparation of financial statements on a replacement cost basis.

(c) A **combination** of these two systems: suggestions of this type have been put forward by many writers.

3.2 Why modified historical cost accounting is still used

It must seem strange, given the criticisms levelled at it, that modified historical cost accounting is still in such widespread use. There are various reasons for this, not the least of which is **resistance to change** in the conservative accounting profession.

Modified historical cost accounts are **easy** to prepare, easy to read and easy to understand. While they do not reflect current values, the revaluation of non-current assets is seen as one of the most important items requiring such an adjustment, and therefore the value of the accounts is improved enormously by such revaluations taking place.

In periods of **low inflation**, historical cost accounts are viewed as a reasonable reflection of the reality of the given situation.

3.3 Current value accounting

The move towards current value accounting has already taken a number of steps. Entities are now permitted to revalue non-current assets such as land and buildings in line with market value, and financial assets and liabilities such as securities and investments can be carried at **fair value**, in accordance with IFRS 9 (see section 2).

These developments, and the use of fair values in acquisition accounting (to measure the assets of the subsidiary and therefore arrive at a realistic goodwill valuation) are relatively uncontroversial. However, there are those who would like fair value to be used more widely as a system of current value. In the US a move is being advocated towards Current Value Accounting (CVA). Under CVA the original cost of an asset would be replaced with its discounted present value ie the present value of its future cash flows. This is obviously suitable for monetary items such as receivables and payables. The expected inflows and outflows would be discounted to present value using an interest rate which reflects the current time value of money. For assets such as vehicles, which do not yield a pre-determined future cash flow, current cost would be a more applicable measure – based either on the current cost of the original asset or on its replacement by a more up-to-date version. For inventories, current replacement cost or net realisable value would be indicated.

3.4 Historical cost accounting: does it have a future?

Investment analysts have argued that historical cost information is out of date and not relevant and that fair value information, based on active market prices, is the best available measure of future cash flows which an asset can be expected to generate.

This argument is heard increasingly in the US, where investors are the most highly-regarded user group for financial information, and the issue is likely to arise in the context of any further IASB/FASB convergence discussions .

We will now go on to discuss two alternative systems which have sought in the past to address the shortcomings of historical cost accounting – **Current purchasing power (CPP)** and **Current cost accounting (CCA)**. We begin by looking at the fundamental difference between these two systems being a different concept of capital maintenance and therefore of profit.

4 Concepts of capital and capital maintenance

FAST FORWARD

The concept of capital selected should be appropriate to the needs of the users of an entity's financial statements.

Most entities use a **financial concept of capital** when preparing their financial statements.

4.1 Concepts of capital maintenance and the determination of profit

First of all, we need to define the different concepts of capital.

4.2 Definitions

Key term

> **Capital**. Under a **financial concept of capital**, such as invested money or invested purchasing power, capital is the net assets or equity of the entity. The financial concept of capital is adopted by most entities. Focusing on the equity ownership of the entity is often referred to as the **proprietary concept of capital**: if we pay all profits out as dividends and inflation exists then in future our business will gradually run down, as our cash will become insufficient to buy replacement inventory.

Under an **operating concept of capital (also known as physical concept of capital)**, such as operating capability, capital is the productive capacity of the entity based on, for example, units of output per day. Capital is looked at as the capacity to maintain a level of assets, by using **replacement cost** for our cost of sales we will set aside enough cash to buy replacement assets.

The definition of profit is also important.

Key term

Profit. The residual amount that remains after expenses (including capital maintenance adjustments, where appropriate) have been deducted from income. Any amount over and above that required to maintain the capital at the beginning of the period is profit.   *(Conceptual Framework)*

The main difference between the two concepts of capital maintenance is the treatment of the **effects of changes in the prices of assets and liabilities** of the entity. In general terms, an entity has maintained its capital if it has as much capital at the end of the period as it had at the beginning of the period. Any amount over and above that required to maintain the capital at the beginning of the period is profit.

(a)   **Financial capital maintenance**: profit is the increase in nominal money capital over the period. This is the concept used in CPP, and used under historical cost accounting.

(b)   **Operating or Physical capital maintenance**: profit is the increase in the physical productive capacity over the period. This is the concept used in CCA.

5 Current purchasing power (CPP)

FAST FORWARD

CPP accounting is a method of accounting for general (not specific) inflation. It does so by expressing asset values in a stable monetary unit, the $ of current purchasing power.

5.1 Capital maintenance in times of inflation

Profit can be measured as the **difference between how wealthy a company is at the beginning and at the end of an accounting period**.

(a)   This wealth can be expressed in terms of the capital of a company as shown in its opening and closing statements of financial position.

(b)   A business which maintains its capital unchanged during an accounting period can be said to have broken even.

(c)   Once **capital has been maintained**, **anything** achieved **in excess represents profit**.

For this analysis to be of any use, we must be able to draw up a company's statement of financial position at the beginning and at the end of a period, so as to place a value on the opening and closing capital. There are particular difficulties in doing this during a **period of rising prices**.

In conventional historical cost accounts, assets are stated in the statement of financial position at the amount it cost to acquire them (less any amounts written off in respect of depreciation or impairment in value). Capital is simply the **difference between assets and liabilities**.

Exam focus point

If prices are rising, it is possible for a company to show a profit in its historical cost accounts despite having identical physical assets and owing identical liabilities at the beginning and end of its accounting period.

For example, consider the following opening and closing statement of financial positions of a company.

	Opening	Closing
	$	$
Inventory (100 items at cost)	500	600
Other net assets	1,000	1,000
Capital	1,500	1,600

Assuming that no new capital has been introduced during the year, and no capital has been distributed as dividends, the profit shown in historical cost accounts would be $100, being the excess of closing capital over opening capital. And yet in physical terms the company is no better off: it still has 100 units of inventory (which cost $5 each at the beginning of the period, but $6 each at the end) and its other net assets are identical. The 'profit' earned has merely enabled the company to keep pace with inflation.

An alternative to the concept of capital maintenance based on historical costs is to express capital in **physical** terms. On this basis, no profit would be recognised in the example above because the physical substance of the company is unchanged over the accounting period. Capital is maintained if at the end of the period the company is in a position to achieve the same physical output as it was at the beginning of the period. You should bear in mind that financial definitions of capital maintenance are not the only ones possible; in theory at least, there is no reason why profit should not be measured as the increase in a company's **physical** capital over an accounting period.

5.2 The unit of measurement

Another way to tackle the problems of capital maintenance in times of rising prices is to look at the **unit of measurement** in which accounting values are expressed.

It is an axiom of conventional accounting, as it has developed over the years, that value should be measured in terms of money. It is also **implicitly assumed** that **money values are stable**, so that $1 at the start of the financial year has the same value as $1 at the end of that year. But when **prices are rising**, this assumption is invalid: **$1 at the end of the year has less value (less purchasing power) than it had one year previously**.

This leads to problems when aggregating amounts which have arisen at different times. For example, a company's non-current assets may include items bought at different times over a period of many years. They will each have been recorded in $s, but the value of $1 will have varied over the period. In effect the **non-current asset figure in a historical cost statement of financial position is an aggregate of a number of items expressed in different units**. It could be argued that such a figure is **meaningless**.

Faced with this argument, one possibility would be to re-state all accounts items in terms of a stable monetary unit. There would be difficulties in practice, but in theory there is no reason why a stable unit ($ CPP = $s of current purchasing power) should not be devised. In this section we will look at a system of accounting (current purchasing power accounting, or CPP) based on precisely this idea.

5.3 Specific and general price changes

We can identify two different types of price inflation.

When prices are rising, it is likely that the **current value of assets will also rise**, but not necessarily by the general rate of inflation. For example, if the replacement cost of a machine on 1 January 20X2 was $5,000, and the general rate of inflation in 20X2 was 8%, we would not necessarily expect the replacement cost of the machine at 31 December 20X2 to be $5,000 plus 8% = $5,400. The rate of price increase on the machinery might have been less than 8% or more than 8%. (Conceivably, in spite of general inflation, the replacement cost of the machinery might have gone down.)

(a) There is **specific price inflation**, which measures price changes over time for a specific asset or group of assets.

(b) There is **general price inflation**, which is the average rate of inflation, which reduces the general purchasing power of money.

To counter the problems of specific price inflation some system of current value accounting may be used (such as current cost accounting). The capital maintenance concepts underlying current value systems do not attempt to allow for the maintenance of real value in money terms.

Current purchasing power (CPP) accounting is based on a different concept of capital maintenance.

Key term

> **CPP** measures profits as the increase in the current purchasing power of equity. Profits are therefore stated after allowing for the declining purchasing power of money due to price inflation.

When applied to historical cost accounting, CPP is a system of accounting which makes adjustments to income and capital values to allow for the general rate of price inflation.

5.4 The principles and procedures of CPP accounting

In CPP accounting, profit is measured after allowing for general price changes. It is a fundamental idea of CPP that capital should be maintained in terms of the same monetary purchasing power, so that:

$$P_{CPP} = D_{CPP} + (E_{t(CPP)} - E_{(t-1)CPP})$$

where P_{CPP} is the CPP accounting profit

          D_{CPP} is distributions to shareholders, re-stated in current purchasing power terms

          $E_{t(CPP)}$ is the total value of assets attributable to the owners of the business entity at the end of the accounting period, restated in current purchasing power terms

          $E_{(t-1)CPP}$ is the total value of the owners' equity at the beginning of the year re-stated in terms of current purchasing power at the end of the year

A current purchasing power $ relates to the value of money on the last day of the accounting period.

Profit in CPP accounting is therefore measured after allowing for **maintenance of equity capital**. To the extent that a company is financed by loans, there is no requirement to allow for the maintenance of the purchasing power of the non-current liabilities. Indeed, as we shall see, the equity of a business can profit from the loss in the purchasing power value of loans.

5.5 Monetary and non-monetary items

Key term

> A **monetary item** is an asset or liability whose amount is fixed by contract or statute in terms of $s, regardless of changes in general price levels and the purchasing power of the currency.

The main examples of monetary items are cash, receivables, payables and non-current liabilities.

Key term

> A **non-monetary item** is an asset or liability whose value is not fixed by contract or statute.

These include land and buildings, plant and machinery and inventory.

In CPP accounting, the monetary items held must be looked at carefully.

(a)   If a company **borrows money in a period of inflation**, the amount of the debt will remain fixed (by law) so that when the debt is eventually paid, it will be paid in $s of a lower purchasing power.

        For example, if a company borrows $2,000 on 1 January 20X5 and repays the loan on 1 January 20X9, the purchasing power of the $2,000 repaid in 20X9 will be much less than the value of $2,000 in 20X5, because of inflation. Since the company by law must repay only $2,000 of principal, it has gained by having the use of the money from the loan for four years. (The lender of the $2,000 will try to protect the value of his loan in a period of inflation by charging a higher rate of interest; however, this does not alter the fact that the loan remains fixed at $2,000 in money value.)

(b)   If a company **holds cash in a period of inflation**, its value in terms of current purchasing power will decline. The company will 'lose' by holding the cash instead of converting it into a non-monetary asset. Similarly, if goods are sold on credit, the amount of the debt is fixed by contract; and in a period of inflation, the current purchasing power of the money from the sale, when it is eventually received, will be less than the purchasing power of the debt, when it was first incurred.

In CPP accounting, it is therefore argued that there are **gains from having monetary liabilities and losses from having monetary assets**.

(a) In the case of **monetary assets**, there is a need to make a charge against profit for the loss in purchasing power, because there will be a need for extra finance when the monetary asset is eventually used for operational activities. For example, if a company has a cash balance of $200, which is just sufficient to buy 100 new items of raw material inventory on 1 January 20X5, and if the rate of inflation during 20X5 is 10%, the company would need $220 to buy the same 100 items on 1 January 20X6 (assuming the items increase in value by the general rate of inflation). By holding the $200 as a monetary asset throughout 20X5, the company would need $20 more to buy the same goods and services on 1 January 20X6 that it could have obtained on 1 January 20X5. $20 would be a CPP loss on holding the monetary asset (cash) for a whole year.

(b) In the case of **monetary liabilities**, the argument in favour of including a 'profit' in CPP accounting is not as strong. By incurring a debt, say, on 1 January 20X5, there will not be any eventual cash input to the business. The 'profit' from the monetary liabilities is a 'paper' profit, and T A Lee, a notable economist, has argued against including it in the CPP statement of profit or loss.

5.6 Example: CPP accounting

Seep Co had the following assets and liabilities at 31 December 20X4.

(a) All non-current assets were purchased on 1 January 20X1 at a cost of $60,000, and they had an estimated life of six years. Straight-line depreciation is used.

(b) Closing inventories have a historical cost value of $7,900. They were bought in the period November-December 20X4.

(c) Receivables amounted to $8,000, cash to $2,000 and short-term payables to $6,000.

(d) There are non-current liabilities of $15,000.

(e) The general price index includes the following information:

Year	Date	Price index
20X1	1 January	100
20X4	30 November	158
20X4	31 December	160
20X5	31 December	180

The historical cost statement of financial position of Seep Co at 31 December 20X4 was as follows.

	$	$
Assets		
Non-current assets at cost		60,000
Less depreciation		40,000
		20,000
Current assets		
Inventories	7,900	
Receivables	8,000	
Cash	2,000	
		17,900
Total assets		37,900

Equity and liabilities
Capital

Equity	16,900
Loan capital	15,000
	31,900
Current liabilities: payables	6,000
Total equity and liabilities	37,900

Required

(a) Prepare a CPP statement of financial position as at 31 December 20X4.

(b) What was the depreciation charge against CPP profits in 20X4?

(c) What must be the value of equity at 31 December 20X5 if Seep Co is to 'break even' and make neither a profit nor a loss in 20X5?

Solution

(a) CPP STATEMENT OF FINANCIAL POSITION AS AT 31 DECEMBER 20X4

	$c	$c
Assets		
Non-current assets, at cost 60,000 × 160/100	96,000	
Less depreciation 40,000 × 160/100	64,000	
		32,000
Inventory* 7,900 × 160/158	8,000	
Receivables**	8,000	
Cash**	2,000	
		18,000
		50,000
Equity and liabilities		
Capital		
Loan capital**		15,000
Equity***		29,000
		44,000
Current liabilities: payables**		6,000
		50,000

Notes

*   Inventories purchased between 1 November and 31 December are assumed to have an average index value relating to the mid-point of their purchase period, at 30 November.

**   Monetary assets and liabilities are not re-valued, because their CPP value is the face value of the debt or cash amount.

***   Equity is a mixture of monetary and non-monetary asset values, and is the balancing figure in this example.

(b) Depreciation in 20X4 would be one sixth of the CPP value of the assets at the end of the year, $1/_6$ of $96,000 = $16,000. Alternatively, it is:

$(1/_6 \times \$60,000) \times 160/100 = \$16,000$

(c) To maintain the capital value of equity in CPP terms during 20X5, the CPP value of equity on 31 December 20X5 will need to be:

$\$29,000 \times 180/160 = \$32,625$

Question

Rice and Price set up in business on 1 January 20X5 with no non-current assets, and cash of $5,000. On 1 January they acquired inventories for the full $5,000, which they sold on 30 June 20X5 for $6,000. On 30 November they obtained a further $2,100 of inventory on credit. The index of the general price level gives the following index figures.

Date	Index
1 January 20X5	300
30 June 20X5	330
30 November 20X5	350
31 December 20X5	360

Calculate the CPP profits (or losses) of Rice and Price for the year to 31 December 20X5.

Answer

The approach is to prepare a CPP statement of profit or loss.

	$c	$c
Sales (6,000 × 360/330)		6,545
Less cost of goods sold (5,000 × 360/300)		6,000
		545
Loss on holding cash for 6 months*	(545)	
Gain by owing payables for 1 month**	60	
		485
CPP profit		60

*   ($6,000 × 360/330) – $6,000 = $c 545
** ($2,100 × 360/350) – $2,100 = $c 60

Note that under historical cost accounting the gross profit would be $1,000 ($6,000 - $5,000).

5.7 The advantages and disadvantages of CPP accounting

5.7.1 Advantages

(a)   The restatement of asset values in terms of a **stable money value** provides **a more meaningful basis of comparison** with other companies. Similarly, provided that previous years' profits are re-valued into CPP terms, it is also possible to compare the current year's results with past performance.

(b)   **Profit** is measured in **'real' terms** and excludes 'inflationary value increments'. This enables better forecasts of future prospects to be made.

(c)   CPP **avoids the subjective valuations** of current value accounting, because a single price index is applied to all non-monetary assets.

(d)   CPP **provides a stable monetary** unit with which to value profit and capital; ie $c.

(e)   Since it is based on historical cost accounting, **raw data is easily verified**, and measurements of value can be readily audited.

5.7.2 Disadvantages

(a)   It is not **clear what $c means**. 'Generalised purchasing power' as measured by a retail price index, or indeed any other general price index, has no obvious practical significance.

> *'Generalised purchasing power has no relevance to any person or entity because no such thing exists in reality, except as a statistician's computation.'*   (T A Lee)

(b)   The use of indices inevitably involves **approximations** in the measurements of value.

(c)   The value **of assets in a CPP statement of financial position has less meaning than a current value statement of financial position**. It cannot be supposed that the CPP value of net assets reflects:

(i)   The general goods and services that could be bought if the assets were released

(ii)   The consumption of general goods and services that would have to be forgone to replace those assets

In this respect, a CPP statement of financial position has similar drawbacks to an historical cost statement of financial position.

6 Current cost accounting (CCA)

FAST FORWARD

CCA is based on a physical concept of capital maintenance. Profit is recognised after the operating capability of the business has been maintained.

6.1 Value to the business (deprival value)

Current cost accounting (CCA) reflects an approach to capital maintenance based on maintaining the **operating capability** of a business. The conceptual basis of CCA is that the value of assets consumed or sold, and the value of assets in the statement of financial position, should be stated at their **value to the business** (also known as 'deprival value').

Deprival value is an important concept, which you may find rather difficult to understand at first, and you should read the following explanation carefully.

Key term

> The **deprival value** of an asset is the loss which a business entity would suffer if it were deprived of the use of the asset.

(a)   A basic assumption in CCA is that 'capital maintenance' should mean maintenance of the 'business substance' or 'operating capability' of the business entity. As we have seen already, it is generally accepted that profit is earned only after a sufficient amount has been charged against sales to ensure that the capital of the business is maintained. In CCA, a **physical** rather than financial definition of capital is used: capital maintenance is measured by the ability of the business entity to keep up the same level of operating capability.

(b)   'Value to the business' is the required method of valuation in current cost accounting, because it reflects the extra funds which would be required to maintain the operating capability of the business entity if it suddenly lost the use of an asset.

Value to the business, or deprival value, can be any of the following values.

(a)   **Replacement cost**: in the case of non-current assets, it is assumed that the replacement cost of an asset would be its net replacement cost (NRC), its gross replacement cost minus an appropriate provision for depreciation to reflect the amount of its life already 'used up'.

(b)   **Net realisable value** (NRV): what the asset could be sold for, net of any disposal costs.

(c)   **Economic value** (EV), or value in use: what the existing asset will be worth to the company over the rest of its useful life.

The choice of deprival value from one of the three values listed will depend on circumstances. In simple terms you should remember that in **CCA deprival value is nearly always replacement cost.**

If the asset is worth replacing, its deprival value will always be net replacement cost. If the asset is not worth replacing, it might have been disposed of straight away, or else it might have been kept in operation until the end of its useful life.

You may therefore come across a statement that deprival value is the **lower of**:

* **Net replacement cost**
* The **higher of net realisable value and economic value**

We have already seen that if an asset is not worth replacing, the deprival value will be NRV or EV. However, there are many assets which will not be replaced either because:

(a)   The asset is **technologically obsolete**, and has been (or will be) superseded by more modern equipment

(b)   The business is **changing the nature of its operations** and will not want to continue in the same line of business once the asset has been used up

Such assets, even though there are reasons not to replace them, would still be valued (usually) at net replacement cost, because this 'deprival value' still provides an estimate of the **operating capability** of the company.

6.2 CCA profits and deprival value

The deprival value of assets is reflected in the CCA statement of profit or loss by the following means.

(a)   **Depreciation** is charged on non-current assets on the basis of **gross replacement cost** of the asset (where NRC is the deprival value).

(b)   Where **NRV or EV** is the deprival value, the charge against CCA profits will be the **loss in value of the asset** during the accounting period; ie from its previous statement of financial position value to its current NRV or EV.

(c)   **Goods sold** are charged at their **replacement cost**. Thus if an item of inventory cost $15 to produce, and sells for $20, by which time its replacement cost has risen to $17, the CCA profit would be $3.

	$
Sales	20
Less replacement cost of goods sold	17
Current cost profit	3

6.3 Example: CCA v accounting for inflation

Suppose that Arthur Smith Co buys an asset on 1 January for $10,000. The estimated life of the asset is five years, and straight-line depreciation is charged. At 31 December the gross replacement cost of the asset is $10,500 (5% higher than on 1 January) but general inflation during the year, as measured by the retail price index, has risen 20%.

(a)   To maintain the value of the business against inflation, the asset should be revalued as follows.

	$
Gross ($10,000 × 120%)	12,000
Depreciation charge for the year (@ 20%)	2,400
Net value in the statement of financial position	9,600

(b)   In CCA, the business maintains its operating capability if we revalue the asset as follows.

	$
Gross replacement cost	10,500
Depreciation charge for the year (note)	2,100
NRC; statement of financial position value	8,400

Note	$
Historical cost depreciation	2,000
CCA depreciation adjustment (5%)	100
Total CCA depreciation cost	2,100

CCA preserves the operating capability of the company but does not necessarily preserve it against the declining value in the purchasing power of money (against inflation). As mentioned previously, CCA is a system which takes account of specific price inflation (changes in the prices of specific assets or groups of assets) but **not of general price inflation**.

A strict view of current cost accounting might suggest that a set of CCA accounts should be prepared from the outset on the basis of deprival values. In practice, current cost accounts are usually prepared by **starting from historical cost accounts and making appropriate adjustments**.

6.4 Current cost adjustments to historical cost profit

In current cost accounting, profit is calculated as follows.

	$
Historical cost profit	X
Less current cost operating adjustments	X
Current cost profit	X

The holding gains, both realised and unrealised, are excluded from current cost profit. The double entry for the debits in the current cost statement of profit or loss is to credit each operating adjustment to a non-distributable current cost reserve.

6.5 The current cost statement of profit or loss

The format of the current cost statement of profit or loss would show the following information, although not necessarily in the order given.

	$	$
Historical cost profit (before interest & taxation)		X
Current cost operating adjustments		
Cost of sales adjustment (COSA)	(X)	
Monetary working capital adjustment (loss or gain) (MWCA)	(X) or X	
Depreciation adjustment	(X)	
		(X)
Current cost operating profit (before interest and taxation)		X
Less interest payable and receivable		(X)
Add gearing adjustment		X
Current cost profit attributable to shareholders		X
Less taxation		(X)
Current cost profit for the year		X

6.6 Cost of sales adjustment (COSA)

The COSA is necessary to **eliminate realised holding gains** on inventory. It represents the difference between the replacement cost and the historical cost of goods sold. The exclusion of holding gains from CC profit is a necessary consequence of the need to maintain operating capability. The COSA represents that portion of the HC profit which must be consumed in replacing the inventory item sold so that trading can continue. Where practical difficulties arise in estimating replacement cost, a simple indexing system can be used.

6.7 Depreciation adjustment

The depreciation adjustment is the **difference between the depreciation charge on the gross replacement cost of the assets and the historical cost depreciation**. This is (as with the COSA) a realised holding gain which is excluded from the CC profit. Where comparison is made with a different asset for the purposes of calculating replacement cost (because of the obsolescence of the old asset), then allowance must be made for different useful lives and different production capabilities.

6.8 Monetary working capital adjustment (MWCA)

Where a company gives or takes credit for the sale or purchase of goods, the goods are paid for at the **end** of the credit period at the replacement cost as at the **beginning** of the credit period. If a company measures profit as the excess of revenue over cost:

(a)   **Outstanding payables protect** the company to some extent from **price changes** because the company lags behind current prices in its payment

(b)   **Outstanding receivables**, in contrast, would be a **burden on profits** in a period of rising prices because sales receipts will always relate to previous months' sales at a lower price/cost/profit level

The MWCA can therefore be **either a gain or a loss**.

6.9 The current cost statement of financial position

In the current cost statement of financial position:

- **Assets** will be valued at their '**value to the business**'.
- **Liabilities** will be valued at their **monetary amount**.
- There will be a current cost reserve to reflect the revaluation surpluses.

6.10 Example: Current cost accounts

At the beginning of a period, Arthur Smith Co has the following statement of financial position.

	$
Assets	
Non-current asset (newly acquired)	10,000
Inventories (newly acquired)	2,000
	12,000
Capital	
Equity	8,000
Loan stock (10% interest)	4,000
	12,000

The company gearing is 33%, in terms of both HC and CCA. During the period, sales of goods amounted to $15,000, the replacement cost of sales was $13,200 and the historical cost of sales was $12,000.

Closing inventories, at replacement cost, were $4,600 and at HC were $4,400. Depreciation is provided for at 10% straight line, and at the end of the period the non-current assets had a gross replacement cost of $11,000. The HC accounts were as follows.

STATEMENT OF PROFIT OR LOSS

	$
Sales	15,000
Less cost of sales	12,000
	3,000
Depreciation	1,000
Profit before interest	2,000
Interest	400
Profit	1,600

CLOSING STATEMENT OF FINANCIAL POSITION

	$
Non-current asset at cost less depreciation	9,000
Inventories	4,400
Cash	200
	13,600
Equity	9,600
Loan stock	4,000
	13,600

Taxation is ignored.

Required

Prepare workings for the CCA accounts. (Depreciation for the period will be based on the end of year value of the non-current asset. All sales and purchases were for cash.)

Solution

The COSA is ($13,200 – $12,000) = $1,200
The depreciation adjustment is: $100
The MWCA is nil (there are no purchases or sales on credit).

Note: The small cash balance in the closing statement of financial position might be regarded as necessary for business purposes and therefore taken up in the MWCA as monetary working capital. In this example, we will treat the $200 as a cash surplus.

	$	$
Historical cost profit (before interest)		2,000
Current cost adjustments		
COSA	1,200	
MWCA	0	
Depreciation	100	
		1,300
Current cost operating profit		700

The gearing adjustment is calculated by multiplying the three current cost adjustments (here $1,300) by the gearing proportion (by the proportion of the gains which is financed by borrowing and which therefore provides additional profits for equity, since the real value of the borrowing is declining in a period of rising prices).

The gearing proportion is the ratio:

$$\frac{\text{Net borrowing}}{\text{Average net operating assets in the year}}$$

Net operating assets consist of non-current assets, inventories and monetary working capital. They are financed partly by net borrowings and partly by equity. The gearing proportion can therefore equally well be expressed as:

$$\frac{\text{Average net borrowing in the period}}{\text{Average equity interests plus average net borrowing in the period}}$$

Equity interests include the current cost reserve, and also any proposed dividends. Average figures are taken as being more representative than end of year figures.

	$
Opening figures	
Net borrowing	4,000
Equity interests	8,000
Equity plus net borrowing	12,000

Closing figures

Since cash is here regarded as a surplus amount, the company is losing value during a period of inflation by holding cash – just as it is gaining by having fixed loans. If cash is not included in MWC, it is:

(a)   Deducted from net borrowings
(b)   Excluded from net operating assets

(Net operating assets consist of non-current assets, long-term trade investments, inventories and monetary working capital.)

The closing figures are therefore as follows.

	$	$
Non-current assets (at net replacement cost $11,000 – $1,100)		9,900
Inventories (at replacement cost)		4,600
Monetary working capital		0
Net operating assets (equals equity interest plus net borrowings)		14,500
Less: net borrowing	4,000	
cash in hand	(200)	
		3,800
Therefore equity interest		10,700

Average figures	Opening	Closing	Average
Net borrowing	$4,000	$3,800	$3,900
Net operating assets	$12,000	$14,500	$13,250

The gearing proportion is: $\dfrac{3,900}{13,250} \times 100\% = 29.43\%$

Exam focus point

> The above example is more complicated than you would meet in the exam. However, it is useful to show all the workings.

Question

Prepare the CCA accounts based on the above example.

Answer

CCA STATEMENT OF PROFIT OR LOSS

	$	$
Historical cost profit before interest		2,000
Current cost adjustments		
COSA	1,200	
MWCA	0	
Depreciation	100	
		(1,300)
Current cost operating profit		700
Interest	(400)	
Gearing adjustment ($1,300 × 29.43%)	383	
		(17)
Current cost profit		683

CCA STATEMENT OF FINANCIAL POSITION (end of year)

	$	$
Non-current assets (net replacement cost)		9,900
Inventories (replacement cost)		4,600
Cash		200
		14,700
Financed by		
Equity at start of year		8,000
Addition to reserves during year		683
Current cost reserve		
Excess of net replacement cost over carrying value (9,900 – 9,000)	900	
Depreciation adjustment	100	
COSA	1,200	
MWCA	0	
	2,200	
Less gearing adjustment	(383)	
	1,817	
Add revaluation of year-end inventories	200	
		2,017
		10,700
Loan stock		4,000
		14,700

6.11 The advantages and disadvantages of current cost accounting

6.11.1 Advantages

(a)   By excluding holding gains from profit, CCA can be used to indicate whether the dividends paid to shareholders will **reduce the operating capability** of the business.

(b)   Assets are valued after management has considered the **opportunity cost** of holding them, and the expected benefits from their future use. CCA is therefore a useful guide for management in deciding whether to hold or sell assets.

(c)   It is **relevant** to the needs of information users in:

(i)   Assessing the stability of the business entity

(ii)   Assessing the vulnerability of the business (eg to a takeover), or the liquidity of the business

(iii)   Evaluating the performance of management in maintaining and increasing the business substance

(iv)   Judging future prospects

(d)   It can be **implemented fairly easily** in practice, by making simple adjustments to the historical cost accounting profits. A current cost statement of financial position can also be prepared with reasonable simplicity.

6.11.2 Disadvantages

(a)   It is impossible to make valuations of EV or NRV without **subjective judgements**. The measurements used are therefore not objective.

(b)   There are several problems to be overcome in deciding how to provide an **estimate of replacement** costs for non-current assets.

(i)   It must be understood from the outset that whereas depreciation based on the historical cost of an asset can be viewed as a means of spreading the cost of the asset over its estimated life, depreciation based on replacement costs does not conform to this traditional accounting view.

(ii)   Depreciation based on replacement costs would appear to be a means of providing that sufficient funds are set aside in the business to ensure that the asset can be replaced at the end of its life. But if it is not certain what technological advances might be in the next few years and how the type of assets required might change between the current time and the estimated time of replacement, it is difficult to argue that depreciation based on today's costs is a valid way of providing for the eventual physical replacement of the asset.

(iii)   It is more correct, however, that depreciation in CCA does not set aside funds for the physical replacement of non-current assets.

'CCA aims to maintain no more and no less than the facilities that are available at the accounting date... despite the fact that the non-current assets which provide those facilities might never be replaced in their existing or currently available form... In simple language, this means charging depreciation on the basis of the current replacement cost of the assets at the time the facilities are used.'
(Mallinson)

(iv)   It may be argued that depreciation based on historical cost is more accurate than replacement cost depreciation, because the historical cost is known, whereas replacement cost is simply an estimate. However, replacement costs are re-assessed each year, so that inaccuracies in the estimates in one year can be rectified in the next year.

(c)   The mixed value approach to valuation means that some assets will be valued at replacement cost, but others will be valued at net realisable value or economic value. It is arguable that the **total assets** will, therefore, have an **aggregate value** which is **not particularly meaningful** because of this mixture of different concepts.

(d)   It can be argued that **'deprival value'** is an **unrealistic concept**, because the business entity has not been deprived of the use of the asset. This argument is one which would seem to reject the fundamental approach to 'capital maintenance' on which CCA is based.

Chapter roundup

- **Comprehensive income** means **all** transactions for the period, other than those between an entity and its owners. As we have seen in Chapter 3, IAS 1 (revised) requires the reporting of comprehensive income.

- The concept of **fair value** has become very important since the issue of IAS 39. Entities are now permitted to remeasure certain financial instruments to fair value. This practice continues under IFRS 9 which will eventually replace IAS 39.

- There are several advantages and disadvantages to using historical cost accounts. A number of alternatives to historical cost accounting are presently under discussion. Some progress has been made and more can be expected in the future.

- The concept of capital selected should be appropriate to the needs of the users of an entity's financial statements.

- CPP accounting is a method of accounting for general (not specific) inflation. It does so by expressing asset values in a stable monetary unit, the $ of current purchasing power.

- CCA is based on a physical concept of capital maintenance. Profit is recognised after the operating capability of the business has been maintained.

Quick quiz

1   Can methods of current value accounting be described as systems for accounting for inflation?

2   Distinguish between specific price inflation and general price inflation.

3   What is an asset's deprival value if it is not worth replacing?

Answers to quick quiz

1   No

2   • Specific price inflation measures price changes over time for a specific asset or group of assets
     • General price inflation measures the continual reduction in the general purchasing power of money

3   The higher of net realisable value and economic value

End of chapter question

Income measurement and capital maintenance concepts (AIA November 2007)

As part of a staff development event, EduInc gave four members of staff from its finance department, April, Ben, Charlie and Deni, $200 each asking them to each make as much profit as they could within the hour. Purely by chance, each person bought an item which cost exactly $200 cash and sold it just before the hour ended for $300 cash when each item's replacement cost was $240. Each person was also asked to produce a profit calculation and statement of financial position to record the events, assuming general prices had increased over the hour by 10%. As an incentive each employee was allowed to keep (as a dividend) the amount calculated as 'profit'.

The statements produced by the four employees have been summarised as follows:

	April $	Ben $	Charlie $	Deni $
Profit calculation				
Sales	300	300	300	300
Less cost of sales	(200)	(200)	(240)	(240)
Operating profit	100	100	60	60
Less inflation adjustment	–	20	–	–
Profit	100	80	60	60
Statements of financial position				
Equity at start	200	200	200	200
Profit	100	80	60	60
Realised holding gain				40
				100
Less inflation adjustment				20
Real profit				80
Less dividend	(100)	(80)	(60)	(60)
				20
	200	200	200	220
Financial capital maintenance reserve				
		20		20
Realised holding gain	–	–	40	–
Equity at end	200	220	240	240
Cash	200	220	240	240

The organiser of the event is confused that despite each employee entering into exactly the same transaction and starting from exactly the same point, they have each produced different calculation of profit and/or statements of financial position.

Required

Provide an explanation of the four different profit measurement and capital maintenance concepts demonstrated above.

(17 marks)

Substance of transactions

Topic list	Syllabus reference
1 Off balance sheet finance explained	11.1, 11.4
2 Substance over form	11.1, 11.4
3 The IASB *Conceptual Framework*	11.1, 11.4
4 Common forms of off balance sheet finance	11.1, 11.4

Introduction

This is a very topical area and has been for some time. Companies (and other entities) have in the past used the **legal form** of a transaction to determine its accounting treatment, when in fact the **substance** of the transaction has been very different. We will look at the question of **substance over form** and the kind of transactions undertaken by entities trying to avoid reporting true substance in Sections 1 and 2.

The main weapon in tackling these abuses is the IASB's *Conceptual Framework for Financial Reporting* because it applies **general definitions** to the elements that make up financial statements. We will look at how this works in Section 3.

In Section 4 common forms of off balance sheet finance are explained through a series of example transactions.

1 Off balance sheet finance explained

The subject of **off balance sheet finance** is a complex one which has plagued the accountancy profession. In practice, off balance sheet finance schemes are often very sophisticated and these are beyond the range of this syllabus.

Key term

Off balance sheet finance is the funding or refinancing of a company's operations in such a way that, under legal requirements and traditional accounting conventions, some or all of the finance may not be shown in its statement of financial position.

'Off balance sheet transactions' are transactions which meet the above objective. These transactions may involve the **removal of assets** from the statement of financial position, as well as liabilities, and they are also likely to have a significant impact on profit or loss.

1.1 Why off balance sheet finance exists

Why might company managers wish to enter into such transactions?

(a)   In some countries, companies traditionally have a lower level of gearing than companies in other countries. Off balance sheet finance is used to **keep gearing low**, probably because of the views of analysts and brokers.

(b)   A company may need to keep its gearing down in order to stay within the terms of **loan covenants** imposed by lenders.

(c)   A quoted company with high borrowings is often expected (by analysts and others) to declare a **rights issue** in order to reduce gearing. This has an adverse effect on a company's share price and so off balance sheet financing is used to reduce gearing and the expectation of a rights issue.

(d)   Analysts' short-term views are a problem for companies **developing assets** which are not producing income during the development stage. Such companies will match the borrowings associated with such developing assets, along with the assets themselves, off balance sheet. They are brought back into the financial statements once income is being generated by the assets. This process keeps return on capital employed higher than it would have been during the development stage.

(e)   In the past, groups of companies have excluded **subsidiaries** from consolidation in an off balance sheet transaction because they carry out completely different types of business and have different characteristics. The usual example is a leasing company (in, say, a retail group) which has a high level of gearing.

You can see from this brief list of reasons that the overriding motivation is to avoid **misinterpretation**. In other words, the company does not trust the analysts or other users to understand the reasons for a transaction and so avoids any effect such transactions might have by keeping them out of the financial statements. Unfortunately, the position of the company is then misstated and the user of the accounts is misled.

You must understand that not all forms of 'off balance sheet finance' are undertaken for cosmetic or accounting reasons. Some transactions are carried out to **limit or isolate risk**, to reduce interest costs and so on. In other words, these transactions are in the best interests of the company, not merely a cosmetic repackaging of figures which would normally appear in the statement of financial position.

1.2 The off balance sheet finance problem

The result of the use of increasingly sophisticated off balance sheet finance transactions is a situation where the users of financial statements do not have a proper or clear view of the **state of the company's affairs**. The disclosures required by national company law and accounting standards did not in the past provide sufficient rules for disclosure of off balance sheet finance transactions and so very little of the true nature of the transaction was exposed.

Whatever the purpose of such transactions, **insufficient disclosure** creates a problem. This problem has been debated over the years by the accountancy profession and other interested parties and some progress has been made (see the later sections of this chapter). However, company collapses during recessions have often revealed much higher borrowings than originally thought, because part of the borrowing was not disclosed in the financial statements.

The main argument used for banning off balance sheet finance is that the true **substance** of the transactions should be shown, not merely the **legal form**, particularly when it is exacerbated by poor disclosure.

2 Substance over form

Key term

> **Substance over form.** The principle that transactions and other events are accounted for and presented in accordance with their substance and economic reality and not merely their legal form.

This is a very important concept. It is used to **determine accounting treatment** in financial statements through accounting standards and so prevent off balance sheet transactions. The following paragraphs give examples of where the principle of substance over form is enforced in various accounting standards.

2.1 IAS 17 *Leases*

In IAS 17, there is an explicit requirement that if the lessor transfers substantially all the **risks and rewards of ownership** to the lessee then, even though the legal title has not necessarily passed, the item being leased should be shown as an asset in the statement of financial position of the lessee and the amount due to the lessor should be shown as a liability.

2.2 IAS 24 *Related party disclosures*

IAS 24 requires financial statements to disclose fully any material transactions undertaken with a related party by the reporting entity, **regardless of any price charged**.

2.3 IAS 11 *Construction contracts*

In IAS 11 there is a requirement to account for **attributable profits** on construction contracts under the accruals convention. However, there may be a problem with realisation, since it is arguable whether we should account for profit which, although attributable to the work done, may not have yet been invoiced to the customer. It is argued that the convention of substance over form is applied to justify ignoring the strict legal position.

2.4 Creative accounting

You may also hear the term **creative accounting** used in the context of reporting the substance of transactions. This can be defined simply as the manipulation of figures for a desired result. Remember, however, that it is very rare for a company, its directors or employees to manipulate results for the purpose of fraud. The major consideration is usually the effect the results will have on the company's share price. Some areas open to abuse (although some of these loopholes have been closed) are given below and you should by now understand how these can distort a company results.

(a)   Income recognition and cut-off
(b)   Impairment of purchased goodwill
(c)   Manipulation of reserves
(d)   Revaluations and depreciation
(e)   Window dressing
(f)   Changes in accounting policy

Question	Creative accounting

Creative accounting, off balance sheet finance and related matters (in particular how ratio analysis can be used to discover these practices) often come up in articles in the financial press. Find a library, preferably a good technical library, which can provide you with copies of back issues of such newspapers or journals and look for articles on creative accounting. You might find it useful to read about the Enron accounting scandal which involved off balance sheet finance and meant that debt was not reported in the financial statements.

3 The IASB *Conceptual Framework*

FAST FORWARD

Make sure that you have memorised the definitions for **assets and liabilities** (and **income** and **expenses**) and the criteria for their **recognition** given in the IASB's *Conceptual Framework*.

The 1989 Framework included substance over form as a qualitative characteristic. The 2011 Conceptual Framework does not specifically mention substance over form but the IASB considers it to be implied in the concept of 'faithful representation'. To account for an item according to its legal form but not its economic substance would not be a faithful representation.

(a)   For the majority of transactions there is **no difference** between the two and therefore no issue.

(b)   For other transactions **substance and form diverge** and the choice of treatment can give different results due to non-recognition of an asset or liability even though benefits or obligations result.

Full disclosure is not enough: all transactions must be **accounted for** correctly, with full disclosure of related details as necessary to give the user of accounts a full understanding of the transactions.

3.1 Relationship to accounting standards

The interaction of the *Conceptual Framework* **with other Standards** is also an important issue. Whichever rules are the more specific should be applied, given that IFRSs should be consistent with the *Conceptual Framework*. Leasing provides a good example: straightforward leases which fall squarely within the terms of IAS 17 should be accounted for without any need to refer to the *Conceptual Framework*, but where their terms are more complex, or the lease is only one element in a larger series of transactions, then the *Conceptual Framework* comes into play.

3.2 Basic principles

How else does the *Conceptual Framework* enforce the substance over form rule? Its main method is to define the elements of financial statements and therefore to give rules for their recognition. The key considerations are whether a transaction has **given rise to new assets and liabilities**, and whether it has **changed any existing assets and liabilities**.

The characteristics of transactions whose substance is not readily apparent are as follows.

(a)   The **legal title** to an item is separated from the ability to enjoy the principal benefits, and the exposure to the main risks associated with it.

(b)   The transaction is **linked to one or more others** so that the commercial effect of the transaction cannot be understood without reference to the complete series.

(c)   The transaction includes **one or more options**, under such terms that it makes it highly likely that the option(s) will be exercised.

3.3 Definitions

As we saw in Chapter 6 these are perhaps the most important definitions.

Key terms

An **asset** is a resource controlled by the entity as a result of past events and from which future economic benefits are expected to flow to the entity.

A **liability** is a present obligation of the entity arising from past events, the settlement of which is expected to result in an outflow from the entity of resources embodying economic benefits.*(Conceptual Framework)*

Identification of **who has the risks** relating to an asset will generally indicate **who has the benefits** and hence **who has the asset**. If an entity is in certain circumstances unable to avoid an **outflow of benefits**, this will provide evidence that it has a liability.

The definitions given in the IASB *Conceptual Framework* of income and expenses are not as important as those of assets and liabilities. This is because income and expenses are **described in terms of changes in assets and liabilities**, ie they are secondary definitions.

Key terms

Income is increases in economic benefits during the accounting period in the form of inflows or enhancements of assets or decreases of liabilities that result in increases in equity, other than those relating to contributions from equity participants.

Expenses are decreases in economic benefits during the accounting period in the form of outflows or depletions of assets or incurrences of liabilities that result in decreases in equity, other than those relating to distributions to equity participants.   *(Conceptual Framework)*

The real importance, then, is the way the *Conceptual Framework* defines assets and liabilities. This forces entities to acknowledge their assets and liabilities regardless of the legal status.

It is not sufficient, however, that the asset or liability fulfils the above definitions; it must also satisfy **recognition criteria** in order to be shown in an entity's accounts.

3.4 Recognition

Key term

Recognition is the process of incorporating in the financial statements an item that meets the definition of an element and satisfies the criteria for recognition set out below. It involves the depiction of the item in words and by a monetary amount and the inclusion of that amount in the statement of financial position or statement of comprehensive income totals.

The next key question is deciding **when** something which satisfies the definition of an asset or liability has to be recognised in the statement of financial position. Where a transaction results in an item that meets the definition of an asset or liability, that item should be recognised in the statement of financial position if:

(a)   It is **probable that a future inflow or outflow** of benefit to or from the entity will occur, *and*
(b)   The item can be **measured at a monetary amount with sufficient reliability.**

This effectively prevents entities abusing the definitions of the elements by recognising items that are vague in terms of likelihood of occurrence and measurability. If this were not in force, entities could **manipulate the financial statements** in various ways, eg recognising assets when the likely future economic benefits cannot yet be determined.

Probability is assessed based on the situation at the reporting date. For example, it is usually expected that some customers of an entity will not pay what they owe. The expected level of non-payment is based on past experience and the receivables asset is reduced by a percentage (the general doubtful debt provision).

Measurement must be reliable, but it does not preclude the use of **reasonable estimates**, which is an essential part of the financial statement preparation.

Even if something does not qualify for recognition now, it may meet the criteria **at a later date**.

3.5 Other standards

The *Conceptual Framework* provides the general guidance for reporting the substance of transactions and preventing off balance sheet finance. The IASB has developed guidance for specific transactions. These were mentioned in Section 2 and they are covered in various parts of this text. You should consider the particular off balance sheet finance problem they tackle as you study them.

- IAS 17 *Leases*
- IAS 18 *Revenue*
- IAS 24 *Related party disclosures*

3.6 Section summary

Important points to remember from the *Conceptual Framework* are:

- Substance over form
- Definitions of assets and liabilities
- Definition of recognition
- Criteria for recognition

4 Common forms of off balance sheet finance

FAST FORWARD ▶ Some of the **major types** of off balance sheet finance include factoring and sale and leaseback.

We will consider how the principles of the *Conceptual Framework* would be applied to these transactions.

- Consignment inventory
- Sale and repurchase agreements
- Sale and leaseback transactions
- Factoring of receivables/debts

Exam focus point

These examples are taken from a UK standard on reporting the substance of transactions, but that standard uses almost the same definitions for assets, liabilities, recognition, etc as the IASB *Conceptual Framework*, and so these notes are applicable internationally. Note also that, in all the cases discussed, there may be situations somewhere between the two extremes given in each.

4.1 Consignment inventory

Consignment inventory is an arrangement where inventory is held by one party (say a distributor) but is owned by another party (for example a manufacturer or a finance company). Consignment inventory is common in the motor trade and is similar to goods sold on a 'sale or return' basis.

To identify the correct treatment, it is necessary to identify the point at which the distributor or dealer acquired the benefits of the asset (the inventory) rather than the point at which legal title was acquired. If the manufacturer has the right to require the return of the inventory, and if that right is likely to be exercised, then the inventory is *not* an asset of the dealer. If the dealer is rarely required to return the inventory, then this part of the transaction will have little commercial effect in practice and should be ignored for accounting purposes. The potential liability would need to be disclosed in the financial statements.

4.1.1 Summary of indications of asset status

The following analysis summarises the range of possibilities in such a transaction.

Indications that the inventory is *not an asset* of the dealer at delivery	Indications that the inventory *is an asset* of the dealer at delivery
Manufacturer can require dealer to **return inventory** (or transfer inventory to another dealer) without compensation.	Manufacturer cannot require dealer to **return or transfer inventory**.
Penalty paid by the dealer to prevent returns/transfers of inventory at the manufacturer's request.	**Financial incentives** given to persuade dealer to transfer inventory at manufacturer's request.
Dealer has unfettered **right to return inventory** to the manufacturer without penalty and actually exercises the right in practice.	Dealer has **no right to return inventory** or is commercially compelled not to exercise its right of return.
Manufacturer bears **obsolescence risk**, eg: • Obsolete inventory is returned to the manufacturer without penalty, or • Financial incentives given by manufacturer to prevent inventory being returned to it (eg on a model change or if it becomes obsolete).	Dealer bears **obsolescence risk**, eg: • Penalty charged if dealer returns inventory to manufacturer, or • Obsolete inventory cannot be returned to the manufacturer and no compensation is paid by manufacturer for losses due to obsolescence.
Inventory **transfer price** charged by manufacturer is based on manufacturer's list price at date of transfer of legal title.	Inventory **transfer price** charged by manufacturer is based on manufacturer's list price at date of delivery.
Manufacturer bears **slow movement risk**, eg: transfer price set independently of time for which dealer holds inventory, and there is no deposit.	Dealer bears **slow movement risk**, eg: • Dealer is effectively charged interest as transfer price or other payments to manufacturer vary with time for which dealer holds inventory, *or* • Dealer makes a substantial interest-free deposit that varies with the levels of inventory held.

4.1.2 Required accounting

The following apply where it is concluded that the inventory **is in substance an asset** of the dealer.

(a)   The inventory should be recognised as such in the dealer's statement of financial position, together with a corresponding liability to the manufacturer.

(b)   Any deposit should be deducted from the liability and the excess classified as a trade payable.

Where it is concluded that the inventory is **not in substance an asset** of the dealer, the following apply.

(a)   The inventory should not be included in the dealer's statement of financial position until the transfer of risks and rewards has crystallised.

(b)   Any deposit should be included under 'other receivables'.

Question
Recognition

Daley Motors Co owns a number of car dealerships throughout a geographical area. The terms of the arrangement between the dealerships and the manufacturer are as follows.

(a)   Legal title passes when the cars are either used by Daley Co for demonstration purposes or sold to a third party.

(b)   The dealer has the right to return vehicles to the manufacturer without penalty. (Daley Co has rarely exercised this right in the past.)

(c)   The transfer price is based on the manufacturer's list price at the date of delivery.

(d)   Daley Co makes a substantial interest-free deposit based on the number of cars held.

Should the asset and liability be recognised by Daley Co at the date of delivery?

Answer

(a)   Legal form is irrelevant
(b)   Yes: only because rarely exercised (otherwise 'no')
(c)   Yes
(d)   Yes: the dealership is effectively forgoing the interest which could be earned on the cash sum

4.2 Sale and repurchase agreements and sale and leaseback transactions

These are arrangements under which the company sells an asset to another person on terms that allow the company to **repurchase the asset** in certain circumstances. A common example is the sale and repurchase of maturing whisky inventories. The key question is whether the transaction is a **straightforward sale**, or whether it is, in effect, a **secured loan**. It is necessary to look at the arrangement to determine who has the rights to the economic benefits that the asset generates, and the terms on which the asset is to be repurchased.

If the seller has the right to the benefits of the **use of the asset**, and the repurchase terms are such that the **repurchase is likely** to take place, the transaction should be accounted for as a **loan**.

4.2.1 Summary of indications of the sale of the asset

The following summary is helpful.

Indications of *sale* of original asset to buyer (nevertheless, the seller may retain a different asset)	Indications of *no sale* of original asset to buyer (secured loan)
	Sale price does not equal **market value** at date of sale.
No commitment for **seller to repurchase** asset, eg call option where there is a real possibility the option will fail to be exercised.	Commitment for **seller to repurchase** asset, eg: • Put and call option with the same exercise price • Either a put or a call option with no genuine commercial possibility that the option will fail to be exercised, *or* • Seller requires asset back to use in its business, or asset is in effect the only source of seller's future sales
Risk of **changes in asset value** borne by buyer such that buyer does not receive solely a lender's return, eg both sale and repurchase price equal market value at date of sale/repurchase.	Risk of **changes in asset value** borne by seller such that buyer receives solely a lender's return, eg: • Repurchase price equals sale price plus costs plus interest • Original purchase price adjusted retrospectively to pass variations in the value of the asset to the seller • Seller provides residual value guarantee to buyer or subordinated debt to protect buyer from falls in the value of the asset
Nature of the asset is such that it will be used over the life of the agreement, and seller has no rights to **determine its use**. Seller has no rights to determine asset's development or future sale.	Seller retains right to **determine asset's use**, development or sale, or rights to profits therefrom.

4.2.2 Required accounting

Where the substance of the transaction is that of a **secured loan**:

(a)   The seller should continue to recognise the original asset and record the proceeds received from the buyer as a liability.

(b)   Interest, however designated, should be accrued.

(c)   The carrying amount of the asset should be reviewed for impairment and written down if necessary.

4.2.3 Sale and leaseback transactions

A sale and leaseback transaction involves the sale of an asset and the leasing back of the same asset. The lease payment and the sale price are usually negotiated as a package.

The accounting treatment depends upon the type of lease involved. If the transaction results in a **finance lease**, then it is in substance a loan from the lessor to the lessee (the lessee has sold the asset and then leased it back), with the asset as security. In this case, any 'profit' on the sale should not be recognised as such, but should be deferred and amortised over the lease term.

If the transaction results in an **operating lease** and the transaction has been conducted at **fair value**, then it can be regarded as a normal sale transaction. The asset is derecognised and any profit on the sale is recognised. The operating lease instalments are treated as lease payments, rather than repayments of capital plus interest.

If the result is an operating lease and the sale price was **below fair value**, this may be being **compensated for by lower rentals** in the future. If this is the case, any loss on sale should be amortised over the period for which the asset is expected to be used. If the sale price was **above fair value** any excess is deferred and amortised over the period for which the asset is expected to be used.

Question   Recognition and sales proceeds

A construction company, Mecanto Co, agrees to sell to Hamlows Bank some of the land within its landbank. The terms of the sale are as follows.

(a)   The sales price is to be at open market value.

(b)   Mecanto Co has the right to develop the land on the basis that it will pay all the outgoings on the land plus an annual fee of 5% of the purchase price.

(c)   Mecanto has the option to buy back the land at any time within the next five years. The repurchase price is based on:

   (i)   original purchase price
   (ii)   expenses relating to the purchase
   (iii) an interest charge of base rate + 2%
   (iv)   less amounts received from Mecanto by Hamlows

(d)   At the end of five years Hamlows Bank may offer the land for sale generally. Any shortfall on the proceeds relative to the agreed purchase price agreed with Mecanto has to be settled by Mecanto in cash.

Should the asset continue to be recognised by Mecanto Co and the sales proceeds treated as a loan?

Answer

(a)   No: the sales price is as for an arm's length transaction.

(b)   Yes: Mecanto has control over the asset.
      Yes: Mecanto has to pay a fee based on cash received.

(c)   Yes: interest is charged on the proceeds paid by Mecanto.
      Yes: the repurchase price is based on the lender's return

(d)   Yes: options ensure that Mecanto bears all the risk (both favourable and unfavourable) of changes in the market value of the land.

4.3 Factoring of receivables/debts

Where debts or receivables are factored, the original creditor **sells the debts to the factor**. The sales price may be fixed at the outset or may be adjusted later. It is also common for the factor to offer a credit facility that allows the seller to draw upon a proportion of the amounts owed.

In order to determine the correct accounting treatment it is necessary to consider whether the benefit of the debts has been passed on to the factor, or whether the factor is, in effect, providing a loan on the security of the receivable balances. If the seller has to **pay interest** on the difference between the amounts advanced to him and the amounts that the factor has received, and if the seller bears the **risks of non-payment** by the debtor, then the indications would be that the transaction is, in effect, a loan.

4.3.1 Summary of indications of appropriate treatment

The following is a summary of indicators of the appropriate treatment.

Indications the debts are *not an asset* of the seller	Indications that the debts are an *asset* of the seller
Transfer is for a **single non-returnable fixed sum**.	**Finance cost varies** with speed of collection of debts, eg: • By adjustment to consideration for original transfer, or • Subsequent transfers priced to recover costs of earlier transfers.
There is **no recourse** to the seller for losses.	There is **full recourse** to the seller for losses.
Factor is paid **all amounts** received from the factored debts (and no more). Seller has no rights to further sums from the factor.	Seller is required to **repay** amounts received from the factor on or before a set date, regardless of timing or amounts of collections from debtors.

4.3.2 Required accounting

Where the seller has retained no significant benefits and risks relating to the debts and has no obligation to repay amounts received from the factors, the receivables should be removed from its statement of financial position and no liability shown in respect of the proceeds received from the factor. A profit or loss should be recognised, calculated as the difference between the carrying amount of the debts and the proceeds received.

Where the seller does retain significant benefits and risks, a gross asset (equivalent in amount to the gross amount of the receivables) should be shown in the statement of financial position of the seller within assets, and a corresponding liability in respect of the proceeds received from the factor should be shown within liabilities. The interest element of the factor's charges should be recognised as it accrues and included in profit or loss with other interest charges. Other factoring costs should be similarly accrued.

Chapter roundup

- The subject of **off balance sheet finance** is a complex one which has plagued the accountancy profession. In practice, off balance sheet finance schemes are often very sophisticated and these are beyond the range of this syllabus.

- Make sure that you have memorised the definitions for **assets and liabilities** (and **income** and **expenses**) and the criteria for their **recognition** given in the IASB's *Conceptual Framework*.

- Some of the **major types** of off balance sheet finance include factoring and sale and leaseback.

Quick quiz

1   Why do companies want to use off balance sheet finance?

2   Describe the concept of substance over form?

3   What are the common features of transactions whose substance is not readily apparent?

4   When should a transaction be recognised?

Answers to quick quiz

1   The overriding motivation is to avoid misinterpretation. However, the result is that users are misled.

2   The principle that transactions and other events are accounted for and presented in accordance with their substance and economic reality rather than merely their legal form.

3   (a)   The legal title is separated from the ability to enjoy benefits.

    (b)   The transaction is linked to others so that the commercial effect cannot be understood without reference to the complete series.

    (c)   The transaction includes one or more options under such terms that it is likely the option(s) will be exercised.

4   When it is probable that a future inflow or outflow of economic benefit to the entity will occur and the item can be measured in monetary terms with sufficient reliability.

End of chapter question

Floatem[21] (AIA November 2008)

Floatem[21](F21) is based in Hong Kong. The company sells a small power boat *The Knotbuster* which it purchases from Sailwell plc (S) a manufacturer based in the South of England. Boats are supplied to Floatem[21] on the following terms:

		Contract Terms
1	Transfer price	Based on the manufactured list price at the date of delivery.
2	Legal title	Will pass to F21 when the boats are either sold to third parties in the ordinary course of business or used as demonstration models.
3	Returns	Both S and F21 have the unconditional option to have the boats returned to S.
4	Damaged goods	S will charge a penalty of 15% of the manufactured price if goods are returned damaged or cannot be sold by S within six months of their return.
5	Deposit	F21 must pay an interest free deposit of 10% of the manufactured price per boat.

The finance director of Floatem[21] is not sure whether the company's stock of *Knotbuster* boats should be included on its statement of financial position as inventory and has asked you for advice. He is particularly confused because the risks and rewards of ownership appear to be shared between the two companies.

Required

Explain the factors for and against treating the stock of boats as an asset of Floatem[21] and advise the finance director.   **(10 marks)**

Accounting for tangible non-current assets

Topic list	Syllabus reference
1 Depreciation accounting	11.2
2 IAS 16 *Property, plant and equipment*	11.2
3 IAS 20 *Government grants*	11.2
4 IAS 40 *Investment property*	11.2
5 IAS 36 *Impairment of assets*	11.2
6 IAS 23 *Borrowing costs*	11.2

Introduction

IAS 16 should be familiar to you from your earlier studies, as should the mechanics of accounting for depreciation, revaluations and disposals of non-current assets. Some questions are given here for revision purposes.

IAS 20 on government grants is a straightforward Standard and you should have few problems with it.

IAS 40 deals with investment properties, which can be treated differently from other property under IAS 16.

IAS 36 on impairment is a topical Standard.

IAS 23 requires certain borrowing costs to be capitalised.

Summary of accounting standards

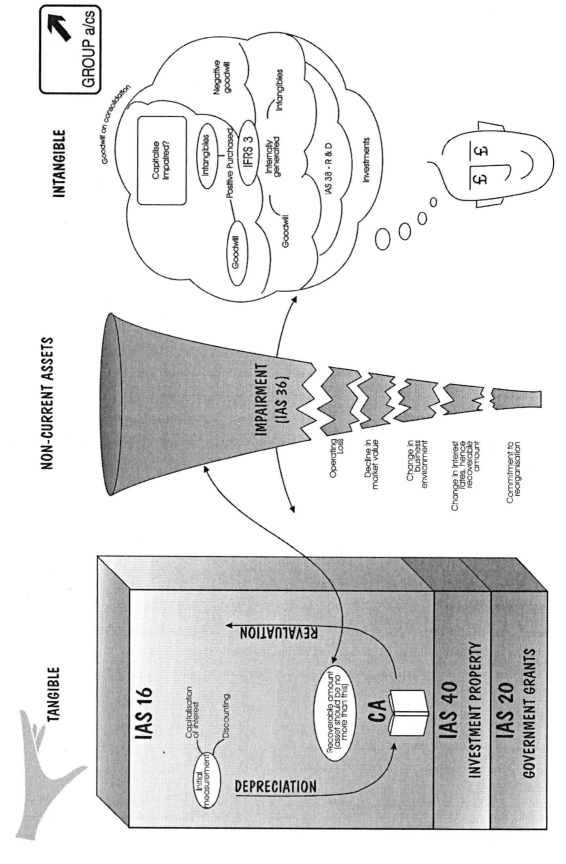

1 Depreciation accounting

Where assets held by an entity have a **limited useful life** for that entity it is necessary to apportion the value of an asset used in a period against the revenue it has helped to create.

1.1 Non-current assets

If an asset's life extends over more than one accounting period, it earns profits over more than one period. It is a **non-current asset**.

With the exception of land held on freehold or very long leasehold, **every non-current asset eventually wears out over time**. Machines, cars and other vehicles, fixtures and fittings, and even buildings do not last for ever. When a business acquires a non-current asset, it will have some idea about how long its useful life will be, and it might decide what to do with it.

(a)   Keep on using the non-current asset until it becomes **completely worn out**, useless, and worthless.

(b)   **Sell off** the non-current asset at the end of its useful life, either by selling it as a second-hand item or as scrap.

Since a non-current asset has a cost, and a limited useful life, and its value eventually declines, it follows that a charge should be made to profit or loss to reflect the use that is made of the asset by the business. This charge is called **depreciation**.

1.2 Scope

Depreciation accounting is governed by IAS 16 *Property, plant and equipment* which we will look at in Section 2 of this chapter. However, this section will deal with some of the IAS 16 definitions concerning depreciation.

Key terms

> **Depreciation** is the result of systematic allocation of the depreciable amount of an asset over its estimated useful life. Depreciation for the accounting period is charged to net profit or loss for the period either directly or indirectly.
>
> **Property, plant and equipment** are tangible items that:
>
> - Are held by for use in the production or supply of goods or services, for rental to others, or for administrative purposes, and
> - Are expected to be used during more than one period.
>
> **Useful life** is one of two things.
>
> - The period over which an asset is expected to be available for use by the entity, *or*
> - The number of production or similar units expected to be obtained from the asset by the entity.
>
> **Depreciable amount** is the cost of an asset or other amount substituted for cost, less the estimated residual value.
>
> *(IAS 16)*

An 'amount substituted for cost' will normally be a **current market value** after a revaluation has taken place.

1.3 Depreciation

IAS 16 requires the depreciable amount of a depreciable asset to be allocated on a **systematic basis** to each accounting period during the useful life of the asset. **Every part of an item of property, plant and equipment with a cost that is significant in relation to the total cost of the item must be depreciated separately**.

One way of defining depreciation is to describe it as a means of **spreading the cost** of a non-current asset over its useful life, and so matching the cost against the full period during which it earns profits for the business. Depreciation charges are an example of the application of the accrual assumption to calculate profits.

There are situations where, over a period, an asset has **increased in value**, ie its current value is greater than the carrying amount in the financial statements. You might think that in such situations it would not be necessary to depreciate the asset. The Standard states, however, that this is irrelevant, and that depreciation should still be charged to each accounting period, based on the depreciable amount, irrespective of a rise in value.

An entity is required to begin depreciating an item of property, plant and equipment when it is available for use and to continue depreciating it until it is derecognised even if it is idle during the period.

1.4 Useful life

The following factors should be considered when **estimating the useful life** of a depreciable asset.

- Expected **physical wear and tear**
- **Obsolescence**
- Legal or other **limits** on the use of the assets

Once decided, the useful life should be **reviewed at least every financial year end** and depreciation rates adjusted for the current and future periods if expectations vary significantly from the original estimates. The effect of the change should be disclosed in the accounting period in which the change takes place.

The assessment of useful life requires **judgement** based on previous experience with similar assets or classes of asset. When a completely new type of asset is acquired (ie through technological advancement or through use in producing a brand new product or service) it is still necessary to estimate useful life, even though the exercise will be much more difficult.

The Standard also points out that the physical life of the asset might be longer than its useful life to the entity in question. One of the main factors to be taken into consideration is the **physical wear and tear** the asset is likely to endure. This will depend on various circumstances, including the number of shifts for which the asset will be used, the entity's repair and maintenance programme and so on. Other factors to be considered include obsolescence (due to technological advances/improvements in production or a reduction in demand for the product or service produced by the asset) and legal restrictions, eg length of a related lease.

1.5 Residual value

In most cases the residual value of an asset is **likely to be immaterial**. If it is likely to be of any significant value, that value must be estimated at the date of purchase or any subsequent revaluation. The amount of residual value should be estimated based on the current situation with other similar assets, used in the same way, which are now at the end of their useful lives. Any expected costs of disposal should be offset against the gross residual value.

1.6 Depreciation methods

Consistency is important. The depreciation method selected should be applied consistently from period to period unless altered circumstances justify a change. When the method *is* changed, the effect should be quantified and disclosed and the reason for the change should be stated.

Various methods of allocating depreciation to accounting periods are available, but whichever is chosen must be applied **consistently** (as required by IAS 1: see Chapter 1), to ensure comparability from period to period. Change of policy is not allowed simply because of the profitability situation of the entity.

You should be familiar with the various **accepted methods of allocating depreciation** and the relevant calculations and accounting treatments, which are revised in questions at the end of this section.

1.7 Disclosure

An accounting policy note should disclose the **valuation bases** used for determining the amounts at which depreciable assets are stated, along with the other accounting policies: see IAS 1.

IAS 16 also requires the following to be disclosed for each major class of depreciable asset.

- **Depreciation methods** used
- **Useful lives** or the depreciation rates used
- **Total depreciation** allocated for the period
- **Gross amount** of depreciable assets and the related accumulated depreciation

1.8 What is depreciation?

The need to depreciate non-current assets arises from the **accruals assumption**. If money is expended in purchasing an asset then the amount expended must at some time be charged against profits. If the asset is one which contributes to an entity's revenue over a number of accounting periods it would be inappropriate to charge any single period (eg the period in which the asset was acquired) with the whole of the expenditure. Instead, some method must be found for spreading the cost of the asset over its useful economic life.

This view of depreciation as a process of allocation of the cost of an asset over several accounting periods is the view adopted by IAS 16. It is worth mentioning here two **common misconceptions** about the purpose and effects of depreciation.

(a) It is sometimes thought that the carrying amount of an asset is equal to its net realisable value and that the object of charging depreciation is to **reflect the fall in value of an asset over its life**. This misconception is the basis of a common, but incorrect, argument which says that freehold properties (say) need not be depreciated in times when property values are rising. It is true that historical cost statements of financial position often give a misleading impression when a property's carrying amount is much below its market value, but in such a case it is open to a business to incorporate a revaluation into its books, or even to prepare its accounts based on current costs. This is a separate problem from that of allocating the property's cost over successive accounting periods.

(b) Another misconception is that depreciation is provided **so that an asset can be replaced at the end of its useful life**. This is not the case.

    (i) If there is no intention of replacing the asset, it could then be argued that there is no need to provide for any depreciation at all.

    (ii) If prices are rising, the replacement cost of the asset will exceed the amount of depreciation provided.

The following questions are for revision purposes only.

A lorry bought for a business cost $17,000. It is expected to last for five years and then be sold for scrap for $2,000. Usage over the five years is expected to be:

Year 1	200 days
Year 2	100 days
Year 3	100 days
Year 4	150 days
Year 5	40 days

Required

Work out the depreciation to be charged each year under:

(a)   The straight-line method
(b)   The reducing balance method (using a rate of 35%)
(c)   The machine hour method

Answer

(a)   Under the straight-line method, depreciation for each of the five years is:

$$\text{Annual depreciation} = \frac{\$(17,000 - 2,000)}{5} = \$3,000$$

(b)   Under the reducing balance method, depreciation for each of the five years is:

Year	Depreciation		
1	35% × $17,000	=	$5,950
2	35% × ($17,000 – $5,950) = 35% × $11,050	=	$3,868
3	35% × ($11,050 – $3,868) = 35% × $7,182	=	$2,514
4	35% × ($7,182 – $2,514) = 35% × $4,668	=	$1,634
5	Balance to bring book value down to $2,000 = $4,668 – $1,634 – $2,000	=	$1,034

(c)   Under the machine hour method, depreciation for each of the five years is calculated as follows.

Total usage (days) = 200 + 100 + 100 + 150 + 40 = 590 days

$$\text{Depreciation per day} = \frac{\$(17,000 - 2,000)}{590} = \$25.42$$

Year	Usage (days)	Depreciation ($) (days × $25.42)
1	200	5,084.00
2	100	2,542.00
3	100	2,542.00
4	150	3,813.00
5	40	1,016.80
		14,997.80

Note: The answer does not come to exactly $15,000 because of the rounding carried out at the 'depreciation per day' stage of the calculation.

Question	Depreciation discussion

(a)   What are the purposes of providing for depreciation?

(b)   In what circumstances is the reducing balance method more appropriate than the straight-line method? Give reasons for your answer.

Answer

(a)   The accounts of a business try to recognise that the cost of a non-current asset is gradually consumed as the asset wears out. This is done by gradually writing off the asset's cost as an expense in profit or loss over several accounting periods. This process is known as depreciation, and is an example of the accruals assumption. IAS 16 *Property, plant and equipment* requires that depreciation should be allocated on a systematic basis to each accounting period during the useful life of the asset.

With regard to the accruals principle, it is fair that the profits should be reduced by the depreciation charge; this is not an arbitrary exercise. Depreciation is not, as is sometimes supposed, an attempt to set aside funds to purchase new non-current assets when required. Depreciation is not generally provided on freehold land because it does not 'wear out' (unless it is held for mining or a similar purpose).

(b)   The reducing balance method of depreciation is used instead of the straight-line method when it is considered fair to allocate a greater proportion of the total depreciable amount to the earlier years and a lower proportion to the later years on the assumption that the benefits obtained by the business from using the asset decline over time.

In favour of this method it may be argued that it links the depreciation charge to the costs of maintaining and running the asset. In the early years these costs are low and the depreciation charge is high, while in later years this is reversed.

Question	Depreciation accounting

A business purchased two rivet-making machines on 1 January 20X5 at a cost of $15,000 each. Each had an estimated life of five years and a nil residual value. The straight-line method of depreciation is used.

Owing to an unforeseen slump in market demand for rivets, the business decided to reduce its output of rivets, and switch to making other products instead. On 31 March 20X7, one rivet-making machine was sold (on credit) to a buyer for $8,000.

Later in the year, however, it was decided to abandon production of rivets altogether, and the second machine was sold on 1 December 20X7 for $2,500 cash.

Prepare the machinery account, accumulated depreciation of machinery account and disposal of machinery account for the accounting year to 31 December 20X7.

Answer

MACHINERY ACCOUNT

		$			$
20X7			*20X7*		
1 Jan	Balance b/f	30,000	31 Mar	Disposal of machinery account	15,000
			1 Dec	Disposal of machinery account	15,000
		30,000			30,000

ACCUMULATED DEPRECIATION OF MACHINERY

		$			$
20X7			*20X7*		
31 Mar	Disposal of machinery account*	6,750	1 Jan	Balance b/f	12,000
1 Dec	Disposal of machinery account**	8,750	31 Dec	Statement of profit or loss***	3,500
		15,500			15,500

*   Depreciation at date of disposal = $6,000 + $750
**   Depreciation at date of disposal = $6,000 + $2,750
***   Depreciation charge for the year = $750 + $2,750

DISPOSAL OF MACHINERY

		$			$
20X7			*20X7*		
31 Mar	Machinery account	15,000	31 Mar	Account receivable (sale price)	8,000
			31 Mar	Accumulated depreciation	6,750
1 Dec	Machinery	15,000	1 Dec	Cash (sale price)	2,500
			1 Dec	Provision for depreciation	8,750
			31 Dec	Profit or loss (loss on disposal)	4,000
		30,000			30,000

You should be able to calculate that there was a loss on the first disposal of $250, and on the second disposal of $3,750, giving a total loss of $4,000.

Workings

1   At 1 January 20X7, accumulated depreciation on the machines will be:

2 machines × 2 years × $\dfrac{\$15,000}{5}$ per machine pa = $12,000, or $6,000 per machine

2   Monthly depreciation is $\dfrac{\$3,000}{12}$ = $250 per machine per month

3   The machines are disposed of in 20X7.

(a)   On 31 March – after three months of the year
Depreciation for the year on the machine = 3 months × $250 = $750

(b)   On 1 December – after 11 months of the year
Depreciation for the year on the machine = 11 months × $250 = $2,750

2 IAS 16 *Property, plant and equipment*

FAST FORWARD

IAS 16 covers all aspects of accounting for property, plant and equipment. This represents the bulk of items which are **'tangible' non-current assets**.

2.1 Scope

IAS 16 should be followed when accounting for property, plant and equipment *unless* another International Accounting Standard requires a **different treatment**.

IAS 16 **does not apply** to the following.

(a)   Biological assets related to agricultural activity
(b)   Mineral rights and mineral reserves, such as oil, gas and other non-regenerative resources

However, the Standard applies to property, plant and equipment used to develop these assets.

2.2 Definitions

The Standard gives a large number of definitions.

Key terms

> **Property, plant and equipment** are tangible assets that:
>
> - Are held for use in the production or supply of goods or services, for rental to others, or for administrative purposes; and
> - Are expected to be used during more than one period.
>
> **Cost** is the amount of cash or cash equivalents paid or the fair value of the other consideration given to acquire an asset at the time of its acquisition or construction.
>
> **Residual value** is the net amount which the entity expects to obtain for an asset at the end of its useful life after deducting the expected costs of disposal.
>
> **Entity specific value** is the present value of the cash flows an entity expects to arise from the continuing use of an asset and from its disposal at the end of its useful life, or expects to incur when settling a liability.
>
> **Fair value** is the price that would be received to sell an asset or paid to transfer a liability in an orderly transaction between market participants at the measurement date.   (IFRS 13)
>
> **Carrying amount** is the amount at which an asset is recognised in the statement of financial position after deducting any accumulated depreciation and accumulated impairment losses.
>
> An **impairment loss** is the amount by which the carrying amount of an asset exceeds its recoverable amount.   (IAS 16)

2.3 Recognition

In this context, recognition simply means incorporation of the item in the business's accounts, in this case as a non-current asset. The recognition of property, plant and equipment depends on two criteria.

(a)   It is probable that **future economic benefits** associated with the asset will flow to the entity
(b)   The cost of the asset to the entity can be **measured reliably**

These recognition criteria apply to **subsequent expenditure** as well as costs incurred initially.

Property, plant and equipment can amount to **substantial amounts** in financial statements, affecting the presentation of the company's financial position and the profitability of the entity, both through depreciation and if an asset is wrongly classified as an expense and taken to profit or loss.

2.3.1 First criterion: future economic benefits

The **degree of certainty** attached to the flow of future economic benefits must be assessed. This should be based on the evidence available at the date of initial recognition (usually the date of purchase). The entity should thus be assured that it will receive the rewards attached to the asset and it will incur the associated risks, which will only generally be the case when the rewards and risks have actually passed to the entity. Until then, the asset should not be recognised.

2.3.2 Second criterion: cost measured reliably

It is generally easy to measure the cost of an asset as the **transfer amount on purchase**, ie what was paid for it. **Self-constructed assets** can also be measured easily by adding together the purchase price of all the constituent parts (labour, material etc) paid to external parties.

2.4 Separate items

Most of the time assets will be identified individually, but this will not be the case for **smaller items**, such as tools, dies and moulds, which are sometimes classified as inventory and written off as an expense.

Major components or spare parts, however, should be recognised as property, plant and equipment.

For very **large and specialised items**, an apparently single asset should be broken down into its composite parts. This occurs where the different parts have different useful lives and different depreciation rates are applied to each part, eg an aircraft, where the body and engines are separated as they have different useful lives.

2.5 Safety and environmental equipment

When such assets as these are acquired they will qualify for recognition where they enable the entity to **obtain future economic benefits** from related assets in excess of those it would obtain otherwise. The recognition will only be to the extent that the carrying amount of the asset and related assets does not exceed the total recoverable amount of these assets.

2.6 Initial measurement

Once an item of property, plant and equipment qualifies for recognition as an asset, it will initially be **measured at cost**.

2.6.1 Components of cost

The Standard lists the components of the cost of an item of property, plant and equipment.

- **Purchase price**, less any trade discount or rebate

- **Import duties** and non-refundable purchase taxes

- **Directly attributable costs** of bringing the asset to working condition for its intended use, eg:
    - The cost of site preparation
    - Initial delivery and handling costs
    - Installation costs
    - Testing
    - Professional fees (architects, engineers)

- Initial estimate of the unavoidable cost of dismantling and removing the asset and restoring the site on which it is located

IAS 16 provides **additional guidance on directly attributable** costs included in the cost of an item of property, plant and equipment.

(a)   These costs bring the asset to the location and working conditions necessary for it to be capable of operating in the manner intended by management, including those costs to test whether the asset is functioning properly.

(b)   They are determined after deducting the net proceeds from selling any items produced when bringing the asset to its location and condition.

The Standard also states that income and related expenses of operations that are **incidental** to the construction or development of an item of property, plant and equipment should be **recognised** in profit or loss.

The following costs **will not be part of the cost** of property, plant or equipment unless they can be attributed directly to the asset's acquisition, or bringing it into its working condition.

- Administration and other general overhead costs
- Start-up and similar pre-production costs
- Initial operating losses before the asset reaches planned performance

All of these will be recognised as an **expense** rather than an asset.

In the case of **self-constructed assets**, the same principles are applied as for acquired assets. If the entity makes similar assets during the normal course of business for sale externally, then the cost of the asset will be the cost of its production under IAS 2 *Inventories*. This also means that abnormal costs (wasted material, labour or other resources) are excluded from the cost of the asset. An example of a self-constructed asset is when a building company builds its own head office.

2.6.2 Exchanges of assets

IAS 16 specifies that exchange of items of property, plant and equipment, regardless of whether the assets are similar, are measured at **fair value, unless the exchange transaction lacks commercial substance** or the fair value of neither of the assets exchanged can be **measured reliably**. If the acquired item is not measured at fair value, its cost is measured at the carrying amount of the asset given up.

Expenditure incurred in replacing or renewing a component of an item of property, plant and equipment must be **recognised in the carrying amount of the item**. The carrying amount of the replaced or renewed component must be derecognised. A similar approach is also applied when a separate component of an item of property, plant and equipment is identified in respect of a major inspection to enable the continued use of the item.

2.7 Measurement subsequent to initial recognition

The Standard offers two possible treatments here, essentially a choice between keeping an asset recorded at **cost** or revaluing it to **fair value**.

(a)   **Cost model.** Carry the asset at its cost less depreciation and any accumulated impairment loss.

(b)   **Revaluation model.** Carry the asset at a revalued amount, being its fair value at the date of the revaluation less any subsequent accumulated depreciation and subsequent accumulated impairment losses. IAS 16 makes clear that the **revaluation model is available only if the fair value of the item can be measured reliably**.

2.7.1 Revaluations

The **market value** of land and buildings usually represents fair value, assuming existing use and line of business. Such valuations are usually carried out by professionally qualified valuers.

In the case of **plant and equipment**, fair value can also be taken as **market value**. Where a market value is not available, however, depreciated replacement cost should be used. There may be no market value where types of plant and equipment are sold only rarely or because of their specialised nature (ie they would normally only be sold as part of an ongoing business).

The frequency of valuation depends on the **volatility of the fair values** of individual items of property, plant and equipment. The more volatile the fair value, the more frequently revaluations should be carried out. Where the current fair value is very different from the carrying value then a revaluation should be carried out.

Most importantly, when an item of property, plant and equipment is revalued, **the whole class of assets to which it belongs should be revalued.**

All the items within a class should be **revalued at the same time**, to prevent selective revaluation of certain assets and to avoid disclosing a mixture of costs and values from different dates in the financial statements. A rolling basis of revaluation is allowed if the revaluations are kept up-to-date and the revaluation of the whole class is completed in a short period of time.

How should any **increase in value** be treated when a revaluation takes place? The debit will be the increase in value in the statement of financial position, but what about the credit? The increase should be recorded as other comprehensive income in the statement of profit or loss and other comprehensive income and credited to a **revaluation surplus in the statement of financial position**, *unless* the increase is reversing a previous decrease which was recognised as an expense in profit or loss. To the extent that this offset is made, the increase is recognised as income in profit or loss; any excess is then recorded as other comprehensive income and taken to the revaluation surplus.

2.8 Example: Revaluation surplus

Binkie Co has an item of land carried in its books at $13,000. Two years ago a slump in land values led the company to reduce the carrying value from $15,000. This was taken as an expense in profit or loss. There has been a surge in land prices in the current year, however, and the land is now worth $20,000.

Account for the revaluation in the current year.

Solution

The double entry is:

DEBIT	Asset value (statement of financial position)	$7,000
CREDIT	Profit or loss (reversing previous downward revaluation)	$2,000
	Revaluation surplus (recognised as other comprehensive income)	$5,000

The case is similar for a **decrease in value** on revaluation. Any decrease should be recognised as an expense, except where it offsets a previous increase recorded as other comprehensive income and credited to a revaluation surplus in owners' equity. Any decrease greater than the previous upwards increase in value must be taken as an expense to profit or loss.

2.9 Example: Revaluation decrease

Let us simply swap round the example given above. The original cost was $15,000, revalued upwards to $20,000 two years ago. The value has now fallen to $13,000.

Account for the decrease in value.

Solution

The double entry is:

DEBIT	Revaluation surplus (recognised as other comprehensive income)	$5,000
DEBIT	Profit or loss (decrease below historic cost)	$2,000
CREDIT	Asset value (statement of financial position)	$7,000

There is a further complication when a **revalued asset is being depreciated**. As we have seen, an upward revaluation means that the depreciation charge will increase. Normally, a revaluation surplus is only realised when the asset is sold, but when it is being depreciated, part of that surplus is being realised as the asset is used. The amount of the surplus realised is the difference between depreciation charged on the revalued amount and the (lower) depreciation which would have been charged on the asset's original cost. **This amount can be transferred to retained (ie realised) earnings but not through profit or loss.** This transfer is recorded in the statement of changes in equity.

2.10 Example: Revaluation and depreciation

Crinckle Co bought an asset for $10,000 at the beginning of 20X6. It had a useful life of five years. On 1 January 20X8 the asset was revalued to $12,000. The expected useful life has remained unchanged (ie three years remain).

Account for the revaluation and state the treatment for depreciation from 20X8 onwards.

Solution

On 1 January 20X8 the carrying amount of the asset is $10,000 - (2 \times \$10,000 \div 5) = \$6,000$. For the revaluation:

DEBIT	Asset value (statement of financial position)	$6,000	
CREDIT	Revaluation surplus (other comprehensive income)		$6,000

The depreciation for the next three years will be $12,000 \div 3 = \$4,000$, compared to depreciation on cost of $10,000 \div 5 = \$2,000$. So each year, the extra $2,000 can be treated as part of the surplus which has become realised:

DEBIT	Revaluation surplus	$2,000	
CREDIT	Retained earnings		$2,000

This is a movement on owner's equity, disclosed in the statement of changes in equity.

2.11 Depreciation

The Standard states:

- The **depreciable amount** of an item of property, plant and equipment should be allocated on a systematic basis over its useful life

- The **depreciation method** used should reflect the pattern in which the asset's economic benefits are consumed by the entity

- The **depreciation charge** for each period should be recognised as an expense unless it is included in the carrying amount of another asset

Land and buildings are dealt with separately even when they are acquired together because land normally has an unlimited life and is therefore not depreciated. In contrast buildings do have a limited life and must be depreciated. Any increase in the value of land on which a building is standing will have no impact on the determination of the building's useful life.

Depreciation is usually treated as an **expense**, but not where it is absorbed by the entity in the process of producing other assets. For example, depreciation of plant and machinery can be incurred in the production of goods for sale (inventory items). In such circumstances, the depreciation is included in the cost of the new assets produced.

2.11.1 Review of useful life

A review of the **useful life** of property, plant and equipment should be carried out **at least at each financial year end** and the depreciation charge for the current and future periods should be adjusted if expectations have changed significantly from previous estimates. Changes are changes in accounting estimates and are accounted for prospectively as adjustments to future depreciation.

2.11.2 Review of depreciation method

The **depreciation method** should also be reviewed **at least at each financial year end** and, if there has been a significant change in the expected pattern of economic benefits from those assets, the method should be changed to suit this changed pattern. When such a change in depreciation method takes place the change should be accounted for as a **change in accounting estimate** and the depreciation charge for the current and future periods should be adjusted.

2.11.3 Impairment of asset values

An **impairment loss** should be treated in the same way as a **revaluation decrease** ie the decrease should be **recognised as an expense in profit or loss**. However, a revaluation decrease (or impairment loss) should be recorded as other comprehensive income and charged directly against any related revaluation surplus to the extent that the decrease does not exceed the amount held in the revaluation surplus in respect of that same asset.

A **reversal of an impairment** loss should be treated in the same way as a **revaluation increase**, ie a revaluation increase should be recognised as income in profit or loss to the extent that it reverses a revaluation decrease or an impairment loss of the same asset previously recognised as an expense in profit or loss.

2.12 Retirements and disposals

When an asset is permanently **withdrawn from use, or sold or scrapped**, and no future economic benefits are expected from its disposal, it should be derecognised.

Gains or losses are the difference between the estimated net disposal proceeds and the carrying amount of the asset. They should be recognised as income or expense in profit or loss.

2.13 Derecognition

An entity is required to **derecognise the carrying amount** of an item of property, plant or equipment that it disposes of on the date the **criteria for the sale of goods** in IAS 18 *Revenue* would be met. This also applies to parts of an asset.

An entity cannot classify as revenue (ie in the top line of the statement of profit or loss and other comprehensive income) a gain it realises on the disposal of an item of property, plant and equipment.

2.14 Disclosure

The Standard has a long list of disclosure requirements, for each class of property, plant and equipment.

(a)   **Measurement bases** for determining the gross carrying amount (if more than one, the gross carrying amount for that basis in each category)

(b)   **Depreciation methods** used

(c)   **Useful lives** or depreciation rates used

(d)   **Gross carrying amount** and accumulated depreciation (aggregated with accumulated impairment losses) at the beginning and end of the period

(e)   **Reconciliation** of the carrying amount at the beginning and end of the period showing:

    (i)   Additions

    (ii)   Disposals

    (iii)   Acquisitions through business combinations (see Chapter 15)

    (iv)   Increases/decreases during the period from revaluations and from impairment losses

    (v)   Impairment losses recognised in profit or loss

    (vi)   Impairment losses reversed in profit or loss

    (vii) Depreciation

    (viii) Net exchange differences (from translation of statements of foreign entity)

    (ix)   Any other movements

The financial statements should also disclose the following.

(a)   Any recoverable amounts of property, plant and equipment

(b)   Existence and amounts of **restrictions on title**, and items pledged as security for liabilities

(c)   Accounting policy for **the estimated costs of restoring the site**

(d)   Amount of expenditures on account of **items in the course of construction**

(e)   Amount of commitments to **acquisitions**

Revalued assets require further disclosures.

(a)   Basis used to revalue the assets

(b)   Effective date of the revaluation

(c)   Whether an independent valuer was involved

(d)   Nature of any indices used to determine replacement cost

(e)   Carrying amount of each class of property, plant and equipment that would have been included in the financial statements had the assets been carried at cost less accumulated depreciation and accumulated impairment losses

(f)   Revaluation surplus, indicating the movement for the period and any restrictions on the distribution of the balance to shareholders

The Standard also **encourages disclosure** of additional information, which the users of financial statements may find useful.

(a)   The carrying amount of temporarily idle property, plant and equipment

(b)   The gross carrying amount of any fully depreciated property, plant and equipment that is still in use

(c)   The carrying amount of property, plant and equipment retired from active use and held for disposal

(d)   The fair value of property, plant and equipment when this is materially different from the carrying amount

The following format (with notional figures) is commonly used to disclose non-current assets movements.

	Total $	Land and buildings $	Plant and equipment $
Cost or valuation			
At 1 January 20X8	50,000	40,000	10,000
Revaluation surplus	12,000	12,000	–
Additions in year	4,000	–	4,000
Disposals in year	(1,000)	–	(1,000)
At 31 December 20X8	65,000	52,000	13,000

	Total $	Land and buildings $	Plant and equipment $
Depreciation			
At 1 January 20X8	16,000	10,000	6,000
Charge for year	4,000	1,000	3,000
Eliminated on disposals	(500)	–	(500)
At 31 December 20X8	19,500	11,000	8,500
Carrying amount			
At 31 December 20X8	45,500	41,000	4,500
At 1 January 20X8	34,000	30,000	4,000

Question — Statement of financial position items

(a)   In a statement of financial position prepared in accordance with IAS 16, what does the carrying amount represent?

(b)   In a set of financial statements prepared in accordance with IAS 16, is it correct to say that the carrying amount figure in a statement of financial position cannot be greater than the market (net realisable) value of the partially used asset as at the reporting date? Explain your reasons for your answer.

Answer

(a)   In simple terms the carrying amount of an asset is the cost of an asset less the 'accumulated depreciation', that is all depreciation charged so far. It should be emphasised that the main purpose of charging depreciation is to ensure that profits are fairly reported. Thus depreciation is concerned with profits in the statement of profit or loss and other comprehensive income rather than the asset value in the statement of financial position. In consequence the carrying amount figure in the statement of financial position can be quite arbitrary. In particular, it does not necessarily bear any relation to the market value of an asset and is of little use for planning and decision making.

An obvious example of the disparity between carrying amount and market value is found in the case of buildings, which may be worth more than ten times as much as their carrying value.

(b)   Carrying amount can in some circumstances be higher than market value (net realisable value). IAS 16 *Property, plant and equipment* states that the value of an asset cannot be greater than its 'recoverable amount'. However, 'recoverable amount' as defined in IAS 16 is the amount recoverable from further use. This may be higher than the market value.

This makes sense if you think of a specialised machine which could not fetch much on the secondhand market but which will produce goods which can be sold at a profit for many years.

Exam focus point

Property and/or other non-current assets are likely to be tested as they have come up on a number of papers.

3 IAS 20 *Government grants*

It is common for entities to receive government grants for various purposes (grants may be called subsidies, premiums, or other names). They may also receive other types of assistance which may be in many forms. The treatment of government grants is covered by IAS 20 *Accounting for government grants and disclosure of government assistance.*

3.1 Scope

IAS 20 does *not* cover the following situations.

- Accounting for government grants in financial statements reflecting the effects of **changing prices**
- Government assistance given in the form of **'tax breaks'**
- Government acting as **part-owner** of the entity

3.2 Definitions

These definitions are given by the Standard.

Key terms

> **Government**. Government, government agencies and similar bodies whether local, national or international.
>
> **Government assistance**. Action by government designed to provide an economic benefit specific to an entity or range of entities qualifying under certain criteria.
>
> **Government grants**. Assistance by government in the form of transfers of resources to an entity in return for past or future compliance with certain conditions relating to the operating activities of the entity. They exclude those forms of government assistance which cannot reasonably have a value placed upon them and transactions with government which cannot be distinguished from the normal trading transactions of the entity.
>
> **Grants related to assets** Government grants whose primary condition is that an entity qualifying for them should purchase, construct or otherwise acquire non-current assets. Subsidiary conditions may also be attached restricting the type or location of the assets or the periods during which they are to be acquired or held.
>
> **Grants related to income** Government grants other than those related to assets.
>
> **Forgivable loans**. Loans which the lender undertakes to waive repayment of under certain prescribed conditions.
>
> **Fair value**. The price that would be received to sell an asset or paid to transfer a liability in an orderly transaction between market participants at the measurement date.

You can see that there are many **different forms** of government assistance: both the type of assistance and the conditions attached to it will vary. Government assistance may have encouraged an entity to undertake something it otherwise would not have done.

How will the receipt of government assistance affect the financial statements?

(a) An appropriate method must be found to account for any **resources transferred**

(b) The extent to which an entity has **benefited** from such assistance during the reporting period should be shown

3.3 Government grants

An entity should not recognise government grants (including non-monetary grants at fair value) until it has **reasonable assurance** that:

- The entity will comply with any **conditions** attached to the grant
- The entity will **actually receive** the grant

Even if the grant has been received, this does not prove that the conditions attached to it have been or will be fulfilled.

It makes no difference in the treatment of the grant whether it is received in cash or given as a reduction in a liability to government, ie the **manner of receipt is irrelevant**.

Any related **contingency** should be recognised under IAS 37 *Provisions, contingent liabilities and contingent assets*, once the grant has been recognised.

In the case of a **forgivable loan** (as defined in key terms above) from government, it should be treated in the same way as a government grant when it is reasonably assured that the entity will meet the relevant terms for forgiveness.

3.3.1 Accounting treatment of government grants

There are two methods which could be used to account for government grants, and the arguments for each are given in IAS 20.

(a)   **Capital approach**: credit the grant directly to shareholders' interests.

(b)   **Income approach**: the grant is credited to the statement of profit or loss over one or more periods.

Question	Capital approach or income approach

Can you think of the different arguments used in support of each method?

Answer

The Standard gives the following arguments in support of each method.

Capital approach

(a)   The grants are a **financing device**, so should be recorded in the statement of financial position. In the statement of profit or loss they would simply offset the expenses which they are financing. No repayment is expected by the government, so the grants should be credited directly to shareholders' interests.

(b)   Grants are **not earned**, they are incentives without related costs, so it would be wrong to take them to the statement of profit or loss.

Income approach

(a)   The grants are **not received from shareholders** so should not be credited directly to shareholders' interests.

(b)   Grants are **not given or received for nothing**. They are earned by compliance with conditions and by meeting obligations. There are therefore, associated costs with which the grant can be matched in the statement of profit or loss as these costs are being compensated by the grant.

(c)   Grants are an extension of **fiscal policies** and so as income taxes and other taxes are charged against income, so grants should be credited to income.

IAS 20 requires grants to be recognised under the **income approach**, ie grants are recognised in profit or loss over the relevant periods to match them with related costs which they have been received to compensate. This should be done on a systematic basis. **Grants should not, therefore, be credited directly to shareholders' interests.**

It would be against the accruals assumption to credit grants to income on a receipts basis, so a **systematic basis of matching** must be used. A receipts basis would only be acceptable if no other basis were available.

It will usually be easy to identify the **costs related to a government grant**, and thereby the period(s) in which the grant should be recognised as income, ie when the costs are incurred. Where grants are received in relation to a depreciating asset, the grant will be recognised over the periods in which the asset is depreciated *and* in the same proportions.

Question   Recognition

Arturo Co receives a government grant representing 50% of the cost of a depreciating asset which costs $40,000. How will the grant be recognised if Arturo Co depreciates the asset:

(a)   Over four years straight line; *or*
(b)   At 40% reducing balance?

The residual value is nil. The useful life is four years.

Answer

The grant should be recognised in the same proportion as the depreciation.

(a)   Straight-line

	Depreciation	Grant income
	$	$
Year 1	10,000	5,000
2	10,000	5,000
3	10,000	5,000
4	10,000	5,000

(b)   Reducing-balance

	Depreciation	Grant income
	$	$
Year 1	16,000	8,000
2	9,600	4,800
3	5,760	2,880
4 (remainder)	8,640	4,320

In the case of **grants for non-depreciable assets**, certain obligations may need to be fulfilled, in which case the grant should be recognised in profit or loss over the periods in which the cost of meeting the obligation is incurred. For example, if a piece of land is granted on condition that a building is erected on it, then the grant should be recognised as income over the building's life.

There may be a **series of conditions** attached to a grant, in the nature of a package of financial aid. An entity must take care to identify precisely those conditions which give rise to costs which in turn determine the periods over which the grant will be earned. When appropriate, the grant may be split and the parts allocated on different bases.

An entity may receive a grant as compensation for expenses or losses which it has **already incurred**. Alternatively, a grant may be given to an entity simply to provide immediate financial support where no future related costs are expected. In cases such as these, the grant received should be recognised as income of the period in which it becomes receivable.

3.3.2 Non-monetary government grants

A non-monetary asset may be transferred by government to an entity as a grant, for example a piece of land, or other resources. The **fair value** of such an asset is usually assessed and this is used to account for both the asset and the grant. Alternatively, both may be valued at a nominal amount.

3.3.3 Presentation of grants related to assets

There are two choices here for how government grants related to assets (including non-monetary grants at fair value) should be shown in the statement of financial position.

(a)   Set up the grant as **deferred income**.
(b)   **Deduct the grant** in arriving at the **carrying amount** of the asset.

These are considered to be acceptable alternatives and we can look at an example showing both.

3.3.4 Example: accounting for grants related to assets

A company receives a 20% grant towards the cost of a new item of machinery, which cost $100,000. The machinery has an expected life of four years and a nil residual value. The expected profits of the company, before accounting for depreciation on the new machine or the grant, amount to $50,000 per annum in each year of the machinery's life.

Solution

The results of the company for the four years of the machine's life would be as follows.

(a)   Reducing the cost of the asset

	Year 1 $	Year 2 $	Year 3 $	Year 4 $	Total $
Profits					
Profit before depreciation	50,000	50,000	50,000	50,000	200,000
Depreciation*	(20,000)	(20,000)	(20,000)	(20,000)	(80,000)
Profit	30,000	30,000	30,000	30,000	120,000

*The depreciation charge on a straight-line basis, for each year, is:

$\frac{1}{4}$ of $(100,000 - 20,000) = $20,000.

STATEMENT OF FINANCIAL POSITION AT YEAR END (EXTRACT)

	$	$	$	$
Non-current asset at cost	80,000	80,000	80,000	80,000
Depreciation	(20,000)	(40,000)	(60,000)	(80,000)
	60,000	40,000	20,000	–

(b)   Treating the grant as deferred income

	Year 1 $	Year 2 $	Year 3 $	Year 4 $	Total $
Profits					
Profit before grant & dep'n	50,000	50,000	50,000	50,000	200,000
Depreciation	(25,000)	(25,000)	(25,000)	(25,000)	(100,000)
Grant	5,000	5,000	5,000	5,000	20,000
Profit	30,000	30,000	30,000	30,000	120,000

STATEMENT OF FINANCIAL POSITION AT YEAR END (EXTRACT)

	Year 1 $	Year 2 $	Year 3 $	Year 4 $
Non-current asset at cost	100,000	100,000	100,000	100,000
Depreciation	(25,000)	(50,000)	(75,000)	(100,000)
	75,000	50,000	25,000	–
Deferred income				
Government grant				
deferred income	15,000	10,000	5,000	–

Whichever of these methods is used, the **cash flows** in relation to the purchase of the asset and the receipt of the grant are often disclosed separately because of the significance of the movements in cash flow.

3.3.5 Presentation of grants related to income

These grants are a credit in profit or loss, but there is a choice in the method of disclosure.

(a) Present as a **separate credit** or under a general heading, eg 'other income'
(b) **Deduct from the related expense**

Some would argue that offsetting income and expenses in the statement of profit or loss is not good practice. Others would say that the expenses would not have been incurred had the grant not been available, so offsetting the two is acceptable. Although both methods are acceptable, disclosure of the grant may be necessary for a **proper understanding** of the financial statements, particularly the effect on any item of income or expense which is required to be separately disclosed.

3.3.6 Government loans

Loans from the government at zero or low interest are accounted for as a government grant.

The benefit is calculated as the difference between the initial carrying amount of the loan (in accordance with IFRS 9) and the proceeds received.

3.3.7 Repayment of government grants

If a grant must be repaid it should be accounted for as a **revision of an accounting estimate** (see IAS 8).

(a) **Repayment of a grant related to income:** apply first against any unamortised deferred income set up in respect of the grant; any excess should be recognised immediately as an expense.

(b) **Repayment of a grant related to an asset**: increase the carrying amount of the asset or reduce the deferred income balance by the amount repayable. The cumulative additional depreciation that would have been recognised to date in the absence of the grant should be immediately recognised as an expense.

It is possible that the circumstances surrounding repayment may require a review of the **asset value** and an impairment of the new carrying amount of the asset.

3.4 Government assistance

Some forms of government assistance are excluded from the definition of government grants.

(a) Some forms of government assistance **cannot reasonably have a value placed on them**, eg free technical or marketing advice, provision of guarantees.

(b)   There are transactions with government which **cannot be distinguished from the entity's normal trading transactions**, eg government procurement policy resulting in a portion of the entity's sales. Any segregation would be arbitrary.

Disclosure of such assistance may be necessary because of its significance; its nature, extent and duration should be disclosed.

3.5 Disclosure

Disclosure is required of the following.

- **Accounting policy** adopted, including method of presentation
- **Nature and extent** of government grants recognised and other forms of assistance received
- **Unfulfilled conditions and other contingencies** attached to recognised government assistance

4 IAS 40 *Investment property*

FAST FORWARD

An entity may own land or a building **as an investment** rather than for use in the business. It may therefore generate cash flows largely independently of other assets which the entity holds.

4.1 Definitions

Consider the following definitions.

Key terms

> **Investment property** is property (land or a building – or part of a building – or both) held (by the owner or by the lessee under a finance lease) to earn rentals or for capital appreciation or both, rather than for:
>
> (a)   Use in the production or supply of goods or services or for administrative purposes, or
> (b)   Sale in the ordinary course of business
>
> **Owner-occupied property** is property held by the owner (or by the lessee under a finance lease) for use in the production or supply of goods or services or for administrative purposes.
>
> **Fair value** is the price that would be received to sell an asset or paid to transfer a liability in an orderly transaction between market participants at the measurement date.
>
> **Cost** is the amount of cash or cash equivalents paid or the fair value of other consideration given to acquire an asset at the time of its acquisition or construction.
>
> **Carrying amount** is the amount at which an asset is recognised in the statement of financial position.
>
> A property interest that is held by a lessee under an **operating lease** may be classified and accounted for as an **investment property**, if and only if the property would otherwise meet the definition of an investment property and the lessee uses the IAS 40 **fair value model**. This classification is available on a property-by-property basis.

Examples of investment property include:

(a)   **land held for long-term capital appreciation** rather than for short-term sale in the ordinary course of business

(b)   A **building** owned by the reporting entity (or held by the entity under a finance lease) and **leased out under an operating lease**

The scope of the Standard was amended in 2008 to include property under construction or development for **future** use as investment property. Previously, until the property was ready to be used as an investment property, IAS 16 applied.

Question   Investment

Rich Co owns a piece of land. The directors have not yet decided whether to build a factory on it for use in its business or to keep it and sell it when its value has risen.

Would this be classified as an investment property under IAS 40?

Answer

Yes. If an entity has not determined that it will use the land either as an owner-occupied property or for short-term sale in the ordinary course of business, the land is considered to be held for capital appreciation.

4.2 The Standard

The objective of IAS 40 is to prescribe the accounting treatment for investment property and related disclosure requirements.

The Standard includes investment property held under a finance lease or leased out under an operating lease. However, the current IAS 40 does not deal with matters covered in IAS 17 *Leases*.

You now know what *is* an investment property under IAS 40. Below are examples of items that are **not investment property**.

Type of non-investment property	Applicable IAS
Property intended for sale in the ordinary course of business	IAS 2 *Inventories*
Property being constructed or developed on behalf of third parties	IAS 11 *Construction contracts*
Owner-occupied property	IAS 16 *Property, plant and equipment*

4.3 Recognition

Investment property should be recognised as an asset when **two conditions** are met.

(a) It is **probable** that the **future economic benefits** that are associated with the investment property will **flow to the entity**.

(b) The **cost** of the investment property can be **measured reliably**.

4.4 Initial measurement

An investment property should be measured initially at its **cost,** including transaction costs.

A property interest held under a lease and classified as an investment property shall be accounted for **as if it were a finance lease**. The asset is recognised at the lower of the fair value of the property and the present value of the minimum lease payments. An equivalent amount is recognised as a liability.

4.5 Measurement subsequent to initial recognition

IAS 40 requires an entity to **choose between two models**.

- **The fair value model**
- **The cost model**

Whatever policy it chooses should be applied to **all of its investment property**.

Where an entity chooses to classify a property held under an **operating lease** as an investment property, there is **no choice**. The **fair value model must be used** for all the entity's investment property, regardless of whether it is owned or leased.

4.5.1 Fair value model

Key term

> After initial recognition, an entity that chooses the **fair value model** should measure all of its investment property at fair value, except in the extremely rare cases where this cannot be measured reliably. In such cases it should apply the IAS 16 cost model.
>
> A gain or loss arising from a change in the fair value of an investment property should be recognised in net **profit or loss** for the period in which it arises.
>
> The fair value of investment property should reflect market conditions at the reporting date.

IAS 40 was the first standard to allow a fair value model for non-financial assets. This is not the same as a revaluation, where increases in carrying amount above a cost-based measure are recognised as other comprehensive income and credited to a revaluation surplus. Under the fair value model all changes in fair value are recognised in profit or loss.

The Standard elaborates on **issues relating to fair value**.

(a)   Fair value assumes that an orderly transaction has taken place between market participants, ie both buyer and seller are reasonably informed about the nature and characteristics of the investment property.

(b)   A buyer participating in an orderly transaction is **motivated but not compelled** to buy. A seller participating in an orderly transaction is neither an over-eager nor a forced seller, nor one prepared to sell at any price or to hold out for a price not considered reasonable in the current market.

(c)   **Fair value is not the same as 'value in use'** as defined in IAS 36 *Impairment of assets*. Value in use reflects factors and knowledge specific to the entity, while fair value reflects factors and knowledge relevant to the market.

(d)   In determining fair value an entity **should not double count assets**. For example, elevators or air conditioning are often an integral part of a building and should be included in the investment property, rather than recognised separately.

(e)   In those rare cases where the **entity cannot determine the fair value of an investment property reliably**, the cost model in **IAS 16** must be applied until the investment property is disposed of. The **residual value must be assumed to be zero**.

4.5.2 Cost model

The cost model is the **cost model in IAS 16**. Investment property should be measured at **depreciated cost, less any accumulated impairment losses**. An entity that chooses the cost model should **disclose the fair value of its investment property**.

4.5.3 Changing models

Once the entity has chosen the fair value or cost model, it should apply it to all its investment property. It **should not change from one model to the other unless the change will result in a more appropriate presentation**. IAS 40 states that it is highly unlikely that a change from the fair value model to the cost model will result in a more appropriate presentation.

4.6 Transfers

Transfers to or from investment property should **only** be made **when there is a change in use**. For example, owner occupation commences so the investment property will be treated under IAS 16 as an owner-occupied property.

When there is a transfer from investment property carried at fair value to owner-occupied property or inventories, the property's cost for subsequent accounting under IAS 16 or IAS 2 should be its fair value at the date of change of use.

Conversely, an owner-occupied property may become an investment property and need to be carried at fair value. An entity should apply IAS 16 up to the date of change of use. It should treat any difference at that date between the carrying amount of the property under IAS 16 and its fair value as a revaluation under IAS 16.

4.7 Disposals

Derecognise (eliminate from the statement of financial position) an investment property on disposal or when it is permanently withdrawn from use and no future economic benefits are expected from its disposal.

Any **gain or loss** on disposal is the difference between the net disposal proceeds and the carrying amount of the asset. It should generally be **recognised as income or expense in profit or loss**.

Compensation from third parties for investment property that was impaired, lost or given up shall be recognised in profit or loss when the compensation becomes receivable.

4.8 Disclosure requirements

These relate to:

- Choice of fair value model or cost model
- Whether property interests held as operating leases are included in investment property
- Criteria for classification as investment property
- Assumptions in determining fair value
- Use of independent professional valuer (encouraged but not required)
- Rental income and expenses
- Any restrictions or obligations

4.8.1 Fair value model – additional disclosures

An entity that adopts this must also disclose a **reconciliation** of the carrying amount of the investment property at the beginning and end of the period.

4.8.2 Cost model – additional disclosures

These relate mainly to the depreciation method. In addition, an entity which adopts the cost model **must disclose the fair value** of the investment property.

4.9 Decision tree

The decision tree below summarises which IAS applies to various kinds of property.

Exam focus
point

> Learn this decision tree – it will help you tackle most of the problems you are likely to meet in the exam!

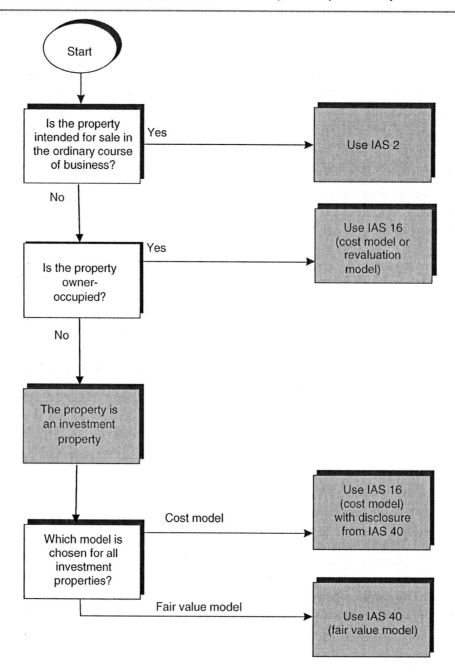

5 IAS 36 *Impairment of assets*

Impairment is determined by comparing the carrying amount of the asset with its recoverable amount.

There is an established principle that assets should not be carried at above their recoverable amount. An entity should write down the carrying amount of an asset to its recoverable amount if the carrying amount of an asset is not recoverable in full. IAS 36 was published in June 1998 and has since been revised. It puts in place a detailed methodology for carrying out impairment reviews and related accounting treatments and disclosures.

5.1 Scope

IAS 36 applies to all tangible, intangible and financial assets except inventories, assets arising from construction contracts, deferred tax assets, assets arising under IAS 19 *Employee benefits* and financial assets within the scope of IFRS 9 *Financial instruments*. This is because those standards already have rules for recognising and measuring impairment. Note also that IAS 36 does not apply to non-current assets held for sale, which are dealt with under IFRS 5 *Non-current assets held for sale and discontinued operations*.

Key terms

> **Impairment loss.** The amount by which the carrying amount of an asset or a cash-generating unit exceeds its recoverable amount.
>
> **Carrying amount.** The amount at which an asset is recognised after deducting any accumulated depreciation (amortisation) and accumulated impairment losses thereon. *(IAS 36)*

The basic principle underlying IAS 36 is relatively straightforward. If an asset's value in the accounts is higher than its realistic value, measured as its 'recoverable amount', the asset is judged to have suffered an impairment loss. It should therefore be reduced in value, by the amount of the **impairment loss**. The amount of the impairment loss should be **written off against profit** immediately.

The main accounting issues to consider are therefore as follows.

(a)   How is it possible to **identify when** an impairment loss may have occurred?

(b)   How should the **recoverable amount** of the asset be measured?

(c)   How should an 'impairment loss' be **reported in the accounts**?

5.2 Identifying a potentially impaired asset

An entity should assess at each reporting date whether there are any indications of impairment to any assets. The concept of **materiality** applies, and only material impairment needs to be identified.

If there are indications of possible impairment, the entity is required to make a formal estimate of the **recoverable amount** of the assets concerned.

IAS 36 suggests how **indications of a possible impairment** of assets might be recognised. The suggestions are based largely on common sense.

(a)   **External sources of information**

(i)   A fall in the asset's market value that is more significant than would normally be expected from passage of time over normal use.

(ii)   A significant change in the technological, market, legal or economic environment of the business in which the assets are employed.

(iii) An increase in market interest rates or market rates of return on investments likely to affect the discount rate used in calculating value in use.

(iv)   The carrying amount of the entity's net assets being more than its market capitalisation.

(b)   **Internal sources of information**: evidence of obsolescence or physical damage, adverse changes in the use to which the asset is put, or the asset's economic performance

Even if there are no indications of impairment, the following assets must **always** be tested for impairment annually.

(a)   An intangible asset with an **indefinite useful life**
(b)   **Goodwill** acquired in a business combination

5.3 Measuring the recoverable amount of the asset

What is an asset's recoverable amount?

The **recoverable amount of an asset** should be measured as the **higher value** of:

(a)   The asset's fair value less costs of disposal; *and*
(b)   Its value in use.   *(IAS 36)*

An asset's fair value less costs of disposal is the price that would be received to sell the asset in an orderly transaction between market participants at the measurement date, less direct disposal costs such as legal expenses.

(a)   If there is **an active market** in the asset, the fair value should be based on the **market price**, or on the price of recent transactions in similar assets.

(b)   If there is **no active market** in the assets it might be possible to **estimate** fair value using best estimates of what market participants might pay in an orderly transaction.

Fair value less costs of disposal **cannot** be reduced, however, by including within costs of disposal any **restructuring or reorganisation expenses**, or any costs that have already been recognised in the accounts as liabilities.

The concept of 'value in use' is very important.

The **value in use** of an asset is measured as the present value of estimated future cash flows (inflows minus outflows) generated by the asset, including its estimated net disposal value (if any) at the end of its expected useful life.

The cash flows used in the calculation should be **pre-tax cash flows** and a **pre-tax discount rate** should be applied to calculate the present value.

The calculation of **value in use** must reflect the following.

(a)   An estimate of the **future cash flows** the entity expects to derive from the asset
(b)   Expectations about **possible variations** in the amount and timing of future cash flows
(c)   The **time value of money**
(d)   The price for bearing the **uncertainty** inherent in the asset, *and*
(e)   **Other factors** that would be reflected in pricing future cash flows from the asset

Calculating a value in use therefore calls for estimates of future cash flows, and the possibility exists that an entity might come up with **over-optimistic estimates** of cash flows. The IAS therefore states the following.

(a)   Cash flow projections should be based on **'reasonable and supportable' assumptions**.

(b)   Projections of cash flows, normally up to a maximum period of five years, should be based on the most **recent budgets or financial forecasts**.

(c)   Cash flow projections beyond this period should be obtained by extrapolating short-term projections, using either a **steady or declining growth rate** for each subsequent year (unless a rising growth rate can be justified). The long-term growth rate applied should not exceed the average long-term growth rate for the product, market, industry or country, unless a higher growth rate can be justified.

5.4 Composition of estimates of future cash flows

These should include the following.

(a)   Projections of **cash inflows** from **continuing use** of the asset

(b)   Projections of **cash outflows** necessarily incurred to **generate the cash inflows** from continuing use of the asset

(c)   **Net cash flows** received/paid on **disposal** of the asset at the end of its useful life

There is an underlying principle that future cash flows should be estimated for the asset in its current condition. Future cash flows relating to restructurings to which the entity is not yet committed, or to future costs to add to, replace part of, or service the asset are excluded.

Estimates of future cash flows should **exclude** the following.

(a)   Cash inflows/outflows from financing activities
(b)   Income tax receipts/payments

The amount of net cash inflow/outflow on **disposal** of an asset should assume an arm's length transaction.

The **discount rate** should be a current pre-tax rate (or rates) that reflects the current assessment of the time value of money and the risks specific to the asset. The discount rate should not include a risk weighting if the underlying cash flows have already been adjusted for risk.

5.5 Recognition and measurement of an impairment loss

The rule for assets at historical cost is:

Rule to learn

> If the recoverable amount of an asset is lower than the carrying amount, the carrying amount should be reduced by the difference (ie the impairment loss) which should be charged as an expense in profit or loss.

The rule for assets held at a revalued amount (such as property revalued under IAS 16) is:

Rule to learn

> The impairment loss is to be treated as a revaluation decrease under the relevant IAS.

In practice this means:

• To the extent that there is a revaluation surplus held in respect of the asset, the impairment loss should be recognised as other comprehensive income and charged to the revaluation surplus.

• Any excess should be charged to profit or loss.

The IAS goes into quite a large amount of detail about the important concept of cash generating units. As a basic rule, the recoverable amount of an asset should be calculated for the **asset individually**. However, there will be occasions when it is not possible to estimate such a value for an individual asset, particularly in the calculation of value in use. This is because cash inflows and outflows cannot be attributed to the individual asset.

If it is not possible to calculate the recoverable amount for an individual asset, the recoverable amount of the asset's cash generating unit should be measured instead.

Key term

A **cash generating unit** is the smallest identifiable group of assets for which independent cash flows can be identified and measured.

Question

Cash generating unit I

Can you think of some examples of cash generating units?

Answer

Here are two possibilities.

(a)   A mining company owns a private railway that it uses to transport output from one of its mines. The railway now has no market value other than as scrap, and it is impossible to identify any separate cash inflows with the use of the railway itself. Consequently, if the mining company suspects an impairment in the value of the railway, it should treat the mine as a whole as a cash generating unit, and measure the recoverable amount of the mine as a whole.

(b)   A bus company has an arrangement with a town's authorities to run a bus service on four routes in the town. Separately identifiable assets are allocated to each of the bus routes, and cash inflows and outflows can be attributed to each individual route. Three routes are running at a profit and one is running at a loss. The bus company suspects that there is an impairment of assets on the loss-making route. However, the company will be unable to close the loss-making route, because it is under an obligation to operate all four routes, as part of its contract with the local authority. Consequently, the company should treat all four bus routes together as a cash generating unit, and calculate the recoverable amount for the unit as a whole.

Question

Cash generating unit II

Minimart belongs to a retail store chain Maximart. Minimart makes all its retail purchases through Maximart's purchasing centre. Pricing, marketing, advertising and human resources policies (except for hiring Minimart's cashiers and salesmen) are decided by Maximart. Maximart also owns five other stores in the same city as Minimart (although in different neighbourhoods) and 20 other stores in other cities. All stores are managed in the same way as Minimart. Minimart and four other stores were purchased five years ago and goodwill was recognised.

What is the cash-generating unit for Minimart?

Answer

In identifying Minimart's cash-generating unit, an entity considers whether, for example:

(a)   Internal management reporting is organised to measure performance on a store-by-store basis.

(b)   The business is run on a store-by-store profit basis or on a region/city basis.

All Maximart's stores are in different neighbourhoods and probably have different customer bases. So, although Minimart is managed at a corporate level, Minimart generates cash inflows that are largely independent from those of Maximart's other stores. Therefore, it is likely that Minimart is a cash-generating unit.

 **Question**

Mighty Mag Publishing Co owns 150 magazine titles of which 70 were purchased and 80 were self-created. The price paid for a purchased magazine title is recognised as an intangible asset. The costs of creating magazine titles and maintaining the existing titles are recognised as an expense when incurred. Cash inflows from direct sales and advertising are identifiable for each magazine title. Titles are managed by customer segments. The level of advertising income for a magazine title depends on the range of titles in the customer segment to which the magazine title relates. Management has a policy to abandon old titles before the end of their economic lives and replace them immediately with new titles for the same customer segment.

What is the cash-generating unit for an individual magazine title?

Answer

It is likely that the recoverable amount of an individual magazine title can be assessed. Even though the level of advertising income for a title is influenced, to a certain extent, by the other titles in the customer segment, cash inflows from direct sales and advertising are identifiable for each title. In addition, although titles are managed by customer segments, decisions to abandon titles are made on an individual title basis.

Therefore, it is likely that individual magazine titles generate cash inflows that are largely independent one from another and that each magazine title is a separate cash-generating unit.

If an active market exists for the output produced by the asset or a group of assets, this asset or group should be identified as a cash generating unit, even if some or all of the output is used internally.

Cash generating units should be identified consistently from period to period for the same type of asset unless a change is justified.

The group of net assets less liabilities that are considered for impairment should be the same as those considered in the calculation of the recoverable amount. (For the treatment of goodwill and corporate assets see below.)

5.6 Example: Recoverable amount and carrying amount

Fourways Co is made up of four cash generating units. All four units are being tested for impairment.

(a)   Property, plant and equipment and separate intangibles would be allocated to be cash generating units as far as possible.

(b)   Current assets such as inventories, receivables and prepayments would be allocated to the relevant cash generating units.

(c)   Liabilities (eg payables) would be deducted from the net assets of the relevant cash generating units.

(d)   The net figure for each cash generating unit resulting from this exercise would be compared to the relevant recoverable amount, computed on the same basis.

5.7 Accounting treatment of an impairment loss

If, and only if, the recoverable amount of an asset is less than its carrying amount in the statement of financial position, an impairment loss has occurred. This loss should be **recognised immediately**.

(a) The asset's **carrying amount** should be reduced to its recoverable amount in the statement of financial position.

(b) The **impairment loss** should be recognised immediately in profit or loss (unless the asset has been revalued in which case the loss is treated as a revaluation decrease; see Paragraph 5.5).

After reducing an asset to its recoverable amount, the **depreciation charge** on the asset should then be based on its new carrying amount, its estimated residual value (if any) and its estimated remaining useful life.

An impairment loss should be recognised for a **cash generating unit** if (and only if) the recoverable amount for the cash generating unit is less than the carrying amount in the statement of financial position for all the assets in the unit. When an impairment loss is recognised for a cash generating unit, the loss should be allocated between the assets in the unit in the following order.

(a) First, to any assets that are obviously damaged or destroyed
(b) Next, to the **goodwill** allocated to the cash generating unit
(c) Then to all other assets in the cash-generating unit, on a *pro rata* basis

In allocating an impairment loss, the carrying amount of an asset should not be reduced below the highest of:

(a) Its fair value less costs of disposal
(b) Its value in use (if determinable)
(c) Zero

Any remaining amount of an impairment loss should be recognised as a liability if required by other IASs.

5.8 Example 1: Impairment loss

A company that extracts natural gas and oil has a drilling platform in the Caspian Sea. It is required by legislation of the country concerned to remove and dismantle the platform at the end of its useful life. Accordingly, the company has included an amount in its accounts for removal and dismantling costs, and is depreciating this amount over the platform's expected life.

The company is carrying out an exercise to establish whether there has been an impairment of the platform.

(a) Its carrying amount in the statement of financial position is $3m.

(b) The company has received an offer of $2.8m for the platform from another oil company. The bidder would take over the responsibility (and costs) for dismantling and removing the platform at the end of its life.

(c) The present value of the estimated cash flows from the platform's continued use is $3.3m.

(d) The carrying amount in the statement of financial position for the provision for dismantling and removal is currently $0.6m.

What should be the value of the drilling platform in the statement of financial position, and what, if anything, is the impairment loss?

Solution

Fair value less costs of disposal	=	$2.8m
Value in use	=	PV of cash flows from use less the carrying amount of the provision/liability = $3.3m – $0.6m = $2.7m
Recoverable amount	=	Higher of these two amounts, ie $2.8m
Carrying amount	=	$3m
Impairment loss	=	$0.2m

The carrying amount should be reduced to $2.8m

5.9 Example 2: Impairment loss

A company has acquired another business for $4.5m: tangible assets are valued at $4.0m and goodwill at $0.5m.

An asset with a carrying amount of $1m is destroyed in a terrorist attack. The asset was not insured. The loss of the asset, without insurance, has prompted the company to assess whether there has been an impairment of assets in the acquired business and what the amount of any such loss is.

The recoverable amount of the business (a single cash generating unit) is measured as $3.1m.

Solution

There has been an impairment loss of $1.4m ($4.5m – $3.1m).

The impairment loss will be recognised in profit or loss. The loss will be allocated between the assets in the cash generating unit as follows.

(a)   A loss of $1m can be attributed directly to the uninsured asset that has been destroyed.

(b)   The remaining loss of $0.4m should be allocated to goodwill.

The carrying amount of the assets will now be $3m for tangible assets and $0.1m for goodwill.

5.10 Reversal of an impairment loss

The annual assessment to determine whether there may have been some impairment should be **applied to all assets**, including assets that have already been impaired in the past.

In some cases, the recoverable amount of an asset that has previously been impaired might turn out to be **higher** than the asset's current carrying amount. In other words, there might have been a reversal of some of the previous impairment loss.

(a)   The reversal of the impairment loss should be **recognised immediately** as income in profit or loss.

(b)   The carrying amount of the asset should be increased to its **new recoverable amount**.

Rule to learn

> An impairment loss recognised for an asset in prior years should be recovered if, and only if, there has been a change in the estimates used to determine the asset's recoverable amount since the last impairment loss was recognised.

The asset cannot be revalued to a carrying amount that is higher than its value would have been if the asset had not been impaired originally, ie its **depreciated carrying amount** had the impairment not taken place. Depreciation of the asset should now be based on its new revalued amount, its estimated residual value (if any) and its estimated remaining useful life.

An exception to this rule is for **goodwill**. An impairment loss for goodwill should not be reversed in a subsequent period.

Question	Reversal of impairment loss

A cash generating unit comprising a factory, plant and equipment etc and associated purchased goodwill becomes impaired because the product it makes is overtaken by a technologically more advanced model produced by a competitor. The recoverable amount of the cash generating unit falls to $60m, resulting in an impairment loss of $80m, allocated as follows.

	Carrying amounts before impairment	Carrying amounts after impairment
	$m	$m
Goodwill	40	
Patent (with no market value)	20	
Tangible non-current assets (market value $60m)	80	60
Total	140	60

After three years, the entity makes a technological breakthrough of its own, and the recoverable amount of the cash generating unit increases to $90m. The carrying amount of the tangible non-current assets had the impairment not occurred would have been $70m.

Required

Calculate the reversal of the impairment loss.

Answer

The reversal of the impairment loss is recognised to the extent that it increases the carrying amount of the tangible non-current assets to what it would have been had the impairment not taken place, ie a reversal of the impairment loss of $10m is recognised and the tangible non-current assets written back to $70m. Reversal of the impairment is not recognised in relation to the goodwill and patent because the effect of the external event that caused the original impairment has not reversed – the original product is still overtaken by a more advanced model.

5.11 Disclosure

IAS 36 calls for substantial disclosure about impairment of assets. The information to be disclosed includes the following.

(a)   For each class of assets, the amount of **impairment losses recognised** and the amount of any **impairment losses recovered** (ie reversals of impairment losses)

(b)   For each individual asset or cash generating unit that has suffered a **significant impairment loss**, details of the nature of the asset, the amount of the loss, the events that led to recognition of the loss, whether the recoverable amount is fair value less costs of disposal or value in use, and if the recoverable amount is value in use, the basis on which this value was estimated (eg the discount rate applied).

In May 2013, IAS 36 was revised to bring the disclosure requirements into line with IFRS 13 *Fair Value Measurement*. Entities must now disclose additional details of the method of determining fair value. (IFRS 13 is not examinable at Paper 11).

5.12 Section summary

The main aspects of IAS 36 to consider are:

- **Indications** of impairment of assets
- **Measuring recoverable amount**, as fair valueless costs of disposal or value in use
- **Measuring value in use**
- **Cash generating units**
- **Accounting treatment** of an impairment loss, for individual assets and cash generating units
- **Reversal** of an impairment loss

6 IAS 23 *Borrowing costs*

FAST FORWARD

IAS 23 looks at the treatment of **borrowing costs**, particularly where the related borrowings are applied to the construction of certain assets. These are what are usually called 'self-constructed assets', where an entity builds its own inventory or non-current assets over a substantial period of time.

6.1 Definitions

Only two definitions are given by the Standard.

Key terms

> **Borrowing costs**. Interest and other costs incurred by an entity in connection with the borrowing of funds.
>
> **Qualifying asset**. An asset that necessarily takes a substantial period of time to get ready for its intended use or sale. *(IAS 23)*

The Standard lists what may be **included in borrowing costs**.

- Interest on bank overdrafts and short-term and long-term borrowings
- Amortisation of discounts or premiums relating to borrowings
- Amortisation of ancillary costs incurred in connection with the arrangement of borrowings
- Finance charges in respect of finance leases recognised in accordance with IAS 17 (See Chapter 20)

The Standard also gives examples of qualifying assets.

- Inventories that require a substantial period of time to bring them to a saleable condition
- Manufacturing plants
- Power generation facilities
- Investment properties
- Intangible assets

Inventories produced in bulk over short periods and on a regular basis are **not qualifying assets**, nor are assets ready for sale or their intended use when purchased.

6.2 Capitalisation

Borrowing costs that are **directly attributable** to the acquisition, construction or production of a qualifying asset should be capitalised as part of the cost of that asset. The standard lays out the criteria for determining which borrowing costs are eligible for capitalisation.

6.2.1 Borrowing costs eligible for capitalisation

Those borrowing costs directly attributable to the acquisition, construction or production of a qualifying asset must be identified. These are the borrowing costs that **would have been avoided** had the expenditure on the qualifying asset not been made. This is obviously straightforward where funds have been borrowed for the financing of one particular asset.

Difficulties arise, however, where the entity uses a **range of debt instruments** to finance a wide range of assets, so that there is no direct relationship between particular borrowings and a specific asset. For example, all borrowings may be made centrally and then lent to different parts of the group or entity. Judgement is therefore required, particularly where further complications can arise (eg foreign currency loans).

Once the relevant borrowings are identified, which relate to a specific asset, then the **amount of borrowing costs available for capitalisation** will be the actual borrowing costs incurred on those borrowings during the period, *less* any investment income on the temporary investment of those borrowings. It would not be unusual for some or all of the funds to be invested before they are actually used on the qualifying asset.

Question	Capitalisation

On 1 January 20X6 Stremans Co borrowed $1.5m to finance the production of two assets, both of which were expected to take a year to build. Work started during 20X6. The loan facility was drawn down and incurred on 1 January 20X6, and was utilised as follows, with the remaining funds invested temporarily.

	Asset A	Asset B
	$'000	$'000
1 January 20X6	250	500
1 July 20X6	250	500

The loan rate was 9% and Stremans Co can invest surplus funds at 7%.

Required

Ignoring compound interest, calculate the borrowing costs which may be capitalised for each of the assets and consequently the cost of each asset as at 31 December 20X6.

Answer

		Asset A	Asset B
		$	$
Borrowing costs			
To 31 December 20X6	$500,000/$1,000,000 × 9%	45,000	90,000
Less investment income			
To 30 June 20X6	$250,000/$500,000 × 7% × 6/12	(8,750)	(17,500)
		36,250	72,500
Cost of assets			
Expenditure incurred		500,000	1,000,000
Borrowing costs		36,250	72,500
		536,250	1,072,500

In a situation where **borrowings are obtained generally**, but are applied in part to obtaining a qualifying asset, then the amount of borrowing costs eligible for capitalisation is found by applying the 'capitalisation rate' to the expenditure on the asset.

The **capitalisation rate** is the weighted average of the borrowing costs applicable to the entity's borrowings that are outstanding during the period, *excluding* borrowings made specifically to obtain a qualifying asset. However, there is a cap on the amount of borrowing costs calculated in this way: it must not exceed actual borrowing costs incurred.

Sometimes one overall weighted average can be calculated for a group or entity, but in some situations it may be more appropriate to use a weighted average for borrowing costs for **individual parts of the group or entity**.

Question   Construction

Acruni Co had the following loans in place at the beginning and end of 20X6.

	1 January 20X6 $m	31 December 20X6 $m
10% Bank loan repayable 20X8	120	120
9.5% Bank loan repayable 20X9	80	80
8.9% debenture repayable 20X7	–	150

The 8.9% debenture was issued to fund the construction of a qualifying asset (a piece of mining equipment), construction of which began on 1 July 20X6.

On 1 January 20X6, Acruni Co began construction of a qualifying asset, a piece of machinery for a hydro-electric plant, using existing borrowings. Expenditure drawn down for the construction was: $£30m on 1 January 20X6, $20m on 1 October 20X6.

Required

Calculate the borrowing costs that can be capitalised for the hydro-electric plant machine.

Answer

Capitalisation rate = weighted average rate = $(10\% \times \frac{120}{120 + 80}) + (9.5\% \times \frac{80}{120 + 80}) = 9.8\%$

$$
\begin{aligned}
\text{Borrowing costs} &= (\$30m \times 9.8\%) + (\$20m \times 9.8\% \times 3/12) \\
&= \$3.43m
\end{aligned}
$$

6.2.2 Carrying amount exceeds recoverable amount

A situation may arise whereby the carrying amount (or expected ultimate cost) of the qualifying asset exceeds its recoverable amount or net realisable value. In these cases, the carrying amount must be **written down or written off**, as required by other IFRSs. In certain circumstances (again as allowed by other IFRSs), these amounts may be written back in future periods.

6.2.3 Commencement of capitalisation

Three events or transactions must be taking place for capitalisation of borrowing costs to be started.

(a)   Expenditure on the asset is being incurred
(b)   Borrowing costs are being incurred
(c)   Activities are in progress that are necessary to prepare the asset for its intended use or sale

Expenditure must result in the payment of cash, transfer of other assets or assumption of interest-bearing liabilities. **Deductions from expenditure** will be made for any progress payments or grants received in connection with the asset. IAS 23 allows the **average carrying amount** of the asset during a period (including borrowing costs previously capitalised) to be used as a reasonable approximation of the expenditure to which the capitalisation rate is applied in the period. Presumably more exact calculations can be used.

Activities necessary to prepare the asset for its intended sale or use extend further than physical construction work. They encompass technical and administrative work prior to construction, eg obtaining permits. They do *not* include holding an asset when no production or development that changes the asset's condition is taking place, eg where land is held without any associated development activity.

6.2.4 Suspension of capitalisation

If active development is **interrupted for any extended periods**, capitalisation of borrowing costs should be suspended for those periods.

Suspension of capitalisation of borrowing costs is not necessary for **temporary delays** or for periods when substantial technical or administrative work is taking place.

6.2.5 Cessation of capitalisation

Once all the activities necessary to prepare the qualifying asset for its intended use or sale are substantially complete, then capitalisation of borrowing costs should cease. This will normally be when **physical construction of the asset is completed**, although minor modifications may still be outstanding.

The asset may be completed in **parts or stages**, where each part can be used while construction is still taking place on the other parts. Capitalisation of borrowing costs should cease for each part as it is completed. The example given by the Standard is a business park consisting of several buildings.

6.2.6 Disclosure

The following should be disclosed in the financial statements in relation to borrowing costs.

(a)   Amount of borrowing costs **capitalised during the period**
(b)   **Capitalisation rate** used to determine the amount of borrowing costs eligible for capitalisation

Chapter roundup

- Where assets held by an entity have a **limited useful life** to that entity it is necessary to apportion the value of an asset used in a period against the revenue it has helped to create.

- IAS 16 covers all aspects of accounting for property, plant and equipment. This represents the bulk of items which are **'tangible' non-current assets**.

- It is common for entities to receive government grants for various purposes (grants may be called subsidies, premiums, or other names). They may also receive other types of assistance which may be in many forms. The treatment of government grants is covered by IAS 20 *Accounting for government grants and disclosure of government assistance*.

- An entity may own land or a building **as an investment** rather than for use in the business. It may therefore generate cash flows largely independently of other assets which the entity holds.

- Impairment is determined by comparing the carrying amount of the asset with its recoverable amount.

- IAS 23 looks at the treatment of **borrowing costs**, particularly where the related borrowings are applied to the construction of certain assets. These are what are usually called 'self-constructed assets', where an entity builds its own inventory or non-current assets over a substantial period of time.

Quick quiz

1   Define depreciation.

2   Which of the following elements can be included in the production cost of a non-current asset?

    (i)   Purchase price of raw materials
    (ii)   Architect's fees
    (iii)   Import duties
    (iv)   Installation costs

3   Market value can usually be taken as fair value.

    True   ☐

    False   ☐

4   Define impairment loss.

5   Investment properties must always be shown at fair value.

    True   ☐

    False   ☐

Answers to quick quiz

1   See Section 1.2

2   All of them.

3   True

4   See Section 5.1

5   False. The cost model may be used, provided it is used consistently.

End of chapter question

Reconciliation (AIA May 2006)

IAS 16 *Property, plant and equipment* requires a reconciliation of the carrying amount at the beginning and end of the period for each class of property, plant and equipment, including details of depreciation.

The statement of financial position of Exivat at the year end 31 December 20X4 includes the following property, plant and equipment values:

	Cost	Accumulated depreciation
	$'000	$'000
Land and buildings	3,000	900
Plant and equipment	2,100	990
Fixtures and fittings	915	546

It is company policy to charge no depreciation in year of disposal and a full year's depreciation in year of acquisition. The company adopts the straight line method of depreciation.

The following events and transactions occurred during the year ended 31 December 20X5.

Land and buildings – On 1 January 20X5 Exivat revalued its existing property to its market value of $3,600,000. The company also purchased additional property for cash at a cost of $300,000. The effective rate of depreciation on land and buildings is 2% per annum on the carrying value of the land and buildings.

Plant and equipment – A piece of equipment that originally cost $1,050,000 and had accumulated depreciation at 31 December 20X4 of $750,000 was sold for $240,000.

Additional plant and equipment acquired during the year cost $1,140,000. The relevant depreciation rate is 10% with a residual value of nil.

Fixtures and fittings – Certain fixtures were considered to be fully impaired and were to be written off. These fixtures originally cost $120,000 and had a written down value of $45,000.

Additional fixtures and fittings were acquired for $105,000 during the year. The relevant depreciation rate is 15% with a residual value of nil.

Required

(a)   Discuss the usefulness of disclosures of the movement in non-current assets.   **(6 marks)**

(b)   Prepare a statement providing reconciliations of the cost/valuation and depreciation of each class of property, plant and equipment at the year ended 31 December 20X5.   **(14 marks)**

(Total = 20 marks)

10

Intangible non-current assets

Topic list	Syllabus reference
1 IAS 38 *Intangible assets*	11.2
2 Goodwill	11.2

Introduction

We begin our examination of intangible non-current assets with a discussion of IAS 38.

Goodwill and its treatment is a controversial area, as is the accounting for items similar to goodwill, such as brands.

1 IAS 38 *Intangible assets*

FAST FORWARD ▶ Intangible assets are defined by IAS 38 as non-monetary assets without physical substance.

1.1 The objectives of the Standard

(a) To establish the criteria for when an intangible asset may or should be **recognised**
(b) To specify how intangible assets should be **measured**
(c) To specify the **disclosure requirements** for intangible assets

1.2 Scope

IAS 38 applies to all intangible assets with certain **exceptions**: deferred tax assets (IAS 12), leases that fall within the scope of IAS 17, financial assets, insurance contracts, assets arising from employee benefits (IAS 19), non-current assets held for sale and mineral rights and exploration and extraction costs for minerals etc (although intangible assets used to develop or maintain these rights are covered by the Standard). It does *not* apply to goodwill acquired in a business combination (when one business purchases another), which is dealt with under IFRS 3 *Business combinations*.

1.2.1 Definition of an intangible asset

The definition of an intangible asset is a key aspect of the Standard, because the rules for deciding whether or not an intangible asset may be **recognised** in the accounts of an entity are based on the definition of what an intangible asset is.

Key term

> An **intangible asset** is an identifiable non-monetary asset without physical substance. The asset must be:
> (a) Controlled by the entity as a result of events in the past, *and*
> (b) Something from which the entity expects future economic benefits to flow.

Examples of items that might be considered as intangible assets include computer software, patents, copyrights, motion picture films, customer lists, franchises and fishing rights. An item should not be recognised as an intangible asset, however, unless it **fully meets the definition** in the Standard. The guidelines go into great detail on this matter.

1.3 Intangible asset: must be identifiable

An intangible asset must be identifiable in order to distinguish it from goodwill. With non-physical items, there may be a problem with **'identifiability'**.

(a) If an intangible asset is **acquired separately through purchase**, there may be a transfer of a legal right that would help to make an asset identifiable.

(b) An intangible asset may be identifiable if it is **separable**, ie if it could be rented or sold separately. However, 'separability' is not an essential feature of an intangible asset.

1.4 Intangible asset: control by the entity

Another element of the definition of an intangible asset is that it must be under the control of the entity as a result of a past event. The entity must therefore be able to enjoy the future economic benefits from the asset, and prevent the access of others to those benefits. A **legally enforceable right** is evidence of such control, but is not always a *necessary* condition.

(a) Control over **technical knowledge or know-how** only exists if it is protected by a **legal right**.

(b) The skill of employees, arising out of the benefits of **training costs**, are most unlikely to be recognisable as an intangible asset, because an entity does not control the future actions of its staff.

(c) Similarly, **market share and customer loyalty** cannot normally be intangible assets, since an entity cannot control the actions of its customers.

1.5 Intangible asset: expected future economic benefits

An item can only be recognised as an intangible asset if economic benefits are expected to flow in the future from ownership of the asset. Economic benefits may come from the **sale** of products or services, or from a **reduction in expenditures** (cost savings).

An intangible asset, when recognised initially, must be measured at **cost**. It should be recognised if, and only if **both** the following occur.

(a) It is probable that the **future economic benefits** that are attributable to the asset will **flow to the entity**.

(b) The **cost can be measured reliably**.

Management has to exercise its judgement in assessing the degree of certainty attached to the flow of economic benefits to the entity. External evidence is best.

(a) If an intangible asset is **acquired separately**, its cost can usually be measured reliably as its purchase price (including incidental costs of purchase such as legal fees, and any costs incurred in getting the asset ready for use).

(b) When an intangible asset is acquired as **part of a business combination** (ie an acquisition or takeover), the cost of the intangible asset is its fair value at the date of the acquisition.

Quoted market prices in an active market provide the most reliable estimate of the fair value of an intangible asset. If no active market exists for an intangible asset, its fair value is the amount that the entity would have paid for the asset, at the acquisition date, in an orderly transaction between market participants, on the basis of the best information available. In determining this amount, an entity should consider the outcome of recent transactions for similar assets. There are techniques for estimating the fair values of unique intangible assets (such as brand names) and these may be used to measure an intangible asset acquired in a business combination.

In accordance with IAS 20, intangible assets acquired by way of government grant and the grant itself may be recorded initially either at cost (which may be zero) or fair value.

1.6 Exchanges of assets

If one intangible asset is exchanged for another, the cost of the intangible asset is measured at fair value unless:

(a) The exchange transaction lacks commercial substance, *or*
(b) The fair value of neither the asset received nor the asset given up can be measured reliably.

Otherwise, its cost is measured at the carrying amount of the asset given up.

1.7 Internally generated goodwill

Rule to learn

> Internally generated goodwill may **not** be recognised as an **asset**.

The Standard deliberately precludes recognition of internally generated goodwill because it requires that, for initial recognition, the cost of the asset rather than its fair value should be capable of being measured reliably and that it should be identifiable and controlled. Thus an asset which is subjective and cannot be measured reliably can not be recognised.

1.8 Research and development costs

1.8.1 Research

Research activities by definition do not meet the criteria for recognition under IAS 38. This is because, at the research stage of a project, it cannot be certain that future economic benefits will probably flow to the entity from the project. There is too much uncertainty about the likely success or otherwise of the project. **Research costs should therefore be written off as an expense as they are incurred**.

Examples of research costs

- Activities aimed at obtaining new knowledge
- The search for, evaluation and final selection of, applications of research findings or other knowledge
- The search for alternatives for materials, devices, products, processes, systems or services
- The formulation, design evaluation and final selection of possible alternatives for new or improved materials, devices, products, systems or services

1.8.2 Development

Development costs **may qualify** for recognition as intangible assets provided that the following **strict criteria** can be demonstrated.

(a) The technical feasibility of completing the intangible asset so that it will be available for use or sale.

(b) Its intention to complete the intangible asset and use or sell it.

(c) Its ability to use or sell the intangible asset.

(d) How the intangible asset will generate probable future economic benefits. Among other things, the entity should demonstrate the existence of a market for the output of the intangible asset or the intangible asset itself or, if it is to be used internally, the usefulness of the intangible asset.

(e) Its ability to measure the expenditure attributable to the intangible asset during its development reliably.

Where **all** of these criteria are met, development costs should be capitalised. Otherwise these costs should be expensed as they are incurred.

In contrast with research costs development costs are incurred at a later stage in a project, and the probability of success should be more apparent. Examples of development costs include the following.

(a) The design, construction and testing of pre-production or pre-use prototypes and models

(b) The design of tools, jigs, moulds and dies involving new technology

(c) The design, construction and operation of a pilot plant that is not of a scale economically feasible for commercial production

(d) The design, construction and testing of a chosen alternative for new or improved materials, devices, products, processes, systems or services

1.8.3 Other internally generated intangible assets

The Standard **prohibits** the recognition of **internally generated brands, mastheads, publishing titles and customer lists** and similar items as intangible assets. These all fail to meet one or more (in some cases all) the definition and recognition criteria and in some cases are probably indistinguishable from internally generated goodwill.

1.8.4 Cost of an internally generated intangible asset

The costs allocated to an internally generated intangible asset should only be costs that can be **directly attributed** or allocated on a reasonable and consistent basis to creating, producing or preparing the asset for its intended use. The principles underlying the costs which may or may not be included are similar to those for other non-current assets and inventory.

The cost of an internally operated intangible asset is the sum of the **expenditure incurred from the date when** the intangible asset first **meets the recognition criteria**. If, as often happens, considerable costs have already been recognised as expenses before management could demonstrate that the criteria have been met, this earlier expenditure should not be retrospectively recognised at a later date as part of the cost of an intangible asset.

Question   Treatment

Doug Co is developing a new production process. During 20X3, expenditure incurred was $100,000, of which $90,000 was incurred before 1 December 20X3 and $10,000 between 1 December 20X3 and 31 December 20X3. Doug Co can demonstrate that, at 1 December 20X3, the production process met the criteria for recognition as an intangible asset. The recoverable amount of the know-how embodied in the process is estimated to be $50,000.

How should the expenditure be treated?

Answer

At the end of 20X3, the production process is recognised as an intangible asset at a cost of $10,000. This is the expenditure incurred since the date when the recognition criteria were met, that is 1 December 20X3. The $90,000 expenditure incurred before 1 December 20X3 is expensed, because the recognition criteria were not met. It will never form part of the cost of the production process recognised in the statement of financial position.

1.9 Recognition of an expense

All expenditure related to an intangible which does not meet the criteria for recognition either as an identifiable intangible asset or as goodwill arising on an acquisition should be **expensed as incurred**. The IAS gives examples of such expenditure.

- Start up costs
- Training costs
- Advertising costs
- Business relocation costs

Prepaid costs for services, for example advertising or marketing costs for campaigns that have been prepared but not launched, can still be recognised as a **prepayment**.

1.10 Measurement of intangible assets subsequent to initial recognition

The Standard allows two methods of valuation for intangible assets after they have been first recognised.

Applying the **cost model**, an intangible asset should be **carried at its cost**, less any accumulated amortisation and less any accumulated impairment losses.

The **revaluation model** allows an intangible asset to be carried at a revalued amount, which is its **fair value** at the date of revaluation, less any subsequent accumulated amortisation and any subsequent accumulated impairment losses.

(a)   The fair value must be able to be measured reliably with reference to an **active market** in that type of asset.

(b)   The **entire class** of intangible assets of that type must be revalued at the same time (to prevent selective revaluations).

(c)   If an intangible asset in a class of revalued intangible assets cannot be revalued because there is **no active market** for this asset, the asset should be carried at its **cost less any accumulated amortisation and impairment losses**.

(d)   Revaluations should be made with such **regularity** that the carrying amount does not differ from that which would be determined using fair value at the reporting date.

Key term

> An **active market** is a market in which all of the following conditions exist:
>
> * The items traded in the market are homogenous
> * Willing buyers and sellers can normally be found at any time
> * Prices are available to the public

Point to note

> This treatment is **not** available for the **initial recognition** of intangible assets. This is because the cost of the asset must be reliably measured.

The guidelines state that there **will not usually be an active market** in an intangible asset; therefore the revaluation model will usually not be available. For example, although copyrights, publishing rights and film rights can be sold, each has a unique sale value. In such cases, revaluation to fair value would be inappropriate. A fair value might be obtainable however for assets such as fishing rights or quotas or taxi cab licences.

Where an intangible asset is revalued upwards to a fair value, the amount of the revaluation should be credited directly to equity under the heading of a **revaluation surplus**.

However, if a revaluation surplus is a **reversal of a revaluation decrease** that was previously charged against income, the increase can be recognised as income in profit or loss.

Where the carrying amount of an intangible asset is revalued downwards, the amount of the **downward revaluation** should be charged as an expense in profit or loss, unless the asset has previously been revalued upwards. A revaluation decrease should be first recognised as other comprehensive income and charged against any previous revaluation surplus in respect of that asset.

Question   Downward revaluation

An intangible asset is measured by a company at fair value. The asset was revalued by $400 in 20X3, and there is a revaluation surplus of $400 in the statement of financial position. At the end of 20X4, the asset is valued again, and a downward valuation of $500 is required.

Required

State the accounting treatment for the downward revaluation.

Answer

In this example, the downward valuation of $500 can first be set against the revaluation surplus of $400. The revaluation surplus will be reduced to 0 and a charge of $100 made as an expense in profit or loss in 20X4.

When the revaluation model is used, and an intangible asset is revalued upwards, the cumulative revaluation **surplus may be transferred to retained earnings** when the surplus is eventually realised. The surplus would be realised when the asset is disposed of. However, the surplus may also be realised over time as the **asset is used** by the entity. The amount of the surplus realised each year is the difference between the amortisation charge for the asset based on the revalued amount of the asset, and the amortisation that would be charged on the basis of the asset's historical cost. The realised surplus in such case should be transferred from revaluation surplus directly to retained earnings, and disclosed in the statement of changes in equity.

1.11 Useful life

An entity should **assess** the useful life of an intangible asset, which may be **finite or indefinite**. An intangible asset has an indefinite useful life when there is **no foreseeable limit** to the period over which the asset is expected to generate net cash inflows for the entity.

Many factors are considered in determining the useful life of an intangible asset, including: expected usage; typical product life cycles; technical, technological, commercial or other types of obsolescence; the stability of the industry; expected actions by competitors; the level of maintenance expenditure required; and legal or similar limits on the use of the asset, such as the expiry dates of related leases. Computer software and many other intangible assets normally have short lives because they are susceptible to technological obsolescence. However, uncertainty does not justify choosing a life that is unrealistically short.

The useful life of an intangible asset that arises from **contractual or other legal rights** should not exceed the period of the rights, but may be shorter depending on the period over which the entity expects to use the asset.

1.12 Amortisation period and amortisation method

An intangible asset with a finite useful life should be amortised over its **expected useful life**.

(a) Amortisation should start when the asset is **available for use**.

(b) Amortisation should cease at the earlier of the date that the asset is classified **as held for sale** in accordance with IFRS 5 *Non-current assets held for sale and discontinued operations* and the date that the asset is **derecognised**.

(c) The amortisation method used should reflect the **pattern in which the asset's future economic benefits are consumed**. If such a pattern cannot be predicted reliably, the straight-line method should be used.

(d) The amortisation charge for each period should normally be recognised **in profit or loss**.

The **residual value** of an intangible asset with a finite useful life is **assumed to be zero** unless a third party is committed to buying the intangible asset at the end of its useful life or unless there is an active market for that type of asset (so that its expected residual value can be measured) and it is probable that there will be a market for the asset at the end of its useful life.

The amortisation period and the amortisation method used for an intangible asset with a finite useful life should be **reviewed at each financial year end**.

1.13 Intangible assets with indefinite useful lives

An intangible asset with an indefinite useful life **should not be amortised**. (IAS 36 requires that such an asset is tested for impairment at least annually.)

The useful life of an intangible asset that is not being amortised should be **reviewed each year** to determine whether it is still appropriate to assess its useful life as indefinite. Reassessing the useful life of an intangible asset as finite rather than indefinite is an indicator that the asset may be impaired and therefore it should be tested for impairment.

Question	Intangible asset

It may be difficult to establish the useful life of an intangible asset, and judgement will be needed. Consider how to determine the useful life of a *purchased* brand name.

Answer

Factors to consider would include the following.

(a)   Legal protection of the brand name and the control of the entity over the (illegal) use by others of the brand name (ie control over pirating)

(b)   Age of the brand name

(c)   Status or position of the brand in its particular market

(d)   Ability of the management of the entity to manage the brand name and to measure activities that support the brand name (eg advertising and PR activities)

(e)   Stability and geographical spread of the market in which the branded products are sold

(f)   Pattern of benefits that the brand name is expected to generate over time

(g)   Intention of the entity to use and promote the brand name over time (as evidenced perhaps by a business plan in which there will be substantial expenditure to promote the brand name)

1.14 Disposals/retirements of intangible assets

An intangible asset should be eliminated from the statement of financial position when it is disposed of or when there is no further expected economic benefit from its future use. On disposal the gain or loss arising from the **difference between the net disposal proceeds and the carrying amount** of the asset should be taken to profit or loss as a gain or loss on disposal (ie treated as income or expense).

1.15 Disclosure requirements

The Standard has fairly extensive disclosure requirements for intangible assets. The financial statements should disclose the **accounting policies** for intangible assets that have been adopted.

For **each class of intangible assets**, disclosure is required of the following.

* The **method of amortisation** used
* The **useful life** of the assets or the amortisation rate used

- The **gross carrying amount**, the **accumulated amortisation** and the **accumulated impairment losses** as at the beginning and the end of the period

- A **reconciliation of the carrying amount** as at the beginning and at the end of the period (additions, retirements/disposals, revaluations, impairment losses, impairment losses reversed, amortisation charge for the period, net exchange differences, other movements)

- The carrying amount of **internally-generated intangible assets**

The financial statements should also disclose the following.

- In the case of intangible assets that are assessed as having an indefinite useful life, the carrying amounts and the reasons supporting that assessment

- For intangible assets acquired by way of a **government grant** and initially recognised at fair value, the **fair value initially recognised**, the **carrying amount**, and whether they are carried under the **cost model** or the **revaluation model** for subsequent remeasurements

- The carrying amount, nature and remaining amortisation period of any intangible asset that is **material to the financial statements of the entity as a whole**

- The existence (if any) and amounts of intangible assets whose **title is restricted** and of intangible assets that have been **pledged as security** for liabilities

- The amount of any **commitments for the future acquisition of intangible assets**

Where intangible assets are accounted for at revalued amounts, disclosure is required of the following.

- The **effective date of the revaluation** (by class of intangible assets)

- The **carrying amount** of revalued intangible assets

- The carrying amount that would have been shown (by class of assets) **if the cost model had been used**, and the amount of amortisation that would have been charged

- The amount of any **revaluation surplus** on intangible assets, as at the beginning and end of the period, and movements in the surplus during the year (and any restrictions on the distribution of the balance to shareholders)

The financial statements should also disclose the amount of research and development expenditure that have been charged as expenses of the period.

1.16 Section summary

- An intangible asset should be recognised if, and only if, it is probable that future economic benefits will flow to the entity and the cost of the asset can be measured reliably.

- An asset is initially recognised at cost and subsequently carried either at cost or revalued amount.

- Costs that do not meet the recognition criteria should be expensed as incurred.

- An intangible asset with a finite useful life should be amortised over its useful life. An intangible asset with an indefinite useful life should not be amortised.

Question   R&D

As an aid to your revision, list the examples given in IAS 38 of activities that might be included in either research or development.

Answer

IAS 38 gives these examples.

Research

- Activities aimed at obtaining new knowledge
- The search for applications of research findings or other knowledge
- The search for product or process alternatives
- The formulation and design of possible new or improved product or process alternatives

Development

- The evaluation of product or process alternatives

- The design, construction and testing of pre-production prototypes and models

- The design of tools, jigs, moulds and dies involving new technology

- The design, construction and operation of a pilot plant that is not of a scale economically feasible for commercial production

2 Goodwill

FAST FORWARD

Purchased goodwill arising on consolidation is retained in the statement of financial position as an intangible asset. It must be reviewed for impairment annually.

2.1 What is goodwill?

Goodwill is **created by good relationships** between a business and its customers.

(a) By building up a **reputation** (by word of mouth perhaps) for high quality products or high standards of service

(b) By **responding promptly and helpfully** to queries and complaints from customers

(c) Through the **personality of the staff** and their attitudes to customers

The value of goodwill to a business might be **extremely significant**. However, goodwill is not usually valued in the accounts of a business at all, and we should not normally expect to find an amount for goodwill in its statement of financial position. As an example, the welcoming smile of the bar staff may contribute more to a bar's profits than the fact that a new electronic cash register has recently been acquired. But, whereas the cash register will be recorded in the accounts as a non-current asset, the value of staff would be ignored for accounting purposes.

On reflection, we might agree with this omission of goodwill from the accounts of a business.

(a) The goodwill is **inherent** in the business but it has not been paid for, and it does not have an 'objective' value. We can guess at what such goodwill is worth, but such guesswork would be a matter of individual opinion, and not based on hard facts.

(b) Goodwill **changes** from day to day. One act of bad customer relations might damage goodwill and one act of good relations might improve it. Staff with a favourable personality might retire or leave to find another job, to be replaced by staff who need time to find their feet in the job, and so on. Since goodwill is continually changing in value, realistically it cannot be recorded in the accounts of the business.

2.2 Purchased goodwill

There is one exception to the general rule that goodwill has no objective valuation. This is **when a business is sold**. People wishing to set up in business have a choice of how to do it – they can either buy their own long-term assets and inventory and set up their business from scratch, or they can buy up an existing business from a proprietor willing to sell it. When a buyer purchases an existing business, he will have to purchase not only its long-term assets and inventory (and perhaps take over its accounts payable and receivable too) but also the goodwill of the business.

Purchased goodwill is shown in the statement of financial position because it has been paid for. It has no tangible substance, and so it is an **intangible non-current asset**.

2.3 How is the value of purchased goodwill decided?

When a business is sold, there is likely to be some purchased goodwill in the selling price. But **how is the amount of this purchased goodwill decided**?

This is not really a problem for accountants, who must simply record the goodwill in the accounts of the new business. The value of the goodwill is a **matter for the purchaser and seller to agree upon in fixing the purchase/sale price**. However, two methods of valuation are worth mentioning here.

(a)   The seller and buyer agree on a price for the business **without specifically quantifying the goodwill**. The purchased goodwill will then be the difference between the price agreed and the value of the identifiable net assets in the books of the new business.

(b)   However, the calculation of goodwill often precedes the fixing of the purchase price and becomes a **central element of negotiation**. There are many ways of arriving at a value for goodwill and most of them are related to the profit record of the business in question.

No matter how goodwill is calculated within the total agreed purchase price, the goodwill shown by the purchaser in his accounts will be **the difference between the purchase consideration and his own valuation of the tangible net assets acquired**. If A values his tangible net assets at $40,000, goodwill is agreed at $21,000 and B agrees to pay $61,000 for the business but values the tangible net assets at only $38,000, then the goodwill in B's books will be $61,000 – $38,000 = $23,000.

2.4 How is goodwill treated in the financial statements?

Exam focus point

> IFRS 3 *Business combinations* covers the treatment of goodwill acquired in a business combination (when one business purchases another) (see Chapters 15 – 17).

Key term

> **Goodwill**. An asset representing the future economic benefits arising from other assets acquired in a business combination that are not individually identified and separately recognised.   *(IFRS 3)*

Goodwill acquired in a business combination is **recognised as an asset** and is initially measured at **cost**. Cost is the excess of the value of the business over the net fair value of the identifiable assets, liabilities and contingent liabilities of that business. The value of the business is made up of the consideration paid by the acquirer for their interest plus the value of the interest not purchased (the non-controlling interest).

After initial recognition goodwill acquired in a business combination is measured **at cost less any accumulated impairment losses**. It is **not amortised**. Instead it is tested for impairment at least annually, in accordance with IAS 36 *Impairment of assets*.

A **bargain purchase** arises when the net fair value of the acquiree's identifiable assets, liabilities and contingent liabilities exceeds the consideration paid by the acquirer plus any non-controlling interest. This results in 'negative goodwill' (although this is not a term used by IFRS 3).

Negative goodwill can arise as the result of **errors** in measuring the fair value of either the cost of the combination or the acquiree's identifiable net assets.

Where there is negative goodwill, an entity should first **reassess** the amounts at which it has measured both the cost of the combination and the acquiree's identifiable net assets. This exercise should identify any errors.

Any negative goodwill remaining should be **recognised immediately in profit or loss** (that is, in the statement of profit or loss).

Question	Characteristics of goodwill

What are the main characteristics of goodwill which distinguish it from other intangible non-current assets? To what extent do you consider that these characteristics should affect the accounting treatment of goodwill? State your reasons.

Answer

Goodwill may be distinguished from other intangible non-current assets by reference to the following characteristics.

(a)   It is incapable of realisation separately from the business as a whole.

(b)   Its value has no reliable or predictable relationship to any costs which may have been incurred.

(c)   Its value arises from various intangible factors such as skilled employees, effective advertising or a strategic location. These indirect factors cannot be valued.

(d)   The value of goodwill may fluctuate widely according to internal and external circumstances over relatively short periods of time.

(e)   The assessment of the value of goodwill is highly subjective.

It could be argued that, because goodwill is so different from other intangible non-current assets it does not make sense to account for it in the same way. Thus the capitalisation and amortisation treatment would not be acceptable. Furthermore, because goodwill is so difficult to value, any valuation may be misleading, and it is best eliminated from the statement of financial position altogether. However, there are strong arguments for treating it like any other intangible non-current asset. This issue remains controversial.

Chapter roundup

- **Intangible assets** are defined by **IAS 38** as non-monetary assets without physical substance.

- **Purchased goodwill** arising on consolidation is retained in the statement of financial position as an intangible asset. It must be reviewed for impairment annually.

Quick quiz

1   Intangible assets can only be recognised in a company's accounts if:

- It is probable that .... will flow to the entity
- The cost can be ....

2   What are the criteria which must be met before development expenditure can be deferred?

3   Start up costs must be expensed.

True ☐

False ☐

4   Peggy buys Phil's business for $30,000. The business assets are a bar valued at $20,000, inventories at $3,000 and receivables of $3,000. What is the value of goodwill?

5   How is purchased goodwill accounted for?

Answers to quick quiz

1　Future economic benefits. Measured reliably.

2　See Para 1.8.2

3　True

4　$30,000 – $20,000 – $3,000 – $3,000 = $4,000

5　Cost less impairment losses

End of chapter question

Intangible assets (AIA May 2007)

EcoSaver is an environmentally friendly aerospace design company based in Europe. The company's year end is 31 December. In 20X2 the company began investigating the prospect of developing a new propulsion system which would, if successful, cut jet-engine carbon emissions by 50%. In the period 20X2-20X3 the Company spent $15m on this research.

Events in subsequent years were as follows:

20X4　　The company's technical director Hank Getrich III was able to convince the Company's board that the previous two years of research had paid off and that he had come up with a technically feasible design (codenamed 'Carbobuster') which he believed could be sold for large sums to aerospace manufacturers for at least the next five years. Hank produced details of the trial run of a prototype which appeared to show the 'Carbobuster' worked. The board promised to make adequate resources available to Hank to complete the project. The total sum spent during the year was made up as follows:

	$m
Services and sundry materials	20
Staff costs associated with the project	15
Expenses associated with the project	10
Proportion of general overheads	6
Training potential 'Carbobuster' technical staff	4
	55

20X5　　The Company incurred completion costs of $5m made up entirely of staff costs associated with the project. Hank produced very convincing details showing strong cash flow projections over the next five years. In September, at a launch party costing $1m, the 'Carbobuster' design was finally marketed.

20X6　　The EcoSaver Plc financial statements were published on 31 March.

　　　　On April 1, the first manufacturer to use the design found it contained a fatal flaw and demanded the immediate return of all monies paid together with costs. The Company asked for confirmation of this from an independent aerospace engineer and, following his confirmation that the design was virtually useless, Hank announced that a change in accounting policy would be necessary.

Required

Explain how the above events would have been dealt with in the financial statements of EcoSaver for the period 20X2 – 20X3 and in each of the three years 20X4, 20X5 and 20X6. [Refer to current standards where appropriate and assume all had been effective for all periods covered by the question.] **(15 marks)**

Events after the reporting period, provisions and contingencies

Topic list	Syllabus reference
1 IAS 10 *Events after the reporting period*	11.2
2 IAS 37 *Provisions, contingent liabilities and contingent assets*	11.2

Introduction

You will have met these Standards in your earlier studies. However, you may be asked in more detail about IAS 37 for Paper 11.

1 IAS 10 *Events after the reporting period*

IAS 10 should be familiar from your earlier studies, but it could still come up in part of a question.

You have already studied IAS 10 *Events after the reporting period*.

Knowledge brought forward from earlier studies

IAS 10 *Events after the reporting period*

Definition

Events after the reporting period are those events, both favourable and unfavourable, that occur between the end of the reporting period and the date on which the financial statements are authorised for issue. Two types of events can be identified:

- Those that provide further evidence of conditions that existed at the end of the reporting period
- Those that are indicative of conditions that arose after the reporting period

Accounting treatment

- **Adjust** assets and liabilities where events after the end of the reporting period provide further evidence of conditions existing at the reporting date.

- **Do not adjust**, but instead disclose, important events after the end of the reporting period that do not affect the condition of assets/liabilities at the end of the reporting period.

- **Equity dividends** for a period declared after the reporting period but before the financial statements are approved should not be recognised as a liability but shown as a note in the financial statements.

Disclosure

- Nature of event
- Estimate of financial effect (or statement that estimate cannot be made)

---

2 IAS 37 *Provisions, contingent liabilities and contingent assets*

As we have seen with regard to events after the reporting period, financial statements must include **all the information necessary for an understanding of the company's financial position**. Provisions, contingent liabilities and contingent assets are 'uncertainties' that must be accounted for consistently if we are to achieve this understanding.

2.1 Objective

IAS 37 *Provisions, contingent liabilities and contingent assets* aims to ensure that appropriate **recognition criteria** and **measurement bases** are applied to provisions, contingent liabilities and contingent assets and that **sufficient information** is disclosed in the **notes** to the financial statements to enable users to understand their nature, timing and amount.

2.2 Provisions

Before IAS 37, there was no accounting standard dealing with provisions. Companies wanting to show their results in the most favourable light used to make large 'one off' provisions in years where a high level of underlying profits was generated. These provisions, often known as 'big bath' provisions, were then available to shield expenditure in future years when perhaps the underlying profits were not as good.

In other words, provisions were used for profit smoothing. Profit smoothing is misleading.

Important

> The key aim of IAS 37 is to ensure that **provisions are made only** where there are valid grounds for them.

IAS 37 views a provision as a liability.

Key terms

> A **provision** is a **liability** of uncertain timing or amount.
>
> A **liability** is a present obligation of the entity arising from past events the settlement of which is expected to result in an outflow from the entity of resources embodying economic benefits.   *(IAS 37)*

The IAS distinguishes provisions from other liabilities such as trade payables and accruals. This is on the basis that for a provision there is **uncertainty** about the timing or amount of the future expenditure. While uncertainty is clearly present in the case of certain accruals the uncertainty is generally much less than for provisions.

2.3 Recognition

IAS 37 states that a provision should be **recognised** as a liability in the financial statements when:

- An entity has a **present obligation** (legal or constructive) as a result of a past event
- It is probable that an outflow of resources embodying economic benefits will be required to settle the obligation
- A **reliable estimate** can be made of the amount of the obligation

2.4 Meaning of obligation

It is fairly clear what a legal obligation is. However, you may not know what a **constructive obligation** is.

Key term

> IAS 37 defines a **constructive obligation** as:
>
> 'An obligation that derives from an entity's actions where:
>
> (a)   by an established pattern of past practice, published policies or a sufficiently specific current statement the entity has indicated to other parties that it will accept certain responsibilities; *and*
>
> (b)   as a result, the entity has created a valid expectation on the part of those other parties that it will discharge those responsibilities.'

| Question | Provision |

In which of the following circumstances might a provision be recognised?

(a)   On 13 December 20X9 the board of an entity decided to close down a division. The accounting date of the company is 31 December. Before 31 December 20X9 the decision was not communicated to any of those affected and no other steps were taken to implement the decision.

(b)   The board agreed a detailed closure plan on 20 December 20X9 and details were given to customers and employees.

(c)   A company is obliged to incur clean up costs for environmental damage (that has already been caused).

(d)   A company intends to carry out future expenditure to operate in a particular way in the future.

Answer

(a)   No provision would be recognised as the decision has not been communicated.

(b)   A provision would be made in the 20X9 financial statements as there is a constructive obligation.

(c)   A provision for such costs is appropriate.

(d)   No present obligation exists and under IAS 37 no provision would be appropriate. This is because the entity could avoid the future expenditure by its future actions, maybe by changing its method of operation.

2.4.1 Probable transfer of economic benefits

For the purpose of the IAS, a transfer of resources embodying economic benefits is regarded as **'probable'** if the event is **more likely than not** to occur. This appears to indicate a probability of more than 50%. However, the Standard makes it clear that where there is a number of similar obligations the probability should be based on considering the population as a whole, rather than one single item.

2.4.2 Example: transfer of economic benefits

If a company has entered into a warranty obligation then the probability of transfer of resources embodying economic benefits may well be extremely small in respect of one specific item. However, when considering the population as a whole the probability of some transfer of economic benefits is quite likely to be much higher. If there is a **greater than 50% probability** of some transfer of economic benefits then a **provision** should be made for the **expected amount**.

2.4.3 Measurement of provisions

Important

> The amount recognised as a provision should be the best estimate of the expenditure required to settle the present obligation at the reporting period.

The estimates will be determined by the **judgement** of the entity's management supplemented by the experience of similar transactions.

Allowance is made for **uncertainty**. Where the provision being measured involves a large population of items, the obligation is estimated by weighting all possible outcomes by their associated probabilities, ie **expected value**.

Parker Co sells goods with a warranty under which customers are covered for the cost of repairs of any manufacturing defect that becomes apparent within the first six months of purchase. The company's past experience and future expectations indicate the following pattern of likely repairs.

% of goods sold	Defects	Cost of repairs if all items suffered from these defects $m
75	None	–
20	Minor	1.0
5	Major	4.0

What is the expected cost of repairs?

Answer

The cost is found using 'expected values' (75% × $nil) + (20% × $1.0m) + (5% × $4.0m) = $400,000.

Where the effect of the **time value of money** is material, the amount of a provision should be the **present value** of the expenditure required to settle the obligation. An appropriate **discount** rate should be used.

The discount rate should be a **pre-tax rate** that reflects current market assessments of the time value of money. **The discount rate(s) should not reflect risks for which future cash flow estimates have been adjusted.**

2.4.4 Future events

Future events which are reasonably expected to occur (for example, new legislation, changes in technology) may affect the amount required to settle the entity's obligation and should be taken into account.

2.4.5 Expected disposal of assets

Gains from the expected disposal of assets should not be taken into account in measuring a provision.

2.4.6 Reimbursements

Some or all of the expenditure needed to settle a provision may be expected to be recovered from a third party. If so, the **reimbursement should be recognised only when it is virtually certain that reimbursement will be received if the entity settles the obligation.**

- The reimbursement should be treated as a separate asset, and the amount recognised should not be greater than the provision itself.

- The provision and the amount recognised for reimbursement may be netted off in the statement of profit or loss.

2.4.7 Changes in provisions

Provisions should be reviewed at the end of each reporting period and adjusted to reflect the current best estimate. If it is no longer probable that a transfer of resources will be required to settle the obligation, the provision should be reversed.

2.4.8 Use of provisions

A provision should be used only for expenditures for which the provision was originally recognised. Setting expenditures against a provision that was originally recognised for another purpose would conceal the impact of two different events.

2.4.9 Future operating losses

Provisions should not be recognised for future operating losses. They do not meet the definition of a liability and the general recognition criteria set out in the Standard.

2.4.10 Onerous contracts

If an entity has a contract that is onerous, the present obligation under the contract **should be recognised and measured** as a provision. An example might be vacant leasehold property.

Key term

> An **onerous contract** is a contract entered into with another party under which the unavoidable costs of fulfilling the terms of the contract exceed any revenues expected to be received from the goods or services supplied or purchased directly or indirectly under the contract and where the entity would have to compensate the other party if it did not fulfil the terms of the contract.

2.5 Examples of possible provisions

It is easier to see what IAS 37 is driving at if you look at examples of those items which are possible provisions under this Standard. Some of these we have already touched on.

(a) **Warranties**. These are argued to be genuine provisions as on past experience it is probable, ie more likely than not, that some claims will emerge. The provision must be estimated, however, on the basis of the class as a whole and not on individual claims. There is a clear legal obligation in this case.

(b) **Major repairs**. In the past it has been quite popular for companies to provide for expenditure on a major overhaul to be accrued gradually over the intervening years between overhauls. Under IAS 37 this is no longer possible as IAS 37 would argue that this is a mere intention to carry out repairs, not an obligation. The entity can always sell the asset in the meantime. The only solution is to treat major assets such as aircraft, ships, furnaces etc as a series of smaller assets where each part is depreciated over shorter lives. Thus any major overhaul may be argued to be replacement and therefore capital rather than revenue expenditure.

(c) **Self insurance**. A number of companies have created a provision for self insurance based on the expected cost of making good fire damage and so on instead of paying premiums to an insurance company. Under IAS 37 this provision is no longer justifiable as the entity has no obligation until a fire or accident occurs. No obligation exists until that time.

(d) **Environmental contamination**. If the company has an environmental policy such that other parties would expect the company to clean up any contamination or if the company has broken current environmental legislation then a provision for environmental damage must be made.

(e) **Decommissioning or abandonment costs**. When an oil company initially purchases an oilfield it is put under a legal obligation to decommission the site at the end of its life. Prior to IAS 37 most oil companies set up the provision gradually over the life of the field so that no one year would be unduly burdened with the cost.

IAS 37, however, insists that a legal obligation exists on the initial expenditure on the field and therefore a liability exists immediately. This would appear to result in a large charge to profit or loss in the first year of operation of the field. However, the IAS takes the view that the cost of purchasing the field in the first place is not only the cost of the field itself but also the costs of putting it right again. Thus all the costs of abandonment may be capitalised.

(f)   **Restructuring**. This is considered in detail below.

2.6 Provisions for restructuring

One of the main purposes of IAS 37 was to target abuses of provisions for restructuring. Accordingly, IAS 37 lays down **strict criteria** to determine when such a provision can be made.

IAS 37 defines a **restructuring** as:

A programme that is planned and is controlled by management and materially changes either:

- The scope of a business undertaken by an entity
- The manner in which that business is conducted

The IAS gives the following **examples** of events that may fall under the definition of restructuring.

- The **sale or termination** of a line of business

- The **closure of business locations** in a country or region or the **relocation** of business activities from one country region to another

- **Changes in management structure**, for example, the elimination of a layer of management

- **Fundamental reorganisations** that have a material effect on the **nature and focus** of the entity's operations

The question is whether or not an entity has an obligation – legal or constructive – at the reporting period. For this to be the case:

- An entity must have a **detailed formal plan** for the restructuring

- It must have **raised a valid expectation** in those affected that it will carry out the restructuring by starting to implement that plan or announcing its main features to those affected by it

A mere management decision is not normally sufficient. Management decisions may sometimes trigger recognition, but only if earlier events such as negotiations with employee representatives and other interested parties have been concluded subject only to management approval.

Where the restructuring involves the **sale of an operation** then IAS 37 states that no obligation arises until the entity has entered into a **binding sale agreement**. This is because until this has occurred the entity will be able to change its mind and withdraw from the sale even if its intentions have been announced publicly.

2.6.1 Costs to be included within a restructuring provision

The IAS states that a restructuring provision should include only the **direct expenditures** arising from the restructuring, which are those that are both:

- **Necessarily entailed** by the restructuring; *and*
- Not associated with the **ongoing activities** of the entity.

The following costs should specifically *not* be included within a restructuring provision.

- **Retraining** or relocating continuing staff
- **Marketing**
- **Investment in new systems** and distribution networks

2.7 Disclosure

Disclosures for provisions fall into two parts.

(a) Disclosure of details of the **change in carrying amount** of a provision from the beginning to the end of the year

(b) Disclosure of the **background** to the making of the provision and the uncertainties affecting its outcome

2.8 Contingent liabilities

Now you understand provisions it will be easier to understand contingent assets and liabilities.

Key term

> IAS 37 defines a **contingent liability** as:
>
> (a) 'A possible obligation that arises from past events and whose existence will be confirmed only by the occurrence or non-occurrence of one or more uncertain future events not wholly within the entity's control.
>
> (b) A present obligation that arises from past events but is not recognised because:
>
>   (i) It is not probable that an outflow of resources embodying economic benefits will be required to settle the obligation.
>
>   (ii) The amount of the obligation cannot be measured with sufficient reliability'.

As a rule of thumb, probable means more than 50% likely. **If an obligation is probable, it is not a contingent liability** – instead, a **provision is needed**.

2.8.1 Treatment of contingent liabilities

Contingent liabilities **should not be recognised in financial statements** but they **should be disclosed**. The required disclosures are:

- A brief description of the nature of the contingent liability
- An estimate of its financial effect
- An indication of the uncertainties that exist
- The possibility of any reimbursement

2.9 Contingent assets

Key term

> IAS 37 defines a **contingent asset** as:
>
> 'A possible asset that arises from past events and whose existence will be confirmed by the occurrence or non-occurrence of one or more uncertain future events not wholly within the entity's control'.

A contingent asset must not be recognised. Only when the realisation of the related economic benefits is **virtually certain** should recognition take place. At that point, **the asset is no longer a contingent asset!**

2.10 Disclosure

2.10.1 Disclosure: contingent liabilities

A **brief description** must be provided of all material contingent liabilities unless they are likely to be remote.

In addition, provide

- An estimate of their **financial effect**
- Details of **any uncertainties**
- The possibility of any reimbursement

2.10.2 Disclosure: contingent assets

Contingent assets must only be disclosed in the notes if they are **probable**. In that case a brief description of the contingent asset should be provided along with an estimate of its likely financial effect.

2.11 'Get out'

IAS 37 permits reporting entities to avoid disclosure requirements relating to provisions, contingent liabilities and contingent assets if they would be expected to **seriously prejudice** the position of the entity in dispute with other parties. However, this should only be employed in **extremely rare** cases. Details of the general nature of the provision/contingencies must still be provided, together with an explanation of why it has not been disclosed.

2.12 Flow chart

You must practise the questions below to get the hang of IAS 37. But first, study the flow chart, taken from IAS 37, which is a good summary of its requirements concerning provisions and contingent liabilities.

Exam focus point

If you learn this flow chart you should be able to deal with most questions you are likely to meet in an exam.

```
                        ┌──────────┐
                        │  Start   │
                        └────┬─────┘
                             │
                             ▼
        ╱─────────────────╲        No        ╱─────────────╲        No
       ╱ Present obligation ╲────────────────▶  Possible     ╲──────────────────────────┐
       │ as a result of an  │                │ obligation?   │                          │
       ╲ obligating event?  ╱                ╲               ╱                          │
        ╲─────────────────╱                   ╲─────────────╱                           │
                │                                    │                                  │
              Yes                                  Yes                                  │
                │                                    │                                  │
                ▼                                    ▼                                  │
        ╱─────────────╲        No          ╱─────────────╲          Yes                │
       ╱   Probable    ╲──────────────────▶   Remote?     ╲────────────────────────────┤
       │   outflow?     │                  ╲               ╱                            │
       ╲               ╱                    ╲─────────────╱                             │
        ╲─────────────╱                          │                                      │
                │                               No                                      │
              Yes                                │                                      │
                │                                │                                      │
                ▼                                │                                      │
        ╱─────────────╲    No (rare)            │                                      │
       ╱   Reliable    ╲─────────────┐          │                                      │
       │   estimate?    │            │          │                                      │
       ╲               ╱             │          │                                      │
        ╲─────────────╱             │          │                                      │
                │                   │          │                                      │
              Yes                   ▼          ▼                                      ▼
                │            ┌──────────────────────┐                        ┌──────────────┐
                ▼            │ Disclose contingent   │                        │  Do nothing  │
        ┌─────────────┐      │      liability        │                        └──────────────┘
        │   Provide   │      └──────────────────────┘
        └─────────────┘
```

Question Recognition of provision

Warren Co gives warranties at the time of sale to purchasers of its products. Under the terms of the warranty the manufacturer undertakes to make good, by repair or replacement, manufacturing defects that become apparent within a period of three years from the date of the sale. Should a provision be recognised?

Answer

Warren Co **cannot avoid** the cost of repairing or replacing all items of product that manifest manufacturing defects in respect of which warranties are given before the reporting date, and a provision for the cost of this should therefore be made.

Warren Co is obliged to repair or replace items that fail within the entire warranty period. Therefore, in respect of **this year's sales**, the obligation provided for at the reporting date should be the cost of making good items for which defects have been notified but not yet processed, **plus** an estimate of costs in respect of the other items sold for which there is sufficient evidence that manufacturing defects **will** manifest themselves during their remaining periods of warranty cover.

Question

After a wedding in 20X0 ten people died, possibly as a result of food poisoning from products sold by Callow Co. Legal proceedings are started seeking damages from Callow but it disputes liability. Up to the date of approval of the financial statements for the year to 31 December 20X0, Callow's lawyers advise that it is probable that it will not be found liable. However, when Callow prepares the financial statements for the year to 31 December 20X1 its lawyers advise that, owing to developments in the case, it is probable that it will be found liable.

What is the required accounting treatment:

(a)   At 31 December 20X0?
(b)   At 31 December 20X1?

Answer

(a)   *At 31 December 20X0*

On the basis of the evidence available when the financial statements were approved, there is no obligation as a result of past events. No provision is recognised. The matter is disclosed as a contingent liability unless the probability of any transfer is regarded as remote.

(b)   *At 31 December 20X1*

On the basis of the evidence available, there is a present obligation. A transfer of economic benefits in settlement is probable.

A provision is recognised for the best estimate of the amount needed to settle the present obligation.

2.13 Section summary

- The objective of IAS 37 is to ensure that appropriate recognition criteria and measurement bases are applied to provisions and contingencies and that sufficient information is disclosed.

- The IAS seeks to ensure that provisions are **only recognised** when a **measurable obligation** exists. It includes detailed rules that can be used to ascertain when an obligation exists and how to measure the obligation.

- The Standard attempts to **eliminate** the **'profit smoothing'** which has gone on before it was issued.

Chapter roundup

- **IAS 10** should be familiar from your earlier studies, but it still could come up in part of a question.

- As we have seen with regard to events after the reporting period, financial statements must include **all the information necessary for an understanding of the company's financial position**. Provisions, contingent liabilities and contingent assets are 'uncertainties' that must be accounted for consistently if we are to achieve this understanding.

Quick quiz

1   Define events occurring after the reporting period.

2   A customer goes bankrupt after the reporting period and his debt must be written off. What type of event is this?

    Adjusting event   ☐

    Non-adjusting event   ☐

3   Inventory is lost in a fire after the reporting period. What type of an event is this?

    Adjusting event   ☐

    Non-adjusting event   ☐

4   A provision is a .... of .... timing or amount.

5   A programme is undertaken by management which converts the previously wholly owned chain of restaurants they ran into franchises. Is this restructuring?

6   Define contingent asset and contingent liability.

Answers to quick quiz

1 Those events, unfavourable and favourable, which occur between the end of the reporting period and the date on which the financial statements are authorised for issue.

2 Adjusting

3 Non-adjusting

4 **Liability** of **uncertain** timing or amount

5 Yes. The manner in which the business is conducted has changed

6 Refer to Paras 2.9 and 2.8 respectively

End of chapter question

Patel (AIA May 2005)

(a) With reference to IAS 37 *Provisions, contingent liabilities and contingent assets* describe the recognition and measurement of provisions and contingencies in published financial statements.

(7 marks)

(b) Provide advice on the accounting treatment of the following items in the accounts of a company, Patel, for the year ended 31 March 20X5:

(i) Patel entered into a two year, fixed price, long run manufacturing contract with a customer on 1 January 20X5. Patel is manufacturing 1,000 units of product per month. The forecast profit when the contract was signed was $10 per unit but due to unforeseen price increases in raw materials used by Patel each unit is anticipated to make a loss of $7.

(ii) The directors of Patel have decided to restructure one of its manufacturing divisions. The cost of the restructuring is significant and could amount to $10 million. The decision to restructure has been agreed and minuted at the directors board meeting in February 20X5.

(6 marks)

(Total = 13 marks)

Related parties; segment information; interim financial reporting

Topic list	Syllabus reference
1 IAS 24 *Related party disclosures*	11.1, 11.2
2 Segment reporting	11.5
3 IAS 34 *Interim financial reporting*	11.3
4 IFRS 1 *First time adoption of international financial reporting standards*	11.1

Introduction

In this chapter, we look at four further accounting standards.

IAS 24 *Related party disclosures* is an important Standard in maintaining the transparency of financial statements.

IFRS 8 *Operating segments* requires quoted entities to provide additional information about their results, breaking them down into different components.

IAS 34 *Interim financial reporting* provides guidance where entities publish interim financial reports.

IFRS 1 *First time adoption of international financial reporting standards* sets out the procedure to be followed where an entity prepares its financial statements under IFRSs for the first time.

1 IAS 24 *Related party disclosures*

IAS 24 is a disclosure statement.

1.1 Introduction

In the absence of information to the contrary, it is assumed that a reporting entity has **independent discretionary power** over its resources and transactions and pursues its activities independently of the interests of its individual owners, managers and others. Transactions are presumed to have been undertaken on an **arm's length basis**, ie on terms such as could have obtained in a transaction with an external party, in which each side bargained knowledgeably and freely, unaffected by any relationship between them.

These assumptions may not be justified when **related party relationships** exist, because the requisite conditions for competitive, free market dealings may not be present. While the parties may endeavour to achieve arm's length bargaining the very nature of the relationship may preclude this occurring.

1.2 Objective

This is the related parties issue and IAS 24 tackles it by ensuring that financial statements contain the disclosures necessary to draw attention to the possibility that the reported financial position and results may have been affected by the existence of related parties and by material transactions with them. In other words, this is a Standard which is primarily concerned with **disclosure**.

1.3 Scope

The Standard requires disclosure of related party transactions and outstanding balances in the **separate financial statements** of a parent, venturer or investor presented in accordance with IAS 27 as well as in consolidated financial statements.

An entity's financial statements disclose related party transactions and outstanding balances with other entities in a group. **Intragroup** transactions and balances are **eliminated** in the preparation of consolidated financial statements.

1.4 Definitions

The following important definitions are given by the Standard. Note that the definitions of **control** and **significant influence** are the same as those given in IFRS 10 and IAS 28.

Key terms

A **related party** is a person or entity that is related to the entity that is preparing its financial statements (in this Standard referred to as the 'reporting entity').

(a) A person or a close member of that person's family is related to a reporting entity if that person:

    (i) Has control or joint control over the reporting entity;

    (ii) Has significant influence over the reporting entity; or

    (iii) Is a member of the key management personnel of the reporting entity or of a parent of the reporting entity.

(b) An entity is related to a reporting entity if any of the following conditions applies:

    (i) The entity and the reporting entity are members of the same group (which means that each parent, subsidiary and fellow subsidiary is related to the others).

**Key terms
(cont'd)**

(ii) One entity is an associate or joint venture of the other entity (or an associate or joint venture of a member of a group of which the other entity is a member).

(iii) Both entities are joint ventures of the same third party.

(iv) One entity is a joint venture of a third entity and the other entity is an associate of the third entity.

(v) The entity is a post-employment benefit plan for the benefit of employees of either the reporting entity or an entity related to the reporting entity. If the reporting entity is itself such a plan, the sponsoring employers are also related to the reporting entity.

(vi) The entity is controlled or jointly controlled by a person identified in (a).

(vii) A person identified in (a)(i) has significant influence over the entity or is a member of the key management personnel of the entity (or of a parent of the entity).

Related party transaction. A transfer of resources, services or obligations between a reporting entity and a related party, regardless of whether a price is charged.

Control. An investor controls an investee when the investor is exposed, or has rights, to variable returns from its involvement with the investee and has the ability to affect those returns through power over the investee.

Significant influence is the power to participate in the financial and operating policy decisions of the investee, but is not control or joint control of those policies. **Joint control** is the contractually agreed sharing of control of an arrangement which exists only when decisions about the relevant activities require unanimous consent of the parties sharing control.

Key management personnel are those persons having authority and responsibility for planning, directing and controlling the activities of the entity, directly or indirectly, including any director (whether executive or otherwise) of that entity.

Close members of the family of an individual are those family members who may be expected to influence, or be influenced by, that individual in their dealings with the entity and include:

(a) That person's children and spouse or domestic partner
(b) Children of that person's spouse or domestic partner; and
(c) Dependants of that person or that person's spouse or domestic partner

(IAS 24, IFRS 10, IAS 28)

The most important point to remember here is that, when considering each possible related party relationship, attention must be paid to the **substance of the relationship, not merely the legal form**.

IAS 24 lists the following which are **not related parties**.

(a) **Two entities simply because they have a director or other key management in common**

(b) **Two venturers, simply because they share joint control over a joint venture.**

(c) Certain other bodies, simply as a result of their **role in normal business dealings** with the entity:

    (i) Providers of finance
    (ii) Trade unions
    (iii) Public utilities
    (iv) Government departments and agencies

(d) **Any single customer, supplier, franchisor, distributor, or general agent** with whom the entity transacts a significant amount of business, simply by virtue of the resulting economic dependence.

However if there are additional circumstances indicating a relationship with control or significant influence then these entities **may** be related parties.

1.5 Disclosure

As noted above, IAS 24 is almost entirely concerned with disclosure and its provisions are meant to **supplement** those disclosure requirements required by national company legislation and other IFRSs.

The Standard lists some **examples** of transactions that are disclosed if they are with a related party:

- Purchases or sales of goods (finished or unfinished)
- Purchases or sales of property and other assets
- Rendering or receiving of services
- Leases
- Transfers of research and development
- Transfers under licence agreements
- Provision of finance (including loans and equity contributions in cash or in kind)
- Provision of guarantees and collateral security
- Settlement of liabilities on behalf of the entity or by the entity on behalf of another party.

Relationships between **parents and subsidiaries** must be **disclosed irrespective** of **whether** any **transactions** have **taken place between** the related parties. An entity must disclose the **name** of its **parent** and, if different, the **ultimate controlling party**. This will enable a reader of the financial statements to be able to form a view about the effects of a related party relationship on the reporting entity.

If neither the parent nor the ultimate controlling party produces financial statements available for public use, the name of the next most senior parent that does so shall also be disclosed.

An entity should disclose **key management personnel compensation** in **total** and for **each** of the following **categories**.

(a) **Short-term employee benefits** (eg, wages, salaries, social security contributions, paid annual leave and paid sick-leave, profit sharing and bonuses and non-monetary benefits such as medical care, housing, cars and free or subsidised goods or services)

(b) **Post-employment benefits** (eg, pensions, other retirement benefits, life insurance and medical care)

(c) **Other long-term benefits** (eg, long-service leave, sabbatical leave, long-term disability benefits and, if they are not payable within 12 months after the end of the period, profit sharing bonuses and deferred compensation)

(d) **Termination benefits**

(e) **Share based payment**

Compensation includes amounts paid on behalf of a parent of the entity in respect of the entity.

Where **transactions have taken place** between related parties, the entity should disclose the **nature** of the related party relationships, as well as information about the **transactions and outstanding balances** necessary for an understanding of the potential effect of the relationship on the financial statements. As a minimum, disclosures must include:

(a) The **amount of the transactions**

(b) The **amount of outstanding balances**, including commitments, *and*

   (i) Their terms and conditions, including whether they are secured, and the nature of the consideration to be provided in settlement

   (ii) Details of any guarantees given or received

(c) Allowances for **doubtful debts** related to the amount of outstanding balances

(d) The **expense** recognised during the period in respect of **bad or doubtful debts** due from related parties

The above disclosures shall be made separately for **each** of the following categories:

- The parent
- Entities with joint control or significant influence over the entity
- Subsidiaries
- Associates
- Joint ventures in which the entity is a venturer
- Key management personnel of the entity or its parent
- Other related parties

Items of a similar nature may be **disclosed in aggregate** *unless* separate disclosure is necessary for an understanding of the effect on the financial statements.

Disclosures that related party transactions were made on terms equivalent to those that prevail in arm's length transactions can be made only if such disclosures can be substantiated.

1.6 Government related entities

A reporting entity is exempt from the disclosure requirements above in relation to related party transactions and outstanding balances, including commitments, with:

(a) A government that has control, joint control or significant influence over the reporting entity; and

(b) Another entity that is a related party because the same government has control, joint control or significant influence over both the reporting entity and the other entity.

1.7 Section summary

IAS 24 is primarily concerned with **disclosure**. You should learn the following.

- **Definitions**: these are very important
- Relationships covered
- Relationships that **may not** necessarily be between related parties
- **Disclosures**: again, very important, representing the whole purpose of the Standard

2 Segment reporting

FAST FORWARD

An important aspect of reporting financial performance is **segment reporting**. This is covered by IFRS 8 *Operating segments*.

2.1 Introduction

Large entities produce a wide range of products and services, often in several different countries. Further information on how the overall results of entities are made up from each of these product or geographical areas will help the users of the financial statements. This is the reason for **segment reporting**.

- The entity's **past performance** will be better understood
- The entity's **risks and returns** may be better assessed
- More **informed judgements** may be made about the entity as a whole

Risks and returns of a **diversified, multinational company** can only be assessed by looking at the individual risks and rewards attached to groups of products or services or in different groups of products or services or in different geographical areas. These are subject to differing rates of profitability, opportunities for growth, future prospects and risks.

Segment reporting is covered by IFRS 8 *Operating segments*, which was issued in November 2006.

2.2 Objective

An entity must disclose information to enable users of its financial statements to evaluate the nature and financial effects of the business activities in which it engages and the economic environments in which it operates.

2.3 Scope

Only entities whose **equity or debt securities are publicly traded** (ie on a stock exchange) need disclose segment information. In group accounts, only **consolidated** segmental information needs to be shown. (The statement also applies to entities filing or in the process of filing financial statements for the purpose of issuing instruments.)

2.4 Definition of operating segment

FAST FORWARD

> Reportable segments are **operating segments** or aggregation of operating segments that meet specified criteria.

You need to learn this definition, as it is crucial to the Standard.

Key term

Operating segment. This is a component of an entity:

(a)   that engages in business activities from which it may earn revenues and incur expenses (including revenues and expenses relating to transactions with other components of the same entity)

(b)   whose operating results are regularly reviewed by the entity's chief operating decision maker to make decisions about resources to be allocated to the segment and assess its performance, *and*

(c)   for which discrete financial information is available.   *(IFRS 8)*

The term 'chief operating decision maker' identifies a function, not necessarily a manager with a specific title. That function is to allocate resources and to assess the performance of the entity's operating segments

2.5 Aggregation

Two or more operating segments may be **aggregated** if the segments have **similar economic characteristics**, and the segments are similar in *each* of the following respects:

- The **nature of the products or services**
- The **nature of the production process**
- The **type or class of customer for their products or services**
- The **methods used to distribute their products or provide their services**, *and*
- If applicable, the **nature of the regulatory environment**

2.6 Determining reportable segments

An entity must report separate information about **each operating segment** that:

(a)   Has been identified as meeting the **definition of an operating segment**; and

(b)   Segment total is **10% or more of total**:

  (i)   **Revenue** (internal and external), *or*

  (ii)   All **segments not reporting a loss** (or all segments in loss if greater), *or*

  (iii)   **Assets**

At least **75% of total external revenue** must be reported by operating segments. Where this is not the case, additional segments must be identified (even if they do not meet the 10% thresholds).

Two or more operating segments **below** the thresholds may be aggregated to produce a reportable segment if the segments have similar economic characteristics, and the segments are similar in a **majority** of the aggregation criteria above.

Operating segments that do not meet **any of the quantitative thresholds** may be reported separately if management believes that information about the segment would be useful to users of the financial statements.

2.6.1 Decision tree to assist in identifying reportable segments

The following decision tree will assist in identifying reportable segments.

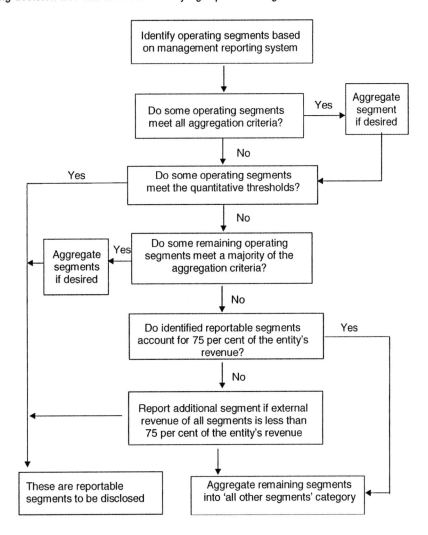

2.7 Disclosures

IFRS 8 **disclosures** are of:

- Operating segment profit or loss
- Segment assets
- Segment liabilities
- Certain income and expense items

Disclosures are also required about the **revenues derived from products or services** and about the **countries** in which revenues are earned or assets held, even if that information is not used by management in making decisions.

Disclosures required by the IFRS are extensive, and best learned by looking at the example and proforma, which follow the list.

(a)   Factors used to identify the entity's reportable segments

(b)   **Types of products and services** from which each reportable segment derives its revenues

(c)   Reportable segment revenues, profit or loss, assets, liabilities and other material items:

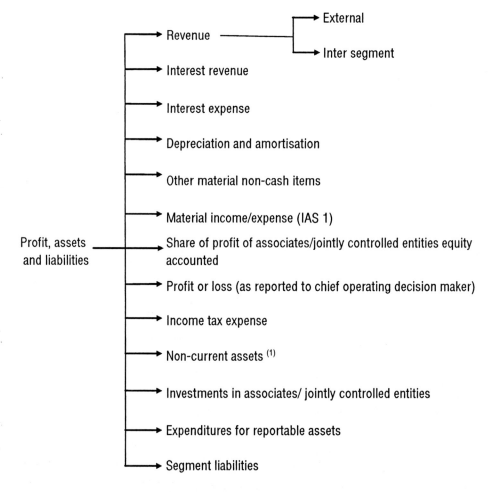

A **reconciliation** of the each of the above material items to the entity's reported figures is required.

Reporting of a measure of **profit or loss** by segment is compulsory. Other items are disclosed if included in the figures reviewed by or regularly provided to the chief operating decision maker.

(d)   **External revenue** by each product and service (if reported basis is not products and services)

(e)   **Geographical information**:

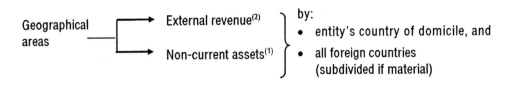

Notes

(1)   Non-current assets excludes financial instruments, deferred tax assets, post-employment benefit assets, and rights under insurance contracts.

(2)   External revenue is allocated based on the customer's location.

(f)   Information about **reliance on major customers** (ie those who represent more than 10% of external revenue)

(g)   Segment asset disclosure is not compulsory if it is not reported internally.

2.7.1 Disclosure example from IFRS 8

The following example is adapted from the IFRS 8 *Implementation Guidance*, which emphasises that this is for illustrative purposes only and that the information must be presented in the most understandable manner in the specific circumstances.

The hypothetical company does not allocate tax expense (tax income) or non-recurring gains and losses to reportable segments. In addition, not all reportable segments have material non-cash items other than depreciation and amortisation in profit or loss. The amounts in this illustration, denominated as dollars, are assumed to be the amounts in reports used by the chief operating decision maker.

	Car parts $	Motor vessel $	Software $	Electronics $	Finance $	All other $	Totals $
Revenues from external customers	3,000	5,000	9,500	12,000	5,000	1,000 [a]	35,500
Intersegment revenues	–	–	3,000	1,500	–	–	4,500
Interest revenue	450	800	1,000	1,500	–	–	3,750
Interest expense	350	600	700	1,100	–	–	2,750
Net interest revenue [b]	–	–	–	–	1,000	–	1,000
Depreciation and amortisation	200	100	50	1,500	1,100	–	2,950
Reportable segment profit	200	70	900	2,300	500	100	4,070
Other material non-cash items:							
Impairment of assets	–	200	–	–	–	–	200
Reportable segment assets	2,000	5,000	3,000	12,000	57,000	2,000	81,000
Expenditure for reportable segment non-current assets	300	700	500	800	600	–	2,900
Reportable segment liabilities	1,050	3,000	1,800	8,000	30,000	–	43,850

(a)   Revenues from segments below the quantitative thresholds are attributable to four operating segments of the company. Those segments include a small property business, an electronics equipment rental business, a software consulting practice and a warehouse leasing operation. None of those segments has ever met any of the quantitative thresholds for determining reportable segments.

(b)   The finance segment derives a majority of its revenue from interest. Management primarily relies on net interest revenue, not the gross revenue and expense amounts, in managing that segment. Therefore, as permitted by IFRS 8, only the net amount is disclosed.

2.7.2 Suggested proforma

INFORMATION ABOUT PROFIT OR LOSS, ASSETS AND LIABILITIES

	Segment A	Segment B	Segment C	All other segments	Inter-segment	Entity total
Revenue – external customers	X	X	X	X	–	X
Revenue – inter segment	X	X	X	X	X	–
	X	X	X	X	(X)	X
Interest revenue	X	X	X	X	(X)	X
Interest expense	(X)	(X)	(X)	(X)	X	(X)
Depreciation and amortisation	(X)	(X)	(X)	(X)	–	(X)
Other material non-cash items	X/(X)	X/(X)	X/(X)	X/(X)	X/(X)	X/(X)
Material income/expense (IAS 1)	X/(X)	X/(X)	X/(X)	X/(X)	X/(X)	X/(X)
Share of profit of associate/JVs	X	X	X	X	–	X
Segment profit before tax	X	X	X	X	(X)	X
Income tax expense	(X)	(X)	(X)	(X)	–	(X)
Unallocated items						X/(X)
Profit for the period						X
Segment assets	X	X	X	X	(X)	X
Investments in associate/JVs	X	X	X	X	–	X
Unallocated assets						X
Entity's assets						X
Expenditures for reportable assets	X	X	X	X	(X)	X
Segment liabilities	X	X	X	X	(X)	X
Unallocated liabilities						X
Entity's liabilities						X

INFORMATION ABOUT GEOGRAPHICAL AREAS

	Country of domicile	Foreign countries	Total
Revenue – external customers	X	X	X
Non-current assets	X	X	X

2.8 Different ways of defining segments

IFRS 8 adopts a managerial approach. The published segment information is based on the way that the company or group is actually managed and an entity's reportable segments (called operating segments) are the ones used in its internal management reports.

The previous Standard, IAS 14 *Segment reporting*, took a different approach. Under IAS 14, a reportable segment was 'a distinguishable component of an entity that is subject to risks and returns that are different from those of other segments'. The directors could use judgement in deciding which parts of an entity should be treated as separate reportable segments, but they were expected to take into account factors such as returns on investment, rates of growth and the potential for future development experienced by different parts of the business. This approach was called the 'risks and returns' approach.

IFRS 8 has been a controversial Standard. Some users claim that the managerial approach to defining segments is too flexible and allows management to hide information, particularly the extent of their overseas operations. Some critics of IFRS 8 would like entities to be required to report segment information by country.

2.9 Advantages and disadvantages of the old and new segment definition approaches

	Advantages	Disadvantages
Risks and Returns approach	• The information can be reconciled to the financial statements • It is a consistent method • The method helps to highlight the profitability, risks and returns of an identifiable segment	• Segment determination is the responsibility of directors and is subjective • Management may report segments which are not consistent for internal reporting and control purposes making its usefulness questionable
Managerial approach (IFRS 8)	• It is cost effective because the marginal cost of reporting segmental data will be low • Users can be sure that the segment data reflects the operational strategy of the business	• The information may be commercially sensitive • The segments may include operations with different risks and returns

2.10 Section summary

IFRS 8 is a **disclosure Standard**.

- **Segment reporting** is necessary for a better understanding and assessment of:
  - Past performance
  - Risks and returns
  - Informed judgements

- IFRS 8 adopts the **managerial approach** to identifying segments

- The standard gives guidance on how segments should be **identified** and **what information should be disclosed** for each

It also sets out **requirements for related disclosures** about products and services, geographical areas and major customers.

3 IAS 34 *Interim financial reporting*

IAS 34 recommends that **entities should produce interim financial reports** and, for entities that do publish such reports, it lays down principles and guidelines for their production.

The following definitions are used in IAS 34.

> **Interim period** is a financial reporting period shorter than a full financial year.
>
> **Interim financial report** means a financial report containing either a complete set of financial statements (as described in IAS 1) or a set of condensed financial statements (as described in this standard) for an interim period. *(IAS 34)*

3.1 Scope

The Standard does **not** make the preparation of interim financial reports **mandatory**, taking the view that this is a matter for governments, securities regulators, stock exchanges or professional accountancy bodies to decide within each country. The IASB does, however, strongly recommend to these institutions, that interim financial reporting should be a requirement for companies whose equity or debt securities are **publicly traded**.

(a)   An interim financial report should be produced by such companies for **at least the first six months of their financial year** (ie a half year financial report)

(b)   The report should be **available no later than 60 days** after the end of the interim period

Thus, a company with a year ending 31 December would be required as a minimum to prepare an interim report for the half year to 30 June and this report should be available before the end of August.

3.2 Minimum components

The proposed Standard specifies the **minimum component elements** of an interim financial report.

*   Condensed statement of financial position

*   Condensed statement of profit or loss and other comprehensive income, presented either as a single condensed statement or two condensed statements

*   Condensed statement of changes in equity

*   Condensed statement of cash flows

*   Selected note disclosures

*   Comparative information for the preceding period

The rationale for requiring only condensed statements and selected note disclosures is that entities need not duplicate information in their interim report that is contained in their report for the previous financial year. Interim statements should **focus more on new events, activities and circumstances**.

3.3 Form and content

Where **full financial statements** are given as interim financial statements, IAS 1 should be used as a guide, otherwise IAS 34 specifies minimum contents.

The **condensed statement of financial position** should include, as a minimum, each of the major components of assets, liabilities and equity as were in the statement of financial position at the end of the previous financial year, thus providing a summary of the economic resources of the entity and its financial structure.

The **condensed statement of profit or loss and other comprehensive income** should include, as a minimum, each of the component items of income and expense as are shown in profit or loss for the previous financial year, together with the earnings per share and diluted earnings per share.

The **condensed statement of cash flows** should show, as a minimum, the three major sub-totals of cash flow as required in statements of cash flows by IAS 7, namely: cash flows from operating activities, cash flows from investing activities and cash flow from financing activities.

The **condensed statement of changes in equity** should include, as a minimum, each of the major components of equity as were contained in the statement of changes in equity for the previous financial year of the entity.

3.3.1 Selected explanatory notes

IAS 34 states that **relatively minor changes** from the most recent annual financial statements need not be included in an interim report. However, the notes to the interim report should include the following (unless the information is contained elsewhere in the report).

(a) A statement that the **same accounting policies and methods of computation** have been used for the interim statements as were used for the most recent annual financial statements. If not, the nature of the differences and their effect should be described. (The accounting policies for preparing the interim report should only differ from those used for the previous annual accounts in a situation where there has been a change in accounting policy since the end of the previous financial year, and the new policy will be applied for the annual accounts of the current financial period.)

(b) Explanatory comments on the **seasonality or 'cyclicality'** of operations in the interim period. For example, if a company earns most of its annual profits in the first half of the year, because sales are much higher in the first six months, the interim report for the first half of the year should explain this fact

(c) The **nature and amount** of items during the interim period affecting assets, liabilities, capital, net income or cash flows, that are unusual, due to their nature, incidence or size

(d) The **issue or repurchase** of equity or debt securities

(e) Nature and amount of any **changes in estimates** of amounts reported in an earlier interim report during the financial year, or in prior financial years if these affect the current interim period

(f) **Dividends paid** on ordinary shares and the dividends paid on other shares

(g) **Segmental results** for the business segments or geographical segments of the entity (see IFRS 8)

(h) Any **significant events since the end of the interim period**

(i) Effect of the **acquisition or disposal** of subsidiaries during the interim period

(j) Any significant change in a **contingent liability or a contingent asset** since the date of the last annual statement of financial position

The entity should also disclose the fact that the interim report has been produced **in compliance with** IAS 34 on interim financial reporting.

Question   Disclosures

Give some examples of the type of disclosures required according to the above list of explanatory notes.

Answer

The following are examples.

- Write-down of inventories to net realisable value and the reversal of such a write-down

- Recognition of a loss from the impairment of property, plant and equipment, intangible assets, or other assets, and the reversal of such an impairment loss

- Reversal of any provisions for the costs of restructuring

- Acquisitions and disposals of items of property, plant and equipment

- Commitments for the purchase of property, plant and equipment

- Litigation settlements

- Corrections of fundamental errors in previously reported financial data

- Any debt default or any breach of a debt covenant that has not been corrected subsequently

- Related party transactions

3.4 Periods covered

The Standard requires that interim financial reports should provide financial information for the following periods or as at the following dates.

(a)   **Statement of financial position data** as at the end of the current interim period, and comparative data as at the end of the most recent financial year

(b)   **Statement of profit or loss and other comprehensive income data** for the current interim period and cumulative data for the current year to date, together with comparative data for the corresponding interim period and cumulative figures for the previous financial year

(c)   **Statement of cash flows data** should be **cumulative** for the current year to date, with comparative cumulative data for the corresponding interim period in the previous financial year

(d)   **Data for the statement of changes in equity** should be for both the current interim period and for the year to date, together with comparative data for the corresponding interim period, and cumulative figures, for the previous financial year

3.5 Materiality

Materiality should be assessed in relation to the interim period financial data. It should be recognised that interim measurements **rely to a greater extent on estimates** than annual financial data.

3.6 Recognition and measurement principles

A large part of IAS 34 deals with recognition and measurement principles, and guidelines as to their practical application. The **guiding principle** is that an entity should use the **same recognition and measurement principles in its interim statements as it does in its annual financial statements**.

This means, for example, that a cost that would not be regarded as an asset in the year-end statement of financial position should not be regarded as an asset in the statement of financial position for an interim period. Similarly, an accrual for an item of income or expense for a transaction that has not yet occurred (or a deferral of an item of income or expense for a transaction that has already occurred) is inappropriate for interim reporting, just as it is for year-end reporting.

Applying this principle of recognition and measurement may result, in a subsequent interim period or at the year-end, in a **remeasurement** of amounts that were reported in a financial statement for a previous interim period. **The nature and amount of any significant remeasurements should be disclosed.**

3.6.1 Revenues received occasionally, seasonally or cyclically

Revenue that is received as an occasional item, or within a seasonal or cyclical pattern, should not be anticipated or deferred in interim financial statements, if it would be inappropriate to anticipate or defer the revenue for the annual financial statements. In other words, the principles of revenue recognition should be applied consistently to the interim reports and year-end reports.

3.6.2 Costs incurred unevenly during the financial year

These should only be anticipated or deferred (ie treated as accruals or prepayments) if it would be appropriate to anticipate or defer the expense in the annual financial statements. For example, it would be appropriate to anticipate a cost for property rental where the rental is paid in arrears, but it would be inappropriate to anticipate part of the cost of a major advertising campaign later in the year, for which no expenses have yet been incurred.

The Standard goes on, in an appendix, to deal with **specific applications** of the recognition and measurement principle. Some of these examples are explained below, by way of explanation and illustration.

3.6.3 Payroll taxes or insurance contributions paid by employers

In some countries these are assessed on an annual basis, but paid at an uneven rate during the course of the year, with a large proportion of the taxes being paid in the early part of the year, and a much smaller proportion paid later on in the year. In this situation, it would be appropriate to use an estimated average annual tax rate for the year in an interim statement, not the actual tax paid. This treatment is appropriate because it reflects the fact that the taxes are assessed on an annual basis, even though the payment pattern is uneven.

3.6.4 Cost of a planned major periodic maintenance or overhaul

The cost of such an event later in the year must not be anticipated in an interim financial statement *unless* there is a legal or constructive obligation to carry out this work. The fact that a maintenance or overhaul is planned and is carried out annually is not of itself sufficient to justify anticipating the cost in an interim financial report.

3.6.5 Other planned but irregularly-occurring costs

Similarly, these costs such as charitable donations or employee training costs, should not be accrued in an interim report. These costs, even if they occur regularly and are planned, are nevertheless discretionary.

3.6.6 Year-end bonus

A year-end bonus should not be provided for in an interim financial statement *unless* there is a constructive obligation to pay a year-end bonus (eg a contractual obligation, or a regular past practice) and the size of the bonus can be reliably measured.

3.6.7 Holiday pay

The same principle applies here. If holiday pay is an enforceable obligation on the employer, then any unpaid accumulated holiday pay may be accrued in the interim financial report.

3.6.8 Non-mandatory intangible assets

The entity might incur expenses during an interim period on items that might or will generate non-monetary intangible assets. IAS 38 *Intangible assets* requires that costs to generate non-monetary intangible assets (eg development expenses) should be recognised as an expense when incurred *unless* the costs form part of an identifiable intangible asset. Costs that were initially recognised as an expense cannot subsequently be treated instead as part of the cost of an intangible asset. IAS 34 states that interim financial statements should adopt the same approach. This means that it would be inappropriate in an interim financial statement to 'defer' a cost in the expectation that it will eventually be part of a non-monetary intangible asset that has not yet been recognised: such costs should be treated as an expense in the interim statement.

3.6.9 Depreciation

Depreciation should only be charged in an interim statement on non-current assets that have been acquired, not on non-current assets that will be acquired later in the financial year.

3.6.10 Tax on income

An entity will include an expense for income tax (tax on profits) in its interim statements. The **tax rate** to use should be the estimated average annual tax rate for the year. For example, suppose that in a particular jurisdiction, the rate of tax on company profits is 30% on the first $200,000 of profit and 40% on profits above $200,000. Now suppose that a company makes a profit of $200,000 in its first half year, and expects to make $200,000 in the second half year. The rate of tax to be applied in the interim financial report should be 35%, not 30%, ie the expected average rate of tax for the year as a whole. This approach is appropriate because income tax on company profits is charged on an annual basis, and an effective annual rate should therefore be applied to each interim period.

As another illustration, suppose a company earns pre-tax income in the first quarter of the year of $30,000, but expects to make a loss of $10,000 in each of the next three quarters, so that net income before tax for the year is zero. Suppose also that the rate of tax is 30%. In this case, it would be inappropriate to anticipate the losses, and the tax charge should be $9,000 for the first quarter of the year (30% of $30,000) and a negative tax charge of $3,000 for each of the next three quarters, if actual losses are the same as anticipated.

Where the tax year for a company does not coincide with its financial year, a separate estimated weighted average tax rate should be applied for each tax year, to the interim periods that fall within that tax year.

Some countries give entities tax credits against the tax payable, based on amounts of capital expenditure or research and development, or similar undertaken. Under most tax regimes, these credits are calculated and granted on an annual basis; therefore, it is appropriate to include anticipated tax credits within the calculation of the estimated average tax rate for the year, and apply this rate to calculate the tax on income for interim periods. However, if a tax benefit relates to a specific one-time event, it should be recognised within the tax expense for the interim period in which the event occurs.

3.6.11 Inventory valuations

Within interim reports, inventories should be valued in the same way as for year-end accounts. It is recognised, however, that it will be necessary to rely more heavily on estimates for interim reporting than for year-end reporting.

In addition, it will normally be the case that the net realisable value of inventories should be estimated from selling prices and related costs to complete and dispose at interim dates.

3.7 Use of estimates

Although accounting information must be reliable and free from material error, it may be necessary to sacrifice some accuracy and reliability for the sake of timeliness and cost-benefits. This is particularly the case with interim financial reporting, where there will be much less time to produce reports than at the financial year end. The proposed standard therefore recognises that estimates will have to be used to a greater extent in interim reporting, to assess values or even some costs, than in year-end reporting.

An appendix to IAS 34 gives some examples of the use of estimates.

(a) **Inventories**. An entity might not need to carry out a full inventory count at the end of each interim period. Instead, it may be sufficient to estimate inventory values using sales margins.

(b) **Provisions**. An entity might employ outside experts or consultants to advise on the appropriate amount of a provision, as at the year end. It will probably be inappropriate to employ an expert to make a similar assessment at each interim date. Similarly, an entity might employ a professional valuer to revalue non-current assets at the year end, whereas at the interim date(s) the entity will not rely on such experts.

(c) **Income taxes**. The rate of income tax (tax on profits) will be calculated at the year end by applying the tax rate in each country/jurisdiction to the profits earned there. At the interim stage, it may be sufficient to estimate the rate of income tax by applying the same 'blended' estimated weighted average tax rate to the income earned in all countries/jurisdictions.

The principle of **materiality** applies to interim financial reporting, as it does to year-end reporting. In assessing materiality, it needs to be recognised that interim financial reports will rely more heavily on estimates than year-end reports. Materiality should be assessed in relation to the interim financial statements themselves, and should be independent of 'annual materiality' considerations.

3.8 Section summary

- IAS 34 in concept makes **straightforward proposals** for the production of interim financial reports by entities.

- It is essential to apply **principles of recognition and measurement** that will prevent entities from 'massaging' the interim figures.

- The **detail** in the **guidelines** is therefore very important, and the application of the recognition and measurement principles to particular valuations and measurements needs to be understood.

4 IFRS 1 *First time adoption of international financial reporting standards*

FAST FORWARD

IFRS 1 sets out the precise way in which companies should implement a **change from local accounting standards (their previous GAAP) to IFRSs.**

4.1 Background and definitions

The standard is intended to ensure that an entity's **first IFRS financial statements** contain **high quality information** that is transparent for users and comparable over all periods presented; provides a suitable starting point for accounting under IFRSs; and can be generated at a cost that does not exceed the benefits to users.

- **Date of transition to IFRSs**. The beginning of the earliest period for which an entity presents full comparative information under IFRSs in its first IFRS financial statements.

- **Deemed cost** An amount used as a surrogate for cost or depreciated cost at a given date.

- **Fair value** The price that would be received to sell an asset or paid to transfer a liability in an orderly transaction between market participants at the measurement date.

- **First IFRS financial statements** The first annual financial statements in which an entity adopts International Financial Reporting Standards (IFRSs), by an explicit and unreserved statement of compliance with IFRSs.

- **First IFRS reporting period** The latest reporting period covered by an entity's first IFRS financial statements.

- **Opening IFRS statement of financial position** An entity's statement of financial position (published or unpublished) at the date of transition to IFRSs.

- **Previous GAAP** The basis of accounting that a first time adopter used immediately before adopting IFRSs.

IFRS 1 **only applies** where an entity prepares IFRS financial statements **for the first time**. Changes in accounting policies made by an entity that already applies IFRSs should be dealt with by applying either IAS 8 or specific transitional requirements in other standards.

4.2 Making the transition to IFRS

An entity should:

(a) Select accounting policies that comply with IFRSs **at the reporting date** for the entity's first IFRS financial statements.

(b) Prepare an **opening IFRS statement of financial position** at the **date of transition to IFRSs.** This is the starting point for subsequent accounting under IFRSs. The date of transition to IFRSs is the beginning of the earliest comparative period presented in an entity's first IFRS financial statements.

(c) **Disclose the effect** of the change in the financial statements.

4.3 Example: Reporting date and opening IFRS statement of financial position

An EU listed company has a 31 December year-end and is required to comply with IFRSs from 1 January 20X5.

Required

What is the date of transition to IFRSs?

Solution

The company's first IFRS financial statements will be for the **year ended 31 December 20X5**.

IFRS 1 requires that at least one year's comparative figures are presented in the first IFRS financial statements. The comparative figures will be for the year ended 31 December 20X4.

Therefore the date of transition to IFRSs is **1 January 20X4** and the company prepares an opening IFRS statement of financial position at this date.

4.4 Preparing the opening IFRS statement of financial position

IFRS 1 states that in its opening IFRS statement of financial position an entity shall:

(a) **Recognise all assets and liabilities** whose recognition is required by IFRSs

(b) Not recognise items as assets or liabilities if IFRSs do not permit such recognition

(c) **Reclassify items** that it recognised under previous GAAP as one type of asset, liability or component of equity, but are a different type of asset, liability or component of equity under IFRSs

(d) **Apply IFRS in measuring** all recognised assets and liabilities

This involves restating the statement of financial position prepared at the same date under the entity's previous GAAP so that it complies with IFRSs in force **at the first reporting date**. In our example above, the company prepares its opening IFRS statement of financial position at **1 January 20X4**, following accounting policies that comply with IFRSs in force at **31 December 20X5**.

The accounting policies that an entity uses in its opening IFRS statement of financial position may differ from those it used for the same date using its previous GAAP. The resulting adjustments are recognised directly **in retained earnings** (in equity) **at the date of transition**. (This is because the adjustments arise from events and transactions before the date of transition to IFRS.)

An entity's **estimates** in accordance with IFRSs at the date of transition to IFRSs must be **consistent** with estimates made at the same date under previous GAAP (after adjustments to reflect any difference in accounting policies) unless there is **objective evidence** that those estimates were **in error.**

4.5 Exemptions from other IFRSs

A business may elect to use **any or all** of a range of exemptions. These enable an entity not to apply certain requirements of specific accounting standards retrospectively in drawing up its opening IFRS statement of financial position. Their purpose is to ensure that the cost of producing IFRS financial statements does not exceed the benefits to users.

4.5.1 Business combinations

Exam focus point

> You may want to come back to this paragraph after you have done Part C of this Text on group accounts.

IFRS 3 need not be applied retrospectively to business combinations that occurred before the date of the opening IFRS statement of financial position. This has the following consequences.

(a) **All acquired assets and liabilities are recognised** other than:

    (i) Some financial assets and financial liabilities derecognised under the previous GAAP (derivatives and special purpose entities must be recognised);

    (ii) Assets (including goodwill) and liabilities that were not recognised under previous GAAP and would not qualify for recognition under IFRSs.

    Any resulting change is recognised by **adjusting retained earnings** (ie equity) unless the change results from the recognition of an intangible asset that was previously subsumed within goodwill.

(b) **Items which do not qualify for recognition** as an asset or liability under IFRSs must be excluded from the opening IFRS statement of financial position. For example, intangible assets that do not qualify for separate recognition under IAS 38 must be reclassified as part of goodwill.

(c) The carrying amount of **goodwill** in the opening IFRS statement of financial position is based on its carrying amount **under previous GAAP**. However, goodwill must be tested for impairment at the transition date.

4.5.2 Property, plant and equipment

An entity may measure an item of property, plant and equipment at its **fair value at the transition** date and then use the fair value as its **deemed** cost at that date.

An entity may use a **previous GAAP revaluation**, or a valuation for the purpose of a privatisation or initial public offering, as the deemed cost at the transition date, so long as the revaluation was **broadly comparable** to fair value or depreciated replacement cost at the date of the valuation.

These exemptions are also available for:

(a)   Investment properties measured under the cost model in IAS 40 *Investment property*

(b)   Intangible assets that meet the recognition criteria and the criteria for revaluation in IAS 38 *Intangible assets*

4.5.3 Compound financial instruments

IAS 32 requires compound financial instruments to be split at inception into separate liability and equity components. If the liability component is no longer outstanding at the date of the transition to IFRSs, the split is not required.

Question   First time adopter

Russell Co will adopt International Financial Reporting Standards (IFRSs) for the first time in its financial statements for the year ended 31 December 20X4.

In its previous financial statements for 31 December 20X2 and 20X3, which were prepared under local GAAP, the company made a number of routine accounting estimates, including accrued expenses. It also recognised a general provision for liabilities, calculated at a fixed percentage of its retained profits for the year. This is required under its local GAAP.

Subsequently, some of the accruals were found to be overestimates and some were found to be underestimates.

Required

Discuss how the matters above should be dealt with in the IFRS financial statements of Russell Co for the year ended 31 December 20X4.

Answer

Provided that the routine accounting estimates have been made in a manner consistent with IFRSs no adjustments are made in the first IFRS financial statements. The only exception to this is if the company has subsequently discovered that these estimates were in material error. Although there were some overestimates and some underestimates, this is probably not the case here.

The general provision is a different matter. This provision would definitely not have met the criteria for recognition under IAS 37 and therefore it will not be recognised in the opening IFRS statement of financial position (1 January 20X3) or at subsequent year-ends.

4.6 Presentation and disclosure

An entity's first IFRS financial statements must include **at least:**

(a) Three statements of financial position;
(b) Two statements of profit or loss and other comprehensive income;
(c) Two statements of profit or loss (if presented);
(d) Two statements of cash flows; and
(e) Two statements of changes in equity and related notes.

An entity must also **explain the effect** of the transition from previous GAAP to IFRSs on its financial position, financial performance and cash flows by providing **reconciliations:**

(a) Of **equity** reported under previous GAAP to equity under IFRSs at the **date of transition** and at the **end of the last period presented in accordance with previous GAAP**

(b) Of profit for the most recent financial statements presented under previous GAAP.

The reconciliations must give sufficient detail to enable users to understand the material adjustments to the statement of financial position and the statement of profit or loss and other comprehensive income.

If an entity presented a statement of cash flows under its previous GAAP, it should also explain the material **adjustments to the statement of cash flows**.

If an entity corrects **errors made under previous GAAP**, the reconciliations must distinguish the correction of errors from changes in accounting policies.

Where **fair value has been used as deemed cost** for a non-current asset in the opening IFRS statement of financial position, the financial statements must disclose the aggregate of fair values and the aggregate adjustments to the carrying amounts reported under previous GAAP for each line in the opening IFRS statement of financial position.

Chapter roundup

- IAS 24 is a disclosure statement.

- An important aspect of reporting financial performance is **segment reporting.** This is covered by IFRS 8 *Operating segments.*

- Reportable segments are **operating segments** or aggregation of operating segments that meet specified criteria.

- IFRS 8 **disclosures** are of:

    - Operating segment profit or loss
    - Segment assets
    - Segment liabilities
    - Certain income and expense items

    Disclosures are also required about the **revenues derived from products or services** and about the **countries** in which revenues are earned or assets held, even if that information is not used by management in making decisions.

- IFRS 1 sets out the precise way in which an entity should implement a **change from old accounting standards (previous GAAP) to IFRSs.**

Quick quiz

1 A managing director of an entity is a related party. True or false?

2 All entities must disclose segment information. True or false?

3 Geographical segment information is not required. True or false?

4 What is the 'date of transition to IFRS' according to IFRS 1?

Answers to quick quiz

1   True. A member of the key management of an entity is a related party of that entity.

2   False. Only entities whose equity or debt securities are publicly traded need disclose segment information.

3   False. Information about revenues from different countries must be disclosed unless it is not available and the cost to develop it would be excessive. It should always be disclosed if it is used by management in making operating decisions.

4   The beginning of the earliest comparative period presented in an entity's first IFRS financial statements.

End of chapter question

Stone Cutter (AIA November 2009)

The following map (not drawn to scale) shows the layout of the Stone Cutter Leisure Complex:

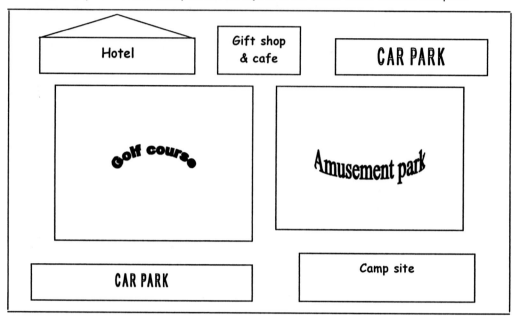

Although the company does not prepare consolidated financial statements, its equity shares are publicly traded on the local stock market.

The operating results of the company are regularly reviewed by a group of directors who, based upon that review, allocate resources to the various parts of the complex. The following operating review was placed in front of those directors on 31 October 2009, the company's year end:

		Operating Review					
		For the year ended 31 October 2009					
	Hotel	Gift shop & cafe	Golf course	Amusement park	Camp site	Other[1]	Total
Number of visitors (thousands)	134		58	228	101		
	$m	$m	$m	$m	$m	$m	$m
Revenue – external	30.82	9.38	12.73	11.39	2.01	0.67	67.00
Revenue – internal			7.04	5.85			12.89
Profit before tax	9.25	4.12	3.70	1.70	1.12	0.67	20.56
Total assets	102.78	5.77	13.98	34.61	2.23		159.37

[1] 'Other' represents income from advertising $0.50m and sundry sales of $0.17m.

All visitors to the complex are allowed to park their cars free of charge in the car parks which have been recently built at a cost of $3.8m. Visitors staying at the hotel and camp site also receive passes to enable them to use the amusement park and golf course. The passes are accounted for at their fair value.

Required

(a) The following refer to Stone Cutter's segment reporting:

(i) The directors are uncertain whether segment information is necessary as the company does not prepare consolidated accounts. Explain to the directors why the IFRS concerning operating segments will apply to the company. **(2 marks)**

(ii) Identify those parts of the complex which will satisfy the IFRS definition of an operating segment. **(3 marks)**

(iii) Explain to what extent each part of the company's activities meets the IFRS criteria for a reportable segment. **(8 marks)**

(iv) One director holds the opinion that, despite being separate components for the purpose of allocating resources, the hotel and gift shop and café should be reported in the financial statements as one segment as the nature of their products and services is similar. Under what circumstances would IFRS allow this aggregation? **(8 marks)**

(v) The directors have decided that one of the company's key development strategies for next year will be to grow its advertising revenue. Advise the directors on how to deal with the advertising revenue of $0.50m and the sundry sales of $0.17m in the presentation of the company's segment information. **(4 marks)**

(vi) The draft financial statements of Stone Cutter show the following:

Profit before tax and discontinued operations $ 17.00m
Total assets $175.00m

Suggest possible explanations for the difference between the above two figures and the figures shown by the Operating Review presented to the directors. **(4 marks)**

(b)   Discuss how the following will be taken into account in the preparation of Stone Cutter's financial statements for the year ended 31 October 2009:

(i)   The standard price of a hotel room is $200 per night but if visitors also purchase a pass for the amusement park the cost is $230. The standard cost of an amusement park pass bought independently is $75. Experience shows that all passes are eventually used although at 31 October 2009, there are 800 passes outstanding.   **(6 marks)**

(ii)   The cost of developing the two car parks includes $2m for freehold land. In deciding upon their treatment in the financial statements, the directors have estimated that the car parks will have to be completely refashioned and resurfaced every ten years but have not yet decided whether to use the cost or the revaluation model to account for the assets. Advise the directors on the accounting implications of each model.   **(5 marks)**

(Total = 40 marks)

13

Partnership accounts

Topic list	Syllabus reference
1 The characteristics of partnerships	11.3
2 Preparing partnership accounts	11.3
3 Retirement or death of a partner	11.3
4 Admission of a partner	11.3
5 Formation of a partnership from two or more sole traders	11.3
6 Simple dissolution of a partnership	11.3
7 Partnership transferred to a company	11.3

Introduction

This chapter deals with partnership accounts. These should be familiar to you from your earlier studies, but at this level exam questions are likely to go into greater depth.

Note that partnerships are not bound by IFRSs and therefore the IAS 1 (revised) requirement to provide a statement of profit or loss and other comprehensive income is not applicable to partnerships. This chapter therefore deals with the presentation of profits or losses in the statement of profit or loss only.

1 The characteristics of partnerships

Partnership can be defined as the relationship which exists between persons carrying on a business in common with a view of profit.

In other words, a partnership is an arrangement between two or more individuals in which they undertake to share the risks and rewards of a joint business operation.

It is usual for a partnership to be established formally by means of a **partnership agreement**. However, if individuals act as though they are in partnership even if no written agreement exists, then it will be presumed that a partnership does exist and that its terms of agreement are reflected in the way the partners conduct the business, ie the way profits have been divided in the past, and so on. In some countries legislation may exist which governs partnerships.

1.1 The partnership agreement

The partnership agreement is a written agreement in which the terms of the partnership are set out, and in particular the financial arrangements as between partners. The items it should cover include the following.

(a)   **Capital.** Each partner puts in a share of the business capital. If there is to be an agreement on how much each partner should put in and keep in the business, as a minimum fixed amount, this should be stated.

(b)   **Profit-sharing ratio.** Partners can agree to share profits in any way they choose. For example, if there are three partners in a business, they might agree to share profits equally but on the other hand, if one partner does a greater share of the work, or has more experience and ability, or puts in more capital, the ratio of profit sharing might be geared to reflect this.

(c)   **Interest on capital.** Partners might agree to pay themselves interest on the capital they put into the business. If they do so, the agreement will state what rate of interest is to be applied.

(d)   **Partners' salaries.** Partners might also agree to pay themselves salaries. These are not salaries in the same way that an employee of the business will be paid a wage or salary, because partners' salaries are an appropriation of profit, and not an expense in the statement of profit or loss of the business. The purpose of paying salaries is to give each partner a satisfactory basic income before the residual profits are shared out.

(e)   **Withdrawals on account of profit.** Partners may draw out their share of profits from the business. However, they might agree to put a limit on how much they should draw out in any period. If so, this limit should be specified in the partnership agreement. To encourage partners to delay making withdrawals from the business until the financial year has ended, the agreement might also be that partners should be charged interest on their withdrawals during the year.

Question   Partners' salaries and profit-sharing

Suppose Bill and Ben are partners sharing profit in the ratio 2:1 and that they agree to pay themselves a salary of $10,000 each. If profits before deducting salaries are $26,000, how much income would each partner receive?

Answer

First, the two salaries are deducted from profit, leaving $6,000 ($26,000 – $20,000).

This $6,000 has to be distributed between Bill and Ben in the ratio 2:1. In other words, Bill will receive twice as much as Ben. You can probably work this out in your head and see that Bill will get $4,000 and Ben $2,000, but we had better see how this is calculated properly.

Add the 'parts' of the ratio together. For our example, 2 + 1 = 3. Divide this total into whatever it is that has to be shared out. In our example, $6,000 ÷ 3 = $2,000. Each 'part' is worth $2,000, so Bill receives 2 × $2,000 = $4,000 and Ben will receive 1 × $2,000 = $2,000.

So the final answer to the question is that Bill receives his salary plus $4,000 and Ben his salary plus $2,000. This could be laid out as follows.

	Bill	Ben	Total
	$	$	$
Salary	10,000	10,000	20,000
Share of residual profits (ratio 2:1)	4,000	2,000	6,000
	14,000	12,000	26,000

1.2 Advantages and disadvantages of trading as a partnership

Operating as a partnership entails certain advantages and disadvantages when compared with both sole traders and limited liability companies.

1.2.1 Partnership v sole trader

The *advantages* of operating as a partnership rather than as a sole trader are practical rather than legal. They include the following.

(a)   Risks are spread across a larger number of people.
(b)   The trader will have access to a wider network of contacts through the other partners.
(c)   Partners should bring to the business not only capital but skills and experience.
(d)   It may well be easier to raise finance from external sources such as banks.

Possible *disadvantages* include the following.

(a)   While the risk is spread over a larger number of people, so are the profits!
(b)   By bringing in more people the former sole trader dilutes control over his business.
(c)   There may be disputes between the partners.

1.2.2 Partnership v limited liability company

Limited liability companies offer limited liability to their owners. This means that the maximum amount that an owner stands to lose in the event that the company becomes insolvent and must pay off its debts is the capital in the business. In the case of partnerships (and sole traders), liability for the debts of the business is unlimited, which means that if the business runs up debts and is unable to pay, the proprietors will become personally liable for the unpaid debts and would be required, if necessary, to sell their private possessions in order to pay for them.

Limited liability is clearly a significant incentive for a partnership to incorporate (become a company). Other advantages of incorporation are that it is easier to raise capital and that the retirement or death of one of its members does not necessitate dissolution and re-formation of the firm.

In practice, however, particularly for small firms, these advantages are more apparent than real. Banks will normally seek personal guarantees from shareholders before making loans or granting an overdraft facility and so the advantage of limited liability is lost to a small owner-managed business.

In addition, a company faces a greater administrative and financial burden arising from:

(a)   Compliance with national company legislation notably in having to prepare annual accounts and have them audited, file annual returns and keep statutory books

(b)   Compliance with national accounting standards and/or IFRSs

(c)   Formation and annual registration costs

2 Preparing partnership accounts

2.1 How does accounting for partnerships differ from accounting for sole traders?

Partnership accounts are identical in many respects to the accounts of sole traders.

(a)   The assets of a partnership are like the assets of any other business, and are accounted for in the same way. The assets side of a partnership statement of financial position is no different from what has been shown in earlier chapters of this Study Text.

(b)   The net profit of a partnership is calculated in the same way as the net profit of a sole trader. The only minor difference is that if a partner makes a loan to the business (as distinct from capital contribution) then interest on the loan will be an expense in the statement of profit or loss, in the same way as interest on any other loan from a person or organisation who is not a partner. We will return to partner loans later in the chapter.

There are two respects in which partnership accounts are different, however.

(a)   The funds put into the business by each partner are shown differently.

(b)   The net profit must be **appropriated** by the partners, ie shared out according to the partnership agreement. This appropriation of profits must be shown in the partnership accounts.

Key term

> **Appropriation of profit** means sharing out profits in accordance with the partnership agreement.

2.2 Funds employed

When a partnership is formed, each partner puts in some capital to the business. These initial capital contributions are recorded in a series of **capital accounts**, one for each partner. (Since each partner is ultimately entitled to repayment of his capital it is clearly vital to keep a record of how much is owed to whom.) The precise amount of initial capital contributed by each partner is a matter for general agreement and there is no question of each partner necessarily contributing the same amount, although this does sometimes happen.

Important

> The balance for the capital account will always be a brought forward credit entry in the partnership accounts, because the capital contributed by proprietors is a liability of the business.

In addition to a capital account, each partner normally has:

(a)   a **current account** and
(b)   a **withdrawals account**

Key term

> A **current account** is used to record the **profits retained in the business** by the partner.

It is, therefore, a sort of capital account, which increases in value when the partnership makes profits, and falls in value when the partner whose current account it is makes drawings out of the business.

The main differences between the capital and current account in accounting for partnerships are as follows.

(a) Whereas the balance on the capital account remains static from year to year (with one or two exceptions), the current account is continually fluctuating up and down, as the partnership makes profits which are shared out between the partners, and as each partner makes withdrawals an account of profit.

(b) A further difference is that when the partnership agreement provides for interest on capital, partners receive interest on the balance in their capital account, but **not on the balance in their current account.**

The withdrawals accounts serve exactly the same purpose as the withdrawals account for a sole trader. Each partner's withdrawals are recorded in a separate account. At the end of an accounting period, each partner's withdrawals are cleared to his current account:

DEBIT   Current account of partner
CREDIT   Withdrawals account of partner

(If the amount of the withdrawals exceeds the balance on a partner's current account, the current account will show a debit balance. However, in normal circumstances, we should expect to find a credit balance on the current accounts.)

The partnership statement of financial position will therefore consist of:

(a) the capital accounts of each partner, *and*
(b) the current accounts of each partner, net of withdrawals on account

This will be illustrated in an example later.

2.3 Loans by partners

In addition, it is sometimes the case that an existing or previous partner will make a loan to the partnership in which case he becomes a creditor of the partnership. In the statement of financial position, such a loan is not included as partners' funds, but is shown separately as a long-term liability (unless repayable within 12 months in which case it is a current liability). This is the case whether or not the loan creditor is also an existing partner.

However, **interest on such loans will be credited to the partner's current account** (if he is an existing partner). This is administratively more convenient, especially when the partner does not particularly want to be paid the loan interest in cash immediately it becomes due. You should bear in mind the following.

(a) Interest on loans from a partner is accounted for as an expense in the statement of profit or loss, and not as an appropriation of profit, even though the interest is added to the current account of the partners.

(b) If there is no interest rate specified, national legislation *may* provide for interest to be paid at a specified percentage on loans by partners.

2.4 Appropriation of net profits

The net profit of a partnership is shared out between them according to the terms of their agreement. This sharing out is shown in an **appropriation account**, which follows on from the statement of profit or loss.

The accounting entries are:

(a)   DEBIT   Statement of profit or loss with net profit c/d
       CREDIT   Appropriation account with net profit b/d

(b)   DEBIT   Appropriation account
       CREDIT   Current accounts of each partner

with an individual share of profits for each partner.

The way in which profit is shared out depends on the terms of the partnership agreement. The steps to take are as follows.

Step 1	Establish the amount of net profit.
Step 2	Appropriate interest on capital and salaries first. Both of these items are an appropriation of profit and are not expenses in the statement of profit or loss.
Step 3	If partners agree to pay interest on their withdrawals during the year: DEBIT Current accounts CREDIT Appropriation of profit account
Step 4	**Residual profits**: these are the difference between net profits (plus any interest charged on withdrawals) and appropriations for interest on capital and salaries is the residual profit. This is shared out between partners in the profit-sharing ratio.
Step 5	Each partner's share of profits is credited to the relevant current account.
Step 6	The balance on each partner's withdrawals account is debited to the relevant current account.

In practice each partner's capital account will occupy a separate ledger account, as will their *current* accounts etc. The examples which follow in this text use the columnar form; they might also ignore the breakdown of net assets employed (non-current and current assets) to help to clarify and simplify the illustrations.

Exam focus point

For examination purposes however, it is customary to represent the details of these accounts side by side, in columnar form, to save time.

    Question   Partnership accounts

Locke, Niece and Munster are in partnership with an agreement to share profits in the ratio 3:2:1. They also agree that:

(a)   all three should receive interest at 12% on capital;

(b)   Munster should receive a salary of $6,000 per annum;

(c)   interest will be charged on withdrawals at the rate of 5% (charged on the end of year withdrawals balances);

(d)   the interest rate on the loan by Locke is 5%.

The statement of financial position of the partnership as at 31 December 20X5 revealed the following.

	$	$
Capital accounts		
Locke	20,000	
Niece	8,000	
Munster	6,000	
		34,000
Current accounts		
Locke	3,500	
Niece	(700)	
Munster	1,800	
		4,600
Loan account (Locke)		6,000
Capital employed to finance net long-term assets and working capital		44,600

Withdrawals on account made during the year to 31 December 20X6 were as follows.

	$
Locke	6,000
Niece	4,000
Munster	7,000

The net profit for the year to 31 December 20X6 was $24,530 before deducting loan interest.

Required

Prepare the appropriation account for the year to 31 December 20X6, and the partners' capital accounts, and current accounts.

Answer

The interest payable by each partner on their withdrawals during the year is:

		$
Locke	5% of $6,000	300
Niece	5% of $4,000	200
Munster	5% of $7,000	350
		850

These payments are debited to the current accounts and credited to the **appropriation** account.

The interest payable to Locke on his loan is:

5% of $6,000 = $300

We can now begin to work out the appropriation of profits.

	$	$
Net profit, less loan interest (deducted in statement of profit or loss $24,530 – $300)		24,230
Add interest on withdrawals		850
		25,080
Less Munster salary		6,000
		19,080
Less interest on capital		
Locke (12% of $20,000)	2,400	
Niece (12% of $ 8,000)	960	
Munster (12% of $ 6,000)	720	
		4,080
		15,000

		$	$
Residual profits			
Locke	(3)	7,500	
Niece	(2)	5,000	
Munster	(1)	2,500	
			15,000

Make sure you remember what the various interest figures represent and that you understand exactly what has been calculated here.

(a) The partners can take withdrawals on account of profit out of the business, but if they do they will be charged interest on it.

(b) The partners have capital tied up in the business (of course, otherwise there would be no business) and they have agreed to pay themselves interest on whatever capital each has put in.

(c) Once all the necessary adjustments have been made to net profit, $15,000 remains and is divided up between the partners in the ratio 3:2:1.

Now the financial statements for the partnership can be prepared.

LOCKE NIECE MUNSTER
APPROPRIATION ACCOUNT
FOR THE YEAR ENDED 31 DECEMBER 20X6

	$	$		$	$
			Net profit b/d		24,230
Salaries: Munster		6,000	Interest on		
Interest on capital			withdrawals:		
Locke	2,400		Current account of:		
Niece	960		Locke	300	
Munster	720		Niece	200	
		4,080	Munster	350	
Residual profits					850
Locke	7,500				
Niece	5,000				
Munster	2,500				
		15,000			
		25,080			25,080

PARTNERS' CURRENT ACCOUNTS

	Locke $	Niece $	Munster $		Locke $	Niece $	Munster $
Balance b/f		700		Balance b/f	3,500		1,800
Interest on withdrawals	300	200	350	Loan interest	300		
Withdrawals	6,000	4,000	7,000	Interest on capital	2,400	960	720
Balance c/f	7,400	1,060	3,670	Salary			6,000
				Residual profits	7,500	5,000	2,500
	13,700	5,960	11,020		13,700	5,960	11,020
				Balance b/f	7,400	1,060	3,670

PARTNERS' CAPITAL ACCOUNTS

	Locke $	Niece $	Munster $
Balance b/f	20,000	8,000	6,000

The statement of financial position of the partners as at 31 December 20X6 would be as follows.

	$	$
Capital accounts		
Locke	20,000	
Niece	8,000	
Munster	6,000	
		34,000
Current accounts		
Locke	7,400	
Niece	1,060	
Munster	3,670	
		12,130
		46,130
Net assets		
As at 31 December 20X5		44,600
Added during the year (applying the business equation, this is the difference between net profits and withdrawals = $24,230 – $17,000)		7,230
Add loan interest added to Locke's current account and not paid out		300
As at 31 December 20X6		52,130
Less long-term payables		
Loan: Locke		(6,000)
		46,130

Again, make sure you understand what has happened here.

(a)   The partners' **capital** accounts have not changed. They were brought forward at $20,000, $8,000 and $6,000, and they are just the same in the new statement of financial position.

(b)   The partners' **current** accounts have changed. The balances brought forward from last year's statement of financial position of $3,500, ($700) and $1,800 have become $7,400, $1,060 and $3,670 in the new statement of financial position. How this came about is shown in the partners' current (ledger) accounts.

(c)   The events recorded in the current accounts are a reflection of how the partnership has distributed its profit, and this was shown in the statement of division of profit.

3 Retirement or death of a partner

FAST FORWARD

Any change in a partnership involves dealing with goodwill. Each existing partner must be credited with their share of goodwill earned to date.

Any changes in a partnership constitution require a new partnership agreement, as the arrangements relating to appropriation of profits and so on are likely to be changed. Legally, the old partnership is usually dissolved and a new partnership created, but from the accounting point of view it is more realistic to make appropriate adjustments in the existing partnership books, rather than to close them off and start afresh.

When an existing partner dies, or decides to retire from the partnership, his share of the partnership assets must be calculated and transferred to him (or to his personal representatives). Unless all the partnership assets and liabilities are correctly valued in the books, the partner's capital and current account total will not show his actual entitlement.

Normally, the true worth of the partnership will exceed the book figure of net assets, and so various assets/liabilities will have to be **revalued** and goodwill taken into account, if only on a temporary basis.

When assets are revalued, any profits or losses on revaluation are entered, in profit sharing ratio, in the partners' capital accounts (rather than their current accounts) unless there is agreement to the contrary.

Usually, since a number of items may be affected, a revaluation account is used to arrive at a total balance of profit or loss on revaluation. This balance is then divided between the partners in the profit sharing ratio in their capital accounts.

Question
Death of a partner

Scrap, Iron and Ore are partners in a scrap metal business, sharing profits in the ratio 5:3:2 respectively. Their capital and current account balances on 1 January 20X3 were as follows.

	Capital accounts $	Current accounts $
Scrap	24,000	9,900
Iron	18,000	4,300
Ore	13,000	(200)

Driving home from a New Year Party, Iron neglected to make a necessary right turn and drove into a river and drowned. On 1 January 20X3 (the date of Iron's death) certain assets of the Scrap, Iron and Ore partnership were revalued. The breakdown of the total assets less current liabilities figure (in the 31 December 20X2 accounts), together with relevant revaluations was as follows.

	Book value $	Valuation $
Property	30,000	45,000
Equipment and machinery (CV)	25,000	20,500
Inventory	30,000	30,000
Trade accounts receivable (one emigrated and could not be traced)	18,000	17,500
Bank	10,000	10,000
	113,000	123,000
Trade accounts payable	(24,000)	(24,000)
Net assets	89,000	99,000

Show the journal entries recording the above revaluations in the partnership books.

Answer

JOURNAL

		$	$
DEBIT	Property	15,000	
CREDIT	Revaluation account		15,000
	Being profit on revaluation		
DEBIT	Revaluation account	5,000	
CREDIT	Equipment and machinery		4,500
	Trade accounts receivable		500
	Being loss on revaluation		
DEBIT	Revaluation account	10,000	
CREDIT	Partners' capital accounts		
	Scrap (5/10)		5,000
	Iron (3/10)		3,000
	Ore (2/10)		2,000

Being net profit on revaluation of assets divided between the partners in profit sharing ratio.

Remember that if the revaluation of the partnership assets had brought about a net decrease in value, then the partners would be debited with the loss.

3.1 Goodwill

In addition to revaluing tangible assets when there is a change in a partnership, the problem of **goodwill** may have to be considered. Goodwill, whether originally purchased (being defined as the excess of the fair market value of the price paid for a business over the fair market value of the individual assets and liabilities acquired) or whether internally generated is dependent on a wide variety of factors, such as business location, reputation, staff personalities and the ability to earn profits or 'super profits' and so on.

Key term

> **Goodwill** is the excess of the price paid for a business over the market value of its individual assets and liabilities.

Goodwill often has to be calculated when fixing the purchase (or sale) price of a business, as well as when a partnership constitution is changed. There are many ways of arriving at a value for goodwill and most of them are related to the profit record of the business.

A partner who retires or dies must be credited with his fair share of the partnership

assets, including goodwill. Just as the profit/loss on revaluation of tangible items was divided between the partners, so the goodwill figure (once calculated per the partnership agreement) has to be entered in the partnership books. The journal entry made in Scrap, Iron and Ore's books (assuming an arbitrary figure for goodwill of $32,000) would be:

JOURNAL

		$	$
DEBIT	Goodwill account	32,000	
CREDIT	Partners' capital accounts:		
	Scrap (5/10)		16,000
	Iron (3/10)		9,600
	Ore (2/10)		6,400
	Being introduction of goodwill into the partnership books		

The partners' capital accounts on 1 January 20X3 are now as follows.

CAPITAL ACCOUNTS

	Scrap $	Iron $	Ore $		Scrap $	Iron $	Ore $
Iron's estate (personal representative's a/c)		30,600		Balance b/d	24,000	18,000	13,000
				Revaluation	5,000	3,000	2,000
				Goodwill	16,000	9,600	6,400
Balances c/f	45,000		21,400				
	45,000	30,600	21,400		45,000	30,600	21,400

The balances on the **deceased partner's** capital and current accounts ($30,600 + $4,300) are transferred to a separate loan account. The total of $34,900 is a liability of the partnership and has to be paid to Iron's personal representative.

A **retiring partner** may take his full entitlement immediately (in cash or in assets) but often will only take part of the amount due, leaving the balance as a loan to the partnership to be repaid over a period of time. Any interest paid on the loan is a chargeable expense in the statement of profit or loss.

3.2 Elimination of goodwill

Once goodwill appears in the books, the partners must decide what to do with it. Whether goodwill is a 'premium paid on acquisition' (when a business is acquired as a going concern) or whether it is internally generated, it is often unstable and is usually difficult to quantify.

There are three principal ways to treat goodwill.

(a)   Retain goodwill in the accounts indefinitely (as an intangible asset) on the basis that the total goodwill of a business tends to increase rather than decrease, and so write-off is unnecessary.

(b)   Retain goodwill in the statement of financial position but review every year for impairment and reduce if necessary by the amount of the impairment.

(c)   Write off goodwill immediately on the grounds of prudence. The goodwill never appears in the statement of financial position and so the fact that goodwill does have some value, however difficult it is to quantify, is ignored.

Option (b) is required by IFRS 3 but partnerships (other than limited liability partnerships) are not subject to IFRSs and so can choose their own policy.

Question   Goodwill

In Scrap, Iron and Ore the two surviving partners decide to continue in partnership sharing profits in the ratio: Scrap 2: Ore 1. If goodwill is to be retained in the books of the new partnership no further entry is required. However, if it is to be eliminated, then the 'new' partners have to bear the write-off in their new profit sharing ratio.

JOURNAL

		$	$
DEBIT	Partners' capital accounts:		
	Scrap (2/3)	21,333	
	Ore (1/3)	10,667	
CREDIT	Goodwill account		32,000
	Being goodwill written off in the partnership books		

4 Admission of a partner

When a prospective partner is due to be admitted to a partnership, the old partners will wish to ensure that they receive their full entitlement to partnership profits up to the date of the change in the constitution. Similarly, the 'new' partner will not wish to bear any losses which may have arisen during the period prior to his admission. Consequently, as in the case of retirement or death of a partner, the partnership assets (including goodwill) will have to be revalued and the new values introduced (and possibly later eliminated) from the partnership books. If the new partner introduces additional capital into the partnership, the total amount of cash/assets he brings in must be credited to his capital account. This account may include (in examination questions at least) an amount he brings in for goodwill.

Question   Admission of a partner

Oil and Grease, equal partners in a vehicle repair business, agree to Detergent becoming a partner on 1 January 20X1. Their capitals are Oil $12,000; Grease $9,000; and Detergent agrees to introduce $3,000 capital and $2,000 for his share of the partnership goodwill. The partners agree to share profits in the ratio Oil 2: Grease 2: Detergent 1, and decide that goodwill should not be shown in the books. What entries should be made to record the admission in the accounts?

Answer

The partners' capital accounts, with goodwill of $10,000 ($2,000 being a one-fifth share of the total goodwill) being introduced and eliminated are as follows.

CAPITAL ACCOUNTS

	Oil $	Grease $	Detergent $		Oil $	Grease $	Detergent $
Goodwill				Balances b/f	12,000	9,000	
Oil (2/5)	4,000			Bank: cash			
Grease (2/5)		4,000		introduced			5,000
Detergent (1/5)			2,000	Goodwill			
				Oil (½)	5,000		
Balances c/f	13,000	10,000	3,000	Grease (½)		5,000	
	17,000	14,000	5,000		17,000	14,000	5,000

Should the old partners wish to withdraw their share of the premium paid by Detergent for goodwill, they can each take out $1,000 (*Debit* Capital accounts *Credit* Cash), thus restoring their capitals to the original amounts.

When tangible assets are revalued on the admission of a new partner, the profit or loss on revaluation must be divided between the old partners. Generally the new values are retained in the books (as indeed goodwill may be), but should the examination question state that 'new values are not be introduced' the profit or loss has to be apportioned between the new partners (as illustrated above).

4.1 Partnership changes during a financial period

If a change in the constitution of a partnership takes place during the financial year the profit and loss appropriation account will have to be prepared in two stages in columnar form. Generally it is assumed that profit is earned evenly over a period (unless otherwise stated), but some points to watch out for are as follows.

(a) If an employee is admitted to partnership in mid-year, his salary while an employee is an expense chargeable wholly against profits of the first part of the year and subsequent withdrawals on account are debited to his current account.

(b) If a partner leaves in mid-year and a loan account is created, interest on the loan account is chargeable as an expense against profits of the last part of the year only.

5 Formation of a partnership from two or more sole traders

When two or more businesses decide to combine their operations (to expand their range of operations, achieve some economies of scale etc) the problems of accounting for the amalgamation will arise.
In respect of partnership accounts typical problems are concerned with *either:*

- Two (or more) sole traders amalgamating to form a partnership; *or*
- A sole trader amalgamating with an existing partnership; *or*
- Two partnerships amalgamating to form a new partnership.

We are concerned with the first of these situations.

Whatever the type of amalgamation, the accounting problems are very much the same. As we have already seen, where a partner retires from, or a new partner is admitted to, a partnership, problems arise in respect of revaluing assets, valuing goodwill, establishing new profit shares, ascertaining new capital introduced, and so on. All these problems of establishing and evaluating assets which are to be brought in, and liabilities which are to be taken over by the new partnership, are relevant to amalgamations.

The old firms' assets and liabilities are **realised** by 'sale' to the new firm, not for cash, but for a share in the capital of the new business, the amount of capital being determined by the value of net assets contributed.

A **revaluation account** is used in each of the old firms' existing set of books to account for and apportion to the sole traders their share of the profit or loss on revaluation of assets and liabilities. A goodwill account (if necessary) is used to introduce (or increase) the goodwill, and to credit the sole traders with their share.

Once both firms have adjusted their asset, liability and capital accounts to take into account the agreed values, the separate books may be **merged**. The traders' agreed capital balances are transferred to the new firm capital accounts and goodwill written off (in new profit sharing ratio) if necessary.

Question	Two sole traders becoming a partnership

Sinner and Gee were two sole traders in the same line of business. On 1 January 20X1 the two firms were to be merged to form Sinnergee, the partners sharing the profits equally. The summarised statements of financial position of the two firms on 31 December 20X0 were as follows.

STATEMENTS OF FINANCIAL POSITION AS AT 31 DECEMBER 20X0

	Sinner $	Gee $
Assets		
Non-current assets		
Property	–	20,000
Plant etc	12,500	–
Current assets		
Trade accounts receivable	12,000	–
Cash	8,000	2,000
Total assets	32,500	22,000
Capital and liabilities		
Current liabilities		
Trade accounts payable	2,500	–
Capital		
Sinner	30,000	
Gee		22,000
Total capital and liabilities	32,500	22,000

The property is to be revalued at $24,000 and the plant at $11,000. Goodwill is agreed at $5,000 for Sinner and $2,500 for Gee, but is not to appear on the books. All assets and liabilities are taken over by the new firm.

Show the capital accounts of the sole traders just before the merger, the partners' capital accounts in the new partnership, and the opening statement of financial position (in draft form) of Sinnergee.

Answer

SINNER: CAPITAL ACCOUNT

	$		$
Revaluation a/c $(12,500 – 11,000)	1,500	Balance b/f	30,000
Transfer to Sinnergee	33,500	Goodwill	5,000
	35,000		35,000

GEE: CAPITAL ACCOUNT

	$		$
		Balance b/f	22,000
		Revaluation a/c	4,000
Transfer to Sinnergee	28,500	Goodwill	2,500
	28,500		28,500

SINNERGEE: CAPITAL ACCOUNTS

	Sinner	Gee		Sinner	Gee
	$	$		$	$
Goodwill w/off 1:1	3,750	3,750	Transfer: old firms	33,500	28,500
Balances c/d	29,750	24,750			
	33,500	28,500		33,500	28,500

SINNERGEE
DRAFT OPENING STATEMENT OF FINANCIAL POSITION

	$	$
Assets		
Non-current assets		
Property	24,000	
Plant etc	11,000	
		35,000
Current assets	12,000	
Trade accounts receivable	10,000	
Cash		22,000
Total assets		57,000
Capital and liabilities		
Capital		
Sinner	29,750	
Gee	24,750	
		54,500
Current liabilities		
Trade account payable		2,500
Total capital and liabilities		57,000

6 Simple dissolution of a partnership

Accounting for a dissolution is a matter of double entry bookkeeping.

We will now examine the sequence of events when the business does *not* continue and the partnership ceases to exist.

Step 1   All assets (except cash) and liabilities are transferred to a realisation account at their book value.

Step 2   Each partner's current account is cleared to his capital account, as the distinction between the two is irrelevant at this stage.

Step 3   As the assets are sold and liabilities are settled, double entry is made between the realisation account and the cash account. Any realisation expenses are debited to the realisation account. If partners take over assets this fact is recorded in their accounts.

Step 4   When all assets are disposed of and all liabilities met, the balance on the realisation account is transferred to the partners' accounts, in their profit sharing ratio. A credit balance on the realisation account represents a profit on dissolution, a debit balance a loss.

Step 5   At this stage the total amount due to the partners should equal the cash balance. The cash is distributed and the partnership is over.

Question   Dissolution

Hop Skip and Jump decide to dissolve their partnership on 1 January 20X2, after an ugly scene at Skip's New Year's Eve party. The statement of financial position of the partnership as at 31 December 20X1, was as follows.

	$	$		$	$
Capital accounts			Current assets		
Hop	21,000		Investments	21,000	
Skip	21,000		Accounts receivable	37,000	
Jump	10,000		Balance at bank	3,000	
		52,000			61,000
Current accounts			Non-current assets at net		
Hop	5,750		book value		
Skip	2,450		Furniture and fittings	20,000	
Jump	2,500		Motor vehicles	16,000	
		10,700			36,000
Loan		15,000			
Accounts payable		19,300			
		97,000			97,000

The loan was repaid, interest already having been paid up to 31 December 20X1. The furniture and fittings were sold for $18,200 and Jump took over a motor vehicle (which had a carrying amount of $5,000) at an agreed valuation of $6,000. The other vehicles were sold for $13,450 after repairs had first been carried out on a faulty transit van by the Gloria Monday Service Station, at a cost of $450. Trade accounts receivable realised only $34,800. Because of large discounts available, trade accounts payable were settled for $17,600. The investments realised $22,300. Dissolution expenses, excluding the transit van repair costs, totalled $750. Hop, Skip and Jump share profits and losses in the ratio 2:2:1.

You are required to show the relevant accounts and the final distribution between the partners.

Answer

The first stage in accounting for the dissolution is:

(a) To combine the capital and current account for each partner, since the distinction between the two is no longer relevant;

(b) To transfer all assets (except cash) and liabilities to a realisation account at their book value. A liability will appear as a credit entry in the realisation account and an asset as a debit entry.

PARTNERSHIP ACCOUNTS

		Hop $	Skip $	Jump $
	Capital account:			
	balance b/f	21,000	21,000	10,000
	Current account:			
	balance b/f	5,750	2,450	2,500
		26,750	23,450	12,500

REALISATION ACCOUNT

	$		$
Furniture and fittings		Loan account	15,000
(CA)	20,000	Trade accounts payable	19,300
Motor vehicles (CA)	16,000		
Investments	21,000		
Trade accounts receivable	37,000		

CASH AND BANK

	$	
Balance b/f	3,000	

The net result of these accounting entries is to clear all the accounts of the partnership, except for the three shown above.

The next stage is to record what happens on the sale of the business assets and settlement of the business debts.

(a) In paying accounts payable and redeeming loans:

DEBIT　　　Realisation account
CREDIT　　Cash and bank account

(b) In selling assets (for cash):

DEBIT　　　Cash and bank account
CREDIT　　Realisation account

(c) Costs incurred in the dissolution (or on realisation):

DEBIT　　　Realisation account
CREDIT　　Cash and bank account

(d) Assets taken out by partners:

DEBIT　　　Partner's account, with the agreed valuation of the asset
CREDIT　　Realisation account

The accounts now appear as follows.

PARTNERS' ACCOUNTS

	Hop $	Skip $	Jump $		Hop $	Skip $	Jump $
Realisation account (vehicle)		6,000		Balance b/f	26,750	23,450	12,500

REALISATION ACCOUNT

	$		$
Furniture and fittings	20,000	Loan account	15,000
Motor vehicles	16,000	Trade accounts payable	19,300
Investments	21,000		
Trade accounts receivable	37,000		
Cash and bank: payments		Cash and bank: proceeds	
Loan account paid off	15,000	Furniture and fittings	18,200
Payables settled	17,600	Motor vehicles	13,450
Transit van repairs	450	Investments	22,300
Realisation expenses	750	From receivables	34,800
Balance (ie balancing figure)	1,250	Jump's account (motor vehicle)	6,000
	129,050		129,050

CASH AND BANK

	$		$
Balance b/f	3,000	Realisation account	
Realisation account		Loan	15,000
Furniture and fittings	18,200	Trade accounts payable	17,600
Motor vehicles	13,450	Transit van repairs	450
Investments	22,300	Expenses	750
Trade accounts receivable	34,800	Balance c/f	57,950
	91,750		91,750

The balances on the various accounts are now as follows.

			$	$	$
CREDIT	Partners' accounts:	Hop		26,750	
		Skip		23,450	
		Jump		6,500	
					56,700
DEBIT	Cash and bank		57,950		
CREDIT	Realisation account				1,250

The balance on the realisation account is the profit or loss on realisation. In this example, there is a profit on realisation.

	Proceeds from realisation $	Book value of assets less liabilities $
Furniture and fittings	18,200	20,000
Motor vehicles (13,450 + 6,000)	19,450	16,000
Investments	22,300	21,000
Trade accounts receivable	34,800	37,000
Loan	(15,000)	(15,000)
Trade accounts payable	(17,600)	(19,300)
Van repairs	(450)	
Expenses	(750)	
	60,950	59,700

Excess of proceeds over carrying values $(60,950 − 59,700) = $1,250.

The next stage is to share the profit or loss on realisation between the partners in the profit sharing ratio. Having done this, the money due to each partner is established, and the partnership accounts are ended by:

(a)   Crediting the bank account
(b)   Debiting the partners' accounts

with the money due to and so paid to each partner.

The final accounts are as follows.

REALISATION ACCOUNT

	$	$		$
Book values			Book values	
Furniture & fittings		20,000	Loan	15,000
Motor vehicles		16,000	Trade accounts payable	19,300
Investments		21,000		
Trade accounts receivable		37,000	Bank	
Bank			Furniture etc	18,200
Loan repaid		15,000	Motor vehicles	13,450
Trade accounts payable		17,600	Trade accounts receivable	34,800
Repairs		450	Investment	22,300
Expenses		750		
Profit on realisation			Jump (vehicle)	6,000
Hop (2)	500			
Skip (2)	500			
Jump (1)	250			
		1,250		
		129,050		129,050

PARTNERS' ACCOUNTS

	Hop $	Skip $	Jump $		Hop $	Skip $	Jump $
Realisation a/c			6,000	Capital b/d	21,000	21,000	10,000
Cash *	27,250	23,950	6,750	Current b/d	5,750	2,450	2,500
				Realisation a/c	500	500	250
	27,250	23,950	12,750		27,250	23,950	12,750

* Balance due to each partner, and so paid out of the partnership's bank account.

CASH AND BANK

	$		$	$
Balance b/d	3,000	Realisation a/c		
		Loan		15,000
Realisation a/c		Trade accounts payable		17,600
Furniture etc	18,200	Repairs		450
Motor vehicles	13,450	Expenses		750
Trade accounts receivable	34,800			
Investment	22,300	Partners' accounts:		
		Hop	27,250	
		Skip	23,950	
		Jump	6,750	
				57,950
	91,750			91,750

Question

Alpha and Beta are in partnership. They share profits equally after Alpha has been allowed a salary of $4,000 pa. No interest is charged on drawings or allowed on current accounts or capital accounts. The trial balance of the partnership at 31 December 20X9 before adjusting for any of the items below, is as follows.

		Dr $'000	Cr $'000
Capital	– Alpha		30
	– Beta		25
Current	– Alpha		3
	– Beta		4
Drawings	– Alpha	4	
	– Beta	5	
Sales			200
Inventory 1 January 20X9		30	
Purchases		103	
Operating expenses		64	
Loan – Beta (10%)			10
– Gamma (10%)			20
Land and buildings		60	
Plant and machinery – cost		70	
– depreciation to 31 December 20X9			40
Receivables and payables		40	33
Bank			11
		376	376

(i) Closing inventory at 31 December was $24,000.

(ii) On 31 December Alpha and Beta agree to take their manager, Gamma, into partnership. Gamma's loan account balance is to be transferred to a capital account as at 31 December. It is agreed that in future Alpha, Beta and Gamma will all share profits equally. Alpha will be allowed a salary of $4,000 as before, and Gamma will be allowed a salary of $5,000 per annum (half of what he received in 20X9 as manager, included in operating expenses).

The three partners agree that the goodwill of the business at 31 December should be valued at $12,000, but is not to be recorded in the books. It is also agreed that land and buildings are to be revalued to a figure of $84,000 and that this revalued figure is to be retained and recorded in the accounts.

(iii) Interest on the loan has not been paid.

(iv) Included in sales are two items sold on 'sale or return' for $3,000 each. Each item had cost the business $1,000. One of these items was in fact returned on 4 January 20Y0 and the other was one formally accepted by the customer on 6 January 20Y0.

Required

Submit with appropriately labelled headings and subheadings:

(a) Partners' capital accounts in columnar form
(b) Partners' current accounts in columnar form
(c) Statement of profit or loss and appropriation account for 20X9
(d) Statement of financial position as at 31 December 20X9

Answer

(a)

PARTNERS' CAPITAL ACCOUNTS

	Alpha $'000	Beta $'000	Gamma $'000		Alpha $'000	Beta $'000	Gamma $'000
Goodwill				Balances b/d	30	25	–
eliminated	4	4	4	Goodwill	6	6	–
Balances c/d	44	39	16	Land revaluation			
				surplus	12	12	–
				Loan account	–	–	20
	48	43	20		48	43	20

(b)

PARTNERS' CURRENT ACCOUNTS

	Alpha $'000	Beta $'000	Gamma $'000		Alpha $'000	Beta $'000	Gamma $'000
Drawings	4	5	–	Balances b/d	3	4	–
Balances c/d	11	8	2	Salary	4	–	–
				Residual profit	8	8	–
				Loan interest	–	1	2
	15	13	2		15	13	2

Note. It is assumed that the adjustment for interest is DR Interest expense CR Partners' current accounts. Interest could have been a cash payment, in which case you could have credited cash instead.

(c)   STATEMENT OF PROFIT OR LOSS AND APPROPRIATION ACCOUNT
FOR THE YEAR ENDED 31 DECEMBER 20X9

	$'000	$'000
Sales (200 – 6)		194
Opening inventory	30	
Purchases	103	
	133	
Closing inventory (24 + 2)	26	
Cost of sales		107
Gross profit		87
Operating expenses	64	
Interest (10% × (10,000 + 20,000))	3	
		67
Net profit		20
Salary – Alpha		4
Residual profit		16
Residual profit appropriated – Alpha ($^1/_2$)	8	
– Beta ($^1/_2$)	8	
		16

Note. No adjustment has to be made in respect of Gamma's salary as manager as this relates entirely to the period *before* he became a partner and so has been properly treated as an *expense* and not as an *appropriation* of profit. However, when an employee is made a partner mid-year, an adjustment is required to differentiate between his salary as an employee and his salary as a partner in apportioning profit to each partnership.

(d) STATEMENT OF FINANCIAL POSITION AS AT 31 DECEMBER 20X9

	$'000	$'000
Non-current assets		
Land and buildings (revalued amount)		84
Plant and machinery – cost		70
– depreciation		40
		30
		114
Current assets		
Inventory (W)	26	
Receivables (W)	34	
		60
		174
Partners' capital accounts		
Alpha	44	
Beta	39	
Gamma	16	
		99
Partners' current accounts		
Alpha	11	
Beta	8	
Gamma	2	
		21
		120
Non-current liabilities		
10% loan – Beta		10
Current liabilities		
Bank overdraft	11	
Payables	33	
		44
		174

Working

Sales made on sale or return can only be treated as sales once the customer accepts the goods. Up to that point, the goods 'sold' are treated as inventory and valued at the lower of cost and net realisable value, as usual. The goods accepted in January will therefore be treated as sold in the next accounting period.

	$'000
∴ Sales: $200,000 – $6,000	194
Inventory: $24,000 + $2,000	26
Receivables: $40,000 – $6,000	34

7 Partnership transferred to a company

7.1 Introduction

This is a fairly common situation since it covers the conversion of a partnership into a limited company as well as a direct sale to outside parties. Often the limited company will be entirely owned by the old partners, ie they will be given shares in the company as part or all of the consideration for their share in the partnership. A partnership will often be 'converted' into a limited company when the business becomes quite large.

BPP LEARNING MEDIA

7.2 Closing off a set of partnership books on sale or conversion to a limited company

This exercise is very similar to a dissolution except that:

(a)   Most of the assets are sold to one buyer and this might include some or all of the cash;

(b)   The assets are not sold for cash alone but a mix of shares, debentures and/or cash.

Accounting is for two basic operations:

(a)   **The sale of the assets to the company**

   (i)   Use a realisation account

   The purchase consideration payable by the company is in effect the sale proceeds. This must be computed – when shares are issued they are always valued at their issued price not the nominal value. As the contract with the company may be agreed before the purchase consideration is received, it is normal to open a personal account for the purchaser, ie the new company.

DEBIT	New company account with the purchase consideration
CREDIT	Realisation account

   The balance on the realisation account is credited/debited to the partners' accounts. (Note, as before, that the capital/current account distinction is meaningless.)

   (ii)   When the company pays the purchase consideration:

DEBIT	Cash
DEBIT	Shares in new company
CREDIT	New company account

   This is merely the discharge of a debt.

(b)   **The distribution of the purchase consideration between the partners**

   (i)   **Transfer shares** and debentures to partners in the agreed proportions

DEBIT	Partners' accounts
CREDIT	Shares in new company (at issue value)
CREDIT	Debentures in new company (at issue value)

   (ii)   Finally transfer cash in or out to close down the partnership accounts

7.3 Opening appropriate accounts in the company's records

The company will place values on the assets it acquires. If the purchase consideration exceeds the value of the net tangible assets, the surplus will be treated as goodwill because it represents the premium paid to acquire those assets. If the reverse is the case (ie negative goodwill) the amount will be credited to a non-distributable reserve.

The accounting treatment centres around a personal account for the vendor, ie the old partnership and again comprises two basic operations.

(a)   **The purchase of the assets**

DEBIT	Sundry assets at agreed values
CREDIT	Vendor (partnership) account

(b)   **The discharge of purchase consideration**

DEBIT	Vendor (partnership) account with elements of purchase consideration
CREDIT	Share capital, share premium, debentures, cash etc

   Any balance on the vendor's account is then transferred to the goodwill or capital reserve.

7.4 Example: Preparing final accounts covering the year in which sale or conversion takes place

A and B trade as partners sharing profits 3:2 and decide to sell their business to X which agrees to pay $16,000 in the form of:

5,000 $1 shares at a premium of 20c
6,000 $1 8% debentures issued at 90c
Cash of $4,600

X is to acquire all the net assets of the partnership with the exception of the cash and the two motor vehicles which A and B are to take over at values of $900 and $600 respectively.

A and B agree that their accounts are to be settled so that:

(a)   they take the ordinary shares in X in profit sharing ratio;
(b)   the debentures are to be taken in the ratio of their capital accounts;

The balance is to be settled by cash transfer.

STATEMENT OF FINANCIAL POSITION OF A AND B AT DATE OF TAKEOVER

	Cost	Dep'n	CV
	$	$	$
Non-current assets			
Freehold property	4,000		4,000
Fixtures and fittings	1,000	500	500
Motor vehicles	2,500	500	2,000
	7,500	1,000	6,500
Current assets			
Inventory		4,000	
Receivables	2,100		
Less: allowance for doubtful debts	100		
Cash		2,000	
		1,000	
			7,000
			13,500

	$	$
Capital accounts		
A	6,000	
B	3,000	
		9,000
Current accounts		
A	1,500	
B	1,500	
		3,000
		12,000
Current liabilities		1,500
		13,500

Required

(a)   Show the ledger accounts reflecting the above transactions in the books of A and B;

(b)   Show the journal entries in the books of X to reflect the takeover assuming that the partnership assets are taken over at book value with the exception of the freehold which is to be valued at $7,000 and the receivables at $1,800;

(c)   Construct the opening statement of financial position of X.

Solution

Numbers in brackets refer to sequence of entries.

(a)   **Books of A and B**

REALISATION ACCOUNT

	$	$		$	$
(1) Freehold property		4,000	(2) Trade payables		1,500
(1) Fixtures and fittings		500	(3) X account – monetary		
(1) Motor vehicles		2,000	value of purchase		
(1) Inventory		4,000	consideration:		
(1) Receivables		2,000	Shares 5,000 @ $1.20	6,000	
Partners' accounts –			Debentures 6,000 @ 90p	5,400	
profit on sale:			Cash	4,600	
(5) A(3)	3,900				16,000
(5) B(2)	2,600		Partners' accounts –		
		6,500	motor vehicles taken		
			over:		
			(4) A	900	
			(4) B	600	
					1,500
		–			
		19,000			19,000

PARTNERS' ACCOUNT

	A $	B $		A $	B $
(4) Realisation account –			Balances b/d:		
motor vehicles taken			Capital accounts	6,000	3,000
over	900	600	Current accounts	1,500	1,500
X account – discharge				7,500	4,500
of purchase			(5) Realisation account –		
consideration:			profit on sale	3,900	2,600
(6) Shares 3:2	3,600	2,400			
(6) Debentures 2:1	3,600	1,800			
(8) Cash	3,300	2,300			
	11,400	7,100		11,400	7,100

CASH ACCOUNT

	$		$
Balance b/d	1,000	Final settlement to close	
(7) X	4,600	down books:	
		(8) A	3,300
		(8) B	2,300
	5,600		5,600

NEW COMPANY'S ACCOUNT – X

	$		$
(3) Realisation account –		Discharge of purchase	
monetary value of		consideration to	
purchase consideration	16,000	partners' accounts:	
		(6) Shares in X	6,000
		(6) Debentures in X	5,400
		(7) Cash	4,600
	16,000		16,000

(b)   X JOURNAL

	Dr $	Cr $
Freehold property	7,000	
Fixtures and fittings	500	
Inventory	4,000	
Receivables	2,100	
Bad debt allowance		300
Trade payables		1,500
A and B partnership account		16,000
Goodwill – balancing figure (see note)	4,200	
	17,800	17,800

Purchase of $11,800 specific net assets from A and B for $16,000, giving rise to $4,200 goodwill.

	Dr	Cr
A and B partnership account	16,000	
Debenture discount	600	
Ordinary share capital		5,000
Share premium account		1,000
8% debentures		6,000
Cash – bank overdraft		4,600
	16,600	16,600

Discharge of purchase consideration, being:

(i)   5,000 ordinary $1 shares issued at a premium of 20c per share
(ii)   6,000 $1 8% debentures
(iii) $4,600 in cash

> **Tutorial note**
>
> The 'goodwill' arising in the new company's accounts is simply the excess of the purchase consideration over the fair values placed on the net tangible assets taken over. This should be contrasted with the 'profit on realisation' in the partnership books, which is the surplus of the sale proceeds over the book values of the assets sold. The two figures will thus not necessarily be the same.

(c)   X OPENING STATEMENT OF FINANCIAL POSITION

	$	$	$
Non-current assets			
Goodwill			4,200
Freehold property at valuation			7,000
Fixtures and fittings at valuation			500
			11,700
Current assets			
Inventory		4,000	
Receivables	2,100		
Less: allowance for doubtful debts	300		
		1,800	
			5,800
			17,500
Capital and reserves			
Ordinary shares of $1, fully paid			5,000
Share premium account		1,000	
Less: debenture discount written off		600	
			400
			5,400

	$	$	$
Non-current liabilities			
8% debentures			6,000
Current liabilities			
Trade payables		1,500	
Bank overdraft		4,600	
			6,100
			17,500

Tutorial note

Partner A now owns 60% of the company's shares and partner B owns 40%. They are effectively still acting as a partnership but through the medium of a company.

Question	Conversion

The AB partnership sells net assets with a book value of $40,000 to Z for consideration of 45,000 $1 shares issued at par. Z values the net assets at $38,000.

(a)   What is the profit on realisation to be shared between the partners?

(b)   What value will be placed on goodwill in Z's books?

(c)   If the shares in Z were issued at a premium of 25c, how many shares would have to be issued?

(d)   What accounting entries would be required in Z's books to record the transfer (assuming shares issued at $1.25)?

Answer

(a) $5,000 (45,000 – 40,000)

(b) $7,000 (45,000 – 38,000)

(c) $\dfrac{45,000}{1.25}$ = 36,000 $1 shares

(d)

		$	$
DEBIT	Sundry assets	38,000	
DEBIT	Goodwill	7,000	
CREDIT	AB partnership account		45,000
DEBIT	AB partnership account	45,000	
CREDIT	Share capital		36,000
CREDIT	Share premium		9,000

7.5 Books carried on without a break

The above example of X assumes that the partnership books are closed off, and new books are opened up for the company. In practice, very often the old books are carried on without a break and amended at the end of the accounting period to reflect the conversion into a company. In this situation the necessary adjusting entries can be made through the partners' accounts since they represent the net assets of the partnership at their existing book values. Hence:

(a)   Any assets or liabilities not taken over must be written out of the books by transfer to the partner concerned, ie

(i)   Assets not taken over:

DEBIT   Partners' account
CREDIT   Asset account

thus reducing both the balance due to the partner and the net assets taken over.

(ii)   Liabilities not taken over:

DEBIT   Liability account
CREDIT   Partner's account

thus extinguishing the liability and increasing the net assets taken over.

(b)   The remaining assets (including goodwill) and liabilities must be increased or reduced to their agreed take-over values. The profit or loss arising will be credited or debited to the partners' accounts in profit sharing ratio. A revaluation account may be used for this purpose if several adjustments are required.

(c)   Open up accounts for each element of the purchase consideration and debit each partner's share to his partner's account.

(d)   Any balances remaining on the partner's accounts will be settled by cash transfers into or out of the business.

(e)   A company cannot distribute profits made prior to the date of its incorporation. Consequently, any pre-incorporation profits should be transferred to a non-distributable reserve or used to write down any goodwill arising on takeover.

7.6 Receivables and payables not taken over

Often the purchaser of a business will not take over the existing receivables and payables (for tax reasons). He may, however, agree to collect the debts and pay off the liabilities on behalf of the vendor, so that the existing purchase and sales ledger are carried on. The transactions affecting the vendor are recorded by means of suspense accounts. The necessary entries would be made as follows.

Receivables

(a)	Debts to be collected	DEBIT	Receivables' account
		CREDIT	Receivables' suspense account
(b)	Cash collected	DEBIT	Cash
		CREDIT	Receivables' account
(c)	Bad debts incurred or discounts allowed	DEBIT	Receivables' suspense account
		CREDIT	Receivables' account
(d)	Amount due to vendor	DEBIT	Receivables' suspense account
		CREDIT	Vendor's account

Payables

(a)	Suppliers to be paid	DEBIT	Payables' suspense account
		CREDIT	Payables' account
(b)	Cash paid	DEBIT	Payables' account
		CREDIT	Cash
(c)	Discounts received	DEBIT	Payables' accounts
		CREDIT	Payables' suspense account
(d)	Amount due from vendor	DEBIT	Vendor's account
		CREDIT	Payables' suspense account

Receivables and payables

When taking over the business of Generous & Co, Generous agreed to collect the receivables of $7,700 and settle the accounts payable of $5,600 on behalf of the former partners. The debts were collected subject to a bad debt of $320 and discount allowed of $150 and out of the proceeds the suppliers were paid subject to discount received of $95.

Record the entries in the books of the company to show the final amount payable to the partners.

Answer

RECEIVABLES' ACCOUNT

	$		$
Receivables' suspense account	7,700	Cash (bal fig)	7,230
		Receivables' suspense account:	
		Bad debt	320
		Discount allowed	150
	7,700		7,700

RECEIVABLES' SUSPENSE ACCOUNT

	$		$
Receivables' account:		Receivables' account	7,700
Bad debt	320		
Discount allowed	150		
Vendor's account (bal fig)	7,230		
	7,700		7,700

VENDOR'S ACCOUNT

	$		$
Payables' suspense account	5,505	Receivables' suspense account	7,230
Balance c/d	1,725		
	7,230		7,230

PAYABLES' ACCOUNT

	$		$
Cash (bal fig)	5,505	Payables' suspense account	5,600
Payables' suspense account –			
discount received	95		
	5,600		5,600

PAYABLES' SUSPENSE ACCOUNT

	$		$
Payables' account	5,600	Payables' account – discount	
		received	95
		Vendor's account (bal fig)	5,505
	5,600		5,600

The balance remaining on the vendor's account represents the final amount payable to the partners.

Note. For statement of financial position purposes any balances on the suspense accounts will cancel out with the corresponding balances on the receivables' and payables' accounts.

7.7 The implications of partnership dissolution and conversion to partners

The commercial reasons for the transfer of a business to a limited company should be understood as this will help you master the accounting entries. The most common situation is that the partners have decided to trade as a limited company rather than a partnership. The business may have grown in size so that a corporate structure is more sensible. Alternatively, the partners may consider that they can increase their customer base if they trade as a company. Last, but by no means least, the partners may consider that it is advantageous from a tax viewpoint to incorporate.

After the conversion, the partners become shareholders in the company. How many shares each receives depends on their relative involvement in the old partnership in terms of past capital contributed and time spent in development of the business.

Question   Conversion to a limited company

John, Keith and Len are in partnership sharing profits in the ratio of 3:2:1 respectively.

A statement of financial position for the partnership as at 31 March 20X3 is shown below.

	$		$	$
Non-current assets		Capital accounts		
Premises	100,000	John		100,000
Plant	52,000	Keith		80,000
Office furniture	27,000	Len		40,000
	179,000			220,000
Current assets		Current account		
Inventory	29,500	John	6,450	
Receivables	51,500	Keith	14,978	
Cash	10,412	Len	2,636	
				18,792
		Trade payables		31,620
	270,412			270,412

Len retired on 31 March 20X3, and John and Keith formed a company, Jake, to take over the business on that date.

Details of the changes agreed were as follows.

(a)   The assets of the business, other than cash, were to be taken over by the company at a valuation of $284,000, but the tangible assets were to be recorded in the books of Jake at the same book value as in the partnership books. Trade payables were to be paid by the partnership.

(b)   The share capital of Jake was:

135,000 ordinary shares of $1 each

(c)   The company raised a 16% debenture loan of $70,000 from a merchant bank.

(d)   Jake paid for its acquisition as follows.

(i)   135,000 ordinary shares issued to John and Keith to satisfy their capital accounts;
(ii)   16% debentures issued to John, Keith and Len to repay their current accounts;
(iii)   the balance in cash.

(e)   The profit/loss on realisation is to be transferred to the current accounts.

Required

(a) Prepare the current accounts of the partners.
(b) Draft journal entries to record these transactions in the books of Jake.
(c) Prepare the cash account of the partnership.
(d) Prepare a statement of financial position for Jake as at 1 April 20X3.

Answer

(a) CURRENT ACCOUNTS

	John $	Keith $	Len $		John $	Keith $	Len $
Balance b/d			2,636	Balance b/d	6,450	14,978	
16% debentures	18,450	22,978	1,364	Realisation a/c	12,000	8,000	4,000
	18,450	22,978	4,000		18,450	22,978	4,000

The 16% debentures issued to partners total $42,792.

(b) JOURNAL ENTRIES

	Dr $	Cr $
Goodwill (bal fig)	24,000	
Premises	100,000	
Plant	52,000	
Furniture	27,000	
Inventory	29,500	
Receivables	51,500	
Vendors – the partnership		284,000

Assets purchased from the partnership and goodwill as the excess of price over book value of assets acquired

	Dr $	Cr $
Vendor	284,000	
Ordinary shares of $1 each		135,000
Share premium account (W2)		45,000
16% debentures (see (a))		42,792
Cash (bal fig)		61,208

Being payment to the vendor

	Dr $	Cr $
Cash	70,000	
16% debentures		70,000

Being debentures issued for cash

(c)   CASH ACCOUNT (PARTNERSHIP)

	$		$
Balance b/d	10,412	Payables	31,620
Cash from Jake	61,208	Len's capital account	40,000
	71,620		71,620

(d) JAKE STATEMENT OF FINANCIAL POSITION AS AT 1 APRIL 20X3

	$	$
Non-current assets		
Tangible assets		
Premises	100,000	
Plant	52,000	
Furniture	27,000	
		179,000
Goodwill		24,000

Current assets

Inventory	29,500
Receivables	51,500
Cash	8,792
	87,792
	292,792

Capital

Share capital

Ordinary shares of $1 each	135,000
	–
Share premium account	45,000
	180,000
16% debentures (70,000 + 42,792)	112,792
	292,792

Workings

(1)   REALISATION ACCOUNT

	$	$		$
Book value of:			Consideration	284,000
Non-current assets		179,000		
Inventory		29,500		
Receivables		51,500		
Profit on realisation				
John 3	12,000			
Keith 2	8,000			
Len 1	4,000			
		24,000		
		284,000		284,000

(2)   Issue of shares – 135,000 shares satisfies balances on John and Keith's accounts.

	$
Balance on capital accounts	180,000
Nominal value of shares issued	(135,000)
Share premium	45,000

Chapter roundup

- Any change in a partnership involves dealing with goodwill. Each existing partner must be credited with their share of goodwill earned to date.

- Accounting for a dissolution is a matter of double entry bookkeeping.

Quick quiz

1   What is a partnership?

2   Is a partner's salary an expense of the partnership?

3   Why might a sole trader take on a partner?

4   What is the difference between a partner's capital account and a partner's current account?

5   How is profit shared between partners?

6   What are the entries required to introduce goodwill into a partnership and subsequently to eliminate it?

7   If tangible assets are revalued on admission of a partner, how is the profit or loss on revaluation treated?

8   Describe the sequence of accounting procedures on dissolution of a partnership.

9   What is the double entry to record:

   (a)   The sale of partnership assets for cash?
   (b)   Dissolution costs incurred?

Answers to quick quiz

1   The relationship which exists between persons carrying on a business in common with a view of profit.

2   No

3   (a)   To spread risk
    (b)   To obtain access to wider network of contacts
    (c)   To obtain extra skills and experience
    (d)   To obtain additional finance

4   Capital account represents long-term capital; current account is used for partners' share of profits and their drawings on account of that profit.

5   According to the partnership agreement.

6   Credit old partners in old profit-sharing ratio
    Debit new partners in new profit-sharing ratio

7   Credited or debited to old partners in old profit-sharing ratios

8   (a)   Combine each partner's capital and current accounts
    (b)   Transfer all assets and liabilities except cash to a realisation account
    (c)   Pay off liabilities (debit realisation account and credit cash)
    (d)   Record sale of assets (debit cash, credit realisation account)
    (e)   Pay costs of realisation (debit realisation account and credit cash)
    (f)   Record takeover of assets by partners
    (g)   Distribute balance to partners (or receive payment from partners with debit balances)

9   See 8 (d) and 8 (e) above.

End of chapter question

Chart and graph (AIA May 2005)

Chart and Graph decided for financial reasons to convert their partnership into a limited liability company, Diagram. The conversion took place on 31 January 20X5 but the accounts have been maintained throughout the year ending 30 April 20X5 for the partnership. The following trial balance, produced after the assessment of gross profit for the year, therefore contains no entries concerning the conversion.

TRIAL BALANCE AS AT 30 APRIL 20X5

	$	$
Capital accounts: Chart		38,000
Graph		35,000
Partners drawings: Chart	15,382	
Graph	8,000	
Directors salaries	5,000	
Inventory at 30 April 20X5	30,000	
Gross profit for year ended 30 April 20X5		167,215
Cash discounts allowed (80% partnership. 20% Company)	1,300	
Company formation expenses	600	
Administration expenses	14,700	
Distribution costs	18,660	
Freehold property	138,000	
Plant and equipment, cost	6,600	
Plant and equipment, accumulated depreciation		2,610
Motor vehicles, at cost	18,900	
Motor vehicles, accumulated depreciation		6,300
Trade receivables	21,475	
Trade payables		46,450
Bank	16,958	
	295,575	295,575

Chart and Graph shared profits in the ratio 4:3 until 31 January 20X5, when the partnership was converted to the company, Diagram. The partners allocated the 200,000 $1 ordinary shares of Diagram in proportion to their partnership capital accounts at the date of conversion. No partners' current accounts were maintained.

The following information is also relevant.

(i) The Freehold property is to be revalued at 31 January 20X5 to $187,000. All other assets and liabilities are to continue at their book value.

(ii) The gross profit was to be shared: Partnership (80%) $133,772
Company (20%) $33,443

(iii) Depreciation is to be based on cost at the following rates:

Plant and equipment 10% straight-line
Motor vehicles 30% reducing balance

(iv) A trade receivable of $3,000 was considered to be doubtful and a provision created to cover the debt. The relevant sale was made in December 20X4.

Required

(a) A statement of profit or loss, commencing with gross profit, for the year ended 30 April 20X5 analysed into the profit attributable to the partnership and the profit attributable to the company.

(12 marks)

(b) Detailed capital accounts for the partners, showing clearly the shares issued to close the partnership accounts.

(5 marks)

(c) A statement of financial position for the company, Diagram, as at 30 April 20X5.

(8 marks)

(Total = 25 marks)

Accounting for taxation

14

Topic list	Syllabus reference
1 Sales tax	11.3
2 Current tax	11.3
3 Deferred tax	11.3
4 Taxation in company accounts	11.3
5 Presentation and disclosure of taxation	11.3

Introduction

In almost all countries entities are taxed on the basis of their trading income. In some countries this may be called corporation or corporate tax, but we will follow the terminology of IAS 12 *Income taxes* and call it income tax.

In Section 1 we will look briefly at sales tax.

There are two aspects of income tax which must be accounted for: **current tax** and **deferred tax**. These will be discussed in Sections 2 and 3 respectively.

Note: Throughout this chapter we will assume a current corporate income tax rate of 30% and a current personal income tax rate of 20%, unless otherwise stated.

1 Sales tax

Sales tax is a tax on the supply of goods and services. Tax is collected at each transfer point in the chain from prime producer to final consumer. Eventually, the consumer bears the tax in full and any tax paid earlier in the chain can be recovered by the trader who paid it.

1.1 Example: Sales tax

A manufacturing company, Alyson Co, purchases raw materials at a cost of $1,000 plus sales tax at 17½%. From the raw materials Alyson Co makes finished products which it sells to a retail outlet, Barry Co, for $1,600 plus sales tax. Barry Co sells the products to customers at a total price of $2,000 plus sales tax. How much sales tax is paid to the tax authorities at each stage in the chain?

Solution

	Value of goods sold $	Sales tax at 17½% $
Supplier of raw materials	1,000	175
Value added by Alyson Co	600	105
Sale to Barry Co	1,600	280
Value added by Barry Co	400	70
Sales to 'consumers'	2,000	350

1.2 How is sales tax collected?

Although it is the final consumer who eventually bears the full tax of $350, the sum is **collected and paid over to the tax authorities by the traders who make up the chain.** Each trader must assume that his customer is the final consumer and must collect and pay over sales tax at the appropriate rate on the full sales value of the goods sold. He is entitled to reclaim sales tax paid on his own purchases (inputs) and so makes a net payment to the tax authorities equal to the tax on value added by himself.

In the example above, the supplier of raw materials collects from Alyson Co sales tax of $175, all of which he pays over. When Alyson Co sells goods to Barry Co sales tax is charged at the rate of 17½% on $1,600 = $280. Only $105, however, is paid by Alyson Co because the company is entitled to deduct sales tax of $175 suffered on its own purchases. Similarly, Barry Co must charge its customers $350 in sales tax but need only pay over the net amount of $70 after deducting the $280 sales tax suffered on its purchase from Alyson Co.

1.3 Registered and non-registered persons

Traders whose sales (outputs) are below a certain minimum need not register for sales tax. Such traders neither charge sales tax on their outputs nor are entitled to reclaim sales tax on their inputs. They are in the same position as a final consumer.

All outputs of registered traders are either taxable or exempt. Traders carrying on exempt activities (such as banks) cannot charge sales tax on their outputs and consequently cannot reclaim sales tax paid on their inputs.

Taxable outputs are usually chargeable at one of **three rates**:

(a)   **Zero-rated** (0%)
(b)   **Standard-rated** (20% in the UK)
(c)   **Lower standard-rated** (5% on items like domestic fuel in the UK)

The tax authorities publish lists of supplies falling into each category. **Persons carrying on taxable activities** (even activities taxable at zero per cent) **are entitled to reclaim sales tax paid on their inputs**.

Some traders carry on a **mixture of taxable and exempt activities**. Such traders need to apportion the sales tax suffered on inputs and **can only reclaim the proportion relating to taxable outputs**.

1.4 Accounting for sales tax

As a general principle the treatment of sales tax in the accounts of a trader should reflect his role as a collector of the tax and **sales tax should not be included in income or in expenditure whether of a capital or of a revenue nature**.

1.4.1 Irrecoverable sales tax

Where the **trader bears the sales tax** himself, as in the following cases, this should be reflected in the accounts.

(a)   **Persons not registered** for sales tax will suffer sales tax on inputs. This will effectively increase the cost of their consumable materials and their non-current assets and must be so reflected in the financial statements, ie shown **inclusive of sales tax**.

(b)   **Registered persons** who also carry on **exempted** activities will have a residue of sales tax which is borne on them. In this situation the costs to which this residue applies will be inflated by the **irrecoverable sales tax**.

(c)   **Non-deductible inputs will be borne** by all traders (examples in the UK are tax on cars bought which are not for resale, client entertaining expenses and provision of domestic accommodation for a company's directors).

Exam focus point

Where sales tax is not recoverable it must be regarded as an inherent part of the cost of the items purchased and included in profit or loss or the statement of financial position as appropriate.

1.5 Further points

Sales tax is charged on the price net of any discount and this general principle is carried to the extent that where a cash discount is offered, sales tax is charged on the net amount **even where the discount is not taken up**.

Most sales tax registered persons are obliged to record sales tax when a supply is received or made (effectively when a credit sales invoice is raised or a purchase invoice recorded). This has the effect that **the net sales tax liability has on occasion to be paid to the tax authorities before all output tax has been paid by customers**. If a debt is subsequently written off, the sales tax element may not be recovered from the tax authorities for six months from the date of sale, even if the customer becomes insolvent.

Some small businesses can join the cash accounting scheme whereby sales tax is only paid to the tax authorities after it is received from customers. This delays recovery of input tax but improves cash flow overall, although it may involve extra record keeping. Irrecoverable debt relief is automatic under this scheme since if sales tax is not paid by the customer it is not due to the tax authorities.

Question

Sunglo Co is preparing accounts for the year ended 31 May 20X9. Included in its statement of financial position as at 31 May 20X8 was a balance for sales tax recoverable of $15,000.

Its summary statement of profit or loss for the year is as follows.

	$'000
Sales (all standard-rated)	500
Purchases (all standard-rated)	120
Gross profit	380
Expenses	(280)
Interest receivable	20
Profit before tax	120

Note. Expenses

	$'000
Wages and salaries	200
Client entertainment expenditure	10
Other (all standard-rated)	70
	280

Payments of $5,000, $15,000 and $20,000 have been made in the year and a repayment of $12,000 was received. What is the balance for sales tax in the statement of financial position as at 31 May 20X9? Assume a 17.5% standard rate of sales tax.

Answer

SUNGLO CO: SALES TAX ACCOUNT

	$		$
Balance b/d	15,000	Sales ($500,000 × 17.5%)	87,500
Purchases ($120,000 × 17.5%)	21,000	Bank	12,000
Other expenses ($70,000 × 17.5%)	12,250		
Bank	40,000		
Balance c/d	11,250		
	99,500		99,500

1.6 Disclosure requirements

The following accounting rules should be followed.

(a)   **Revenue** shown in the statement of profit or loss should **exclude** sales tax on taxable outputs. If gross revenue must be shown then the sales tax in that figure must also be shown as a deduction in arriving at the revenue exclusive of sales tax.

(b)   **Irrecoverable sales tax** allocated to non-current assets and other items separately disclosed should be **included in their cost** where material and practical.

(c)   The **net amount due to (or from) the tax authorities** should be **included in the total for payables** (or receivables), and need not be separately disclosed.

2 Current tax

 Current tax is the amount payable to the tax authorities in relation to the trading activities of the period.

2.1 Introduction

You may have assumed until now that accounting for income tax was a very simple matter for companies. You would calculate the amount of tax due to be paid on the company's taxable profits and (under the classical system):

DEBIT   Tax charge (statement of profit or loss)
CREDIT   Tax liability (statement of financial position)

with this amount.

Indeed, this aspect of corporate taxation – **current tax** – *is* ordinarily straightforward. Complexities arise, however, when we consider the future tax consequences of what is going on in the accounts now. This is an aspect of tax called **deferred tax**, which we will look at in the next section.

2.2 IAS 12 *Income taxes*

IAS 12 covers both current and deferred tax. The parts relating to current tax are fairly brief, because this is the simple and uncontroversial area of tax.

2.3 Definitions

These are some of the definitions given in IAS 12. We will look at the rest later.

Key terms

> **Accounting profit**. Net profit or loss for a period before deducting tax expense.
>
> **Taxable profit (tax loss)**. The profit (loss) for a period, determined in accordance with the rules established by the taxation authorities, upon which income taxes are payable (recoverable).
>
> **Tax expense (tax income)**. The aggregate amount included in the determination of net profit or loss for the period in respect of current tax and deferred tax.
>
> **Current tax**. The amount of income taxes payable (recoverable) in respect of the taxable profit (tax loss) for a period. *(IAS 12)*

Before we go any further, let us be clear about the difference between current and deferred tax.

(a)   **Current tax** is the amount *actually payable* to the tax authorities in relation to the trading activities of the entity during the period.

(b)   **Deferred tax** is an *accounting measure*, used to match the tax effects of transactions with their accounting impact and thereby produce less distorted results.

You should understand this a little better after working through Section 3.

2.4 Recognition of current tax liabilities and assets

IAS 12 requires any **unpaid tax** in respect of the current or prior periods to be recognised as a **liability**.

Conversely, any **excess tax** paid in respect of current or prior periods over what is due should be recognised as an asset.

Question

In 20X8 Darton Co had taxable profits of $120,000. In the previous year (20X7) income tax on 20X7 profits had been estimated as $30,000.

Required

Calculate tax payable and the charge for 20X8 if the tax due on 20X7 profits was subsequently agreed with the tax authorities as:

(a) $35,000
(b) $25,000

Any under- or over-payments are not settled until the following year's tax payment is due.

Answer

(a)

	$
Tax due on 20X8 profits ($120,000 × 30%)	36,000
Underpayment for 20X7	5,000
Tax charge and liability	41,000

(b)

	$
Tax due on 20X8 profits (as above)	36,000
Overpayment for 20X7	(5,000)
Tax charge and liability	31,000

Alternatively, the rebate due could be shown separately as income in the statement of profit or loss and other comprehensive income and as an asset in the statement of financial position. An offset approach like this is, however, most likely.

Taking this a stage further, IAS 12 also requires recognition as an asset of the benefit relating to any tax loss that can be **carried back** to recover current tax of a previous period. This is acceptable because it is probable that the benefit will flow to the entity *and* it can be reliably measured.

2.5 Example: Tax losses carried back

In 20X7 Eramu Co paid $50,000 in tax on its profits. In 20X8 the company made tax losses of $24,000. The local tax authority rules allow losses to be carried back to offset against current tax of prior years.

Required

Show the tax charge and tax liability for 20X8.

Solution

Tax repayment due on tax losses = 30% × $24,000 = $7,200.
The double entry will be:

DEBIT	Tax receivable (statement of financial position)	$7,200	
CREDIT	Tax repayment (statement of profit or loss)		$7,200

The tax receivable will be shown as an asset until the repayment is received from the tax authorities.

2.6 Measurement

Measurement of current tax liabilities (assets) for the current and prior periods is very simple. They are measured at the **amount expected to be paid to (recovered from) the tax authorities**. The tax rates (and tax laws) used should be those enacted (or substantively enacted) by the reporting date.

2.7 Recognition of current tax

Normally, current tax is recognised as income or expense and included in the net profit or loss for the period, except in three cases.

(a) Tax arising from a **business combination** which is an acquisition is treated differently.

(b) Tax arising from a transaction or event which is recognised as **other comprehensive income and accumulated in equity** (in the same or a different period).

(c) Tax arising from a transaction or event which is recognised directly in equity (in the same or a different period).

The rule in cases (b) and (c) is logical. If a transaction or event is charged or credited to other comprehensive income or directly to equity, rather than to profit or loss, then the related tax should be also. An example of case (c) is where, under IAS 8, an adjustment is made to the **opening balance of retained earnings** due to either a change in accounting policy that is applied retrospectively, or to the correction of a material prior period error.

2.8 Presentation

In the statement of financial position, **tax assets and liabilities** should be shown separately from other assets and liabilities.

Current tax assets and liabilities can be **offset**, but this should happen only when certain conditions apply.

(a) The entity has a **legally enforceable right** to set off the recognised amounts.

(b) The entity intends to settle the amounts on a **net basis**, or to realise the asset and settle the liability at the same time.

The **tax expense (income)** related to the profit or loss from ordinary activities should be shown in the statement of profit or loss.

The **disclosure requirements** of IAS 12 are extensive and we will look at these later in the chapter.

3 Deferred tax

FAST FORWARD

Deferred tax is an accounting measure used to match the tax effects of transactions with their accounting impact. It is unlikely that complicated numerical questions will be set in the exam so concentrate on **understanding** deferred tax.

You may already be aware from your studies of taxation that accounting profits and taxable profits are not the same. There are several reasons for this but they may conveniently be considered under two headings.

(a) **Permanent differences** arise because certain expenditure, such as entertainment of UK customers, is not allowed as a deduction for tax purposes although it is quite properly deducted in arriving at accounting profit. Similarly, certain income (such as UK dividend income) is not subject to tax, although it forms part of accounting profit.

(b) **Temporary differences** arise because certain items are included in the accounts of a period which is different from that in which they are dealt with for taxation purposes.

Deferred taxation is the tax attributable to timing differences.

Key term

> **Deferred tax.** Estimated future tax consequences of transactions and events recognised in the financial statements of the current and previous periods.

Deferred taxation is therefore a means of ironing out the tax inequalities arising from timing differences.

(a) In years when **corporation tax is saved** by temporary differences such as accelerated capital allowances, a charge for deferred taxation is made in the statement of profit or loss and a provision set up in the statement of financial position.

(b) In years when **temporary differences reverse**, because the depreciation charge exceeds the tax allowances available, a deferred tax credit is made in the statement of profit or loss and the statement of financial position provision is reduced.

You should be clear in your mind that the tax actually payable to the tax authorities is the **tax liability**. The credit balance on the deferred taxation account represents an estimate of tax saved because of temporary differences but expected ultimately to become payable when those differences reverse.

The following are the main categories in which temporary differences can occur.

(a) **Accelerated capital allowances.** Tax deductions for the cost of a non-current asset are accelerated or decelerated, ie received before or after the cost of the non-current asset is recognised in the statement of profit or loss.

(b) **Pension liabilities** are accrued in the financial statements but are allowed for tax purposes only when paid or contributed at a later date (pensions are not in the Paper 11 syllabus).

(c) **Interest charges or development costs** are capitalised in the statement of financial position but are treated as revenue expenditure and allowed as incurred for tax purposes.

(d) **Intragroup profits in inventory**, unrealised at group level, are reversed on consolidation.

(e) **Revaluations.** An asset is revalued in the financial statements but the revaluation gain becomes taxable only if and when the asset is sold.

(f) **Unrelieved tax losses.** A tax loss is not relieved against past or present taxable profits but can be carried forward to reduce future taxable profits.

(g) **Unremitted earnings of subsidiaries.** The unremitted earnings of subsidiary and associated undertakings and joint ventures are recognised in the group results but will be subject to further taxation only if and when remitted to the parent undertaking.

Deferred taxation is therefore an accounting convention which is introduced in order to apply the accruals concept to income reporting where timing differences occur. However, **deferred tax assets** are not included in accounts as a rule, because it would not be prudent, given that the recovery of the tax is uncertain.

3.1 Basis of provision

A comprehensive tax allocation system is one in which deferred taxation is computed for every instance of temporary differences: **full provision**. The opposite extreme would be the **nil provision** approach ('**flow through** method'), where only the tax payable in the period would be charged to that period. There is also a middle course called **partial provision** where the effect of timing differences is accepted for to the extent that it is probable that a liability or an asset will crystallise.

The **probability** that a liability or asset would crystallise was assessed by the directors on the basis of **reasonable assumptions**. They had to take into account all relevant information available up to the date on which they approved the financial statements, and also their intentions for the future. Ideally, financial projections of future plans had to be made for a number (undefined) of years ahead. The directors' judgement had to be exercised with prudence.

If a company predicted, for example, that capital expenditure would **continue at the same rate** for the foreseeable future, so that capital allowances and depreciation would remain at the same levels, then no originating or reversing differences of any significance to the continuing trend of the tax charge would arise and so no change to the provision for deferred tax needed to be made (unless there were other significant temporary differences).

3.2 The three different methods compared

Under the **flow-through method**, the tax liability recognised is the expected legal tax liability for the period (ie no provision is made for deferred tax). The main **advantages** of the method are that it is straightforward to apply and the tax liability recognised is closer to many people's idea of a 'real' liability than that recognised under either full or partial provision.

The main **disadvantages** of flow-through are that it can lead to large fluctuations in the tax charge and that it does not allow tax relief for long-term liabilities to be recognised until those liabilities are settled. The method is not used internationally.

The **full provision method** has the **advantage** that it is consistent with general international practice. It also recognises that each temporary difference at the reporting date has an effect on future tax payments. If a company claims an accelerated capital allowance on an item of plant, future tax assessments will be bigger than they would have been otherwise. Future transactions may well affect those assessments still further, but that is not relevant in assessing the position at the reporting date. The **disadvantage** of full provision is that, under certain types of tax system, it gives rise to large liabilities that may fall due only far in the future. The full provision method is the one prescribed by IAS 12.

The **partial provision method** addresses this disadvantage by providing for deferred tax only to the extent that it is expected to be paid in the foreseeable future. This has an obvious intuitive appeal, but its effect is that deferred tax recognised at the reporting date includes the tax effects of future transactions that have not been recognised in the financial statements, and which the reporting company has neither undertaken nor even committed to undertake at that date. It is difficult to reconcile this with the IASB's *Conceptual Framework*, which defines assets and liabilities as arising from past events.

Exam focus point

> You need to understand the concept of deferred tax, it is unlikely that you will need to perform detailed calculations.

It is important that you understand the issues properly so consider the example below.

3.3 Example: The three methods compared

Suppose that Pamella Co begins trading on 1 January 20X7. In its first year it makes profits of $5m, the depreciation charge is $1m and the capital allowances on those assets is $1.5m. The rate of income tax is 33%.

Solution: Flow through method

The tax liability for the year is 33% $(5.0 + 1.0 − 1.5)m = $1.485m. The potential deferred tax liability of 33% × ($1.5m − $1m) is completely ignored and no judgement is required on the part of the preparer.

Solution: Full provision

The tax liability is $1.485m again, but the debit in the statement of profit or loss is increased by the deferred tax liability of 33% × $0.5m = $165,000. The total tax charge is therefore $1,650,000 which is an effective tax rate of 33% on accounting profits (ie 33% × $5.0m). Again, no judgement is involved in using this method.

Solution: Partial provision

Is a deferred tax provision necessary under partial provision? It is now necessary to look ahead at future capital expenditure plans. Will tax allowances exceed depreciation over the next few years? If *yes*, no provision for deferred tax is required. If *no*, then a reversal is expected, ie there is a year in which depreciation is greater than tax allowances. The deferred tax provision is made on the maximum reversal which will be created, and any not provided is disclosed by note.

If we assume that the review of expected future capital expenditure under the partial method required a deferred tax charge of $82,500 (33% × $250,000), we can then summarise the position.

3.4 Summary

The methods can be compared as follows.

Method	Provision $	Disclosure $
Flow-through	–	–
Full provision	165,000	–
Partial provision	82,500	82,500

3.5 IAS 12 *Income tax*

IAS 12 requires entities to provide for temporary differences on a **full, rather than partial provision basis.**

3.6 Objective

The objective of IAS 12 is to ensure that:

(a)   Future tax consequences of past transactions and events are recognised as liabilities or assets in the financial statements

(b)   The financial statements disclose any other special circumstances that may have an effect on future tax charges

3.7 Scope

The IAS applies **to all financial statements that are intended to give a true and fair view** of a reporting entity's financial position and profit or loss (or income and expenditure) for a period. The IAS applies to taxes calculated on the basis of taxable profits, including withholding taxes paid on behalf of the reporting entity.

3.8 Recognition of deferred tax assets and liabilities

Remember!

> **Deferred tax** should be recognised in respect of **all temporary differences that have originated but not reversed by the reporting date**.
>
> Deferred tax should **not be recognised on permanent differences.**

 Question   Timing differences

Can you remember some examples of temporary differences?

Answer

- Accelerated capital allowances
- Pension liabilities accrued but taxed when paid
- Interest charges and development costs capitalised but allowed for tax purposes when incurred
- Unrealised intra-group inventory profits reversed on consolidation
- Revaluation gains
- Tax losses
- Unremitted earnings of subsidiaries, associates and joint ventures recognised in group results

Key term

Permanent differences. Differences between an entity's taxable profits and its results as stated in the financial statements that arise because certain types of income and expenditure are non-taxable or disallowable, or because certain tax charges or allowances have no corresponding amount in the financial statements.

3.8.1 Allowances for non-current asset expenditure

Deferred tax **should be recognised** when the **allowances** for the cost of a non-current asset are **received before or after the cost of the non-current asset is recognised in the statement of profit or loss.** However, if and when **all conditions** for retaining the allowances have been met, the **deferred tax should be reversed**.

If an asset is not being depreciated (and has not otherwise been written down to a carrying amount less than cost), the temporary difference is the amount of tax allowances received.

Most tax allowances are received on a **conditional basis**, ie they are repayable (for example, via a balancing charge) if the assets to which they relate are sold for more than their tax written-down value. However, some, such as industrial buildings allowances, are repayable only if the assets to which they relate are sold within a specified period. Once that period has expired, all conditions for retaining the allowance have been met. At that point, deferred tax that has been recognised (ie on the excess of the allowance over any depreciation) is reversed.

Question

Tax allowances

An industrial building qualifies for a tax allowance when purchased in 20X1. The building is still held by the company in 20Z6. What happens to the deferred tax?

Answer

All the conditions for retaining tax allowances have been met. This means that the temporary differences have become permanent and the deferred tax recognised should be reversed. Before the 25-year period has passed, deferred tax should be provided on the difference between the amount of the industrial building allowance and any depreciation charged on the asset.

3.9 Measurement – discounting

IAS 12 states that deferred tax and liabilities **should not be discounted** because of the complexities and difficulties involved.

3.10 Section summary

- Deferred tax is tax relating to temporary differences.
- Full provision must be made for temporary differences.

Exam focus point

Questions on deferred tax for Paper 11 should be fairly straightforward. It is likely to be tested as part of a larger question rather than a question in its own right.

4 Taxation in company accounts

FAST FORWARD

The statement of financial position liability for tax payable is the tax charge for the year. In the statement of profit or loss the tax charge for the year is adjusted for transfers to or from deferred tax and for prior year under- or over-provisions.

We have now looked at the components of taxation in company accounts. There are two main aspects to be learned:

(a) Taxation on profits in the statement of profit or loss
(b) Taxation payments due, shown as a liability in the statement of financial position

You should note that taxation on other comprehensive income is also disclosed in the statement of profit or loss and other comprehensive income, however this is unlikely to feature at the Paper 11 level.

4.1 Taxation on profits

The tax on profit on ordinary activities is calculated by **aggregating**:

(a) **Income tax** on taxable profits
(b) **Transfers to or from deferred taxation**
(c) Any **under-provision or over-provision** of income tax on profits of previous years

When income tax on profits is calculated for the statement of profit or loss, **the calculation is only an estimate of what the company thinks its tax liability will be. In subsequent dealings with the tax authorities, a different income tax charge might eventually be agreed.**

The difference between the estimated tax on profits for one year and the actual tax charge finally agreed for the year is made as an adjustment to taxation on profits in the following year, **resulting in the disclosure of either an underprovision or an overprovision of tax**.

Question

Tax payable

In the accounting year to 31 December 20X3, Neil Down Co made an operating profit before taxation of $110,000.

Income tax on the operating profit has been estimated as $45,000. In the previous year (20X2) income tax on 20X2 profits had been estimated as $38,000 but it was subsequently agreed at $40,500.

A transfer to the credit of the deferred taxation account of $16,000 will be made in 20X3.

Required

(a) Calculate the tax on profits for 20X3 for disclosure in the accounts.
(b) Calculate the amount of tax payable.

BPP
LEARNING MEDIA

Answer

(a)

	$
Income tax on profits	45,000
Deferred taxation	16,000
Underprovision of tax in previous year $(40,500 – 38,000)	2,500
Tax on profits for 20X3	63,500

(b)

	$
Tax payable on 20X3 profits	45,000

4.2 Taxation in the statement of financial position

It should already be apparent from the previous examples that the income tax charge in the statement of profit or loss will not be the same as income tax liabilities in the statement of financial position.

In the statement of financial position, there are several items which we might expect to find.

(a) **Amounts underprovided/overprovided in the prior year**. These will appear as debits/credits to the tax payable account.

(b) If no tax is payable (or very little), then there might be an **income tax recoverable asset** disclosed in current assets (income tax is normally recovered by offset against the tax liability for the year).

(c) There will usually be a **liability for tax**, possibly including the amounts due in respect of previous years but not yet paid.

(d) We may also find a **liability on the deferred taxation account**. Deferred taxation is shown under 'non-current' in the statement of financial position.

Question

Tax charge

For the year ended 31 July 20X4 Norman Kronkest Co made taxable trading profits of $1,200,000 on which income tax is payable at 30%.

(a) A transfer of $20,000 will be made to the deferred taxation account. The balance on this account was $100,000 before making any adjustments for items listed in this paragraph.

(b) The estimated tax on profits for the year ended 31 July 20X3 was $80,000, but tax has now been agreed at $84,000 and fully paid.

(c) Tax on profits for the year to 31 July 20X4 is payable on 1 May 20X5.

(d) In the year to 31 July 20X4 the company made a capital gain of $60,000 on the sale of some property. This gain is taxable at a rate of 30%.

Required

(a) Calculate the tax charge for the year to 31 July 20X4.

(b) Calculate the tax liabilities in the statement of financial position of Norman Kronkest as at 31 July 20X4.

Answer

(a)

Tax charge for the year	$
(i) Tax on trading profits (30% of $1,200,000)	360,000
Tax on capital gain	18,000
Deferred taxation	20,000
	398,000
Underprovision of taxation in previous years $(84,000 – 80,000)	4,000
Tax charge on profit for the period	402,000

(ii)   *Note.* The statement of profit or loss will show the following.

	$
Profit before taxation	1,260,000
Income tax expense	(402,000)
Profit for the year	858,000

(b)

Deferred taxation	$
Balance brought forward	100,000
Transferred from profit or loss	20,000
Deferred taxation in the statement of financial position	120,000

The tax liability is as follows.

Payable on 1 May 20X5

	$
Tax on profits (30% of $1,200,000)	360,000
Tax on capital gain (30% of $60,000)	18,000
Due on 1 May 20X5	378,000

Summary

	$
Current liabilities	
Tax, payable on 1 May 20X5	378,000
Non-current liabilities	
Deferred taxation	120,000
	498,000

Note: It may be helpful to show the journal entries for these items.

		$	$
DEBIT	Tax charge (statement of profit or loss)	402,000	
CREDIT	Tax payable		*382,000
	Deferred tax		20,000

* This account will show a debit balance of $4,000 until the underprovision is recorded, since payment has already been made: (360,000 + 18,000 + 4,000).

5 Presentation and disclosure of taxation

IAS 12 contains rules for comprehensive presentation and disclosure of taxation items, which are summarised here.

5.1 Presentation of tax assets and liabilities

These should be **presented separately** from other assets and liabilities in the statement of financial position. Deferred tax assets and liabilities should be distinguished from current tax assets and liabilities.

In addition, deferred tax assets/liabilities should *not* be classified as current assets/ liabilities, where an entity makes such a distinction.

There are only limited circumstances where **current tax** assets and liabilities may be **offset**. This should only occur if two things apply.

(a)   The entity has a legally enforceable right to set off the recognised amounts.

(b)   The entity intends either to settle on a net basis, or to realise the asset and settle the liability simultaneously.

Similar criteria apply to the **offset of deferred tax assets and liabilities**.

5.2 Presentation of tax expense

The tax expense or income related to the profit or loss for the year should be presented in the **statement of profit or loss**.

5.3 Disclosure

As you would expect, the major components of tax expense or income should be disclosed separately. These will generally include the following.

(a)   **Current tax expense** (income)

(b)   Any adjustments recognised in the period for **current tax of prior periods** (ie for over-/under-statement in prior years)

(c)   Amount of **deferred tax expense (income)** relating to the origination and reversal of **temporary differences**

(d)   Amount of the benefit arising from a previously unrecognised tax loss, tax credit or temporary difference of a prior period that is used to **reduce current tax expense**

(e)   Amount of the benefit from a previously unrecognised tax loss, tax credit or temporary difference of a prior period that is used to **reduce deferred tax expense**

(f)   Deferred tax expense arising from the **write-down**, or reversal of a previous write-down, of a deferred tax asset

(g)   Amount of tax expense (income) relating to those **changes in accounting policies** and **errors** which are included in the determination of net profit or loss for the period in accordance with IAS 8, because they cannot be accounted for retrospectively.

There are substantial additional disclosures required by the Standard. All these items should be shown separately.

(a)   Aggregate current and deferred tax relating to items that are charged or credited to **equity**

(b)   The amount of income tax relating to each component of other comprehensive income

(c)   An explanation of the relationship between **tax expense (income)** and **accounting profit** in *either* or *both* of the following forms:

    (i)   A numerical reconciliation between tax expense (income) and the product of accounting profit multiplied by the applicable tax rate(s), disclosing also the basis on which the applicable tax rate(s) is (are) computed, *or*

    (ii)   A numerical reconciliation between the average effective tax rate and the applicable tax rate, disclosing also the basis on which the applicable tax rate is computed

(d)   An explanation of **changes in the applicable tax rate(s)** compared to the previous accounting period

(e)   The amount (and expiry date, if any) of **deductible temporary differences**, unused tax losses, and unused tax credits for which no deferred tax is recognised in the statement of financial position

(f)   In respect of each type of **temporary difference**, and in respect of each type of **unused tax loss** and **unused tax credit**:

    (i)   The amount of the deferred tax assets and liabilities recognised in the statement of financial position for each period presented

    (ii)   The amount of the deferred tax income or expense recognised in the statement of profit or loss, if this is not apparent from the changes in the amounts recognised in the statement of financial position

(g)   In respect of **discontinued operations**, the tax expense relating to:

    (i)   The gain or loss on discontinuance

    (ii)   The profit or loss from the ordinary activities of the discontinued operation for the period, together with the corresponding amounts for each prior period presented

In addition, an entity should disclose the amount of a deferred tax asset and the nature of the evidence supporting its recognition, when:

(a)   The utilisation of the deferred tax asset is dependent on future taxable profits in excess of the profits arising from the reversal of existing taxable temporary differences, *and*

(b)   The entity has suffered a loss in either the current or preceding period in the tax jurisdiction to which the deferred tax asset relates.

Chapter roundup

- **Current tax** is the amount payable to the tax authorities in relation to the trading activities of the period.

- **Deferred tax** is an accounting measure, used to match the tax effects of transactions with their accounting impact. It is unlikely that complicated numerical questions will be set in the exam so concentrate on **understanding** deferred tax.

- The statement of financial position liability for tax payable is the tax charge for the year. In the statement of profit or loss the tax charge for the year is adjusted for transfers to or from deferred tax and for prior year under- or over-provisions.

- IAS 12 contains rules for comprehensive presentation and disclosure of taxation items, which are summarised here.

Quick quiz

1   What is the sales tax at 20% on sales of $5,000, if 10% are zero-rated?

2   The tax expense related to the profit for the year should be shown in the statement of profit or loss.

   True   ☐

   False ☐

3   Deferred tax liabilities are the amounts of income taxes payable in future periods in respect of

   ....

4   Give three examples of taxable temporary differences.

5   Which of the following methods of accounting for deferred tax is adopted by IAS 12?

   A   Flow-through method
   B   Differential method
   C   Full provision method
   D   Partial provision method

Answers to quick quiz

1   $900 [(90% × $5,000) × 20%]

2   True

3   Taxable temporary differences

4   Any three of:

- Interest revenue received in arrears
- Depreciation accelerated for tax purposes
- Development costs capitalised in the statement of financial position
- Prepayments
- Sale of goods revenue recognised before the cash is received

5   C

End of chapter question

Deferred tax (AIA November 2007)

Dee For has recently qualified as a pilot and is now intending to set up a private company in the near future to run small charter passenger flights from her home town. Most of her business plan has been written but she has recently learned that the company's forecast statements of profit or loss and other comprehensive income and financial position may be incorrect as she has not taken into account the likely impact of deferred tax on those financial statements. She has therefore asked you for help and, following a meeting, the following facts come to light:

(i)   The aircraft would cost $1m. It would have a life of five years after which, it would have no residual value and will then be scrapped. Depreciation will be on a straight-line basis.

(ii)   The government of the country in which she lives has recently introduced a scheme for new entrepreneurs which provides a tax allowance on capital expenditure of this type of 25% per annum using the reducing balance method. In this country, depreciation is not a deductible expense for tax purposes. Also in this country, a balancing adjustment is allowed whenever the asset is sold or scrapped.

(iii)   Corporate income tax is currently set at 30%. It has remained unchanged for many years now and the government has indicated there are no plans to change it.

(iv)   The company's forecast annual accounting profit before tax is $2m per annum over the next five years.

Required

(a)   Demonstrate the impact of the above on the company's forecast statements of profit or loss and statement of financial position for each of the next five years by comparing the 'nil provision' method with the 'full provision method'.   **(12 marks)**

(b)   Explain the 'partial provision' method and whether it could apply to Dee For's company.   **(3 marks)**

(c)   Explain how your answer to a) would be affected by a government announcement that it intends to increase the corporate income tax rate in the near future.   **(2 marks)**

(Total = 17 marks)

Introduction to groups

Topic list	Syllabus reference
1 Group accounts	11.3
2 Consolidated and separate financial statements	11.3
3 Content of group accounts and group structure	11.3
4 Group accounts: the related parties issue	11.3

Introduction

Consolidation is an extremely important area of the syllabus for both Paper 11 and Paper 13.

For Paper 11, you will cover the basic principles of consolidation and learn to prepare simple group accounts. The more complex aspects of consolidation will be examined in Paper 13.

The key to consolidation questions in the examination is to adopt a logical approach and to practise as many questions as possible.

In this chapter we will look at the major definitions in consolidation. These matters are fundamental to your comprehension of group accounts, so make sure you can understand them and then **learn them**.

1 Group accounts

FAST FORWARD

Many large businesses consist of several companies controlled by one central or administrative company. Together these companies are called a **group**. The controlling company, called the **parent** or **holding company**, will own some or all of the shares in the other companies, called **subsidiaries**.

1.1 Introduction

There are many reasons for businesses to operate as groups; for the goodwill associated with the names of the subsidiaries, for tax or legal purposes and so forth. In many countries, company law requires that the results of a group should be presented as a whole. Unfortunately, it is not possible simply to add all the results together and this chapter and those following will teach you how to **consolidate** all the results of companies within a group.

In traditional accounting terminology, a **group of companies** consists of a **parent company** and one or more **subsidiary companies** which are controlled by the parent company.

1.2 Accounting standards

In May 2011 the IASB issued a number of new or revised standards related to group accounting. We will be looking at five accounting standards in this and the next three chapters.

- IAS 27 (revised) *Separate financial statements*
- IFRS 3 *Business combinations*
- IFRS 10 *Consolidated financial statements (revised in June 2012)*
- IFRS 12 *Disclosure of interests in other entities (revised in June 2012)*
- IAS 28 *Investments in associates and joint ventures*

These standards are all concerned with different aspects of group accounts, but there is some overlap between them, particularly between IFRS 10 and IAS 27.

In this and the next chapter we will concentrate on IAS 27 and IFRS 10, which covers the basic group definitions and consolidation procedures of a parent-subsidiary relationship. First of all, however, we will look at all the important definitions involved in group accounts, which **determine how to treat each particular type of investment** in group accounts.

1.3 Definitions

We will look at some of these definitions in more detail later, but they are useful here in that they give you an overview of all aspects of group accounts.

Exam focus point

All the definitions relating to group accounts are extremely important. You must **learn them** and **understand** their meaning and application.

Key terms

Control. An investor controls an investee when the investor is exposed, or has rights, to variable returns from its involvement with the investee and has the ability to affect those returns through power over the investee.

Power. Existing rights that give the current ability to direct the relevant activities of the investee.

Subsidiary. An entity that is controlled by another entity .

Parent. An entity that controls one or more entities.

Group. A parent and its subsidiaries.

(IFRS 10)

Key terms (cont'd)

Associate. An entity over which an investor has significant influence and which is neither a subsidiary nor an interest in a joint venture. *(IFRS 10)*

Significant influence is the power to participate in the financial and operating policy decisions of an investee but is not control or joint control of those policies. *(IAS 28)*

We can summarise the different types of investment *and* the required accounting for them as follows.

Investment	Criteria	Required treatment in group accounts
Subsidiary	Control	Full consolidation
Associate	Significant influence	Equity accounting (see Chapter 18)
Investment which is none of the above	Asset held for accretion of wealth	As for single company accounts per IFRS 9

1.4 Investments in subsidiaries

The important point here is **control**. In most cases, this will involve the holding company or parent owning a majority of the ordinary shares in the subsidiary (to which normal voting rights are attached). There are circumstances, however, when the parent may own only a minority of the voting power in the subsidiary, *but* the parent still has control.

IFRS 10 provides a definition of control and identifies three separate elements of control:

An investor controls an investee if and only if it has all of the following:

(1) Power over the investee
(2) Exposure to, or rights to, variable returns from its involvement with the investee; and
(3) The ability to use its power over the investee to affect the amount of the investor's returns

If there are changes to one or more of these three elements of control, then an investor should reassess whether it controls an investee.

Power (as defined under Key Terms) can be obtained directly from ownership of the majority of voting rights or can be derived from other rights, such as:

- Rights to appoint, reassign or remove key management personnel who can direct the relevant activities

- Rights to appoint or remove another entity that directs the relevant activities

- Rights to direct the investee to enter into, or veto changes to, transactions for the benefit of the investor

- Other rights, such as those specified in a management contract

Exam focus point

You should learn the contents of the above paragraph as you may be asked to explain or apply them in the exam.

1.4.1 Accounting treatment in group accounts

IFRS 10 requires a parent to present consolidated financial statements, in which the accounts of the parent and subsidiary (or subsidiaries) are combined and presented **as a single entity**.

1.5 Investments in associates

This type of investment is something less than a subsidiary, but more than a simple investment. The key criterion here is **significant influence**. This is defined as the 'power to participate', but *not* to 'control' (which would make the investment a subsidiary).

Significant influence can be determined by the holding of voting rights (usually attached to shares) in the entity. IAS 28 states that if an investor holds **20% or more** of the voting power of the investee, it can be presumed that the investor has significant influence over the investee, *unless* it can be clearly shown that this is not the case.

Significant influence can be presumed *not* to exist if the investor holds **less than 20%** of the voting power of the investee, unless it can be demonstrated otherwise.

The **existence of significant influence** is evidenced in one or more of the following ways.

(a)   Representation on the **board of directors** (or equivalent) of the investee
(b)   Participation in the **policy making process**
(c)   **Material transactions** between investor and investee
(d)   Interchange of management personnel
(e)   Provision of essential technical information

1.5.1 Accounting treatment in group accounts

IAS 28 requires the use of the **equity method** of accounting for investments in associates. This method will be explained in detail in Chapter 18.

Question	Treatments

The section summary after this question will give an augmented version of the table given in Paragraph 1.3 above. Before you look at it, see if you can write out the table yourself.

1.6 Disclosure

(a)   Disclosure requirements previously contained in other standards have been brought together in IFRS 12. The standard requires disclosure of the significant judgments and assumptions made in determining the nature of an interest in another entity or arrangement, and in determining the type of joint arrangement in which an interest is held

(b)   Information about interests in subsidiaries, associates, joint arrangements and structured entities that are not controlled by an investor

1.6.1 Disclosure of subsidiaries

The following disclosures are required in respect of subsidiaries

(a)   The interest that non-controlling interests have in the group's activities and cash flows including the name of the relevant subsidiaries, their principle place of business and the interest and voting rights of non-controlling interests

(b)   Nature and extent of significant restrictions on an investor's ability to use group assets and liabilities

(c)   Nature of the risks associated with an entity's interests in consolidated structured entities such as the provision of financial support

(d)   Consequences of changes in ownership interest in a subsidiary (whether control is lost or not)

1.6.2 Disclosure of associates

(a)   Nature, extent and financial effect of an entity's interests in associates, including the name of the investee, principal place of business, the investor's interest in the investee, method of accounting for the investee and restrictions on the investee's ability to transfer funds to the investor

(b)   Risks associated with an interest in an associate

(c)   Summarised financial information

1.7 Section summary

Investment	Criteria	Required treatment in group accounts
Subsidiary	Control (> 50% rule)	Full consolidation (IFRS 10)
Associate	Significant influence (20%+ rule)	Equity accounting (IAS 28)
Investment which is none of the above	Asset held for accretion of wealth	As for single company accounts (IFRS 9)

2 Consolidated and separate financial statements

IFRS 10 requires a parent to present **consolidated** financial statements.

2.1 Introduction

Key term

> **Consolidated financial statements.** The financial statements of a group in which assets, liabilities, equity, income, expenses and cash flows of the parent and its subsidiaries are presented as those of a single economic entity.
> *(IFRS 10)*

When a parent issues consolidated financial statements, it should consolidate **all subsidiaries**, both foreign and domestic.

2.2 Exemption from preparing group accounts

A parent **need not present** consolidated financial statements if and only if all of the following hold:

(a)   The parent is itself a **wholly-owned subsidiary** or it is a **partially owned subsidiary** of another entity and its other owners, including those not otherwise entitled to vote, have been informed about, and do not object to, the parent not presenting consolidated financial statements

(b)   Its securities are **not publicly traded**

(c)   It is **not in the process of issuing securities** in public securities markets; and

(d)   The **ultimate or intermediate parent** publishes consolidated financial statements that comply with International Financial Reporting Standards

A parent that does not present consolidated financial statements must comply with the IAS 27 rules on separate financial statements (discussed later in this section).

2.3 Potential voting rights

An entity may own share warrants, share call options, or other similar instruments that are **convertible into ordinary shares** in another entity. If these are exercised or converted they may give the entity voting power or reduce another party's voting power over the financial and operating policies of the other entity (potential voting rights). The **existence and effect** of potential voting rights, including potential voting rights held by another entity, should be considered when assessing whether an entity has control over another entity (and therefore has a subsidiary).

2.4 Exclusion of a subsidiary from consolidation

The rules on exclusion of subsidiaries from consolidation are necessarily strict, because this is a common method used by entities to manipulate their results. If a subsidiary which carries a large amount of debt can be excluded, then the gearing of the group as a whole will be improved. In other words, this is a way of taking debt **out of the statement of financial position**.

IAS 27 did originally allow a subsidiary to be excluded from consolidation where **control is intended to be temporary**. This exclusion was then removed by IFRS 5.

Subsidiaries held for sale are accounted for in accordance with IFRS 5 *Non-current assets held for sale and discontinued operations*.

It has been argued in the past that subsidiaries should be excluded from consolidation on the grounds of **dissimilar activities**, ie the activities of the subsidiary are so different to the activities of the other companies within the group that to include its results in the consolidation would be misleading. IAS 27 and IFRS 10 both reject this argument: exclusion on these grounds is not justified because better (relevant) information can be provided about such subsidiaries by consolidating their results and then giving additional information about the different business activities of the subsidiary.

The previous version of IAS 27 permitted exclusion where the subsidiary operates under **severe long-term restrictions** and these significantly impair its ability to transfer funds to the parent. This exclusion has now been **removed**. Control must actually be lost for exclusion to occur.

2.5 Different reporting dates

In most cases, all group companies will prepare accounts to the same reporting date. One or more subsidiaries may, however, prepare accounts to a different reporting date from the parent and the bulk of other subsidiaries in the group.

In such cases the subsidiary may prepare additional statements to the reporting date of the rest of the group, for consolidation purposes. If this is not possible, the subsidiary's accounts may still be used for the consolidation, *provided that* the gap between the reporting dates is **three months or less**.

Where a subsidiary's accounts are drawn up to a different accounting date, **adjustments should be made** for the effects of significant transactions or other events that occur between that date and the parent's reporting date.

2.6 Uniform accounting policies

Consolidated financial statements should be prepared using **the same accounting policies** for like transactions and other events in similar circumstances.

Adjustments must be made where members of a group use different accounting policies, so that their financial statements are suitable for consolidation.

2.7 Date of inclusion/exclusion

IFRS 10 requires the results of subsidiary undertakings to be included in the consolidated financial statements from:

(a)   The date of 'acquisition', ie the **date on which the investor obtains control of the investee**, to
(b)   The date of 'disposal', ie the **date the investor loses control of the investee**.

Once an investment is no longer a subsidiary, it should be treated as an associate under IAS 28 (if applicable) or as an investment under IFRS 9 (see Chapter 21).

2.8 Accounting for subsidiaries and associates in the parent's separate financial statements

A parent company will usually produce its own single company financial statements and these should be prepared in accordance with IAS 27 (revised) *Separate financial statements*. In these statements, investments in subsidiaries and associates included in the consolidated financial statements should be *either*:

(a)   Accounted for at **cost**, *or*
(b)   In accordance with **IFRS 9** (see Chapter 21).

Where subsidiaries are **classified as held for sale** in accordance with IFRS 5 they should be accounted for in accordance with IFRS 5 (see Chapter 9).

2.9 Disclosure – individual financial statements

Where a parent chooses to take advantage of the exemptions from preparing consolidated financial statements (see above) the **separate financial statements** must disclose:

(a)   The fact that the financial statements are separate financial statements; that the exemption from consolidation has been used; the name and country of incorporation of the entity whose consolidated financial statements that comply with IFRSs have been published; and the address where those consolidated financial statements are obtainable

(b)   A list of significant investments in subsidiaries, jointly controlled entities and associates, including the name, country of incorporation, proportion of ownership interest and, if different, proportion of voting power held

(c)   A description of the method used to account for the investments listed under (b).

When a parent prepares separate financial statements in addition to consolidated financial statements, the separate financial statements must disclose:

(a)   The fact that the statements are separate financial statements and the reasons why they have been prepared if not required by law

(b)   Information about investments and the method used to account for them, as above.

2.10 Section summary

You should learn:

*   **Definitions**
*   Rules for **exemption** from preparing consolidated financial statements
*   **Disclosure**

3 Content of group accounts and group structure

FAST FORWARD   It is important to distinguish between the parent company **individual accounts** and the **group accounts**.

3.1 Introduction

The information contained in the individual statements of a parent company and each of its subsidiaries does not give a picture of the group's total activities. A **separate set of group statements** can be prepared from the individual ones. Remember that a group has no separate (legal) existence, except for accounting purposes.

Consolidated financial statements are one form of group accounts which combines the information contained in the separate accounts of a holding company and its subsidiaries as if they were the accounts of a single entity. 'Group accounts' and 'consolidated accounts' are terms often used synonymously.

In simple terms a set of consolidated accounts is prepared by **adding together** the assets and liabilities of the parent company and each subsidiary. The **whole** of the assets and liabilities of each company are included, even though some subsidiaries may be only partly owned. The 'equity and liabilities' section of the statement of financial position will indicate how much of the net assets are attributable to the group and how much to outside investors in partly owned subsidiaries. These **outside investors** are known as the **non-controlling interest**.

Key term

> **Non-controlling interest.** The equity in a subsidiary not attributable, directly or indirectly, to a parent.
> *(IFRS 3, IAS 27)*

Non-controlling interest should be presented in the consolidated statement of financial position **within equity, separately from the parent shareholders' equity**.

Most parent companies present their own individual accounts and their group accounts in a single **package**. The package typically comprises the following.

- **Parent company financial statements**, which will include' investments in subsidiary undertakings' as an asset in the statement of financial position, and income from subsidiaries (dividends) in the statement of profit or loss
- **Consolidated statement of financial position**
- **Consolidated statement of profit or loss and other comprehensive income** (or separate statement of profit or loss)
- **Consolidated statement of cash flows**

It may not be necessary to publish all of the parent company's financial statements, depending on local or national regulations.

3.2 Group structure

With the difficulties of definition and disclosure dealt with, let us now look at group structures. The simplest are those in which a parent company has only a **direct interest** in the shares of its subsidiary companies. For example:

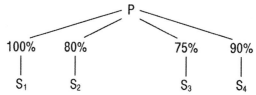

S_1 Co is a wholly owned subsidiary of P Co. S_2 Co, S_3 Co and S_4 Co are partly owned subsidiaries; a proportion of the shares in these companies is held by outside investors.

Often a parent will have **indirect holdings** in its subsidiary companies. This can lead to more complex group structures.

P Co owns 51% of the equity shares in S Co, which is therefore its subsidiary. S Co in its turn owns 51% of the equity shares in SS Co. SS Co is therefore a subsidiary of S Co and consequently a subsidiary of P Co. SS Co would describe S Co as its parent (or holding) company and P Co as its ultimate parent company.

Note that although P Co can control the assets and business of SS Co by virtue of the chain of control, its interest in the assets of SS Co is only 26%. This can be seen by considering a dividend of $100 paid by SS Co: as a 51% shareholder, S Co would receive $51; P Co would have an interest in 51% of this $51 = $26.01.

	Question	Consolidated accounts

During the time until your examination you should obtain as many sets of the published accounts of large companies in your country as possible. Examine the accounting policies in relation to subsidiary and associated companies and consider how these policies are shown in the accounting and consolidation treatment. Consider the effect of any disposals during the year. Also, look at all the disclosures made relating to fair values, goodwill etc and match them to the disclosure requirements outlined in this chapter and in subsequent chapters on IFRS 3 and IAS 28.

Alternatively (or additionally) you should attempt to obtain such information from the financial press.

Exam focus point

You will not be tested on complex group structures in Paper 11. Your exam will not feature sub-subsidiaries, but you will meet this topic again in Paper 13.

4 Group accounts: the related parties issue

 FAST FORWARD

Parent companies and subsidiaries are **related parties** as per IAS 24. Bear in mind that this relationship can be exploited.

IAS 24 draws attention to the significance of related party relationships and transactions – that transactions between the parties may not be 'at arm's length' and that users of the accounts must be made aware of this, as it may affect their view of the financial statements.

4.1 Individual company accounts

The relationship between a parent and a subsidiary is the most obvious example of a related party relationship and it offers a number of opportunities for manipulating results. Some of these may be aimed at improving the parent's individual financial statements.

Any of the following could take place:

- The subsidiary sells goods to the parent company at an artificially low price. This increases parent company profit while reducing profit in the subsidiary, thus increasing profit available for distribution to parent company shareholders at the expense of the non-controlling interest.

- The parent sells goods to the subsidiary at an artificially high price. This has the same result as above.

- The subsidiary makes a loan to the parent at an artificially low rate of interest or the parent makes a loan to the subsidiary at an artificially high rate of interest. The loans will be cancelled on consolidation but the interest payments will transfer profits from the subsidiary to the parent.

- The parent can sell an asset to the subsidiary at an amount in excess of its carrying amount. This again serves to transfer profit (and cash) to the parent.

4.2 Consolidated accounts

The transactions above seek to improve the **individual** parent company accounts at the expense of the individual subsidiary accounts. Dividends are paid to shareholders on the basis of these individual company financial statements, not the consolidated financial statements.

The tightening up of the opportunities for excluding a subsidiary from consolidation under IAS 27 have reduced the opportunities for improving the appearance of the **consolidated** financial statements. Prior to this, a number of possibilities could be exploited:

- A group could obtain loans via a subsidiary, which was not then consolidated. The loan would not appear in the consolidated statement of financial position and group gearing (% of capital provided by loans) would appear lower than it actually was.

- Sale and leaseback transactions could be carried out in which assets were sold to a non-consolidated subsidiary and leased back under an operating lease. This enabled the asset and its associated borrowings to be removed from the statement of financial position.

4.3 Disposal of subsidiaries

While the situations above are all concerned with improving the appearance of the parent company or group financial statements at the expense of those of the subsidiary, there may be occasions where the **opposite** is the intention.

For instance, when a parent company has decided to dispose of its shares in a poorly-performing subsidiary, it may seek to enhance the results of that subsidiary for the purpose of selling at a profit. In this case, transactions such as those at 4.1 above may be undertaken in the other direction – to transfer profit from the **parent** to the **subsidiary**.

4.4 Effect on trading

Even where no related party transactions have taken place, the parent/subsidiary relationship can still affect how the parties do business. For instance if, prior to acquisition by the parent, the subsidiary had a major customer or supplier who was a competitor of the parent, that trading arrangement can be expected to cease. The subsidiary may itself have been a competitor of the parent, in which case it may now have had to withdraw from certain markets in favour of the parent.

Look out for any of these issues in a consolidated accounts question.

Chapter roundup

- Many large businesses consist of several companies controlled by one central or administrative company. Together these companies are called a **group**. The controlling company, called the **parent** or **holding company**, will own some or all of the shares in the other companies, called **subsidiaries**.

- IFRS 10 requires a parent to present **consolidated** financial statements.

- It is important to distinguish between the parent company **individual accounts** and the **group accounts**.

- Parent companies and subsidiaries are **related parties** as per IAS 24. Bear in mind that this relationship can be exploited.

Quick quiz

1   Define a 'subsidiary'.

2   When can control be assumed?

3   What accounting treatment does IFRS 10 require of a parent company?

4   When is a parent exempted from preparing consolidated financial statements?

5   Under what circumstances should subsidiaries be excluded from consolidation?

6   How should an investment in a subsidiary be accounted for in the separate financial statements of the parent?

7   What is a non-controlling interest?

Answers to quick quiz

1 An entity that is controlled by another entity.

2 When the investor has rights to variable returns from the investee and is able to affect those returns by its power over the investee.

3 The accounts of parent and subsidiary are combined and presented as a single entity.

4 When the parent is itself a wholly owned subsidiary, or a partially owned subsidiary and the non-controlling interests do not object, when its securities are not publicly traded and when its ultimate or intermediate parent publishes IFRS-compliant financial statements.

5 Very rarely, if at all. See Section 2.4.

6 (a) At cost, or
   (b) In accordance with IFRS 9.

7 The equity in a subsidiary not attributable, directly or indirectly, to a parent.

End of chapter question

Usefulness

Explain why consolidated financial statements are useful to the users of financial statements (as opposed to just the parent company's separate (entity) financial statements).

The consolidated statement of financial position

16

Introduction

This chapter introduces the **basic procedures** required in consolidation and gives a formal step plan for carrying out a statement of financial position consolidation. This step procedure should be useful to you as a starting guide for answering any question, but remember that you cannot rely on it to answer the question for you.

Each question must be approached and **answered on its own merits**. Examiners often put small extra or different problems in because, as they are always reminding students, it is not possible to 'rote-learn' consolidation.

The **method of consolidation** shown here uses schedules for workings (retained earnings, non-controlling interest etc) rather than the ledger accounts used in some other texts. This is because we believe that ledger accounts lead students to 'learn' the consolidation journals without thinking about what they are doing – always a dangerous practice in consolidation questions.

There are plenty of questions in this chapter – work through *all* of them carefully.

1 IFRS 10 Summary of consolidation procedures

IFRS 10 sets out the basic procedures for preparing consolidated financial statements.

1.1 Basic procedure

The financial statements of a parent and its subsidiaries are **combined on a line-by-line basis** by adding together like items of assets, liabilities, equity, income and expenses.

The following steps are then taken, in order that the consolidated financial statements should **show financial information about the group as if it was a single entity**.

(a)   The carrying amount of the parent's **investment in each subsidiary** and the parent's **portion of equity** of each subsidiary are **eliminated or cancelled**

(b)   **Non-controlling interests in the net income of consolidated subsidiaries** are adjusted against group income, to arrive at the net income attributable to the owners of the parent

(c)   **Non-controlling interests** in the net assets of consolidated subsidiaries should be presented separately in the consolidated statement of financial position

Other matters to be dealt with include the following.

(a)   **Goodwill on consolidation** should be dealt with according to IFRS 3
(b)   **Dividends paid** by a subsidiary must be accounted for

IFRS 10 states that all intragroup balances and transactions, and the resulting **unrealised profits**, should be **eliminated in full. Unrealised losses** resulting from intragroup transactions should also be eliminated *unless* cost can be recovered. This will be explained later in this chapter.

1.2 Cancellation and part cancellation

The preparation of a consolidated statement of financial position, in a very simple form, consists of two procedures.

(a)   Take the individual accounts of the parent company and each subsidiary and **cancel out items** which appear as an asset in one company and a liability in another.

(b)   Add together all the uncancelled assets and liabilities throughout the group.

Items requiring cancellation may include the following.

(a)   The asset **'shares in subsidiary companies'** which appears in the parent company's accounts will be matched with the liability 'share capital' in the subsidiaries' accounts.

(b)   There may be **intra-group trading** within the group. For example, S Co may sell goods on credit to P Co. P Co would then be a receivable in the accounts of S Co, while S Co would be a payable in the accounts of P Co.

1.3 Example: Cancellation

P Co regularly sells goods to its one subsidiary company, S Co, which it has owned since S Co's incorporation. The statement of financial position of the two companies on 31 December 20X6 are given below.

STATEMENT OF FINANCIAL POSITION AS AT 31 DECEMBER 20X6

	P Co $	S Co $
Assets		
Non-current assets		
Property, plant and equipment	35,000	45,000
Investment in 40,000 $1 shares in S Co at cost	40,000	
	75,000	

	P Co $	S Co $
Current assets		
Inventories	16,000	12,000
Receivables: S Co	2,000	
Other	6,000	9,000
Cash at bank	1,000	
Total assets	100,000	66,000
Equity and liabilities		
Equity		
40,000 $1 ordinary shares		40,000
70,000 $1 ordinary shares	70,000	
Retained earnings	16,000	19,000
	86,000	59,000
Current liabilities		
Bank overdraft		3,000
Payables: P Co		2,000
Payables: Other	14,000	2,000
Total equity and liabilities	100,000	66,000

Required

Prepare the consolidated statement of financial position of P Co at 31 December 20X6.

Solution

The cancelling items are:

(a) P Co's asset 'investment in shares of S Co' ($40,000) cancels with S Co's liability 'share capital' ($40,000);

(b) P Co's asset 'receivables: S Co' ($2,000) cancels with S Co's liability 'payables: P Co' ($2,000).

The remaining assets and liabilities are added together to produce the following consolidated statement of financial position.

P CO
CONSOLIDATED STATEMENT OF FINANCIAL POSITION AS AT 31 DECEMBER 20X6

Assets	$	$
Non-current assets		
Property, plant and equipment		80,000
Current assets		
Inventories	28,000	
Receivables	15,000	
Cash at bank	1,000	
		44,000
Total assets		124,000
Equity and liabilities		
Equity		
70,000 $1 ordinary shares	70,000	
Retained earnings	35,000	
	105,000	
Current liabilities		
Bank overdraft	3,000	
Payables	16,000	
		19,000
Total equity and liabilities		124,000

Note the following

(a)   P Co's bank balance is **not netted off** with S Co's bank overdraft. To offset one against the other would be less informative and would conflict with the principle that assets and liabilities should not be netted off.

(b)   The share capital in the consolidated statement of financial position is the **share capital of the parent company alone**. This must *always* be the case, no matter how complex the consolidation, because the share capital of subsidiary companies must *always* be a wholly cancelling item.

1.4 Part cancellation

An item may appear in the statements of financial position of a parent company and its subsidiary, but not at the same amounts.

(a)   The parent company may have acquired **shares in the subsidiary** at a price **greater or less than their par value**. The asset will appear in the parent company's accounts at cost, while the liability will appear in the subsidiary's accounts at par value. This raises the issue of **goodwill**, which is dealt with later in this chapter.

(b)   Even if the parent company acquired shares at par value, it **may not** have **acquired all the shares of the subsidiary** (so the subsidiary may be only partly owned). This raises the issue of **non-controlling interests**, which are also dealt with later in this chapter.

(c)   The inter-company trading balances may be out of step because of **goods or cash in transit**.

(d)   One company may have **issued loan stock** of which a **proportion only** is taken up by the other company.

The following question illustrates the techniques needed to deal with items (c) and (d) above. The procedure is to **cancel as far as possible**. The remaining uncancelled amounts will appear in the consolidated statement of financial position.

(a)   **Uncancelled loan stock** will appear as a **liability of the group**.

(b)   **Uncancelled balances on intra-group accounts** represent **goods or cash in t**ransit, which will appear in the consolidated statement of financial position.

Question	Cancellation

The statements of financial position of P Co and of its subsidiary S Co have been made up to 30 June. P Co has owned all the ordinary shares and 40% of the loan stock of S Co since its incorporation.

P CO
STATEMENT OF FINANCIAL POSITION AS AT 30 JUNE

	$	$
Assets		
Non-current assets		
Property, plant and equipment	120,000	
Investment in S Co, at cost		
80,000 ordinary shares of $1 each	80,000	
$20,000 of 12% loan stock in S Co	20,000	
		220,000
Current assets		
Inventories	50,000	
Receivables	40,000	
Current account with S Co	18,000	
Cash	4,000	
		112,000
Total assets		332,000

	$	$
Equity and liabilities		
Equity		
Ordinary shares of $1 each, fully paid	100,000	
Retained earnings	95,000	
		195,000
Non-current liabilities		
10% loan stock		75,000
Current liabilities		
Payables	47,000	
Taxation	15,000	
		62,000
Total equity and liabilities		332,000

S CO
STATEMENT OF FINANCIAL POSITION AS AT 30 JUNE

	$	$
Assets		
Property, plant and equipment		100,000
Current assets		
Inventories	60,000	
Receivables	30,000	
Cash	6,000	
		96,000
Total assets		196,000
Equity and liabilities		
Equity		
80,000 ordinary shares of $1 each, fully paid	80,000	
Retained earnings	28,000	
		108,000
Non-current liabilities		
12% loan stock		50,000
Current liabilities		
Payables	16,000	
Taxation	10,000	
Current account with P Co	12,000	
		38,000
Total equity and liabilities		196,000

The difference on current account arises because of goods in transit.

Required

Prepare the consolidated statement of financial position of P Co.

Answer

P CO
CONSOLIDATED STATEMENT OF FINANCIAL POSITION AS AT 30 JUNE

	$	$
Assets		
Non-current assets		
Property, plant and equipment (120,000 + 100,000)		220,000
Current assets		
Inventories (50,000 + 60,000)	110,000	
Goods in transit (18,000 – 12,000)	6,000	
Receivables (40,000 + 30,000)	70,000	
Cash (4,000 + 6,000)	10,000	
		196,000
Total assets		416,000
Equity and liabilities		
Equity		
Ordinary shares of $1 each, fully paid (parent)	100,000	
Retained earnings (95,000 + 28,000)	123,000	
		223,000
Non-current liabilities		
10% loan stock	75,000	
12% loan stock (50,000 × 60%)	30,000	
		105,000
Current liabilities		
Payables (47,000 + 16,000)	63,000	
Taxation (15,000 + 10,000)	25,000	
		88,000
Total equity and liabilities		416,000

Note especially how:

(a)   The uncancelled loan stock in S Co becomes a liability of the group
(b)   The goods in transit is the difference between the current accounts ($18,000 – $12,000)
(c)   The investment in S Co's shares is cancelled against S Co's share capital

2 Non-controlling interests

FAST FORWARD

In the consolidated statement of financial position it is necessary to distinguish **non-controlling interests** from those net assets attributable to the group and financed by shareholders' equity.

2.1 Introduction

It was mentioned earlier that the total assets and liabilities of subsidiary companies are included in the consolidated statement of financial position, even in the case of subsidiaries which are only partly owned. A proportion of the net assets of such subsidiaries in fact belongs to investors from outside the group (**non-controlling interests**).

IFRS 3 allows two alternative ways of calculating non-controlling interest in the group statement of financial position. Non-controlling interest can be valued at:

(a)   Its proportionate share of the fair value of the subsidiary's net assets; or

(b)   Full (or fair) value (usually based on the market value of the shares held by the non-controlling interest).

The following example shows non-controlling interest calculated at its proportionate share of the subsidiary's net assets. This is the method you will be required to use in Paper 11.

2.2 Example: non-controlling interest

P Co has owned 75% of the share capital of S Co since the date of S Co's incorporation. Their latest statements of financial position are given below.

P CO
STATEMENT OF FINANCIAL POSITION

	$	$
Assets		
Non-current assets		
Property, plant and equipment	50,000	
30,000 $1 ordinary shares in S Co at cost	30,000	
		80,000
Current assets		45,000
Total assets		125,000
Equity and liabilities		
Equity		
80,000 $1 ordinary shares	80,000	
Retained earnings	25,000	
		105,000
Current liabilities		20,000
Total equity and liabilities		125,000

S CO
STATEMENT OF FINANCIAL POSITION

	$	$
Assets		
Property, plant and equipment		35,000
Current assets		35,000
Total assets		70,000
Equity and liabilities		
Equity		
40,000 $1 ordinary shares	40,000	
Retained earnings	10,000	
		50,000
Current liabilities		20,000
Total equity and liabilities		70,000

Required

Prepare the consolidated statement of financial position.

Solution

All of S Co's net assets are consolidated despite the fact that the company is only 75% owned. The amount of net assets attributable to non-controlling interests is calculated as follows.

	$
Non-controlling share of share capital (25% × $40,000)	10,000
Non-controlling share of retained earnings (25% × $10,000)	2,500
	12,500

Of S Co's share capital of $40,000, $10,000 is included in the figure for non-controlling interest, while $30,000 is cancelled with P Co's asset 'investment in S Co'.

Of S Co's retained earnings of $10,000, $2,500 is included in the figure for non-controlling interest, while $7,500 is included in group retained earnings.

The consolidated statement of financial position can now be prepared.

P GROUP
CONSOLIDATED STATEMENT OF FINANCIAL POSITION

	$	$
Assets		
Property, plant and equipment		85,000
Current assets		80,000
Total assets		165,000
Equity and liabilities		
Equity attributable to owners of the parent		
Share capital	80,000	
Retained earnings $(25,000 + (75% × $10,000))	32,500	
		112,500
Non-controlling interest		12,500
		125,000
Current liabilities		40,000
Total equity and liabilities		165,000

2.3 Procedure

(a) Aggregate the assets and liabilities in the statement of financial position ie 100% P + 100% S irrespective of how much P actually owns.

This shows the amount of net assets **controlled** by the group.

(b) Share capital is that of the parent only.

(c) Balance of subsidiary's reserves are consolidated (after cancelling any intra-group items).

(d) Calculate the non-controlling interest share of the subsidiary's net assets (share capital plus reserves).

Question

Set out below are the draft statement of financial position of P Co and its subsidiary S Co. You are required to prepare the consolidated statement of financial position. The non-controlling interest is valued at its proportional share of the fair value of the subsidiary's net assets.

P CO

	$	$
Assets		
Non-current assets		
Property, plant and equipment		31,000
Investment in S Co		
12,000 $1 ordinary shares at cost	12,000	
$8,000 10% loan stock at cost	8,000	
		20,000
		51,000
Current assets		21,000
Total assets		72,000
Equity and liabilities		
Equity		
Ordinary shares of $1 each	40,000	
Retained earnings	22,000	
		62,000
Current liabilities		10,000
Total equity and liabilities		72,000

S CO

	$	$
Assets		
Property, plant and equipment		34,000
Current assets		32,000
Total assets		66,000
Equity and liabilities		
Equity		
Ordinary shares of $1 each	20,000	
Revaluation surplus	6,000	
Retained earnings	4,000	
		30,000
Non-current liabilities		
10% loan stock		26,000
Current liabilities		10,000
Total equity and liabilities		66,000

Answer

The group structure is:

P Co
| 60%
↓
S Co

Partly cancelling items are the components of P Co's investment in S Co, ie ordinary shares, loan stock. Non-controlling shareholders have an interest in 40% (8,000/20,000) of S Co's ordinary shares, including reserves.

You should now aggregate the assets and liabilities and produce workings for non-controlling interest, revaluation surplus and retained earnings as follows.

Workings

1	*Revaluation surplus*	
		$
	P Co	–
	Share of S Co's revaluation surplus (60% × 6,000)	3,600
		3,600

2	*Retained earnings*	
		$
	P Co	22,000
	Share of S Co's retained earnings (60% × 4,000)	2,400
		24,400

3	*Non-controlling interest*	
		$
	S Co's net assets (66,000 – 36,000)	30,000
	× 40%	12,000

The results of the workings are now used to construct the consolidated statement of financial position.

P GROUP
CONSOLIDATED STATEMENT OF FINANCIAL POSITION

	$	$
Assets		
Property, plant and equipment		65,000
Current assets		53,000
Total assets		118,000
Equity and liabilities		
Equity attributable to owners of the parent		
Ordinary shares of $1 each	40,000	
Revaluation surplus (W1)	3,600	
Retained earnings (W2)	24,400	
		68,000
Non-controlling interest (W3)		12,000
		80,000
Non-current liabilities		
10% loan stock (26,000 – 8,000)		18,000
Current liabilities		20,000
Total equity and liabilities		118,000

Notes

(a) S Co is a subsidiary of P Co because P Co owns 60% of its ordinary capital.

(b) As always, the share capital in the consolidated statement of financial position is that of the parent company alone. The share capital in S Co's statement of financial position was partly cancelled against the investment shown in P Co's statement of financial position, while the uncancelled portion was credited to non-controlling interest.

(c) The figure for non-controlling interest comprises the interest of outside investors in the share capital and reserves of the subsidiary. The uncancelled portion of S Co's loan stock is not shown as part of non-controlling interest but is disclosed separately as a liability of the group.

3 Dividends paid by a subsidiary

When a subsidiary company pays a **dividend** during the year the accounting treatment is not difficult. Suppose S Co, a 60% subsidiary of P Co, pays a dividend of $1,000 on the last day of its accounting period. Its total reserves before paying the dividend stood at $5,000.

(a) $400 of the dividend is paid to non-controlling shareholders. The cash leaves the group and will not appear anywhere in the consolidated statement of financial position.

(b) The parent company receives $600 of the dividend, debiting cash and crediting profit or loss. This will be cancelled on consolidation.

(c) The remaining balance of retained earnings in S Co's statement of financial position ($4,000) will be consolidated in the normal way. The group's share (60% × $4,000 = $2,400) will be included in group retained earnings in the statement of financial position; the non-controlling interest share (40% × $4,000 = $1,600) is credited to the non-controlling interest account in the statement of financial position.

However, the situation is more complicated when a subsidiary pays a dividend shortly after acquisition and some of that dividend is deemed to been paid from pre-acquisition profits. This situation is considered in Section 10.

4 Goodwill arising on consolidation

FAST FORWARD

> **Goodwill** is the excess of the amount transferred plus the amount of the non-controlling interests over fair value of the net assets of the subsidiary.

4.1 Accounting

To begin with, **we will examine the entries made by the parent company in its own statement of financial position when it acquires shares.**

When a company P Co wishes to **purchase shares** in a company S Co it must pay the previous owners of those shares. The most obvious form of payment would be in **cash**. Suppose P Co purchases all 40,000 $1 shares in S Co and pays $60,000 cash to the previous shareholders in consideration. The entries in P Co's books would be:

DEBIT	Investment in S Co at cost	$60,000	
CREDIT	Bank		$60,000

However, the previous shareholders might be prepared to accept some other form of consideration. For example, they might accept an agreed number of **shares** in P Co. P Co would then issue new shares in the agreed number and allot them to the former shareholders of S Co. This kind of deal might be attractive to

P Co since it avoids the need for a heavy cash outlay. The former shareholders of S Co would retain an indirect interest in that company's profitability via their new holding in its parent company.

Continuing the example, suppose that instead of $60,000 cash the shareholders of S Co agreed to accept one $1 ordinary share in P Co for every two $1 ordinary shares in S Co. P Co would then need to issue and allot 20,000 new $1 shares. How would this transaction be recorded in the books of P Co?

The former shareholders of S Co have presumably agreed to accept 20,000 shares in P Co because they consider each of those shares to have a value of $3. This gives us the following method of recording the transaction in P Co's books.

DEBIT	Investment in S Co	$60,000	
CREDIT	Share capital		$20,000
	Share premium account		$40,000

The amount which P Co records in its books as the cost of its investment in S Co may be more or less than the book value of the assets it acquires. Suppose that S Co in the previous example has nil reserves and nil liabilities, so that its share capital of $40,000 is balanced by tangible assets with a book value of $40,000. For simplicity, assume that the book value of S Co's assets is the same as their market or fair value.

Now when the directors of P Co agree to pay $60,000 for a 100% investment in S Co they must believe that, in addition to its tangible assets of $40,000, S Co must also have intangible assets worth $20,000. This amount of $20,000 paid over and above the value of the tangible assets acquired is called **goodwill arising on consolidation** (sometimes **premium on acquisition**).

Following the normal cancellation procedure the $40,000 share capital in S Co's statement of financial position could be cancelled against $40,000 of the 'investment in S Co' in the statement of financial position of P Co. This would leave a $20,000 debit uncancelled in the parent company's accounts and this $20,000 would appear in the consolidated statement of financial position under the caption 'Intangible non-current assets: goodwill arising on consolidation'.

4.2 Goodwill and pre-acquisition profits

Up to now we have assumed that S Co had nil retained earnings when its shares were purchased by P Co. Assuming instead that S Co had earned profits of $8,000 in the period before acquisition, its statement of financial position just before the purchase would look as follows.

	$
Total assets	48,000
Share capital	40,000
Retained earnings	8,000
	48,000

If P Co now purchases all the shares in S Co it will acquire total assets worth $48,000 at a cost of $60,000. Clearly in this case S Co's intangible assets (goodwill) are being valued at $12,000. It should be apparent that any earnings retained by the subsidiary **prior to its acquisition** by the parent company must be **incorporated in the cancellation** process so as to arrive at a figure for goodwill arising on consolidation. In other words, not only S Co's share capital, but also its **pre-acquisition** retained earnings, must be cancelled against the asset 'investment in S Co' in the accounts of the parent company. The uncancelled balance of $12,000 appears in the consolidated statement of financial position.

The consequence of this is that **any pre-acquisition retained earnings of a subsidiary company are not aggregated with the parent company's retained earnings** in the consolidated statement of financial position. The figure of consolidated retained earnings comprises the retained earnings of the parent company plus the **post-acquisition retained earnings only of subsidiary companies**. The post-acquisition retained earnings are simply retained earnings now *less* retained earnings at acquisition.

4.3 Example: Goodwill and pre-acquisition profits

Sing Co acquired the ordinary shares of Wing Co on 31 March when the draft statements of financial position of each company were as follows.

SING CO
STATEMENT OF FINANCIAL POSITION AS AT 31 MARCH

	$
Assets	
Non-current assets	
Investment in 50,000 shares of Wing Co at cost	80,000
Current assets	40,000
Total assets	120,000
Equity and liabilities	
Equity	
Ordinary shares	75,000
Retained earnings	45,000
Total equity and liabilities	120,000

WING CO
STATEMENT OF FINANCIAL POSITION AS AT 31 MARCH

	$
Current assets	60,000
Equity	
50,000 ordinary shares of $1 each	50,000
Retained earnings	10,000
	60,000

Prepare the consolidated statement of financial position as at 31 March.

Solution

The technique to adopt here is to produce a new working: 'Goodwill'. A proforma working is set out below.

Goodwill

	$	$
Consideration transferred		X
Net assets acquired as represented by:		
Ordinary share capital	X	
Share premium	X	
Retained earnings on acquisition	X	
		(X)
Goodwill		X

Applying this to our example the working will look like this.

	$	$
Consideration transferred		80,000
Net assets acquired as represented by:		
Ordinary share capital	50,000	
Retained earnings on acquisition	10,000	
		(60,000)
Goodwill		20,000

SING CO
CONSOLIDATED STATEMENT OF FINANCIAL POSITION AS AT 31 MARCH

	$
Assets	
Non-current assets	
Goodwill arising on consolidation (W)	20,000
Current assets (40,000 + 60,000)	100,000
	120,000
Equity	
Ordinary shares	75,000
Retained earnings	45,000
	120,000

4.4 Goodwill and non-controlling interest

Now let us look at what would happen if Sing Co had obtained less than 100% of the shares of Wing Co.

If Sing Co had paid $70,000 for 80% of the shares in Wing Co, the goodwill working would be as follows:

	$
Consideration transferred	70,000
Non-controlling interest (60,000 × 20%)	
Net assets acquired	(60,000)
Goodwill	22,000

4.5 Impairment of goodwill

Goodwill arising on consolidation is subjected to an annual impairment review and impairment may be expressed as an amount or as a percentage. The double entry to write off the impairment is:
Dr Group retained earnings   Cr Goodwill.

4.6 Gain on a bargain purchase

Goodwill arising on consolidation is one form of **purchased goodwill**, and is governed by IFRS 3. As explained in an earlier chapter IFRS 3 requires that goodwill arising on consolidation should **be capitalised in the consolidated statement of financial position** and **reviewed for impairment every year**.

Goodwill arising on consolidation is the difference between the cost of an acquisition and the value of the subsidiary's net assets acquired. This difference can be **negative**: the aggregate of the fair values of the separable net assets acquired may **exceed** what the parent company paid for them. This is often referred to as negative goodwill. IFRS 3 refers to this as a 'bargain purchase'. In this situation:

(a)   An entity should first **re-assess** the amounts at which it has measured both the cost of the combination and the acquiree's identifiable net assets. This exercise should **identify any errors.**

(b)   Any **excess remaining** should be **recognised immediately in profit or loss**.

4.7 Forms of consideration

The consideration paid by the parent for the shares in the subsidiary can take different forms and this will affect the calculation of goodwill. Here are some examples:

4.7.1 Contingent consideration

The parent acquired 60% of the subsidiary's $100m share capital on 1 January 20X6 for a cash payment of $150m and a further payment of $50m on 31 March 20X7 if the subsidiary's post acquisition profits have exceeded an agreed figure by that date.

In the financial statements for the year to 31 December 20X6 $50m will be added to the cost of the combination, discounted as appropriate.

IFRS 3 requires the acquisition-date **fair value** of contingent consideration to be recognised as part of the consideration for the acquiree. In an examination question students will be told the acquisition-date fair value or told how to calculate it.

The acquirer may be required to pay contingent consideration in the form of equity or of a debt instrument or cash. A debt instrument should be presented as under IAS 32. Contingent consideration can also be an asset, if the consideration has already been transferred and the acquirer has the right to require the return of some of it, if certain considerations are met.

Note: The previous version of IFRS 3 only required contingent consideration to be recognised if it was **probable** that it would become payable. IFRS 3 revised dispenses with this requirement – **all contingent consideration is now recognised**. It is possible that the fair value of the contingent consideration may change after the acquisition date. If this is due to additional information obtained that affects the position at acquisition date goodwill should be remeasured. If the change is due to events after the acquisition date (such as a higher earnings target has been met, so more is payable) it should be accounted for under IAS 39 if the consideration is in the form of a financial instrument (such as loan notes) or under IAS 37 as an increase in a provision if it is cash. Any equity instrument is not remeasured.

4.7.2 Deferred consideration

An agreement may be made that part of the consideration for the combination will be paid at a future date. This consideration will therefore be discounted to its present value using the acquiring entity's cost of capital.

Example

The parent acquired 75% of the subsidiary's 80m $1 shares on 1 Jan 20X6. It paid $3.50 per share and agreed to pay a further $108m on 1 Jan 20X7.

The parent company's cost of capital is 8%.

In the financial statements for the year to 31 December 20X6 the cost of the combination will be as follows:

	$m
80m shares × 75% × $3.50	210
Deferred consideration:	
$108m × 1/1.08	100
Total consideration	310

At 31 December 20X6, the cost of the combination will be unchanged but $8 will be charged to finance costs, being the unwinding of the discount on the deferred consideration.

4.7.3 Share exchange

The parent has acquired 12,000 $1 shares in the subsidiary by issuing 5 of its own $1 shares for every 4 shares in the subsidiary. The market value of the parent company's shares is $6.

Cost of the combination:

	$
12,000 × 5/4 × $6	90,000

Note that this is credited to the share capital and share premium of the parent company as follows:

	Dr	Cr
Investment in subsidiary	90,000	
Share capital ($12,000 × 5/4)		15,000
Share premium ($12,000 × 5/4 × 5)		75,000

4.7.4 Expenses and issue costs

Expenses of the combination, such as lawyers and accountants fees are written off as incurred. However, IFRS 3 requires that the costs of issuing equity are treated as a deduction from the proceeds of the equity issue. Share issue costs will therefore be debited to the share premium account. Issue costs of financial instruments are deducted from the proceeds of the financial instrument.

4.8 Adjustments to goodwill

At the date of acquisition the parent recognises the assets, liabilities and contingent liabilities of the subsidiary at their fair value at the date when control is acquired. It may be that some of these assets or liabilities had not previously been recognised by the acquiree.

For instance, the subsidiary may have tax losses brought forward, but had not recognised these as an asset because it could not foresee future profits against which they could be offset. If it now appears that taxable profits will be forthcoming, the deferred tax asset can be recognised.

An entity has acquired a 60% interest in another entity which has brought forward tax losses unutilised of $200,000. The tax losses can now be utilised.

The adjustment will be:

	Dr	Cr
Deferred tax (subsidiary)	200,000	
Goodwill (effectively)		200,000

5 A technique of consolidation

FAST FORWARD

We have now looked at the topics of cancellation, non-controlling interests and goodwill arising on consolidation. It is time to set out an approach to be used in tackling **consolidated statements of financial position**.

(1)   Aggregate the assets and liabilities on the statement of financial position. Cancel common items.
(2)   Calculate goodwill.
(3)   Calculate non-controlling interest.
(4)   Calculate retained earnings.

Question   Consolidated statement of financial position

The draft statements of financial position of Ping Co and Pong Co on 30 June 20X4 were as follows.

PING CO
STATEMENT OF FINANCIAL POSITION AS AT 30 JUNE 20X4

	$	$
Assets		
Non-current assets		
Property, plant and equipment	50,000	
20,000 ordinary shares in Pong Co at cost	30,000	
		80,000
Current assets		
Inventory	3,000	
Receivables	16,000	
Cash	2,000	
		21,000
Total assets		101,000

	$	$
Equity and liabilities		
Equity		
Ordinary shares of $1 each	45,000	
Revaluation surplus	12,000	
Retained earnings	26,000	
		83,000
Current liabilities		
Owed to Pong Co	8,000	
Trade payables	10,000	
		18,000
Total equity and liabilities		101,000

PONG CO
STATEMENT OF FINANCIAL POSITION AS AT 30 JUNE 20X4

	$	$
Assets		
Property, plant and equipment		40,000
Current assets		
Inventory	8,000	
Owed by Ping Co	10,000	
Receivables	7,000	
		25,000
Total assets		65,000
Equity and liabilities		
Equity		
Ordinary shares of $1 each	25,000	
Revaluation surplus	5,000	
Retained earnings	28,000	
		58,000
Current liabilities		
Trade payables		7,000
Total equity and liabilities		65,000

Ping Co acquired its investment in Pong Co on 1 July 20X1 when the retained earnings of Pong Co stood at $6,000. There have been no changes in the share capital or revaluation surplus of Pong Co since that date. At 30 June 20X4 Pong Co had invoiced Ping Co for goods to the value of $2,000 which had not been received by Ping Co.

There is no impairment of goodwill. It is group policy to value non-controlling interest at its proportionate share of the subsidiary's identifiable net assets.

Prepare the consolidated statement of financial position of Ping Co as at 30 June 20X4.

Answer

1   **Agree current accounts.**

Ping Co has goods in transit of $2,000 making its total inventory $3,000 + $2,000 = $5,000 and its liability to Pong Co $8,000 + $2,000 = $10,000.

Cancel common items: these are the current accounts between the two companies of $10,000 each.

2 **Calculate goodwill.**

Goodwill

	$	$
Consideration transferred		30,000
Non-controlling interest (W3)		7,200
		37,200
Net assets acquired as represented by:		
Ordinary share capital	25,000	
Revaluation surplus on acquisition	5,000	
Retained earnings on acquisition	6,000	
		(36,000)
Goodwill		1,200

This goodwill must be capitalised in the consolidated statement of financial position.

3 **Calculate non-controlling interest.**

(a) *at acquisition*

	$
Pong Co's net assets (W2)	36,000
× 20%	7,200

(b) *at year end*

	$
Pong Co's net assets (65,000 – 7,000)	58,000
× 20%	11,600

4 **Calculate consolidated reserves.**

Consolidated revaluation surplus

	$
Ping Co	12,000
Share of Pong Co's post acquisition revaluation surplus	–
	12,000

Consolidated retained earnings

	Ping	Pong
	$	$
Retained earnings per question	26,000	28,000
Less pre-acquisition		(6,000)
		22,000
Share of Pong: 80% × $22,000	17,600	
	43,600	

5 **Prepare the consolidated statement of financial position.**

PING CO
CONSOLIDATED STATEMENT OF FINANCIAL POSITION AS AT 30 JUNE 20X4

	$	$
Assets		
Non-current assets		
Property, plant and equipment ($50,000 + $40,000)		90,000
Intangible asset: goodwill		1,200
Current assets		
Inventories ($5,000 + $8,000)	13,000	
Receivables ($16,000 + $7,000)	23,000	
Cash	2,000	
		38,000
Total assets		129,200

Equity and liabilities
Equity

Ordinary shares of $1 each	45,000	
Revaluation surplus	12,000	
Retained earnings	43,600	
		100,600
Non-controlling interest		11,600
		112,200
Current liabilities		
Trade payables ($10,000 + $7,000)		17,000
Total equity and liabilities		129,200

6 Intra-group trading

Intra-group trading can give rise to **unrealised profit** which is eliminated on consolidation.

6.1 Unrealised profit

Any receivable/payable balances outstanding between the companies are cancelled on consolidation. No further problem arises if all such intra-group transactions are **undertaken at cost**, without any mark-up for profit.

However, each company in a group is a separate trading entity and may wish to treat other group companies in the same way as any other customer. In this case, a company (say A Co) may buy goods at one price and sell them at a higher price to another group company (B Co). The accounts of A Co will quite properly include the profit earned on sales to B Co; and similarly B Co's statement of financial position will include inventories at their cost to B Co, ie at the amount at which they were purchased from A Co.

This gives rise to two problems.

(a)   Although A Co makes a profit as soon as it sells goods to B Co, the group does not make a sale or achieve a profit until an outside customer buys the goods from B Co.

(b)   Any purchases from A Co which remain unsold by B Co at the year end will be included in B Co's inventory. Their value in the statement of financial position will be their cost to B Co, which is not the same as their cost to the group.

The objective of consolidated accounts is to present the financial position of several connected companies as that of a single entity, the group. This means that **in a consolidated statement of financial position the only profits recognised should be those earned by the group** in providing goods or services to outsiders; and similarly, inventory in the consolidated statement of financial position should be valued at cost to the group.

Suppose that a parent company P Co buys goods for $1,600 and sells them to a wholly owned subsidiary S Co for $2,000. The goods are in S Co's inventory at the year end and appear in S Co's statement of financial position at $2,000. In this case, P Co will record a profit of $400 in its individual accounts, but from the group's point of view the figures are:

Cost	$1,600
External sales	nil
Closing inventory at cost	$1,600
Profit/loss	nil

If we add together the figures for retained earnings and inventory in the individual statements of financial position of P Co and S Co the resulting figures for consolidated retained earnings and consolidated inventory will each be overstated by $400. A **consolidation adjustment** is therefore necessary as follows.

DEBIT   Group retained earnings
CREDIT   Group inventory (statement of financial position)

with the amount of **profit unrealised** by the group.

Question

Unrealised profit

P Co acquired all the shares in S Co one year ago when the reserves of S Co stood at $10,000. Draft statements of financial position for each company are as follows.

	P Co $	P Co $	S Co $	S Co $
Assets				
Non-current assets				
Property, plant and equipment	80,000			40,000
Investment in S Co at cost	46,000			
		126,000		
Current assets		40,000		30,000
Total assets		166,000		70,000
Equity and liabilities				
Equity				
Ordinary shares of $1 each	100,000		30,000	
Retained earnings	45,000		22,000	
		145,000		52,000
Current liabilities		21,000		18,000
Total equity and liabilities		166,000		70,000

During the year S Co sold goods to P Co for $50,000, the profit to S Co being 20% of selling price. At the end of the reporting period, $15,000 of these goods remained unsold in the inventories of P Co. At the same date, P Co owed S Co $12,000 for goods bought and this debt is included in the trade payables of P Co and the receivables of S Co. The goodwill arising on consolidation has been impaired. The amount of the impairment is $1,500.

Required

Prepare a draft consolidated statement of financial position for P Co.

Answer

1   *Goodwill*

	$	$
Consideration transferred		46,000
Net assets acquired as represented by		
Share capital	30,000	
Retained earnings	10,000	
		(40,000)
Goodwill		6,000

2   Retained earnings

	P Co	S Co
	$	$
Retained earnings per question	45,000	22,000
Unrealised profit: 20% × $15,000		(3,000)
Pre-acquisition		(10,000)
		9,000
Share of S Co	9,000	
Goodwill impairment loss	(1,500)	
	52,500	

P CO
CONSOLIDATED STATEMENT OF FINANCIAL POSITION

	$	$
Assets		
Non-current assets		
Property, plant and equipment	120,000	
Goodwill (6,000 – 1,500)	4,500	
		124,500
Current assets (W1)		55,000
Total assets		179,500
Equity and liabilities		
Equity		
Ordinary shares of $1 each	100,000	
Retained earnings	52,500	
		152,500
Current liabilities (W2)		27,000
Total equity and liabilities		179,500

Workings

1   Current assets

	$	$
In P Co's statement of financial position		40,000
In S Co's statement of financial position	30,000	
Less S Co's current account with P Co cancelled	(12,000)	
		18,000
		58,000
Less unrealised profit excluded from inventory valuation		(3,000)
		55,000

2   Current liabilities

	$
In P Co's statement of financial position	21,000
Less P Co's current account with S Co cancelled	(12,000)
	9,000
In S Co's statement of financial position	18,000
	27,000

6.2 Non-controlling interests in unrealised intra-group profits

A further problem occurs where a subsidiary company which is **not wholly owned is involved in intra-group trading** within the group. If a subsidiary S Co is 75% owned and sells goods to the parent company for $16,000 cost plus $4,000 profit, ie for $20,000 and if these items are unsold by P Co at the end of the reporting period, the 'unrealised' profit of $4,000 earned by S Co and charged to P Co will be partly owned by the non-controlling interest of S Co.

The correct treatment of these intragroup profits is to remove the whole profit, charging the non-controlling interest with their proportion.

Entries to learn

DEBIT	Group retained earnings
DEBIT	Non-controlling interest
CREDIT	Group inventory (statement of financial position)

6.3 Example: non-controlling interests and intra-group profits

P Co has owned 75% of the shares of S Co since the incorporation of that company. During the year to 31 December 20X2, S Co sold goods costing $16,000 to P Co at a price of $20,000 and these goods were still unsold by P Co at the end of the year. Draft statements of financial position of each company at 31 December 20X2 were as follows.

	P Co		S Co	
Assets	$	$	$	$
Non-current assets				
Property, plant and equipment	125,000		120,000	
Investment: 75,000 shares in S Co at cost	75,000		–	
		200,000		120,000
Current assets				
Inventories	50,000		48,000	
Trade receivables	20,000		16,000	
		70,000		64,000
Total assets		270,000		184,000
Equity and liabilities	$	$	$	$
Equity				
Ordinary shares of $1 each fully paid	80,000		100,000	
Retained earnings	150,000		60,000	
		230,000		160,000
Current liabilities		40,000		24,000
Total equity and liabilities		270,000		184,000

Required

Prepare the consolidated statement of financial position of P Co at 31 December 20X2. It is the group policy to value the non-controlling interest at its proportionate share of the subsidiary's net assets.

Solution

The profit earned by S Co but unrealised by the group is $4,000 of which $3,000 (75%) is attributable to the group and $1,000 (25%) to the non-controlling interest. Remove the whole of the profit loading, charging the non-controlling interest with their proportion.

	P Co $	S Co $
Retained earnings		
Per question	150,000	60,000
Less unrealised profit		(4,000)
		56,000
Share of S Co: $56,000 × 75%	42,000	
	192,000	
Non-controlling interest		
S Co's net assets (184,000 – 24,000)		160,000
Unrealised profit		(4,000)
		156,000
× 25%		39,000

P CO

CONSOLIDATED STATEMENT OF FINANCIAL POSITION AS AT 31 DECEMBER 20X2

	$	$
Assets		
Property, plant and equipment		245,000
Current assets		
Inventories $(50,000 + 48,000 – 4,000)	94,000	
Trade receivables	36,000	
		130,000
Total assets		375,000
Equity and liabilities		
Equity		
Ordinary shares of $1 each	80,000	
Retained earnings	192,000	
		272,000
Non-controlling interest		39,000
		311,000
Current liabilities		64,000
Total equity and liabilities		375,000

7 Intra-group sales of non-current assets

FAST FORWARD ➤ As well as engaging in trading activities with each other, group companies may on occasion wish to transfer non-current assets.

7.1 Accounting treatment

In their individual accounts the companies concerned will treat the transfer just like a sale between unconnected parties: the selling company will record a profit or loss on sale, while the purchasing company will record the asset at the amount paid to acquire it, and will use that amount as the basis for calculating depreciation.

On consolidation, the usual **'group entity' principle applies**. The consolidated statement of financial position must show assets at their cost to the group, and any depreciation charged must be based on that cost. Two consolidation adjustments will usually be needed to achieve this.

(a) An adjustment to alter retained earnings and non-current assets cost so as to remove any element of unrealised profit or loss. This is similar to the adjustment required in respect of unrealised profit in inventory.

(b) An adjustment to alter retained earnings and accumulated depreciation is made so that consolidated depreciation is based on the asset's cost to the group.

In practice, these steps are combined so that the retained earnings of the entity making the unrealised profit are debited with the unrealised profit less the additional depreciation.

The double entry is as follows.

(a) Sale by parent

| DEBIT | Group retained earnings |
| CREDIT | Non-current assets |

with the profit on disposal, less the additional depreciation.

(b) Sale by subsidiary

DEBIT	Group retained earnings (P's share of S)
DEBIT	Non-controlling interest (NCI's share of S)
CREDIT	Non-current assets

with the profit on disposal, less additional depreciation

7.2 Example: intra-group sale of non-current assets

P Co owns 60% of S Co and on 1 January 20X1 S Co sells plant costing $10,000 to P Co for $12,500. The companies make up accounts to 31 December 20X1 and the balances on their retained earnings at that date are:

P Co after charging depreciation of 10% on plant	$27,000
S Co including profit on sale of plant	$18,000

Required

Show the working for consolidated retained earnings.

Solution

Retained earnings

	P Co $	S Co $
Per question	27,000	18,000
Disposal of plant		
Profit		(2,500)
Depreciation: 10% × $2,500		250
		15,750
Share of S Co: $15,750 × 60%	9,450	
	36,450	

Notes

1   The non-controlling interest in the retained earnings of S Co is 40% × $15,750 = $6,300.

2   The asset is written down to cost and depreciation on the 'profit' element is removed. The group profit for the year is thus reduced by a net (($2,500 – $250) × 60%) = $1,350.

8 Summary: consolidated statement of financial position

Purpose	To show the net assets which P controls and the ownership of those assets.
Net assets	Always 100% P plus 100% S providing P holds a majority of voting rights.
Share capital	P only.
Reason	Simply reporting to the parent company's shareholders in another form.
Retained earnings	100% P plus group share of post-acquisition retained earnings of S less consolidation adjustments.
Reason	To show the extent to which the group actually owns total assets less liabilities.
Non-controlling interest	NCI share of S's consolidated net assets, or valuation at fair value.
Reason	To show the equity in a subsidiary not attributable to the parent.

9 Acquisition of a subsidiary during its accounting period

FAST FORWARD

When a parent company acquires a subsidiary during its accounting period the only accounting entries made at the time will be those recording the **cost of acquisition in the parent company's books**.

9.1 Accounting problem

As we have already seen, at the end of the accounting year it will be necessary to prepare consolidated accounts.

The subsidiary company's accounts to be consolidated will show the subsidiary's profit or loss for the whole year. For consolidation purposes, however, it will be necessary to distinguish between:

(a) Profits earned before acquisition
(b) Profits earned after acquisition

In practice, a subsidiary company's profit may not accrue evenly over the year; for example, the subsidiary might be engaged in a trade, such as toy sales, with marked seasonal fluctuations. Nevertheless, the assumption can be made that **profits accrue evenly** whenever it is impracticable to arrive at an accurate split of pre- and post-acquisition profits.

Once the amount of pre-acquisition profit has been established the appropriate consolidation workings (goodwill, retained earnings) can be produced.

Bear in mind that in calculating **non-controlling interests** at the year end, where it is calculated on the basis of the NCI share of net assets the distinction between pre– and post-acquisition profits is irrelevant. The non-controlling shareholders are simply credited with their share of the subsidiary's total net assets at the end of the reporting period.

Where the non-controlling interest id based on fair value it is worthwhile to summarise what happens on consolidation to the retained earnings figures extracted from a subsidiary's statement of financial position. Suppose the accounts of S Co, a 60% subsidiary of P Co, show retained earnings of $20,000 at the end of the reporting period, of which $14,000 were earned prior to acquisition. The figure of $20,000 will appear in the consolidated statement of financial position as follows.

	$
Non-controlling interests working: their share of total retained earnings at the end of the reporting period (40% × $20,000)	8,000
Goodwill working: group share of pre-acquisition retained earnings (60% × $14,000)	8,400
Consolidated retained earnings working: group share of post-acquisition retained earnings (60% × $6,000)	3,600
	20,000

Question   **Acquisition**

Hinge Co acquired 80% of the ordinary shares of Singe Co on 1 April 20X5. On 31 December 20X4 Singe Co's accounts showed a share premium account of $4,000 and retained earnings of $15,000. The statements of financial position of the two companies at 31 December 20X5 are set out below. Neither company has paid any dividends during the year. Non-controlling interest should be valued at its proportionate share of net assets.

You are required to prepare the consolidated statement of financial position of Hinge Co at 31 December 20X5. There has been no impairment of goodwill.

HINGE CO
STATEMENT OF FINANCIAL POSITION AS AT 31 DECEMBER 20X5

	$	$
Assets		
Non-current assets		
Property, plant and equipment	32,000	
16,000 ordinary shares of 50c each in Singe Co	50,000	
		82,000
Current assets		85,000
Total assets		167,000
Equity and liabilities		
Equity		
Ordinary shares of $1 each	100,000	
Share premium account	7,000	
Retained earnings	40,000	
		147,000
Current liabilities		20,000
Total equity and liabilities		167,000

SINGE CO
STATEMENT OF FINANCIAL POSITION AS AT 31 DECEMBER 20X5

	$	$
Assets		
Property, plant and equipment		30,000
Current assets		43,000
Total assets		73,000
Equity and liabilities		
Equity		
20,000 ordinary shares of 50c each	10,000	
Share premium account	4,000	
Retained earnings	39,000	
		53,000
Current liabilities		20,000
Total equity and liabilities		73,000

Answer

Singe Co has made a profit of $24,000 ($39,000 – $15,000) for the year. In the absence of any direction to the contrary, this should be assumed to have arisen evenly over the year; $6,000 in the three months to 31 March and $18,000 in the nine months after acquisition. The company's pre-acquisition retained earnings are therefore as follows.

	$
Balance at 31 December 20X4	15,000
Profit for three months to 31 March 20X5	6,000
Pre-acquisition retained earnings	21,000

The balance of $4,000 on share premium account is all pre-acquisition.

The consolidation workings can now be drawn up.

1   *Goodwill*

	$	$
Consideration transferred		50,000
Non-controlling interest (W2)		7,000
Net assets acquired		57,000
represented by		
Ordinary share capital	10,000	
Retained earnings (pre-acquisition)	21,000	
Share premium	4,000	
		(35,000)
Goodwill		22,000

2   *Non-controlling interest at acquisition*

	$	$
Share capital	10,000	
Share premium	4,000	
Retained earnings 31.12.X4	15,000	
Earnings 3 months to 31.03.X5	6,000	
		35,000
NCI 20%		7,000

3   *Non-controlling interest at reporting date*

	$
Singe Co net assets (73,000 – 20,000)	53,000
× 20%	10,600

4   *Retained earnings*

	Hinge Co $	Singe Co $
Per question	40,000	39,000
Pre-acquisition (see above)		(21,000)
		18,000
Share of Singe: $18,000 × 80%	14,400	
	54,400	

5   *Share premium account*

	$
Hinge Co	7,000
Share of Singe Co's post-acquisition share premium	–
	7,000

HINGE CO
CONSOLIDATED STATEMENT OF FINANCIAL POSITION AS AT 31 DECEMBER 20X5

	$	$
Assets		
Property, plant and equipment		62,000
Goodwill (W1)		22,000
Current assets		128,000
Total assets		212,000
Equity and liabilities		
Equity		
Ordinary shares of $1 each	100,000	
Reserves		
Share premium account (W5)	7,000	
Retained earnings (W4)	54,400	
		161,400
Non-controlling interest (W3)		10,600
		172,000
Current liabilities		40,000
Total equity and liabilities		212,000

9.2 Example: Pre-acquisition losses of a subsidiary

As an illustration of the entries arising when a subsidiary has pre-acquisition *losses*, suppose P Co acquired all 50,000 $1 ordinary shares in S Co for $20,000 on 1 January 20X1 when there was a debit balance of $35,000 on S Co's retained earnings. In the years 20X1 to 20X4 S Co makes profits of $40,000 in total, leaving a credit balance of $5,000 on retained earnings at 31 December 20X4. P Co's retained earnings at the same date are $70,000.

Solution

The consolidation workings would appear as follows.

1   *Goodwill*

	$	$
Consideration transferred		20,000
Net assets acquired		
as represented by		
Ordinary share capital	50,000	
Retained earnings	(35,000)	
		(15,000)
Goodwill		5,000

2   *Retained earnings*

	P Co	S Co
	$	$
At the end of the reporting period	70,000	5,000
Pre-acquisition loss		35,000
		40,000
S Co – share of post-acquisition retained earnings		
(40,000 × 100%)	40,000	
	110,000	

10 Pre-acquisition dividends

The revisions made to IAS 27 *Consolidated and separate financial statements* in 2008 simplified this area. There is no longer any need to identify whether a subsidiary's dividends are paid from pre- or post-acquisition earnings. Any dividends received by a parent from a subsidiary, jointly controlled entity or associate are recognised as income in the parent's separate financial statements (and cancelled out as intra-group income in the consolidated statement of comprehensive income).

11 Fair values in acquisition accounting

Fair values are very important in calculating goodwill.

11.1 Goodwill

To understand the importance of fair values in the acquisition of a subsidiary consider again what we mean by goodwill.

Key term

> **Goodwill.** The excess of the fair value of the consideration transferred plus the amount of the non-controlling interests over the fair value of the identifiable net assets of the acquiree on the acquisition date.

The **statement of financial position of a subsidiary company** at the date it is acquired may not be a guide to the fair value of its net assets. For example, the market value of a freehold building may have risen greatly since it was acquired, but it may appear in the statement of financial position at historical cost less accumulated depreciation.

11.2 What is fair value?

Fair value is defined as follows by IFRS 3 and various other standards (including IFRS 13) – it is an important definition.

Key term

> **Fair value.** The price that would be received to sell an asset or paid to transfer a liability in an orderly transaction between market participants at the measurement date.

We will look at the requirements of IFRS 3 regarding fair value in more detail below. First let us look at some practical matters.

11.3 Fair value adjustment calculations

Until now we have calculated goodwill as the difference between the consideration transferred and the **book value (carrying amount)** of net assets acquired by the group. If this calculation is to comply with the definition above we must ensure that the book value of the subsidiary's net assets is the same as their **fair value**.

There are two possible ways of achieving this.

(a) The **subsidiary company** might **incorporate any necessary revaluations** in its own books of account. In this case, we can proceed directly to the consolidation, taking asset values and reserves figures straight from the subsidiary company's statement of financial position.

(b) The **revaluations** may be made as a **consolidation adjustment without being incorporated** in the subsidiary company's books. In this case, we must make the necessary adjustments to the subsidiary's statement of financial position as a working. Only then can we proceed to the consolidation.

Note: Remember that when depreciating assets are revalued there may be a corresponding alteration in the amount of depreciation charged and accumulated.

11.4 Example: fair value adjustments

P Co acquired 75% of the ordinary shares of S Co on 1 September 20X5. At that date the fair value of S Co's non-current assets was $23,000 greater than their carrying amount, and the balance of retained earnings was $21,000. The statements of financial position of both companies at 31 August 20X6 are given below. S Co has not incorporated any revaluation in its books of account.

P CO

STATEMENT OF FINANCIAL POSITION AS AT 31 AUGUST 20X6

	$	$
Assets		
Non-current assets		
Property, plant and equipment	63,000	
Investment in S Co at cost	51,000	
		114,000
Current assets		82,000
Total assets		196,000
Equity and liabilities		
Equity		
Ordinary shares of $1 each	80,000	
Retained earnings	96,000	
		176,000
Current liabilities		20,000
Total equity and liabilities		196,000

S CO

STATEMENT OF FINANCIAL POSITION AS AT 31 AUGUST 20X6

	$	$
Assets		
Property, plant and equipment		28,000
Current assets		43,000
Total assets		71,000
Equity and liabilities		
Equity		
Ordinary shares of $1 each	20,000	
Retained earnings	41,000	
		61,000
Current liabilities		10,000
Total equity and liabilities		71,000

If S Co had revalued its non-current assets at 1 September 20X5, an addition of $3,000 would have been made to the depreciation charged for 20X5/X6.

Required

Prepare P Co's consolidated statement of financial position as at 31 August 20X6. Non-controlling interest is to be valued at its proportionate share of the fair value of the subsidiary's identifiable net assets.

Solution

P CO CONSOLIDATED STATEMENT OF FINANCIAL POSITION AS AT 31 AUGUST 20X6

	$	$
Non-current assets		
Property, plant and equipment $(63,000 + 48,000)*	111,000	
Goodwill (W1)	3,000	
		114,000
Current assets		125,000
		239,000

	$	$
Equity and liabilities		
Equity		
Ordinary shares of $1 each	80,000	
Retained earnings (W3)	108,750	
		188,750
Non-controlling interest (W2)		20,250
		209,000
Current liabilities		30,000
		239,000

* (28,000 + 23,000 – 3,000)

1 Goodwill

	$	$
Consideration transferred		51,000
Non-controlling interest (64,000 × 25%)		16,000
		67,000
Net assets acquired as represented by		
Ordinary share capital	20,000	
Retained earnings	21,000	
Fair value adjustment	23,000	
		(64,000)
Goodwill		3,000

2 Non-controlling interest at reporting date

	$
S Co's net assets (71,000 – 10,000)	61,000
Fair value adjustment (23,000 – 3,000)	20,000
	81,000
× 25%	20,250

3 Retained earnings

	P Co	S Co
	$	$
Per question	96,000	41,000
Pre acquisition profits		(21,000)
Depreciation adjustment		(3,000)
Post acquisition S Co		17,000
Group share in S Co		
($17,000 × 75%)	12,750	
Group retained earnings	108,750	

Question   Fair value

An asset is recorded in S Co's books at its historical cost of $4,000. On 1 January 20X5 P Co bought 80% of S Co's equity. Its directors attributed a fair value of $3,000 to the asset as at that date. It had been depreciated for two years out of an expected life of four years on the straight line basis. There was no expected residual value. On 30 June 20X5 the asset was sold for $2,600. What is the profit or loss on disposal of this asset to be recorded in S Co's accounts and in P Co's consolidated accounts for the year ended 31 December 20X5?

Answer

S Co: Carrying amount at disposal (at historical cost) = $4,000 × 1½/4 = $1,500
       ∴ Profit on disposal = $1,100 (depreciation charge for the year = $500)

P Co: Carrying amount at disposal (at fair value) = $3,000 × 1½/2 = $2,250
       ∴ Profit on disposal for consolidation = $350 (depreciation for the year = $750).

The non-controlling interest would be credited with 20% of both the profit on disposal and the depreciation charge as part of the one line entry in the consolidated statement of profit or loss .

11.5 IFRS 3 Fair values

IFRS 3 sets out **general principles** for arriving at the fair values of a subsidiary's assets and liabilities. The acquirer should recognise the acquiree's identifiable assets, liabilities and contingent liabilities at the acquisition date only if they satisfy the following criteria:

(a) In the case of an **asset other than an intangible asset** it is **probable** that any associated **future economic benefits** will flow to the acquirer, and its fair value can be **measured reliably.**

(b) In the case of a **liability other than a contingent liability** it is probable that an **outflow** of resources embodying economic benefits will be required to settle the obligation, and its fair value can be **measured reliably**.

(c) In the case of an **intangible asset** or a **contingent liability**, its fair value can be measured reliably.

However, IFRS 3 sets out a number of exceptions to these general principles. The ones which you are most likely to meet in the exam are dealt with below.

The acquiree's identifiable assets and liabilities might include assets and liabilities **not previously recognised** in the acquiree's financial statements. For example, a tax benefit arising from the acquiree's tax losses that was not recognised by the acquiree may be recognised by the group if the acquirer has future taxable profits against which the unrecognised tax benefit can be applied.

11.5.1 Restructuring and future losses

An acquirer **should not recognise liabilities for future losses** or other costs expected to be incurred as a result of the business combination.

IFRS 3 explains that a plan to restructure a subsidiary following an acquisition is not a present obligation of the acquiree at the acquisition date. Neither does it meet the definition of a contingent liability. Therefore an acquirer **should not recognise a liability for** such **a restructuring plan** as part of allocating the cost of the combination unless the subsidiary was already committed to the plan before the acquisition.

This **prevents creative accounting**. An acquirer cannot set up a provision for restructuring or future losses of a subsidiary and then release this to the profit or loss in subsequent periods in order to reduce losses or smooth profits.

11.5.2 Intangible assets

The acquiree may have **intangible assets**, such as development expenditure. These can be recognised separately from goodwill only if they are **identifiable**. An intangible asset is identifiable only if it:

(a) Is **separable**, ie capable of being separated or divided from the entity and sold, transferred, or exchanged, either individually or together with a related contract, asset or liability, or

(b) Arises from contractual or other legal rights

IFRS 3 explains that an acquirer recognises acquired identifiable intangible assets (such as internally generated brand names, patents or customer relationships), that the acquiree did not recognise as an asset in its financial statements.

11.5.3 Contingent liabilities

Contingent liabilities of the acquirer are **recognised** if their **fair value can be measured reliably**. This is a departure from the normal rules in IAS 37; contingent liabilities are not normally recognised, but only disclosed.

After their initial recognition, the acquirer should measure contingent liabilities that are recognised separately at the higher of:

(a)   The amount that would be recognised in accordance with IAS 37
(b)   The amount initially recognised

11.5.4 Cost of a business combination

The general principle is that the acquirer should measure the cost of a business combination as the total of the **fair values**, at the date of acquisition, **of assets transferred by the acquirer**, liabilities incurred or assumed, and equity instruments issued by the acquirer, in exchange for control of the acquiree.

Sometimes all or part of the cost of an acquisition is deferred (ie, does not become payable immediately). The fair value of any deferred consideration is determined by **discounting** the amounts payable to their **present value** at the date of exchange.

Where equity instruments (eg, ordinary shares) of a quoted entity form part of the cost of a combination, the **published price** at the date of exchange normally provides the best evidence of the instrument's fair value and except in rare circumstances this should be used.

Future losses or other costs expected to be incurred as a result of a combination should not be included in the cost of the combination.

Costs **attributable** to the combination, for example professional fees and administrative costs, should not be included: they are recognised as an expense when incurred. **Costs of issuing debt instruments and equity shares** are covered by IAS 32 *Financial instruments: presentation*, which states that such costs should **reduce the proceeds from the debt issue or the equity issue**.

Question	Goodwill on consolidation

On 1 September 20X7 Tyzo Co acquired 6 million $1 shares in Kono Co at $2.00 per share. At that date Kono Co produced the following interim financial statements.

	$m		$m
Property, plant and equipment		Trade payables	3.2
(note 1)	16.0	Taxation	0.6
Inventories (note 2)	4.0	Bank overdraft	3.9
Receivables	2.9	Long-term loans	4.0
Cash in hand	1.2	Share capital ($1 shares)	8.0
		Retained earnings	4.4
	24.1		24.1

Notes

1   The following information relates to the property, plant and equipment of Kono Co at 1 September 20X7.

	$m
Gross replacement cost	28.4
Net replacement cost (gross replacement cost less depreciation)	16.8
Economic value	18.0
Net realisable value	8.0

2   The inventories of Kono Co which were shown in the interim financial statements are raw materials. They would have cost $4.2 million to replace at 1 September 20X7.

3   On 1 September 20X7 Tyzo Co took a decision to rationalise the group so as to integrate Kono Co. The costs of the rationalisation were estimated to total $3.0 million and the process was due to start on 1 March 20X8. No provision for these costs has been made in the financial statements given above.

4   Kono Co has disclosed a contingent liability of $200,000 in its interim financial statements relating to litigation

5   Tyzo Group values the non-controlling interest using the proportion of net assets method.

Required

Compute the goodwill on consolidation of Kono Co that will be included in the consolidated financial statements of the Tyzo Co group for the year ended 31 December 20X7, explaining your treatment of the items mentioned above. You should refer to the provisions of relevant accounting standards.

Answer

GOODWILL ON CONSOLIDATION OF KONO CO

	$m	$m
Consideration ($2.00 × 6m)		12.0
Non-controlling interest (25% × 13.2)		3.3
		15.3
Fair value of net assets acquired		
Share capital	8.0	
Pre-acquisition reserves	4.4	
Fair value adjustments		
Property, plant and equipment (16.8 – 16.0)	0.8	
Inventories (4.2 – 4.0)	0.2	
Contingent liability	(0.2)	
		(13.2)
Goodwill		2.1

Notes on treatment

(a)   Share capital and pre-acquisition profits represent the book value (carrying amount) of the net assets of Kono Co at the date of acquisition. Adjustments are then required to this book value in order to give the fair value of the net assets at the date of acquisition. For short-term monetary items, fair value is their carrying amount on acquisition.

(b)   IFRS 3 states that the fair value of property, plant and equipment should be determined by market value or, if information on a market price is not available (as is the case here), then by reference to depreciated replacement cost, reflecting normal business practice. The net replacement cost (ie $16.8m) represents the gross replacement cost less depreciation based on that amount, and so further adjustment for extra depreciation is unnecessary.

(c)   Raw materials should be valued at their replacement cost of $4.2m.

(d)   The rationalisation costs cannot be reported in pre-acquisition results under IFRS 3 as they are not a liability of Kono Co at the acquisition date.

(e)   The contingent liability should be included as part of the acquisition net assets of Kono even though it is not deemed probable and therefore has not been recognised in Kono's individual accounts. However, the disclosed amount is not necessarily the fair value at which a third party would assume the liability. If the probability is low, then the fair value is likely to be lower than $200,000.

11.5.5 Example: Cost of a business combination

Rather than pay cash for Kono Co's shares, Tyzo has funded the acquisition by issuing 4.5m of its own shares to Kono Co's shareholders.

Tyzo's shares have a market value of $3. The costs of the share issue amounted to $500,000 and Tyzo paid a total of $750,000 to lawyers and accountants to carry out the combination.

Calculate the goodwill.

Solution

	$
Consideration:	
Share issue (4.5m × $3)	13.5
Non-controlling interest (as above)	3.3
Net assets acquired (as above)	(13.2)
Goodwill	3.6

Note: The share issue costs are debited to share premium and the $750,000 expenses are written off.

11.6 Goodwill arising on acquisition

Goodwill should be carried in the statement of financial position at **cost less any accumulated impairment losses**. Refer back to Paragraph 4.10 for more detail on this.

Chapter roundup

- IFRS 10 sets out the basic procedures for preparing consolidated financial statements.

- In the consolidated statement of financial position it is necessary to distinguish **non-controlling interests** from those net assets attributable to the group and financed by shareholders' equity.

- **Goodwill** is the excess of the amount transferred plus the amount of non-controlling interests over the fair value of the net assets of the subsidiary.

- We have now looked at the topics of cancellation, non-controlling interests and goodwill arising on consolidation. It is time to set out an approach to be used in tackling **consolidated statements of financial position**.

- Intra-group trading can give rise to **unrealised profit** which is eliminated on consolidation.

- As well as engaging in trading activities with each other, group companies may on occasion wish to **transfer non-current assets**.

- When a parent company acquires a subsidiary during its accounting period the only accounting entries made at the time will be those recording the **cost of the acquisition in the parent company's books**.

- **Fair values** are very important in calculating goodwill.

Quick quiz

1   Chicken Co owns 80% of Egg Co. Egg Co sells goods to Chicken Co at cost plus 50%. The total invoiced sales to Chicken Co by Egg Co in the year ended 31 December 20X9 were $900,000 and, of these sales, goods which had been invoiced at $60,000 were held in inventory by Chicken Co at 31 December 20X9. What is the reduction in aggregate group gross profit?

2   Major Co, which makes up its accounts to 31 December, has an 80% owned subsidiary Minor Co. Minor Co sells goods to Major Co at a mark-up on cost of 33.33%. At 31 December 20X8, Major had $12,000 of such goods in its inventory and at 31 December 20X9 had $15,000 of such goods in its inventory.

   What is the amount by which the consolidated profit attributable to Major Co's shareholders should be adjusted in respect of the above?

   Ignore taxation

   A $1,000 Debit
   B $800 Credit
   C $750 Credit
   D $600 Debit

3   Goodwill is always positive. True or false?

4   What entries are made in the workings to record the pre-acquisition profits of a subsidiary?

5   Describe the requirement of IFRS 3 in relation to the revaluation of a subsidiary company's assets to fair value at the acquisition date.

6   What guidelines are given by IFRS 3 in relation to valuing land and buildings fairly?

Answers to quick quiz

1    $60,000 \times \dfrac{50}{150} = $20,000$

2   D $(15,000 - 12,000) \times \dfrac{33.3}{133.3} \times 80\%$

3   False. Goodwill can be negative if the purchaser has 'got a bargain'.

4   See Para 4.2

5   See Para 11.5

6   Market value is the best guideline.

End of chapter question

Barcelona and Madrid

Barcelona acquired 60% of Madrid's ordinary share capital on 30 June 20X2 at a price $1.06 per share. The balance on Madrid's retained earnings at that date was $104m and the general reserve stood at $11m.

Their respective statements of financial position as at 30 September 20X6 are as follows:

	Barcelona $m	Madrid $m
Non-current assets:		
Property, plant & equipment	2,848	354
Patents	45	–
Investment in Madrid	159	–
	3,052	354
Current assets		
Inventories	895	225
Trade and other receivables	1,348	251
Cash and cash equivalents	212	34
	2,455	510
	5,507	864
Equity		
Share capital (20c ordinary shares)	920	50
General reserve	775	46
Retained earnings	2,086	394
	3,781	490
Non-current liabilities		
Long-term borrowings	558	168
Current liabilities		
Trade and other payables	1,168	183
Current portion of long-term borrowings	–	23
	1,168	206
	5,507	864

Annual impairment tests have revealed cumulative impairment losses relating to recognised goodwill of $17m to date.

Required

Produce the consolidated statement of financial position for the Barcelona Group as at 30 September 20X6. It is the group policy to value the non-controlling interest at its proportionate share of the fair value of the subsidiary's identifiable net assets. **(10 marks)**

17

The consolidated statement of profit or loss

Topic list	Syllabus reference
1 The consolidated statement of profit or loss	11.3
2 The consolidated statement of profit or loss and other comprehensive income	11.3

Introduction

This chapter deals with the consolidated statement of profit or loss and the consolidated statement of profit or loss and other comprehensive income, including adjustments for intra-group transactions.

Most of the consolidation adjustments will involve the **statement of profit or loss**, so that is the focus of this chapter.

1 The consolidated statement of profit or loss

The source of the consolidated statement of profit or loss is the individual statements of profit or loss of the separate companies in the group.

1.1 Consolidation procedure

It is customary in practice to prepare a working paper (known as a **consolidation schedule**) on which the individual statements of profit or loss are set out side by side and totalled to form the basis of the consolidated statement of profit or loss.

Exam focus point

In an examination it is very much quicker not to do this. Use workings to show the calculation of complex figures such as the non-controlling interest and show the derivation of others on the face of the statement of profit or loss, as shown in our examples.

In the consolidated statement of profit or loss non-controlling interest is brought in as a one-line adjustment at the end of the statement.

1.2 Simple example: consolidated statement of profit or loss

P Co acquired 75% of the ordinary shares of S Co on that company's incorporation in 20X3. The summarised statements of profit or loss and movement on retained earnings of the two companies for the year ending 31 December 20X6 are set out below.

	P Co	S Co
	$	$
Revenue	75,000	38,000
Cost of sales	30,000	20,000
Gross profit	45,000	18,000
Administrative expenses	14,000	8,000
Profit before tax	31,000	10,000
Income tax expense	10,000	2,000
Profit for the year	21,000	8,000
Note: Movement on retained earnings		
Retained earnings brought forward	87,000	17,000
Profit for the year	21,000	8,000
Retained earnings carried forward	108,000	25,000

Required

Prepare the consolidated statement of profit or loss and extract from the statement of changes in equity showing retained earnings and non-controlling interest.

Solution

P CO
CONSOLIDATED STATEMENT OF PROFIT OR LOSS
FOR THE YEAR ENDED 31 DECEMBER 20X6

	$
Revenue (75 + 38)	113,000
Cost of sales (30 + 20)	50,000
Gross profit	63,000
Administrative expenses (14 + 8)	22,000
Profit before tax	41,000
Income tax expense (10 + 2)	12,000
Profit for the year	29,000
Profit attributable to:	
Owners of the parent	27,000
Non-controlling interest ($8,000 × 25%)	2,000
	29,000

STATEMENT OF CHANGES IN EQUITY (EXTRACT)

	Retained Earnings $	Non-controlling Interest $	Total Equity $
Balance at 1 January 20X6	99,750	4,250	104,000
Total comprehensive income for the year	27,000	2,000	29,000
Balance at 31 December 20X6	126,750	6,250	133,000

Notice how the non-controlling interest is dealt with.

(a)   Down to the line **'profit for the year'** the **whole** of S Co's results is included without reference to group share or non-controlling share. The profit is then split between the owners of the parent company and the non-controlling interest. The non-controlling interest is calculated as the NCI share of the subsidiary's profit for the year.

(b)   The non-controlling share ($4,250) of S Co's retained earnings brought forward (17,000 × 25%) is **excluded** from group retained earnings. This means that the carried forward figure of $126,750 is the figure which would appear in the statement of financial position for group retained earnings.

This last point may be clearer if we construct the working for group retained earnings.

Group retained earnings

	P Co $	S Co $
At year-end	108,000	25,000
Less pre-acquisition retained earnings		–
		25,000
S Co – share of post acquisition retained earnings (25,000 × 75%)	18,750	
	126,750	

The non-controlling share of S Co's retained earnings comprises the non-controlling interest in the $17,000 profits brought forward plus the non-controlling interest ($2,000) in $8,000 retained profits for the year.

We will now look at the complications introduced by **intra-group trading**, **intra-group dividends** and **pre-acquisition profits** in the subsidiary.

1.3 Intra-group trading

Intra-group sales and purchases are eliminated from the consolidated statement of profit or loss.

Like the consolidated statement of financial position, the consolidated statement of profit or loss should deal with the results of the group as those of a single entity. When one company in a group sells goods to another an identical amount is added to the sales revenue of the first company and to the cost of sales of the second. Yet as far as the entity's dealings with outsiders are concerned no sale has taken place.

The consolidated figures for sales revenue and cost of sales should represent **sales to**, and **purchases from, outsiders**. An adjustment is therefore necessary to reduce the sales revenue and cost of sales figures by the value of intra-group sales during the year.

We have also seen in an earlier chapter that any unrealised profits on intra-group trading should be excluded from the figure for group profits. This will occur whenever goods sold at a profit within the group remain in the inventory of the purchasing company at the year end. The best way to deal with this is to **calculate the unrealised profit on unsold inventories at the year end and reduce consolidated gross profit by this amount**. Cost of sales will be the balancing figure.

1.4 Example: Intra-group trading

Suppose in our earlier example that S Co had recorded sales of $5,000 to P Co during 20X6. S Co had purchased these goods from outside suppliers at a cost of $3,000. One half of the goods remained in P Co's inventory at 31 December 20X6. Prepare the revised consolidated statement of profit or loss.

Solution

The consolidated statement of profit or loss for the year ended 31 December 20X6 would now be as follows.

	$
Revenue (75 + 38 – 5)	108,000
Cost of sales (30 + 20 – 5 + 1*)	(46,000)
Gross profit (45 + 18 – 1*)	62,000
Administrative expenses	(22,000)
Profit before taxation	40,000
Income tax expense	(12,000)
Profit for the year	28,000
Profit attributable to:	
Owners of the parent	26,250
Non-controlling interest (8,000 – 1,000) × 25%	1,750
	28,000

Note:

Retained earnings brought forward	99,750
Profit for the year	26,250
Retained earnings carried forward	126,000

*Unrealised profit: ½ × ($5,000 – $3,000)

An adjustment will be made for the unrealised profit against the inventory figure in the consolidated statement of financial position.

1.5 Intra-group dividends

In our example so far we have assumed that S Co retains all of its after-tax profit. It may be, however, that S Co distributes some of its profits as dividends. As before, the **non-controlling interest** in the subsidiary's profit should be calculated immediately after the figure of after-tax profit. For this purpose, no account need be taken of how much of the non-controlling interest is to be distributed by S Co as dividend.

Note that group retained earnings are only adjusted for dividends paid to the parent company shareholders. Dividends paid by the subsidiary to the parent are cancelled on consolidation and dividends paid to the non-controlling interest are replaced by the allocation to the non-controlling interest of their share of the profit for the year of the subsidiary.

1.6 Pre-acquisition profits

Only the **post acquisition** profits of the subsidiary are brought into the consolidated statement of profit or loss.

As explained above, the figure for retained earnings carried forward must be the same as the figure for retained earnings in the consolidated statement of financial position. We have seen in previous chapters that retained earnings in the consolidated statement of financial position comprise:

(a)   The **whole of the parent company's** retained earnings

(b)   A **proportion of the subsidiary company's** retained earnings. The proportion is the **group's share of post-acquisition retained earnings** in the subsidiary. From the total retained earnings of the subsidiary we must therefore **exclude** both the **non-controlling share** of total retained earnings and the **group's share of pre-acquisition** retained earnings.

A **similar procedure is necessary in the consolidated statement of profit or loss** if it is to link up with the consolidated statement of financial position. Previous examples have shown how the non-controlling share of profits is excluded in the statement of profit or loss. Their share of profits for the year is deducted from profit after tax, while the figure for profits brought forward in the consolidation schedule includes only the group's proportion of the subsidiary's profits.

In the same way, when considering examples which include pre-acquisition profits in a subsidiary, the figure for profits brought forward should include only the group's share of the post-acquisition retained profits. If the subsidiary is **acquired during the accounting year**, it is therefore necessary to apportion its profit for the year between pre-acquisition and post-acquisition elements. The part year method is used.

With the part-year method, the entire statement of profit or loss of the subsidiary is split between pre-acquisition and post-acquisition amounts. Only the post-acquisition figures are included in the consolidated statement of profit or loss.

Question   Acquisition

P Co acquired 60% of the $100,000 equity of S Co on 1 April 20X5. The statements of profit or loss of the two companies for the year ended 31 December 20X5 are set out below.

	P Co	S Co	S Co ($^9/_{12}$)
	$	$	$
Revenue	170,000	80,000	60,000
Cost of sales	65,000	36,000	27,000
Gross profit	105,000	44,000	33,000
Other income – dividend received S Co	3,600		
Administrative expenses	43,000	12,000	9,000
Profit before tax	65,600	32,000	24,000
Income tax expense	23,000	8,000	6,000
Profit for the year	42,600	24,000	18,000

Note

Dividends (paid 31 December)	12,000	6,000	
Profit retained	30,600	18,000	
Retained earnings brought forward	81,000	40,000	
Retained earnings carried forward	111,600	58,000	

Prepare the consolidated statement of profit or loss and the retained earnings and non-controlling interest extracts from the statement of changes in equity.

Answer

The shares in S Co were acquired three months into the year. Only the post-acquisition proportion (9/12ths) of S Co's statement of profit or loss is included in the consolidated statement of profit or loss. This is shown above for convenience.

P CO CONSOLIDATED STATEMENT OF PROFIT OR LOSS
FOR THE YEAR ENDED 31 DECEMBER 20X5

	$
Revenue (170 + 60)	230,000
Cost of sales (65 + 27)	(92,000)
Gross profit	138,000
Administrative expenses (43 + 9)	(52,000)
Profit before tax	86,000
Income tax expense (23 + 6)	(29,000)
Profit for the year	57,000
Profit attributable to:	
Owners of the parent	49,800
Non-controlling interest (18 × 40%)	7,200
	57,000

STATEMENT OF CHANGES IN EQUITY

	Retained earnings	Non-controlling interest
	$	$
Balance at 1 January 20X5	81,000	–
Dividends paid (6,000 – 3,600)	(12,000)	(2,400)
Total comprehensive income for the year	49,800	7,200
Added on acquisition of subsidiary (W)	–	58,400
Balance at 31 December 20X5	118,800	63,200

* All of S Co's profits brought forward are pre-acquisition.

Working

	$
Added on acquisition of subsidiary:	
Share capital	100,000
Retained earnings brought forward	40,000
Profits Jan-March 20X5 (24,000 – 18,000)	6,000
	146,000
Non-controlling share 40%	58,400

Question

The following information relates to Brodick Co and its subsidiary Lamlash Co for the year to 30 April 20X7.

	Brodick Co $'000	Lamlash Co $'000
Revenue	1,100	500
Cost of sales	(630)	(300)
Gross profit	470	200
Administrative expenses	(105)	(150)
Dividend from Lamlash Co	24	–
Profit before tax	389	50
Income tax expense	(65)	(10)
Profit for the year	324	40

Note

Dividends paid	200	30
Profit retained	124	10
Retained earnings brought forward	460	106
Retained earnings carried forward	584	116

Additional information

(a) The issued share capital of the group was as follows.

   Brodick Co   : 5,000,000 ordinary shares of $1 each.
   Lamlash Co : 1,000,000 ordinary shares of $1 each.

(b) Brodick Co purchased 80% of the issued share capital of Lamlash Co in 20X0. At that time, the retained earnings of Lamlash stood at $56,000.

Required

Insofar as the information permits, prepare the Brodick group consolidated statement of profit or loss for the year to 30 April 20X7, and extracts from the statement of changes in equity showing retained earnings and non-controlling interest.

Answer

BRODICK GROUP
CONSOLIDATED STATEMENT OF PROFIT OR LOSS
FOR THE YEAR TO 30 APRIL 20X7

	$'000
Revenue (1,100 + 500)	1,600
Cost of sales (630 + 300)	(930)
Gross profit	670
Administrative expenses (105 + 150)	(255)
Profit before tax	415
Income tax expense (65 + 10)	(75)
Profit for the year	340

Profit attributable to:

	$
Owners of the parent	332
Non-controlling interest (W1)	8
	340

STATEMENT OF CHANGES IN EQUITY

	Non-controlling interest $'000	Retained earnings $'000
Balance brought forward (W3)/(W2)	221	500
Dividends paid (30,000 – 24,000)	(6)	(200)
Total comprehensive income for the year	8	332
Balance carried forward	223	632

Workings

1   *Non-controlling interests*

	$'000
In Lamlash (20% × 40)	8

2   *Retained earnings brought forward*

	Brodick Co $'000	Lamlash Co $'000
Per question	460	106
Less pre-aqn		(56)
		50
Share of Lamlash: 80% × 50	40	
	500	

3   *Non-controlling interest brought forward*

	$'000
Share capital	1,000
Retained earnings brought forward	106
	1,106
Non-controlling share 20%	221

1.7 Section summary

The table below summarises the main points about the consolidated statement.

Purpose	To show the results of the group for an accounting period as if it were a single entity.
Revenue to profit for year	100% P + 100% S (excluding adjustments for intra-group transactions).
Reason	To show the results of the group which were controlled by the parent company.
Intra-group sales	Strip out intra-group activity from both sales revenue and cost of sales.
Unrealised profit on intra-group sales	(a) Goods sold by P. Increase cost of sales by unrealised profit. (b) Goods sold by S. Increase cost of sales by full amount of unrealised profit and decrease non-controlling interest by their share of unrealised profit.
Depreciation	If the value of S's non-current assets have been subjected to a fair value uplift then any additional depreciation must be charged in the consolidated statement of profit or loss. The non-controlling interest will need to be adjusted for their share.
Transfer of non-current assets	Expenses must be increased by any profit on the transfer and reduced by any additional depreciation arising from the increased carrying value of the asset.

Non-controlling interests	S's profit after tax (PAT)	X
	Less: * unrealised profit	(X)
	* profit on disposal of non-current assets	(X)
	additional depreciation following FV uplift	(X)
	Add: ** additional depreciation following disposal of	
	non-current assets	X
		X
	NCI%	X
	* Only applicable if sales of goods and non-current assets made by subsidiary.	
	** Only applicable if sale of non-current assets made by subsidiary.	
Reason	To show the extent to which profits generated through P's control are in fact owned by other parties.	
Reserves carried forward	As per the calculations for the statement of financial position.	

2 The consolidated statement of profit or loss and other comprehensive income

The consolidated statement of profit or loss and other comprehensive income is produced using the consolidated statement of profit or loss as a basis.

The only items of other comprehensive income that you are likely to meet in the exam are revaluation gains and losses, so a consolidated statement of profit or loss and other comprehensive income will be easy to produce once you have done the statement of profit or loss.

We will take the last question and add an item of comprehensive income to illustrate this.

2.1 Example: Consolidated statement of profit or loss and other comprehensive income

The consolidated statement of profit or loss of the Brodrick Group is as in the answer to the last question. In addition, Lamlash made a $200,000 revaluation gain on one of its properties during the year.

2.2 Solution

BRODRICK GROUP
CONSOLIDATED STATEMENT OF COMPREHENSIVE INCOME FOR THE YEAR TO 30 APRIL 20X7

	$'000
Revenue	1,600
Cost of sales	(930)
Gross profit	670
Administrative expenses	(255)
Profit before tax	415
Income tax expense	(75)
Profit for the year	340
Other comprehensive income:	
Gain on property revaluation	200
Total comprehensive income for the year	540
Profit attributable to:	
Owners of the parent	332
Non-controlling interest	8

Total comprehensive income attributable to:

Owners of the parent (332 + (200 × 80%))	492
Non-controlling interest (8 + (200 × 20%))	48
	540

2.3 Consolidated statement of profit or loss and other comprehensive income (separate statement)

If we were using the two-statement format (as explained in Chapter 3) we would produce a separate statement of profit or loss and statement of comprehensive income.

2.4 Example: Other comprehensive income

BRODRICK GROUP
CONSOLIDATED STATEMENT OF PROFIT OR LOSS AND OTHER COMPREHENSIVE INCOME

Profit for the year	340
Other comprehensive income:	
Gain on property revaluation	200
Total comprehensive income for the year	540
Total comprehensive income attributable to:	
Owners of the parent (332 + (200 × 80%))	492
Non-controlling interest (8 + (200 × 20%)	48
	540

2.5 Consolidated statement of changes in equity

These amounts would appear in the consolidated statement of changes in equity as follows:

	Retained earnings $'000	Revaluation surplus $'000	Total $'000	Non-controlling interest $'000	Total $'000
Total comprehensive income for the year	332	160	492	48	540

Chapter roundup

- The source of the consolidated statement of profit or loss is the individual statements of profit or loss of the separate companies in the group.

- In the consolidated statement of profit or loss non-controlling interest is brought in as a one-line adjustment at the end of the statement.

- Intra-group sales and purchases are eliminated from the consolidated statement of profit or loss.

- Only the **post acquisition** profits of the subsidiary are brought into the consolidated statement of profit or loss.

- The consolidated statement of profit or loss and other comprehensive income is produced using the consolidated statement of profit or loss as a basis.

Quick quiz

1   Where does unrealised profit on intra-group trading appear in the statement of profit or loss?

2   At the beginning of the year a 75% subsidiary transfers a non-current asset to the parent for $500,000. Its carrying value was $400,000 and it has 4 years of useful life left. How is this accounted for at the end of the year in the consolidated statement of profit or loss?

3   Barley Co has owned 100% of the issued share capital of Oats Co for many years. Barley Co sells goods to Oats Co at cost plus 20%. The following information is available for the year:

Revenue   – Barley Co $460,000
             – Oats Co $120,000

During the year Barley Co sold goods to Oats Co for $60,000 of which $18,000 were still held in inventory by Oats at the year end.

At what amount should revenue appear in the consolidated statement of profit or loss?

Answers to quick quiz

1   As a deduction from consolidated gross profit and increase to cost of sales.

2

	$
Unrealised profit	100,000
Additional depreciation (100 ÷ 4)	(25,000)
Net charge to profit or loss	75,000

	DR	CR
	$	$
Non-current asset		100,000
Additional depreciation	25,000	
Group profit (75%)	56,250	
Non-controlling interest (25%)	18,750	
	100,000	100,000

3   Revenue: $460,000 + $120,000 – $60,000 = $520,000

End of chapter question

Fallowfield and Rusholme

Fallowfield acquired a 60% holding in Rusholme three years ago when Rusholme's retained earnings balance stood at $16,000. Both businesses have been very successful since the acquisition and their respective statements of profit or loss for the year ended 30 June 20X8 are as follows:

	Fallowfield	Rusholme
	$	$
Revenue	403,400	193,000
Cost of sales	(201,400)	(92,600)
Gross profit	202,000	100,400
Distribution costs	(16,000)	(14,600)
Administrative expenses	(24,250)	(17,800)
Dividends from Rusholme	15,000	
Profit before tax	176,750	68,000
Income tax expense	(61,750)	(22,000)
Profit for the year	115,000	46,000

STATEMENT OF CHANGES IN EQUITY (EXTRACT)

	Fallowfield Retained earnings	Rusholme Retained earnings
	$	$
Balance at 1 July 20X7	163,000	61,000
Dividends	(40,000)	(25,000)
Profit for the year	115,000	46,000
Balance at 30 June 20X8	238,000	82,000

Additional information

During the year Rusholme sold some goods to Fallowfield for $40,000, including 25% mark up. Half of these items were still in inventories at the year-end.

Required

Produce the consolidated statement of profit or loss of Fallowfield Co and its subsidiary for the year ended 30 June 20X8, and an extract from the statement of changes in equity, showing retained earnings. Goodwill is to be ignored. **(15 marks)**

Accounting for associates

Topic list	Syllabus reference
1 Accounting for associates	11.3
2 The equity method	11.3
3 Statement of profit or loss and statement of financial position	11.3

Introduction

In this chapter we deal with the treatment of associates in the consolidated financial statements. An associate is an entity in which an investor has significant influence, rather than control. The equity method is used to account for associates.

As the group's share of profit in the associate appears under profit or loss rather than other comprehensive income, we have concentrated on the separate statement of profit or loss.

1 Accounting for associates

FAST FORWARD

Accounting for associates is covered by IAS 28 *Investments in associates and joint ventures*. The investing company does not have control, as it does with a subsidiary, but it does have **significant influence**.

1.1 Definitions

We looked at some of the important definitions in Chapter 15; these are repeated here with some additional important terms.

Key terms

> **Associate**. An entity over which an investor has significant influence.
>
> **Significant influence** is the power to participate in the financial and operating policy decisions of the investee but is not control or joint control of those policies.
>
> **Equity method**. A method of accounting whereby the investment is initially recognised at cost and adjusted thereafter for the post-acquisition change in the investor's share of net assets of the investee. The investor's profit or loss includes it's share of the investee's profit or loss and the investor's other comprehensive income includes its share of the investee's other comprehensive income.

We have already looked at how the **status** of an investment in an associate should be determined. Go back to Section 1 of Chapter 15 to revise it. (Note that, as for an investment in a subsidiary, any **potential voting rights** should be taken into account in assessing whether the investor has **significant influence** over the investee.)

IAS 28 requires all investments in associates to be accounted for in the consolidated accounts using the equity method, *unless* the investment is classified as 'held for sale' in accordance with IFRS 5 in which case it should be accounted for under IFRS 5 (see Chapter 5), or the exemption in the paragraph below applies.

An investor is exempt from applying the equity method if:

(a)   It is a parent exempt from preparing consolidated financial statements under IFRS 10, or

(b)   All of the following apply:

    (i)   The investor is a **wholly-owned subsidiary** or it is a **partially owned subsidiary** of another entity and its other owners, including those not otherwise entitled to vote, have been informed about, and do not object to, the investor not applying the equity method;

    (ii)   The investor's securities are **not publicly traded**

    (iii)   It is **not in the process of issuing securities** in public securities markets; and

    (iv)   The **ultimate or intermediate parent** produces consolidated financial statements available for public use that comply with International Financial Reporting Standards.

IAS 28 **does not allow** an investment in an associate to be excluded from equity accounting when an investee operates under severe long-term restrictions that significantly impair its ability to transfer funds to the investor. Significant influence must be lost before the equity method ceases to be applicable.

The use of the equity method should be **discontinued** from the date that the investor **ceases to have significant influence**.

From that date, the investor shall account for the investment in accordance with IFRS 9 *Financial instruments*. The carrying amount of the investment at the date that it ceases to be an associate shall be regarded as its cost on initial measurement as a financial asset under IFRS 9.

1.2 Separate financial statements of the investor

If an investor **issues consolidated financial statements** (because it has subsidiaries), an investment in an associate should be *either*:

(a)   Accounted for at **cost**, or
(b)   In accordance with **IFRS 9** (at fair value)

in its separate financial statements.

If an investor that does *not* **issue consolidated financial statements** (ie it has no subsidiaries) but has an investment in an associate this should similarly be included in the financial statements of the investor either at cost, or in accordance with IFRS 9 (see Chapter 21).

2 The equity method

2.1 Application of the equity method: consolidated accounts

Many of the procedures required to apply the equity method are the same as are required for full consolidation. In particular, **intra-group unrealised profits** must be excluded.

2.1.1 Consolidated statement of profit or loss

The basic principle is that the investing company (X Co) should take account of its **share of the earnings** of the associate, Y Co, whether or not Y Co distributes the earnings as dividends. X Co achieves this by adding to consolidated profit the group's share of Y Co's profit after tax.

Notice the difference between this treatment and the **consolidation** of a subsidiary company's results. If Y Co were a subsidiary X Co would take credit for the whole of its sales revenue, cost of sales etc and would then make a one-line adjustment to remove any non-controlling share.

Under equity accounting, the associate's sales revenue, cost of sales and so on are *not* **amalgamated** with those of the group. Instead the group share only of the associate's profit after tax for the year is added to the group profit.

2.1.2 Consolidated statement of financial position

A figure for **investment in associates** is shown which at the time of the acquisition must be stated at cost. This amount will increase (decrease) each year by the amount of the group's share of the associated company's profit (loss) for the year.

2.2 Example: Associate

P Co, a company with subsidiaries, acquires 25,000 of the 100,000 $1 ordinary shares in A Co for $60,000 on 1 January 20X8. In the year to 31 December 20X8, A Co earns profits after tax of $24,000, from which it pays a dividend of $6,000.

How will A Co's results be accounted for in the individual and consolidated accounts of P Co for the year ended 31 December 20X8?

Solution

In the **individual accounts** of P Co, the investment will be recorded on 1 January 20X8 at cost. Unless there is an impairment in the value of the investment (see below), this amount will remain in the individual statement of financial position of P Co permanently. The only entry in P Co's individual statement of profit or loss will be to record dividends received. For the year ended 31 December 20X8, P Co will:

DEBIT	Cash	$1,500	
CREDIT	Income from shares in associates		$1,500

In the **consolidated accounts** of P Co equity accounting principles will be used to account for the investment in A Co. Consolidated profit after tax will include the group's share of A Co's profit after tax (25% × $24,000 = $6,000). To the extent that this has been distributed as dividend, it is already included in P Co's individual accounts and will automatically be brought into the consolidated results. That part of the group's share of profit in the associate which has not been distributed as dividend ($4,500) will be brought into consolidation by the following adjustment.

DEBIT	Investment in associates	$4,500
CREDIT	Share of profit of associates	$4,500

The asset 'Investment in associates' is then stated at $64,500, being cost plus the group share of post-acquisition retained profits.

3 Statement of profit or loss and statement of financial position

3.1 Consolidated statement of profit or loss

FAST FORWARD

In the **consolidated statement of profit or loss** the investing group takes credit for its **share of the after-tax profits** of associates, whether or not they are distributed as dividends.

A **consolidation schedule** may be used to prepare the consolidated statement of profit or loss of a group with associates. The treatment of associates' profits in the following example should be studied carefully.

3.2 Illustration

The following **consolidation schedule** relates to the P Co group, consisting of the parent company, an 80% owned subsidiary (S Co) and an associate (A Co) in which the group has a 30% interest.

CONSOLIDATION SCHEDULE

	Group $'000	P Co $'000	S Co $'000	A Co $'000
Revenue	1,400	600	800	300
Cost of sales	770	370	400	120
Gross profit	630	230	400	180
Administrative expenses	290	110	180	80
	340	120	220	100
Interest receivable	30	30	–	–
	370	150	220	100
Interest payable	(20)	–	(20)	–
Share of profit of associate (57× 30%)	17	–	–	
	367	150	200	100
Income tax expense	(145)	(55)	(90)	(43)
Profit for the year	222	95	110	57
Non-controlling interest (110× 20%)	(22)			
	200			

Note the following

(a) Group sales revenue, group gross profit and costs such as depreciation etc exclude the sales revenue, gross profit and costs etc of associated companies.

(b) The group share of the associated company profits is credited to group profit or loss. If the associated company has been acquired during the year, it would be necessary to deduct the pre-acquisition profits (remembering to allow for tax on current year profits).

(c) The non-controlling interest will only ever apply to subsidiary companies.

3.3 Pro-forma consolidated statement of profit or loss

The following is a **suggested layout** (using the figures given in the illustration above) for the consolidated statement of profit or loss for a company having subsidiaries as well as associates.

	$'000
Revenue	1,400
Cost of sales	(770)
Gross profit	630
Other income: interest receivable	30
Administrative expenses	(290)
Finance costs	(20)
Share of profit of associate	17
Profit before tax	367
Income tax expense	(145)
Profit for the year	222
Profit attributable to:	
Owners of the parent	200
Non-controlling interest	22
	222

3.4 Consolidated statement of financial position

FAST FORWARD

In the consolidated statement of financial position the investment in associates should be shown as:

- **Cost of the investment in the associate**; plus
- Group share of post acquisition profits; less
- Any amounts paid out as dividends; less
- Any amount written off the investment

As explained earlier, the consolidated statement of financial position will contain an **asset 'Investment in associates'**. The amount at which this asset is stated will be its original cost plus the group's share of any **profits earned since acquisition** which have not been distributed as dividends.

3.5 Example: Consolidated statement of financial position

On 1 January 20X6 the net tangible assets of A Co amount to $220,000, financed by 100,000 $1 ordinary shares and revenue reserves of $120,000. P Co, a company with subsidiaries, acquires 30,000 of the shares in A Co for $75,000. During the year ended 31 December 20X6 A Co's profit after tax is $30,000, from which dividends of $12,000 are paid.

Show how P Co's investment in A Co would appear in the consolidated statement of financial position at 31 December 20X6.

Solution

CONSOLIDATED STATEMENT OF FINANCIAL POSITION
AS AT 31 DECEMBER 20X6 (extract)

	$
Non-current assets	
Investment in associates	
Cost	75,000
Group share of post-acquisition retained profits	
(30% × $18,000)	5,400
	80,400

Question

Set out below are the draft accounts of Parent Co and its subsidiaries and of Associate Co. Parent Co acquired 40% of the equity capital of Associate Co three years ago when the latter's reserves stood at $40,000.

SUMMARISED STATEMENTS OF FINANCIAL POSITION

	Parent Co & subsidiaries $'000	Associate Co $'000
Property, plant and equipment	220	170
Investment in Associate at cost	60	–
Loan to Associate Co	20	–
Current assets	100	50
	400	220
Share capital ($1 shares)	250	100
Retained earnings	150	100
	400	200
Loan from Parent Co	-	20
	400	220

SUMMARISED STATEMENTS OF PROFIT OR LOSS

	Parent Co & subsidiaries $'000	Associate Co $'000
Profit before tax	95	80
Income tax expense	35	30
Net profit for the year	60	50

You are required to prepare the summarised consolidated accounts of Parent Co.

Notes

(1)   Assume that the associate's assets/liabilities are stated at fair value.
(2)   Assume that there are no non-controlling interests in the subsidiary companies.

Answer

PARENT CO
CONSOLIDATED STATEMENT OF PROFIT OR LOSS

	$'000
Net profit	95
Share of profits of associated company (50 × 40%)	20
Profit before tax	115
Income tax expense	(35)
Profit attributable to the owners of Parent Co	80

PARENT CO
CONSOLIDATED STATEMENT OF FINANCIAL POSITION

	$'000
Assets	
Property, plant and equipment	220
Investment in associate (see note)	104
Current assets	100
Total assets	424

Equity and liabilities	$'000
Share capital	250
Retained earnings (W)	174
Total equity and liabilities	424

Note	
	$'000
Investment in associate	
Cost of investment	60
Share of post-acquisition retained earnings (W)	24
Loan to associate	20
	104

(IAS 28 (38) states that any long-term interests that in substance are part of the entity's net investment in the associate should be included as part of 'investments in associate'. In the example above the loan to the associate has been treated as part of the net investment).

Working

Retained earnings	Parent & Subsidiaries $'000	Associate $'000
Per question	150	100
Pre-acquisition		40
Post-acquisition		60
Group share in associate		
($60 × 40%)	24	
Group retained earnings	174	

Question   Associate II

Alfred Co bought a 25% shareholding on 31 December 20X8 in Grimbald Co at a cost of $38,000.

During the year to 31 December 20X9 Grimbald Co made a profit before tax of $82,000 and the taxation charge on the year's profits was $32,000. A dividend of $20,000 was paid on 31 December out of these profits.

Calculate the entries for the associate which would appear in the consolidated accounts of the Alfred group, in accordance with the requirements of IAS 28.

Answer

CONSOLIDATED STATEMENT OF PROFIT OR LOSS

	$
Group share of profit of associate (82,000 × 25%)	20,500
Less taxation (32,000 × 25%)	(8,000)
Share of profit of associate	12,500

CONSOLIDATED STATEMENT OF FINANCIAL POSITION

	$
Investment in associate	45,500

Working

	$
Cost of investment	38,000
Share of post-acquisition retained earnings ((82,000 – 32,000 – 20,000) × 25%)	7,500
	45,500

The following points are also relevant and are similar to a parent-subsidiary consolidation situation.

(a)   Use financial statements drawn up to the **same reporting date.**

(b)   If this is impracticable, adjust the financial statements for **significant transactions/ events** in the intervening period. The difference between the reporting date of the associate and that of the investor must be no more than three months.

(c)   Use **uniform accounting policies** for like transactions and events in similar circumstances, adjusting the associate's statements to reflect group policies if necessary.

3.6 'Upstream' and 'downstream' transactions

'Upstream' transactions are, for example, sales of assets from an associate to the investor. 'Downstream' transactions are, for example, sales of assets from the investor to an associate.

Profits and losses resulting from 'upstream' and 'downstream' transactions between an investor (including its consolidated subsidiaries) and an associate are eliminated to the extent of the investor's interest in the associate. This is very similar to the procedure for eliminating intra-group transactions between a parent and a subsidiary. The important thing to remember is that **only the group's share is eliminated**.

3.7 Example: Downstream transaction

A Co, a parent with subsidiaries, holds 25% of the equity shares in B Co. During the year, A Co makes sales of $1,000,000 to B Co at cost plus a 25% mark-up. At the year-end, B Co has all these goods still in inventories.

Solution

A Co has made an unrealised profit of $200,000 (1,000,000 × 25/125) on its sales to the associate. The group's share (25%) of this must be eliminated:

DEBIT   Cost of sales (consolidated profit or loss) $50,000
CREDIT   Investment in associate (consolidated statement of financial position) $50,000

Because the sale was made to the associate, the group's share of the unsold inventory forms part of the investment in the associate at the year-end. If the associate had made the sale to the parent, the adjustment would have been:

DEBIT   Cost of sales (consolidated profit or loss) $50,000
CREDIT   Inventories (consolidated statement of financial position) $50,000

3.8 Associate's losses

When the equity method is being used and the investor's share of losses of the associate equals or exceeds its interest in the associate, the investor should **discontinue** including its share of further losses. The investment is reported at nil value. The interest in the associate is normally the carrying amount of the investment in the associate, but it also includes any other long-term interests, for example, long term receivables or loans.

After the investor's interest is reduced to nil, **additional losses** should only be recognised where the investor has incurred obligations or made payments on behalf of the associate (for example, if it has guaranteed amounts owed to third parties by the associate).

3.9 Impairment losses

IAS 39 deals with the impairment of financial assets recognised in accordance with IFRS 9. It sets out a list of indications that a financial asset (including an associate) may have become impaired. Any impairment loss is recognised in accordance with IAS 36 *Impairment of assets* for each associate individually.

In the case of an associate, any impairment loss will be deducted from the carrying amount in the statement of financial position.

The working would be as follows.

	$
Cost of investment	X
Share of post-acquisition retained earnings	X
	X
Impairment loss	(X)
Investment in associate	X

Exam focus point

It is not unusual in an exam to have both an associate and a subsidiary to account for in a consolidation.

Question   Consolidated statement of financial position

The statements of financial position of J Co and its investee companies, P Co and S Co, at 31 December 20X5 are shown below.

STATEMENTS OF FINANCIAL POSITION AS AT 31 DECEMBER 20X5

	J Co $'000	P Co $'000	S Co $'000
Non-current assets			
Freehold property	1,950	1,250	500
Plant and machinery	795	375	285
Investments	1,500	–	–
	4,245	1,625	785
Current assets			
Inventory	575	300	265
Trade receivables	330	290	370
Cash	50	120	20
	955	710	655
Total assets	5,200	2,335	1,440
Equity and liabilities			
Equity			
Share capital – $1 shares	2,000	1,000	750
Retained earnings	1,460	885	390
	3,460	1,885	1,140
Non-current liabilities			
12% loan stock	500	100	
Current liabilities			
Trade payables	680	350	300
Bank overdraft	560	–	–
	1,240	350	300
Total equity and liabilities	5,200	2,335	1,440

Additional information

(a)   J Co acquired 600,000 ordinary shares in P Co on 1 January 20X0 for $1,000,000 when the retained earnings of P Co were $200,000.

(b)   At the date of acquisition of P Co, the fair value of its freehold property was considered to be $400,000 greater than its value in P Co's statement of financial position. P Co had acquired the property in January 20W0 and the buildings element (comprising 50% of the total value) is depreciated on cost over 50 years.

(c)   J Co acquired 225,000 ordinary shares in S Co on 1 January 20X4 for $500,000 when the retained earnings of S Co were $150,000.

(d)   P Co manufactures a component used by both J Co and S Co. Transfers are made by P Co at cost plus 25%. J Co held $100,000 inventory of these components at 31 December 20X5 and S Co held $80,000 at the same date.

(e)   The goodwill in P Co is impaired and should be fully written off. An impairment loss of $92,000 is to be recognised on the investment in S Co.

(f)   Non-controlling interest is valued at proportionate share of net assets.

Required

Prepare, in a format suitable for inclusion in the annual report of the J Group, the consolidated statement of financial position at 31 December 20X5.

Answer

J GROUP CONSOLIDATED STATEMENT OF FINANCIAL POSITION AS AT 31 DECEMBER 20X5

	$'000
Non-current assets	
Freehold property (W2)	3,570.00
Plant and machinery (795 + 375)	1,170.00
Investment in associate (W9)	475.20
	5,215.20
Current assets	
Inventory (W3)	855.00
Receivables (W4)	620.00
Cash (50 + 120)	170.00
	1,645.00
Total assets	6,860.20
Equity and liabilities	
Equity	
Share capital	2,000.00
Retained earnings (W10)	1,778.12
	3,778.12
Non-controlling interest (W11)	892.08
	4,670.20
Non-current liabilities	
12% loan stock (500 + 100)	600.00
Current liabilities (W5)	1,590.00
Total equity and liabilities	6,860.20

Workings

1   *Group structure*

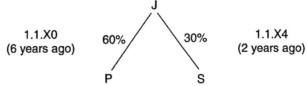

	1.1.X0 (6 years ago)	60%	J	30%	1.1.X4 (2 years ago)
			P	S	

2   *Freehold property*

	$'000
J Co	1,950
P Co	1,250
Fair value adjustment	400
Additional depreciation (400 × 50% ÷ 40) × 6 years (20X0-20X5)	(30)
	3,570

3   *Inventory*

	$'000
J Co	575
P Co	300
PUP (100 × $^{25}/_{125}$)	(20)
	855

4   *Receivables*

	$'000
J Co	330
P Co	290
	620

5   *Current liabilities*

	$'000
J Co: bank overdraft	560
trade payables	680
P Co: trade payables	350
	1,590

6   *Unrealised profit (PUP)*

	$'000
On sales to J (parent co) 100 × 25/125	20.0
On sales to S (associate) 80 × 25/125 × 30%	4.8
	24.8

7   *Fair value adjustments*

	Difference at acquisition $'000	Difference now $'000
Property	400	400
Additional depreciation: 200 × 6/40	–	(30)
	400	370

∴ Charge $30,000 to retained earnings

8 Goodwill

	$'000	$'000
P Co		
Consideration transferred		1,000
Non-controlling interest (1,600 × 40%)		640
		1,640
Net assets acquired		
Share capital	1,000	
Retained earnings	200	
Fair value adjustment	400	
		(1,600)
Goodwill at acquisition		40
Impairment loss		(40)
		0

9 Investment in associate

	$'000
Cost of investment	500.00
Share of post-acquisition profit (390 – 150) × 30%	72.00
Less PUP	(4.80)
Less impairment loss	(92.00)
	475.20

10 Retained earnings

	J	P	S
	$'000	$'000	$'000
Retained earnings per question	1,460.0	885.0	390.0
Adjustments			
Unrealised profit (W6)		(24.8)	
Fair value adjustments (W7)		(30.0)	
		830.2	390.0
Less pre-acquisition reserves		(200.0)	(150.0)
	1,460.0	630.2	240.0
P: 60% × 630.2	378.1		
S: 30% × 240	72.0		
Less impairment losses : P (W8)	(40.0)		
S	(92.0)		
	1,778.1		

11 Non-controlling interest at reporting date

	$'000
Net assets of P Co	1,885.0
Fair value adjustment (W11)	370.0
Less PUP: sales to J Co	(20.0)
sales to S Co (80 × $^{25}/_{125}$ × 30%)	(4.8)
	2,230.2
Non-controlling interest (40%)	892.08

Chapter roundup

- Accounting for associates is covered by IAS 28 *Investments in associates and joint ventures*. The investing company does not have control, as it does with a subsidiary, but it does have **significant influence**.

- In the **consolidated statement of profit or loss** the investing group takes credit for its **share of the after-tax profits** of associates, whether or not they are distributed as dividends.

- In the **consolidated statement of financial position**, the investment in associates should be shown as:

  - **Cost of the investment in the associate**; plus
  - Group share of post-acquisition profits; less
  - Any amounts paid out as dividends; less
  - Any amount written off the investment

Quick quiz

1   Define an associate.

2   How should associates be accounted for in the separate financial statements of the investor?

3   What is the effect of the equity method on the consolidated statement of profit or loss and statement of financial position?

Answers to quick quiz

1   An entity over which an investor has significant influence.

2   Either at cost or in accordance with IFRS 9.

3   (a)   *Consolidated statement of profit or loss.* Investing company includes its share of the earnings of the associate, by adding its share of profit after tax.

  (b)   *Consolidated statement of financial position.* Investment in an associate is initially included in assets at cost. This will increase or decrease each year according to whether the associated company makes a profit or loss.

End of chapter question

Hever

Hever has held shares in two companies, Spiro and Aldridge, for a number of years. As at 31 December 20X4 they have the following statements of financial position:

	Hever $'000	Spiro $'000	Aldridge $'000
Non-current assets			
Property, plant & equipment	370	190	260
Investments	218	–	–
	588	190	260
Current assets:			
Inventories	160	100	180
Trade receivables	170	90	100
Cash	50	40	10
	380	230	290
	968	420	550
Equity			
Share capital ($1 ords)	200	80	50
Share premium	100	80	30
Retained earnings	568	200	400
	868	360	480
Current liabilities			
Trade payables	100	60	70
	968	420	550

You ascertain the following additional information:

(1) The 'investments' in the statement of financial position comprise solely Hever's investment in Spiro ($128,000) and in Aldridge ($90,000).

(2) The 48,000 shares in Spiro were acquired when Spiro's retained earnings balance stood at $20,000.

The 15,000 shares in Aldridge were acquired when that company had a retained earnings balance of $150,000.

(3) When Hever acquired its shares in Spiro the fair value of Spiro's net assets equalled their book values with the following exceptions:

	$'000
Property, plant and equipment	50 higher
Inventories	20 lower (sold during 20X4)

Depreciation arising on the fair value adjustment to non-current assets since this date is $5,000.

(4) During the year, Hever sold inventories to Spiro for $16,000, which originally cost Hever $10,000. Three-quarters of these inventories have subsequently been sold by Spiro.

(5) No impairment losses on goodwill had been necessary by 31 December 20X4.

Required

Produce the consolidated statement of financial position for the Hever group (incorporating the associate). It is the group policy to value the non-controlling interest at its proportionate share of the fair value of the subsidiary's identifiable net assets. **(25 marks)**

Accounting for specialised transactions

Inventories and construction contracts

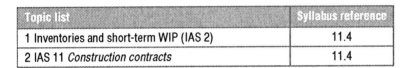

Topic list	Syllabus reference
1 Inventories and short-term WIP (IAS 2)	11.4
2 IAS 11 *Construction contracts*	11.4

Introduction

You have encountered inventory and its valuation in your earlier studies.
Inventory and short-term work-in-progress valuation has a direct impact on a
company's gross profit and it is usually a material item in any company's
accounts. This is therefore an important subject area. If you have any doubts
about accounting for inventories and methods of inventory valuation you would
be advised to go back to your earlier study material and revise this topic.

Section 1 of this chapter goes over some of this ground again, concentrating
on the effect of IAS 2. Section 2 goes on to discuss a new area, construction
contracts, which are effectively long-term work in progress. You should find
this topic fairly logical as long as you work through the examples and questions
carefully.

1 Inventories and short-term WIP (IAS 2)

Most of this is revision. However, you should be aware that the use of LIFO is prohibited under IAS 2.

1.1 Introduction

In most businesses the value put on inventory is an important factor in the determination of profit. Inventory valuation is, however, a highly subjective exercise and consequently a wide variety of different methods are used in practice.

1.2 IAS 2 *Inventories*

IAS 2 lays out the required accounting treatment for inventories (sometimes called stocks) under the historical cost system. The major area of contention is the cost **value of inventory** to be recorded. This is recognised as an asset of the entity until the related revenues are recognised (ie the item is sold) at which point the inventory is recognised as an expense (ie cost of sales). Part or all of the cost of inventories may also be expensed if a write-down to **net realisable value** is necessary. IAS 2 also provides guidance on the cost formulae that are used to assign costs to inventories.

In other words, the fundamental accounting assumption of **accruals** requires costs to be matched with associated revenues. In order to achieve this, costs incurred for goods which remain unsold at the year end must be carried forward in the statement of financial position and matched against future revenues.

1.3 Scope

The following items are **excluded** from the scope of the Standard.

(a)   Work in progress under **construction contracts** (covered by IAS 11 *Construction contracts*, see Section 2)

(b)   **Financial instruments** (ie shares, bonds)

(c)   **Biological assets**

Certain inventories are exempt from the Standard's **measurement rules**, ie those held by:

(a)   Producers of **agricultural and forest products**
(b)   **Commodity-broker traders**

1.4 Definitions

The Standard gives the following important definitions.

Key terms

> **Inventories** are assets:
>
> • Held for sale in the ordinary course of business;
>
> • In the process of production for such sale; *or*
>
> • In the form of materials or supplies to be consumed in the production process or in the rendering of services.
>
> **Net realisable value** is the estimated selling price in the ordinary course of business less the estimated costs of completion and the estimated costs necessary to make the sale.   *(IAS 2)*
>
> **Fair value** is the price that would be received to sell an asset or paid to transfer a liability in an orderly transaction between market participants at the measurement date.

Inventories can **include** any of the following.

(a) **Goods purchased and held for resale**, eg goods held for sale by a retailer, or land and buildings held for resale

(b) **Finished goods** produced

(c) **Work-in-progress** being produced

(d) Materials and supplies awaiting use in the production process (**raw materials**)

1.5 Measurement of inventories

The Standard states that '**inventories should be measured at the lower of cost and net realisable value**'.

Exam focus point

This is a very important rule and you will be expected to apply it in the exam.

1.6 Cost of inventories

The cost of inventories will consist of all costs of:

(a) **Purchase**
(b) **Costs of conversion**
(c) **Other costs** incurred in bringing the inventories to their **present location and condition**

1.6.1 Costs of purchase

The Standard lists the following as comprising the costs of purchase of inventories:

- **Purchase price** *plus*

- **Import duties** and other taxes *plus*

- Transport, handling and any other cost **directly attributable** to the acquisition of finished goods, services and materials *less*

- **Trade discounts**, rebates and other similar amounts

1.6.2 Costs of conversion

Costs of conversion of inventories consist of two main parts.

(a) Costs **directly related** to the units of production, eg direct materials, direct labour

(b) Fixed and variable **production overheads** that are incurred in converting materials into finished goods, allocated on a systematic basis.

You may have come across the terms 'fixed production overheads' or 'variable production overheads' elsewhere in your studies. The Standard defines them as follows.

Key terms

Fixed production overheads are those indirect costs of production that remain relatively constant regardless of the volume of production, eg the cost of factory management and administration.

Variable production overheads are those indirect costs of production that vary directly, or nearly directly, with the volume of production, eg indirect materials and labour. *(IAS 2)*

The Standard emphasises that fixed production overheads must be allocated to items of inventory on the basis of the **normal capacity of the production facilities**. This is an important point.

(a) **Normal capacity** is the expected achievable production based on the average over several periods/seasons, under normal circumstances.

(b) The above figure should take account of the capacity lost through **planned maintenance**.

(c) If it approximates to the normal level of activity then the **actual level of production** can be used.

(d) **Low production** or **idle plant** will *not* result in a higher fixed overhead allocation to each unit.

(e) **Unallocated overheads** must be recognised as an expense in the period in which they were incurred.

(f) When production is **abnormally high**, the fixed production overhead allocated to each unit will be reduced, so avoiding inventories being stated at more than cost.

(g) The allocation of variable production overheads to each unit is based on the **actual use** of production facilities.

1.6.3 Other costs

Any other costs should only be recognised if they are incurred in bringing the inventories to their **present location and condition**.

The Standard lists types of cost which **would not be included** in cost of inventories. Instead, they should be recognised as an **expense** in the period they are incurred.

(a) **Abnormal amounts** of wasted materials, labour or other production costs

(b) **Storage costs** (except costs which are necessary in the production process before a further production stage)

(c) **Administrative overheads** not incurred to bring inventories to their present location and conditions

(d) **Selling costs**

1.6.4 Techniques for the measurement of cost

Two techniques are mentioned by the Standard, both of which produce results which **approximate to cost**, and so both of which may be used for convenience.

(a) **Standard costs** are set up to take account of normal production values: amount of raw materials used, labour time etc. They are reviewed and revised on a regular basis.

(b) **Retail method**: this is often used in the retail industry where there is a large turnover of inventory items, which nevertheless have similar profit margins. The only practical method of inventory valuation may be to take the total selling price of inventories and deduct an overall average profit margin, thus reducing the value to an approximation of cost. The percentage will take account of reduced price lines. Sometimes different percentages are applied on a department basis.

1.7 Cost formulae

Cost of inventories should be assigned by **specific identification** of their individual costs for:

(a) Items that are **not ordinarily interchangeable**
(b) Goods or services produced and segregated for **specific projects**

Specific costs should be attributed to individual items of inventory when they are segregated for a specific project, but not where inventories consist of a large number of interchangeable (ie identical or very similar) items. In the latter case the rule is as specified below.

1.7.1 Interchangeable items

Rule to learn

> The cost of inventories should be assigned by using the **first-in, first-out (FIFO)** or **weighted average cost** formulae. The LIFO formula (last in, first out) is **not permitted** by IAS 2.

You should be familiar with these methods from your Paper 1 studies. Under the weighted average cost method, a recalculation can be made after each purchase, **or alternatively only at the period end**.

IAS 2 explains that an entity should use **the same cost formula for all inventories having similar nature and use to the entity.** For inventories with different nature or use (for example, certain commodities used in one business segment and the same type of commodities used in another business segment), different cost formulae may be justified. A difference in geographical location of inventories (and in the respective tax rules), by itself, is not sufficient to justify the use of different cost formulae.

1.8 Net realisable value (NRV)

As a general rule assets should not be carried at amounts greater than those expected to be realised from their sale or use. In the case of inventories this amount could fall below cost when items are **damaged or become obsolete**, or where the **costs to completion have increased** in order to make the sale.

In fact we can identify the principal situations in which **NRV is likely to be less than cost**, ie where there has been:

(a)   An **increase in costs** or a **fall in selling price**
(b)   A **physical deterioration** in the condition of inventory
(c)   **Obsolescence** of products
(d)   A decision as part of the company's marketing strategy to manufacture and sell products at a **loss**
(e)   **Errors in production or purchasing**

A write-down of inventories would normally take place on an item by item basis, but similar or related items may be **grouped together**. This grouping together is acceptable for, say, items in the same product line, but it is not acceptable to write-down inventories based on a whole classification (eg finished goods) or a whole business.

The assessment of NRV should take place **at the same time** as estimates are made of selling price, using the most reliable information available. Fluctuations of price or cost should be taken into account if they relate directly to **events after the reporting period**, which confirm conditions existing at the end of the period.

The reasons why inventory is held must also be taken into account. Some inventory, for example, may be held to satisfy a firm contract and its NRV will therefore be the **contract price**. Any additional inventory of the same type held at the period end will, in contrast, be assessed according to general sales prices when NRV is estimated.

NRV must be reassessed at the end of each period and compared again with cost. If the NRV has risen for inventories held over the end of more than one period, then the previous write-down must be **reversed** to the extent that the inventory is then valued at the lower of cost and the new NRV. This may be possible when selling prices have fallen in the past and then risen again.

On occasion a write-down to NRV may be of such size, incidence or nature that it must be **disclosed separately**.

1.9 Recognition as an expense

The following treatment is required **when inventories are sold**.

(a)   The **carrying amount** is recognised as an expense in the period in which the related revenue is recognised.

(b)   The amount of any **write-down of inventories** to NRV and all losses of inventories are recognised as an expense in the period the write-down or loss occurs.

(c)   The amount of any **reversal of any write-down of inventories**, arising from an increase in NRV, is recognised as a reduction in the amount of inventories recognised as an expense in the period in which the reversal occurs.

1.10 Disclosure

The financial statements should disclose the following.

(a)   **Accounting policies** adopted in measuring inventories, including the cost formula used

(b)   **Total carrying amount of inventories** and the carrying amount in classifications appropriate to the entity

(c)   **Carrying amount** of inventories carried at fair value less costs to sell

(d)   The amount of inventories **recognised as an expense** in the period

(e)   The amount of any **write-down** of inventories **recognised as an expense** in the period

(f)   The amount of any **reversal of any write-down** that is recognised as a reduction in the amount of inventories recognised as an expense in the period

(g)   **Circumstances or events** that led to the reversal of a write-down of inventories

(h)   Carrying amount of inventories **pledged as security for liabilities**

This information is of great relevance to users of financial statements, particularly the change in assets from period to period. The Standard lists common **classifications for inventories**.

- Merchandise
- Production supplies
- Materials
- Work-in-progress
- Finished goods

The financial statements must also disclose *either:*

(a)   The **cost of inventories** recognised as an expense during the period, *or*

(b)   The **operating costs**, applicable to revenues, recognised as an expense during the period, classified by their nature

The choice reflects differences in **the way the statement of profit or loss part of the statement of profit or loss and other comprehensive income can be presented**.

Where the entity discloses the amount of **operating costs** applicable to the revenues of the period, classified by their nature, then the costs recognised as an expense will be disclosed for:

(a)   Raw materials and consumables
(b)   Labour costs
(c)   Other operating costs
(d)   The net change in inventories for the period

You are the accountant at Water Pumps Co, and you have been asked to calculate the valuation of the company's inventory at cost at its year end of 30 April 20X5.

Water Pumps manufactures a range of pumps. The pumps are assembled from components bought by Water Pumps (the company does not manufacture any parts).

The company does not use a standard costing system, and work in progress and finished goods are valued as follows.

(a)   Material costs are determined from the product specification, which lists the components required to make a pump.

(b)   The company produces a range of pumps. Employees record the hours spent on assembling each type of pump, this information is input into the payroll system which prints the total hours spent each week assembling each type of pump. All employees assembling pumps are paid at the same rate and there is no overtime.

(c)   Overheads are added to the inventory value in accordance with IAS 2 *Inventories*. The financial accounting records are used to determine the overhead cost, and this is applied as a percentage based on the direct labour cost.

For direct labour costs, you have agreed that the labour expended for a unit in work in progress is half that of a completed unit.

The draft accounts show the following materials and direct labour costs in inventory.

	Raw materials	Work in progress	Finished goods
Materials ($)	74,786	85,692	152,693
Direct labour ($)		13,072	46,584

The costs incurred in April, as recorded in the financial accounting records, were as follows.

	$
Direct labour	61,320
Selling costs	43,550
Depreciation and finance costs of production machines	4,490
Distribution costs	6,570
Factory manager's wage	2,560
Other production overheads	24,820
Purchasing and accounting costs relating to production	5,450
Other accounting costs	7,130
Other administration overheads	24,770

For your calculations assume that all work in progress and finished goods were produced in April 20X5 and that the company was operating at a normal level of activity.

Required

Calculate the value of overheads which should be added to work in progress and finished goods in accordance with IAS 2 *Inventories*.

Note: You should include details and a description of your workings and all figures should be calculated to the nearest $.

Answer

Calculation of overheads for inventories

Production overheads are as follows.

	$
Depreciation/finance costs	4,490
Factory manager's wage	2,560
Other production overheads	24,820
Accounting/purchasing costs	5,450
	37,320

Direct labour = $61,320

$\therefore$ Production overhead rate = $\dfrac{37,320}{61,320}$ = 60.86%

Inventory valuation

	Raw materials $	WIP $	Finished goods $	Total $
Materials	74,786	85,692	152,693	313,171
Direct labour	–	13,072	46,584	59,656
Production overhead (at 60.86% of labour)	–	7,956	28,351	36,307
	74,786	106,720	227,628	409,134

2 IAS 11 *Construction contracts*

FAST FORWARD

At this stage of your studies, the most difficult part of IAS 11 is the mastering of the **valuation and disclosure clauses**.

2.1 Introduction

Imagine that you are the accountant at a construction company. Your company is building a large tower block that will house offices, under a contract with an investment company. It will take three years to build the block and over that time you will obviously have to pay for building materials, wages of workers on the building, architects' fees and so on. You will receive periodic payments from the investment company at various predetermined stages of the construction. How do you decide, in each of the three years, **what to include as income and expenditure** for the contract in the statement of profit or loss and other comprehensive income?

This is the problem tackled by IAS 11 *Construction contracts*.

2.2 Example: construction contract

A numerical example might help to illustrate the problem. Suppose that a contract is started on 1 January 20X5, with an estimated completion date of 31 December 20X6. The final contract price is $1,500,000. In the first year, to 31 December 20X5:

(i)   Costs incurred amounted to $600,000.

(ii)   Half the work on the contract was completed.

(iii) Certificates of work completed have been issued, to the value of $750,000. (*Note.* It is usual, in a construction contract, for a qualified person such as an architect or engineer to inspect the work completed, and if it is satisfactory, to issue certificates. This will then be the notification to the customer that progress payments are now due to the contractor. Progress payments are commonly the amount of valuation on the work certificates issued, minus a precautionary retention of 10%.)

(iv) It is estimated with reasonable certainty that further costs to completion in 20X6 will be $600,000.

What is the contract profit in 20X5, and what entries would be made for the contract at 31 December 20X5 if:

(a) Profits are deferred until the completion of the contract?
(b) A proportion of the estimated revenue and profit is recognised in 20X5?

Solution

(a) If profits were deferred until the completion of the contract in 20X6, the revenue and profit recognised on the contract in 20X5 would be nil, and the value of work in progress on 31 December 20X5 would be $600,000. IAS 11 takes the view that this policy is unreasonable, because in 20X6, the total profit of $300,000 would be recorded. Since the contract revenues are earned throughout 20X5 and 20X6, a profit of nil in 20X5 and $300,000 in 20X6 would be contrary to the accruals concept of accounting.

(b) **It is fairer to recognise revenue and profit throughout the duration of the contract.**

As at 31 December 20X5 revenue of $750,000 should be matched with cost of sales of $600,000 , leaving an attributable profit for 20X5 of $150,000.

The only statement of financial position entry as at 31 December 20X5 is a receivable of $750,000 recognising that the company is owed this amount for work done to date. No balance remains for work in progress, the whole $600,000 having been recognised in cost of sales.

2.3 What is a construction contract?

A contract which needs IAS 11 treatment does not have to last for a period of more than one year. The main point is that the contract activity **starts in one financial period and ends in another**, thus creating the problem: to which of two or more periods should contract income and costs be allocated? In fact the definition given in the IAS of a construction contract is very straightforward.

Key term

> **Construction contract.** A contract specifically negotiated for the construction of an asset or a combination of assets that are closely interrelated or interdependent in terms of their design, technology and function or their ultimate purpose or use.
> *(IAS 11)*

The Standard differentiates between fixed price contracts and cost plus contracts.

Key terms

> **Fixed price contract.** A contract in which the contractor agrees to a fixed contract price, or a fixed rate per unit of output, which in some cases is subject to cost escalation clauses.
>
> **Cost plus contract.** A construction contract in which the contractor is reimbursed for allowable or otherwise defined costs, plus a percentage of these costs or a fixed fee.

Construction contracts may involve the building of one asset, eg a bridge, or a series of interrelated assets eg an oil refinery. They may also include **rendering of services** (eg architects) or restoring or demolishing an asset.

2.4 Combining and segmenting construction contracts

The Standard lays out the factors which determine whether the construction of a **series of assets** under one contract should be treated as several contracts.

(a)   **Separate proposals** are submitted for each asset

(b)   **Separate negotiations** are undertaken for each asset; the customer can accept/reject each individually

(c)   **Identifiable costs and revenues** can be separated for each asset

There are also circumstances where a **group of contracts** should be treated as **one single construction contract**.

(a)   The group of contracts are negotiated as a **single package**

(b)   Contracts are **closely interrelated**, with an overall profit margin

(c)   The contracts are performed **concurrently** or **in a single sequence**

2.5 Contract revenue

Contract revenue will be the **amount specified in the contract**, subject to variations in the contract work, incentive payments and claims *if* these will probably give rise to revenue and *if* they can be reliably measured. The result is that contract revenue is measured at the **fair value** of received or receivable revenue.

The Standard elaborates on the types of uncertainty, which depend on the outcome of future events, that affect the **measurement of contract revenue**.

*   An **agreed variation** (increase/decrease)
*   **Cost escalation clauses** in a fixed price contract (increase)
*   **Penalties** imposed due to delays by the contractor (decrease)
*   **Number of units** varies in a contract for fixed prices per unit (increase/decrease)

In the case of any variation, claim or incentive payment, two factors should be assessed to determine whether contract revenue should be recognised.

(a)   Whether it is **probable** that the customer will accept the variation/claim, or that the contract is sufficiently advanced that the performance criteria will be met

(b)   Whether the amount of the revenue can be **measured reliably**

2.6 Contract costs

Contract costs consist of:

(a)   Costs relating **directly** to the contract

(b)   Costs attributable to general contract activity which can be **allocated** to the contract, such as insurance, cost of design and technical assistance not directly related to a specific contract and construction overheads

(c)   Any other costs which can be **charged to the customer** under the contract, which may include general administration costs and development costs

Costs that **relate directly** to a specific contract include the following.

*   **Site labour costs**, including site supervision
*   Costs of **materials** used in construction
*   **Depreciation** of plant and equipment used on the contract
*   Costs of **moving** plant, equipment and materials to and from the contract site

- Costs of **hiring** plant and equipment
- Costs of **design and technical assistance** that are directly related to the contract
- Estimated costs of **rectification and guarantee work**, including expected warranty costs
- **Claims from third parties**

General contract activity costs should be **allocated systematically and rationally**, and all costs with similar characteristics should be treated **consistently**. The allocation should be based on the **normal level** of construction activity. Borrowing costs may be attributed in this way (see IAS 23: Chapter 9).

Some costs **cannot be attributed** to contract activity and so the following should be **excluded** from construction contract costs.

- **General administration costs** (unless reimbursement is specified in the contract)
- **Selling costs**
- **R&D** (unless reimbursement is specified in the contract)
- **Depreciation** of idle plant and equipment not used on any particular contract

2.7 Recognition of contract revenue and expenses

Revenue and costs associated with a contract should be recognised according to the stage of completion of the contract at the end of the reporting period, but *only when* the **outcome of the activity can be estimated reliably**. This is often known as the **percentage of completion method**.

If a loss is predicted on a contract, then it should be recognised immediately. A reliable estimate of the outcome of a construction contract can only be made when **certain conditions** have been met, and these conditions will be different for fixed price and cost plus contracts.

(a) **Fixed price contracts**

    (i)   Probable that economic benefits of the contract will flow to the entity

    (ii)   Total contract revenue can be reliably measured

    (iii) Stage of completion at the period end and costs to complete the contract can be reliably measured

    (iv) Costs attributable to the contract can be identified clearly and be reliably measured (actual costs can be compared to previous estimates)

(b) **Cost plus contracts**

    (i)   Probable that economic benefits of the contract will flow to the entity

    (ii)   Costs attributable to the contract (whether or not reimbursable) can be identified clearly and be reliably measured

The **percentage of completion method** is an application of the accruals assumption. Contract revenue is matched to the contract costs incurred in reaching the stage of completion, so revenue, costs and profit are attributed to the proportion of work completed.

We can **summarise** the treatment as follows.

(a) Recognise **contract revenue** as revenue in the accounting periods in which the work is performed

(b) Recognise **contract costs** as an expense in the accounting period in which the work to which they relate is performed

(c) Any **expected excess** of total contract costs over total contract revenue should be recognised as an expense immediately

(d) Any costs incurred which relate to **future activity** should be recognised as an asset if it is probable that they will be recovered (often called contract work-in-progress, ie amounts due from the customer)

(e) Where amounts have been recognised as contract revenue, but their **collectability** from the customer becomes doubtful, such amounts should be recognised as an expense, not a deduction from revenue

2.8 When can reliable estimates be made?

IAS 11 only allows contract revenue and costs to be recognised when the outcome of the contract can be predicted, ie when it is probable that the economic benefits attached to the contract will flow to the entity. IAS 11 states that this can only be when a contract has been agreed which establishes the following.

- The **enforceable rights** of each party in respect of the asset to be constructed
- The **consideration** that is to be exchanged
- **Terms and manner of settlement**

In addition, the entity should have an **effective internal financial budgeting and reporting system**, in order to review and revise the estimates of contract revenue and costs as the contract progresses.

2.9 Determining the stage of completion

How should you decide on the stage of completion of any contract? The Standard lists several methods.

- **Proportion of contract costs incurred** for work carried out to date
- **Surveys** of work carried out
- **Physical proportion** of the contract work completed

2.10 Example: Stage of completion

Centrepoint Co have a fixed price contract to build a tower block. The initial amount of revenue agreed is $220m. At the beginning of the contract on 1 January 20X6 the initial estimate of the contract costs is $200m. At the end of 20X6 the estimate of the total costs has risen to $202m.

During 20X7 the customer agrees to a variation which increases expected revenue from the contract by $5m and causes additional costs of $3m. At the end of 20X7 there are materials stored on site for use during the following period which cost $2.5m.

It is decided to determine the stage of completion of the contract by calculating the proportion that contract costs incurred for work to date bear to the latest estimated total contract costs. The contract costs incurred at the end of each year were 20X6: $52.52m, 20X7: $154.2m (including materials in store), 20X8 $205m.

Required

Calculate the stage of completion for each year of the contract and show how revenues, costs and profits will be recognised in each year.

Solution

The financial data for each year end during the construction period can be summarised as follows.

	20X6	20X7	20X8
	$'000	$'000	$'000
Initial amount of revenue agreed in the contract	220,000	220,000	220,000
Variation	–	5,000	5,000
Total contract revenue	220,000	225,000	225,000
Contract costs incurred to date	52,520	154,200	205,000
Contract costs to complete	149,480	50,800	–
Total estimated contract costs	202,000	205,000	205,000
Estimated profit	18,000	20,000	20,000
Stage of completion	26.0%	74.0%	100.0%

The stage of completion has been calculated using the formula:

$$\frac{\text{Contract costs incurred to date}}{\text{Total estimated contract costs}}$$

The stage of completion in 20X7 is calculated by deducting the $2.5m of materials held for the following period from the costs incurred up to that year end, ie:

$154.2m – $2.5m = $151.7m. $151.7m/$205m = 74%.

Revenue, expenses and profit will be recognised as follows.

		To date $'000	Recognised in prior years $'000	Recognised in current year $'000
20X6	Revenue ($220m × 26%)	57,200		
	Costs ($202m × 26%)	(52,520)		
		4,680		
20X7	Revenue ($225m × 74%)	166,500	57,200	109,300
	Costs ($205m × 74%)	(151,700)	(52,520)	(99,180)
		14,800	4,680	10,120
20X8	Revenue ($225m × 100%)	225,000	166,500	58,500
	Costs ($205m × 100%)	(205,000)	(151,700)	(53,300)
		20,000	14,800	5,200

You can see from the above example that, when the stage of completion is determined using the contract costs incurred to date, only contract costs reflecting the work to date should be included in costs incurred to date.

(a) Exclude costs relating to **future activity**, eg cost of materials delivered but not yet used

(b) Exclude payments made to subcontractors **in advance** of work performed

2.11 Outcome of the contract cannot be predicted reliably

When the contract's outcome cannot be predicted reliably the following treatment should be followed.

(a) Only recognise revenue to the extent of contract costs incurred which are expected to be **recoverable**

(b) Recognise contract costs as an **expense** in the period they are incurred

This **no profit/no loss approach** reflects the situation near the beginning of a contract, ie the outcome cannot be reliably estimated, but it is likely that costs will be recovered.

Contract costs which **cannot be recovered** should be recognised as an expense straight away. IAS 11 lists the following situations where this might occur.

- The contract is **not fully enforceable**, ie its validity is seriously questioned

- The completion of the contract is subject to the outcome of **pending litigation or legislation**

- The contract relates to properties which will probably be **expropriated or condemned**

- The customer is **unable to meet its obligations** under the contract

- The contractor **cannot complete** the contract or in any other way meet its obligations under the contract

Where these **uncertainties cease to exist**, contract revenue and costs should be recognised as normal, ie by reference to the stage of completion.

2.12 Recognition of expected losses

Any loss on a contract should be **recognised as soon as it is foreseen**. The loss will be the amount by which total expected contract revenue is exceeded by total expected contract costs. The loss amount is not affected by whether work has started on the contract, the stage of completion of the work or profits on other contracts (unless they are related contracts treated as a single contract).

2.13 Changes in estimates

The effect of any change in the estimate of contract revenue or costs or the outcome of a contract should be accounted for as a **change in accounting estimate** under IAS 8 *Accounting policies, changes in accounting estimates and errors.*

2.14 Example: Changes in estimates

The example below shows the effect of a change in estimate of costs on the figures that appear in the financial statements.

Battersby Co enters into a three-year contract.

Estimated revenue = $20,000
Estimated total cost = $16,000

However, during Year 2, management revises its estimate of total costs incurred and thus the outcome of the contract. As a result, during Year 2, a loss is recognised on the contract for the year, even though the contract will still be profitable overall.

	Year 1 $	Year 2 $	Year 3 $
Estimated revenue	20,000	20,000	20,000
Estimated total cost	(16,000)	(18,000)	(18,000)
Estimated total profit	4,000	2,000	2,000
Cost incurred to date	$8,000	$13,500	$18,000
Percentage of completion	50%	75%	100%
Recognised profit/(loss) for year	$2,000	($500)	$500
Cumulative recognised profit	$2,000	$1,500	$2,000

Progress billings of $8,000, $8,000 and $4,000 are made on the last day of each year and are received in the first month of the following year. The statement of financial position asset at the end of each year is:

	Year 1 $	Year 2 $	Year 3 $
Costs incurred	8,000	13,500	18,000
Recognised profits	2,000	2,000	2,500
(Recognised losses)	–	(500)	(500)
(Progress billings)	(8,000)	(16,000)	(20,000)
Amount recognised as an asset/(liability)	2,000	(1,000)	0

In addition, at each year end, the entity recognises a trade receivable for the amount outstanding at the end of the year of $8,000, $8,000 and $4,000.

2.15 Disclosures

The following should be disclosed under IAS 11:

- Contract revenue recognised as **revenue in the period**
- **Methods used** to determine the **contract revenue**
- **Methods used** to determine **stage of completion** of contracts which are in progress

For **contracts in progress** at the end of the reporting period, show the following.

- **Total costs incurred** and recognised profits (less recognised losses) to date
- **Advances** received
- **Retentions** (progress billings not paid until the satisfaction of certain conditions)

The gross amounts due from customers for contract work must be shown as an **asset**. The gross amount due to customers for contract work must be shown as a **liability**. These balances are calculated as follows:

	$
Contract costs incurred to date	X
Recognised profits/(losses) to date	X
	X
Progress billings to date	(X)
Amounts due from/(to) customers	X/(X)

> **Note:** This represents unbilled revenue. Unpaid billed revenue will be included in trade receivables.

Any **contingent gains or losses**, eg due to warranty costs, claims, penalties or possible losses, should be disclosed in accordance with IAS 37 *Provisions, contingent liabilities and contingent assets*.

2.16 Example: Disclosure

Suppose that Tract Ore Co finishes its first year of operations in which all contract costs were paid in cash and all progress billings and advances were received in cash. For contracts W, X and Z only:

(a) Contract costs include costs of materials purchased for use in the contract which have not been used at the period end; *and*

(b) Customers have advanced sums to the contractor for work not yet performed.

The relevant figures for all contracts at the end of Tract Ore's first year of trading are as follows.

	V $m	W $m	X $m	Y $m	Z $m	Total $m
Contract revenue recognised	37.7	135.2	98.8	52.0	14.3	338.0
Contract expenses recognised	(28.6)	(117.0)	(91.0)	(65.0)	(14.3)	(315.9)
Expected losses recognised	–	–	–	10.4	7.8	18.2
Recognised profits less recognised losses	9.1	18.2	7.8	(23.4)	(7.8)	3.9
Contract costs incurred in the period	28.6	132.6	117.0	65.0	26.0	369.2
Contract expenses recognised	(28.6)	(117.0)	(91.0)	(65.0)	(14.3)	(315.9)
Contract expenses that relate to future activity recognised as an asset	–	15.6	26.0	–	11.7	53.3
Contract revenue	37.7	135.2	98.8	52.0	14.3	338.0
Progress billings	(26.0)	(135.2)	(98.8)	(46.8)	(14.3)	(321.1)
Unbilled contract revenue	11.7	–	–	5.2	–	16.9
Advances	–	20.8	5.2	–	6.5	32.5

Required

Show the figures that should be disclosed under IAS 11.

Solution

Following IAS 11, the required disclosures would be as follows.

	$m
Contract revenue recognised in the period	338.0
Contract costs incurred and recognised profits (less recognised losses) to date (W)	373.1
Advances received	32.5
Gross amount due from customers for contract work: asset (W)	57.2
Gross amount due to customers for contract work: liability (W)	(5.2)

Workings

These amounts are calculated as follows.

	V $m	W $m	X $m	Y $m	Z $m	Total $m
Contract costs incurred	28.6	132.6	117.0	65.0	26.0	369.2
Recognised profits less recognised losses	9.1	18.2	7.8	(23.4)	(7.8)	3.9
	37.7	150.8	124.8	41.6	18.2	373.1
Progress billings	(26.0)	(135.2)	(98.8)	(46.8)	(14.3)	(321.1)
Due from customers	11.7	15.6	26.0		3.9	57.2
Due to customers				(5.2)		(5.2)

2.17 Section summary

In valuing long-term contracts and the other disclosures required under IAS 11, an organised approach is essential. The following suggested method breaks the process down into five logical steps.

Step 1 **Compare the contract value** and the **total costs** expected to be incurred on the contract. If a loss is foreseen (that is, if the costs to date plus estimated costs to completion exceed the contract value) then it must be charged against profits. If a loss has already been charged in previous years, then only the difference between the loss as previously and currently estimated need be charged.

Step 2 Using the percentage completed to date (or other formula given in the question), calculate sales revenue **attributable** to the contract for the period (for example, percentage complete × total contract value, less of course, revenue taken in previous periods).

Step 3 **Calculate the cost of sales** on the contract for the period.

	$
Total contract costs × percentage complete	
(or follow instructions in question)	X
Less any costs charged in previous periods	(X)
	X
Add foreseeable losses in full (not previously charged)	X
Cost of sales on contract for the period	X

Step 4 **Deduct the cost of sales** for the period as calculated above (including any foreseeable loss) from sales revenue calculated at step 2 to give profit (loss) recognised for the period.

Step 5 **Calculate amounts due to/from** customers as per the working on the previous page.

2.18 Summary of accounting treatment

The following summarises the accounting treatment for long-term contracts – **make sure that you understand it.**

2.18.1 Statement of profit or loss

(a) **Revenue and costs**

   (i) Sales revenue and associated costs should be recorded in profit or loss as the contract activity progresses.

   (ii) Include an appropriate proportion of total contract value as sales revenue.

   (iii) The costs incurred in reaching that stage of completion are matched with this sales revenue, resulting in the reporting of results which can be attributed to the proportion of work completed.

   (iv) Sales revenue is the value of work carried out to date.

(b) **Profit recognised in the contract**

   (i) It must reflect the proportion of work carried out.

   (ii) It should take into account any known inequalities in profitability in the various stages of a contract.

2.18.2 Statement of financial position

(a) **Current asset/liability**

	$
Costs incurred to date	X
Recognised profits/(losses) to date	(X)
	X
Progress billings to date	(X)
Amount due from/(to) customers	X/(X)

(b) **Receivables**

	$
Unpaid progress billings	X

(c) **Payables.** Where (a) gives a net 'amount due to customers' this amount should be included in payables under 'payments on account'.

The main business of Santolina Co is construction contracts. At the end of September 20X3 there are two uncompleted contracts on the books, details of which are as follows.

CONTRACT	A	B
Date commenced	1.9.X3	1.4.X1
Expected completed date	23.12.X3	23.12.X3
	$	$
Final contract price	70,000	290,000
Costs to 30.9.X3	21,000	210,450
Value of work certified to 30.9.X3	20,000	230,000
Progress billings to 30.9.X3	20,000	210,000
Cash received to 30.9.X3	18,000	194,000
Estimated costs to completion at 30.9.X3	41,000	20,600

Required

Prepare calculations showing the amounts to be included in the statement of financial position at 30 September 20X3 in respect of the above contracts.

Answer

Contract A is a short-term contract and will be included in the statement of financial position as work-in-progress at cost less amounts received and receivable $(21,000 – 20,000) ie $1,000.

Contract B is a long-term contract and will be included in the statement of financial position at cost plus recognised profit less progress billings.

The estimated final profit is:

	$
Final contract price	290,000
Less: costs to date	(210,450)
estimated future costs	(20,600)
Estimated final profit	58,950

The recognised profit is found as follows.

$$\text{Estimated final profit} \times \frac{\text{Work certified}}{\text{Total contract price}}$$

$$\$58,950 \times \frac{230,000}{290,000}$$

Recognised profit = 46,753

Gross amounts due from customers for contract work

CONTRACT B

	$
Costs to date	210,450
Recognised profit	46,753
Anticipated loss	–
	257,203
Progress billings	(210,000)
Amounts due from customers	47,203
Trade receivables (210-194)	16,000

Question   IAS 11 calculations

Haggrun Co has two contracts in progress, the details of which are as follows.

	Happy (profitable) $'000	Grumpy (loss-making) $'000
Total contract price	300	300
Costs incurred to date	90	150
Estimated costs to completion	135	225
Progress payments invoiced and received	116	116

Required

Show extracts from the statements of profit or loss and statement of financial position for each contract, assuming they are both:

(a)   40% complete; *and*
(b)   36% complete.

Answer

Happy contract

(a)   40% complete

	$'000
Statement of profit or loss	
Sales revenue (40% × 300)	120
Cost of sales (40% × 225)	(90)
Gross profit	30
Statement of financial position	
Amount due from customers (90 + 30 − 116)	4

(b)   36% complete

	$'000
Statement of profit or loss	
Sales revenue (36% × 300)	108
Cost of sales (36% × 225)	(81)
Gross profit	27
Statement of financial position	
Amount due to customers (90 + 27 − 116)	1

Grumpy contract

(a)   40% complete

Working

	$'000	$'000
Total contract price		300
Less: costs to date	150	
estimated costs to completion	225	
		(375)
Foreseeable loss		(75)

	$'000
Statement of profit or loss	
Sales revenue (40% × 300)	120
Cost of sales (40% × 375)	(150)
	(30)
Provision for future losses (bal fig)	(45)
Gross loss	(75)
Statement of financial position	
Amounts due to customers (150 – 75 – 116)	(41)

(b) 36% complete

	$'000
Statement of profit or loss	
Sales revenue (36% × 300)	108
Cost of sales (36% × 375)	(135)
	(27)
Provision for future losses (balancing figure)	(48)
Gross loss	(75)
Statement of financial position	
Amount due to customers (150 – 75 –116)	41

Chapter roundup

- Most of this is revision. However, you should be aware that the use of LIFO is prohibited under IAS 2.

- At this stage of your studies, the most difficult part of IAS 11 is the mastering of the **valuation and disclosure clauses**.

Quick quiz

1 Net realisable value = Selling price less ....and ....

2 Which inventory costing method is allowed under IAS 2?

    (a)   FIFO
    (b)   LIFO

3 Any expected loss on a construction contract must be recognised, in full, in the year it was identified.

    True   ☐

    False   ☐

4 List the five steps to be taken when valuing construction contracts.

5 Which line items in the statements of profit or loss and other comprehensive income and statement of financial position are potentially affected by construction contracts?

Answers to quick quiz

1   Net realisable value = selling price less costs to completion and costs necessary to make the sale

2   (a) FIFO. LIFO is not allowed.

3   True

4   See Paragraph 2.17

5   Statement of profit or loss and other comprehensive income: revenue and cost of sales
    Statement of financial position: inventories, receivables, payables

End of chapter question

Construction contracts (AIA May 2007)

Archit Co is a construction company specialising in the building of bridges. Until recently, the company had only built small structures which were started and finished usually within one year. However, on 1 April 20X6 the company signed its largest contract yet – the construction of a large bridge spanning a river which will take three years to complete. The board are not sure how this new contract will impact on the company's financial statements and have therefore asked you to explain it to them. The following details have been extracted from the project's contract notes (note: 20X8 and 20X9 figures are estimates):

Bridge Project

Contract price:	€15m
Contract signed:	1 April 20X6
Work commenced:	22 May 20X6

	As at 31 March		
	20X7	*20X8*	*20X9*
	€'000	*€'000*	*€'000*
Invoiced to customers	4,500	3,750	6,750
Cash received from customers	4,000	3,500	7,500
Total costs incurred during the year	3,250	2,900	3,600
Estimated future costs to complete	6,500	3,600	–
Cost of materials in store (included in 'total costs' above)	300	400	–

The board have been advised to use the most common method to determine the stage of completion of the project; which is, by calculating the proportion that contract costs incurred to date bear to the total estimated contract costs.

Required

Calculate the figures that should appear in the company's statements of profit or loss and other comprehensive income and statement of financial position for each of the above three years in respect of the above contract. [Calculate all figures to the nearest €000]

(15 marks)

Accounting for leases

Topic list	Syllabus reference
1 Types of lease	11.4
2 Lessees	11.4
3 Lessors	11.4

Introduction

Leasing transactions are extremely common so this is an important practical subject. **Lease accounting is regulated by IAS 17**, which was introduced because of abuses in the use of lease accounting by companies.

These companies effectively 'owned' an asset and 'owed' a debt for its purchase, but showed neither the asset nor the liability in the statement of financial position because they were not required to do so. This is an example of **'off balance sheet finance'**.

1 Types of lease

A finance lease is a means of acquiring the long-term use of an asset whereas an operating lease is a short-term rental agreement. Substance over form must be applied when accounting for leases.

1.1 What is a lease?

Where goods are acquired other than on immediate cash terms, arrangements have to be made in respect of the future payments on those goods. In the simplest case of **credit sales**, the purchaser is allowed a period of time (say one month) to settle the outstanding amount and the normal accounting procedure in respect of receivables/payables will be adopted. An alternative arrangement would be to enter into a leasing agreement (some types of lease are called **hire purchase agreements** in some countries).

IAS 17 *Leases* standardises the accounting treatment and disclosure of assets held under lease.

In a leasing transaction there is a **contract** between the lessor and the lessee for the hire of an asset. The lessor retains legal ownership but conveys to the lessee the right to use the asset for an agreed period of time in return for specified rentals. IAS 17 defines a lease and recognises two types.

Key terms

> **Lease.** An agreement whereby the lessor conveys to the lessee in return for rent the right to use an asset for an agreed period of time.
>
> **Finance lease.** A lease that transfers substantially all the risks and rewards incident to ownership of an asset. Title may or may not eventually be transferred.
>
> **Operating lease.** A lease other than a finance lease.   *(IAS 17)*

A **finance lease** may be a **hire purchase agreement**. (The difference is that under a hire purchase agreement the customer eventually, after paying an agreed number of instalments, becomes entitled to exercise an option to purchase the asset. Under other leasing agreements, ownership remains forever with the lessor.)

In this chapter the **user** of an asset will often be referred to simply as the **lessee**, and the **supplier** as the **lessor**. You should bear in mind that identical requirements apply in the case of hirers and vendors respectively under hire purchase agreements.

To expand on the definition above, a finance lease should be presumed if at the inception of a lease the **present value of the minimum lease payments** is approximately equal to the **fair value of the leased asset**.

The present value should be calculated by using the **interest rate implicit in the lease**.

Key terms

> **Minimum lease payments.** The payments over the lease term that the lessee is or can be required to make, excluding contingent rent, costs for services and taxes to be paid by and be reimbursed to the lessor, together with:
>
> (a)   For a lessee, any amounts guaranteed by the lessee or by a party related to the lessee
> (b)   For a lessor, any residual value guaranteed to the lessor by one of the following.
>
> > (i)   The lessee
> > (ii)   A party related to the lessee
> > (iii) An independent third party financially capable of meeting this guarantee
>
> However, if the lessee has the option to purchase the asset at a price which is expected to be sufficiently lower than fair value at the date the option becomes exercisable for it to be reasonably certain, at the inception of the lease, that the option will be exercised, the minimum lease payments comprise the minimum payments payable over the lease term to the expected date of exercise of this purchase option and the payment required to exercise it.

Interest rate implicit in the lease

The discount rate that, at the inception of the lease, causes the aggregate present value of:

(a)   The minimum lease payments, *and*

(b)   The unguaranteed residual value

to be equal to the sum of

(a)   The fair value of the leased asset, *and*

(b)   Any initial direct costs.

Initial direct costs are **incremental costs** that are directly attributable to **negotiating** and **arranging** a lease, except for such costs incurred by manufacturer or dealer lessors. Examples of initial direct costs include amounts such as **commissions, legal fees** and relevant internal costs.

Lease term. The non-cancellable period for which the lessee has contracted to lease the asset together with any further terms for which the lessee has the option to continue to lease the asset, with or without further payment, when at the inception of the lease it is reasonably certain that the lessee will exercise the option.

A **non-cancellable lease** is a lease that is cancellable only in one of the following situations.

(a)   Upon the occurrence of some remote contingency

(b)   With the permission of the lessor

(c)   If the lessee enters into a new lease for the same or an equivalent asset with the same lessor

(d)   Upon payment by the lessee of an additional amount such that, at inception, continuation of the lease is reasonably certain

The **inception of the lease** is the earlier of the date of the lease agreement and the date of commitment by the parties to the principal provisions of the lease. As at this date:

(a)   A lease is classified as either an operating lease or a finance lease; *and*

(b)   In the case of a finance lease, the amounts to be recognised at the start of lease term are determined.

Economic life is *either:*

(a)   The period over which an asset is expected to be economically usable by one or more users, *or*

(b)   The number of production or similar units expected to be obtained from the asset by one or more users.

Useful life is the estimated remaining period, from the beginning of the lease term, without limitation by the lease term, over which the economic benefits embodied in the asset are expected to be consumed by the entity.

Guaranteed residual value is:

(a)   For a lessee, that part of the residual value which is guaranteed by the lessee or by a party related to the lessee (the amount of the guarantee being the maximum amount that could, in any event, become payable).

(b)   For a lessor, that part of the residual value which is guaranteed by the lessee or by a third party unrelated to the lessor who is financially capable of discharging the obligations under the guarantee.

Unguaranteed residual value is that portion of the residual value of the leased asset, the realisation of which by the lessor is not assured or is guaranteed solely by a party related to the lessor.

Key terms (cont'd)

Gross investment in the lease is the aggregate of:

(a) The minimum lease payments receivable by the lessor under a finance lease, *and*
(b) Any unguaranteed residual value accruing to the lessor.

Net investment in the lease is the gross investment in the lease discounted at the interest rate implicit in the lease.

Unearned finance income is the difference between:

(a) The gross investment in the lease, *and*
(b) The net investment in the lease.

The **lessee's incremental borrowing rate of interest** is the rate of interest the lessee would have to pay on a similar lease or, if that is not determinable, the rate that, at the inception of the lease, the lessee would incur to borrow over a similar term, and with a similar security, the funds necessary to purchase the asset.

Contingent rent is that portion of the lease payments that is not fixed in amount but is based on a factor other than just the passage of time (eg percentage of sales, amount of usage, price indices, market rates of interest).

(IAS 17)

There are further definitions in IAS 17, but (fortunately!) these go beyond the scope of your syllabus.

1.2 Accounting for leases: lessees and lessors

Operating leases do not really pose an accounting problem. The lessee pays amounts periodically to the lessor and these are **charged to profit or loss** (as an expense in the statement of profit or loss). The lessor treats the leased asset as a non-current asset and depreciates it in the normal way. Rentals received from the lessee are credited to profit or loss (as income in the statement of profit or loss) in the lessor's books.

For assets held under **finance leases** (including hire purchase) this accounting treatment would not disclose the reality of the situation. If a **lessor** leases out an asset on a finance lease, the asset will probably never be seen on his premises or used in his business again. It would be inappropriate for a lessor to record such an asset as a non-current asset. In reality, what he owns is a **stream of cash flows receivable** from the lessee. **The asset is an amount receivable rather than a non-current asset**.

Similarly, a **lessee** may use a finance lease to fund the 'acquisition' of a major asset which he will then use in his business perhaps for many years. **The substance of the transaction is that he has acquired a non-current asset**, and this is reflected in the accounting treatment prescribed by IAS 17, even though in law the lessee may never become the owner of the asset.

Exam focus point

Questions on leasing could involve a discussion of the reasons for the different accounting treatments of operating and finance leases, from the perspectives of both the lessor and the lessee. Practical questions could involve preparation of the relevant ledger accounts and/or extracts from the financial statements.

The following summary diagram should help you when deciding whether a lease is an operating lease or a finance lease.

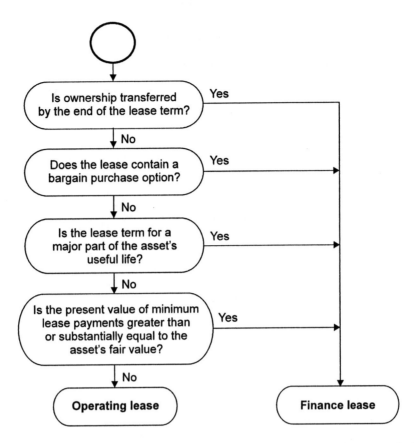

IAS 17 states that when classifying a lease of **land and buildings** an entity should treat each element separately. Land normally has an indefinite economic life. This means that a lease of land is almost always an operating lease, because the lease term will be much shorter than the useful life of the land.

2 Lessees

You must learn the **disclosure requirements of IAS 17** for both lessors and lessees.

2.1 Accounting treatment

IAS 17 requires that, when an asset changes hands under a **finance lease, lessor and lessee should account for the transaction as though it were a credit sale**. In the lessee's books therefore:

DEBIT   Asset account
CREDIT   Lessor (liability) account

The amount to be recorded in this way is the **lower of** the **fair value** and the **present value** of the **minimum lease payments**.

IAS 17 states that it is not appropriate to show liabilities for leased assets as deductions from the leased assets. A distinction should be made between **current and non-current** lease liabilities, if the entity makes this distinction for other liabilities.

The asset should be **depreciated** (on the bases set out in IASs 16 and 38) over the shorter of:

(a)   The lease term
(b)   The asset's useful life

If there is reasonable certainty of eventual ownership of the asset, then it should be depreciated over its useful life.

2.2 Apportionment of rental payments

When the lessee makes a rental payment it will comprise two elements.

(a)   An **interest charge** on the finance provided by the lessor. This proportion of each payment is interest payable and interest receivable in the accounts of the lessee and lessor respectively.

(b)   A repayment of part of the **capital cost** of the asset. In the lessee's books this proportion of each rental payment must be debited to the lessor's account to reduce the outstanding liability. In the lessor's books, it must be credited to the lessee's account to reduce the amount owing (the debit of course is to cash).

The accounting problem is to decide what proportion of each instalment paid by the lessee represents interest, and what proportion represents a repayment of the capital advanced by the lessor. There are two apportionment methods you may encounter:

(a)   The **actuarial method**
(b)   The **sum-of-the-digits method**

Exam focus point

In theory, the aim is that the interest charge should reduce over the lease term in line with the liability. In practice, the sum of digits method approximates to the actuarial method, and the examiner has indicated that both methods are examinable.

The **actuarial method** is the best and most scientific method. It derives from the common-sense assumption that the interest charged by a lessor company will equal the rate of return desired by the company, multiplied by the amount of capital it has invested.

(a)   At the beginning of the lease the capital invested is equal to the fair value of the asset (less any initial deposit paid by the lessee).

(b)   This amount reduces as each instalment is paid. It follows that the interest accruing is greatest in the early part of the lease term, and gradually reduces as capital is repaid. In this section, we will look at a simple example of the actuarial method.

The **sum-of-the-digits** method approximates to the actuarial method, splitting the total interest (without reference to a rate of interest) in such a way that the greater proportion falls in the earlier years.

2.3 Example: Apportionment methods

On 1 January 20X0 Bacchus Co, wine merchants, buys a small bottling and labelling machine from Silenus Co under a finance lease. The cash price of the machine was $7,710 while the amount to be paid was $10,000. The agreement required the immediate payment of a $2,000 deposit with the balance being settled in four equal annual instalments commencing on 31 December 20X0. The charge of $2,290 represents interest of 15% per annum, calculated on the remaining balance of the liability during each accounting period. Depreciation on the plant is to be provided for at the rate of 20% per annum on a straight-line basis assuming a residual value of nil.

You are required to show the breakdown of each instalment between interest and capital.

Solution

Actuarial method

Interest is calculated as 15% of the outstanding *capital* balance at the beginning of each year. The outstanding capital balance reduces each year by the capital element comprised in each instalment. The outstanding capital balance at 1 January 20X0 is $5,710 ($7,710 fair value less $2,000 deposit).

	Total $	Capital $	Interest $
Capital balance at 1 Jan 20X0		5,710	
1st instalment			
(interest = $5,710 × 15%)	2,000	1,144	856
Capital balance at 1 Jan 20X1		4,566	
2nd instalment			
(interest = $4,566 × 15%)	2,000	1,315	685
Capital balance at 1 Jan 20X2		3,251	
3rd instalment			
(interest = $3,251 × 15%)	2,000	1,512	488
Capital balance at 1 Jan 20X3		1,739	
4th instalment			
(interest = $1,739 × 15%)	2,000	1,739	261
	8,000		2,290
Capital balance at 1 Jan 20X4		–	

Sum of digits method

	$
Total finance charge to be allocated	
Lease payments	10,000
Cash price of machine	(7,710)
Finance charge	2,290

Number of interest bearing periods (n) = 4

The sum of digits is calculated as $\dfrac{n(n + 1)}{2}$ therefore in this case $\dfrac{4 \times 5}{2} = 10$

A proportion of the finance charge is then allocated to each interest bearing period as follows:

Year ended 31 December 20X0	4/10 × 2,290	916
Year ended 31 December 20X1	3/10 × 2,290	687
Year ended 31 December 20X2	2/10 × 2,290	458
Year ended 31 December 20X3	1/10 × 2,290	229

The capital balance is therefore as follows over the term of the lease:

	Total $	Capital $	Interest $
1 January 20X0		5,710	
1st instalment	2,000	(1,084)	916
Capital balance at 1 January 20X1		4,626	
2nd instalment	2,000	(1,313)	687
Capital balance at 1 January 20X2		3,313	
3rd instalment	2,000	(1,542)	458
Capital balance at 1 January 20X3		1,771	
4th instalment	2,000	(1,771)	229
	8,000	Nil	2,290

2.4 Disclosure requirements for lessees

IAS 17 requires the following disclosures by lessees in respect of finance leases.

(a)　The **net carrying amount** at the end of the reporting period for each class of asset

(b)　A **reconciliation** between the total of future minimum lease payments at the end of the reporting period, and their present value. In addition, an entity should disclose the total of minimum lease payments at the reporting date, and their present value, for each of the following periods.

　　(i)　Not later than one year
　　(ii)　Later than one year and not later than five years
　　(iii)　Later than five years

(c)　**Contingent rents** recognised in income for the period

(d)　Total of **future minimum sublease payments** expected to be received under non-cancellable subleases at the reporting date

(e)　A **general description** of the lessee's material leasing arrangements including, but not limited to, the following.

　　(i)　The basis on which contingent rent payments are determined

　　(ii)　The existence and terms of renewal or purchase options and escalation clauses

　　(iii)　Restrictions imposed by lease arrangements, such as those concerning dividends, additional debt, and further leasing

IAS 17 encourages (but does not require) further disclosures, as appropriate.

2.5 Example: Lessee disclosures

These disclosure requirements will be illustrated for Bacchus Co. We will assume that Bacchus Co makes up its accounts to 31 December and uses the actuarial method to apportion finance charges.

Solution

The company's accounts for the first year of the lease, the year ended 31 December 20X0, would include the information given below.

STATEMENT OF FINANCIAL POSITION AS AT 31 DECEMBER 20X0 (EXTRACTS)

	$	$
Non-current assets		
Assets held under finance leases		
Plant and machinery at cost	7,710	
Less accumulated depreciation (20% × $7,710)	(1,542)	
		6,168
Current liabilities		
Obligations under finance leases		1,315
Non-current liabilities		
Obligations under finance leases		
$(1,512 + 1,739)		3,251

(Notice that only the outstanding **capital** element is disclosed under liabilities, ie the total of the minimum lease payments with future finance charges separately deducted.)

STATEMENT OF PROFIT OR LOSS
FOR THE YEAR ENDED 31 DECEMBER 20X0 (EXTRACT)

	$
Interest payable and similar charges	
Interest on finance leases	856

For **operating leases** the disclosures are as follows.

(a)   The total of future minimum lease payments under non-cancellable operating leases for each of the following periods:

  (i)   Not later than one year
  (ii)   Later than one year and not later than five years
  (iii) Later than five years

(b)   The total of future minimum sublease payments expected to be received under non-cancellable subleases at the reporting date

(c)   Lease and sublease payments recognised in income for the period, with separate amounts for minimum lease payments, contingent rents, and sublease payments

(d)   A general description of the lessee's significant leasing arrangements including, but not limited to, the following.

  (i)   The basis on which contingent rent payments are determined

  (ii)   The existence and terms of renewal or purchase options and escalation clauses

  (iii) Restrictions imposed by lease arrangements, such as those concerning dividends, additional debt, and further leasing

The following diagram gives a useful summary of the **accounting treatment for a finance lease by a lessee**.

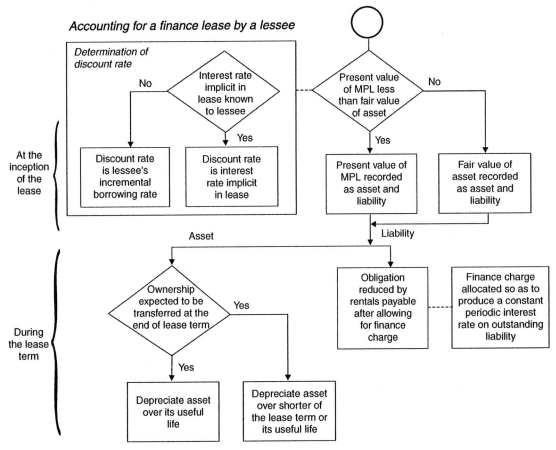

Accounting for a finance lease by a lessee

MPL = Minimum lease payments

3 Lessors

3.1 Accounting treatment: finance leases

In principle, accounting for a **finance lease** by a **lessor** is a **mirror image of the entries for the lessee**. The asset is recorded in the lessor's books as a receivable, *not* as a non-current asset, as follows.

DEBIT   Lessee (receivable) account
CREDIT   Non-current assets

The **income derived** from the lease is spread over accounting periods so as to give a constant periodic rate of return for the lessor. The complex methods of achieving this are beyond the scope of your syllabus, but they are based on the lessor's net investment in respect of the finance lease. You will look at these complex methods later in your studies.

3.2 Accounting treatment: operating leases

An **asset** held for use in operating leases by a lessor should be recorded as a non-current asset and depreciated over its useful life. The basis for depreciation should be consistent with the lessor's policy on similar non-lease assets and follow the guidance in IAS 16.

Income from an operating lease, excluding charges for services such as insurance and maintenance, should be recognised on **a straight-line basis** over the period of the lease, even if the receipts are not on such a basis, unless another systematic and rational basis is more representative of the time pattern in which the benefit from the leased asset is receivable.

Indirect costs should be treated in one of two ways.

(a)   **Deferred** and allocated to income over the lease term in proportion to the recognition of rent income

(b)   Recognised as an **expense** in the period they are incurred

Lessors should refer to IAS 36 on **impairment** in order to determine whether a leased asset has become impaired.

A lessor who is a **manufacturer or dealer** should not recognise any selling profit on entering into an operating lease because it is not the equivalent of a sale.

3.3 Lessors' disclosures for operating leases

The following should be disclosed.

(a)   For each class of asset, the **gross carrying amount**, the accumulated depreciation and accumulated impairment losses at the reporting date:

(i)   Depreciation recognised in income for the period
(ii)   Impairment losses recognised in income for the period
(iii)   Impairment losses reversed in income for the period

(b)   The **future minimum lease payments** under non-cancellable operating leases in the aggregate and for each of the following periods:

(i)   Not later than one year
(ii)   Later than one year and not later than five years
(iii)   Later than five years

(c)   Total **contingent rents** recognised in income

(d)   A **general description** of the lessor's significant leasing arrangements

The accounts of Silenus Co for the year ended 31 December 20X0 would show the information given below.

STATEMENT OF FINANCIAL POSITION AS AT 31 DECEMBER 20X0 (EXTRACTS)

	$
Current assets	
Receivables	
Net investment in finance leases (note)	4,566

NOTES TO THE STATEMENT OF FINANCIAL POSITION

	$
Net investment in finance leases	
Falling due within one year	1,315
Falling due after more than one year	3,251
	4,566

3.4 Sale and leaseback transactions

Under this type of transaction, the holder of an asset **sells it** to another party and then immediately **leases it back again**. The sale price and the rental agreed are dependent upon each other, negotiated as a package. The treatment depends on the type of lease which results.

For **finance leases**, any apparent profit on sale should not be recognised immediately as income, but should be deferred and amortised over the lease term. The transaction is effectively the raising of finance secured on an asset that continues to be held and is not disposed of.

For **operating leases**, any profit on sale is recognised immediately if the transaction was carried out at **fair value** (ie this is a normal sale). For transactions which are not at fair value, the following rules apply.

(a) **Sale price is below fair value**: recognise profit/loss immediately *unless* the loss is compensated by rentals below market value, in which case defer and amortise the loss in proportion to the rental payments over the period the asset is used.

(b) **Sale price is above fair value**: defer and amortise the excess above fair value over the period the asset is used.

(c) **Fair value is less than carrying amount**: the loss (fair value less carrying amount) should be recognised immediately.

Question	Lessor

Leisure Services Co are electrical wholesalers. On 2 May 20X3, they purchased on credit from TV Suppliers Co ten television sets for a total of $1,600. They offered these for sale for cash at $240 each or under a finance lease for a cash deposit of $40 and eight quarterly instalments of $30 each, the first instalment being payable after three months (at the end of which ownership would transfer to the buyer). In the week ended 16 June 20X3 they sold two sets for cash and four under leases for which the cash deposits were paid at the time of sale.

On 1 December 20X3 Leisure Services Co installed one of their sets permanently on their own premises in a closed circuit television installation to detect theft.

You are required to prepare the necessary accounts (except cash and TV Suppliers Co) with dates and narrations in the ledger of Leisure Services Co to record the above transactions, balance them and prepare the statement of profit or loss part of a statement of profit or loss and other comprehensive income up to 31 December 20X3.

Note: The amount of finance interest earned in the period, calculated using the actuarial method and an implicit interest rate of 4.5%, can be included in the statement of profit or loss after sales.

Answer

Lease receivable – 4 sets leased June 2003

	Receivable b/f	Interest 4.5%	Repayment	Receivable c/f
FV ($240 × 4)	960			
Deposit × 4	(160)			
Q/E Sep 2003	800	36	(120)	716
Q/E Dec 2003	716	32	(120)	628

Capital element in first instalment = $(120 – 36) = $84
Capital element in second instalment = $(120 – 32) = $88

Ledger accounts

NON-CURRENT ASSETS

20X3		$			
1 Dec	Purchases: closed circuit TV	160			

LEASE RECEIVABLES

20X3		$	20X3		$
16 May	Sales (4 × $240)	960	16 May	Bank: deposits	160
			16 Aug	Bank: 1st instalment	84
			16 Nov	Bank: 2nd instalment	88
			31 Dec	Balance c/f	628
		960			960

SALES

20X3		$	20X3		$
31 Dec	Statement of profit or loss	1,440	16 May	Lease receivables	960
				Cash (2 × $240)	480
		1,440			1,440

PURCHASES

20X3		$	20X3		$
2 May	Payables	1,600	1 Dec	Non-current assets	160
			31 Dec	Statement of profit or loss	1,440
		1,600			1,600

LEASE INTEREST RECEIVABLE

20X3		$	20X3		$
31 Dec	Statement of profit or loss	68	16 Aug	Bank: 1st instalment	36
			16 Nov	Bank: 2nd instalment	32
		68			68

STATEMENT OF PROFIT OR LOSS TO 31 DECEMBER 20X3

	$	$
Sales		1,440
Lease interest receivable		68
		1,508
Purchases	1,440	
Less closing inventory (3 × $160)	(480)	
Cost of sales		960)
Gross profit		548

Chapter roundup

- A finance lease is a means of acquiring the long-term use of an asset whereas an operating lease is a short-term rental agreement. Substance over form must be applied when accounting for leases.

- You must also learn the **disclosure requirements of IAS 17** for both lessors and lessees.

Quick quiz

1   (a)   ....leases transfer substantially all the risks and rewards of ownership.

    (b)   ....leases are usually short-term rental agreements with the lessor being responsible for the repairs and maintenance of the asset.

2   A business acquires an asset under a finance lease. What is the double entry?

3   List the disclosures required under IAS 17 for lessees.

4   A lorry has an expected useful life of six years. It is acquired under a four-year finance lease. Over which period should it be depreciated?

5   A company leases a photocopier under an operating lease which expires in June 20X2. Its office is leased under an operating lease due to expire in January 20X3. How should past and future operating leases be disclosed in its 31 December 20X1 accounts?

Answers to quick quiz

1   (a)   Finance leases
    (b)   Operating leases

2   DEBIT   Asset account
    CREDIT   Lessor (liability) account

3   See Para 2.4.

4   The four-year term, unless eventual ownership of the lorry is reasonably certain, in which case it should be depreciated over its useful life of six years

5   The total operating lease rentals charged to profit or loss should be disclosed. The payments committed to should be disclosed analysing them between those falling due in the next year and those falling between the second to fifth years.

End of chapter question

Construction First (AIA May 2009)

Construction First provides finance and financial solutions to companies in the construction industry. On 1 January 20X7 the company agreed to finance the lease of equipment costing $145,080 to Bodge Brothers over its useful life of five years at an annual rental of $39,000 payable annually in arrears. The interest rate associated with this transaction is 10% and Construction First incurred direct costs of $2,761 in setting up the lease.

Construction First agreed with the manufacturer of the equipment to pay the amount owing in three equal six-monthly instalments beginning on 31 January 20X7.

Required

Show the entries that would appear in Construction First's statement of profit or loss and statement of financial position (balance sheet) for the year ended 31 December 20X8 together with comparative figures and an appropriate disclosure note.   **(14 marks)**

Financial instruments

Topic list	Syllabus reference
1 Financial instruments	11.4
2 Presentation of financial instruments	11.4
3 Recognition of financial instruments	11.4
4 Measurement of financial instruments	11.4

Introduction

Financial instruments is a very complex issue, but you will only be asked
straightforward questions about the basic issues in the Paper 11 exam.
Presentation issues are important but the fundamental questions of
recognition and measurement of financial instruments are not tackled until
Paper 13, so you should skim read Sections 3 and 4. IFRS 7: *Financial
instruments: disclosure* however is examinable.

1 Financial instruments

Financial instruments can be very complex.

Exam focus point

Although the very complexity of this topic makes it a highly likely subject for an exam question in Paper 13, there are limits as to how complex and detailed a question the examiner can set at Paper 11 with any realistic expectation of students being able to answer it! You should, therefore, concentrate on the essential points.

1.1 Introduction

If you read the financial press you will probably be aware of **rapid international expansion** in the use of financial instruments. These vary from straightforward, traditional instruments, eg bonds, through to various forms of so-called 'derivative instruments'.

We can perhaps summarise the reasons why a project on accounting for financial instruments was considered necessary as follows.

(a) The **significant growth of financial instruments** over recent years has outstripped the development of guidance for their accounting.

(b) The topic is of **international concern**, other national standard-setters are involved as well as the IASB.

(c) There have been a number of **high-profile disasters** involving derivatives which, while not caused by accounting failures, have raised questions about accounting and disclosure practices.

Two Standards are relevant:

(a) IAS 32 *Financial instruments: presentation*, which deals with:

(i) The classification of financial instruments between liabilities and equity
(ii) Presentation of certain compound instruments, and

(b) IFRS 7 *Financial instruments: disclosures*, which revised, simplified and incorporated disclosure requirements previously included in IAS 32

IAS 32 is not within the examinable standards list for Paper 11, however it does provide the basic rules on the presentation of financial instruments so is covered in this chapter.

There are two other standards on financial instruments - IAS 39 *Financial instruments: recognition and measurement* and IFRS 9 *Financial instruments* which are outside the scope of the Paper 11 syllabus, but you will study these at Paper 13.

1.2 Definitions

The most important definitions are common to both Standards.

Key terms

Financial instrument. Any contract that gives rise to both a financial asset of one entity and a financial liability or equity instrument of another entity.

Financial asset. Any asset that is:

(a) Cash

(b) An equity instrument of another entity

(c) A contractual right to receive cash or another financial asset from another entity; or to exchange financial instruments with another entity under conditions that are potentially favourable to the entity, *or*

(d) A contract that will or may be settled in the entity's own equity instruments and is:

    (i) A non-derivative for which the entity is or may be obliged to receive a variable number of the entity's own equity instruments; *or*

    (ii) A derivative that will or may be settled other than by the exchange of a fixed amount of cash or another financial asset for a fixed number of the entity's own equity instruments.

Financial liability. Any liability that is:

(a) A contractual obligation:

    (i) To deliver cash or another financial asset to another entity, *or*

    (ii) To exchange financial instruments with another entity under conditions that are potentially unfavourable; *or*

(b) A contract that will or may be settled in the entity's own equity instruments and is:

    (i) A non-derivative for which the entity is or may be obliged to deliver a variable number of the entity's own equity instruments; *or*

    (ii) A derivative that will or may be settled other than by the exchange of a fixed amount of cash or another financial asset for a fixed number of the entity's own equity instruments.

Equity instrument. Any contract that evidences a residual interest in the assets of an entity after deducting all of its liabilities.

Fair value is the price that would be received to sell an asset or paid to transfer a liability in an orderly transaction between market participants at the measurement date.

Derivative. A financial instrument or other contract with all three of the following characteristics.

(a) Its value changes in response to the change in a specified interest rate, financial instrument price, commodity price, foreign exchange rate, index of prices or rates, credit rating or credit index, or other variable (sometimes called the 'underlying');

(b) It requires no initial net investment or an initial net investment that is smaller than would be required for other types of contracts that would be expected to have a similar response to changes in market factors; *and*

(c) It is settled at a future date. *(IAS 32 and IFRS 9)*

These definitions are very important – particularly the first three – so learn them.

We should clarify some points arising from these definitions. First, one or two terms above should be themselves defined.

(a) A '**contract**' need not be in writing, but it must comprise an agreement that has 'clear economic consequences' and which the parties to it cannot avoid, usually because the agreement is enforceable in law.

(b) An '**entity**' here could be an individual, partnership, incorporated body or government agency.

1.2.1 Financial assets and liabilities

The definitions of **financial assets** and **financial liabilities** may seem rather circular, referring as they do to the terms financial asset and financial instrument. The point is that there may be a chain of contractual rights and obligations, but it will lead ultimately to the receipt or payment of cash *or* the acquisition or issue of an equity instrument.

Examples of **financial assets** include:

- Trade receivables
- Options
- Shares (when held as an investment)

Examples of **financial liabilities** include:

- Trade payables
- Debenture loans payable
- Redeemable preference (non-equity) shares
- Forward contracts standing at a loss

As we have already noted, financial instruments include both of the following.

(a) **Primary instruments**: eg receivables, payables and equity securities

(b) **Derivative instruments**: eg financial options, futures and forwards, interest rate swaps and currency swaps, **whether recognised or unrecognised**

IAS 32 makes it clear that the following items are *not* financial instruments.

(a) **Physical assets**, eg inventories, property, plant and equipment, leased assets and **intangible assets** (patents, trademarks etc)

(b) **Prepaid expenses**, deferred revenue and most warranty obligations

(c) Liabilities or assets that are **not contractual** in nature

(d) Contractual rights/obligations that **do not involve transfer of a financial asset**, for example, commodity futures contracts

Question	Definitions

Can you give the reasons why physical assets and prepaid expenses do not qualify as financial instruments?

Answer

Refer to the definitions of financial assets and liabilities given above.

(a) **Physical assets**: control of these creates an opportunity to generate an inflow of cash or other assets, but it does not give rise to a present right to receive cash or other financial assets.

(b) **Prepaid expenses**: the future economic benefit is the receipt of goods/services rather than the right to receive cash or other financial assets.

Contingent rights and obligations meet the definition of financial assets and financial liabilities respectively, even though many do not qualify for recognition in financial statements. This is because the contractual rights or obligations exist because of a past transaction or event (for example, assumption of a guarantee).

1.3 Derivatives

A **derivative** is a financial instrument that **derives** its value from the price or rate of an underlying item. Common **examples** of derivatives include the following:

(a) **Forward contracts**: agreements to buy or sell an asset at a fixed price at a fixed future date

(b) **Futures contracts**: similar to forward contracts except that contracts are standardised and traded on an exchange

(c) **Options**: rights (but not obligations) for the option holder to exercise at a pre-determined price; the option writer loses out if the option is exercised

(d) **Swaps**: agreements to swap one set of cash flows for another (normally interest rate or currency swaps)

The nature of derivatives often gives rise to **particular problems**. The **value** of a derivative (and the amount at which it is eventually settled) depends on **movements** in an underlying item (such as an exchange rate). This means that settlement of a derivative can lead to a very different result from the one originally envisaged. A company which has derivatives is exposed to **uncertainty and risk** (potential for gain or loss) and this can have a very material effect on its financial performance, financial position and cash flows.

Yet because a derivative contract normally has **little or no initial cost**, under traditional accounting it **may not be recognised** in the financial statements at all. Alternatively, it may be recognised at an amount which bears no relation to its current value. This is clearly **misleading** and leaves users of the financial statements unaware of the **level of risk** that the company faces. IAS 32 and IAS 39 were developed in order to correct this situation.

1.4 Section summary

- Two accounting standards are relevant:
    - **IAS 32**: Financial instruments: presentation
    - **IFRS 7**: *Financial instruments: disclosures*

- The definitions of **financial asset, financial liability** and **equity instrument** are fundamental to the standards.

- Financial instruments include:
    - **Primary** instruments
    - **Derivative** instruments

2 Presentation of financial instruments

FAST FORWARD The objective of IAS 32 is to establish principles for presenting financial instruments as liabilities or equity and for offsetting financial assets and financial liabilities.

2.1 Scope

IAS 32 should be applied in the presentation and disclosure of **all types of financial instruments**, whether recognised or unrecognised.

Certain items are **excluded** for example subsidiaries, associates and joint ventures, pensions and insurance contracts.

2.2 Liabilities and equity

The main thrust of IAS 32 here is that financial instruments should be presented according to their **substance, not merely their legal form**. In particular, entities which issue financial instruments should classify them (or their component parts) as **either financial liabilities, or equity**.

The classification of a financial instrument as a liability or as equity depends on the following.

(a)   The **substance of the contractual arrangement** on initial recognition

(b)   The definitions of a **financial liability** and an **equity instrument**

How should a **financial liability be distinguished from an equity instrument**? The critical feature of a **liability** is an **obligation** to transfer economic benefit. Therefore, a financial instrument is a financial liability if there is a **contractual obligation** on the issuer either to deliver cash or another financial asset to the holder or to exchange another financial instrument with the holder under potentially unfavourable conditions to the issuer.

The financial liability exists **regardless of the way in which the contractual obligation will be settled**. The issuer's ability to satisfy an obligation may be restricted, eg by lack of access to foreign currency, but this is irrelevant as it does not remove the issuer's obligation or the holder's right under the instrument.

Where the above critical feature is *not* met, then the financial instrument is an **equity instrument**. IAS 32 explains that although the holder of an equity instrument may be entitled to a *pro rated* share of any distributions out of equity, the issuer does *not* have a contractual obligation to make such a distribution.

Although substance and legal form are often **consistent with each other**, this is not always the case. In particular, a financial instrument may have the legal form of equity, but in substance it is in fact a liability. Other instruments may combine features of both equity instruments and financial liabilities.

For example, many entities issue **preferred shares** which must be **redeemed** by the issuer for a fixed (or determinable) amount at a fixed (or determinable) future date. Alternatively, the holder may have the right to require the issuer to redeem the shares at or after a certain date for a fixed amount. In such cases, the issuer has an **obligation**. Therefore, the instrument is a **financial liability** and should be classified as such.

The classification of the financial instrument is made when it is **first recognised** and this classification will continue until the financial instrument is removed from the entity's statement of financial position.

2.3 Compound financial instruments

Compound instruments are split into **equity** and **liability** components and presented in the statement of financial position accordingly.

Some financial instruments contain both a liability and an equity element. In such cases, IAS 32 requires the component parts of the instrument to be **classified separately**, according to the substance of the contractual arrangement and the definitions of a financial liability and an equity instrument.

One of the most common types of compound instrument is **convertible debt**. This creates a primary financial liability of the issuer and grants an option to the holder of the instrument to convert it into an equity instrument (usually ordinary shares) of the issuer. This is the economic equivalent of the issue of conventional debt plus a warrant to acquire shares in the future.

Although in theory there are several possible ways of calculating the split, IAS 32 requires the following method.

Step 1   Calculate the value for the liability component.

Step 2   Deduct this from the instrument as a whole to leave a residual value for the equity component.

The reasoning behind this approach is that an entity's equity is its residual interest in its assets amount after deducting all its liabilities.

The **sum of the carrying amounts** assigned to liability and equity will always be equal to the carrying amount that would be ascribed to the instrument **as a whole**.

2.4 Example: valuation of compound instruments

Rathbone Co issues 2,000 convertible bonds at the start of 20X2. The bonds have a three-year term, and are issued at par with a face value of $1,000 per bond, giving total proceeds of $2,000,000. Interest is payable annually in arrears at a nominal annual interest rate of 6%. Each bond is convertible at any time up to maturity into 250 common shares.

When the bonds are issued, the prevailing market interest rate for similar debt without conversion options is 9%. At the issue date, the market price of one common share is $3. The dividends expected over the three-year term of the bonds amount to 14c per share at the end of each year. The risk-free annual interest rate for a three-year term is 5%.

Required

What is the value of the equity component in the bond?

Solution

The liability component is valued first, and the difference between the proceeds of the bond issue and the fair value of the liability is assigned to the equity component. The present value of the liability component is calculated using a discount rate of 9%, the market interest rate for similar bonds having no conversion rights, as shown.

	$
Present value of the principal: $2,000,000 payable at the end of three years ($2m × 0.772)*	1,544,000
Present value of the interest: $120,000 payable annually in arrears for three years ($120,000 × 2.531)*	303,720
Total liability component	1,847,720
Equity component (balancing figure)	152,280
Proceeds of the bond issue	2,000,000

* These figures can be obtained from discount and annuity tables.

The split between the liability and equity components remains the same throughout the term of the instrument, even if there are changes in the **likelihood of the option being exercised**. This is because it is not always possible to predict how a holder will behave. The issuer continues to have an obligation to make future payments until conversion, maturity of the instrument or some other relevant transaction takes place.

Question   Compound instruments

On 1 January 20X1, EFG issued 10,000 5% convertible bonds at their par value of $50 each. The bonds will be redeemed on 1 January 20X6. Each bond is convertible at the option of the holder at any time during the five year period. Interest on the bond will be paid annually in arrears.

The prevailing market interest rate for similar debt without conversion options at the date of issue was 6%.

At what value should the equity element of the financial instrument be recognised in the financial statements of EFG at the date of issue?

Answer

> **Top tip.** The method to use here is to find the present value of the principal value of the bond, $500,000 (10,000 × $50) and the interest payments of $25,000 annually (5% × $500,000) at the market rate for non-convertible bonds of 6%, using the discount factor tables. The difference between this total and the principal amount of $500,000 is the equity element.

	$
Present value of principal $500,000 × 0.747	373,500
Present value of interest $25,000 × 4.212	105,300
Liability value	478,800
Principal amount	500,000
Equity element	21,200

2.5 Interest, dividends, losses and gains

As well as looking at statement of financial position presentation, IAS 32 considers how financial instruments affect the statement of profit or loss and other comprehensive income and changes in equity. The treatment varies according to whether interest, dividends, losses or gains relate to a financial liability or an equity instrument.

(a) Interest, dividends, losses and gains relating to a financial instrument (or component part) classified as a **financial liability** should be recognised as **income or expense** in profit or loss.

(b) Distributions to holders of a financial instrument classified as an **equity instrument** should be **recognised in equity**.

(c) **Transaction costs** of an equity transaction shall be accounted for as a **deduction from equity** (unless they are directly attributable to the acquisition of a business).

2.6 Section summary

- Issuers of financial instruments must classify them as **liabilities** or **equity**.
- The **substance** of the financial instrument is more important than its **legal form**.
- The **critical feature of a financial liability** is the contractual obligation to deliver cash or another financial asset.
- **Compound instruments** are split into equity and liability parts and presented accordingly.
- **Interest, dividends, losses and gains** are treated according to whether they relate to a financial liability or an equity instrument.

Question

Classification

During the financial year ended 28 February 20X5, MN issued redeemable preference shares with a coupon rate of 8%. The shares are redeemable on 28 February 20X9 at premium of 10%.

Identify whether the shares should be classified as a financial liability or equity, **explaining in not more than 40 words each** the reason for your choice.

BPP
LEARNING MEDIA

Answer

The shares are a **financial liability**. The preference shares require regular distributions to the holders but more importantly have the debt characteristic of being redeemable. Therefore according to IAS 32 *Financial instruments: presentation* they must be classified as debt.

3 Recognition of financial instruments

IFRS 9 *Financial instruments* establishes principles for recognising and measuring financial assets and liabilities.

3.1 Scope

IFRS 9 issued in November 2009 replaced parts of IAS 39 with respect to recognition, derecognition, classification and measurement of financial assets and liabilities. This standard is a work in progress and will fully replace IAS 39 in time.

IAS 39 and IFRS 9 apply to **all entities** and to **all types of financial instruments except** those specifically excluded, for example investments in subsidiaries, associates and joint ventures. Note that neither IAS 39 nor IFRS 9 are on the examinable documents list for Paper 11, but the principles discussed briefly in this section are useful for an understanding of the recognition of financial instruments.

3.2 Initial recognition

A financial asset or financial liability should be recognised in the statement of financial position when the reporting entity becomes a party to the contractual provisions of the instrument.

Point to note

An important consequence of this is that all derivatives should be recognised in the statement of financial position.

Notice that this is **different** from the recognition criteria in the *Conceptual Framework* and in most other standards. Items are normally recognised when there is a probable inflow or outflow of resources and the item has a cost or value that can be measured reliably.

3.3 Example: Initial recognition

An entity has entered into two separate contracts:

(a)   A firm commitment (an order) to buy a specific quantity of iron

(b)   A forward contract to buy a specific quantity of iron at a specified price on a specified date provided delivery of iron is not taken

Contract (a) is a **normal trading contract**. The entity does not recognise a liability for the iron until the goods have actually been delivered. (Note that this contract is not a financial instrument because it involves a physical asset, rather than a financial asset.)

Contract (b) is a **financial instrument**. Under IFRS 9, the entity recognises a financial liability (an obligation to deliver cash) on the **commitment date**, rather than waiting for the closing date in which the exchange takes place.

Note that planned future transactions, no matter how likely, are not assets and liabilities of an entity – the entity has not yet become a party to the contract.

3.4 Derecognition

Derecognition is the removal of a previously recognised financial instrument from an entity's statement of financial position.

An entity should derecognise a **financial asset** when:

(a) The **contractual rights** to the cash flows from the financial asset **expire**; *or*

(b) It **transfers the financial asset or substantially all the risks and rewards of ownership** of the financial asset to another party.

Question   Examples

Can you think of an example of a situation in which:

(a) An entity has transferred substantially all the risks and rewards of ownership?
(b) An entity has retained substantially all the risks and rewards of ownership?

Answer

IFRS 9 includes the following examples.

(a) (i) An unconditional sale of a financial asset

    (ii) A sale of a financial asset together with an option to repurchase the financial asset at its fair value at the time of repurchase

(b) (i) A sale and repurchase transaction where the repurchase price is a fixed price or the sale price plus a lender's return

    (ii) A sale of a financial asset together with a total return swap that transfers the market risk exposure back to the entity

Exam focus point

> The principle here is that of **substance over form**.

An entity should derecognise a **financial liability** when it is **extinguished** – ie, when the obligation specified in the contract is discharged or cancelled or expires.

On derecognition, the amount to be included in net profit or loss for the period is calculated as follows.

Formula to learn

	$	$
Carrying amount of asset/liability (measured at the date of derecognition) allocated to the part derecognised		X
Less: Consideration received/paid for the part derecognised (including any new asset obtained less any new liability assumed)	X	
		(X)
Difference to net profit/loss		X

3.5 Section summary

- All financial assets and liabilities should be recognised in the statement of financial position, including derivatives.

- Financial assets should be derecognised when the rights to the cash flows from the asset expire or where substantially all the risks and rewards of ownership are transferred to another party.

- Financial liabilities should be derecognised when they are extinguished.

4 Measurement of financial instruments

FAST FORWARD

All financial instruments should be initially measured at fair value which usually equals cost.

4.1 Initial measurement

Financial instruments are initially measured at the **fair value** of the consideration given or received (ie, cost). **Transaction costs** that are **directly attributable** to the acquisition or issue of a financial instrument which is classified as measured at amortised cost increase this amount for a financial asset and decrease this amount for a financial liability.

4.2 Subsequent measurement

For the purposes Paper 11, the only category of financial assets and liabilities that we need to concern ourselves with are those that are measured at amortised cost.

Key terms

> **Amortised cost of a financial asset or financial liability** is the amount at which the financial asset or liability is measured at initial recognition minus principal repayments, plus or minus the cumulative amortisation using the effective interest method of any difference between that initial amount and the maturity amount, and minus any reduction (directly or through the use of an allowance account) for impairment or uncollectability.
>
> The **effective interest method** is a method of calculating the amortised cost of a financial instrument and of allocating the interest income or interest expense over the relevant period.
>
> The **effective interest rate** is the rate that exactly discounts estimated future cash payments or receipts through the expected life of the financial instrument to the net carrying amount. *(IAS 39)*

4.3 Example: Financial asset at amortised cost

On 1 January 20X1 Abacus Co purchases a debt instrument for its fair value of $1,000. The debt instrument is due to mature on 31 December 20X5. The instrument has a principal amount of $1,250 and the instrument carries fixed interest at 4.72% that is paid annually. The effective rate of interest is 10%.

How should Abacus Co account for the debt instrument over its five-year term?

Solution

Abacus Co will receive interest of $59 (1,250 × 4.72%) each year and $1,250 when the instrument matures.

Abacus must allocate the discount of $250 and the interest receivable over the five year term at a constant rate on the carrying amount of the debt. To do this, it must apply the effective interest rate of 10%.

The following table shows the allocation over the years.

Year	Amortised cost at beginning of year	Interest income for year (@ 10%)	Interest received during year (cash in-flow)	Amortised cost at end of year
	$	$	$	$
20X1	1,000	100	(59)	1,041
20X2	1,041	104	(59)	1,086
20X3	1,086	109	(59)	1,136
20X4	1,136	113	(59)	1,190
20X5	1,190	119	(1,250 + 59)	–

Each year the carrying amount of the financial asset is increased by the interest income for the year and reduced by the interest actually received during the year.

Investments whose **fair value cannot be reliably measured** should be measured at **cost**.

4.4 Example: Financial liability at amortised cost

Galaxy Co issues a bond for $503,772 on 1 January 20X2. No interest is payable on the bond, but it will be held to maturity and redeemed on 31 December 20X4 for $600,000. The effective interest rate on the bond is 6%.

Solution

The bond is a 'deep discount' bond and is a financial liability of Galaxy Co. It is measured at amortised cost. Although there is no interest as such, the difference between the initial cost of the bond and the price at which it will be redeemed is the finance cost of 6% which is the effective interest rate. This must be allocated over the term of the bond at a constant rate on the carrying amount.

The following table shows the allocation over the years.

Year	Amortised cost at beginning of year	Interest expense for year (@ 6%)	Interest paid during year (cash out-flow)	Amortised cost at end of year
	$	$	$	$
20X2	503,772	30,226	(0)	533,998
20X3	533,998	32,040	(0)	566,038
20X4	566,038	33,962	(600,000)	0

The charge to profit or loss in year 1 is $30,226 (503,772 × 6%)

The balance outstanding at 31 December 20X2 is $533,998

Question   Financial liabilities measured at amortised cost

On 1 January 20X3 Deferred issued $600,000 loan notes. Issue costs were $200. The loan notes do not carry interest, but are redeemable at a premium of $152,389 on 31 December 20X4. The effective finance cost of the loan notes is 12%.

What is the finance cost in respect of the loan notes for the year ended 31 December 20X4?

Answer

The premium on redemption of the loan notes represents a finance cost. The effective rate of interest must be applied so that the debt is measured at amortised cost.

At the time of issue, the loan notes are recognised at their net proceeds of $599,800 (600,000 – 200).

The finance cost for the year ended 31 December 20X4 is $80,613, calculated as follows:

	B/f	Interest @ 12%	C/f
	$	$	$
20X3	599,800	71,976	671,776
20X4	671,776	80,613	752,389

Finance liabilities measured at amortised cost

On 1 January 20X5, an entity issued a debt instrument with a coupon rate of 3.5% at a par value of $6,000,000. The directly attributable costs of issue were $120,000. The debt instrument is repayable on 31 December 20Y1 at a premium of $1,100,000.

What is the total amount of the finance cost associated with the debt instrument?

Answer

	$
Issue costs	120,000
Interest $6,000,000 \times 3.5\% \times 7$ years	1,470,000
Premium on redemption	1,100,000
Total finance cost	2,690,000

Chapter roundup

- Financial instruments can be very complex.

- The objective of IAS 32 is to establish principles for presenting financial instruments as liabilities or equity and for offsetting financial assets and financial liabilities.

- **Compound instruments** are split into **equity** and **liability** components and presented in the statement of financial position accordingly.

- IFRS 9 *Financial instruments* establishes principles for recognising and measuring financial assets and liabilities.

- All financial instruments should be initially measured at fair value which usually equals cost.

Quick quiz

1   Which issues are dealt with by IAS 32?

2   Define the following.

    (a)   Financial asset
    (b)   Financial liability
    (c)   Equity instrument

3   What is the critical feature used to identify a financial liability?

4   How should compound instruments be classified by the issuer?

5   When should a financial asset be de-recognised?

6   How are financial instruments initially measured?

Answers to quick quiz

1   Classification between liabilities and equity; presentation.

2   See Key Terms, Paragraph 1.2

3   The contractual obligation to deliver cash or another financial asset to the holder.

4   By calculating the present value of the liability component and then deducting this from the instrument as a whole to leave a residual value for the equity component.

5   Financial assets should be derecognised when the rights to the cash flows from the asset expire or where substantially all the risks and rewards of ownership are transferred to another party.

6   Fair value which usually equals cost.

End of chapter question

Financial instruments (AIA November 2007)

Just Crisps is a small public limited company planning to launch a new product in 20X8. Up until now the company has financed its operations with equity, held by the company's original shareholders, but the new product will require the issue of a debt instrument. Unfortunately, the company's finance director is unsure how the debt would be accounted for in the company's financial statements and has asked you for guidance. The following facts have come to your attention:

- The company plans to issue 40,000 $100 bonds which will mature in five years' time.

- The maximum interest rate Just Crisps can afford to pay is 6% per annum but investors could receive 10% per annum on an investment with similar risk and maturity.

Required

(a)   The finance director is surprised to learn that the company is likely to receive a principal sum of only $3,393,600 as a maximum and not the $4,000,000 she had hoped for. Explain, with calculations, why this is the case. **(5 marks)**

The following table has been provided for your use:

	Present value of $1 Discount rate	
	6%	10%
Periods 1	0.943	0.909
2	0.890	0.826
3	0.840	0.751
4	0.792	0.683
5	0.747	0.621

(b)   Following the above explanation, the finance director announces that she wishes to account for the rolled-up interest of $606,400 by allocating it equally to each of the five years over which the debt will be outstanding but is told that this is not the 'interest method' favoured by the IASB. Explain why the IASB favours the 'interest method' and show, with calculations, its effect on the company's statements of profit or loss and other comprehensive income and financial position for each of the five years. **(10 marks)**

(Total = 15 marks)

P
A
R
T

E

Financial analysis

Statements of cash flows

Topic list	Syllabus reference
1 IAS 7 *Statement of cash flows*	11.5
2 Preparing a statement of cash flows	11.5
3 Interpretation of statements of cash flows	11.5

Introduction

You have already covered much of the material on statements of cash flows in your earlier studies. Much of this is repeated here for revision. You will tackle group statements of cash flows only when you reach Paper 13.

The importance of the distinction between cash and profit and the scant attention paid to this by the statement of profit or loss has resulted in the development of statements of cash flows.

This chapter adopts a systematic approach to the preparation of statements of cash flows in examinations; you should learn this method and you will then be equipped for any problems in the exam itself.

The third section of the chapter looks at the information which is provided by statements of cash flows and how it should be analysed.

1 IAS 7 *Statement of cash flows*

A statement of cash flows is a useful addition to a company's financial statements as a measure of performance.

1.1 Introduction

It has been argued that 'profit' does not always give a useful or meaningful picture of a company's operations. Readers of a company's financial statements might even be **misled by a reported profit figure**.

(a)   Shareholders might believe that if a company makes a profit after tax, of say, $100,000 then this is the amount which it could afford to **pay as a dividend**. Unless the company has **sufficient cash** available to stay in business and also to pay a dividend, the shareholders' expectations would be wrong.

(b)   Employees might believe that if a company makes profits, it can afford to **pay higher wages** next year. This opinion may not be correct: the ability to pay wages depends on the **availability of cash**.

(c)   Survival of a business entity depends not so much on profits as on its **ability to pay its debts when they fall due**. Such payments might include 'revenue' items such as material purchases, wages, interest and taxation and so on, but also capital payments for new non-current assets and the repayment of loan capital when this falls due (for example, on the redemption of debentures).

From these examples, it may be apparent that a company's performance and prospects depend not so much on the 'profits' earned in a period, but more realistically on liquidity or **cash flows**.

1.2 Funds flow and cash flow

Some countries, either currently or in the past, have required the disclosure of additional statements based on **funds flow** rather than cash flow. However, the definition of 'funds' can be very vague and such statements often simply require a rearrangement of figures already provided in the statements of financial position and statement of profit or loss. By contrast, a statement of cash flows is unambiguous and provides information which is additional to that provided in the rest of the accounts. It also lends itself to organisation by activity and not by statement of financial position classification.

Statements of cash flows are frequently given as an **additional statement**, supplementing the statements of financial position, statement of profit or loss and other comprehensive income, and related notes.

Exam focus point

The group aspects of statements of cash flows (and certain complex matters) have been excluded as they are beyond the scope of your syllabus.

1.3 Objective of IAS 7

The aim of IAS 7 is to provide information to users of financial statements about the entity's **ability to generate cash and cash equivalents**, as well as indicating the cash needs of the entity. The statement of cash flows provides *historical* information about cash and cash equivalents, classifying cash flows between operating, investing and financing activities.

1.4 Scope

A statement of cash flows should be presented as an **integral part** of an entity's financial statements. All types of entity can provide useful information about cash flows as the need for cash is universal, whatever the nature of their revenue-producing activities. Therefore **all entities are required by the Standard to produce a statement of cash flows**.

1.5 Benefits of cash flow information

The use of statements of cash flows is very much **in conjunction** with the rest of the financial statements. Users can gain further appreciation of the change in net assets, of the entity's financial position (liquidity and solvency) and the entity's ability to adapt to changing circumstances by affecting the amount and timing of cash flows. Statements of cash flows **enhance comparability** as they are not affected by differing accounting policies used for the same type of transactions or events.

Cash flow information of a historical nature can be used as an indicator of the amount, timing and certainty of future cash flows. Past forecast cash flow information can be **checked for accuracy** as actual figures emerge. The relationship between profit and cash flows can be analysed as can changes in prices over time.

1.6 Definitions

The Standard gives the following definitions, the most important of which are **cash** and **cash equivalents**.

Key terms

> **Cash** comprises cash on hand and demand deposits.
>
> **Cash equivalents** are short-term, highly liquid investments that are readily convertible to known amounts of cash and which are subject to an insignificant risk of changes in value.
>
> **Cash flows** are in-flows and out-flows of cash and cash equivalents.
>
> **Operating activities** are the principal revenue-producing activities of the entity and other activities that are not investing or financing activities.
>
> **Investing activities** are the acquisition and disposal of non-current assets and other investments not included in cash equivalents.
>
> **Financing activities** are activities that result in changes in the size and composition of the equity capital and borrowings of the entity. *(IAS 7)*

1.7 Cash and cash equivalents

The Standard expands on the definition of cash equivalents: they are not held for investment or other long-term purposes, but rather to meet short-term cash commitments. To fulfil the above definition, an investment's **maturity date should normally be within three months from its acquisition date**. It would usually be the case then that equity investments (ie shares in other companies) are *not* cash equivalents. An exception would be where preferred shares were acquired with a very close maturity date.

Loans and other borrowings from banks are classified as investing activities. In some countries, however, **bank overdrafts** are repayable on demand and are treated as part of an entity's total cash management system. In these circumstances an overdrawn balance will be included in cash and cash equivalents. Such banking arrangements are characterised by a balance which fluctuates between overdrawn and credit.

Movements between different types of cash and cash equivalent are not included in cash flows. The investment of surplus cash in cash equivalents is part of cash management, not part of operating, investing or financing activities.

1.8 Presentation of a statement of cash flows

IAS 7 requires statements of cash flows to report cash flows during the period classified by **operating, investing and financing activities**.

1.9 Example: simple statement of cash flows

Flail Co commenced trading on 1 January 20X1 with a medium-term loan of $21,000 and a share issue which raised $35,000. The company purchased non-current assets for $21,000 cash, and during the year to 31 December 20X1 entered into the following transactions.

(a)   Purchases from suppliers were $19,500, of which $2,550 was unpaid at the year end.
(b)   Wages and salaries amounted to $10,500, of which $750 was unpaid at the year end.
(c)   Interest on the loan of $2,100 was fully paid in the year and a repayment of $5,250 was made.
(d)   Sales revenue was $29,400, including $900 receivables at the year end.
(e)   Interest on cash deposits at the bank amounted to $75.
(f)   A dividend of $4,000 was proposed as at 31 December 20X1.

You are required to prepare a historical statement of cash flows for the year ended 31 December 20X1.

Solution

FLAIL CO
STATEMENT OF CASH FLOWS FOR
THE YEAR ENDED 31 DECEMBER 20X1

	$	$
Cash flows from operating activities		
Cash received from customers ($29,400 – $900)	28,500	
Cash paid to suppliers and employees		
($19,500 – $2,550 + ($10,500 – $750)	(26,700)	
Interest paid	(2,100)	
Net cash used in operating activities		(300)
Cash flows from investing activities		
Purchase of non-current assets	(21,000)	
Interest received	75	
Net cash used in investing activities		(20,925)
Cash flows from financing activities		
Issue of shares	35,000	
Proceeds from medium-term loan	21,000	
Repayment of medium-term loan	(5,250)	
Net cash from financing activities		50,750
Net increase in cash and cash equivalents		29,525
Cash and cash equivalents at 1 January 20X1		–
Cash and cash equivalents at 31 December 20X1		29,525

Note that the dividend is only proposed and so there is no related cash flow in 20X1.

The managers of Flail Co have the following information in respect of projected cash flows for the year to 31 December 20X2.

(a) Non-current asset purchases for cash will be $3,000.

(b) Further expenses will be:

   (i) purchases from suppliers – $18,750 ($4,125 owed at the year end);
   (ii) wages and salaries – $11,250 ($600 owed at the year end);
   (iii) loan interest – $1,575.

(c) Sales revenue will be $36,000 ($450 receivables at the year end).

(d) Interest on bank deposits will be $150.

(e) A further capital repayment of $5,250 will be made on the loan.

(f) A dividend of $5,000 will be proposed and last year's final dividend paid.

(g) Income taxes of $2,300 will be paid in respect of 20X1.

Prepare the cash flow forecast for the year to 31 December 20X2.

Answer

FLAIL CO
STATEMENT OF FORECAST CASH FLOWS FOR
THE YEAR ENDING 31 DECEMBER 20X2

	$	$
Cash flows from operating activities		
Cash received from customers ($36,000 + $900 – $450)	36,450	
Cash paid to suppliers and employees ($18,750 + $2,550 – $4,125 + $11,250 + $750 – $600)	(28,575)	
Interest paid	(1,575)	
Taxation	(2,300)	
Net cash paid from operating activities		4,000
Cash flow from investing activities		
Purchase of non-current assets	(3,000)	
Interest received	150	
Net cash used in investing activities		(2,850)
Cash flows from financing activities		
Repayment of medium-term loan	(5,250)	
Dividend payment	(4,000)	
Net cash used in financing activities		(9,250)
Forecast net decrease in cash and cash equivalents		(8,100)
Cash and cash equivalents as at 31 December 20X1		29,525
Forecast cash and cash equivalents as at 31 December 20X2		21,425

1.10 Activities

The manner of presentation of cash flows between operating, investing and financing activities **depends on the nature of the entity**. By classifying cash flows between different activities in this way users can see the impact on cash and cash equivalents of each one, and their relationships with each other. We can look at each in more detail.

1.10.1 Operating activities

This is perhaps the key part of the statement of cash flows because it shows whether, and to what extent, companies can **generate cash from their operations**. It is these operating cash flows which must, in the end pay for all cash outflows relating to other activities, ie paying loan interest, dividends and so on.

Most of the components of cash flows from operating activities will be those items which **determine the profit or loss of the entity**, ie they relate to the main revenue-producing activities of the entity. The Standard gives the following as examples of cash flows from operating activities.

- Cash receipts from the sale of goods and the rendering of services
- Cash receipts from royalties, fees, commissions and other revenue
- Cash payments to suppliers for goods and services
- Cash payments to and on behalf of employees

Certain items may be included in the profit or loss for the period which do *not* relate to operational cash flows, for example the profit or loss on the sale of a piece of plant will be included in profit or loss, but the cash flows will be classed as **investing**.

1.10.2 Investing activities

The cash flows classified under this heading show the extent of new investment in **assets which will generate future profit and cash flows**. The Standard gives the following examples of cash flows arising from investing activities.

- Cash payments to acquire property, plant and equipment, intangibles and other non-current assets, including those relating to capitalised development costs and self-constructed property, plant and equipment
- Cash receipts from sales of property, plant and equipment, intangibles and other non-current assets
- Cash payments to acquire shares or debentures of other entities
- Cash receipts from sales of shares or debentures of other entities
- Cash advances and loans made to other parties
- Cash receipts from the repayment of advances and loans made to other parties

1.10.3 Financing activities

This section of the statement of cash flows shows the share of cash which the entity's capital providers have claimed during the period. This is an indicator of **likely future interest and dividend payments**. The standard gives the following examples of cash flows which might arise under this heading.

- Cash proceeds from issuing shares
- Cash payments to owners to acquire or redeem the entity's shares
- Cash proceeds from issuing debentures, loans, notes, bonds, mortgages and other short or long-term borrowings
- Principal repayments of amounts borrowed under finance leases

The final item needs more explanation. Where the reporting entity uses an asset held under a finance lease, the amounts to go in the statement of cash flows as financing activities are repayments of the **principal (capital)** rather than the **interest**. The interest paid will be shown under operating activities.

1.11 Example: Finance lease rental

The notes to the financial statements of Hayley Co show the following in respect of obligations under finance leases.

Year ended 30 June	20X5	20X4
	$'000	$'000
Amounts payable within one year	12	8
Within two to five years	110	66
	122	74
Less finance charges allocated to future periods	(14)	(8)
	108	66

Interest paid on finance leases in the year to 30 June 20X5 amounted to $6m. Additions to tangible non-current assets acquired under finance leases were shown in the non-current asset note at $56,000.

Required

Calculate the capital repayment to be shown in the statement of cash flows of Hayley Co for the year to 30 June 20X5.

Solution

OBLIGATIONS UNDER FINANCE LEASES

	$'000		$'000
Capital repayment (bal fig)	14	Bal 1.7.X4	66
Bal 30.6.X5	108	Additions	56
	122		122

1.12 Reporting cash flows from operating activities

The Standard offers a choice of method for this part of the statement of cash flows.

(a) **Direct method**: disclose major classes of gross cash receipts and gross cash payments

(b) **Indirect method**: profit or loss is adjusted for the effects of transactions of a non-cash nature, any deferrals or accruals of past or future operating cash receipts or payments, and items of income or expense associated with investing or financing cash flows

The **direct method is the preferred method** because it discloses information, not available elsewhere in the financial statements, which could be of use in estimating future cash flows. The example below shows both methods.

1.12.1 Using the direct method

There are different ways in which the **information about gross cash receipts and payments** can be obtained. The most obvious way is simply to extract the information from the accounting records. This may be a laborious task, however, and the indirect method below may be easier. The example and question above used the direct method.

1.12.2 Using the indirect method

This method is undoubtedly **easier** from the point of view of the preparer of the statement of cash flows. The profit or loss for the period is adjusted for the following.

(a) Changes during the period in inventories, operating receivables and payables
(b) Non-cash items, eg depreciation, provisions, profits/losses on the sales of assets
(c) Other items, the cash flows from which should be classified under investing or financing activities.

A **proforma** of such a calculation, taken from the IAS, is as follows and this method may be more common in the exam. (The proforma has been amended to reflect changes to IFRS.)

	$
Cash flows from operating activities	
Profit before taxation	X
Adjustments for:	
Depreciation	X
Investment income	(X)
Interest expense	X
	X
Increase in trade and other receivables	(X)
Decrease in inventories	X
Decrease in trade payables	(X)
Cash generated from operations	X
Interest paid	(X)
Income taxes paid	(X)
Net cash from operating activities	X

It is important to understand why **certain items are added and others subtracted**. Note the following points.

(a) Depreciation is not a cash expense, but is deducted in arriving at profit. It makes sense, therefore, to eliminate it by adding it back.

(b) By the same logic, a loss on a disposal of a non-current asset (arising through underprovision of depreciation) needs to be added back and a profit deducted.

(c) An increase in inventories means less cash – you have spent cash on buying inventory.

(d) An increase in receivables means the company's customers have not paid as much, and therefore there is less cash within the company.

(e) If the company pays off payables, causing the figure to decrease, again it must have less cash.

1.12.3 Indirect versus direct

The direct method is encouraged where the necessary information is not too costly to obtain, but IAS 7 does not require it. In practice, the indirect method is more commonly used, since it is quicker and easier.

1.13 Interest and dividends

Cash flows from interest and dividends received and paid should each be **disclosed separately**. Each should be classified in a consistent manner from period to period as either operating, investing or financing activities.

Dividends paid by the entity can be classified in **one of two ways**.

(a) As a **financing cash flow**, showing the cost of obtaining financial resources.

(b) As a component of **cash flows from operating activities** so that users can assess the entity's ability to pay dividends out of operating cash flows.

1.14 Taxes on income

Cash flows arising from taxes on income should be **separately disclosed** and should be classified as cash flows from operating activities *unless* they can be specifically identified with financing and investing activities.

Taxation cash flows are often **difficult to match** to the originating underlying transaction, so most of the time all tax cash flows are classified as arising from operating activities.

1.15 Components of cash and cash equivalents

The components of cash and cash equivalents should be disclosed and a **reconciliation** should be presented, showing the amounts in the statement of cash flows reconciled with the equivalent items reported in the statement of financial position.

It is also necessary to disclose the **accounting policy** used in deciding the items included in cash and cash equivalents, in accordance with IAS 1 *Presentation of financial statements*, but also because of the wide range of cash management practices worldwide.

1.16 Other disclosures

All entities should disclose, together with a **commentary by management**, any other information likely to be of importance, for example:

(a) Restrictions on the use of or access to any part of cash equivalents

(b) The amount of undrawn borrowing facilities which are available

(c) Cash flows which increased operating capacity compared to cash flows which merely maintained operating capacity

(d) Cash flows arising from each reported industry and geographical segment

1.17 Example of a statement of cash flows

In the next section we will look at the procedures for preparing a statement of cash flows. First, look at this **example**, adapted from the example given in the Standard.

1.17.1 Direct method

STATEMENT OF CASH FLOWS (DIRECT METHOD)
YEAR ENDED 31 DECEMBER 20X7

	$m	$m
Cash flows from operating activities		
Cash receipts from customers	30,330	
Cash paid to suppliers and employees	(27,600)	
Cash generated from operations	2,730	
Interest paid	(270)	
Income taxes paid	(900)	
Net cash from operating activities		1,560
Cash flows from investing activities		
Purchase of property, plant and equipment	(900)	
Proceeds from sale of equipment	20	
Interest received	200	
Dividends received	200	
Net cash used in investing activities		(480)
Cash flows from financing activities		
Proceeds from issue of share capital	250	
Proceeds from long-term borrowings	250	
Dividends paid*	(1,290)	
Net cash used in financing activities		(790)
Net increase in cash and cash equivalents		290
Cash and cash equivalents at beginning of period (Note)		120
Cash and cash equivalents at end of period (Note)		410

* This could also be shown as an operating cash flow

1.17.2 Indirect method

STATEMENT OF CASH FLOWS (INDIRECT METHOD)
YEAR ENDED 31 DECEMBER 20X7

	$m	$m
Cash flows from operating activities		
Profit before taxation	3,570	
Adjustments for:		
Depreciation	450	
Investment income	(500)	
Interest expense	400	
	3,920	
Increase in trade and other receivables	(500)	
Decrease in inventories	1,050	
Decrease in trade payables	(1,740)	
Cash generated from operations	2,730	
Interest paid	(270)	
Income taxes paid	(900)	
Net cash from operating activities		1,560
Cash flows from investing activities		
Purchase of property, plant and equipment	(900)	
Proceeds from sale of equipment	20	
Interest received	200	
Dividends received	200	
Net cash used in investing activities		(480)
Cash flows from financing activities		
Proceeds from issue of share capital	250	
Proceeds from long-term borrowings	250	
Dividends paid*	(1,290)	
Net cash used in financing activities		(790)
Net increase in cash and cash equivalents		290
Cash and cash equivalents at beginning of period (Note)		120
Cash and cash equivalents at end of period (Note)		410

* This could also be shown as an operating cash flow

1.17.3 Notes

The following note is required to both versions of the statement.

Note: Cash and cash equivalents

Cash and cash equivalents consist of cash on hand and balances with banks, and investments in money market instruments. Cash and cash equivalents included in the statement of cash flows comprise the following statement of financial position amounts.

	20X7	20X6
	$m	$m
Cash on hand and balances with banks	40	25
Short-term investments	370	95
Cash and cash equivalents	410	120

The company has undrawn borrowing facilities of $2,000m of which only $700m may be used for future expansion.

2 Preparing a statement of cash flows

> You must be able to prepare a statement of cash flows by both the indirect and the direct methods.

2.1 Introduction

In essence, preparing a statement of cash flows is very straightforward. You should therefore simply learn the format and apply the steps noted in the example below. Note that the following items are treated in a way that might seem confusing, but the treatment is logical if you **think in terms of cash**.

(a) **Increase in inventory** is treated as **negative** (in brackets). This is because it represents a cash **outflow**; cash is being spent on inventory.

(b) An **increase in receivables** would be treated as **negative** for the same reasons; more receivables means less cash.

(c) By contrast an **increase in payables has a positive cash flow impact** because cash is being retained and not used to settle accounts payable.

2.2 Example: Preparation of a statement of cash flows

Kane Co's statement of profit or loss for the year ended 31 December 20X2 and statements of financial position at 31 December 20X1 and 31 December 20X2 were as follows.

KANE CO
STATEMENT OF PROFIT OR LOSS FOR THE YEAR ENDED 31 DECEMBER 20X2

	$'000	$'000
Sales		720
Raw materials consumed	70	
Staff costs	94	
Depreciation	118	
Loss on disposal of non-current asset	18	
		300
Operating profit		420
Interest payable		28
Profit before tax		392
Taxation		124
Profit for the year		268

There was no other comprehensive income in the year.

KANE CO
STATEMENT OF FINANCIAL POSITION AS AT 31 DECEMBER

	20X2		20X1	
	$'000	$'000	$'000	$'000
Assets				
Non-current assets				
Cost	1,596		1,560	
Depreciation	318		224	
		1,278		1,336
Current assets				
Inventory	24		20	
Trade receivables	76		58	
Bank	48		56	
		148		134
Total assets		1,426		1,470

	20X2		20X1	
	$'000	$'000	$'000	$'000
Equity and liabilities				
Equity				
Share capital	360		340	
Share premium	36		24	
Retained earnings	686		490	
		1,082		854
Non-current liabilities				
Long-term loans		200		500
Current liabilities				
Trade payables	12		6	
Taxation	132		110	
		144		116
		1,426		1,470

During the year, the company paid $90,000 for a new piece of machinery, and a dividend of $72,000 was paid.

Required

Prepare a statement of cash flows for Kane Co for the year ended 31 December 20X2 in accordance with the requirements of IAS 7, using the indirect method.

Solution

Step 1   **Set out the proforma statement of cash flows** with the headings required by IAS 7. You should leave plenty of space. Ideally, use three or more sheets of paper, one for the main statement, one for the notes and one for your workings. It is obviously essential to know the formats very well.

Step 2   Begin with the **cash flows from operating activities** as far as possible. When preparing the statement from statements of financial position, you will usually have to calculate such items as depreciation, loss on sale of non-current assets, profit for the year and tax paid (see Step 4). Note that you may not be given the tax charge in the statement of profit or loss. You will then have to assume that the tax paid in the year is last year's year-end provision and calculate the charge as the balancing figure.

Step 3   Calculate the cash flow figures for **dividends paid, purchase or sale of non-current assets, issue of shares and repayment of loans** if these are not already given to you (as they may be).

Step 4   If you are not given the profit figure, open up a **working**. Using the opening and closing balances of retained earnings, the taxation charge and dividends paid, you will be able to calculate profit for the year as the balancing figure to put in the cash flows from operating activities section.

Step 5   You will now be able to **complete the statement** by slotting in the figures given or calculated.

KANE CO
STATEMENT OF CASH FLOWS FOR THE YEAR ENDED 31 DECEMBER 20X2

	$'000	$'000
Cash flows from operating activities		
Profit before tax	392	
Depreciation charges	118	
Loss on sale of tangible non-current assets	18	
Interest expense	28	
Increase in inventories	(4)	
Increase in receivables	(18)	
Increase in payables	6	
Cash generated from operations	540	
Interest paid	(28)	
Dividends paid	(72)	
Tax paid (110 + 124 − 132)	(102)	
Net cash from operating activities		338
Cash flows from investing activities		
Payments to acquire property, plant and equipment	(90)	
Receipts from sales of property, plant and equipment (W)	12	
Net cash used in investing activities		(78)
Cash flows from financing activities		
Issues of share capital (360 + 36 − 340 − 24)	32	
Long-term loans repaid (500 − 200)	(300)	
Net cash used in financing activities		(268)
Decrease in cash and cash equivalents		(8)
Cash and cash equivalents at 1.1.X2		56
Cash and cash equivalents at 31.12.X2		48

Working: non-current asset disposals

COST

	$'000		$'000
At 1.1.X2	1,560	At 31.12.X2	1,596
Purchases	90	Disposals (balance)	54
	1,650		1,650

ACCUMULATED DEPRECIATION

	$'000		$'000
At 31.12.X2	318	At 1.1.X2	224
Depreciation on disposals		Charge for year	118
(balance)	24		
	342		342

	$'000
Carrying amount of disposals	30
Net loss reported	(18)
Proceeds of disposals	12

Prepare a cash flow statement

Set out below are the financial statements of Emma Co. You are the financial controller, faced with the task of preparing a statement of cash flows in accordance with IAS 7 *Statement of cash flows*.

EMMA CO

STATEMENT OF PROFIT OR LOSS AND OTHER COMPREHENSIVE INCOME FOR THE YEAR ENDED 31 DECEMBER 20X2

	$'000
Revenue	2,553
Cost of sales	1,814
Gross profit	739
Other income: interest received	25
Distribution costs	125
Administrative expenses	264
	350
Interest paid	75
Profit before tax	300
Income tax expense	140
Profit for the year	160
Other comprehensive income	
Revaluation surplus	9
Total comprehensive income for the year	169

EMMA CO

STATEMENTS OF FINANCIAL POSITION AS AT 31 DECEMBER

	20X2	20X1
Assets	$'000	$'000
Non-current assets		
Tangible assets	380	305
Intangible assets	250	200
Investments	–	25
Current assets		
Inventories	150	102
Receivables	390	315
Short-term investments	50	–
Cash in hand	2	1
Total assets	1,222	948

	20X2	20X1
	$'000	$'000
Equity and liabilities		
Equity		
Share capital ($1 ordinary shares)	200	150
Share premium account	160	150
Revaluation surplus	100	91
Retained earnings	160	100
Non-current liabilities		
Long-term loan	170	50
Current liabilities		
Trade payables	127	119
Bank overdraft	185	
Taxation	120	110
Total equity and liabilities	1,222	948

The following information is available.

(a) The proceeds of the sale of non-current asset investments amounted to $30,000.

(b) Fixtures and fittings, with an original cost of $85,000 and a carrying value of $45,000, were sold for $32,000 during the year.

(c) The following information relates to property, plant and equipment.

	31.12.20X2	31.12.20X1
	$'000	$'000
Cost	720	595
Accumulated depreciation	340	290
Carrying amount	380	305

(d) 50,000 $1 ordinary shares were issued during the year at a premium of 20c per share.

(e) The short-term investments are highly liquid and are close to maturity.

(f) A dividend of $100,000 was paid in the year.

Required

Prepare a statement of cash flows for the year to 31 December 20X2 using the format laid out in IAS 7.

Answer

EMMA CO
STATEMENT OF CASH FLOWS FOR THE YEAR ENDED 31 DECEMBER 20X2

	$'000	$'000
Cash flows from operating activities		
Profit before tax	300	
Depreciation charge (W1)	90	
Loss on sale of property, plant and equipment (45 – 32)	13	
Profit on sale of non-current asset investments	(5)	
Interest expense (net)	50	
(Increase)/decrease in inventories	(48)	
(Increase)/decrease in receivables	(75)	
Increase/(decrease) in payables	8	
Cash generated from operations	333	
Interest paid	(75)	
Dividends paid	(100)	
Tax paid (110 + 140 – 120)	(130)	
Net cash from operating activities		28
Cash flows from investing activities		
Payments to acquire property, plant and equipment (W2)	(201)	
Payments to acquire intangible non-current assets	(50)	
Receipts from sales of property, plant and equipment	32	
Receipts from sale of non-current asset investments	30	
Interest received	25	
Net cash flows from investing activities		(164)
Cash flows from financing activities		
Issue of share capital	60	
Long-term loan	120	
Net cash flows from financing		180
Increase in cash and cash equivalents (Note)		44
Cash and cash equivalents at 1.1.X2 (Note)		(177)
Cash and cash equivalents at 31.12.X2 (Note)		(133)

NOTES TO THE STATEMENT OF CASH FLOWS

Note: analysis of the balances of cash and cash equivalents as shown in the statement of financial position

	20X2 $'000	20X1 $'000	Change in year $'000
Cash in hand	2	1	1
Short term investments	50	–	50
Bank overdraft	(185)	(178)	(7)
	(133)	(177)	44

Workings

1   *Depreciation charge*

	$'000	$'000
Depreciation at 31 December 20X2		340
Depreciation 31 December 20X1	290	
Depreciation on assets sold (85 – 45)	40	
		250
Charge for the year		90

2   *Purchase of property, plant and equipment*

PROPERTY, PLANT AND EQUIPMENT (COST)

	$'000		$'000
1.1.X2 Balance b/d	595	Disposals	85
Revaluation	9		
Purchases (bal fig)	201	31.12.X2 Balance c/d	720
	805		805

3 Interpretation of statements of cash flows

FAST FORWARD

IAS 7 *Statement of cash flows* was introduced to provide users with an evaluation of the ability of an entity to generate cash and cash equivalents and of its needs to utilise those cash flows.

3.1 Introduction

So what kind of information does the statement of cash flows, along with its notes, provide?

Some of the main areas where IAS 7 should provide information not found elsewhere in the financial statements are as follows.

(a)   The **relationships between profit and cash** can be seen clearly and analysed accordingly.
(b)   **Cash equivalents** are highlighted, giving a better picture of the liquidity of the company.
(c)   **Financing inflows and outflows must be shown, rather than simply passed through reserves**.

One of the most important things to realise at this point is that it is wrong to try to assess the health or predict the death of a reporting entity solely on the basis of a single indicator. When analysing cash flow data, the **comparison should not just be between cash flows and profit, but also between cash flows over a period of time** (say three to five years).

Cash is not synonymous with profit on an annual basis, but you should also remember that the 'behaviour' of profit and cash flows will be very different. **Profit is smoothed out** through accruals, prepayments, provisions and other accounting conventions. This does not apply to cash, so the **cash flow figures** are likely to be **'lumpy'** in comparison. You must distinguish between this disparity and the trends which will appear over time.

The **relationship between profit and cash flows will vary constantly**. Note that healthy companies do not always have reported profits exceeding operating cash flows. Similarly, unhealthy companies can have operating cash flows well in excess of reported profit. The value of comparing them is in determining the extent to which earned profits are being converted into the necessary cash flows.

Profit is not as important as the extent to which a company can **convert its profits into cash on a continuing basis**. This process should be judged over a period longer than one year. The cash flows should be compared with profits over the same periods to decide how successfully the reporting entity has converted earnings into cash.

Cash flow figures should also be considered in terms of their specific relationships with each other over time. A form of **'cash flow gearing'** can be determined by comparing operating cash flows and financing flows, particularly borrowing, to establish the extent of dependence of the reporting entity on external funding.

Other relationships can be examined.

(a)   Operating cash flows and investment flows can be related to match cash recovery from investment to investment.

(b)   Investment can be compared to distribution to indicate the proportion of total cash outflow designated specifically to investor return and reinvestment.

(c)   A comparison of tax outflow to operating cash flow minus investment flow will establish a 'cash basis tax rate'.

The 'ratios' mentioned above can be monitored **inter- and intra-firm** and the analyses can be undertaken in monetary, general price-level adjusted, or percentage terms.

3.2 The advantages of cash flow accounting

The advantages of cash flow accounting are as follows.

(a)   Survival in business depends on the **ability to generate** cash. Cash flow accounting directs attention towards this critical issue.

(b)   Cash flow is **more comprehensive** than 'profit' which is dependent on accounting conventions and concepts.

(c)   **Creditors** (long- and short-term) are more interested in an entity's ability to repay them than in its profitability. Whereas 'profits' might indicate that cash is likely to be available, cash flow accounting is more direct with its message.

(d)   Cash flow reporting provides a better means of **comparing the results** of different companies than traditional profit reporting.

(e)   Cash flow reporting **satisfies the needs of all users** better.

(i)   For **management**, it provides the sort of information on which decisions should be taken (in management accounting, 'relevant costs' to a decision are future cash flows); traditional profit accounting does not help with decision-making.

(ii)   For **shareholders and auditors**, cash flow accounting can provide a satisfactory basis for stewardship accounting.

(iii)   As described previously, the information needs of **creditors and employees** will be better served by cash flow accounting.

(f)   Cash flow forecasts are **easier to prepare**, as well as more useful, than profit forecasts.

(g)   They can in some respects be **audited more easily** than accounts based on the accruals concept.

(h)   The accruals concept is confusing, and cash flows are **more easily understood**.

(i)   Cash flow accounting should be both retrospective, and also include a forecast for the future. This is of **great information value** to all users of accounting information.

(j)   **Forecasts** can subsequently be **monitored** by the publication of variance statements which compare actual cash flows against the forecast.

Question

Disadvantages

Can you think of some possible disadvantages of cash flow accounting?

Answer

The main disadvantages of cash accounting are essentially the advantages of accruals accounting (proper matching of related items). There is also the practical problem that few businesses keep historical cash flow information in the form needed to prepare a historical statement of cash flows and so extra record keeping is likely to be necessary.

3.3 Criticisms of IAS 7

The inclusion of **cash equivalents** has been criticised because it does not reflect the way in which businesses are managed: in particular, the requirement that to be a cash equivalent an investment has to be within three months of maturity is considered **unrealistic**.

The management of assets similar to cash (ie 'cash equivalents') is not distinguished from other investment decisions.

Chapter roundup

- A statement of cash flows is a useful addition to a company's financial statements as a measure of performance.

- You must be able to prepare a statement of cash flows by both the indirect and the direct methods.

- IAS 7 *Statement of cash flows* was introduced to provide users with an evaluation of the ability of an entity to generate cash and cash equivalents and of its needs to utilise those cash flows.

Quick quiz

1 What is the aim of a statement of cash flows?

2 The standard headings in IAS 7 *Statement of cash flows* are:

- O................. a................

- I.................. a..................

- F.................. a....................

- Net................. in C..................... and ....

3 Cash equivalents are current asset investments which will mature or can be redeemed within three months of the year end.

True ☐

False ☐

4 Why are you more likely to encounter the indirect method as opposed to the direct method?

5 List five advantages of cash flow accounting.

Answers to quick quiz

1   To indicate an entity's ability to generate cash and cash equivalents

2   • Operating activities
    • Investing activities
    • Financing activities
    • Net increase (decrease) in cash and cash equivalents

3   False. See the definition in Section 1.6 if you are not sure about this.

4   The indirect method utilises figures which appear in the financial statements. The figures required for the direct method may not be readily available.

5   See Section 3.2

End of chapter question

Statement of cash flows (AIA November 2007)

From its rural base, A1sourcing provides payroll and book-keeping services for over five thousands clients. The company now plans to expand into banking and finance services but feels to do so it may have to relocate to a major city. This has prompted worries about the company's current cash flow position, especially the cash flow from its present operations, and whether the cash flow is sufficient to support such a relocation and expansion.

The directors of A1sourcing require cash flow information quickly and have asked you to provide a calculation of the company's net cash flow from operating activities for the year ended 31 October 20X7. Unfortunately, the urgency of the request has meant that the company's statement of profit or loss and other comprehensive income is not yet available. However, they have provided you with the following information:

Summarised draft statements of financial position as at 31 October.

	20X7		20X6	
	$'000		$'000	
Assets				
Non-current assets				
Property, plant and equipment at cost		1,240		1,016
Less depreciation		276		232
		964		784
Current assets				
Receivables	380		319	
Cash at bank	64		1	
		444		320
Total assets		1,408		1,104
Equity and liabilities				
Equity				
Share capital		600		400
Share premium		140		60
Retained earnings		224		86
		964		546
Non-current liabilities				
Long-term bond		120		280
Deferred taxation		72		44
		192		324
Current liabilities				
Trade payables		212		146
Bank overdraft		–		56
Taxation payable		40		32
		252		234
		1,408		1,104

Additional cash flow information:

(i)   Property, plant and equipment costing $52,000, and in respect of which $32,000 depreciation had been provided, was disposed of during the year. The items were sold for $16,000. Operating profit includes any profits or losses on disposal.

(ii)   The company paid a dividend of $40,000 during the year.

(iii)   A finance charge of $15,000 has been recognised as an expense for the year. The actual cash payment was $12,000.

(iv)   The tax charge of $88,000 includes deferred tax of $28,000.

(v)   Part of the bond was repaid during the year. This incurred a redemption penalty of $8,000 which has been written off against income.

Required

(a)   Prepare a statement of cash flows in accordance with IAS 7 to calculate the company's net cash flow from operating activities. (Note: a full statement of cash flows showing 'cash flow from investing activities' and 'cash flow from financing activities' is NOT required in answer to this part of the question.)   **(12 marks)**

(b)   Comment on whether the 'net cash flow from operating activities' calculated in (i) above is sufficient to support the proposed relocation.   **(8 marks)**

(Total = 20 marks)

Interpretation of financial statements

Topic list	Syllabus reference
1 The broad categories of ratio	11.5
2 Profitability and return on capital	11.5
3 Liquidity, gearing/leverage and working capital	11.5
4 Shareholders' investment ratios	11.5
5 Accounting policies and the limitations of ratio analysis	11.5
6 Presentation of financial performance	11.5

Introduction

You may remember some of the **basic interpretation of accounts** you studied for Paper 1. This chapter recaps and develops the calculation of ratios and covers more complex accounting relationships. More importantly, perhaps, this chapter looks at how ratios can be analysed, interpreted and how the results should be presented to management.

1 The broad categories of ratio

Your syllabus requires you to **appraise and communicate** the position and prospects of a business based on given and prepared statements and ratios.

If you were to look at a statement of financial position or statement of profit or loss and other comprehensive income, how would you decide whether the company was doing well or badly? Or whether it was financially strong or financially vulnerable? And what would you be looking at in the figures to help you to make your judgement?

Ratio analysis involves **comparing one figure against another** to produce a ratio, and assessing whether the ratio indicates a weakness or strength in the company's affairs.

1.1 The broad categories of ratio

Broadly speaking, basic ratios can be grouped into five categories.

- Profitability and return
- Long-term solvency and stability
- Short-term solvency and liquidity
- Efficiency (turnover ratios)
- Shareholders' investment ratios

Within each heading we will identify a number of standard measures or ratios that are normally calculated and generally accepted as meaningful indicators. One must stress however that each individual business must be considered separately, and a ratio that is meaningful for a manufacturing company may be completely meaningless for a financial institution. **Try not to be too mechanical** when working out ratios and constantly think about what you are trying to achieve.

The key to obtaining meaningful information from ratio analysis is **comparison**. This may involve comparing ratios over time within the same business to establish whether things are improving or declining, and comparing ratios between similar businesses to see whether the company you are analysing is better or worse than average within its specific business sector.

It must be stressed that ratio analysis on its own is not sufficient for interpreting company accounts, and that there are **other items of information** which should be looked at, for example:

(a)   The content of any **accompanying commentary** on the accounts and other statements

(b)   The age and nature of the **company's assets**

(c)   **Current and future developments** in the company's markets, at home and overseas, recent acquisitions or disposals of a subsidiary by the company

(d)   **Unusual** items separately disclosed in the financial statements

(e)   Any other **noticeable features** of the report and accounts, such as events after the reporting period, contingent liabilities, a modified auditors' opinion, the company's taxation position, and so on

1.2 Example: Calculating ratios

To illustrate the calculation of ratios, the following **draft** statement of financial position and statement of profit or loss figures will be used.

FURLONG CO STATEMENT OF PROFIT OR LOSS
FOR THE YEAR ENDED 31 DECEMBER 20X8

	Notes	20X8	20X7
		$	$
Revenue	1	3,095,576	1,909,051
Operating profit	1	359,501	244,229
Interest	2	17,371	19,127
Profit before taxation		342,130	225,102
Income tax expense		74,200	31,272
Profit after taxation		267,930	193,830
Earnings per share		12.8c	9.3c

There was no other comprehensive income in the period.

FURLONG CO STATEMENT OF FINANCIAL POSITION
AS AT 31 DECEMBER 20X8

	Notes	20X8		20X7	
		$	$	$	$
Assets					
Non-current assets					
Property, plant and equipment			802,180		656,071
Current assets					
Inventory		64,422		86,550	
Receivables	3	1,002,701		853,441	
Cash at bank and in hand		1,327		68,363	
			1,068,450		1,008,354
Total assets			1,870,630		1,664,425
Equity and liabilities					
Equity					
Ordinary shares 10c each	5	210,000		210,000	
Share premium account		48,178		48,178	
Retained earnings		630,721		393,791	
			888,899		651,969
Non-current liabilities					
10% loan stock 20X4/20Y0			100,000		100,000
Current liabilities	4		881,731		912,456
Total equity and liabilities			1,870,630		1,664,425

NOTES TO THE ACCOUNTS

		20X8	20X7
		$	$
1	*Sales revenue and profit*		
	Sales revenue	3,095,576	1,909,051
	Cost of sales	2,402,609	1,441,950
	Gross profit	692,967	467,101
	Administrative expenses	333,466	222,872
	Operating profit	359,501	244,229
	Depreciation charged	151,107	120,147

		20X8	20X7
2	*Interest*		
	Payable on bank overdrafts and other loans	8,115	11,909
	Payable on loan stock	10,000	10,000
		18,115	21,909
	Receivable on short-term deposits	744	2,782
	Net payable	17,371	19,127
3	*Receivables*	$	$
	Amounts falling due within one year		
	Trade receivables	884,559	760,252
	Prepayments and accrued income	97,022	45,729
		981,581	805,981
	Amounts falling due after more than one year		
	Trade receivables	21,120	47,460
	Total receivables	1,002,701	853,441
4	*Current liabilities*		
	Trade payables	627,018	545,340
	Accruals and deferred income	102,279	297,264
	Corporate taxes	108,000	37,200
	Other taxes	44,434	32,652
		881,731	912,456
5	*Share capital*		
	Issued and fully paid ordinary shares of 10c each	210,000	210,000
6	*Dividends paid*		
	Ordinary dividends paid	31,000	16,800

2 Profitability and return on capital

In our example, the company made a profit in both 20X8 and 20X7, and there was an increase in profit between one year and the next:

- Of 52% before taxation
- Of 39% after taxation

Profit before taxation is generally thought to be a better figure to use than profit after taxation, because there might be unusual variations in the tax charge from year to year which would not affect the underlying profitability of the company's operations.

Another profit figure that should be calculated is PBIT, **profit before interest and tax**. This is the amount of profit which the company earned before having to pay interest to the providers of loan capital. By providers of loan capital, we usually mean longer-term loan capital, such as debentures and medium-term bank loans, which will be shown in the statement of financial position as non-current liabilities.

Formula to learn

> **Profit before interest and tax** is therefore:
>
> (a) The profit on ordinary activities before taxation; *plus*
> (b) Interest charges on long-term loan capital.

Published financial statements do not always give sufficient detail on interest payable to determine how much is interest on long-term finance. We will assume in our example that the whole of the interest payable ($18,115, note 2) relates to long-term finance.

PBIT in our example is therefore:

	20X8 $	20X7 $
Profit on ordinary activities before tax	342,130	225,102
Interest payable	18,115	21,909
PBIT	360,245	247,011

This shows a 46% growth between 20X7 and 20X8.

2.1 Return on capital employed (ROCE)

It is impossible to assess profits or profit growth properly without relating them to the **amount of funds (capital) that were employed in making the profits**. The most important profitability ratio is therefore return on capital employed (ROCE), which states the profit as a percentage of the amount of capital employed.

Formula to learn

$$ROCE = \frac{\text{Profit before interest and taxation}}{\text{Capital employed}} \times 100\%$$

Capital employed = Shareholders' equity plus non-current liabilities (*or* total assets less current liabilities)

The underlying principle is that we must **compare like with like**, and so if capital means share capital and reserves plus non-current liabilities and debt capital, profit must mean the profit earned by all this capital together. This is PBIT, since interest is the return for loan capital.

In our example, capital employed = 20X8 $1,870,630 – $881,731 = $988,899
20X7 $1,664,425 – $912,456 = $751,969

These total figures are the total assets less current liabilities figures for 20X8 and 20X7 in the statement of financial position.

	20X8	20X7
ROCE	$\dfrac{\$360,245}{\$988,899} = 36.4\%$	$\dfrac{\$247,011}{\$751,969} = 32.8\%$

What does a company's ROCE tell us? What should we be looking for? There are three comparisons that can be made.

(a) The **change in ROCE from one year to the next** can be examined. In this example, there has been an increase in ROCE by about four percentage points from its 20X7 level.

(b) The **ROCE being earned by other companies**, if this information is available, can be compared with the ROCE of this company. Here the information is not available.

(c) A comparison of the ROCE with **current market borrowing rates** may be made.

(i) What would be the cost of extra borrowing to the company if it needed more loans, and is it earning a ROCE that suggests it could make profits to make such borrowing worthwhile?

(ii) Is the company making a ROCE which suggests that it is getting value for money from its current borrowing?

(iii) Companies are in a risk business and commercial borrowing rates are a good independent yardstick against which company performance can be judged.

In this example, if we suppose that current market interest rates, say, for medium-term borrowing from banks, are around 10%, then the company's actual ROCE of 36% in 20X8 would not seem low. On the contrary, it might seem high.

However, it is easier to spot a low ROCE than a high one, because there is always a chance that the company's non-current assets, especially property, are **undervalued** in its statement of financial position, and so the capital employed figure might be unrealistically low. If the company had earned a ROCE, not of 36%, but of, say only 6%, then its return would have been below current borrowing rates and so disappointingly low.

2.2 Return on equity (ROE)

Return on equity gives a more restricted view of capital than ROCE, but it is based on the same principles.

Formula to learn

$$\text{ROE} = \frac{\text{Profit after tax and preferred dividend}}{\text{Ordinary share capital and other equity}} \times 100\%$$

In our example, ROE is calculated as follows.

	20X8	20X7
ROE	$\dfrac{\$267,930}{\$888,899} = 30.1\%$	$\dfrac{\$193,830}{\$651,969} = 29.7\%$

ROE is **not a widely-used ratio**, however, because there are more useful ratios that give an indication of the return to shareholders, such as earnings per share, dividend per share, dividend yield and earnings yield, which are described later.

2.3 Analysing profitability and return in more detail: the secondary ratios

We often sub-analyse ROCE, to find out more about why the ROCE is high or low, or better or worse than last year. There are two factors that contribute towards a return on capital employed, both related to sales revenue.

(a) **Profit margin**. A company might make a high or low profit margin on its sales. For example, a company that makes a profit of 25c per $1 of sales is making a bigger return on its revenue than another company making a profit of only 10c per $1 of sales.

(b) **Asset turnover**. Asset turnover is a measure of how well the assets of a business are being used to generate sales. For example, if two companies each have capital employed of $100,000 and Company A makes sales of $400,000 per annum whereas Company B makes sales of only $200,000 per annum, Company A is making a higher revenue from the same amount of assets (twice as much asset turnover as Company B) and this will help A to make a higher return on capital employed than B. Asset turnover is expressed as 'x times' so that assets generate x times their value in annual sales. Here, Company A's asset turnover is 4 times and B's is 2 times.

Profit margin and asset turnover together explain the ROCE and if the ROCE is the primary profitability ratio, these other two are the secondary ratios. The relationship between the three ratios can be shown mathematically.

Formula to learn

Profit margin × Asset turnover = ROCE

Therefore $\dfrac{\text{PBIT}}{\text{Sales}} \times \dfrac{\text{Sales}}{\text{Capital employed}} = \dfrac{\text{PBIT}}{\text{Capital employed}}$

In our example:

		Profit margin		Asset turnover		ROCE
(a)	20X8	$\dfrac{\$360,245}{\$3,095,576}$	×	$\dfrac{\$3,095,576}{\$988,899}$	=	$\dfrac{\$360,245}{\$988,899}$
		11.64%	×	3.13 times	=	36.4%
(b)	20X7	$\dfrac{\$247,011}{\$1,909,051}$	×	$\dfrac{\$1,909,051}{\$751,969}$	=	$\dfrac{\$247,011}{\$751,969}$
		12.94%	×	2.54 times	=	32.8%

In this example, the company's improvement in ROCE between 20X7 and 20X8 is attributable to a higher asset turnover. Indeed the profit margin has fallen a little, but the higher asset turnover has more than compensated for this.

It is also worth commenting on the change in sales revenue from one year to the next. You may already have noticed that Furlong achieved sales growth of over 60% from $1.9 million to $3.1 million between 20X7 and 20X8. This is very strong growth, and this is certainly one of the most significant items in the financial statements.

2.3.1 A warning about comments on profit margin and asset turnover

It might be tempting to think that a high profit margin is good, and a low asset turnover means sluggish trading. In broad terms, this is so. But there is a trade-off between profit margin and asset turnover, and you cannot look at one without allowing for the other.

(a) A **high profit margin** means a high profit per $1 of sales, but if this also means that sales prices are high, there is a strong possibility that sales revenue will be depressed, and so asset turnover lower.

(b) A **high asset turnover** means that the company is generating a lot of sales, but to do this it might have to keep its prices down and so accept a low profit margin per $1 of sales.

Consider the following.

Company A		Company B	
Sales revenue	$1,000,000	Sales revenue	$4,000,000
Capital employed	$1,000,000	Capital employed	$1,000,000
PBIT	$200,000	PBIT	$200,000

These figures would give the following ratios.

ROCE	=	$\dfrac{\$200,000}{\$1,000,000}$	= 20%	ROCE	=	$\dfrac{\$200,000}{\$1,000,000}$	= 20%
Profit margin	=	$\dfrac{\$200,000}{\$1,000,000}$	= 20%	Profit margin	=	$\dfrac{\$200,000}{\$4,000,000}$	= 5%
Asset turnover	=	$\dfrac{\$1,000,000}{\$1,000,000}$	= 1	Asset turnover	=	$\dfrac{\$4,000,000}{\$1,000,000}$	= 4

The companies have the same ROCE, but it is arrived at in a very different fashion. Company A operates with a low asset turnover and a comparatively high profit margin whereas company B carries out much more business, but on a lower profit margin. Company A could be operating at the luxury end of the market, while company B is operating at the popular end of the market.

2.4 Gross profit margin, net profit margin and profit analysis

Depending on the format of the statement of profit or loss, you may be able to calculate the gross profit margin as well as the net profit margin. **Looking at the two together** can be quite informative.

For example, suppose that a company has the following summarised results for two consecutive years.

	Year 1	Year 2
	$	$
Revenue	70,000	100,000
Cost of sales	42,000	55,000
Gross profit	28,000	45,000
Expenses	21,000	35,000
Net profit	7,000	10,000

Although the net profit margin is the same for both years at 10%, the gross profit margin is not.

In year 1 it is: $\dfrac{\$28,000}{\$70,000}$ =   40%

and in year 2 it is: $\dfrac{\$45,000}{\$100,000}$ =   45%

The improved gross profit margin has not led to an improvement in the net profit margin. This is because expenses as a percentage of sales have risen from 30% in year 1 to 35% in year 2.

3 Liquidity, gearing/leverage and working capital

3.1 Long-term solvency: debt and gearing ratios

Debt ratios are concerned with **how much the company owes in relation to its size**, whether it is getting into heavier debt or improving its situation, and whether its debt burden seems heavy or light.

(a)   When a company is heavily in debt banks and other potential lenders may be unwilling to advance further funds.

(b)   When a company is earning only a modest profit before interest and tax, and has a heavy debt burden, there will be very little profit left over for shareholders after the interest charges have been paid. And so if interest rates were to go up (on bank overdrafts and so on) or the company were to borrow even more, it might soon be incurring interest charges in excess of PBIT. This might eventually lead to the liquidation of the company.

These are two big reasons why companies should keep their debt burden under control. There are four ratios that are particularly worth looking at, the debt ratio, gearing ratio, interest cover and cash flow ratio.

3.2 Debt ratio

Formula to learn

> The **debt ratio** is the ratio of a company's total debts to its total assets.

(a)   Assets consist of non-current assets at their carrying value, plus current assets.
(b)   Debts consist of all payables, whether they are due within one year or after more than one year.

You can ignore long-term provisions and liabilities, such as deferred taxation.

There is no absolute guide to the maximum safe debt ratio, but as a very general guide, you might regard 50% as a safe limit to debt. In practice, many companies operate successfully with a higher debt ratio than this, but 50% is nonetheless a helpful benchmark. In addition, if the debt ratio is over 50% and getting worse, the company's debt position will be worth looking at more carefully.

In the case of Furlong the debt ratio is as follows.

	20X8	20X7
Total debts	$ (881,731 + 100,000)	$ (912,456 + 100,000)
Total assets	$1,870,630	$1,664,425
	= 52%	= 61%

In this case, the debt ratio is quite high, mainly because of the large amount of current liabilities. However, the debt ratio has fallen from 61% to 52% between 20X7 and 20X8, and so the company appears to be improving its debt position.

3.3 Gearing/leverage

Capital gearing or leverage is concerned with a company's **long-term capital structure**. We can think of a company as consisting of non-current assets and net current assets (ie working capital, which is current assets minus current liabilities). These assets must be financed by long-term capital of the company, which is one of two things.

(a)   Issued share capital which can be divided into:

  (i)   Ordinary shares plus other equity (eg reserves)
  (ii) Non-redeemable preference shares (unusual)

(b)   Long-term debt including redeemable preference shares

Preference share capital is normally classified as a non-current liability in accordance with IAS 32, and preference dividends (paid or accrued) are included in finance costs in profit or loss.

The **capital gearing ratio** is a measure of the proportion of a company's capital that is debt. It is measured as follows.

Formula to learn

$$\text{Capital gearing} = \frac{\text{Interest bearing debt} \times 2}{\text{Shareholders' equity} + \text{total prior charge capital}} \times 100\%$$

As with the debt ratio, there is **no absolute limit** to what a gearing ratio ought to be. A company with a gearing ratio of more than 50% is said to be high-geared (whereas low gearing means a gearing ratio of less than 50%). Many companies are high geared, but if a high-geared company is becoming increasingly high geared, it is likely to have difficulty in the future when it wants to borrow even more, unless it can also boost its shareholders' capital, either with retained profits or by a new share issue.

Leverage is an alternative term for gearing; the words have the same meaning. Note that leverage (or gearing) can be looked at conversely, by calculating the proportion of total assets financed by equity, and which may be called the equity to assets ratio. It is calculated as follows.

Formula to learn

$$\text{Equity to assets ratio} = \frac{\text{Shareholders' equity}}{\text{Shareholders' equity} + \text{Interest bearing debt}} \times 100\%$$

or

$$\frac{\text{Shareholders' equity}}{\text{Total assets less current liabilities}}$$

In the example of Furlong, we find that the company, although having a high debt ratio because of its current liabilities, has a low gearing ratio. It has no preference (or preferred) share capital and its only long-term debt is the 10% loan stock. The equity to assets ratio is therefore high.

	20X8	20X7
Gearing ratio	$100,000	$100,000
	$988,899	$751,969
	= 10%	= 13%
Equity to assets ratio	$651,969	
	$88,899	$751,969
	= 90%	= 87%

As you can see, the equity to assets ratio is the mirror image of gearing.

3.4 The implications of high or low gearing/leverage

We mentioned earlier that **gearing or leverage** is, amongst other things, an attempt to **quantify the degree of risk involved in holding equity shares in a company**, risk both in terms of the company's ability to remain in business and in terms of expected ordinary dividends from the company. The problem with a highly geared company is that by definition there is a lot of debt. Debt generally carries a fixed rate of interest (or fixed rate of dividend if in the form of preferred shares), hence there is a given (and large) amount to be paid out from profits to holders of debt before arriving at a residue available for distribution to the holders of equity. The riskiness will perhaps become clearer with the aid of an example.

	Company A $'000	Company B $'000	Company C $'000
Ordinary shares	600	400	300
Retained earnings	200	200	200
Revaluation surplus	100	100	100
	900	700	600
6% preference shares (redeemable)	–	–	100
10% loan stock	100	300	300
Capital employed	1,000	1,000	1,000
Gearing ratio	10%	30%	40%
Equity to assets ratio	90%	70%	60%

Now suppose that each company makes a profit before interest and tax of $50,000, and the rate of tax on company profits is 30%. Amounts available for distribution to equity shareholders will be as follows.

	Company A $'000	Company B $'000	Company C $'000
Profit before interest and tax	50	50	50
Interest/preference dividend	10	30	36
Taxable profit	40	20	14
Taxation at 30%	12	6	4
Profit for the period	28	14	10

If in the subsequent year profit before interest and tax falls to $40,000, the amounts available to ordinary shareholders will become as follows.

	Company A $'000	Company B $'000	Company C $'000
Profit before interest and tax	40	40	40
Interest/preference dividend	10	30	36
Taxable profit	30	10	4
Taxation at 30%	9	3	1
Available for ordinary shareholders	21	7	31

Note the following.

	%	%	%
Gearing ratio	10	30	40
Equity to assets ratio	90	70	60
Change in PBIT	–20	–20	–20
Change in profit available for ordinary shareholders	–25	–50	–70

The more highly geared the company, the greater the risk that little (if anything) will be available to distribute by way of dividend to the ordinary shareholders. The example clearly displays this fact in so far as the more highly geared the company, the greater the percentage change in profit available for ordinary shareholders for any given percentage change in profit before interest and tax. The relationship similarly holds when profits increase, and if PBIT had risen by 20% rather than fallen, you would find that once again the largest percentage change in profit available for ordinary shareholders (this means an increase) will be for the highly geared company. This means that there will be greater **volatility** of amounts available for ordinary shareholders, and presumably therefore greater volatility in dividends paid to those shareholders, where a company is highly geared. That is the risk: you may do extremely well or extremely badly without a particularly large movement in the PBIT of the company.

The risk of a company's ability to remain in business was referred to earlier. Gearing or leverage is relevant to this. A highly geared company has a large amount of interest to pay annually (assuming that the debt is external borrowing rather than preference shares). If those borrowings are **'secured'** in any way (and debentures in particular are secured), then the **holders of the debt are perfectly entitled to force the company** to **realise assets to pay their interest** if funds are not available from other sources. Clearly the more highly geared a company the more likely this is to occur when and if profits fall.

3.5 Interest cover

The interest cover ratio shows whether a company is earning enough profits before interest and tax to pay its interest costs comfortably, or whether its interest costs are high in relation to the size of its profits, so that a fall in PBIT would then have a significant effect on profits available for ordinary shareholders.

Formula to learn

$$\text{Interest cover} = \frac{\text{Profit before interest and tax}}{\text{Interest charges}}$$

An interest cover of two times or less would be low, and should really exceed three times before the company's interest costs are to be considered within acceptable limits.

Returning first to the example of Companies A, B and C, the interest cover was as follows.

		Company A	Company B	Company C
(a)	When PBIT was $50,000 =	$50,000	$50,000	$50,000
		$10,000	$30,000	$30,000
		5 times	1.67 times	1.67 times
(b)	When PBIT was $40,000 =	$40,000	$40,000	$40,000
		$10,000	$30,000	$30,000
		4 times	1.33 times	1.33 times

Note: Although redeemable preference share capital is included as debt for the gearing ratio or leverage, it is usual to exclude redeemable preference share dividends from 'interest' charges. We also look at all interest payments, even interest charges on short-term debt, and so interest cover and gearing do not quite look at the same thing.

Both B and C have a low interest cover, which is a warning to ordinary shareholders that their profits are highly vulnerable, in percentage terms, to even small changes in PBIT.

Question   Interest cover

Returning to the example of Furlong in Paragraph 1.2, what is the company's interest cover?

Answer

Interest payments should be taken gross, from the note to the accounts, and not net of interest receipts as shown in the statement of profit or loss.

	20X8	20X7
PBIT	360,245	247,011
Interest payable	18,115	21,909
	= 20 times	= 11 times

Furlong has more than sufficient interest cover. In view of the company's low gearing, this is not too surprising and so we finally obtain a picture of Furlong as a company that does not seem to have a debt problem, in spite of its high (although declining) debt ratio.

3.6 Cash flow ratio

The cash flow ratio is the ratio of a company's **net cash inflow to its total debts**.

(a)   **Net cash inflow** is the amount of cash which the company has coming into the business from its operations. A suitable figure for net cash inflow can be obtained from the statement of cash flows.

(b)   **Total debts** are short-term and long-term payables, including provisions. A distinction can be made between debts payable within one year and other debts and provisions.

Obviously, a company needs to be earning enough cash from operations to be able to meet its foreseeable debts and future commitments, and the cash flow ratio, and changes in the cash flow ratio from one year to the next, provide a **useful indicator of a company's cash position**.

3.7 Short-term solvency and liquidity

Profitability is of course an important aspect of a company's performance and gearing or leverage is another. Neither, however, addresses directly the key issue of *liquidity*.

Key term

> **Liquidity** is the amount of cash a company can put its hands on quickly to settle its debts (and possibly to meet other unforeseen demands for cash payments too).

Liquid funds consist of:

(a) Cash

(b) Short-term investments for which there is a ready market

(c) Fixed-term deposits with a bank or other financial institution, for example a six-month high-interest deposit with a bank

(d) Trade receivables (because they will pay what they owe within a reasonably short period of time)

(e) Bills of exchange receivable (because like ordinary trade receivables, these represent amounts of cash due to be received within a relatively short period of time)

In summary, **liquid assets are current asset items that will or could soon be converted into cash, and cash itself.** Two common definitions of liquid assets are:

(a) All current assets without exception
(b) All current assets with the exception of inventories

A company can obtain liquid assets from sources other than sales of goods and services, such as the issue of shares for cash, a new loan or the sale of non-current assets. But a company cannot rely on these at all times, and in general, obtaining liquid funds depends on making sales revenue and profits. Even so, profits do not always lead to increases in liquidity. This is mainly because funds generated from trading may be immediately invested in non-current assets or paid out as dividends. You should refer back to the chapter on statements of cash flows to examine this issue.

The reason why a company needs liquid assets is so that it can meet its debts when they fall due. Payments are continually made for operating expenses and other costs, and so there is a **cash cycle** from trading activities of cash coming in from sales and cash going out for expenses.

3.8 The cash cycle

To help you to understand liquidity ratios, it is useful to begin with a brief explanation of the cash cycle. The cash cycle describes **the flow of cash out of a business and back into it again as a result of normal trading operations**.

Cash goes out to pay for supplies, wages and salaries and other expenses, although payments can be delayed by taking some credit. A business might hold inventory for a while and then sell it. Cash will come back into the business from the sales, although customers might delay payment by themselves taking some credit.

The main points about the cash cycle are as follows.

(a) The timing of cash flows in and out of a business does not coincide with the time when sales and costs of sales occur. **Cash flows out can be postponed by taking credit. Cash flows in can be delayed by having receivables.**

(b) **The time between making a purchase and making a sale also affects cash flows.** If inventories are held for a long time, the delay between the cash payment for inventory and cash receipts from selling it will also be a long one.

(c) **Holding inventories and having receivables can therefore be seen as two reasons why cash receipts are delayed.** Another way of saying this is that if a company invests in working capital, its cash position will show a corresponding decrease.

(d) Similarly, **taking credit from creditors can be seen as a reason why cash payments are delayed.** The company's liquidity position will worsen when it has to pay the suppliers, unless it can get more cash in from sales and receivables in the meantime.

The liquidity ratios and working capital turnover ratios are used to test a company's liquidity, length of cash cycle, and investment in working capital.

3.9 Liquidity ratios: current ratio and quick ratio

The 'standard' test of liquidity is the **current ratio**. It can be obtained from the statement of financial position.

Formula to learn

$$\text{Current ratio} = \frac{\text{Current assets}}{\text{Current liabilities}}$$

The idea behind this is that a company should have enough current assets that give a promise of 'cash to come' to meet its future commitments to pay off its current liabilities. Obviously, a **ratio in excess of 1 should be expected**. Otherwise, there would be the prospect that the company might be unable to pay its debts on time. In practice, a ratio comfortably in excess of 1 should be expected, but what is 'comfortable' varies between different types of businesses.

Companies are not able to convert all their current assets into cash very quickly. In particular, some manufacturing companies might hold large quantities of raw material inventories, which must be used in production to create finished goods inventory. These might be warehoused for a long time, or sold on lengthy credit. In such businesses, where inventory turnover is slow, most inventories are not very 'liquid' assets, because the cash cycle is so long. For these reasons, we calculate an additional liquidity ratio, known as the quick ratio or acid test ratio.

The **quick ratio**, or **acid test ratio**, is calculated as follows.

Formula to learn

$$\text{Quick ratio} = \frac{\text{Current assets less inventory}}{\text{Current liabilities}}$$

This ratio should ideally be **at least 1** for companies with a slow inventory turnover. For companies with a fast inventory turnover, a quick ratio can be comfortably less than 1 without suggesting that the company could be in cash flow trouble.

Both the current ratio and the quick ratio offer an indication of the company's liquidity position, but the absolute figures **should not be interpreted too literally**. It is often theorised that an acceptable current ratio is 1.5 and an acceptable quick ratio is 0.8, but these should only be used as a guide. Different businesses operate in very different ways. A supermarket group, for example, might have a current ratio of 0.52 and a quick ratio of 0.17. Supermarkets have low receivables (people do not buy groceries on credit), low cash (good cash management), medium inventories (high inventories but quick turnover, particularly in view of perishability) and very high payables.

Compare this with a manufacturing and retail organisation, with a current ratio of 1.44 and a quick ratio of 1.03. Such businesses operate with liquidity ratios closer to the standard.

What is important is the **trend** of these ratios. From this, one can easily ascertain whether liquidity is improving or deteriorating. If a supermarket has traded for the last 10 years (very successfully) with current ratios of 0.52 and quick ratios of 0.17 then it should be supposed that the company can continue in business with those levels of liquidity. If in the following year the current ratio were to fall to 0.38 and the quick ratio to 0.09, then further investigation into the liquidity situation would be appropriate. It is the relative position that is far more important than the absolute figures.

Don't forget the other side of the coin either. A current ratio and a quick ratio can become **bigger than they need to be**. A company that has large volumes of inventories and receivables might be over-investing in working capital, and so tying up more funds in the business than it needs to. This would suggest poor management of receivables (credit) or inventories by the company.

3.10 Efficiency ratios: control of receivables and inventories

A rough measure of the average length of time it takes for a company's customers to pay what they owe is the accounts receivable collection period.

Formula to learn

The estimated average accounts receivable collection period is calculated as:

$$\frac{\text{Trade receivables}}{\text{Sales}} \times 365 \text{ days}$$

The figure for sales should be taken as the sales revenue figure in the statement of profit or loss. The trade receivables are not the total figure for receivables in the statement of financial position, which includes prepayments and non-trade receivables. The trade receivables figure will be itemised in an analysis of the receivable total, in a note to the accounts.

The estimate of the accounts receivable collection period is **only approximate**.

(a) The statement of financial position value of receivables might be abnormally high or low compared with the 'normal' level the company usually has.

(b) Sales revenue is exclusive of sales taxes, but receivables in the statement of financial position are inclusive of sales tax. We are not strictly comparing like with like.

Sales are usually made on 'normal credit terms' of payment within 30 days. A collection period significantly in excess of this might be representative of poor management of funds of a business. However, some companies must allow generous credit terms to win customers. Exporting companies in particular may have to carry large amounts of receivables, and so their average collection period might be well in excess of 30 days.

The **trend of the collection period over time** is probably the best guide. If the collection period is increasing year on year, this is indicative of a poorly managed credit control function (and potentially therefore, a poorly managed company).

3.11 Accounts receivable collection period: examples

Using the same types of company as examples, the collection period for each of the companies was as follows.

Company	$\frac{\text{Trade receivables}}{\text{sales}}$	Collection period ($\times 365$)	Previous year	Collection period ($\times 365$)
Supermarket	$\frac{\$5,016\text{K}}{\$284,986\text{K}} =$	6.4 days	$\frac{\$3,997\text{K}}{\$290,668\text{K}} =$	5.0 days
Manufacturer	$\frac{\$458.3\text{m}}{\$2,059.5\text{m}} =$	81.2 days	$\frac{\$272.4\text{m}}{\$1,274.2\text{m}} =$	78.0 days
Sugar refiner and seller	$\frac{\$304.4\text{m}}{\$3,817.3\text{m}} =$	29.3 days	$\frac{\$287.0\text{m}}{\$3,366.3\text{m}} =$	31.1 days

The differences in collection period reflect the differences between the types of business. Supermarkets have hardly any trade receivables at all, whereas the manufacturing companies have far more. The collection periods are fairly constant from the previous year for all three companies.

3.12 Inventory turnover period

Another ratio worth calculating is the inventory turnover period. This is another estimated figure, obtainable from published accounts, which indicates the average number of days that items of inventory are held for. As with the average receivable collection period, however, it is only an approximate estimated figure, but one which should be reliable enough for comparing changes year on year.

Formula to learn

> The inventory turnover period is calculated as:
>
> $$\frac{\text{Inventory}}{\text{Cost of sales}} \times 365 \text{ days}$$

This is another measure of how vigorously a business is trading. A lengthening inventory turnover period from one year to the next indicates:

(a)   A slowdown in trading; *or*

(b)   A build-up in inventory levels, perhaps suggesting that the investment in inventories is becoming excessive.

Generally the **higher the inventory turnover the better**, ie the lower the turnover period the better, but several aspects of inventory holding policy have to be balanced.

(a)   Lead times
(b)   Seasonal fluctuations in orders
(c)   Alternative uses of warehouse space
(d)   Bulk buying discounts
(e)   Likelihood of inventory perishing or becoming obsolete

Presumably if we add together the inventory turnover period and receivables collection period, this should give us an indication of how soon inventory is converted into cash. Both receivables collection period and inventory turnover period therefore give us a further indication of the company's liquidity.

3.13 Example: inventory turnover period

The estimated inventory turnover periods for a supermarket are as follows.

Company	$\dfrac{\text{Inventory}}{\text{Cost of sales}}$	Inventory turnover period (days × 365)		Previous year		
Supermarket	$\dfrac{\$15,554K}{\$254,571K}$	22.3 days		$\dfrac{\$14,094K}{\$261,368K}$ ×	365 =	19.7 days

3.14 Accounts payable payment period

Formula to learn

> **Accounts payable payment period** is ideally calculated by the formula:
>
> $$\frac{\text{Trade accounts payable}}{\text{Purchases}} \times 365 \text{ days}$$

It is rare to find purchases disclosed in published accounts and so **cost of sales serves as an approximation**. The payment period often helps to assess a company's liquidity; an increase is often a sign of lack of long-term finance or poor management of current assets, resulting in the use of extended credit from suppliers, increased bank overdraft and so on.

Question	Liquidity and working capital

Calculate liquidity and working capital ratios from the accounts of TEB Co, a business which provides service support (cleaning etc) to customers worldwide. Comment on the results of your calculations.

	20X7 $m	20X6 $m
Sales revenue	2,176.2	2,344.8
Cost of sales	1,659.0	1,731.5
Gross profit	517.2	613.3
Current assets		
Inventories	42.7	78.0
Receivables (note 1)	378.9	431.4
Short-term deposits and cash	205.2	145.0
	626.8	654.4
Current liabilities		
Loans and overdrafts	32.4	81.1
Tax on profits	67.8	76.7
Accruals	11.7	17.2
Payables (note 2)	487.2	467.2
	599.1	642.2
Net current assets	27.7	12.2
Notes		
1 Trade receivables	295.2	335.5
2 Trade payables	190.8	188.1

Answer

	20X7	20X6
Current ratio	$\dfrac{626.8}{599.1} = 1.05$	$\dfrac{654.4}{642.2} = 1.02$
Quick ratio	$\dfrac{584.1}{599.1} = 0.97$	$\dfrac{576.4}{642.2} = 0.90$
Accounts receivable collection period	$\dfrac{295.2}{2,176.2} \times 365 = 49.5$ days	$\dfrac{335.5}{2,344.8} \times 365 = 52.2$ days
Inventory turnover period	$\dfrac{42.7}{1,659.0} \times 365 = 9.4$ days	$\dfrac{78.0}{1,731.5} \times 365 = 16.4$ days
Accounts payable payment period	$\dfrac{190.8}{1,659.0} \times 365 = 42.0$ days	$\dfrac{188.1}{1,731.5} \times 365 = 40.0$ days

The company's current ratio is a little lower than average but its quick ratio is better than average and very little less than the current ratio. This suggests that inventory levels are strictly controlled, which is reinforced by the low inventory turnover period. It would seem that working capital is tightly managed, to avoid the poor liquidity which could be caused by a long receivables collection period and comparatively high payables.

The company in the exercise is a service company and hence it would be expected to have very low inventory and a very short inventory turnover period. The similarity of receivables collection period and payables payment period means that the company is passing on most of the delay in receiving payment to its suppliers.

Question   Operating cycle

(a)   Calculate the operating cycle for Moribund plc for 20X2 on the basis of the following information.

		$
Inventory:	raw materials	150,000
	work in progress	60,000
	finished goods	200,000
Purchases		500,000
Trade accounts receivable		230,000
Trade accounts payable		120,000
Sales		900,000
Cost of goods sold		750,000

Tutorial note. You will need to calculate inventory turnover periods (total year end inventory over cost of goods sold), receivables as daily sales, and payables in relation to purchases, all converted into 'days'.

(b)   List the steps which might be taken in order to improve the operating cycle.

Answer

(a)   The operating cycle can be found as follows.

Inventory turnover period:

$$\frac{\text{Total closing inventory} \times 365}{\text{Cost of goods sold}}$$

plus

Accounts receivable collection period:

$$\frac{\text{Closing trade receivables} \times 365}{\text{Sales}}$$

less

Accounts payable payment period:

$$\frac{\text{Closing trade payables} \times 365}{\text{Purchases}}$$

	20X2
Total closing inventory ($)	410,000
Cost of goods sold ($)	750,000
Inventory turnover period	199.5 days
Closing receivables ($)	230,000
Sales ($)	900,000
Receivables collection period	93.3 days
Closing payables ($)	120,000
Purchases ($)	500,000
Payables payment period	(87.6 days)
Length of operating cycle (199.5 + 93.3 – 87.6)	205.2 days

(b)   The steps that could be taken to reduce the operating cycle include the following.

(i)   Reducing the raw material inventory turnover period.

(ii) Reducing the time taken to produce goods. However, the company must ensure that quality is not sacrificed as a result of speeding up the production process.

(iii)   Increasing the period of credit taken from suppliers. The credit period already seems very long – the company is allowed three months credit by its suppliers, and probably could not be increased. If the credit period is extended then the company may lose discounts for prompt payment.

(iv)   Reducing the finished goods inventory turnover period.

(v)   Reducing the receivables collection period. The administrative costs of speeding up debt collection and the effect on sales of reducing the credit period allowed must be evaluated. However, the credit period does already seem very long by the standards of most industries. It may be that generous terms have been allowed to secure large contracts and little will be able to be done about this in the short term.

4 Shareholders' investment ratios

FAST FORWARD

These are the ratios which help equity shareholders and other investors to assess the value and quality of an investment in the ordinary shares of a company.

They are:

(a)   Earnings per share
(b)   Dividend per share
(c)   Dividend cover
(d)   P/E ratio
(e)   Dividend yield

The value of an investment in ordinary shares in a company **listed on a stock exchange** is its market value, and so investment ratios must have regard not only to information in the company's published accounts, but also to the current price, and the fourth and fifth ratios involve using the share price.

4.1 Earnings per share

It is possible to calculate the return on each ordinary share in the year. This is the earnings per share (EPS). Earnings per share is the amount of net profit for the period that is attributable to each ordinary share which is outstanding during all or part of the period (see Chapter 24).

4.2 Dividend per share and dividend cover

The **dividend per share** in cents is self-explanatory, and clearly an item of some interest to shareholders.

Formula to learn

Dividend cover is a ratio of: $\dfrac{\text{Earnings per share}}{\text{Dividend per (ordinary) share}}$

It shows the **proportion of profit for the year that is available for distribution to shareholders that has been paid (or proposed) and what proportion will be retained in the business to finance future growth.** A dividend cover of 2 times would indicate that the company had paid 50% of its distributable profits as dividends, and retained 50% in the business to help to finance future operations. Retained profits are an important source of funds for most companies, and so the dividend cover can in some cases be quite high.

A **significant change** in the dividend cover from one year to the next would be worth looking at closely. For example, if a company's dividend cover were to fall sharply between one year and the next, it could be that its profits had fallen, but the directors wished to pay at least the same amount of dividends as in the previous year, so as to keep shareholder expectations satisfied.

4.3 P/E ratio

Key term

> The **Price/Earnings (P/E) ratio** is the ratio of a company's current share price to the earnings per share.

A high P/E ratio indicates strong shareholder **confidence** in the company and its future, eg in profit growth, and a lower P/E ratio indicates lower confidence.

The P/E ratio of one company can be compared with the P/E ratios of:

(a) Other companies in the same business sector
(b) Other companies generally

It is often used in **stock exchange reporting** where prices are readily available.

4.4 Dividend yield

Dividend yield is the return a shareholder is currently expecting on the shares of a company.

Formula to learn

> $$\text{Dividend yield} = \frac{\text{Dividend on the share for the year}}{\text{Current market value of the share (ex div)}} \times 100\%$$

(a) The dividend per share is taken as the dividend for the previous year.
(b) Ex-div means that the share price does *not* include the right to the most recent dividend.

Shareholders look for **both dividend yield and capital growth**. Obviously, dividend yield is therefore an important aspect of a share's performance.

Question

Dividend yield

In the year to 30 September 20X8, an advertising agency declares an interim ordinary dividend of 7.4c per share and a final ordinary dividend of 8.6c per share. Assuming an ex div share price of 315 cents, what is the dividend yield?

Answer

The total dividend per share is (7.4 + 8.6) = 16 cents

$$\frac{16}{315} \times 100 = 5.1\%$$

5 Accounting policies and the limitations of ratio analysis

FAST FORWARD ▶

> We discussed the disclosure of accounting policies in our examination of IAS 1. The choice of accounting policy and the effect of its implementation are almost as important as its disclosure in that the results of a company can be altered significantly by the choice of accounting policy.

5.1 The effect of choice of accounting policies

Where accounting standards allow alternative treatment of items in the accounts, then the accounting policy note should declare which policy has been chosen. It should then be applied consistently.

You should be able to think of examples of how the choice of accounting policy can affect the financial statements eg whether to revalue property in IAS 16.

5.2 Changes in accounting policy

The effect of a change of accounting policy is treated as a prior year adjustment according to IAS 8 (see Chapter 5). This means that the comparative figures are adjusted for the change in accounting policy for comparative purposes and an adjustment is made to the opening balances for the current year.

Under **consistency of presentation** in IAS 1, any change in policy may only be made if it can be justified on the grounds that the new policy is preferable to the one it replaces because it will give a fairer presentation of the result and of the financial position of a reporting entity.

The problem with this situation is that the directors may be able to **manipulate the results** through change(s) of accounting policies. This would be done to avoid the effect of an old accounting policy or gain the effect of a new one. It is likely to be done in a sensitive period, perhaps when the company's profits are low or the company is about to announce a rights issue. The management would have to convince the auditors that the new policy was much better, but it is not difficult to produce reasons in such cases.

The effect of such a change is very **short-term**. Most analysts and sophisticated users will discount its effect immediately, except to the extent that it will affect any dividend (because of the effect on distributable profits). It may help to avoid breaches of banking covenants because of the effect on certain ratios.

Obviously, the accounting policy for any item in the accounts could only be changed once in quite a long period of time. Auditors would not allow another change, even back to the old policy, unless there was a wholly exceptional reason.

The managers of a company can choose accounting policies **initially** to suit the company or the type of results they want to achieve. Any changes in accounting policy must be justified, but some managers might try to change accounting policies just to manipulate the results.

5.3 Limitations of ratio analysis

The consideration of how accounting policies may be used to manipulate company results leads us to some of the other limitations of ratio analysis. These can be summarised as follows.

(a) Availability of comparable information
(b) Use of historical/out of date information
(c) Ratios are not definitive – they are only a guide
(d) Interpretation needs careful analysis and should not be considered in isolation
(e) It is a subjective exercise
(f) It can be subject to manipulation
(g) Ratios are not defined in standard form

In the exam, always bear these points in mind; you may even be asked to discuss such limitations, but in any case they should have an impact on your analysis of a set of results.

6 Presentation of financial performance

**Exam focus
point**

Examination questions on financial performance may try to simulate a real life situation. A set of accounts could be presented and you may be asked to prepare a report on them, addressed to a specific interested party, such as a bank.

You should begin your report with a heading showing who it is from, the name of the addressee, the subject of the report and a suitable date.

A good approach is often to head up a **'schedule of ratios and statistics'** which will form an appendix to the main report. Calculate the ratios in a logical sequence, dealing in turn with operating and profitability ratios, use of assets (eg turnover period for inventories, collection period for receivables), liquidity and gearing/leverage.

As you calculate the ratios you are likely to be struck by **significant fluctuations and trends**. These will form the basis of your comments in the body of the report. The report should begin with some introductory comments, setting out the scope of your analysis and mentioning that detailed figures have been included in an appendix. You should then go on to present your analysis under any categories called for by the question (eg separate sections for management, shareholders and creditors, or separate sections for profitability and liquidity).

Finally, look out for opportunities to **suggest remedial action** where trends appear to be unfavourable. Questions sometimes require you specifically to set out your advice and recommendations.

6.1 Planning your answers

This is as good a place as any to stress the importance of planning your answers. This is particularly important for 'wordy' questions. While you may feel like breathing a sigh of relief after all that number crunching, you should not be tempted to 'waffle'. The best way to avoid going off the point is to **prepare an answer plan**. This has the advantage of making you think before you write and structure your answer logically.

The following approach may be adopted when preparing an answer plan.

(a)   Read the question **requirements**.

(b)   **Skim through the question** to see roughly what it is about.

(c)   Read through the question carefully, **underlining any key words**.

(d)   Set out the **headings** for the main parts of your answer. Leave space to insert points within the headings.

(e)   **Jot down points** to make within the main sections, underlining points on which you wish to expand.

(f)   Write your **full answer**.

You should allow yourself the full time allocation for written answers, that is 1.8 minutes per mark. If, however, you run out of time, a clear answer plan with points in note form will earn you more marks than an introductory paragraph written out in full.

Question

The following information has been extracted from the recently published accounts of DG.

EXTRACTS FROM THE STATEMENTS OF PROFIT OR LOSS TO 30 APRIL

	20X9	20X8
	$'000	$'000
Sales	11,200	9,750
Cost of sales	8,460	6,825
Net profit before tax	465	320
This is after charging:		
Depreciation	360	280
Debenture interest	80	60
Interest on bank overdraft	15	9
Audit fees	12	10

STATEMENTS OF FINANCIAL POSITION AS AT 30 APRIL

	20X9		20X8	
	$'000	$'000	$'000	$'000
Assets				
Non-current assets		1,850		1,430
Current assets				
Inventory	640		490	
Receivables	1,230		1,080	
Cash	80		120	
		1,950		1,690
Total assets		3,800		3,120
Equity and liabilities				
Equity				
Ordinary share capital	800		800	
Retained earnings	1,245		875	
		2,045		1,675
Non-current liabilities				
10% debentures		800		600
Current liabilities				
Bank overdraft	110		80	
Payables	750		690	
Taxation	30		20	
Accruals	65		55	
		955		845
Total equity and liabilities		3,800		3,120

The following ratios are those calculated for DG, based on its published accounts for the previous year, and also the latest industry average ratios:

	DG 30 April 20X8	Industry average
ROCE (capital employed = equity and debentures)	16.70%	18.50%
Profit/sales	3.90%	4.73%
Asset turnover	4.29	3.91
Current ratio	2.00	1.90
Quick ratio	1.42	1.27
Gross profit margin	30.00%	35.23%
Accounts receivable collection period	40 days	52 days
Accounts payable payment period	37 days	49 days
Inventory turnover (times)	13.90	18.30
Gearing	26.37%	32.71%

Required

(a)   Calculate comparable ratios (to two decimal places where appropriate) for DG for the year ended 30 April 20X9. All calculations must be clearly shown.

(b)   Write a report to your board of directors analysing the performance of DG, comparing the results against the previous year and against the industry average.

Answer

(a)

	20X8	20X9	Industry average
ROCE	$\dfrac{320+60}{2,275}=16.70\%$	$\dfrac{465+80}{2,845}=19.16\%$	18.50%
Profit/sales	$\dfrac{320+60}{9,750}=3.90\%$	$\dfrac{465+80}{11,200}=4.87\%$	4.73%
Asset turnover	$\dfrac{9,750}{2,275}=4.29\text{x}$	$\dfrac{11,200}{2,845}=3.94\text{x}$	3.91x
Current ratio	$\dfrac{1,690}{845}=2.00$	$\dfrac{1,950}{955}=2.04$	1.90
Quick ratio	$\dfrac{1,080+120}{845}=1.42$	$\dfrac{1,230+80}{955}=1.37$	1.27
Gross profit margin	$\dfrac{9,750-6,825}{9,750}=30.00\%$	$\dfrac{11,200-8,460}{11,200}=24.46\%$	35.23%
Accounts receivable collection period	$\dfrac{1,080}{9,750}\times365=40\text{days}$	$\dfrac{1,230}{11,200}\times365=40\text{days}$	52 days
Accounts payable payment period	$\dfrac{690}{6,825}\times365=37\text{days}$	$\dfrac{750}{8,460}\times365=32\text{days}$	49 days
Inventory turnover (times)	$\dfrac{6,825}{490}=13.9\text{x}$	$\dfrac{8,460}{640}=13.2\text{x}$	18.30x
Gearing	$\dfrac{600}{2,275}=26.37\%$	$\dfrac{800}{2,845}=28.12\%$	32.71%

(b)   REPORT

To: Board of Directors
From: Accountant   Date: xx/xx/xx
Subject: Analysis of performance of DG

This report should be read in conjunction with the appendix attached which shows the relevant ratios (from part (a)).

(i)   **Trading and profitability**

Return on capital employed has improved considerably between 20X8 and 20X9 and is now higher than the industry average.

Net income as a proportion of sales has also improved noticeably between the years and is also now marginally ahead of the industry average. Gross margin, however, is considerably lower than in the previous year and is only some 70% of the industry average. This suggests either that there has been a change in the cost structure of DG or that there has been a change in the method of cost allocation between the periods. Either way, this is a marked change that requires investigation. The company may be in a period of transition as sales have increased by nearly 15% over the year and it would appear that new non-current assets have been purchased.

Asset turnover has declined between the periods although the 20X9 figure is in line with the industry average. This reduction might indicate that the efficiency with which assets are used has deteriorated or it might indicate that the assets acquired in 20X9 have not yet fully contributed to the business. A longer-term trend would clarify the picture.

(ii) **Liquidity and working capital management**

The current ratio has improved slightly over the year and is marginally higher than the industry average. It is also in line with what is generally regarded as satisfactory (2:1).

The quick ratio has declined marginally but is still better than the industry average. This suggests that DG has no short-term liquidity problems and should have no difficulty in paying its debts as they become due.

Receivables as a proportion of sales is unchanged from 20X8 and are considerably lower than the industry average. Consequently, there is probably little opportunity to reduce this further and there may be pressure in the future from customers to increase the period of credit given. The period of credit taken from suppliers has fallen from 37 days' purchases to 32 days' and is much lower than the industry average; thus, it may be possible to finance any additional receivables by negotiating better credit terms from suppliers.

Inventory turnover has fallen slightly and is much slower than the industry average and this may partly reflect stocking up ahead of a significant increase in sales. Alternatively, there is some danger that the inventory could contain certain obsolete items that may require writing off. The relative increase in the level of inventory has been financed by an increased overdraft which may reduce if the inventory levels can be brought down.

The high levels of inventory, overdraft and receivables compared to that of payables suggests a labour intensive company or one where considerable value is added to bought-in products.

(iii) **Gearing**

The level of gearing has increased only slightly over the year and is below the industry average. Since the return on capital employed is nearly twice the rate of interest on the debentures, profitability is likely to be increased by a modest increase in the level of gearing.

Signed: Accountant

Chapter roundup

- Your syllabus requires you to **appraise and communicate** the position and prospects of a business based on given and prepared statements and ratios.

- These are the ratios which help equity shareholders and other investors to assess the value and quality of an investment in the ordinary shares of a company.

- We discussed the disclosure of accounting policies in our examination of IAS 1. The choice of accounting policy and the effect of its implementation are almost as important as its disclosure in that the results of a company can be altered significantly by the choice of accounting policy.

Quick quiz

1   List the main categories of ratio.

2   Brainstorm a list of sources of information which would be useful in interpreting a company's accounts.

3   ROCE is $\dfrac{\text{Profit before interest and tax}}{\text{Capital employed}} \times 100\%$

      True   ☐

      False   ☐

4   Company Q has a net profit margin of 7%. Briefly comment on this.

5   The debt ratio is a company's long-term debt divided by its net assets.

      True   ☐

      False   ☐

6   The cash flow ratio is the ratio of:

      A   Gross cash inflow to total debt
      B   Gross cash inflow to net debt
      C   Net cash inflow to total debt
      D   Net cash inflow to net debt

7   List the formulae for:

      (a)   Current ratio
      (b)   Quick ratio
      (c)   Accounts receivable collection period
      (d)   Inventory turnover period

8   List six limitations of ratio analysis.

Answers to quick quiz

1   See Section 1.1.

2   There are a number of sources (see Section 1.1). Information on competitors and the economic climate are further items of information.

3   True.

4   You should be careful here. You have very little information. This is a low margin but you need to know what industry the company operates in. 7% may be good for a major retailer.

5   False (see Section 3.2).

6   C (see Section 3.6).

7   See Sections 3.9, 3.10 and 3.12.

8   Compare your list to that in Section 5.3.

End of chapter question

Interpretation (AIA May 2007)

The United Reindeer Co manufactures specialised cold weather equipment. The market for this type of equipment is extremely competitive and, as a result, the company has regular difficulty in maintaining market share.

The company's recent draft accounts show a significant increase in its short-term borrowing. Consequently, the finance director is worried about having to approach the bank for an increase in its overdraft facility and has asked you – an employee in the company's finance department – to write a report for the board to identify the questions the bank is likely to ask. The finance director is planning to ask the bank to increase the overdraft facility from €1.1m to €4.0m.

The company's draft statements of profit or loss and other comprehensive income and financial position are as follows:

UNITED REINDEER CO
STATEMENT OF PROFIT OR LOSS AND OTHER COMPREHENSIVE INCOME FOR THE YEAR ENDED 31 MARCH 20X7

	Note	20X7 €m	20X6 €m
Revenue		33.1	31.6
Operating profit	1	4.0	4.4
Investment income		–	0.1
		4.0	4.5
Interest	2	1.0	0.7
Profit before tax		3.0	3.8
Tax		1.7	2.0
Profit after tax		1.3	1.8

There was no other comprehensive income in the period.

UNITED REINDEER CO
STATEMENT OF FINANCIAL POSITION
AT 31 MARCH 20X7

	Note	20X7 €m	20X6 €m
ASSETS			
Non-current assets			
Property, plant and equipment	3	25.5	24.8
Current assets	4	13.1	11.3
Total assets		38.6	36.1
Equity and liabilities			
Equity	5	24.3	24.1
Non-current liabilities			
8% loan stock 20Y0		7.5	7.5
Current liabilities	6	6.8	4.5
Total equity and liabilities		38.6	36.1

Notes to the accounts

1   *Operating costs*

	20X7 €m	20X6 €m
Cost of sales	23.4	22.1
Administrative expenses	5.7	5.1

2   *Interest*

	20X7 €m	20X6 €m
8% loan stock 20Y0	0.6	0.6
Short-term bank borrowing	0.4	0.1

3   *Property, plant and equipment, at cost*

	20X7 €m	20X6 €m
Freehold land and buildings	9.0	9.0
Plant and equipment	16.5	15.8

4   *Current assets*

	20X7 €m	20X6 €m
Inventory	7.0	5.6
Trade receivables	5.3	4.0
Prepayments and accrued income	0.8	0.2
Short-term securities	–	1.5
	13.1	11.3

5   *Equity*

	20X7 €m	20X6 €m
Ordinary shares of €1 each	11.3	11.3
Share premium account	3.8	3.8
Retained earnings	9.0	8.3
Profit for the year	1.3	1.8
Dividend for the year	(1.1)	(1.1)
	24.3	24.1

6   *Current liabilities*

	20X7	*20X6*
	€m	€m
Bank overdraft (unsecured)	3.2	1.0
Trade payables	1.9	1.5
Tax payable	1.7	2.0
	6.8	4.5

The following information is also available:

(i)   A revaluation exercise showed the freehold land and buildings had a fair market value of €15m at the 31 March 20X7. These assets have been used as collateral to secure the long term loan.

(ii)   There were no disposals of plant and equipment during the year but additions totalled €2m.

Required

(a)   Calculate appropriate ratios to be used in your report to the finance director.   **(10 marks)**

(b)   Prepare a report for the finance director of the United Reindeer Co, to highlight:

    (i)   The main areas you think the bank will wish to investigate (explain why you feel the bank will wish to investigate these areas), and

    (ii)   Any additional information you think the bank will require.

Note. Assume domestic inflation in the company's main area of operations is 3% pa.   **(10 marks)**

(Total = 20 marks)

Earnings per share

Topic list	Syllabus reference
1 IAS 33 *Earnings per share*	11.5
2 Basic EPS	11.5
3 Effect on EPS of changes in capital structure	11.5
4 Diluted EPS	11.5
5 Presentation, disclosure and other matters	11.5

Introduction

Earnings per share (EPS) is widely used by investors as a measure of a company's performance and is of particular importance in:

(a) **Comparing the results** of a company over a **period of time**

(b) **Comparing the performance** of one company's equity against the performance of **another company's equity**, and also against the returns obtainable from loan stock and other forms of investment.

The purpose of any earnings yardstick is to achieve as far as possible clarity of meaning, comparability between one company and another, one year and another, and attributability of profits to the equity shares. IAS 33 *Earnings per share* goes some way to ensuring that all these aims are achieved.

1 IAS 33 *Earnings per share*

> IAS 33 is a fairly straightforward Standard. Make sure you follow all the calculations through and you should then be able to tackle questions easily.

1.1 Objective

The objective of IAS 33 is to improve the **comparison** of the performance of different entities in the same period and of the same entity in different accounting periods by prescribing methods for determining the number of shares to be included in the calculation of earnings per share and other amounts per share and by specifying their presentation.

1.2 Definitions

The following definitions are given in IAS 33, some of which are given in other IFRSs.

Key terms

> **Ordinary shares**: an equity instrument that is subordinate to all other classes of equity instruments.
>
> **Potential ordinary share**: a financial instrument or other contract that may entitle its holder to ordinary shares.
>
> **Warrants or options**: financial instruments that give the holder the right to purchase ordinary shares.
>
> **Financial instrument**: any contract that gives rise to both a financial asset of one entity and a financial liability or equity instrument of another entity.
>
> **Equity instrument**: any contract that evidences a residual interest in the assets of an entity after deducting all of its liabilities. *(IAS 33)*

1.2.1 Ordinary shares

There may be more than one class of ordinary shares, but ordinary shares of the same class will have the same rights to receive dividends. Ordinary shares participate in the net profit for the period **only after other types of shares**, eg preference shares.

1.2.2 Potential ordinary shares

IAS 33 identifies the following examples of financial instruments and other contracts generating potential ordinary shares.

(a) **Debt or equity instruments**, including preference shares, that are convertible into ordinary shares

(b) **Share warrants and options**

(c) **Employee plans** that allow employees to receive ordinary shares as part of their remuneration and other share purchase plans

(d) Shares that would be issued upon the satisfaction of **certain conditions** resulting from contractual arrangements, such as the purchase of a business or other assets

1.3 Scope

IAS 33 has the following scope restrictions.

(a) Only companies with (potential) ordinary shares which are **publicly traded** need to present EPS (including companies in the process of being listed).

(b)   EPS need only be presented on the basis of **consolidated results** where the parent's results are shown as well.

(c)   Where companies **choose** to present EPS, even when they have no (potential) ordinary shares which are traded, they must do so in accordance with IAS 33.

2 Basic EPS

FAST FORWARD

You should know how to calculate **basic EPS**.

2.1 Measurement

Basic EPS should be calculated by dividing the **net profit** or loss for the period attributable to ordinary shareholders by the **weighted average number of ordinary shares** outstanding during the period.

$$\text{Basic EPS} = \frac{\text{Net profit/(loss) attributable to ordinary shareholders}}{\text{Weighted average number of ordinary shares outstanding during the period}}$$

2.2 Earnings

Earnings includes **all items of income and expense** (including tax and non-controlling interests) *less* net profit attributable to **preference shareholders**, including preference dividends.

Preference dividends deducted from net profit consist of:

(a)   Preference dividends on non-cumulative preference shares declared in respect of the period

(b)   The full amount of the required preference dividends for cumulative preference shares for the period, *whether or not* they have been declared (*excluding* those paid/declared during the period in respect of previous periods)

2.3 Per share

The number of ordinary shares used should be the weighted average number of ordinary shares during the period. This figure (for all periods presented) should be **adjusted for events**, other than the conversion of potential ordinary shares, that have changed the number of shares outstanding without a corresponding change in resources.

The **time-weighting factor** is the number of days the shares were outstanding compared with the total number of days in the period; a reasonable approximation is usually adequate.

2.4 Example: Weighted average number of shares

Justina Co, a listed company, has the following share transactions during 20X7.

Date	Details	Shares issued	Treasury shares*	Shares outstanding
1 January 20X7	Balance at beginning of year	200,000	30,000	170,000
31 May 20X7	Issue of new shares for cash	80,000	–	250,000
1 December 20X7	Purchase of treasury shares	–	25,000	225,000
31 December 20X7	Balance at year end	280,000	55,000	225,000

*   Treasury shares are an entity's own shares acquired. In some countries own shares cannot be held, but must be cancelled on acquisition.

Required

Calculate the weighted average number of shares outstanding for 20X7.

Solution

The weighted average number of shares can be calculated in two ways.

(a) $(170,000 \times 5/12) + (250,000 \times 6/12) + (225,000 \times 1/12) = 214,583$ shares
(b) $(170,000 \times 12/12) + (80,000 \times 7/12) - (25,000 \times 1/12) = 214,583$ shares

2.5 Consideration

Shares are usually included in the weighted average number of shares from the **date consideration is receivable** which is usually the date of issue; in other cases consider the specific terms attached to their issue (consider the substance of any contract). The treatment for the issue of ordinary shares in different circumstances is as follows.

Consideration	Start date for inclusion
In exchange for cash	When cash is receivable
On the voluntary reinvestment of dividends on ordinary or preferred shares	The dividend payment date
As a result of the conversion of a debt instrument to ordinary shares	Date interest ceases accruing
In place of interest or principal on other financial instruments	Date interest ceases accruing
In exchange for the settlement of a liability of the entity	The settlement date
As consideration for the acquisition of an asset other than cash	The date on which the acquisition is recognised
For the rendering of services to the entity	As services are rendered

Ordinary shares issued as **purchase consideration** in an acquisition should be included as of the date of acquisition because the acquired entity's results will also be included from that date.

If ordinary shares are **partly paid**, they are treated as a fraction of an ordinary share to the extent they are entitled to dividends relative to fully paid ordinary shares.

Contingently issuable shares (including those subject to recall) are included in the computation when all necessary conditions for issue have been satisfied.

Question   Basic EPS

Flame Co is a company with a called up and paid up capital of 100,000 ordinary shares of $1 each and 20,000 10% preferred shares of $1 each. The company manufactures gas appliances. During its financial year to 31 December the company had to pay $50,000 compensation and costs arising from an uninsured claim for personal injuries suffered by a customer while on the company premises.

The gross profit was $200,000. Flame Co paid the required preferred share dividend and declared an ordinary dividend of 42c per share. Assuming an income tax rate of 30% on the given figures show the trading results and EPS of the company.

Answer

FLAME CO
TRADING RESULTS FOR YEAR TO 31 DECEMBER

	$	$
Gross profit		200,000
Expense		(50,000)
Profit before tax		150,000
Tax at 30%		(45,000)
Profit for the financial year		105,000
Dividends		
Preferred *		2,000
Ordinary		42,000

EARNINGS PER SHARE

$$\frac{103,000^*}{100,000} = 103c$$

*($105,000 – $2,000 preferred div = $103,000)

3 Effect on EPS of changes in capital structure

FAST FORWARD

You also need to know how to deal with EPS following changes in capital structure.

3.1 Introduction

We looked at the effect of issues of new shares or buy-backs of shares on basic EPS above. In these situations, the corresponding figures for EPS for the previous year will be comparable with the current year because, as the weighted average number of shares has risen or fallen, there has been a **corresponding increase or decrease in resources**. Money has been received when shares were issued, and money has been paid out to repurchase shares. It is assumed that the sales or purchases have been made at full market price.

3.2 Example: Earnings per share with a new issue

On 30 September 20X2, Boffin Co made an issue at full market price of 1,000,000 ordinary shares. The company's accounting year runs from 1 January to 31 December. Relevant information for 20X1 and 20X2 is as follows.

	20X2	20X1
Shares in issue as at 31 December	9,000,000	8,000,000
Profits after tax and preferred dividend	$3,300,000	$3,280,000

Required

Calculate the EPS for 20X2 and the corresponding figure for 20X1.

Solution

	20X2	20X1
Weighted average number of shares		
9/12 months × 8 million	6,000,000	
3/12 months × 9 million	2,250,000	
	8,250,000	8,000,000
Earnings	$3,300,000	$3,280,000
EPS	40 cents	41 cents

In spite of the increase in total earnings by $20,000 in 20X2, the EPS is not as good as in 20X1, because there was extra capital employed for the final 3 months of 20X2.

There are other events, however, which change the number of shares outstanding, **without a corresponding change in resources**. In these circumstances it is necessary to make adjustments so that the current and prior period EPS figures are comparable.

Four such events are considered by IAS 33.

(a)   **Capitalisation or bonus issue** (sometimes called a stock dividend)
(b)   Bonus element in any other issue, eg a **rights issue** to existing shareholders
(c)   **Share split**
(d)   **Reverse share split** (consolidation of shares)

3.3 Capitalisation/bonus issue and share split/reverse share split

These two types of event can be considered together as they have a similar effect. In both cases, ordinary shares are issued to existing shareholders for **no additional consideration**. The number of ordinary shares has increased without an increase in resources.

This problem is solved by **adjusting the number of ordinary shares outstanding before the event** for the proportionate change in the number of shares outstanding as if the event had occurred at the beginning of the earliest period reported.

3.4 Example: Earnings per share with a bonus issue

Greymatter Co had 400,000 shares in issue, until on 30 September 20X2 it made a bonus issue of 100,000 shares. Calculate the EPS for 20X2 and the corresponding figure for 20X1 if total earnings were $80,000 in 20X2 and $75,000 in 20X1. The company's accounting year runs from 1 January to 31 December.

Solution

	20X2	20X1
Earnings	$80,000	$75,000
Shares at 1 January	400,000	400,000
Bonus issue	100,000	100,000
Shares	500,000	500,000
EPS	16c	15c

The number of shares for 20X1 must also be adjusted if the figures for EPS are to remain comparable.

3.5 Rights issue

A rights issue of shares is an issue of new shares to existing shareholders **at a price below the current market value**. The offer of new shares is made on the basis of x new shares for every y shares currently held; for example, a 1 for 3 rights issue is an offer of one new share at the offer price for every three shares currently held. This means that there is a bonus element included.

To arrive at figures for EPS when a rights issue is made, we need to calculate first of all the **theoretical ex-rights price**. This is a weighted average value per share, and is perhaps explained most easily with a numerical example.

3.6 Example: Theoretical ex-rights price

Suppose that Egghead Co has 10,000,000 shares in issue. It now proposes to make a 1 for 4 rights issue at a price of $3 per share. The market value of existing shares on the final day before the issue is made is $3.50 (this is the 'with rights' value). What is the theoretical ex-rights price per share?

Solution

	$
Before issue 4 shares, value $3.50 each	14.00
Rights issue 1 share, value $3	3.00
Theoretical value of 5 shares	17.00

Theoretical ex-rights price = $\dfrac{\$17.00}{5}$ = $3.40 per share

Note that this calculation can alternatively be performed using the total value and number of outstanding shares.

3.7 Procedures

The procedures for calculating the EPS for the current year and a corresponding figure for the previous year are now as follows.

(a) The **EPS for the corresponding previous period** should be multiplied by the following fraction. (**Note:** The market price on the last day of quotation is taken as the fair value immediately prior to exercise of the rights, as required by the standard.)

Formula to learn

$$\frac{\text{Theoretical ex-rights price}}{\text{Market price on last day of quotation (with rights)}}$$

(b) To obtain the **EPS for the current year** you should:

(i) multiply the number of shares before the rights issue by the fraction of the year before the date of issue and by the following fraction

Formula to learn

$$\frac{\text{Market price on last day of quotation with rights}}{\text{Theoretical ex-rights price}}$$

(ii) Multiply the number of shares after the rights issue by the fraction of the year after the date of issue and add to the figure arrived at in (i)

The total earnings should then be divided by the total number of shares so calculated.

3.8 Example: Earnings per share with a rights issue

Brains Co had 100,000 shares in issue, but then makes a 1 for 5 rights issue on 1 October 20X2 at a price of $1. The market value on the last day of quotation with rights was $1.60.

Calculate the EPS for 20X2 and the corresponding figure for 20X1 given total earnings of $50,000 in 20X2 and $40,000 in 20X1.

Solution

Calculation of theoretical ex-rights price:

	$
Before issue 5 shares, value × $1.60	8.00
Rights issue 1 share, value × $1.00	1.00
Theoretical value of 6 shares	9.00

Theoretical ex-rights price = $\dfrac{\$9}{6}$ = $1.50

EPS for 20X1

EPS as calculated before taking into account the rights issue = 40c ($40,000 divided by 100,000 shares).

$$EPS = \frac{1.50}{1.60} \times 40c = 37\tfrac{1}{2}c$$

(Remember: this is the corresponding value for 20X1 which will be shown in the financial statements for Brains Co at the end of 20X2.)

EPS for 20X2

Number of shares before the rights issue was 100,000. 20,000 shares were issued.

Stage 1:	$100,000 \times {}^{9}/_{12} \times \dfrac{1.60}{1.50}$	80,000
Stage 2:	$120,000 \times {}^{3}/_{12}$	30,000
		110,000

$$EPS = \frac{\$50,000}{110,000} = 45\tfrac{1}{2}c$$

The figure for total earnings is the actual earnings for the year.

Question   Rights issue

Marcoli Co has produced the following net profit figures for the years ending 31 December.

	$m
20X6	1.1
20X7	1.5
20X8	1.8

On 1 January 20X7 the number of shares outstanding was 500,000. During 20X7 the company announced a rights issue with the following details.

Rights: 1 new share for each 5 outstanding (100,000 new shares in total)
Exercise price: $5.00
Last date to exercise rights: 1 March 20X7

The market (fair) value of one share in Marcoli immediately prior to exercise on 1 March 20X7 = $11.00.

Required

Calculate the EPS for 20X6, 20X7 and 20X8.

Answer

Computation of theoretical ex-rights price

This computation uses the total fair value and number of shares.

$$\frac{\text{Fair value of all outstanding shares} + \text{total received from exercise of rights}}{\text{No shares outstanding prior to exercise} + \text{no shares issued in exercise}}$$

$$= \frac{(\$11.00 \times 500,000) + (\$5.00 \times 100,000)}{500,000 + 100,000} = \$10.00$$

Computation of EPS

		20X6 $	20X7 $	20X8 $
20X6	EPS as originally reported $\dfrac{\$1,100,000}{500,000}$	2.20		
20X6	EPS restated for rights issue $\dfrac{\$1,100,000}{500,000} \times \dfrac{10}{11}$	2.00		
20X7	EPS including effects of rights issue $\dfrac{\$1,500,000}{(500,000 \times 2/12 \times 11/10) + (600,000 \times 10/12)}$		2.54	
20X8	$\text{EPS} = \dfrac{\$1,800,000}{600,000}$			3.00

4 Diluted EPS

FAST FORWARD **Diluted EPS** is complicated, but you should be able to deal with a fairly straightforward situation.

4.1 Introduction

At the end of an accounting period, a company may have in issue some **securities** which do not (at present) have any 'claim' to a share of equity earnings, but **may give rise to such a claim in the future**. These securities include:

(a) A **separate class of equity shares** which at present is not entitled to any dividend, but will be entitled after some future date

(b) **Convertible loan stock** or **convertible preferred shares** which give their holders the right at some future date to exchange their securities for ordinary shares of the company, at a pre-determined conversion rate

(c) **Options** or **warrants**

In such circumstances, the future number of ordinary shares in issue might increase, which in turn results in a fall in the EPS. In other words, a **future increase** in the **number of ordinary shares will cause a dilution or 'watering down' of equity**, and it is possible to calculate a **diluted earnings per share** (ie the EPS that would have been obtained during the financial period if the dilution had already taken place). This will indicate to investors the possible effects of a future dilution.

4.2 Earnings

The earnings calculated for basic EPS should be adjusted by the **post-tax** (including deferred tax) effect of:

(a) Any **dividends** on dilutive potential ordinary shares that were deducted to arrive at earnings for basic EPS

(b) **Interest recognised** in the period for the dilutive potential ordinary shares

(c) Any **other changes in income or expenses** (fees and discount, premium accounted for as yield adjustments) that would result from the conversion of the dilutive potential ordinary shares

The conversion of some potential ordinary shares may lead to changes in **other income or expenses**. For example, the reduction of interest expense related to potential ordinary shares and the resulting increase in net profit for the period may lead to an increase in the expense relating to a non-discretionary employee profit-sharing plan. When calculating diluted EPS, the net profit or loss for the period is adjusted for any such consequential changes in income or expense.

4.3 Per share

The number of ordinary shares is the weighted average number of ordinary shares calculated for basic EPS plus the weighted average number of ordinary shares that would be issued on the conversion of all the **dilutive potential ordinary shares** into ordinary shares.

It should be assumed that dilutive ordinary shares were converted into ordinary shares at the **beginning of the period** or, if later, at the actual date of issue. There are two other points.

(a)   The computation assumes the most **advantageous conversion rate** or exercise rate from the standpoint of the holder of the potential ordinary shares.

(b)   **Contingently issuable** (potential) ordinary shares are treated as for basic EPS; if the conditions have not been met, the number of contingently issuable shares included in the computation is based on the number of shares that would be issuable if the end of the reporting period was the end of the contingency period. Restatement is not allowed if the conditions are not met when the contingency period expires.

4.4 Example: Diluted EPS

In 20X7 Farrah Co had a basic EPS of 105c based on earnings of $105,000 and 100,000 ordinary $1 shares. It also had in issue $40,000 15% Convertible Loan Stock which is convertible in two years' time at the rate of four ordinary shares for every $5 of stock. The rate of tax is 30%. In 20X7 gross profit of $200,000 and expenses of $50,000 were recorded, including interest payable of $6,000.

Required

Calculate the diluted EPS.

Solution

Diluted EPS is calculated as follows.

Step 1   **Number of shares**: the additional equity on conversion of the loan stock will be
          $40,000 \times 4/5 = 32,000$ shares

Step 2   **Earnings**: Farrah Co will save interest payments of $6,000 but this increase in profits will be
          taxed. Hence the earnings figure may be recalculated:

	$
Gross profit	200,000
Expenses (50,000 – 6,000)	(44,000)
Profit before tax	156,000
Tax expense (30%)	(46,800)
Earnings	109,200

Step 3   **Calculation**: Diluted EPS = $\dfrac{\$109,200}{132,000} = 82.7c$

Step 4   **Dilution**: the dilution in earnings would be 105c – 82.7c = 22.3c per share

Question

Ardent Co has 5,000,000 ordinary shares of 25 cents each in issue, and also had in issue in 20X4:

(a) $1,000,000 of 14% convertible loan stock, convertible in three years' time at the rate of two shares per $10 of stock

(b) $2,000,000 of 10% convertible loan stock, convertible in one year's time at the rate of three shares per $5 of stock

The total earnings in 20X4 were $1,750,000.

The rate of income tax is 35%.

Required

Calculate the basic EPS and diluted EPS.

Answer

(a) Basic EPS = $\dfrac{\$1,750,000}{5 \text{ million}}$ = 35 cents

(b) We must decide which of the potential ordinary shares (ie the loan stocks) are dilutive (ie would decrease the EPS if converted).

For the 14% loan stock, incremental EPS = $\dfrac{0.65 \times \$140,000}{200,000 \text{ shares}}$

= 45.5c

For the 10% loan stock, incremental EPS = $\dfrac{0.65 \times \$200,000}{1.2\text{m shares}}$

= 10.8c

The effect of converting the 14% loan stock is therefore to **increase** the EPS figure, since the incremental EPS of 45.5c is greater than the basic EPS of 35c. The 14% loan stock is not dilutive and is therefore excluded from the diluted EPS calculation.

The 10% loan stock is dilutive.

Diluted EPS = $\dfrac{\$1.75\text{m} + \$0.13\text{m}}{5\text{m} + 1.2\text{m}}$ = 30.3c

4.5 Treatment of options

It should be assumed that options are exercised and that the assumed proceeds would have been received from the issue of shares at **fair value**. Fair value for this purpose is calculated on the basis of the average price of the ordinary shares during the period.

Options and other share purchase arrangements are dilutive when they would result in the issue of ordinary shares for **less than fair value**. The amount of the dilution is fair value less the issue price. In order to calculate diluted EPS, each transaction of this type is treated as consisting of two parts.

(a) A contract to issue a certain number of ordinary shares at their **average market price** during the period. These shares are fairly priced and are assumed to be neither dilutive nor antidilutive. They are ignored in the computation of diluted earnings per share.

(b)   A contract to issue the remaining ordinary shares for **no consideration**. Such ordinary shares generate no proceeds and have no effect on the net profit attributable to ordinary shares outstanding. Therefore, such shares are dilutive and they are added to the number of ordinary shares outstanding in the computation of diluted EPS.

To the extent that **partly paid shares** are not entitled to participate in dividends during the period, they are considered the equivalent of **warrants** or **options**.

Performance-based employee share options are treated as **contingently issuable shares** because their issue is contingent upon satisfying specified conditions in addition to the passage of time.

Question   Options

Brand Co has the following results for the year ended 31 December 20X7.

Net profit for year	$1,200,000
Weighted average number of ordinary shares outstanding during year	500,000 shares
Average fair value of one ordinary share during year	$20.00
Weighted average number of shares under option during year	100,000 shares
Exercise price for shares under option during year	$15.00

Required

Calculate both basic and diluted earnings per share.

Answer

	Per share	Earnings $	Shares
Net profit for year		1,200,000	
Weighted average shares outstanding during 20X7			500,000
Basic earnings per share	2.40		
Number of shares under option			100,000
Number of shares that would have been issued At fair value: (100,000 × $15.00/$20.00)			(75,000) *
Diluted earnings per share	2.29	1,200,000	525,000

* The earnings have not been increased as the total number of shares has been increased only by the number of shares (25,000) deemed for the purpose of the computation to have been issued for no consideration.

4.6 Dilutive potential ordinary shares

According to IAS 33, potential ordinary shares should be treated as dilutive when, and only when, their conversion to ordinary shares would **decrease net profit per share** from continuing operations. This point was illustrated in the question above.

4.7 Restatement

If the number of ordinary or potential ordinary shares outstanding **increases** as a result of a capitalisation, bonus issue or share split, or decreases as a result of a reverse share split, the calculation of basic and diluted EPS for all periods presented should be **adjusted retrospectively**.

If these changes occur **after the reporting date** but before the financial statements are authorised for issue, the calculations per share for the financial statements and those of any prior period should be based on the **new number of shares** (and this should be disclosed).

In addition, basic and diluted EPS of all periods presented should be adjusted for the effects of **material errors**, and adjustments resulting from **changes** in **accounting policies**, dealt with in accordance with IAS 8.

An entity **does not restate diluted EPS** of any prior period for changes in the assumptions used or for the conversion of potential ordinary shares into ordinary shares outstanding.

Entities are encouraged to disclose a description of ordinary share transactions or potential ordinary share transactions, other than capitalisation issues and share splits, which occur **after the reporting period** when they are of such importance that non-disclosure would affect the ability of the users of the financial statements to make proper evaluations and decisions (see IAS 10). Examples of such transactions include the following.

(a)   Issue of shares for cash

(b)   Issue of shares when the proceeds are used to repay debt or preferred shares outstanding at the reporting date

(c)   Redemption of ordinary shares outstanding

(d)   Conversion or exercise of potential ordinary shares, outstanding at the reporting date, into ordinary shares

(e)   Issue of warrants, options or convertible securities

(f)   Achievement of conditions that would result in the issue of contingently issuable shares

EPS amounts are not adjusted for such transactions occurring after the reporting period because such transactions **do not affect the amount of capital used** to produce the net profit or loss for the period.

5 Presentation, disclosure and other matters

FAST FORWARD ❯❯   IAS 33 contains the following requirements on presentation and disclosure.

5.1 Presentation

Basic and diluted EPS should be presented by an entity on the **face of the statement of profit or loss and other comprehensive income** for each class of ordinary share that has a different right to share in the net profit for the period. The basic and diluted EPS should be presented with **equal prominence** for all periods presented.

Exam focus point

> Disclosure must still be made where the EPS figures (basic and/or diluted) are **negative** (ie a loss per share).

5.2 Disclosure

An entity should disclose the following.

(a)   The amounts used as the **numerators** in calculating basic and diluted EPS, and a **reconciliation** of those amounts to the net profit or loss for the period

(b)   The weighted average number of ordinary shares used as the **denominator** in calculating basic and diluted EPS, and a **reconciliation** of these denominators to each other

5.3 Alternative EPS figures

An entity may present **alternative EPS figures if it wishes**. However, IAS 33 lays out certain rules where this takes place.

(a)   The weighted average number of shares as calculated under IAS 33 **must** be used.

(b)   A **reconciliation** must be given between the component of profit used in the alternative EPS (if it is not a line item in the statement of profit or loss and other comprehensive income) and the line item for profit reported in the statement of profit or loss and other comprehensive income.

(c)   Basic and diluted EPS must be shown with **equal prominence**.

5.4 Significance of earnings per share

Earnings per share (EPS) is one of the most frequently quoted statistics in financial analysis. Because of the widespread use of the price earnings **(P/E) ratio** as a yardstick for investment decisions, it became increasingly important.

It seems that reported and forecast EPS can, through the P/E ratio, have a **significant effect on a company's share price**. Thus, a share price might fall if it looks as if EPS is going to be low. This is not very rational, as EPS can depend on many, often subjective, assumptions used in preparing a historical statement, namely the statement of profit or loss and other comprehensive income. It does not necessarily bear any relation to the value of a company, and of its shares. Nevertheless, the market is sensitive to EPS.

EPS has also served as a means of assessing the **stewardship and management** role performed by company directors and managers. Remuneration packages might be linked to EPS growth, thereby increasing the pressure on management to improve EPS. The danger of this, however, is that management effort may go into distorting results to produce a favourable EPS.

Chapter roundup

- IAS 33 is a fairly straightforward Standard. Make sure you follow all the calculations through and you should then be able to tackle questions easily.

- You should know how to calculate **basic EPS**.

- You also need to know how to deal with EPS following changes in capital structure.

- **Diluted EPS** is complicated, but you should be able to deal with a fairly straightforward situation.

- IAS 33 contains the following requirements on presentation and disclosure.

Quick quiz

1   How is basic EPS calculated?

2   Give the formula for the 'bonus element' of a rights issue.

3   Define 'dilutive potential ordinary share'.

4   Which numerator is used to decide whether potential ordinary shares are dilutive?

5   Why is the numerator adjusted for convertible bonds when calculating diluted EPS?

Answers to quick quiz

1    $$\frac{\text{Net profit / (loss) attributable to ordinary shareholders}}{\text{Weighted average number of ordinary shares outstanding during the period}}$$

2    $$\frac{\text{Actual cum} - \text{rights price}}{\text{Theoretical ex} - \text{rights price}}$$

3   See Paragraph 4.1

4   Net profit from continuing operations only

5   Because the issue of shares will affect earnings (the interest will no longer have to be paid)

End of chapter question

Sadler (AIA May 2004)

The statement of profit or loss and other comprehensive income of Sadler for the year ended 30 April 20X4 was as follows.

	$'000	$'000
Sales		110,120
Cost of sales		67,890
Gross profit		42,230
Distribution costs	9,450	
Administration expenses	12,920	22,370
		19,860
Interest received		870
		20,730
Interest payable		4,521
Profit before taxation		16,209
Income tax expense		8,274
Profit for the year		7,935

There was no other comprehensive income in the period.

Note. There were no discontinued operations during the year.

During the year the company has expanded its activities considerably, requiring a rights issue of $1 ordinary shares by the company. On 1 December 20X3 the company made the rights issue of one ordinary share for every four held at a price of $4.20. The relevant market price for the ordinary shares was $5.40.

The opening number of ordinary shares was 17,625,000 at 1 May 20X3.

There were also 2,100,000 6% cumulative preference shares of $1 each in issue throughout the year. These preference shares are convertible into ordinary shares during 2006 at the rate of one ordinary share for each three preference shares.

Required

(a)   Calculate the basic earnings per share and the diluted earnings per share for Sadler plc for the year ended 30 April 20X4 in line with the requirements of IAS 33 *Earnings per share*.   **(12 marks)**

(b)   Comment on the adjustments that would be required to the previous year's reported earnings per share figures to make them comparable with those of the current year.   **(3 marks)**

(c)   Discuss the importance of the performance measures calculated in (a) and those commented upon in (b).   **(10 marks)**

(Total = 25 marks)

Answers to end of chapter questions

Chapter 1 – Revision of accounting concepts

(a) **The business entity concept**

This concept means that accountants regard a business as a separate entity, distinct from its owners or managers. The concept applies whether the business is a limited liability company (and so recognised in law as a separate entity) or a sole proprietorship or partnership (in which case the business is not separately recognised by the law).

(b) **The money measurement concept**

This concept states that accounts will only deal with those items to which a monetary value can be attributed. For example, in the statement of financial position of a business monetary values can be attributed to such assets as machinery (eg the original cost of the machinery; or the amount it would cost to replace the machinery) and inventories (eg the original cost of the goods, or, theoretically, the price at which the goods are likely to be sold).

The money measurement concept introduces limitations to the subject-matter of accounts. A business may have intangible assets such as the flair of a good manager or the loyalty of its workforce. These may be important enough to give it a clear superiority over an otherwise identical business, but because they cannot be evaluated in monetary terms they do not appear anywhere in the accounts.

(c) **The historical cost convention**

A basic principle of accounting (some writers include it in the list of fundamental accounting assumptions) is that resources are normally stated in accounts at historical cost, ie at the amount which the business paid to acquire them. An important advantage of this procedure is that the objectivity of accounts is maximised: there is usually objective, documentary evidence to prove the amount paid to purchase an asset or pay an expense.

In general, accountants prefer to deal with costs, rather than with 'values'. This is because valuations tend to be subjective and to vary according to what the valuation is for. For example, suppose that a company acquires a machine to manufacture its products. The machine has an expected useful life of four years. At the end of two years the company is preparing a statement of financial position and has to decide what monetary amount to attribute to the asset.

Numerous possibilities might be considered.

(i) The original cost (historical cost) of the machine

(ii) Half of the historical cost, on the ground that half of its useful life has expired

(iii) The amount the machine might fetch on the second-hand market

(iv) The amount it would cost to replace the machine with an identical machine

(v) The amount it would cost to replace the machine with a more modern machine incorporating the technological advances of the previous two years

(vi) The machine's economic value, ie the amount of the profits it is expected to generate for the company during its remaining life

All of these valuations have something to commend them, but the great advantage of the first two is that they are based on a figure (the machine's historical cost) which is objectively verifiable. (Some authors regard objectivity as an accounting concept in its own right.) The subjective judgement involved in the other valuations, particularly (f), is so great as to lessen the reliability of any accounts in which they are used.

(d)   **Stable monetary unit**

The financial statements which an accountant prepares must be expressed in terms of a monetary unit (eg in the UK the £, in the USA the $). It is assumed that the value of this unit remains constant.

In practice, of course, the value of the unit is not usually constant and comparisons between the accounts of the current year and those of previous years may be misleading.

(e)   **Objectivity**

An accountant must show objectivity in his work. This means he should try to strip his conclusions of any personal opinion or prejudice and should be as precise and as detailed as the situation warrants. The result of this should be that any number of accountants will give the same answer independently of each other.

In practice, objectivity is difficult. Two accountants faced with the same accounting data may come to different conclusions as to the correct treatment. It was to combat subjectivity that accounting standards were developed.

(f)   **The realisation concept**

The realisation concept states that revenue and profits are not anticipated but are recognised by inclusion in profit or loss only when *realised* in the form either of cash or other assets, the ultimate cash realisation of which can be assessed with reasonable certainty. Provision is made for all known liabilities (expenses and losses) whether the amount of these is known with certainty or is a best estimate in the light of the information available.

There are some exceptions to the rule, notably for land and buildings. With dramatic rises in property prices in some countries, it has been a common practice to revalue land and buildings periodically to a current value, to avoid having a misleading statement of financial position. Even if the sale of the property is not contemplated, such revaluations create an unrealised profit, which is recognised as other comprehensive income:

DEBIT   Land and buildings account
CREDIT   Other comprehensive income (revaluation surplus)

This profit is sometimes known as a *holding gain*, because it is a profit which arises in the course of holding the asset as a result of its increase in value above cost.

In spite of such exceptions, however, the realisation principle has long been accepted by all practising accountants and it is standard practice that only profits realised at the reporting date should be included in the top half of the statement of profit or loss and other comprehensive income (the statement of profit or loss).

Unfortunately there is no standard definition of realised profits and losses; it could be said that they are such profits or losses of a company as fall to be treated as realised in accordance with principles generally accepted at the time when the accounts are prepared, with respect to the determination for accounting purposes of realised profits.

(g)   **The duality concept**

This convention underpins double entry bookkeeping. Every transaction has two effects. For example, if goods are purchased for cash, the accounts must reflect both the purchase and the payment of cash.

Chapter 2 – Operating structure

International Financial Reporting Standards Foundation (IFRS Foundation):

The IFRS Foundation has overall responsibility for the international standard setting process. Its objectives include the development of high quality accounting standards and the convergence of these international standards with national standards. The Trustees who govern the IFRS Foundation are responsible for fundraising for the standard setting process and appointing members of the other standard setting bodies.

International Accounting Standards Board (IASB):

The IASB has complete responsibility for all technical matters and comprises at present 15 members all who have extensive experience and expertise in technical accounting matters and accounting standard preparation. The IASB is responsible for the preparation and publication of discussion documents for public comment and Exposure Drafts leading to the issuing of International Financial Reporting Standards (IFRSs) as well as the IFRS themselves. The Board works closely with the IFRS Advisory Council on major projects, agenda decisions and setting work priorities.

International Financial Reporting Standards Advisory Council (IFRSAC):

The IFRSAC provides a forum for the participation by organisations and individuals with an interest in international financial reporting, having diverse geographical and functional backgrounds with the objective of:

- Giving advice to the IASB on agenda decisions and priorities in the IASB work;

- Informing the IASB of the views of the organisations and individuals on the Council on major standard setting projects; and

- Giving other advice to the IASB or the IFRS Foundation.

It is comprised of a wide range of representatives from user groups, preparers, financial analysts, academics, auditors, regulators, professional accounting bodies and investor groups that are affected by and interested in the IASB's work.

International Financial Reporting Standards Interpretations Committee (IFRSIC):

The IFRSIC members are appointed by the Trustees of the IFRS Foundation. The role of the IFRSIC is to:

- Interpret the application of IFRS and provide timely guidance on financial reporting issues;
- Ensure its work is in accordance with the IASB convergence objective;
- Publish, after clearance by the IASB, draft Interpretations for public comment;
- Report to the IASB and obtain its approval for the issue of a final interpretation.

Chapter 3 – Eat^z

This question requires an understanding of IAS 1 *Presentation of financial statements* (syllabus section 11.3) and in particular the format requirements for the statement of profit or loss. It takes an uncommon approach in that it requires the presentation to comply with the reporting of the nature of income and expenses rather than the more traditional reporting according to their function.

EAT² LTD STATEMENT OF PROFIT OR LOSS
FOR THE YEAR ENDED 31 DECEMBER 20X7

	Workings	€m
Revenue	W1	46.75
Other operating income		0.35
Increase in inventory		1.20
Wage costs capitalised during the year	W6	0.20
Raw materials	W2	(24.20)
Operating costs	W3	(2.18)
Staff costs	W4	(12.95)
Depreciation	W5	(2.20)
Operating profit		6.97
Finance costs		(0.17)
Profit before tax		6.80
Taxation		(2.90)
Profit for the year		3.90

Workings

1	Sales revenue	
	Sales	48.10
	Less returns inwards	(1.35)
		46.75
2	Raw material	
	Purchases	25.00
	Returns outwards	(1.25)
	Carriage inwards	0.45
		24.20
3	Operating costs	
	Administrative expenses	0.50
	Distribution expenses	0.30
	Hire of delivery lorries	0.95
	Audit fees	0.10
	Doubtful debts [€16.30m × 2%]	0.33
		2.18
4	Staff costs	
	Warehouse employees' wages	5.05
	Warehouse employees' wages capitalised	0.20
	Salesmen's salaries	3.20
	Administrative employment costs	3.00
	Directors' salaries	1.50
		12.95

5 Depreciation is calculated as €11m × 20% = €2.20m. There is no need to allocate it to administration and distribution when using the alternative 'nature' method of presentation.

6 Wages capitalised have to be shown separately (ie added back) as they are included in 'staff costs' to show total wages paid during the year.

7 Dividends paid can be disregarded. They require recognition in the statement of changes in equity.

Chapter 4 – Revenue recognition

This question tests the candidate's knowledge of the requirements of IAS 18 *Revenue recognition* and its application to specific events. It also examines the standard's link with the IASB's *Conceptual Framework* (syllabus section 11.1).

Wholesale

As with all revenue recognition issues, the answer to this question may hinge on intentions. Does Nanotech intend to repurchase? Does Asteroid intend to sell? Given that the equipment is 'at the cutting edge of technology' and that it is to be used 'mainly for display', the former appears to be more appropriate. The IASB *Conceptual Framework* would therefore require the obligation to repurchase to be shown as a liability.

The agreement contains the word 'sale' but, given the above, it appears to be a loan transaction and not a sale.

In this respect, Nanotech should continue to include it in inventory in its statement of financial position and the €150,000 will be shown as a short-term secured loan rather than revenue.

The statement of profit or loss and other comprehensive income for the year ended 31 March 20X7 will include a finance charge determined by the expected period of the 'loan'. Assuming this is twelve months, the finance charge would be €7,500 (€30,000 × 3/12).

Whether the inventory should be disclosed as being 'on consignment' will depend on its materiality.

Franchise

With annual costs of €40,000 but income of only €27,000 the remaining 4 years of the franchise life would be loss-making. Some of the initial fee must therefore be an 'up-front' receipt of revenue and should, as such, be deferred over the remaining 4 years. The question is 'How to do this?'

The *Conceptual Framework* approach is to calculate the appropriate liability. As Nanotech will receive €27,000 pa and the normal value of the service is €48,000, the initial fee must include a payment in advance of €21,000 pa; ie €84,000 (€21,000 × 4) over the remainder of the contract. This amount would be shown as a liability (deferred income) and €166,000 (€250,000 – €84,000) included in income in year 1.

However, it could be argued that the liability only extends to the cost of the future provision; ie:

Mark up = 20% (40,000 cost: 48,000 sales value)

Therefore advance payment of 21,000pa would have a (pro rata) cost of:

21,000 × 100/120 = 17,500 pa

Over the remaining 4 years this amounts to a liability of 17,500 × 4 = 70,000.

Therefore 70,000 would be shown as a liability and 180,000 as income.

There is some debate about whether the above liabilities satisfy the *Conceptual Framework's* definition of a liability. Particular attention would have to be given to the terms of the contract. In particular, concerning the refundability of the initial fee.

Publications

Each Nannytek publication produces monthly income of €15,000 (€180,000/12) with costs of €10,000 per month. As above, the IASB *Conceptual Framework* requires initial consideration of the amount of the liability. As above this could be either:

(a) €135,000 (€180,000 – (€15,000 × 3 months) with €45,000 recognised as income – based on the value of the service to be provided; or

(b) €90,000 (€180,000 – €10,000 × 9 months) with €90,000 recognised in income – based on the cost of the service to be provided.

Chapter 5 – IFRS 5

(a) It is important for users of financial statements that they have information relating to the likely performance of a reporting entity and the resources that will be employed in achieving that performance. IFRS 5 ensures that users receive the most suitable details of the resources (usually either a single non-current asset or a set of net assets referred to as a disposal group) that will not be employed in the ongoing activities of the business but 'whose carrying amount will be recovered principally through a sale transaction rather than through continuing use'. This will help in any assessment of the continuing activities of the business and provide details of non-current assets which will not produce long term profits or cash flows but will generate a single cash flow in the short term and a single profit or loss.

Non-current assets held for sale are presented separately from other assets in the statement of financial position. They are not depreciated.

(b) (i) The closure of the factory does not result in the disposal of a separate major line of business or geographical area of operation nor is the factory being held for sale. The closure therefore does not appear to result in a need to classify any of the performance of Goddard as discontinued in these circumstances. Nothing has been discontinued, merely production reduced to a more competitive level until demand returns.

(ii) The office stationery supply business will probably be considered to represent a separate major line of business and should therefore be classified as a discontinued operation with separate disclosure of its activities in the statement of profit or loss as required by IFRS 5. Its disposal will probably have been a single co-ordinated plan, further confirming the business as a discontinued operation.

Chapter 6 – Framework

This question requires a discussion of the role and content of that part of the conceptual framework dealing with its scope (syllabus section 11.1). It is focussed on an EFRAG Discussion Paper's attempt to stimulate debate about whether the *Conceptual Framework* should apply to non profit-oriented entities as well as profit-oriented entities. It mentions the convergence debate because of its current importance but the required discussion is a general one concerning the scope of any such conceptual framework for financial reporting.

The current *Conceptual Frameworks* of the IASB and FASB are focussed on private sector business entities, as does the convergence project, and therefore do not encompass the likes of charities and non-profit public sector bodies.

In support of Milo:

(i) There is evidence that some national standard setters consider non profit–oriented entities to be just as important as profit-oriented entities as their conceptual frameworks cater for both. So the idea is not totally without support around the world.

(ii) One of the main features of the last twenty years or so has been the introduction of performance based accountability into both profit-oriented and non profit-oriented sectors. The financial position of both sectors is also of growing concern. It would follow from this that common concepts and principles could be developed.

Many public sector bodies use IFRS for reporting purposes; e.g. concerning the recognition of liabilities.

(iii) If the above development continues then it may be best to develop a framework that applies to both sectors from the beginning. If a framework develops which concentrates on one rather than the other then costly and disruptive changes may have to be made in future.

There may also be lessons both sectors can learn from each other by developing a common framework.

In support of Domna:

(i) The performance of a non profit-oriented entity is likely to be measured in terms of the quality of its contribution to society. The performance of a profit-oriented entity is not measured in this way. It is measured in terms of the returns it makes and in an assessment of its future cash flow potential. This focus on returns and the future cash flows therefore colours the type of information it produces. Concepts and principles to reflect this will therefore be very different to that for a non profit-oriented entity.

(ii) Risk is assessed in very different ways. A profit-oriented entity has shareholders whose risk is assessed and measured in a different way to those interested in the affairs of a non profit-oriented entity whose stakeholders may be interested more in eg environmental or employment risk than in financial risk. Objectives of financial reporting would therefore vary greatly.

(iii) The IASB's activities are in accordance with the constitution of its overseeing body the IFRS Foundation which seeks to develop financial statements and other financial reporting to aid economic decision making in the world's capital markets. This is a major statement which focuses on, although undefined, profit-oriented entities.

Chapter 7 – Income measurement and capital maintenance concepts

This question requires a discussion to demonstrate understanding of the various income measurement and capital maintenance concepts (syllabus section 11.1).

If we assume no transactions with owners during a period (ie dividends or new equity capital) then the difference between net assets at the start of the period and net assets at the end will equal the profits and losses for the period. How those net assets are valued is therefore crucially important in determining the profits and losses.

However, to provide quality information, we must be very careful how we distinguish operational (realised) gains and losses from non-operational (unrealised) gains and losses.

April   This approach refers to historical cost accounting. Its main claimed advantage is that it reduces subjectivity to a minimum.

It is a financial capital maintenance (FCM) approach; ie 'capital' represents the amount of 'money' invested by the owner and must be maintained at that amount as a minimum.

Any increase in capital (net assets) above that minimum can therefore be distributed as dividend (ie $100).

No adjustment is made for inflation during the period.

Without an adjustment for inflation (or specific prices rises), the HC results of a firm experiencing volatility in the price of its inputs may be difficult to interpret; eg as explained below, profits may be overdistributed.

Ben This is another FCM approach known as 'current purchasing power' (CPP). It is different to April's idea in that the focus is on maintaining the purchasing power of the owner's opening capital. The idea being that owners would be interested in knowing whether the purchasing power of their investment had been maintained.

Once this opening capital has been maintained (in terms of purchasing power) any further increase in capital (net assets) may be distributed as a dividend (ie $80).

Purchasing power has been maintained because the ending capital ($220) will, generally, purchase the same quantity of goods as the opening capital ($200).

Charlie This approach is different to April's and Ben's in that the emphasis is on maintaining the physical capital. It is therefore known as a physical capital maintenance approach (PCM).

The idea is **that the starting capital** ($200) represents a physical asset (cash $200 which could buy an item of inventory $200) and that for the 'firm' to maintain its operating capability it must be left with either an equivalent physical asset or enough resources to enable it to purchase an equivalent asset (ie $240).

Again, once this has been achieved then any capital in excess of this 'physical maintenance figure' may be distributed ($60).

Deni This approach is a combination of the above three and is known as 'real capital maintenance', 'real income', 'real terms accounting' and various other titles.

The idea is that the profit statement and statement of financial position serve slightly different objectives. The profit statement is considered to show the maximum distribution possible if the firm is to maintain its physical operating capability whereas the statement of financial position reflects whether the owners have maintained the purchasing power of their investment in the firm.

Chapter 8 – Floatem[21]

This question requires a knowledge of the debate concerning substance over form and its application to consignment stock (syllabus section 11.4. It could also apply to section 11.1's coverage of revenue recognition).

Factors concerning the treatment of the stock as inventory of the dealer Floatem[21] (F21) rather than the manufacturer (S).

In favour

- Transfer price is based on the manufactured list price at the date of delivery.

  The price is settled and so S has no further opportunity to adjust the selling price.

- There is a penalty for goods returned either damaged or which appear to be obsolete (ie cannot be sold within six months of their return).

- Interest-free deposit means that it is costing F21 (ie the interest forgone on the deposit) to have the boats in its inventory.

Against

- Option to return boats to S.

  Both companies have the same option therefore it suggests S hasn't totally transferred ownership.

Note: the transfer of legal title is irrelevant as we are considering the recognition of economic substance over legal form.

Advice: on balance it would appear that the boats should be included as inventory in the statement of financial position of Floatem[21].

Chapter 9 – Reconciliation

(a)   These disclosures are important to users of financial statements because users can:

    (i)   Clearly determine which type of non-current assets a business employs in its activities.

    (ii)   Appreciate if the values attached to the non-current assets are historic, which may be out of date, or more up to date valuations.

    (iii)   Gauge the age of the non-current assets in use from the accumulated depreciation.

    (iv)   Appreciate the investment of the company in long term assets and the reduction in capacity from disposals or impairments.

(b)   *Property Plant and Equipment*

	Buildings $'000	Fixtures and Equipment $'000	Fittings $'000	Total $'000
Cost/valuation				
1 January 20X5	3,000	2,100	915	6,015
Revaluation	600	–	–	600
Acquisitions	300	1,140	105	1,545
Disposals	–	(1,050)	(120)	(1,170)
31 December 20X5	3,900	2,190	900	6,990
Depreciation				
1 January 20X5	900	990	546	2,436
Revaluation	(900)	–	–	(900)
Charge for the year	78	219	135	432
Disposals	–	(750)	(75)	(825)
31 December 20X5	78	459	606	1,143
Carrying amount				
31 December 20X5	3,822	1,731	294	5,847
1 January 20X5	2,100	1,110	369	3,579

Chapter 10 – Intangible assets

This question mainly tests candidates' knowledge and ability to apply the requirements of IAS 38 *Intangible assets*. However it also examines its potential link with IAS 8 *Accounting policies, changes in accounting estimates and errors*, IAS 10 *Events after the reporting period* and IAS 36 *Impairment of assets* (syllabus sections 11.2 and 11.1).

20X2 – 20X3 IAS 38 would require the $15m expenditure to be written off as an expense. It is original investigation – into the prospect of developing a new propulsion system. Once written off the expenditure cannot then be capitalised in future.

20X4   All indications are that there is a commercially viable project; in that (IAS 38): it appears technically feasible, EcoSaver plc intends to complete and sell the design, future economic benefits appear probable, the board made resources available to complete the design, and expenditure can be reliably measured.

      Only $45m would be capitalised. The remaining $10m (overheads and staff training) must be written off as an expense.

      No amortisation will be provided as the project is not complete.

20X5   The extra $5m staff costs will be capitalised. As the project is complete and has been marketed the company may amortise over five years; ie $50m/5 = $10m pa.

The launch party costs of $1m will be written off.

The event on April 1 20X6 will not affect the financial statements as it happened after the date the accounts were published (and therefore signed). Therefore IAS 10 does not apply.

20X6   This is not, as Hank suggests, a change in accounting policy as it is not the result of a decision to provide more relevant and reliable information (IAS 8).

However, it could be looked upon as the correction of a prior period error under IAS 8; in that such an error arises from '...failure to use, or misuse of, reliable information that...could reasonably be expected to have been obtained and taken into account...' (para 5). The fact that the manufacturer and independent engineer could spot the flaw seems to suggest that reliable information could have been obtained. If this view is accepted then the opening comparative figure for retained earnings have been overstated and will have to be reduced by the asset's carrying value of $40m ($50m – $10m).

However, if the intention in IAS 8 is that an error occurs only in the 'use... or misuse...' of information that is first and foremost reliable, then the April 1 event will result in the carrying amount of the design ($40m) being impaired and therefore must be written down to zero (via profit or loss) under IAS 36.

Chapter 11 – Patel

(a)   A **provision** is a liability of uncertain timing or amount. It is considered to be a sub-class of liability, not a separate element as defined in the *Conceptual Framework for Financial Reporting*.

Provisions should only be recognised if:

(i)   There is a present obligation from past events; and,

(ii)   It is probable that an outflow of resources embodying economic benefits will be required to settle the obligation; and

(iii)   It is possible to reliably estimate the obligation.

A provision should be measured at the best estimate of the expenditure required to settle the present obligation at the end of the reporting period. Where a large population of items is involved, expected values should be used. Where the effect of the time value of money is material, a provision should be discounted to present value.

Contingent liabilities exist where the existence of the liability or the transfer of economic benefits is less than 50% probable. Such contingent items should be disclosed in the notes to the accounts but they are not to be recognised in the financial statements. If the possibility of transfer is remote then no note is required.

Contingent assets are assets that are dependent on uncertain future events outside the entity's control. They are not to be recognised in the financial statements but should be disclosed as a note when the inflow of economic benefits is probable; otherwise ignore.

(b)   (i)   Patel has a contract in which the unavoidable costs of meeting the obligations exceed the economic benefits expected to be received from the contract. This is referred to as an onerous contract and requires a provision under IAS 37. A provision is required amounting to 21 months at $7,000 per month; a total of $147,000.

(ii)   There is no legal or constructive obligation at the reporting date. No expectations have been raised, through for example the issue of redundancy notices to employees. The recording of the management decision is not sufficient commitment to establish the need for a provision. It is unlikely that a disclosure of a contingent liability would be required.

Chapter 12 – Stone Cutter

This case study question is mainly concerned with IFRS8 Operating segments (syllabus 11.5) but also requires, in part (b), knowledge of IAS 18 *Revenue* (syllabus 11.2) and IAS 16 *Property, plant and equipment* (syllabus 11.1).

(a)   (i)   IFRS8 applies to the separate or individual financial statements of an entity (and to the consolidated financial statements of a group with a parent) whose debt or equity instruments are traded in a public market.

            The non-consolidated nature of Stone Cutter's financial statements should not therefore concern the directors as the company shares are quoted on a public market and therefore IFRS 8 applies.

     (ii)   An operating segment is a component of the company:

- That engages in business activity from which it may earn revenues and incur expenses;

- Whose operating results are regularly reviewed by the chief operating decision maker to make decisions about segment funding and resource allocations, and

- For which discrete financial information is available.

            As the car parks are free of charge they will not satisfy the above. All other parts of the complex will satisfy the definition.

    (iii)   The company should report separately information about an operating segment that meets any of the following three criteria:

	Revenue1	Profit2	Assets3	Individually reportable?
	%	%	%	
Hotel	38.6	45.0	64.5	✓
Gift shop & cafe	11.7	20.0	3.6	✓
Golf course	24.7	18.0	8.8	✓
Amusement park	21.6	8.3	21.7	✓
Camp site	2.6	5.5	1.4	no
Other	0.8	3.3		no

1   reported revenue, including internal sales, is 10% or more of the combined revenue, internal and external, of all operating segments

2   its reported profit is 10% or more of the combined reported profit of all operating segments (none of the segments are loss making; if they were special rules would apply)

3   its assets are 10% or more of the combined assets of all operating segments.

    (iv)   IFRS 8 would only allow the directors to aggregate two or more operating segments into a single segment if:

- Aggregation was consistent with the core principle of the IFRS; ie that of enabling users to evaluate the nature and financial effects of the types of business activities in which Stone Cutter engages and the economic environments in which it operates;

            Likely to be met as there is one economic environment and the provision of accommodation and refreshments is similar and, taken together, different from the other components.

- The hotel and gift shop and café have similar economic characteristics; and
  They may be similar in that one component may very well drive the other.

- The two components are similar in terms of each of the following:

  - the nature of their products and services,
    directors believe this to be the case

  - the nature of their production process (which in Stone Cutter's case may refer to the way in which the services are marketed/developed etc), probably quite similar

  - the type or class of customer for their products and services, to a large extent may be the same customers

  - the methods used to distribute their products and provide their services; and more than likely that these functions will be combined

  - if applicable, the nature of the regulatory environment.
    will in all probability be the same.

  Despite the operating review showing that the hotel and gift shop and café have very different profitability ratios, these ratios are a function of the way the company has allocated revenues, costs and assets, in that the profitability of one may be due to the assets of the other (eg visitors may spend money in the gift shop because they are staying in the hotel). It would appear, on balance that the director has a good case. However, more information will be required in respect of the above.

(v)   'Other revenue' does not meet any of the quantitative thresholds mentioned in (iii) above for recognition as a reportable segment and would therefore normally be shown as 'all other segments'. However, IFRS 8 allows such segments to be considered reportable and separately disclosed, if the directors believe that information about the segment would satisfy the core principle of being useful to users of the financial statements.

The growth of advertising revenue is one of management's key strategies, so much will depend upon whether management see its separate reporting as meeting the above criteria. Doing so would leave sundry sales of $0.17m to be shown as 'all other segments'.

(vi)   This question concerns the reconciliation required by IFRS

Profit before tax: possible reasons for the difference:

- Depreciation on head office not allocated;
- Amortisation of intangibles not allocated.

Total assets: possible reasons for difference:

- Car park development of $3.8m not included as a segment asset;
- Goodwill in statement of financial position not allocated to segments;
- Head office not included as a segment asset.

(b)   (i)   IFRIC 13 Customer Loyalty Programmes concluded in June 2007 that the approach recommended in IAS18 para 13 was the correct treatment; ie some of the consideration received for the sale of the hotel room should be allocated to the granting of the passes and recognised as deferred revenue until the company fulfils its obligations – that is, when the pass is used by the visitor. IFRIC requires the consideration allocated to the pass to be measured by reference to its fair value as follows:

Fair value of hotel room without pass	200.00
Fair value of pass sold independently	75.00
	275.00

Consideration allocated to pass: 75/275 × 230 = $62.73

There are 800 passes outstanding so deferred revenue is:
800 × 62.73 = $50,181.

This amount should be shown as a liability in the statement of financial position.

Tutorial Note: IFRIC 13 is not an examinable document at Paper 11; the reference is included here for information only.

(ii) Upon initial recognition, the freehold land and the car park surface should be recognised as two separate assets; at costs of $2m and $1.8 respectively.

Only the car park surface will be depreciated.

When measuring subsequent to initial recognition, the directors can choose either the cost or the revaluation model as their accounting policy but must, when chosen, apply that policy consistently across each entire class of asset (NB: IAS 16 is quite clear that the revaluation model is only allowed if the fair value of the asset – the car park – can be measured reliably.)

The cost model would result in the car parks being carried at cost of $1.8m less accumulated depreciation (probably using straight line) and any accumulated impairment losses.

Using the revaluation model the car parks would be accounted for at their fair value at the date of revaluation (eg the amount for which they could be sold to an independent car park operator) less any subsequent accumulated depreciation and subsequent accumulated impairment losses.

When the car parks are resurfaced they will be accounted for as an asset disposal and acquisition of a new asset.

Other matters which may have to be considered before the statement of financial position is prepared include:

Component of cost: to ensure all costs included are relevant to bringing the asset into a usable condition.

Any borrowing costs to capitalise?

Chapter 13 – Chart and graph

(a)

	Partnership (9 months) $	(3 months) Company $
Gross profit	133,772	33,443
Directors salaries		(5,000)
Cash discounts	(1,040)	(260)
Company formation expenses		(600)
Administration expenses	(11,025)	(3,675)
Distribution costs	(13,995)	(4,665)
Depreciation – P and E	(495)	(165)
Depreciation – MV	(2,835)	(945)
Provision for doubtful debts	(3,000)	
	101,382	18,133
Chart 4/7		57,933
Graph 3/7		43,449

(b)   **Partners' Capital Accounts**

CHART

	$'000		$'000
Drawings	15,382	Balance bf	38,000
		Profit share	57,933
Ordinary shares	108,551	Freehold property	28,000
	123,933		123,933

Partners' Capital Accounts

GRAPH

	$'000		$'000
Drawings	8,000	Balance bf	35,000
		Profit share	43,449
Ordinary shares	91,449	Freehold property	21,000
	99,449		99,449

(c)   DRAFT STATEMENT OF FINANCIAL POSITION AS AT 30 APRIL 20X5

	$	$
Non-current assets		
Freehold property		187,000
Plant and equipment, cost	6,600	
Plant and equipment, depreciation	(3,270)	3,330
Motor vehicle, cost	18,900	
Motor vehicle, depreciation	(10,080)	
		8,820
		199,150
Current assets		
Inventory	30,000	
Trade receivables	21,475	
Provision for doubtful debts	(3,000)	
Bank	16,958	
		65,433
		264,583
Ordinary share capital		200,000
Retained earnings		18,133
		218,133
Trade payables		46,450
		264,583

Chapter 14 – Deferred tax

This question examines candidates' understanding of the requirements of IAS 12 and the sometimes debated alternatives of partial provision and nil provision (syllabus section 11.3).

(a)   Statements of profit or loss and other comprehensive income

Nil provision

Under this approach, no provision is made for deferred tax. The tax charge for years 1 – 5 will therefore be as shown in W1 below.

Full provision

	1	2	3	4	5
	$'000	$'000	$'000	$'000	$'000
Profit before tax	2,000	2,000	2,000	2,000	2,000
Tax charge as below (W1)	585.0	603.6	617.7	628.5	565.2
Deferred tax charge (W2)	15.0	(3.6)	(17.7)	(28.5)	34.8
	600	600	600	600	600
Profit after tax	1,400	1,400	1,400	1,400	1,400

Statements of financial position: provisions in each year will be recognised as in W2 below.

W1   *Calculation of annual tax liability*

	1	2	3	4	5
	$'000	$'000	$'000	$'000	$'000
Accounting profit before tax	2,000	2,000	2,000	2,000	2,000
Add depreciation	200	200	200	200	200
	2,200	2,200	2,200	2,200	2,200
Less tax allowances	(250)	(188)	(141)	(105)	(316)
Taxable profit	1,950	2,012	2,059	2,095	1,884
Tax @ 30%	585.0	603.6	617.7	628.5	565.2

W2   *Calculation of deferred tax charge and provision*

Yr		Charge to income for depn	Tax allow	Difference	Tax rate	Deferred tax charge	Deferred tax provision
	Asset	$'000	$'000	$'000		$'000	$'000
1	cost	1,000	1,000				
	Depn/tax allowance	(200)	(250)	50	30%	15.0	15.0
		800	750				
2		(200)	(188)	(12)	30%	(3.6)	11.4
		600	562				
3		(200)	(141)	(59)	30%	(17.7)	(6.3)
		400	421				
4		(200)	(105)	(95)	30%	(28.5)	(34.8)
		200	316				
5		(200)	(316)	116	30%	34.8	–
		–	–				

(b)   IAS 12 requires the full provision approach.

The 'partial provision' approach would require the recognition of deferred tax provisions only to the extent that it is expected that a liability will actually arise in the future; ie future capital expenditure commitments would have to be examined to determine whether the provision/liability (eg $15,000 above) will ever have to be settled.

Advantages of partial provision:

- Large balances which may never become liabilities in practice are not built up.
- It presents a more realistic view of the expected liabilities of a company.

Disadvantages of partial provision:

- Greater subjectivity in the calculation of the provision.

(c)   IAS 12 requires use of the 'liability' method. This is in keeping with the IASB's asset/liability approach to reporting.

The deferred tax provision would be adjusted as the tax rate changes thus recognising in the statement of financial position the actual amount which the company expects to pay. This would require a note to be maintained of the provision's history so that an adjustment could be made to the previous provisions.

Chapter 15 – Usefulness

The main reason for preparing consolidated accounts is that groups operate as a single economic unit, and it is not possible to understand the affairs of the parent company without taking into account the financial position and performance of all the companies that it controls. The directors of the parent company should be held fully accountable for all the money they have invested on their shareholders behalf, whether that has been done directly by the parent or via a subsidiary.

There are also practical reasons why parent company accounts cannot show the full picture. The parent company's own financial statements only show the original cost of the investment and the dividends received from the subsidiary. As explained below, this hides the true value and nature of the investment in the subsidiary, and, without consolidation, could be used to manipulate the reported results of the parent.

- The cost of the investment will include a premium for goodwill, but this is only quantified and reported if consolidated accounts are prepared.

- A controlling interest in a subsidiary can (normally) be achieved with a 51% interest. The full value of the assets controlled by the group is only shown through consolidation when the non-controlling interest is taken into account.

- Without consolidation, the assets and liabilities of the subsidiary are disguised.

  - A subsidiary could be very highly geared, making its liquidity and profitability volatile.

  - A subsidiary's assets might consist of intangible assets, or other assets with highly subjective values.

- The parent company controls the dividend policy of the subsidiary, enabling it to smooth out profit fluctuations with a steady dividend. Consolidation reveals the underlying profits of the group.

- Over time the net assets of the subsidiary should increase, but the cost of the investment will stay fixed and will soon bear no relation to the true value of the subsidiary.

Chapter 16 – Barcelona and Madrid

CONSOLIDATED STATEMENT OF FINANCIAL POSITION AS AT 30 SEPTEMBER 20X6

	$m
Non-current assets	
Property, plant & equipment (2,848 + 354)	3,202
Patents	45
Goodwill (W2)	43
	3,290
Current assets	
Inventories (895 + 225)	1,120
Trade and other receivables (1,348 + 251)	1,599
Cash and cash equivalents (212 + 34)	246
	2,965
	6,255

	$m
Equity attributable to owners of the parent	
Share capital	920
General reserve (W4)	796
Retained earnings (W3)	2,243
	3,959
Non-controlling interest (490 × 40%)	196
	4,155
Non-current liabilities	
Long-term borrowings (558 + 168)	726
Current liabilities	
Trade and other payables (1,168 + 183)	1,351
Current portion of long-term borrowings	23
	1,374
	6,255

Workings

1 *Group structure*

Barcelona

| 60% (30.6.X2)

Madrid

2 *Goodwill*

	$m	$m
Consideration transferred (250m × 60% × $1.06)		159
Non-controlling interest at acquisition (165 × 40%)		66
Net assets at acquisition:		
Share capital	50	
General reserve	11	
Retained earnings	104	
		(165)
Goodwill at acquisition		60
Impairment losses to date		(17)
Goodwill at end of reporting period		43

Goodwill – alternative working

	$m	$m
Consideration transferred		159
Net assets at acquisition (as above)	165	
Group share 60%		(99)
Goodwill at acquisition		60
Impairment		17
Goodwill at end of reporting period		43

3 *Retained earnings*

	Barcelona	Madrid
	$m	$m
Per question	2,086	394
Pre-acquisition	–	(104)
	2,086	290
Madrid – share of post acquisition earnings		
(290 × 60%)	174	
Less: goodwill impairment losses to date	(17)	
	2,243	

4   General reserve

	Barcelona $m	Madrid $m
Per question	775	46
Pre-acquisition	–	(11)
	775	35
Madrid – share of post acquisition general reserve (35 × 60%)	21	
	796	

Chapter 17 – Fallowfield and Rusholme

CONSOLIDATED STATEMENT OF PROFIT OR LOSS FOR THE YEAR ENDED 30 JUNE 20X8

	$
Revenue (403,400 + 193,000 – 40,000)	556,400
Cost of sales (201,400 + 92,600 – 40,000 + 4,000)	(258,000)
Gross profit	298,400
Distribution costs (16,000 + 14,600)	(30,600)
Administrative expenses (24,250 + 17,800)	(42,050)
Profit before tax	225,750
Income tax expense (61,750 + 22,000)	(83,750)
Profit for the year	142,000
Profit attributable to:	
Owners of the parent	125,200
Non-controlling interest (W2)	16,800
	142,000

STATEMENT OF CHANGES IN EQUITY (EXTRACT)

	Retained earnings $
Balance at 1 July 20X7 (W3)	190,000
Dividends	(40,000)
Profit for the year	125,200
Balance at 30 June 20X8 (W4)	275,200

Workings

1   Group structure

        Fallowfield
           | 60%   3 years ago
           | Pre-acquisition ret'd earnings: $16,000
        Rusholme

2   Non-controlling interest

	$
Rusholme – profit for the period	46,000
Less: PUP (40,000 × ½ × 25/125)	4,000
	42,000
Non-controlling share 40%	16,800

3 *Retained earnings brought forward*

	Fallowfield	*Rusholme*
	$	$
Per question	163,000	61,000
Pre-acquisition retained earnings	–	(16,000)
	163,000	45,000
Rusholme – share of post acquisition retained earnings		
(45,000 × 60%)	27,000	
	190,000	

4 *Retained earnings carried forward*

	Fallowfield	*Rusholme*
	$	$
Per question	238,000	82,000
PUP	–	(4,000)
Pre-acquisition retained earnings		(16,000)
	238,000	62,000
Rusholme – share of post acquisition retained earnings		
(62,000 × 60%)	37,200	
	275,200	

Chapter 18 – Hever

CONSOLIDATED STATEMENT OF FINANCIAL POSITION AS AT 31 DECEMBER 20X4

	$'000
Non-current assets	
Property, plant & equipment (370 + 190 + (W3) 45)	605
Goodwill (W4)	2
Investment in associate (W5)	165
	772
Current assets	
Inventories (160 + 100 – (W2) 1.5)	258.5
Trade receivables (170 + 90)	260
Cash (50 + 40)	90
	608.5
	1,380.5
Equity attributable to owners of the parent	
Share capital	200
Share premium reserve	100
Retained earnings (W7)	758.5
	1,058.5
Non-controlling interest (W6)	162
	1,220.5
Current liabilities	
Trade payables (100 + 60)	160
	1,380.5

Workings

1   *Group structure*

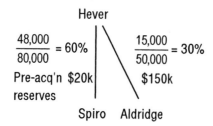

Hever

$\dfrac{48,000}{80,000} = 60\%$ $\dfrac{15,000}{50,000} = 30\%$

Pre-acq'n $20k $150k
reserves

Spiro   Aldridge

∴ In the absence of information to the contrary, Spiro is a subsidiary, and Aldridge an associate of Hever.

2   *Unrealised profit on inventories*

Mark-up = 6,000 ∴ ¼ × 6,000 = $1,500

3   *Fair values – adjustment to net assets*

	At Acquisition	Movement	At reporting date
Property, plant and equipment	50	(5)	45
Inventories	(20)	20	0
	30	15	45

4   *Goodwill on consolidation – Spiro*

	$'000	$'000
Consideration transferred		128
Non-controlling interest (210 × 40%)		84
Net assets at acquisition		
Share capital	80	
Retained earnings	20	
Share premium	80	
Fair value adjustments (W3)	30	
		(210)
Goodwill arising on consolidation		2

Goodwill – alternative working

	$'000	$'000
Consideration transferred		128
Net assets	210	
Group share 60%		(126)
Goodwill arising on consolidation		2

5   *Investment in associate*

	$'000
Cost of associate	90
Share of post-acquisition retained reserves ((400 – 150) × 30%)	75
	165

6   *Non-controlling interest*

	$'000	$'000
Net assets	360	
Fair value adjustment (W3)	45	
	405	
Non-controlling share (40%)		162

7 *Retained earnings*

	Hever $'000	Spiro $'000	Aldridge $'000
Per question	568	200	400
PUP (W2)	(1.5)	–	–
Fair value adjustment (W3)		15	
Pre-acquisition retained earnings		(20)	(150)
		195	250
Spiro – share of post acquisition earnings (195 × 60%)	117		
Aldridge – share of post acquisition earnings (250 × 30%)	75		
Less: goodwill impairment losses to date	(0)		
Less: impairment losses on associate to date	(0)		
	758.5		

Chapter 19 – Construction contracts

This question tests candidates' knowledge and application of the requirements of IAS 11 *Construction contracts* (syllabus section 11.4).

STATEMENT OF PROFIT OR LOSS AND OTHER COMPREHENSIVE INCOME

	For the year ended 31 March		
	20X7 €'000	20X8 €'000	20X9 €'000
Revenue (W3)	4,545	4,305	6,150
Cost of sales (W4)	2,954	2,799	3,997
Net profit	1,591	1,506	2,153

STATEMENT OF FINANCIAL POSITION AS AT 31 MARCH

	As at 31 March		
	20X7 €'000	20X8 €'000	20X9 €'000
Current assets			
Inventories: amounts due from customers on contracts (W5)	341	997	–
Receivables: amounts recoverable on contracts (W6)	500	250	–

Workings

1 The contract is expected to make an overall profit so we do not have to consider the possibility of having to provide for a loss.

2 IAS 11 uses a cumulative approach to calculating cumulative percentage of completion; as follows:

$$20X7: \frac{\text{total costs incurred to date}}{\text{total estimated costs to complete}} = \frac{3,250-300}{9,750} = 30.3\%$$

$$20X8: = \frac{3,250+2,900-400}{9,750} = 59.0\%$$

$$20X9: = 100.0\%$$

				€'000
3	Revenue: 20X7	15m × 30.3%	=	4,545
	20X8	15m × 59% = 8,850 – 4,545	=	4,305
	20X9	15m × 100% = 15,000 – 8,850	=	6,150

4	Cost:	20X7	$9,750 \times 30.3\%$	=	2,954
		20X8	$9,750 \times 59\% = 5,753 - 2,954$	=	2,799
		20X9	$9,750 \times 100\% = 9,750 - 5,753$	=	3,997

5 Inventories: amounts due from customers on contracts [note: in practice, this information would be disclosed by way of a note]

	20X7	20X8	20X9
Costs to date	3,250	6,150	9,750
Profit to date	1,591	3,097	5,250
Less progress billings	(4,500)	(8,250)	(15,000)
	341	997	–

6 Receivables: amounts recoverable on contracts

	20X7	20X8	20X9
Brought forward	–	500	750
Progress billings (invoices)	4,500	3,750	6,750
Cash received	(4,000)	(3,500)	(7,500)
	500	750	–

Note. For information: the question only asks for the figures which appear in the financial statements. In the company's books, the above contract will be recorded as follows:

Ledger account

	20X7	20X8	20X9
	€'000	€'000	€'000
Contract in progress at cost			
Costs to date	3,250	6,150	9,750
Cost of sales to date	(2,954)	5,753)	9,750)
DR	296	397	–
Contract in progress at fair value			
Brought forward	–	4,545	8,850
Revenue for the year	4,545	4,305	6,150
DR	4,545	8,850	15,000
Progress billing			
Brought forward	–	4,500	8,250
Accounts receivable (amounts invoiced)	4,500	3,750	6,750
CR	4,500	8,250	15,000
Net of above balances	341	997	–

Note. The above net figures are equivalent to the amounts shown for 'Inventories: amounts due from customers on contracts' in the statement of financial position.

Chapter 20 – Construction First

This question requires the application of knowledge concerning accounting for finance leases under IAS17 (section 11.4) in the accounts of the lessor.

CONSTRUCTION FIRST STATEMENT OF PROFIT OR LOSS FOR THE YEAR ENDED 31 DECEMBER 20X8

	Workings	20X8 $	20X7 $
Interest received	1	12,363	14,784

CONSTRUCTION FIRST STATEMENT OF FINANCIAL POSITION AS AT 31 DECEMBER 20X8

	Workings	20X8 $	20X7 $
Current assets			
Net investment in finance lease (note x)	1	96,988	123,625
Current liabilities			
Trade payables (145,080/3)	2	–	48,360

Note x	20X8 $	20X7 $
Net investment in finance lease		
Receivable within one year	29,301*	26,637*
Receivable after more than one year	67,687	96,988
	96,988	123,625

* [39,000 – 9,699] / [39,000 – 12,363]

Workings

1   Calculation of interest received and receivable outstanding at end of each year.

		$
1 Jan 20X7	Cost of equipment	145,080
	Direct costs of lease	2,761
		147,841
	Interest @ 10%	14,784
		162,625
	Less cash received	(39,000)
31 Dec 20X7	Balance outstanding	123,625
	Interest @ 10%	12,363
		135,988
	Less cash received	(39,000)
31 Dec 20X8	Balance outstanding	96,988
For information only		
	Interest @ 10%	9,699
		106,687
	Less cash received	(39,000)
31 Dec 20X9	Balance outstanding	67,687
	Interest @ 10%	6,769
		74,456
	Less cash received	(39,000)
31 Dec 20Y0	Balance outstanding	35,456
	Interest @ 10%	3,544
		39,000
	Less cash received	39,000
31 Dec 20Y1	Balance outstanding	–

2   Calculation of liability as at 31 December 20X7:

Construction First has agreed to pay for the equipment over three equal six-monthly instalments beginning on 31 January 20X7. The second payment will have been made on 31 July 20X7 and the final payment on 31 January 20X8. As at 31 December 20X7 there is therefore one payment outstanding.

Chapter 21 – Financial instruments

This question examines candidates' understanding of the method, favoured by the IASB, to allocate finance costs for a simple debt instrument (syllabus section 11.4).

(a)   The interest rate ('coupon rate') on this bond is less than that available on a debt of similar risk and maturity. Therefore, to attract investors, Just Crisps will have to issue the bonds at a price less than their face value of $100; ie they will be issued at a discount. The $3,393,600 is calculated as follows:

	per $100 bond $	Discount factor	Present value $
Annual interest @ 6%	60	3.790	22.74
Repayment of principal	100	0.621	62.10
			84.84

Total amount received: 40,000 bonds × $84.84 = 3,393,600

(b)   The 'interest method' of finance cost allocation ensures that the interest charge in the statement of profit or loss and other comprehensive income reflects the true cost of borrowing at the time the loan contract was signed; ie the market rate of interest on debt of a similar risk and maturity (10%).

The finance cost and liability in the statement of financial position will be calculated as follows:

Year	Debt at start of year $	Finance charge @10% $	Interest paid $	Discount amortised to profit or loss $	Debt at end of year $
1	3,393,600	339,360	(240,000)	99,360	3,492,960
2	3,492,960	349,296	(240,000)	109,296	3,602,256
3	3,602,256	360,226	(240,000)	120,226	3,722,482
4	3,722,482	372,248	(240,000)	132,248	3,854,730
5	3,854,730	385,473	(240,000)	145,473	4,000,203

NB: the debt at end-year should be $4,000,000. The extra 203 is due to rounding error and is not significant.

Chapter 22 – Statement of cash flows

This question examines the candidate's ability to prepare and interpret a basic statement of cash flows in an individual company (syllabus section 11.5).

(a)   A1sourcing
       Extract from the statement of cash flows
       For the year ended 31 October 20X7

	$'000
Cash flows from operating activities	
Profit before tax (W1)	266
Depreciation charge for the year (W2)	76
Loss on disposal of assets (W3)	4
Finance charge	15
Redemption penalty	8
	369
Increase in receivables	(61)
Increase in payables	66
Cash generated from operations	374
Interest paid	(12)
Income tax paid (W4)	(52)
Net cash flow from operating activities	310

(b)   To examine whether the net cash flow from operating activities is sufficient to support the proposed relocation and expansion we must first consider the other uses to which the cash flow has been put:

	$'000
Net capital expenditure (W5)	260
Bond repayment (W6)	171
	431
Extent to which financed by new issue of shares	(280)
Net cash requirement to finance capital expenditure and bond	151
Dividend	40
Overall net cash requirement	191
Net cash flow from operating activities	310
Increase in cash at bank	119

The above shows that the company's overall net cash requirement during the year was easily met by available cash flow from operations. However, the company would have to forecast future cash flow and consider relocation costs and any likely future capital commitments before deciding whether future cash flows would be sufficient to fund the relocation.

Also, the above shows that net capital expenditure was financed by a new issue of shares and that much of the net cash flow from operating activities was used to repay part of the bond. The company would have to balance the likelihood of these events recurring* with the need to fund the above relocation costs.

* The company would also need to consider the likely impact of this on the equity/debt gearing ratio (down from 1.95:1 to 8:1).

Workings

1   *Calculation of 'profit before tax'*

	$'000
Retained earnings at 31.10.X7	224
Retained earnings at 31.10.X6	(86)
Increase in retained earnings during the year	138
Add dividend paid	40
Profit for the year	178
Tax charge in statement of profit or loss	88
Profit for the year before tax	266

2   *Calculation of depreciation charge for the year*

	$'000
Accumulated depreciation: at 31.10.X7	276
at 31.10.X6	232
Net increase for the year	44
Depreciation on disposals	32
Depreciation charge for the year	76

3   *Calculation of profit or loss on disposal*

Proceeds from disposal		16
Cost of assets	52	
Less depreciation	(32)	
		20
Loss on disposal		4

4   *Tax paid calculation*

Opening balances

	$'000
Deferred tax	44
Income tax	32
	76
Tax charge	88
	164
Closing balances:	
Deferred tax	72
Income tax	40
	112
Tax paid (164 – 112)	52

5   *Calculation of net capital expenditure*

	$'000
Closing balance 31.10.X7	1,240
Opening balance 31.10.X6	1,016
	224
Cost of disposals	52
Capital expenditure during year	276
Less proceeds from disposal of assets	(16)
	260

6   *Calculation of bond repayment*

	$'000
Liability at start of year	280
Add amortised interest (Finance charge $15,000 – cash paid $12,000)	3
	283
Redemption penalty	8
	291
Liability at year end	(120)
	171

Chapter 23 – Interpretation

This question examines a candidate's ability to interpret and report on the financial statements of a manufacturing company which uses historical costs as the basis of its financial reporting (syllabus section 11.5).

Note: The following shows the main points to be covered by the report

To: Finance director
From: Finance department
Date: May 20X7

Re: Main areas bank may investigate re request for increased overdraft facility

Main areas for investigation

Profitability

- Revenue is up 4.7%. This is just ahead of inflation (say 3 – 4%) showing output has not increased significantly.

  The bank would want to know whether this was due to poor management or an attempt to boost sales by cutting prices (which clearly hasn't worked)

- Operating profit has dropped from 13.9% of sales to 12.1%. This is quite worrying as interest cover has also fallen from 6.4 times to 4.0 times. ROCE has also fallen from 7.58% to 5.37%

  The bank would be interested in knowing what effect this would have on the company's dividend. It would also wish to see more long-term figures and projections. Is this an increasing trend?

Liquidity

- Acid test shows worsening liquidity. Down from 1.27 to 0.9. Bank would want to know what the trend is like.

- Inventory turnover has slowed from 3.95 to 3.34.

  Given the competitive nature of the market, the bank would want to know about slow moving inventory and possible inefficiencies in management.

- Receivables recovery has increased from 46 days to 58 days. The bank would want to know whether this is due to poor credit control or unique circumstances.

- Cash flow analysis shows that the disposal of short-term securities has been used, in the main, to finance the purchase of plant and machinery. Short-term borrowings have been used to finance the increase in working capital. The bank would want to know what plans the company has for the plant and machinery and whether there are any future capital requirements.

Additional information

The bank would also want to know:

- How the company intends to pay off the overdraft. Will require cash flow forecasts.

- Whether the company would be prepared to secure the overdraft on freehold land and buildings.

- What the company intends to do with the overdraft. If it intends to continue increasing working capital it could appear to be a poor credit risk for the bank.

APPENDIX

	20X7	*20X7*

Liquidity ratio (acid test)

$$\frac{\text{Current assets} - \text{inventory}}{\text{Current liabilities}}$$

$\dfrac{13.1 - 7.0}{6.8} = 0.9$ $\qquad$ $\dfrac{11.3 - 5.6}{4.5} = 1.27$

Receivables turnover

$$\frac{\text{Trade receivables}}{\text{Revenue}} \times 365$$

$\dfrac{5.3}{33.1} = 58 \text{ days}$ $\qquad$ $\dfrac{4.0}{31.6} = 46 \text{ days}$

Inventory turnover

$$\frac{\text{Cost of sales}}{\text{Inventory}} \times 365$$

$\dfrac{23.4}{7.0} = 3.34 \text{ times}$ $\qquad$ $\dfrac{22.1}{5.6} = 3.95 \text{ times}$

Return on capital employed

Using shareholders' funds

$$\frac{\text{Profit after tax}}{\text{Average shareholders' funds}}$$

$\dfrac{1.3}{(24.3 + 24.1)/2} = 5.37\%$ $\qquad$ $\dfrac{1.8}{(24.1 + 23.4)/2} \quad 7.58\%$

Gearing

$$\frac{\text{Long-term debt}}{\text{Shareholders' funds}}$$

$\dfrac{7.5}{24.3} = 0.31 \text{ or } 30.86\%$ $\qquad$ $\dfrac{7.5}{24.1} = 0.31 \text{ or } 31.12\%$

Interest cover

$$\frac{\text{Profit before interest}}{\text{Interest}}$$

$\dfrac{4.0}{1.0} = 4.0 \text{ times}$ $\qquad$ $\dfrac{4.5}{0.7} = 6.4 \text{ times}$

Cash flow 20X7

	€m
Net cash flow from operating activities	
Operating profit	4.0
Depreciation	1.3
Increase in inventory	(1.4)
Increase in receivables and prepayments	(1.9)
Increase in trade payables	0.4
Net cash inflow from operating activities	2.4
Interest paid	(1.0)
Tax paid	(2.0)
Acquisition of plant and machinery	(2.0)
Disposal of short-term securities	1.5
	(1.1)
Dividends paid	(1.1)
Increase in short-term borrowings	(2.2)

Chapter 24 – Sadler

(a)

	$'000
Profit after tax	7,935
Preference dividend ($2,100,000 × 6%)	(126)
Profit attributable to ordinary shares	7,809

Theoretical ex-rights price:

Ordinary shares	Price $	$
4	5.40	21.60
1	4.20	4.20
$\frac{5}{}$		25.80

Theoretical ex-rights price = $\$\dfrac{25.80}{5 \text{ shares}} = \$5.16$

Weighted average number of shares:

7/12 × 17,625,000 × $5.40/$5.16	10,759,448
5/12 × 22,031,250	9,179,688
	19,939,136

Basic earnings per share = $\dfrac{\$7,809,000}{19,939,136 \text{ shares}} = 39.16c$

Add additional ordinary shares, 2,100,000 × 1/3 = 700,000

Diluted earnings per share = $\dfrac{\$7,809,000}{19,939,136 + 700,000} = 37.84c$

(b) For comparative purposes adjustments are required where the change in shares in issue is not matched by a change in resources. An example is with a bonus issue of shares. The adjustment required by Sadler relates to the bonus element of the rights issue of shares.

Comparable EPS = Previous year reported EPS × $\dfrac{\$5.16}{\$5.40}$

(c) The importance of the measures as indicators of financial performance is often dependent on the level of understanding by the user of the problems involved in assessing the relevant level of earnings and the weighted average number of shares. They are clearly seen by financial analysts as being important, with EPS figures being widely published in the financial press. They give shareholders for example important data on the level of earnings of their investment and being computed on a consistent basis, this level can be compared for different investments and different periods. The trend analysis is dependent on the type of adjustments discussed in (b) above. Problems encountered by users of the EPS ratio include:

- Understanding the weighting of shares in issue during the year.

- Appreciating the 'no consideration' concept for options.

- Dealing with exceptional items. Many companies issue alternative EPS figures excluding exceptional items.

- Assessing the probability of the possible dilution actually occurring.

- Understanding the 'ranking' process for the dilution computation.

Exam question bank

AIA May 2005

1 Drill

Drill is a manufacturer of machine tools and is at present contemplating an issue of $2,000,000 10% Debenture loan stock (redeemable 20Y5) in order to finance an improvement in the production facilities. This proposal has caused some consternation to the directors of the company and they have asked for your comments and advice on this matter. The directors are also concerned about Drill's financial performance and position compared with the industrial average for companies operating in the same business sector and have requested that you analyse Drill's accounts for comparison with these averages.

Draft summary financial statements for Drill, together with typical ratios for companies in the machine tool industry are as follows:

Typical industrial ratios in recent years have been:

Gross profit to sales	34%
Operating profit to net assets employed	22.5%
Operating profit to sales	13%
Current ratio	2.5:1
Liquidity ratio	1.2:1
Average age trade receivables	30 days
Average age of inventory	73 Days
Interest cover	8 times
Net Asset turnover	1.73 times
Debt to equity	53.6%

DRILL STATEMENTS OF PROFIT OR LOSS FOR THE YEARS ENDED 31 DECEMBER 20X4 AND 20X3

	20X4	20X3
	$'000	$'000
Revenue	23,500	20,500
Cost of sales	(16,000)	(14,000)
Gross profit	7,500	6,500
Distribution costs	(2,000)	(1,900)
Administrative expenses	(3,000)	(2,600)
Interest paid	(500)	(300)
Profit before tax	2,000	1,700
Income tax	(1,200)	(1,020)
Profit for the year	800	680

There was no other comprehensive income in either year.

Dividends paid	525	280

DRILL STATEMENTS OF FINANCIAL POSITION AS AT 31 DECEMBER 20X4 AND 20X3

	20X4		20X3	
	$'000	$'000	$'000	$'000
Non-current assets:				
Property, Plant and Equipment (CV)		6,315		5,600
Investments		800		750
		7,115		6,350
Current assets				
Inventory	5,100		3,200	
Trade receivables	2,900		1,900	
Prepayments	100		100	
Bank	600		590	
		8,700		5,790
		15,815		12,140
Equity				
Ordinary shares, 50c each.		350	350	
Retained earnings		6,365	6,090	
		6,715	6,440	
Non-current liabilities				
8% Debenture loan stock		5,500	3,300	
Current liabilities		3,600	2,400	
		15,815	12,140	

Note. The following were balances as at 31 December 20X2:

Inventory	$2,500,000
Trade receivables	$1,700,000

Required

(a)   Compute the industrial ratios for Drill for both 20X4 and 20X3.   **(10 marks)**

(b)   Comment on the financial performance and position of Drill and provide the directors with advice on the proposed debenture issue.   **(15 marks)**

(Total = 25 marks)

2 Current and deferred tax

Describe the accounting treatment required by IAS 12 *Income taxes* for:

(a)   Current taxes   **(3 marks)**
(b)   Deferred taxes   **(7 marks)**

(Total = 10 marks)

3 Jackie and Jeff

IAS 24 *Related party disclosures* requires disclosures about related parties and the reporting entity's transactions with related parties.

Required

(a) Discuss the need for business entities to disclose information concerning transactions with related parties. **(5 marks)**

(b) In the following example, identify any related party relationships and state any additional factors to consider or additional information you may require to determine the full extent of these relationships.

Jackie and Jeff (who are wife and husband) are the directors and majority shareholders of the company, Coupland. This company makes purchases from Passmores, a company controlled by Jeff's brother, Graham. Graham is a director of Passmores but he holds no shares in Coupland. Neither Jackie nor Jeff holds shares in Passmores. **(5 marks)**

(Total = 10 marks)

AIA November 2005

4 Petiam

Petiam commenced a new business project on 1 January 20X5 that required a significant initial cash outflow. The project only generates small cash in-flows during the first two years of the three-year period of the project. The majority of the cash in-flows occur on completion of the project which is planned for 1 January 20X8. To match these cash flows the company has raised finance in the form of a 3-year bond. The bond of $50m was issued on 1 January at a discount of 40%. The bond pays a nominal interest of 2% per annum, payable on 31 December each year, and is to be repaid in full ($50m) on 1 January 20X8.

Note. The effective interest rate on the bond is 20% per annum.

Required

(a) Describe how this bond should be accounted for during the three years it is in issue. **(5 marks)**

(b) Calculate the finance charges relating to the bond for 20X5, 20X6 and 20X7, and the liability that should be recognised as at 31 December 20X6. **(5 marks)**

(Total = 10 marks)

AIA May 2006

5 Hoodurz

The following trial balance has been extracted from the books of Hoodurz as at 31 March 20X6:

	$'000	$'000
Administrative expenses	210	
Ordinary share capital, $1 per share		600
Trade receivables	470	
Bank overdraft		80
Provision for warranty claims		205
Distribution costs	420	
Non-current asset investments	560	
Investment income		75
Interest paid	10	
Property, at cost	200	
Plant and equipment, at cost	550	
Plant and equipment, accumulated depreciation (at 31.3.20X6)		220
Retained earnings (at 31.3.20X5)		80
Loans (repayable 31.12.20Y0)		100
Purchases	960	
Inventories (at 31.3.20X5)	150	
Trade payables		260
Sales		2,010
20X4/20X5 final dividend paid	65	
20X5/20X6 interim dividend paid	35	
	3,630	3,630

The following information is relevant

(i)   The trial balance figures include the following amounts for a disposal group that has been classified as 'held for sale' under IFRS 5 *'Non-current assets held for sale and discontinued operations'*:

	$'000
Plant and equipment, at cost	150
Plant and equipment, accumulated depreciation	15
Trade receivables	70
Bank (overdraft)	10
Trade payables	60
Sales	370
Inventories (at 31.3.20X5)	25
Purchases	200
Administration expenses	55
Distribution costs	60

The disposal group had no inventories at the date classified as 'held for sale'.

(ii)   Inventories (excluding the disposal group) at 31.3.20X6 were valued at $160,000

(iii)   The depreciation charges for the year have already been accrued.

(iv)   The income tax for the year ended 31.3.20X6 is estimated to be $74,000. This includes $14,000 in relation to the disposal group.

(v)   The provision for warranty claims is to be increased by $16,000. This is classified as an administration expense.

(vi)   Staff bonuses totalling $20,000 for administration and $20,000 for distribution are to be accrued.

(vii) The property was acquired during February 20X6; therefore depreciation for the year ended 31.3.20X6 is immaterial. The directors have chosen to use the revaluation model for such an asset. The fair value of the property at 31.3.20X6 is $280,000.

Required

Prepare for Hoodurz:

(a)   A statement of profit or loss and other comprehensive income for the year ended 31 March 20X6; and   **(10 marks)**

(b)   A statement of financial position as at 31 March 20X6.   **(20 marks)**

Both statements should comply as far as possible with relevant International Financial Reporting Standards. No notes to the statements are required nor is a statement of changes in equity, but all workings should be clearly shown.

(Total = 30 marks)

6 Revenue recognition

Explain how revenue should be recognised under IAS 18 *Revenue recognition* in each of the following cases:

Case 1: Goods have been sold to customers under normal trade terms but the selling company provides free storage facilities for customers who do not want to take immediate delivery of the goods. The customer can request delivery at any time.   **(4 marks)**

Case 2: Advertising services are provided under a special promotion so that if a customer takes out a contract for 24 monthly advertisements and pays the fees in advance they will only have to pay for 23 advertisements with the last being free.   **(4 marks)**

Case 3: Goods have been sold, and invoiced, that are subject to installation and inspection conditions.   **(4 marks)**

(Total = 12 marks)

AIA November 2006

7 Locator Group

The Locator Group is an unlisted, medium-sized entity which designs and manufactures a wide range of navigational equipment for both military and civil use. The company is a leader in its field and is currently considering a stock-market listing as part of its future expansion plans.

The company's CEO is enthusiastic about financial reporting (the company's financial statements often gain high praise for their quality) and is concerned that a listing – which would require compliance with International Financial Reporting Standards – may have an adverse effect on users' understanding. He has therefore asked you to carry out an initial study to establish the likely effect that such a listing would have on the appearance of the company's statement of financial position.

The following shows the company's draft statement of financial position for its year ended 31 October 20X6:

	€m	€m
Fixed assets		
Intangible assets		4.3
Property, plant and equipment (Note 1)		12.6
Investments (Note 2)		2.0
		18.9
Current assets		
Stocks	1.2	
Debtors	4.8	
Cash	1.8	
	7.8	
Current liabilities		
Trade creditors	4.9	
Proposed dividends (Note 3)	0.5	
	5.4	
Net current assets		2.4
Total assets less current liabilities		21.3
Long-term loans (Note 4)		9.0
Net assets		12.3
Capital and reserves		
Share capital (Note 5)		8.0
Retained earnings		4.3
		12.3

Notes

(1)   PPE includes a photo-embossing machine bought by the company on 1 November 20X4 for €500,000. It has an expected life of 5 years and nil residual value. The company has used the machine continuously since purchase but is now actively looking for a buyer as the machine has become surplus to requirements. The machine's market value (before selling costs of €20,000) is expected to be €220,000. A sale is expected within the next 6 months.

(2)   An investment of €2m in property (including a land element €1.5m with a life of 50 years) was made on 1 November 20X5. At 31 October 20X6, the property's fair value had increased to €2.3m. The CEO has indicated that he would like the company to adopt the fair value model allowed by *IAS 40 Investment Property.*

(3)   The proposed dividend relates to equity shares and was declared on 5 November 20X6. There is no preference dividend outstanding.

(4)   A 4% loan note was issued during October 20X6. It is due to be repaid in five annual instalments beginning 1 January 20X7.

(5)   Share capital includes €0.4m 6% preference shares redeemable at the discretion of the holders on or before 1 April 20X8.

Required

(a)   Redraft the above statement of financial position to comply, where appropriate, with the presentation favoured by International Financial Reporting Standards.   **(15 marks)**

(b)   Explain any adjustments which have to be made to the figures in the draft statement of financial position to comply with International Financial Reporting Standards.   **(8 marks)**

(Total = 23 marks)

8 Jupiter Aviation

Jupiter Aviation is owned by two partners, Alex Luthaw and Sue Perman. The firm operates a number of small, light passenger aircraft which it uses to run pleasure flights. The two partners are now at the next stage of their business development plan and are considering expanding the business into the corporate travel sector; this would involve the acquisition of a small jet aircraft. The following is a transcript of the most recent partners' meeting.

Alex: I'm worried about how we're going to pay for this jet, Sue. We've two options – outright purchase and leasing.

Sue: You're right to be worried, Alex. Our statement of financial position shows partners' capital of €4m and debt of €2m. Which means our debt to capital ratio is already 0.5:1. Jupiter has poor cash flow. We just don't have enough buying power to pay €3.5m for a jet outright.

Alex: Leasing it is then. I've got the lease terms here. We would pay €1m annually in advance for four years.

Sue: And the rate of interest?

Alex: Well, Jupiter's cost of borrowing is 10% but there's something in the lease called 'implicit interest rate' which is 9.7%.

Sue: Either way, there's not much difference. Okay, I agree – we'll go for the lease. Also, as we won't actually own the jet, there'll be no impact on our statement of financial position. We can just put the rentals through the accounts as expenses.

Alex: I'm not happy with that, Sue. Jupiter's statement of financial position should be as transparent as possible. If we're going to have a contractual obligation for four years, it should be recognised. And we should use something called the 'actuarial method' to do so.

Sue: Okay, I can see we disagree. We'll ask Arthur* for advice.

* Arthur is the firm's accountant.

Required

You are Arthur. Draft a memorandum to the partners of Jupiter Aviation to advise on and demonstrate the possible financial reporting implications of each partner's preferred method of accounting for the lease.

(17 marks)

9 Infinite Leisure Group

Infinite Leisure Group owns and operates a number of pubs and clubs across Europe and South East Asia. Since inception the group has made exclusive use of the cost model for the purpose of its annual financial reporting. This has led to a number of shareholders expressing concern about what they see as a consequent lack of clarity and quality in the group's financial statements.

The CEO does not support use of the alternative to the cost model (the revaluation model) believing it produces volatile information. However she is open to persuasion and so, as an example of the impact of a revaluation policy, has asked you to carry out an analysis (using data concerning "Soo$_z$" - one of the group's nightclubs sold during the year to 31 October 20X6) to show the impact the revaluation model would have had on the group's financial statements had the model been adopted from the day the club was acquired.

The following extract has been taken from the company's asset register:

Outlet: "Soo²"	
Acquisition data	
Date acquired	1 November 20X1
Total cost	€10.24m
Cost components	
Plant and equipment	
Cost	€0.24m
Economic life	six years
Residual value	nil
Property	
Buildings	
Cost	€7.0m
Economic life	50 years
Land	
Cost	€3.0m
Updates	
1 November 20X3	Replacement cost of plant & equipment €0.42m. No fair value available (mainly specialised audio visual equipment). No change to economic life.
	Property revaluation €13m (land €4m, buildings €9m). Future Economic life as at 1 Nov 20X3 50 years.
Disposal	
Date committed to a plan to sell	January 20X6
Date sold	June 20X6
Net sale price	€9.1m
Sale price components	
Plant and equipment	€0.1m
Property	€9.0m

Note. The group accounts for property and plant and equipment as separate non-current assets in its statement of financial position using straight-line depreciation.

Required

Prepare an analysis to show the impact on Infinite Leisure's financial statements for each year the "Soo²" nightclub was owned had the revaluation model been in place from the day the nightclub was acquired.

(15 marks)

10 Werit group

The Werit group promotes itself as being a 'leading edge' recruitment agency with a turnover in excess of €200m and profits of €30m. It is currently recruiting itself for the post of finance director and has set applicants a number of questions based upon events from its last year of operations ending on 31 October 20X6. The following extract has been taken from the applicants' question paper:

Potential liabilities: *IAS 37 Provisions Contingent Liabilities and Contingent Assets*

(a) After many years of fine service to both the group and the industry, finance director Sean Head was dismissed by the group on 17 September 20X6. His contract stipulates that he is to receive his annual salary (€500,000) until 31 October 20X7; with the proviso that, should he obtain employment with another recruitment agency, the group has the right to terminate the agreement.

(b) In March 20X5 the agency was asked to recommend a design and marketing executive to Costalotto a company building coastal retirement homes in Spain. The agency's suggested choice began work with Costalotto in May 20X5. In April 20X6 the agency received an angry fax from the CEO of Costalotto. Not only had the marketing executive falsified all of his qualifications but his first construction, a block of cliff-top luxury apartments, has collapsed into the sea. A law firm has launched a legal action against the agency claiming negligence. However, the agency's own lawyers have indicated that, so long as due process can be proved, Costalotto will probably lose the case.

(c) In August 20X6 the agency's human resource department began to organise the forthcoming Christmas party. It is an annual event held as a goodwill gesture for both staff and clients. It is to be a spectacular event costing an estimated €100,000.

Required

You are applying for the post of finance director with The Werit group. Provide answers to the above questions advising the group on how best to account for the three events in its accounts for the year ended 31 October 20X6.   **(15 marks)**

AIA May 2007

11 Government grants

Amy, Suki and Kun are three friends who have recently set up a model agency ASK Models. The agency has recently received a government grant of €30,000 in respect of office furniture and photography and lighting equipment costing €75,000. The friends estimate that owing to the nature of the business these assets will only have a life of five years. They now have to decide how to account for the grant and in a recent meeting each made comments as follows:

Amy   We had to spend the money anyway, so the grant is like a windfall gain. Pure profit in other words. So I suggest we simply credit the whole amount to our profits.

Suki   We can't do that, Amy, because it doesn't sound like revenue – which, if I remember my business studies lectures correctly, is what we should be crediting to profits. I suggest, because all three of us will gain from the grant, that we just credit the whole amount to equity.

Kun   I think both of you are wrong. Surely, the grant effectively reduces the cost of the assets so should be recognised over those assets' lives.

Required

(a) Which of the three friends is correct? Explain your answer. Assuming ASK Models wishes to use international accounting standards, prepare calculations to show how the agency should account for the government grant.   **(6 marks)**

(b) Briefly explain why the other two friends are incorrect.   **(4 marks)**

(Total = 10 marks)

AIA November 2007

12 Blissopia

The Blissopia Leisure Group consists of three divisions:

Blissopia 1, which operates mainstream bars;
Blissopia 2, which operates large restaurants; and
Blissopia 3, which operates one hotel – the Eden.

Divisions 1 and 2 have been trading very successfully and there are no indications of any potential impairment. It is a different matter with the Eden however. The Eden is a 'boutique' hotel and was acquired on 1 November 20X6 for $6.90m. The fair value (using net selling price) of the hotel's net assets at that date and their carrying amount at the year-end were as follows:

	1.11.X6 Fair value $m	31.10.X7 Carrying amount $m
Land and buildings	3.61	3.18
Plant and equipment	0.90	0.81
Cash	1.40	1.12
Vehicles	0.10	0.09
Trade receivables	0.34	0.37
Trade payables	(0.60)	(0.74)
	5.75	4.83

The following facts were discovered following an impairment review as at 31 October 20X7:

(i)   During August 20X7, a rival hotel commenced trading in the same location as the Eden. The Blissopia Leisure Group expects hotel revenues to be significantly affected and has calculated the value-in-use of the Eden to be $3.52m.

(ii)   The company owning the rival hotel has offered to buy the Eden (including all of the above net assets) for $4m. Selling costs would be approximately $50,000.

(iii) One of the hotel vehicles was severely damaged in an accident whilst being used by an employee to carry shopping home from a supermarket. The vehicle's carrying value at 31 October 20X7 was $30,000 and insurers have indicated that as it was being used for an uninsured purpose the loss is not covered by insurance. The vehicle was subsequently scrapped.

(iv)   A corporate client, owing $40,000, has recently gone into liquidation. Lawyers have estimated that the company will only receive 25% of the amount outstanding.

Required

Prepare a memo for the directors of the Blissopia Leisure Group explaining how the group should account for the impairment to the Eden Hotel's assets as at 31 October 20X7. **(15 marks)**

AIA May 2008

13 Jack Matelot

(a) During 20X6, Jack Matelot set up a company JTM to construct and refurbish marinas in various ports around Europe. The company's first accounting period ended on 31 October 20X6 and during that period JTM won a contract to refurbish a small marina in St Malo, France. During the year ended 31 October 20X7, the company won a further two contracts in Barcelona, Spain and Faro, Portugal. The following extract has been taken from the company's contract notes as at 31 October 20X7:

Contract:	Barcelona €m	Faro €m	St Malo €m
Contract value	12.24	10.00	15.00
Work certified:			
To 31 October 20X6	–	–	6.00
Year to 31 October 20X7	6.50	0.50	3.00
To date	6.50	0.50	9.00
Payments received:			
To 31 October 20X6			5.75
Year to 31 October 20X7	3.76	–	1.75
To date	3.76	–	7.50
Invoices sent to client:			
To 31 October 20X6	–	–	6.00
Year to 31 October 20X7	5.00	0.50	2.76
To date	5.00	0.50	8.76
Costs incurred:			
To 31 October 20X6	–	–	6.56
Year to 31 October 20X7	11.50	1.50	3.94
To date	11.50	1.50	10.50
Estimated costs to complete:			
As at 31 October 20X6			5.44
As at 31 October 20X7	4.00	5.50	1.50

Notes

Barcelona: Experiencing difficulties. Although JTM does not anticipate any cost increases, the client has offered to increase contract value by €0.76m as compensation.

Faro: No problems.

St Malo: Work has slowed down during 20X7. However, company feels it can continue profitably.

The company uses the value of work certified to estimate the percentage completion of each contract.

Required

For each contract, calculate the profit or loss attributable to the year ended 31 October 20X7 and show how it would be recognised in the company's statement of financial position at that date. (show your workings clearly). **(25 marks)**

(b)   As JTM's 20X7 accounts were being prepared, it became evident that the St Malo contract had slowed down due to a dispute with a neighbouring marina which claimed that the JTM refurbishment had damaged part of its quayside. The company has been told that the cost of repairing the damage would be €150,000. Jack Matelot believes it is a fair estimate and, in the interests of completing the contract on time, has decided to settle the claim. He is not unduly concerned about the amount involved as such eventualities are adequately covered by insurance.

Required

How should this event be dealt with in the 20X7 accounts?   **(5 marks)**

(c)   During 20X7, Jack Matelot had two major worries; i) the operating performance of JTM had not been as good as expected, and ii) the planned disposal of surplus property (to finance the agreed acquisition of a competitor MoriceMarinas and the payment of a dividend) had not been successful. As a result of these circumstances, Jack had been warning shareholders not to expect a dividend for 20X7. However, during November 20X7, the property was unexpectedly disposed of for €5m; which enabled the payment of a 20X7 dividend of €1m and the acquisition of MoriceMarinas for €4m.

Required

How should the above events be dealt with in the 20X7 accounts?   **(10 marks)**

(Total = 40 marks)

14 Accounting regulation

You have been given the task of preparing a briefing paper for a group of prospective accounting students on the subject of accounting regulation. Each of the students has an 'economics' background and so they are all used to hearing advocates of a 'free-market' approach tell them that accounting information is like any other good; in that, if there is a demand for that information it will be supplied and that a regulation of the market (by means of accounting standards) leads to the supply of non-optimal information. Part of your task therefore is to convince the students of the need for accounting regulation.

Required

(a)   Briefly outline the arguments of those who believe it is necessary to regulate accounting practice.

(6 marks)

(b)   Explain why regulation is necessary if a company enters into transactions which are with a related party. Provide an example of such a transaction.   **(8 marks)**

(c)   To what extent does IAS 34 *Interim financial reporting* attempt to regulate the interim reporting of companies?   **(6 marks)**

(Total = 20 marks)

15 Cher Price

Cher Price runs a very profitable internet based fashion retail business. Her company's capital structure, which has remained unchanged for several years, is as follows:

	£'000
Ordinary shares of £1 each	5,000
Share premium	1,300
5% £1 irredeemable preference shares	1,000
4% convertible loan stock	1,000

The most favourable terms for conversion of the loan stock are 125 ordinary shares for every £100 of loan stock.

Cher is currently considering an expansion of the business which would require an injection of a further £3m of capital but is unsure whether the money should be raised by way of a new issue of ordinary shares (current market value £1.50) or by issuing more convertible loan stock. Both types of issue would be on the same terms as those currently in existence. Her main concern is over the effect of any further capital injection on the company's earnings per share.

The company's average profit after tax (of 30%) is £2m which represents a 25% return on capital employed.

Required

(a)   Calculate the diluted earnings per share figure assuming the company:

    (i)   Issues ordinary shares, and

    (ii)   Issues convertible loan stock.   **(7 marks)**

(b)   Based upon your calculations above, what advice would you give Cher Price concerning the proposed financing of the expansion?   **(3 marks)**

        (Total = 10 marks)

16 Tree

The following shows a chronological list of events concerning a food retailing company Tree plc and the planned disposal of one of its supermarkets in Spain:

31 August 20X7   The board of Tree Plc meet and agree to dispose of the supermarket as soon as possible. The directors have decided to change the company's management strategy – as a result, the supermarket no longer fits in with their future plans. The finance director notes that he may have found a buyer and that tentative discussions suggest a sale may be completed before the 31 December 20X7.

31 October 20X7   The company's financial year end. The carrying amount of the supermarket at this date is €30m; although its value-in-use is estimated to be €20m.

10 November 20X7   The accounts of the company are approved by the directors. An announcement is made that the company is now actively negotiating the sale of the supermarket and that a contract may be signed imminently to sell it for €16m after costs of disposal. Unaudited accounts show that the supermarket is likely to break even during the period between 1 November 20X7 and its likely date of sale.

Required

Explain how the above asset (the supermarket) should be dealt with in Tree Plc's financial statements ended 31 October 20X7.   **(10 marks)**

AIA November 2008

17 Ofkin Company

The Ofkin Company is a medium-size retailer of high street fashions. It is 14 February 20X8 and, as the company's Chief Finance Officer, you are currently considering the draft financial statements for the year ended 2 February 20X8. The following extracts have been taken from the company's draft accounts:

		Statement of financial position As at 2 February		
		Notes	**20X8** **€m**	20X7 **€m**
ASSETS AND LIABILITIES				
Non-current assets				
Property, plant and equipment		1	**47.61**	34.05
Intangible assets		2	**3.62**	3.62
Investments		3	**4.20**	1.50
Deferred tax assets		4	**0.80**	2.40
			56.23	41.57
Current assets				
Inventories			**32.39**	30.16
Trade and other receivables			**51.38**	43.74
Cash and short term deposits			**7.39**	7.23
			91.16	81.13
Total assets			**147.39**	122.70

		Notes	**20X8** **€m**	20X7 **€m**
Current liabilities				
Bank overdrafts			**(3.14)**	(2.23)
Unsecured bank loans			**(10.03)**	–
Trade and other payables			**(57.06)**	(50.63)
Current tax liability		4	**(5.32)**	(5.98)
			(75.55)	(58.84)
Non-current liabilities				
Corporate bond		5	**(34.93)**	(33.94)
Provisions		6	**(5.60)**	(1.27)
Other liabilities		7	**(5.69)**	(8.00)
			(46.22)	(43.21)
Total liabilities			**(121.77)**	(102.05)
Net assets			**25.62**	20.65
EQUITY				
Share capital		8	**2.47**	2.61
Share premium		8	**0.70**	0.60
Capital redemption reserve		8	**0.53**	0.38
Fair value reserve			**0.28**	–
Retained earnings			**21.64**	17.06
Total equity			**25.62**	20.65

Notes

1 Property, plant and equipment

	Freehold Property	Leasehold Property	Plant and Equipment	Total
	€m	€m	€m	€m
Cost				
At February 20X7	7.63	1.06	64.26	72.95
Additions			17.96	17.96
Revaluation	0.28			0.28
Disposals	(0.50)	–	(2.01)	(2.51)
At February 20X8	7.41	1.06	80.21	88.68
Depreciation				
At February 20X7	0.91	0.16	37.83	38.90
Provided during the year			3.86	3.86
Disposals	(0.06)	–	(1.63)	(1.69)
At February 20X8	0.85	0.16	40.06	41.07
Carrying amount at February 20X8	6.56	0.90	40.15	47.61

Property, plant and equipment were disposed of for a cash consideration of €1.5m

2 The recoverable amount of goodwill on 2 February 20X8 was measured on the basis of value-in-use. As this exceeded carrying value no impairment loss was recognised.

3 During the year the company increased its investment in an unlisted equity security. This security does not have a quoted price in an active market and its fair value cannot be reliably measured.

4 Tax expense reported in the statement of profit or loss   €13.33m
   Corporation taxes paid during the year   €12.39m

5 On 12 January 20X7 the company issued €40m five-year 6% bonds. The amount received was €33.94m. The bonds pay interest annually and yield 10% to maturity. The 'interest method' is used by the company to determine the annual cost and the carrying amount of the bond.

6 Provisions are made for the costs of the future rentals or estimated exit cost of leases of unoccupied premises to which the company is committed.

7 On the last day of the 20X7 accounting period, the company leased plant and equipment with a fair value of €8m. Rental of €0.8m is paid at the start of each quarter beginning on the first day of the accounting period ending 2 February 20X8. The interest rate implied in the lease is 3.51% per quarter.

8 During the year the company purchased for cancellation (against retained earnings) 150,000 of its own ordinary shares of €1 each in the open market at a cost of €1.8m.

   On 18 July 20X7 the company issued 10,000 ordinary shares of €1 each for cash consideration of €110,000.

9 During the year the company paid dividends of €10.44m.

10 During the year interest of €0.18m was received.

Required

(a)   Prepare the company's statement of cash flows for the year ended 2 February 20X8 in accordance with IAS7 using the indirect method.

[A statement showing an analysis of net debt is not required.]   **(30 marks)**

(b)   The following facts come to light during your consideration of the draft accounts:

(i)   The year end inventory figure includes damaged stock at a net realisable value of €2m. The stock originally cost €3m but, owing to a sudden change in demand, has been sold today for €3.5m. The normal selling price of this stock is €4.2m.

(ii)   Several large shareholders have expressed their disappointment with the level of dividends paid during the year. As a result, your Chief Executive Officer has proposed to pay a further dividend of €2.5m within one week.

Required

Explain the changes, if any, you will have to make to the statement of cash flows for the year ended 2 February 20X8 as a result of the above.   **(7 marks)**

(c)   Directors' minutes show that on 31 January 20X8, the board was considering investing €1.7m in a liquid investment with a maturity date of 6 May 20X8.

Required

If the investment had been made, explain the impact it would have had on the statement of cash flows for the year ended 2 February 20X8.   **(3 marks)**

(Total = 40 marks)

18 Smallman

For many years, Smallman Plc had been in business providing building equipment to the construction industry. This trade had been very successful but in March 20X6 the company decided to extend its business by also offering building and maintenance services. On 1 July 20X6 the company won its first sub-contract – a one year €700,000 deal to provide building work as part of a contract worth €30m to the main contractor. The contract notes were as follows:

Contract 1

	Year end 31 December 20X6 €m	Year end 31 December 20X7 €m
Sales value recognised	0.50	0.20
Cost of goods sold	(0.35)	(0.17)
Profit recognised	0.15	0.03

The accounting treatment adopted by the company with respect to Contract 1 is to include work certified as sales and costs incurred as cost of goods sold.

In August 20X7, the main contractor ceased trading and Smallman agreed to take over the main contract. Details are as follows:

Contract value	€25m
Estimated costs to complete	€20m
Length of contract	3 years
Percentage complete at 31 December 20X7	30%
20X7 Work certified	€10m
20X7 Costs incurred	€6m

BPP
LEARNING MEDIA

In its 20X7 accounts, the company has followed its normal practice and included €10m work certified in revenue and €6m costs incurred in cost of goods sold. The draft statement of profit or loss for 20X7 is as follows:

	2007 €m	2006 €m
Sales	56.20	37.50
Cost of goods sold	(45.50)	(25.60)
	10.70	11.90
Income tax (at 30%)	(3.20)	(3.60)
Profit for the year	7.50	8.30

The company now wishes to change its accounting policy to the percentage-of-completion method.

Other inventory

During 20X7 the company also discovered that the opening figure for inventory included stock valued at €450,000 which had in fact been sold during December 20X6.

Note: Reserves at 1 January 2006 were €1.40m.

Required

(a) Explain whether the company's change to a percentage-of-completion method will qualify as a change in accounting policy under IFRS. **(3 marks)**

(b) Prepare the statement of profit or loss and retained earnings figures for 20X6 and 20X7 adjusted, where necessary, for the above events. **(12 marks)**

(Total = 15 marks)

19 Cumulus

Cumulus PLC owns and operates a number of 'high-fashion luxury goods' retail outlets around the world. The outlets are either large stand-alone high street stores or smaller shops located in hotel foyers and shopping malls. The company's finance director has recently learned that during 20X7 the company's CEO sanctioned the spending of €30m on three properties. All properties are still held at the year-end but have different uses and purposes. A review of the company's property portfolio revealed the following:

Property portfolio extracts

Property		Price	Description
(i)	Riverside, Bangkok	€17m	Money spent to date on construction of a hotel. CEO's intention is to lease the building on completion to a major hotel chain.
(ii)	Paris	€8m	Five acres of land. Speculative acquisition. Near to a large supermarket. Directors are not sure what to do with the land. Possible uses include construction of a new retail outlet for the company or retention for possible sale when land values increase.
(iii)	Pandacan, Manila	€5m	High-street premises. Intention is to open a retail outlet. Acquired as part of long-term plans to expand company's presence in the Philippines.

Required

Explain to the finance director how the above properties should be dealt with in the company's statement of financial position as at the year-end. **(10 marks)**

AIA May 2009

20 Apollo[21]

Apollo[21] is a renewable energy company which designs and supplies solar technology for commercial and residential buildings. The company was founded in 20X4 and has since experienced rapid growth at a time when its financial reporting systems have been under pressure due to the adoption of IFRS. A period of relative calm has now given the company's CEO the chance to ascertain whether all relevant IFRS have been followed in an appropriate fashion.

As a newly recruited member of the company's finance team, you have been given the task of investigating the accounting policies used to prepare the company's statement of profit or loss. The following is an extract from the company's most recent statement:

APOLLO[21] DRAFT STATEMENT OF PROFIT OR LOSS FOR THE YEAR ENDED 31 OCTOBER 20X8

	€m
Sales	24.00
Cost of sales	(13.70)
Gross profit	10.30
Administration and distribution overheads	(6.90)
Net profit for the period	3.40

On investigation the following facts are discovered:

(i)   Solar panels costing €1.2m to design and manufacture were delivered to a customer during September 20X8. Installation was due to take place during October but owing to bad weather will not now take place until November. Installation costs will amount to a further €0.2m. The total contract value of €2.1m, which has all been received in advance, has been included in sales. The cost of design and manufacture has been included in cost of sales.

Sales also includes advertising revenue of €0.36m received in July 20X8 from several customers who have agreed to advertise in Apollo[21]'s trade brochure from 1 August 20X8 to 31 January 20Y0. As the revenue represents fees received in advance the customers will receive free advertising from 1 December 20X9 to 31 January 20Y0.

Equipment costing €0.06m and with a sales value of €0.10m are in stock at the year end awaiting delivery to a customer who does not wish to take delivery until December 20X8 and has therefore taken advantage of Apollo[21]'s free storage facility.   **(10 marks)**

(ii)   Apollo[21] has a reputation as a keen promoter of environmental protection and during October 20X7 was shocked to learn that emissions from its factory making solar panel casings had been polluting the atmosphere for several years. On discovering the facts and with agreement of the whole board the CEO made an immediate public announcement that a programme to introduce new equipment to reduce the harmful effects would begin in the following month, November 20X7. After an investment appraisal exercise which involved the use of an annual discount rate of 6% contracts were signed on 1 November 20X7 which committed the company to a two year programme of development resulting in the following instalment expenditures on new equipment which the company plans to have operational by 31 October 20X9:

€2m due to be paid 31 October 20X8.

€4m due to be paid 31 October 20X9.

In an attempt to follow international accounting standards the company included a provision of €6m with a corresponding asset of €6m in its statement of financial position as at 31 October 20X7.

This type of equipment has a useful life of 10 years and is usually depreciated on a straight-line basis. Although installation has not yet been completed the company has included depreciation of €600,000 in cost of sales.

(12 marks)

(iii) The company has a loyal and highly skilled workforce. In fact the CEO often refers to the staff as his main asset, often promoting the company with the slogan "Our staff are our strength". Staff turnover is very low and the company has spent €3m this year on maintaining and improving their skills. On the basis that this staff 'asset' is improved every year, the company has capitalised these costs as an intangible asset. On 1 November 20X7 the carrying amount of this 'asset' was €7m.

On 18 July 20X7 the company began a project codenamed "Daystar" to develop a new generation of solar panels. The following events and transactions refer to this project.

Year to:	Event	€m
31 October 20X7	Market research costs	0.25
	Search for alternative materials and processes	0.33
		0.58
31 October 20X8		
Period to 15 August 20X8	Search for alternative materials and processes	0.45
	Design evaluation	0.18
15 August	Directors announce encouraging news that design tests on the *Daystar* have proved positive and demonstrate their firm belief that significant sales will be generated from January 20X9 onwards.	
Period from 16 August to 31 October	Design, construction and testing of prototype costs	0.34
		0.97

Costs of €0.58m were written off to profit or loss in 20X7. However, on the basis that a feasible project appears to have been developed during 20X8 costs of €0.97m have been capitalised.

(10 marks)

(iv) In June 20X7 the company made a decision to sell a specialised piece of equipment. A buyer was identified, a reasonable price was agreed and management were firmly committed to the plan. However, due to circumstances beyond the control of Apollo[21] the sale did not take place. At 31 October 20X8 the asset was still being used although managers were still actively looking for a buyer and committed to its sale. Carrying value information is as follows:

At June 20X7	€1.30m
At 31 October 20X7	€1.20m
At 31 October 20X8	€1.00m

Depreciation has been included in distribution overheads.

Also at 31 October 20X8, the equipment's net realisable value was €300,000 and its value in use was €420,000.

Required

Redraft the statement of profit or loss to take account, where necessary, of the above discoveries. Explain any adjustments and, where no adjustment is necessary, explain why.

(8 marks)

(Total = 40 marks)

21 Glyn and Scott

Glyn and Scott are two Australian based floor layers who trade as partners in the firm 'Floors⁴All'. They share profits in the ratio 2:1. The statement of financial position of the firm at the most recent year end is shown below:

Floors⁴All Statement of Financial Position As at 31 March 20X9			
	$'000	$'000	$'000
Non-current assets			
Property			750
Fixtures, fittings and equipment			25
Motor vehicles			147
			922
Current assets			
Inventory		32	
Trade receivables		96	
Short term deposit		88	
Cash		43	
			259
Total assets			1,181
Current liabilities			
Trade payables			124
Non-current liabilities			
Bank loan			250
Total liabilities			374
Partners' accounts	Glyn	Scott	
	$'000	$'000	$'000
Capital	300	200	
Current accounts	176	131	
	476	331	
Total partners' accounts			807
			1,181

The business is due to go through a period of expansion and in order to take advantage of favourable tax laws, the partners have decided to convert their firm into a limited company on 1 April 20X9 with the name 'Floors⁴All Pty. Ltd.'. The terms of the conversion are as follows:

(i) The new company will pay $1.5m for the firm. This will be made up as follows:

900,000 $1 shares at par to be taken by the partners in their profit sharing ratio.

400,000 $1 2% debentures issued at par and to be taken by the partners in proportion to their capital accounts.

$200,000 cash. The partners have negotiated a bank facility for the new company should it be required as a result of the conversion.

(ii) All of the firm's net assets will be taken over by the new company with the exception of cash and a delivery van. The van will be taken over by Scott at a value of $30,000.

(iii) For the purpose of its opening statement of financial position, the new company will value property at $1,000,000, fixtures, fittings and equipment at $20,000, remaining motor vehicles at $93,000 and trade receivables at $80,000. Other assets and liabilities taken over will be valued at their book value. The bank loan will be secured on the property.

Required

(a)   Prepare the following accounts in the books of Floors⁴All to reflect the above transactions:

Realisation account

Partners joint capital and current accounts   **(10 marks)**

(b)   Prepare the opening statement of financial position of Floors⁴All Pty. Ltd. as at 1 April 20X9. (Any goodwill arising on conversion should be shown in the statement of financial position at its initial carrying value. Ignore goodwill impairment.)   **(8 marks)**

(Total = 18 marks)

22 ˢLink Provision

ˢLink Provision is a leading Pan-European provider of supply chain management services. The entire scope of the company's operations is the provision of contract logistical services in four main areas: manufacturing, industrial, retail and transport.

In the UK, which accounts for 68% of the company's revenue, the management structure has developed along service lines so that a different managing director is responsible for each of the above four main areas. In the rest of Europe the management structure has developed along four geographical lines so that a different managing director is responsible for the company's operations in each of France/Spain, Germany, Central Europe and Eastern Europe. Each of these segments produces an equivalent amount of revenue.

In its financial statements for the year ended 31 December 20X8 the company complied with the requirements of *IAS14 Segment reporting*. The main board now believes that the company's internal reporting system is too cumbersome and wishes to change to a more streamlined approach that will also help the company to comply with the requirements of IFRS 8 *Operating segments* effective from 1 January 20X9.

Required

(a)   Explain the factors the company will have considered in determining its segment reporting practices in the 20X8 accounts.   **(8 marks)**

(b)   Explain the impact IFRS8 will have on the company's choice of a new internal reporting system.
                                                            (8 marks)

(Total = 16 marks)

AIA November 2009

23 Sky Construction

Sky Construction builds tower blocks. The company has one contract currently under way and is considering whether to submit a tender for a second fixed-price $100m contract to build a new tower block which the developer has called 'Yucca Island'. It is hoped work will begin at the start of the company's financial year which is 1 January 20X0 and it is estimated it will take three years to complete the contract. The company directors have been presented with the following contract schedule showing estimated values for work certified and costs expected to be incurred during each year of the contract's life:

Contract : Yucca Island Revenues and costings (estimates)					
	Note	*20X0*	*20X1*	*20X2*	*Total*
Revenue		$m	$m	$m	$m
Work certified	i	15.00	40.00	45.00	100.00
Costings					
Labour	ii	4.65	13.95	12.40	31.00
Materials	iii	6.88	17.20	18.92	43.00
Depreciation of plant and equipment	iv	1.20	1.20	1.20	3.60
Depreciation of fixtures and fittings	v	0.60	0.60	0.60	1.80
Hire and transport of equipment	vi	0.26	0.74	0.50	1.50
Design	vi	2.20	–	–	2.20
General administration	vii	1.60	1.60	1.60	4.80
Borrowing	viii	–	–	–	–

Notes

(i)   A qualified architect regularly inspects work completed to date. The architect then issues certificates of work completed which the company subsequently uses to demand progress payments from the developer. Normal practice is for the developer to retain 10% upon payment. The company determines the stage of completion of contracts by calculating the proportion that contract costs incurred for the work done to date bear to the latest estimated total contract costs.

(ii)   'Labour' includes $150,000 per annum cost of site supervision.

(iii)   At the end of each year of the first two years, inventory at a cost of $300,000 will be in store on the site. This cost is included in materials.

(iv)   Depreciation has been calculated for a full year. Plant and equipment lies idle for approximately one month of the year due to holidays.

(v)   Refers to depreciation of head office fixtures and fittings.

(vi)   All of the company's design costs and two-thirds of its costs of hiring and transporting equipment are applicable to the Yucca Island contract although the company has allocated all of these costs equally between the two contracts.

(vii)   One-quarter of the general administration costs can be charged to the developer.

(viii) Borrowing costs are not included in the above schedule as the company is not sure how to account for them.

The company expects to have the following draw down loan facilities in place at the start of 2010:

　　　　　8% bank loan repayable 20X3　　　$20m

　　　　　9.5% bank loan repayable 20X4　　$30m

The company expects to partly finance construction of Yucca Island using these existing borrowings. Draw downs are expected to occur as follows:

　　　　　1 January 20X0　　　$5m

　　　　　1 January 20X1　　　$15m

　　　　　1 January 20X2　　　$8m

Required

Calculate the estimated percentage stage of completion and profit to be recognised for each year of the Yucca Island contract. Explain your workings.

(15 marks)

24 Hackemov

Hackemov, a public liability company, operates a number of specialist sports goods shops. The appointment of a new CEO has resulted in a company reorganisation during its current financial year to 31 October 20X7. The following events affected the retail side of the company:

(i) On 15 October 20X7 the company accepted an offer for the sale of its North Plain shop which was well above its carrying value. However, the shop has been subject to a sudden surge resulting in a backlog of orders which it will not be able to complete until February 20X8. The prospective buyer does not intend to use the shop for sports goods and has therefore agreed to delay transfer of ownership of the shop until the backlog has been removed.

(ii) Following the Olympic Games in 20X6, the company's Downstream Plain shop noticed a large increase in sales of specialist long distance running shoes. Sales volume remained high as the manufacturer of the shoes offered a one year warranty on any manufacturing defects; extended to two years by Hackemov. During the six months to 31 October 20X7, Hackemov began to receive a number of complaints; not only concerning manufacturing defects but also personal injuries as a result of the defects.

Required

How should the above events be accounted for in Hackemov's financial statements for the year ended 31 October 20X6.

(15 marks)

25 Bald Hill

Bald Hill is an environmental protection company. On 1 November 20X0 the company purchased monitoring equipment for $960,000. It is estimated that the equipment will last for seven years, at the end of which it will be sold for $120,000. The company depreciates such equipment on a straight-line basis; although the government allows depreciation for tax purposes at 25% per annum on a reducing balance basis.

The company pays income tax at 30% and has forecast an annual profit before tax of $1.6m for the foreseeable future.

Required

Prepare Bald Hill's statement of profit or loss showing profit before tax, income taxes and profit after tax for the two years ended 31 October 20X1 and 20X2.

(15 marks)

26 Pearl Waters

Pearl Waters is a public liability company with a number of assets in its statement of financial position collectively referred to as 'property'. The properties are located in various parts of China. They have been acquired for a variety of reasons and this has led the CEO to believe they should be accounted for in different ways. The following is a summary of the company's property assets:

	Costs $m	
Wuhan	10	Land: acquired initially to build a manufacturing plant for use by the company's production division but directors are not sure whether to do this or to keep the land in its undeveloped state and to sell it when land values rise. Its current market value is $16m.

	Costs $m	
Nanchang	11	Buildings: a collection of buildings purchased by the company's property investment division to be sold as soon as possible in the ordinary course of business.
Lhasa	15	$15m represents the construction costs to date of a leisure complex being constructed for a client by the company's construction division.
Beijing	13	$13m represents the costs to date of the company's new head office.

Required

Explain how the above properties should be accounted for in Pearl Water's statement of financial position.

(15 marks)

Additional practice question

27 Pumice

On 1 October 20X5 Pumice acquired the following non-current investments:

- 80% of the equity share capital of Silverton at a cost of $13.6 million
- 50% of Silverton's 10% loan notes at par
- 1.6 million equity shares in Amok at a cost of $6.25 each.

The summarised draft statements of financial position of the three companies at 31 March 20X6 are:

	Pumice $'000	Silverton $'000	Amok $'000
Non-current assets			
Property, plant and equipment	20,000	8,500	16,500
Investments	26,000	nil	1,500
	46,000	8,500	18,000
Current assets	15,000	8,000	11,000
Total assets	61,000	16,500	29,000
Equity and liabilities			
Equity			
Equity shares of $1 each	10,000	3,000	4,000
Retained earnings	37,000	8,000	20,000
	47,000	11,000	24,000
Non-current liabilities			
8% loan note	4,000	nil	nil
10% loan note	nil	2,000	nil
Current liabilities	10,000	3,500	5,000
Total equity and liabilities	61,000	16,500	29,000

The following information is relevant:

(i) The fair values of Silverton's assets were equal to their carrying amounts with the exception of land and plant. Silverton's land had a fair value of $400,000 in excess of its carrying amount and plant had a fair value of $1.6 million in excess of its carrying amount. The plant had a remaining life of four years (straight-line depreciation) at the date of acquisition.

(ii) In the post acquisition period Pumice sold goods to Silverton at a price of $6 million. These goods had cost Pumice $4 million. Half of these goods were still in the inventory of Silverton at 31 March 20X6. Silverton had a balance of $1.5 million owing to Pumice at 31 March 20X6 which agreed with Pumice's records.

(iii) The net profit after tax for the year ended 31 March 20X6 was $2 million for Silverton and $8 million for Amok. Assume profits accrued evenly throughout the year.

(iv) An impairment test at 31 March 20X6 concluded that consolidated goodwill was impaired by $400,000 and the investment in Amok was impaired by $200,000.

(v) No dividends were paid during the year by any of the companies.

(vi) It is group policy to value the non-controlling interest at acquisition at its proportionate share of the fair value of the subsidiary's identifiable net assets.

Required

(a) Discuss how the investments purchased by Pumice on 1 October 20X5 should be treated in its consolidated financial statements. **(5 marks)**

(b) Prepare the consolidated statement of financial position for Pumice as at 31 March 20X6.

(20 marks)

(Total = 25 marks)

AIA May 2010

28 Toro

Toro is a company manufacturing transmission systems to the automotive industry. The company had experienced a period of rapid growth in the past however due to current economic conditions for the first time they are noticing a decrease in the number of orders being placed. This has led to the company reducing its cost base with the result that the remaining staff have found themselves under increasing pressure trying to deal with the work load. The company is in the process of finalising the financial statements for the year ended 31 March 2010 and have asked you to look at some outstanding issues with the company's non-current assets. You have been provided with the following information:

Land and building (extract)

The balance at 1 April 2009 is as follows:

		Land $000	Buildings $000
Offices			
	– valuation	135	524
	– accumulated depreciation	–	21

The depreciation policy is to write assets off over their estimated useful lives on a straight line basis with depreciation charged on a monthly basis. There has been no depreciation charged in the current year. Land and buildings are treated as one asset category but for revaluation purposes are treated separately. Valuations are carried out every three years and were last carried out on 31 March 2007. Toro does not make a transfer from the revaluation reserve to the retained earnings for additional depreciation.

Details of the revaluation reserve and estimated remaining useful life at 31 March 2007 are as follows:

Land	Buildings $000	Estimated useful $000	Life
Offices	56	53	50 years

(i)   At 31 March 2010 a valuation of all of Toro's land and buildings was carried out by a professionally qualified valuer. The results of the valuation are given below:

	Land $000	Buildings $000
Offices	120	400

This has not been recorded in Toro's accounting records.

The following information is also relevant:

On 30 June 2009 Toro entered into an agreement to sell one of its offices for $100,000. Details of the office premises were as follows:

	Land $000	Buildings $000
Valuation at 31 March 2007	26	56
Revaluation reserve at 31 March 2007	8	13
Accumulated depreciation at 31 March 2009	–	15
Estimated fair value at 30 June 2009	28	47

No adjustment has been made for this transaction in Toro's accounting records.

(ii)   At 1 April 2009 there was a balance of $150,000 deferred income relating to government grants. Of this $70,000 relates to plant and machinery that is being depreciated over a 10-year period on a straight line basis. These assets were acquired on 1 April 2006. The balance of $80,000 relates to a grant of $160,000 received from a regional development fund on 1 April 2008. The conditions of the grant were that employment levels at one of Toro's factories must be kept at or above an agreed level for a period of 24 months. Unfortunately, due to the decline in sales orders a number of workers were made redundant at the factory on 30 September 2009 and the number of qualifying employees fell below the agreed number. The company has not notified the government department responsible for awarding grant assistance of the breach of the grant conditions although news of the redundancies was reported in the local press. In the year ended 31 March 2009 $80,000 was deducted from the wages expense in the statement of profit or loss in respect of this grant.

(iii)   Included in the plant register are details of a warehouse that Toro built on some land it recently acquired. Toro had originally intended to use the warehouse in the course of its own business, however given the decline in sales the board agreed to rent out the property to a third party. The company entered into a 5 year rental agreement on 1 February 2010. The costs relating to this project are shown below.

	$
Land	40,000
Build cost	80,000
General overheads	20,000
Professional fees	15,000
Borrowing costs	5,000
Total costs	160,000

A valuer surveyed the building as part of the three-year valuation exercise at $240,000.

(iv) Toro has gained a reputation as being at the forefront of transmission system design in the automotive industry and has generated a significant proportion of its revenue by patenting technology it has developed in-house. Currently Toro is investing a considerable amount of time and money researching transmission systems for a new generation electric vehicle. The board believes because of increasing fuel costs and government intervention that by 2020 the electric car will be used for the majority of short journeys and are determined to keep their position as a market leader.

The following costs have been incurred:

In the year ended 31 March:	
2009 Researching new circuits for use in electric transmission systems (including staff costs of $60,000)	$130,000
2010 Designing new transmission system	$100,000
Developing and testing prototype	$120,000
Application for patent	$30,000

Toro treated the research costs incurred in 2009 as an expense in the statement of profit or loss however a note in the plant register suggests that the entry should be reversed in the year ended 31 March 2010 and that both the $130,000 and the current year's expenditure of $250,000 should be capitalised and matched with future revenues. The board is aware that their competitors are developing similar transmission systems but the development team is extremely confident that the system will be commercially successful.

Required

Show the entries needed to account for each of the above in the company's financial statements at the year end and explain fully to the finance director the reasons for your decision.

(marks will be allocated as follows:)

(i)	**(9 marks)**
(ii)	**(5 marks)**
(iii)	**(3 marks)**
(iv)	**(3 marks)**

(Total = 20 marks)

29 Pyne

(a) Due to ongoing problems with one of its suppliers Pyne Limited ('Pyne') acquired 70% of the ordinary shares of Syne Limited ('Syne') on 1 October 2007 in an attempt to secure future supplies. The retained earnings and share premium account of Syne at the date of acquisition were $300,000 and $1,000,000 respectively. The financial statements of the two companies at 30 September 2009 were as follows:

STATEMENT OF FINANCIAL POSITION AS AT 30 SEPTEMBER 2009

	Pyne $'000	Syne $'000
Non current assets		
Property, plant and equipment	10,000	4,000
Investment in Syne	2,400	–
	12,400	4,000
Current assets		
Inventories	1,800	1,200
Trade receivables	1,600	600
Cash and cash equivalents	200	400
	3,600	2,200
Total assets	16,000	6,200
Equity and liabilities		
Equity shares of $1 each	2,000	1,200
Share premium	1,200	1,000
Retained earnings	9,800	1,400
	13,000	3,600
Non current liabilities		
10% Debenture 2011-13	1,000	800
Current liabilities	2,000	1,800
Total equity and liabilities	16,000	6,200

STATEMENTS OF PROFIT OR LOSS FOR THE YEAR ENDED 30 SEPTEMBER 2009

	Pyne $'000	Syne $'000
Revenue	10,000	5,000
Cost of sales	(7,600)	(3,400)
Gross profit	2,400	1,600
Other income	240	–
Distribution costs	(500)	(100)
Administration expenses	(300)	(180)
Finance costs	(100)	(100)
Profit before taxation	1,740	1,220
Income tax expense	(500)	(400)
Profit for the year	1,240	820

You have been provided with the following additional information:

1.   The trade receivables of Syne at 30 September 2009 include $100,000 due from Pyne.

       However Pyne's corresponding trade payable is included in current liabilities as $80,000. The goods had been received at 30 September but the transaction had not been recorded in Pyne's records due to an administrative delay in processing the most recent delivery note.

2.   During the year the total sales value of goods transferred from Syne to Pyne was $700,000. The inventory of Pyne at 30 September includes goods bought from Syne for $200,000. Syne applied its normal mark up of 25% on the sale of these goods.

3.   On 1 January 2009 Syne sold a piece of equipment to Pyne for $230,000. Syne had purchased the equipment in 2004 for $400,000. The depreciation policy of both companies is to depreciate equipment over a total useful life of 10 years using the straight line method. When assets are transferred it is group policy to depreciate over the remaining useful life. A full year's charge is made in the year of acquisition and none in the year of disposal.

4.   At the date of acquisition the fair values were equal to their carrying amounts.

5.   A review of goodwill as at 30 September 2009 indicated that goodwill was impaired by $150,000.

6.   Syne paid a dividend of $240,000 to Pyne during the year.

7.   Pyne has a policy of accounting for any non-controlling interest as a proportion of the subsidiary's net assets.

Required

Prepare the consolidated statement of financial position as at 30 September 2009 and the consolidated statements of profit or loss for the year ended 30 September 2009.

(27 marks)

(b)   Pyne has three other major suppliers it deals with. During the year it purchased materials from Levee at a cost of $400,000. Levee has a 16% shareholding in Pyne and during the year had provided an unsecured loan at an interest rate of 10%. The loan was repaid in August 2009. A director of Levee, who is also a shareholder, sits on the board of Pyne and receives a remuneration of $15,000 for his duties.

       Pyne also purchased supplies of $200,000 from Devere and $300,000 from Vivre. There are no shareholdings between either of these two companies and the Pyne group although both companies also have commercial dealings with Syne.

Required

Explain how the above should be shown in the financial statements for the year ended 30 September 2009.

(3 marks)

(Total = 30 marks)

30 Ferrar

Ferrar plc is a public company whose principal business, until recently, was the manufacture of high quality door and window locks for the domestic market, however because of increased competition from overseas manufacturers the board of directors decided to expand their existing product range to include the manufacture of complete security systems suitable for both the domestic and commercial markets. This strategy required a significant investment in both new manufacturing equipment and staff development during the year ended 31 December 2009. Initial signs are that the decision appears to have been successful with revenues showing a 25% increase however the latest financial statements have just been published and the company's share price has fallen despite the stock market remaining stable. Understandably the board of directors is concerned by the market's reaction and has asked you to review the financial statements given below:

STATEMENT OF FINANCIAL POSITION AS AT 31 DECEMBER 2009

	2009 $000	2008 $000
Non current assets	43,000	19,700
Current assets		
Inventories	5,000	3,000
Trade receivables	8,300	6,000
Other receivables	500	600
Cash and cash equivalents	–	500
	13,800	10,100
Total assets	56,800	29,800
Equity and liabilities		
Equity shares of $1 each	10,000	8,000
Share premium	3,800	1,000
Retained earnings	8,200	6,500
	22,000	15,500
Non current liabilities		
10% Debenture 2011–13	10,000	10,000
11% Debenture 2015–17	10,000	–
Current liabilities		
Trade creditors	14,000	3,800
Other creditors	800	500
	14,800	4,300
Total equity and liabilities	56,800	29,800

STATEMENTS OF PROFIT OR LOSS FOR THE YEAR 31 DECEMBER 2009

	2009	2008
	$000	$000
Revenue	40,000	32,000
Cost of sales	30,000	23,000
Gross profit	10,000	9,000
Distribution costs	3,200	3,000
Administration expenses	1,300	1,000
Finance costs	2,200	1,000
Profit before taxation	3,300	4,000
Income tax expense	1,000	1,200
Profit for the year	2,300	2,800
Dividends paid	600	480

To finance the expansion the company successfully completed a 1 for 4 rights issue on 1 January 2009 at a price of $2.40. The market price at that date was $2.75.

Required

(a) Calculate the following six ratios for each of the two years ended 31 December 2009:

   (i)   Return on total capital employed
   (ii)   Gross profit percentage
   (iii)   Current ratio
   (iv)   Accounts receivable days
   (v)   Inventory days
   (vi)   Accounts payable days

   and comment on the changes in the company's results, as shown by the movement in these ratios, suggesting *two possible causes* for the change in each one.   **(18 marks)**

(b) Calculate the earnings per share for each of the years ending 30 September.   **(7 marks)**

(Total = 25 marks)

31 Convergence

As part of their convergence program the International Accounting Standards Board (IASB) and the US Financial Accounting Standards Board (FASB) recently announced that they are to harmonise the international accounting standards that deal with off-balance sheet activity in response to the recent financial crisis.

In the announcement Sir David Tweedie, chairman of the IASB, went on to explain that the fact that harmonising international accounting standards is such a complicated business is also what makes it necessary.

Required

(a) Explain what is meant by off-balance sheet finance and outline the particular problems it causes to users of accounting information.

(b) Evaluate how successful the IASB *Conceptual Framework for Financial Reporting* is in dealing with this area.

(10 marks)

32 Nemix

You have recently joined the staff of Nemix Plc, a company specialising in the extraction of on-shore heavy oils, and are assisting in the preparation of the financial statements for the year ended 30 September 2009. The financial controller has approached you concerned with the high level of lease payments being charged through the statement of profit or loss and has asked you to look into it. On further investigation it becomes apparent that your predecessor has failed to apply the principles of IAS 17 *Leases* and has treated all lease payments made in the year as expenses in the statement of profit or loss.

Your initial review has highlighted three leases where you believe the accounting treatment to be incorrect:

(i)   On 1 October 2008 Nemix entered into a non-cancellable five year operating lease for a machine valued at $200,000 which had an estimated life of twenty years. The terms of the lease were that Nemix paid six half yearly payments of $11,000 (1 October and 1 March) commencing on 1 October 2008.

(ii)   On 30 September 2008 Nemix entered into a five year non-cancellable finance lease for a high specification drill bit. The legal fees incurred in arranging the lease amounted to $3,000 and were settled in full on 30 September 2008. The cost price of the asset was $150,000 and the annual lease payments were $40,000 commencing on 30 September 2008. There is a secondary indefinite period to the lease which involves Nemix paying a nominal payment. Nemix plan to take advantage of this. The interest rate implicit is the lease is given as 16.88%. Nemix depreciate plant and equipment using the straight line method of depreciation over the assets useful life in accordance with IAS 16. The plant has a useful life of ten years with an expected scrap value of $13,000 at that date.

(iii)   On January 2009 Nemix entered into a sale and leaseback agreement to sell its head office to Finance Co. The property had a carrying value of $4.6m at that time and had a useful life of 25 years. Nemix immediately leased the property back for a period of 25 years for a payment of $300,000 per annum and was responsible for all on going maintenance to the building. The market value of the property at the date of sale and the present value of the minimum lease payments was $6.1m. (For the purpose of this exercise ignore the split between land and buildings.)

Required

Prepare a paper for the financial controller outlining the main requirements of IAS 17 and detailing how the two leases detailed in (i) and (ii) above should be accounted for in the financial statements for the year ended 30 September 2009. Also explain how any gain/(loss) on the sale and leaseback transaction described in (iii) should be dealt with.

(marks will be allocated as follows:)

(i)   **(4 marks)**

(ii)   **(8 marks)**

(iii)   **(3 marks)**

(Total = 15 marks)

Exam answer bank

1 Drill

(a) **Industrial ratios for Drill**

	20X4	20X3
Gross profit to sales	$\frac{7,500}{23,500} = 31.9\%$	$\frac{6,500}{20,500} = 31.7\%$
Operating profit to net assets employed	$\frac{2,500}{12,215} = 20.5\%$	$\frac{2,000}{9,740} = 20.5\%$
Operating profit to sales	$\frac{2,500}{23,500} = 10.6\%$	$\frac{2,000}{20,500} = 9.8\%$
Current ratio	8,700:3,600 = 2.4:1	5,790:2,400 = 2.4:1
Liquidity ratio	3,600:3,600 = 1.0:1	2,590:2,400 = 1.1:1
Average age of trade receivables	$\frac{2,400}{23,500} \times 365 = 37$	$\frac{1,800}{20,500} \times 365 = 32$
Average age of inventory	$\frac{4,150}{16,000} \times 365 = 95$	$\frac{2,850}{14,000} \times 365 = 74$
Interest cover	$\frac{2,500}{500} = 5$	$\frac{2,000}{300} = 6.7$
Net asset turnover	$\frac{23,500}{12,215} = 1.9$	20,500/9,740 = 2.1
Debt to equity	$\frac{5,500}{6,715} = 81.9\%$	$\frac{3,300}{6,440} = 51.2\%$

(b) The operating performance of Drill has improved in absolute terms with an additional $500,000 profit being achieved in 20X4 when compared to 20X3 but the level of profit achieved per $ of sales is below that of the industry average at both the gross profit and operating profit levels. The company should review its product pricing policy with the average for the industry and also review its cost management in an effort to achieve at least the industry norm. In particular the directors should instigate a review of the administration costs which have increased by over 15% compared with an increase in distribution costs of only just over 5%. The directors should also review their distribution policy; the dividends paid during the year account for 65.6% of the profit for 20X4 while the distribution in 20X3 was only 41.2% of the profit for the year.

The liquidity of the company does not appear to give cause for concern and providing the industry as a whole is not experiencing cash flow problems then the cash position of Drill would appear to be adequate. There is a need however to monitor both the credit control and inventory control procedures to ensure the planned expansion of the working capital is planned and not a result of weak controls and/or management.

These developments could affect the longer term liquidity position of the company and need to be reviewed as a matter of urgency.

The overall financing of the company is the major cause for concern and will affect the directors' decision on the new debenture issue. The level of debt finance compared with equity finance is now well above the industry average, having been below the average in 20X3. The new issue of debentures would make this position even worse and could affect the perception of the company by trade and loan creditors.

With the level of dividends currently being paid it may be possible to meet the finance requirements for the improvements through a share rights issue. This is something that the directors should consider in reaching their decision.

I suggest that a cash management review be undertaken which should include a forecast of the cash flows for the company over the next few years. It may also be useful for the directors to review the company's statement of cash flows to assess the level of cash generated by the company's operating activities.

The overall conclusion is likely to be that the issue of more debt finance would not be a good idea and that alternatives should be investigated. Eg share issue.

2 Current and deferred tax

(a) Current taxes should be recognised in the period in which the taxes are incurred. Assets for taxes relating to a loss in the period should only be recognised if the loss can be recovered against the current tax of a previous period. Taxes should be charged/credited to profit or loss unless matching to other comprehensive income or equity is appropriate.

(b) The deferred tax provision should be calculated on the full provision basis. A deferred tax liability is recognised as the amount of income taxes payable in future periods in respect of taxable temporary differences. These temporary differences include differences from the revaluation of non-current assets. The provision should not be based on discounted figures.

A deferred tax asset requires the existence of probable taxable profits and should be measured as the amount of income taxes recoverable in the future. Such assets can be in respect of, (1) deductible temporary differences, (2) the carry forward of unused tax losses, and, (3) the carry forward of unused tax credits.

Deferred tax is measured at tax rates expected to apply when the deferred tax liability is settled or an asset is realised. The deferred tax should be reported in the same financial statement as the transaction or event to which they are related.

3 Jackie and Jeff

(a) While related party transactions may be a normal feature of commerce and business the existence of related party relationships may affect the reported profit or loss of entities involved in such transactions. Related parties may enter into transactions that would not be undertaken by unrelated parties. The existence of the relationship may also affect transactions between a reporting entity and unrelated parties.

Related party disclosures highlight the possibility that the entity's financial performance and financial position might have been affected by existence of related parties, with transactions not reflecting the values that would have been part of a normal arms length transaction. IAS 24 therefore requires disclosure of the nature of any related party relationships and details of transactions and outstanding balances between related parties.

(b) Jackie and Jeff are related parties of Coupland because they are directors. Graham is a related party of Passmores as he is a director. If Jeff and Graham are close family members (they can influence each other in company dealings) then:

(i) Jeff would be a related party of Passmores.

(ii) Graham would be a related party of Coupland.

(iii) Coupland and Passmores would be related parties of each other as they are controlled by close family members.

It would be necessary to assess whether Jackie and Graham are close family members to further classify related parties.

4 Petiam

(a) While Petiam may be correct in arranging the bond to have cash outflows which are in line with the relevant cash inflows of the business project the entity should not account for the bond based on these cash flows. The charges to profit or loss for each of the three years should include a fair allocation of the finance charges that are incurred on the bond. This includes the discount given on the bond at its initial issue. This discount will add to the overall finance cost of the bond and should not be allocated to the period in which the bond is repaid. The bond will then be recognised in the statement of financial position at the end of each year at its amortised cost, being the initial funds received plus finance charges recognised less the payments of the nominal interest. The calculations and measurements in part (b) show how this would affect the finance charges and the level of liability recognised during the life of the bond.

(b) Allocation of finance charges ($20m + (3 × $.5m) = $21.5m) based on implicit rate of interest.

	Opening Balance $'000	Effective rate of interest $'000	Nominal interest paid $'000	Closing Balance $'000
20X5	30,000	6,000	(500)	35,500
20X6	35,500	7,100	(500)	42,100
20X7	42,100	8,400*	(500)	50,000
		21,500		

* There is a rounding difference of $20,000

		$m
Finance charges:	20X5	6.0
	20X6	7.1
	20X7	8.4

Liability at 31 December 20X6 $42.1m

5 Hoodurz

(a) STATEMENT OF PROFIT OR LOSS AND OTHER COMPREHENSIVE INCOME FOR THE YEAR ENDED 31 MARCH 20X6

	Continuing operations $'000	Discontinued operations $'000	Total $'000
Revenue	1,640	370	2,010
Cost of sales (150 + 960 −160)	(725)	(225)	(950)
Gross profit	915	145	1,060
Distribution costs (420 + 20)	(380)	(60)	(440)
Administrative expenses (210 + 16 + 20)	(191)	(55)	(246)
Finance income	75	–	75
Finance costs	(10)	–	(10)
Profit before tax	409	30	439
Income tax expense	(60)	(14)	(74)
Profit after tax	349	16	365
Other comprehensive income			
Revaluation surplus	80	–	80
Total comprehensive income	429	16	445

(b)   STATEMENT OF FINANCIAL POSITION AS AT 31 MARCH 20X6

	$'000	$'000
Non-current assets		
Property, at valuation		280
Plant and Equipment, at cost (550 – 150)	400	
Plant and equipment, accumulated depreciation (220 – 15)	(205)	195
Investments		560
		1,035
Current assets		
Inventory	160	
Trade receivables (470 – 70)	400	560
Assets held for sale		215
		1,810
Equity		
Ordinary shares		600
Revaluation surplus		80
Retained earnings (see working)		345
		1,025
Non-current liabilities		
Loans	100	
Provisions for warranty claims (205 + 16)	221	321
Current liabilities		
Tax (74 – 14])	60	
Bank overdraft (80 – (10))	90	
Trade payables (260 – 60)	200	
Accrual (staff bonus)	40	390
Liabilities held for sale (60 + 14)		74
		1,810

Working

	$'000
Retained earnings b/f	80
Profit for the year	365
Dividends paid (65 + 35)	(100)
Retained earnings c/f	345

6 Revenue recognition

Case 1

Revenue should be recognised notwithstanding that physical delivery has not been completed so long as there is every expectation that delivery will be made.

The specific goods are available to the customer for delivery at any time.

The selling company appears to have no further significant performance obligations.

Provided the buyer specifically acknowledges the use of the free storage facilities is at their request revenue should be recognised at date of billing not date of delivery.

Case 2

Revenue should be recognised when the service is completed.

The service is considered completed when the related advertisement appears before the public.

The total revenue should be allocated over the twenty four months of the contract not the twenty three months when payment is received.

This may require recognition of prepayments.

Case 3

When goods have been supplied subject to conditions, the conditions must be met before revenue is recognised.

In these circumstances revenue is normally recognised when the buyer accepts delivery, and installation and inspection is complete.

However revenue may be recognised on delivery if:

- Installation is simple; or
- Inspection is only performed to finalise the contract price.

7 Locator Group

This question aims to assess the candidate's ability to prepare a statement of financial position and explain the adjustments necessary to comply with IFRS. Main topic: IFRS 5 Non-current Assets held for sale and discontinued operations, IAS 1 _Presentation of financial statements_ (syllabus sections 11.1 and 11.3).

LOCATOR GROUP
STATEMENT OF FINANCIAL POSITION AS AT 31 OCTOBER 20X6

			€m	€m
(a)	ASSETS			
	Non-current assets			
	Property, plant and equipment	(b1)	12.3	
	Intangible assets		4.3	
	Investments	(b2)	2.3	
				18.9
	Current assets			
	Inventories		1.2	
	Trade receivables		4.8	
	Non-current asset held-for-sale	(b3)	0.2	
	Cash		1.8	
				8.0
	Total assets			26.9
	EQUITY AND LIABILITIES			
	Capital and reserves			
	Share capital	(b4)	7.6	
	Retained earnings	(b5)	5.0	
				12.6
	Non-current liabilities			
	4% loan note	(b6)	7.2	
	6% redeemable preference shares	(b4)	0.4	
				7.6

	€m	€m
Current liabilities		
Trade and other payables	4.9	
Current portion of 4% loan note (b6)	1.8	
		6.7
Total equity and liabilities		26.9

(b) (1) IFRS5 requires that non-current assets held-for-sale should be measured at the lower of their carrying amount and fair value less selling costs.

	€K
Cost of photo-embossing machine	500
Depreciation to date 2 × €100K p.a.	200
Carrying amount	300
Net fair value	200
Write off to profit or loss	100

PPE is therefore 12.6 – (carrying amount at time of reclassification) 0.3 = 12.3

(2) Investment property is revised to fair value (as allowed by IAS 40). As the change is to 'fair value' (as opposed to 'revaluation') the change is recognised in profit or loss for the year.

(3) The photo-embossing machine is now shown in current assets at fair value (see 1) as it is held-for-sale.

(4) As the preference shares can be redeemed at the holder's discretion there exists a contractual obligation. They must therefore be accounted for as a financial liability (IAS 32).

(5) Retained earnings

	€m
Figure per draft statement of financial position	4.3
PPE: loss on write down to fair value (see 1)	(0.1)
Investment in property: increase to fair value (see 2)	0.3
Proposed equity dividend (declared after reporting date and therefore excluded from financial statements– IAS 10)	0.5
	5.0

(6) The current portion of the long-term loan note (9.0/5) has been included in current liabilities.

(7) The purpose of IAS 1 *Presentation of financial statements* is to aid comparability. Disclosure requirements are detailed in the section headed 'Structure and Content'. The standard favours (their use is not obligatory) a presentation which, inter alia, moves the emphasis away from the Anglo-Saxon concentration on equity to a presentation which identifies 'total assets' and 'total equity and liabilities'.

8 Jupiter Aviation

This question aims to test the candidate's understanding of the accounting for leases by a lessee.
Main topic: *Accounting for leases* (syllabus sections 11.3 and 11.4).

MEMORANDUM

To: Jupiter Aviation
From: Arthur
Date: November 20X6
Subject: Accounting implications of jet leasing

As Jupiter Aviation is established as a partnership, there is no overriding regulation governing the style and content of the annual accounts. In principle, therefore both treatments are possible.

Sue's proposal

Sue's proposed accounting treatment is the appropriate method for what is referred to as an operating lease. The contract is accounted for, in substance, as a rental agreement. Rentals are expensed as incurred. There would therefore be no effect on Jupiter's statement of financial position and consequently no effect on gearing.

Alex's proposal

Alex's proposal is more complicated in its effect and refers to what is known as a 'finance lease'. In substance, such a lease would transfer substantially all the risks and rewards of ownership to Jupiter. The test would be whether the present value of the minimum lease payments is substantially equivalent to the fair value of the jet. This is the case (Note 1).

Normal accounting practice (ie if Jupiter was an entity required to use IAS 17 *Leases*) would be for the lease to be accounted for in accordance with its commercial substance. In effect, a loan has been raised to acquire the asset and would be accounted for by including the capital element of the future lease payments in the statement of financial position as a liability (Note 2). The corresponding mirror image of this liability would be the jet accounted for as a non-current asset and depreciated (Note 3).

Impact on financial statements

As you can see lease capitalisation results in higher overall expense initially. Over the four years however, the interest charge diminishes and in years 3 and 4 overall expense is lower.

As mentioned earlier, lease capitalisation results in the recognition of an asset and a liability. As the lease is an interest bearing liability it will increase Jupiter's gearing initially from 0.5:1 to 1.375:1 (Note 5). Of course, as you can see in (2) this liability diminishes over the years and so will the gearing ratio.

Cash flow

Jupiter's cash flows will be the same however the partnership decides to account for the transaction. As there is no regulation governing accounting for partnerships, the decision on how to account for the transaction should therefore be based on a consideration of transparency versus expediency.

Notes

1   Fair value of jet: €3.5m

       PV of future lease payments

       €1m + (€1m × 2.487) = €3.487m

2

Year	Opening liability €m	Annual rental (in advance) €m	Net opening liability €m	Implicit interest @ 9.7% €m	Closing liability €m
1	3.500	1	2.500	0.243	2.743
2	2.743	1	1.743	0.169	1.912
3	1.912	1	0.912	0.088	1.000
4	1.000	1	–	–	–

3   Asset on statement of financial position at start of year 1 at cost = €3.5m
Assuming the economic life is 4 years amortisation = €875k p.a.

4   Impact on profits

Year		Operating lease €m			Finance lease €m
1	Rent	1.0		Amortisation	0.875
				Finance charge	0.243
					1.118
2	Rent	1.0		Amortisation	0.875
				Finance charge	0.169
					1.044
3	Rent	1.0		Amortisation	0.875
				Finance charge	0.088
					0.963
4	Rent	1.0		Amortisation	0.875
				Finance charge	–
					0.875
	Total	4.0			4.000

5   Impact of lease capitalisation on gearing:

Before lease capitalisation the gearing is (debt) €2m : (partners capital) €4m = 0.5:1.
After lease capitalisation the gearing will be (debt) €5.5m : (partner's capital) €4m = 1.375:1.

9 Infinite Leisure Group

The question aims to assess the candidate's understanding of the methods and problems associated with the revaluation approach. Main topic: IAS 16 *Property, plant and equipment* (syllabus section 11.1).

IMPACT OF REVALUATION MODEL ON INFINITE LEISURE'S FINANCIAL STATEMENTS – SOO NIGHTCLUB

	SFP Asset €m	Statement of profit or loss Expense €m	SFP Revaluation surplus €m	SPLOCI Other comp. income €m
Plant and equipment				
1 Nov X1 Cost	0.240			
Dep. 02	0.040	0.040		
31 Oct X2	0.200			
Dep. 03	0.040	0.040		
31 Oct X3	0.160			
1 Nov X3 Revaluation (€0.42m × 4/6)	0.120		0.120	0.120
	0.280			
Dep. 04 (€0.42m/6)	0.070	0.070		
31 Oct X4	0.210		0.120	
Dep. 05	0.070	0.070		
31 Oct X5	0.140		0.120	
Sale	0.100			
Loss on sale	0.040	0.040		
Transfer to realised reserves			0.120	
31 Oct X6	–			

	SFP Asset €m	Statement of profit or loss Expense €m	SFP Revaluation surplus €m	SPLOCI Other comp. income €m
Property				
1 Nov X1 Cost	10.000			
Dep. 02 (€7m/50)	0.140	0.140		
31 Oct X2	9.860			
Dep. 03	0.140	0.140		
31 Oct X3	9.720			
1 Nov X3 Revaluation (€4m + €9m)	3.280		3.280	3.280
	13.000			
Dep. 04 (€9m/50)	0.180	0.180		
31 Oct X4	12.820		3.280	
Dep. 05	0.180	0.180		
31 Oct X5	12.640		3.280	
Sale	9.000			
Loss on sale	3.640	3.640		
Transfer to realised reserves			3.280	
31 Oct X6	–		–	

Note. Infinite Leisure did not become committed to a plan to sell Sooz until January 20X6. If it had been so committed prior to November 20X5, IFRS5 *Non-current Assets Held for Sale and Discontinued Operations* would have become active for the year ended 31 October 20X5.

10 Werit group

This question aims to assess the candidate's ability to apply the requirements of IAS 37 to a business-type scenario. Main topic: IAS 37 *Provisions, contingent liabilities and contingent assets* (syllabus section 11.2).

(a) The Werit group obviously has a contractual obligation to Sean Head of €500,000 as at 31 October 20X6 and a reliable estimate can be made of the amount involved; thereby satisfying two of IAS 37's three recognition criteria. The third, however, may be problematic. Is it *probable* that the group will be required to settle the obligation?

The directors must take all the facts into account. Sean Head has provided 'fine service to both the group and the industry'. If they consider that re-employment is probable then no liability exists and the group will account for payments as they are made.

If directors believe it unlikely that re-employment will happen then a liability does exist at 31 October 20X6.

(b) As stated by the agency's lawyers, the probability of a future transfer of economic benefits (ie future cash outflow) is low. Also, there is no present obligation and a reliable estimate cannot be made. Therefore a provision should not be recognised.

However, as there is a lawsuit in progress, a possible obligation exists which should be disclosed by way of a note, unless the chance of occurrence is remote; in which case no disclosure is required.

(c) This identifies the inconsistencies in IAS 37. It is probable that an outflow will take place and the amount can be measured with sufficient reliability; but is there a present obligation? There is clearly not a *legal* obligation so is there a *constructive* obligation?

A simple intention to make payment for the Christmas party is, by itself, not enough to justify making a provision. There must be an obligation to do so. This obligation must have arisen as a result of a past event.

So, is the fact that Christmas parties are annual events, a 'past event' which gives rise to a present obligation? A constructive obligation is one which is established by an established pattern of past practice and, as a result, has created a valid expectation on the part of others; such that the agency would have no **realistic** alternative but to go ahead with the payment. On the basis that the party is to be spectacular, an annual event and aimed at creating goodwill with both staff and clients, *it would appear that a provision is required.*

However, if it could be contended that the party could be cancelled without harming the reputation or prospects of the agency then *realistically* the agency could do so *and it would appear that a provision is not required.* Also, the past event and present obligation must be linked; ie they should refer to the same circumstance. In this case, the present obligation is in respect of the *future* Christmas party not the past.

In the event the decision may be made on the basis of whether the amount of €100,000 is material or not.

11 Government grants

This questions examines a candidate's ability to discuss and apply the requirements of IAS 20 Accounting for government grants and disclosure of government assistance (syllabus section 11.2).

(a) Kun is correct in that IAS 20 requires that grants for the purchase of non-current assets should be recognised over their useful lives.

IAS 20 permits two approaches:

(1) Write-off the grant against the cost of the non-current asset and depreciate the reduced cost figure. If the country's law requires that such assets are shown at cost, this approach would not be available.

(2) Treat the grant as deferred income and transfer a proportion each year to offset the higher (than in 1) above) depreciation charge.

Calculation

		€
–	Plant and equipment (75,000 – 30,000)	45,000
	Less depreciation (45.000/5)	(9,000)
		36,000
–	Deferred income	30,000
	Written into income (30,000/5)	(6,000)
		24,000
	Plant and equipment	75,000
	Depreciation (75,000/5)	15,000)
		60,000

(b) **Amy** is incorrect to suggest that the whole amount is included in income. It is not actually a 'windfall gain'. The accruals concept would require that the grant is recognised in income in such a way that it is matched with the expenditure (ie depreciation) towards which it contributes.

Suki is incorrect to suggest that the whole amount is included in equity. The grant is not part of an equity transaction; ie it is received from an external source.

12 Blissopia

This question examines candidates' ability to apply the requirements of IAS 36 to a case involving a cash generating unit (syllabus section 11.2).

memo

To: Directors
From:
Date:
Re: Impairment review of the Eden Hotel

Relevant standard IAS 36 *Impairment of assets*

Under the standard, assets should be carried at no more than their recoverable amount. In the case of the Eden, 'assets' refers to the whole division – as a 'cash generating unit' (CGU).

The 'recoverable amount' of the hotel is the higher of its fair value less costs of disposal ($3.95m) and its value-in-use ($3.52m) ie $3.95m.

The carrying amount of the CGU is $5.98m ie book value of assets $4.83m plus goodwill on acquisition $1.15m (Cost $6.90m – fair value of assets acquired $5.75m).

The Eden is therefore impaired by $2.03m. This amount must be written off as an expense to profit or loss and allocated to the net assets as follows:

1   To assets with specific impairment
2   Goodwill
3   Other assets pro rata

Using this approach the impairment of $2.03m will be allocated to assets as follows:

In above order	Carrying value 31.10.X7	Impairment	New carrying value
Trade receivables	0.37	0.03	0.34
Vehicles	0.09	0.03	0.06
Goodwill	1.15	1.15	–
Land and buildings₁	3.18	0.65	2.53
Plant and equipment₁	0.81	0.17	0.64
Cash (not impaired)	1.12	–	1.12
Trade payables (not impaired)	(0.74)	=	(0.74)
	5.98	2.03	3.95

1   The remaining impairment $0.82m is allocated to land and buildings and plant and equipment on a pro rata basis; ie:

Land and buildings $3.18/3.99 \times 0.82 = 0.65$
Plant and equipment $0.81/3.99 \times 0.82 = 0.17$.

13 Jack Matelot

This case study question examines the application of IAS 11 (syllabus section 11.4), IAS 37 and IAS 10 (syllabus section 11.2), IAS 1 (syllabus section 11.3), and IFRS 5 (syllabus section 11.1).

(a)   **Step 1**   The first task is to estimate whether each contract will make an overall profit or loss at the end of each year:

	Barcelona €m	Faro €m	St Malo €m
20X6			
Contract value			15.00
Estimated total costs to complete			12.00
Estimated overall profit			3.00
20X7			
Original contract value	12.24	10.00	15.00
Revision	0.76		
	13.00		
Estimated total costs to complete	(15.50)	(7.00)	(12.00)
Estimated overall profit/(loss)	(2.50)	3.00	3.00

Step 2   Assuming the above outcomes have been estimated reliably, the next task is to estimate the percentage completion of each contract's contract activity; using the value of work certified as the basis (note IAS 11 requires this calculation to be made on a cumulative basis; ie 'to date'):

	Barcelona	Faro	St Malo
20X6			
Work certified to date/contract value			40%
20X7			
Work certified to date/contract value	n/a (losses)	5%	60%

Step 3 We can now produce the figures for inclusion in the 20X7 statement of profit or loss (remembering that the St Malo contract will have had profits recognised in 20X6; and IAS 11 requires use of a cumulative calculation):

	€m	€m	€m
Revenue to date (ie to 31 October 20X7)	6.50	0.50	9.00
Less revenue recognised in 20X6	–	–	6.00
Revenue for 20X7	6.50	0.50	3.00
Profit/loss for 20X7			
Barcelona (full loss provided)	2.50		
Faro (5% = work not sufficiently advanced)		–	
St Malo (to date: 60% × €3.0m)			1.80
Less 2006 (40% × €3.0m)			1.20
			(0.60)
Cost of sales for 20X7	9.00	0.50	2.40

Being:

Cost of sales to date (9.00 – 1.80) =	7.20
Less cost of sales 20X6 (6.00 – 1.20) =	(4.80)
	2.40

Step 4 The statement of financial position figures can now be calculated:

The gross amounts due from customers for contract work must be shown as an asset.

Costs incurred to date	11.50	1.50	10.5
Recognised profits/(losses) to date	(2.50)	–	1.8
Progress billings to date	(5.0)	(0.5)	(8.67)
Amount due from customers	4.0	1.0	3.54

Accounts receivable (this account shows the amount of cash actually outstanding and receivable from the client).

Progress billings	5.00	0.50	8.76
Cash received to date	(3.76)	–	(7.50)
	1.24	0.50	1.26

Contracts in progress at cost (this account shows the cost of work-in-progress not yet charged to cost of sales)

Costs incurred to date	Dr	11.50	1.50	10.50
Less cost of sales to date	Cr	(9.00)	(0.50)	(7.20)

(b) IAS 37 aims to ensure that only genuine obligations are recognised in the financial statements. At first sight, the repair cost of €150,000 looks as if it should be a provision in the accounts of JTM as there is a past event, which has created a legal or constructive (not clear which it is in this case) obligation, and the amount can be estimated reliably. However, as the repair is covered by insurance, an outflow of resources will not take place. The amount and circumstances should therefore be disclosed as a contingent liability as JTM would have to settle privately if the insurance company refused to pay up.

(c) The planned disposal of the property would be disclosed in the 20X7 accounts as being held-for-sale under IFRS 5. The disposal price of €5m could possibly affect the amount shown as it is an adjusting event under IAS 10 providing further evidence of conditions existing at the reporting date.

IFRS 5 would require the property to be measured at the lower of carrying amount and fair value less selling costs and disclosed separately on the face of the statement of financial position.

The dividend of €1m is a non-adjusting event but must be disclosed in notes to the accounts.

Whether the acquisition of MoriceMarinas should be recognised depends upon the circumstances. It is an event after the reporting period and so its recognition depends (under IAS 10) upon whether the conditions existed at that date. If the acquisition had been 'agreed' in that a purchase agreement has been signed then it may qualify for recognition as a provision under IAS 37 as an obligation may have existed at that date. If it is simply an agreement between the directors to acquire the company then it would not be recognised under IAS 37 as the condition (ie an obligation) would not have existed at that date.

14 Accounting regulation

This question requires students to demonstrate an understanding of the arguments for the regulation of financial accounting, the application of 'regulation' to related party transactions and the difficulties of achieving 'regulation' in the context of interim financial reports (syllabus sections 11.1, 11.2 and 11.3).

The following is written from the point of view of a briefing paper which opposes the 'freemarket' approach:

(a)   The absence of effective regulation has been blamed for many failures in accounting; such as the Wall Street Crash in 1929, the GEC/AEI debacle of the 1960s and more recently the WorldCom/Enron catastrophe. Advocates of regulation propose that:

      (i)   Regulation leads to uniformity (or at least standardisation) which in turn provides for greater comparability between entities.

      (ii)   A 'free' market for information cannot be efficient and such inefficiencies lead to the provision of information which may therefore not be the best available.

      (iii)   Without adequate regulation there is no way of knowing whether the information investors are using is in any way fraudulent. Investors and other users need to be able to have faith in the information.

      (iv)   Regulation is needed to protect those who have less power (to demand information) than others.

(b)   Related party transactions are a normal feature of business. However, a company may enter into the transaction on more favourable terms than it would have done had the party not been related. Regulation is necessary so that these transactions are fully disclosed thereby providing transparency in the financial statements figures. Without such disclosure it is possible that investors may not truly interpret the financial performance and position of the business.

Related party transactions would include sales, purchases, asset transfers, remuneration payments, goods transfers, loans etc by a company to or from any party which (IAS 24 *Related party disclosures*):

      (i)   Has control or joint control over the company

      (ii)   Has significant influence over the company

      (iii)   Is key management personnel of the company

      (iv)   Is a member of the same group

      (v)   Is an associate or joint venture of the company

      (vi)   Is, together with the company, a joint venture of a third party

(vii) Is a joint venture of a third party when the company is an associate of the same third party, or vice versa

(viii) Is a post employment benefits plan for the benefit of employees of the company or an entity related to the company

(ix) Is controlled or jointly controlled or significantly influenced by an individual who controls, jointly controls, significantly influences or is key management personnel of the company.

(x) Where a member of key management personnel controls, jointly controls, significantly influences or is key management personnel of the company.

(c) The regulation is not as strict as for annual reporting owing to the nature and timeliness of the report. Indeed, entities are not required (by IFRS) to produce such reports. Where entities do produce such reports:

(i) IAS 34 does not identify which entities should produce a report (although it encourages publicly traded entities to do so).

(ii) The standard does not establish how frequently the reports should be produced (although it encourages publicly traded entities to at least produce half-yearly reports).

(iii) The standard does not legislate for how soon after the interim reporting period the reports should be published (although for publicly traded entities it suggests no later than 60 days after the end of the period).

15 Cher Price

This question requires the calculation of diluted earnings per share to comply with IAS 33 (syllabus section 11.5).

(a) *Method of financing expansion*

	Ordinary shares £'000	Convertible loan stock £'000
Profit attributable to ordinary shareholders:		
Average after-tax profit	2,000	2,000
Increase due to return on planned investment (£3m × 25%)	750	750
Additional interest net of tax relief	–	(84)
	2,750	2,666
Preference dividend (£1m × 5%)	(50)	(50)
Interest saved on conversion		
Original issue unchanged (£1m × 4%)	40	
Original issue plus new issue (£4m × 4%)		160
Tax relief on interest saved	(12)	(48)
	2,728	2,728

	Ordinary shares	Convertible loan stock
Number of ordinary shares		
Original number in issue	5,000	5,000
New issue (£3m/£1.50)	2,000	
Conversion (£1m × 125/100)	1,250	
Conversion (£4m × 125/100)		5,000
	8,250	10,000
Diluted earnings per share	0.33p	0.27p

(b) It would appear that the company's performance would be better represented by a financing using ordinary shares. However, the apparent dichotomy between the conversion rate of 125 shares per £100 stock and the current share price of £1.50 needs to be addressed; ie at present the company's actions mean that, by using loan stock, the lender (upon conversion) would receive

(£3m × 125/100) 3,750,000 shares which, with a market value of £1.50 each, would be worth £5,625,000! Clearly the company must consider whether the conversion rate of 125 shares per £100 stock needs to be significantly reduced.

16 Tree

This question requires a knowledge of IFRS 5 and its application to the case study (section 11.1).

Step 1 As with all assets, the supermarket must be tested for impairment.

There is a possible indication of impairment as the supermarket is only breaking even in the period after the year end.

Its carrying amount (€30m) must be compared with its recoverable amount (€20m)*.

Its new carrying amount would therefore normally be €20m with €10m written off to profit or loss.

*The higher of net realisable value (€16m) and value-in-use (€20m)

Step 2 The further issue here is, should the supermarket be treated as being an asset 'held-for-sale'?

An asset is held-for-sale' if its carrying amount is recovered principally through sale rather than continuing use*:

Criteria (as at 31 October 20X7)	Circumstances	
Commitment to a plan to sell?	Approved on 31 August 20X7; ie before the year-end.	✓
Active programme to find a buyer and complete the sale process	On 31 August 20X7, the finance director noted he may have found a buyer. On 10 November 20X7, it was announced that the company was in active negotiations to sell.	✓
Supermarket must be actively marketed at a reasonable price in relation to its fair value.	As above. Disposal looks highly probable. See below – €16m looks like a 'reasonable price'.	✓
Disposal should be expected to occur within one year.	By 31 December 20X7	✓
Should be no indication of any plan to significantly change the plan to sell.	None given in question. Supermarket is only breaking even after 1 November 20X7 so none is likely.	✓

Branch Ltd should be dealt with in the 31 October 20X7 accounts as held-for-sale.

* Sale price is €16m and value-in-use is €20m. Common sense would seem to suggest that Tree plc should therefore hold on to the supermarket. However, owing to a change in the 'group's management strategy', the decision has been made to sell.

Step 3 As the supermarket is to be treated as 'held-for-sale' it must be reported at the lower of carrying amount (€20m) and fair value less costs of disposal (€16m).

Step 4 The supermarket asset will be written down by €14m. This impairment loss will be allocated to any individually reported assets in accordance with IAS 36.

The supermarket (non-current asset) will not be depreciated.

After the above 'allocation' any individually reported assets will be shown separately in the statement of financial position.

17 Ofkin Company

This extensive case study question primarily examines the requirements of IAS 7 Statement of Cash Flows (Section 11.5) as far as the standard relates to the affairs of a single company. To produce the statement of cash flows, the question also requires a basic understanding of:

Section 11.2   IAS 16 *Property, plant and equipment*, IAS 36 *Impairment of assets*, IAS 38 *Intangible assets*, IAS 37 *Provisions, contingent liabilities and Contingent assets.*

Section 11.3   IAS 12, *Income taxes.*

Section 11.4   IAS 17: *Finance leases*, IAS 32 *Financial instruments.*

Part (b) requires a knowledge of:

Section 11.2   IAS 10 *Events after the reporting period*, IAS 37 *Provisions, contingent liabilities and Contingent assets.*

Section 11.5   IAS 7 *Statement of cash flows.*

(a)

OFKIN GROUP
STATEMENT OF CASH FLOWS
FOR THE FINANCIAL YEAR ENDED 2 FEBRUARY

	Workings	20X8 €m
Cash flows from operating activities		
Operating profit before interest	1	34.25
Depreciation	Per question note 1	3.86
Profit on disposal of property, plant and equipment	2	(0.68)
Increase in inventories	Per statement of financial position	(2.23)
Increase in trade and other receivables	Per statement of financial position	(7.64)
Increase in trade and other payables	Per statement of financial position	6.43
Increase in provisions for future rentals	Per statement of financial position and question note 6	4.33
		___
Cash generated from operations		38.32
Corporation taxes paid	4	(12.39)
Net cash from operating activities		25.93

	Workings	20X8 €m
Cash flows from investing activities		
Proceeds from sale of property, plant and equipment.	Per question note 1	1.50
Acquisition of property, plant and equipment.	Per question note 1	(17.96)
Purchase of investments.	3	(2.70)
Net cash from investing activities		(19.16)
Cash flows from financing activities		
Proceeds from issue of share capital	Per question note 8 and working note 7	0.11
Proceeds of unsecured bank loans	Per statement of financial position	10.03
Repurchase of own shares	Per question note 8	(1.80)
Interest paid on bond	Per working note 5	(2.40)
Payment of finance lease liability	Per working note 6	(2.31)
Finance charge on lease	Per working note 6	(0.89)
Interest received	Per question note 10	0.18
Dividends paid	Per question note 9	(10.44)
Net cash from financing activities		(7.52)
Net decrease in cash and cash equivalents		(0.75)
Opening cash and cash equivalents	See analysis of net debt	5.00
Closing cash and cash equivalents	See analysis of net debt	4.25

Analysis of net debt for information only

	February 20X7 €m	Cash flow €m	Other non-cash changes €m	January 20X8 €m
Cash and short-term deposits	7.23			7.39
Bank overdrafts	(2.23)			(3.14)
Cash and cash equivalents	5.00	(0.75)		4.25
Unsecured bank loans	–	(10.03)	–	(10.03)
Corporate bond	(33.94)	–	(0.99)	(34.93)
Finance leases	(8.00)	2.31		(5.69)
Total net debt	(36.94)	(8.47)	(0.99)	(46.40)

Workings

1   To calculate 'operating profit before interest' we must reconstitute the retained earnings figure. We must do this because the question does not provide us with a statement of profit or loss.

Retained earnings		€m
As at 2 February 2007	Per statement of financial position	17.06
Purchase of ordinary shares for cancellation	Per question note 8. See also working note 7	(1.80)
Dividends paid	Per question note 9	(10.44)
Profit for the year	BALANCING FIGURE	16.82
As at 2 February 2008	Per statement of financial position	21.64
Profit for the year	**From above**	16.82
Add:		
Tax expense reported in statement of profit or loss	Per working note 4 below and per question note 4	13.33
Finance charge in respect of bond	Per working note 5	3.39
Finance charge in respect of finance lease	Per working note 6	0.89

		€m
		34.43
Deduct:		
Interest received	Per question note 10	0.18
Profit before interest		34.25

2 Profit on disposal of property, plant and equipment

		€m
Cost of disposals	Per question note 1	2.51
Depreciation on disposals	Per question note 1	1.69
Carrying value of disposals		0.82
Proceeds	Per question note 1	1.50
Profit on disposal		0.68

3 Due to the circumstances of no quoted price and unreliability of measurement, the investment must be carried at cost. The increase in carrying value must therefore be all as a result of a purchase during the year.

4 Corporation tax and deferred tax.
We could just use the figures given in note 4 of the question to compile the statement. However, students may want to produce a reconciliation so that they are comfortable with the figures. This is as follows:

Corporation tax:		€m
Tax paid	Per question note 4	12.39
Liability carried forward	Per statement of financial position	5.32
		17.71
Liability brought forward	Per statement of financial position	5.98
Expensed to statement of profit or loss		11.73
Deferred tax:		
Reduction in asset assumed this is all written off to statement of profit or loss	Per statement of financial position	1.60
Tax expense reported in statement of profit or loss	Per question note 4	13.33

5 The increase in the carrying value of the bond is made up as follows:

Opening balance @ 10% per annum €33.94m × 10% (to statement of profit or loss)	Per statement of financial position and question note 5	3.39
Interest paid €40m × 6%	Per question note 5	2.40
Increase in carrying value of bond	Per statement of financial position	0.99

6 The finance lease will have been accounted for as follows:

Qtr	Liability at start	Rental paid at start of quarter	Liability during the quarter	Finance charge @3.51% per quarter	Liability at end of quarter
	€m	€m	€m	€m	€m
1	*8.00	0.80	7.20	0.25	7.45
2	7.45	0.80	6.65	0.23	6.88
3	6.88	0.80	6.08	0.21	6.29
4	6.29	0.80	5.49	0.20	*5.69
		3.20		0.89	

* per statement of financial position
Payment of finance lease liability is therefore €3.20m − €0.89m = €2.31m

7	**For information only**	Share capital	Share premium	Capital redemption reserve fund
		€m	€m	€m
	Opening balance per statement of financial position	2.61	0.60	0.38
	Issue of new shares per question note 8	0.01	0.10	
	Shares purchased for cancellation per question note 8. Note: the cash consideration of €1.80m is written off retained earnings.	(0.15)		0.15
	Closing balance per statement of financial position	2.47	0.70	0.53

Note: No action is required as a result of Note 2 of the question. This is acceptable practice.

(b) (i) Normally, the inventory figure in the accounts would be adjusted to cost of €3m as the inventory's net realisable value has turned out to be higher than cost. If this was the case, then 'operating profit before interest and tax' and 'increase in inventories' would both increase by €1m. There would be no change in 'net cash from operating activities' as, of course, there is no cash effect.

However, the question explicitly states that there has been a 'sudden change in demand'. It appears therefore that the fact this event was 'sudden' means it would not provide further evidence of conditions existing at the end of the reporting period (IAS 10).

Overall, it would appear no action is required in the statement of cash flows.

(ii) The proposed dividend cannot be recognised in the accounts as a liability as it does not meet IAS 37's criteria for an obligation. Therefore there is no impact on the statement of cash flows.

(c) IAS 7 would 'normally' require that the investments are dealt with as changes in 'investing activities' rather than as changes in 'cash and cash equivalents' as they mature more than three months from the date of acquisition.

However, IAS 7 only offers guidance in this respect and the final treatment must rest upon the approach taken to treasury management by the company. It may not be commercially appropriate or reflect underlying economic reality to treat them as being for investing purposes.

18 Smallman

This question requires an application of the requirements of IAS 8 *Accounting policies, changes in accounting estimates and errors* (syllabus section 11.1) to a company undertaking a construction contract for the first time. It therefore requires an understanding of which events constitute a change in accounting policy and knowledge of how to apply the standard in practice to the statement of profit or loss and retained earnings figures.

It also requires a basic knowledge of the requirements of IAS 11 *Construction contracts* (syllabus section 11.4).

(a) The company has changed its accounting policy for construction contracts from 'profit-to-date' to 'percentage of completion'. However it should not count as a change in policy as in the past the event was immaterial in 20X6 (profit from contract in 20X6 was only 2% of total profit).

(b) STATEMENT OF PROFIT OR LOSS

	Workings	20X7 €m	20X6 €m
Sales	W1	53.70	37.50
Cost of goods sold	W2	(45.05)	(26.05)
Profit before tax		8.65	11.45
Income tax	W4	(2.59)	(3.46)
Profit for the year		6.06	7.99
Retained earnings			
Opening retained earnings:			
As previously reported [20X7:€1.40m + €8.30]		9.70	1.40
Adjustment for prior period error			
[€0.45m – tax €0.14m]	W4	(0.31)	
As restated		9.39	1.40
Profit for the year	See above	6.06	7.99
Closing retained earnings		15.45	9.39

Workings

		20X7	20X6
1	*Sales*		
	Per draft accounts	56.20	37.50
	less Construction sales using old policy	(10.00)	
		46.20	
	add Construction sales using new policy W3	7.50	
	Adjusted sales figures	53.70	37.50
2	*Cost of goods sold*		
	Per draft accounts	45.50	25.60
	less Construction costs using old policy	(6.00)	
		39.50	
	add Construction costs using new policy W3	6.00	
		45.50	25.60
	Inventory adjustment See question	(0.45)	0.45
	Adjusted cost of goods sold figure	45.05	26.05
3	*Construction contract:*		
	Contract value	25.0	
	Estimated costs to complete	(20.0)	
	Estimated total profit	5.0	

The question does not indicate any problems therefore it is appropriate to use the percentage of completion method:

Construction sales will be recognised as €25m × 30% = €7.50m

Construction cost of goods sold will be recognised as €20m × 30% = €6m

		20X7	20X6
4	*Income tax*		
	Per draft accounts	3.20	3.60
	Net reduction in sales [€2.50 × 30%]*	(0.75)	
	Inventory adjustment [€0.45 × 30%]	0.14	(0.14)
	Adjusted income tax figure	2.59	3.46

*Note that costs have not changed therefore it is assumed that all of the net change in sales will result in a tax saving.

19 Cumulus

This question requires an understanding of IAS 40 Investment property (section 11.2). It is important to demonstrate an understanding not only of how to account for properties which *do* satisfy the criteria for treatment as investment properties but also how to account for those which *don't*.

(i) This will be classed as an investment property (and thereby dealt with under IAS 40).

It qualifies as an investment property because the company is not in the hotel business. Cash flows from the hotel will therefore be independent of the company's other cash flows; ie cash flows are from rental rather than from the company's ordinary course of business.

IAS 40 states that investment property includes property that is being constructed for future use as an investment property.

IAS 40 allows measurement at either:

- Depreciated cost (under IAS 16 with disclosure similar to IAS 40) or
- Fair value (with unrealised holding gains and losses taken to income).

(ii)   This will be classed as an investment property under IAS 40.

If, at the end of the reporting period, the directors haven't been able to decide what to do with the land (i.e. whether to use it in the business or hold it for sale) then it is deemed to be held for capital appreciation.

As before, IAS 40 allows either:

- Depreciated cost (under IAS 16 with disclosure similar to IAS 40) or
- Fair value (with unrealised holding gains and losses taken to income).

(iii)   This is definitely not an investment property as future cash flows will be generated in the ordinary course of business.

IAS 40 does not therefore apply.

The property must be accounted for under IAS 16 Property, Plant and Equipment (using either depreciated cost: cost model or revalued amount: revaluation model (with unrealised holding gains and losses recognised in other comprehensive income).

20 Apollo[21]

This case study question examines the understanding and application of IAS 18 (section 11.1) in part (i); IAS 37 and IAS 16 (section 11.2) in part (ii); IAS 38 (section 11.2) and IAS 1 (section 11.3) in part (iii) and IFRS 5 (section 11.1) in part (iv). Candidates are expected to be able to explain their adjustments.

DRAFT STATEMENT OF PROFIT OR LOSS			Adjusted Statement of profit or loss	Explanation
		€m	€m	
Sales		24.00		
Solar panels	(i)	– 0.30		1
Advertising revenue	(i)	– 0.30		2
Equipment held for customers	(i)	–		3
			23.40	
Cost of goods sold		13.70		
Depreciation	(ii)	– 0.60		4
			13.10	
Gross profit			10.30	
Finance cost re provision	(ii)		– 0.32	5
Training costs	(iii)		– 3.00	
Research and development costs	(iii)			
			– 0.63	

DRAFT STATEMENT OF PROFIT OR LOSS		€m	Adjusted Statement of profit or loss €m	Explanation
Administration and distribution overheads		6.90		
	(iv)	− 0.20	− 6.70	8
Equipment impairment	(iv)		− 1.00	9
Amended loss for the period			− 1.35	

Explanations

1   As the installation is a significant part of the contract (14.3% of total costs), this should be accounted for using the percentage of completion method. A proportion of the sales value should be carried forward to be recognised when installation takes place next year; ie €0.2m/ €1.4m × €2.1m = €0.30m.

  If installation had been straightforward (and insignificant) then it may have been possible to recognise all revenue on delivery – but this is not the case with this contract.

  Also the amount involved can be reliably measured as it has all been received in advance.

  Costs f €1.2m can be left in cost of sales as they represent the cost of work done to date.

2   It is incorrect to recognise all of the advertising revenue in 20X8 as much of the service has not yet been provided. Revenue should be recognised over the whole length of the contact (18 months) and not just the period that is paid for (16 months – with 2 months being free). Revenue must be reduced by the amount relevant to future periods; ie 15mths/18mths × €0.36m = €0.30m.

3   This treatment is acceptable. It is the customer who has decided to delay delivery and take advantage of Apollo[21]'s free facility. Apollo[21] has no further performance duties.

4   The company is quite correct to have set up a provision and associated asset in 20X7. The transfer of economic benefits was virtually certain, a reliable estimate had been made of the amounts involved (there is no indication in the question that the estimated expenditure in 20X8 was inaccurate) and the company appears to have a constructive obligation (it is a keen promoter of the environment and a public announcement has been made supported by the whole board). It therefore complies with IAS 37.

  However, its calculation of the asset and liability is incorrect. This is a significant expenditure lasting over two years and therefore requires the use of present values.

  The asset/liability at 31 October 20X7 should therefore have been €5.45m as follows:

	€m
Instalment: 31 October 20X8 €2m × 0.9433	1.89
31 October 20X9 €4m × 0.8900	3.56
	5.45

  Under IAS 16 depreciation does not begin until the asset is available for use. In this case this will not be until 31 October 20X9. Therefore charging depreciation in 20X8 is incorrect and €600,000 must be deducted from cost of sales.

5   The use of present values results in the liability increasing over time. This 'unwinding' of the discount represents a finance cost to be shown in the statement of profit or loss:

	€m
PV at 31 October 2008 of instalment due 31 October 20X9 (€4m × 0.9433)	3.77
Liability at 1 November 20X7	5.45
Instalment paid 31 October 20X8	(2.00)
Liability at 31 October 20X8	(3.77)
Finance cost (unwinding discount)	0.32

6   To be recognised as an intangible asset under IAS 38, items must be identifiable, controlled by the entity and be able to provide future economic benefits. There is nothing in the question to suggest that the company can control the future actions of its staff therefore the costs cannot be capitalised. The €3m incurred this year will be written off and the €7m carried in the statement of financial position must be dealt with as a prior period adjustment under IAS 1.

7   It is correct to write off the costs of €0.58m in 20X7 as the IAS 38 recognition criteria such as technical feasibility and intention to complete have not been demonstrated.

However it is incorrect to treat all of the 20X8 costs as an asset. Technical feasibility, intention to complete, sales ability and reliable measurement of development costs were not demonstrated until 15 August 20X8. Therefore €0.63m should be written off.

The post 15 August 20X8 costs of €0.34m can be capitalised. However, amortisation will not begin until the Daystar project is complete and producing economic benefits; i.e. from January 20X9.

8   This still qualifies as a non-current asset available for sale under IFRS 5 because, despite being more than a year since the company first made a decision to sell, the sale fell through due to circumstances outside the control of the company.

Under IFRS 5 non-current assets available-for-sale must not be depreciated even if still used. Depreciation charged in 20X7 from June to October (€0.10m) must therefore be adjusted as a prior period error under IAS1. Depreciation of €0.20m for 20X8 must be added back.

9   Under IFRS5 the asset must be shown at the lower of carrying amount (€1.30m after adding back depreciation in 8 above) and fair value* (€0.30m). An impairment write off of €1.00m must be made.

* Assume fair value [FV] is net realisable value [NRV] (price that would be received to sell an asset in an orderly transaction between market participants at the measurement date in accordance with IFRS 13). IAS 36 which requires assets to be shown at their recoverable amount (ie higher of NRV and value in use) does not apply to IFRS 5.

21 Glyn and Scott

This question involves the conversion of a partnership into a limited company (section 11.3). It requires knowledge of how to close down the books of the partnership and how this is reflected in the opening statement of financial position of the new company.

(a)

Realisation a/c

	$'000		$'000
Property	750	Trade payables	124
Fixtures, fittings & equip	25	Bank loan	250
Motor vehicles	147		374
Inventory	32		
Trade receivables	96		
Short term deposit	88	Floors⁴All 'consideration'	1,500
	1,138		
		Scott a/c Vehicle taken over	30
Partners accounts:			
Profit on conversion:			
Glyn (2) 511			
Scott (1) 255			
	766		
	1,904		1,904

Partners' accounts

	Glyn $'000	Scott $'000		Glyn $'000	Scott $'000
Realisation a/c		30	Balances b/d:		
			Capital	300	200
Floors⁴All 'allocation of consideration':			Current	176	131
Shares 2:1	600	300			
Debentures 3:2	240	160	Realisation a/c		
			Profit on conversion	511	255
Cash a/c settlement	147	96			
	987	586		987	586

Cash a/c for information			
	$000		$000
Balance b/d	43	Partners' accounts final settlement	
Floors⁴All	200	Glyn	147
		Scott	96
	243		243

Floors⁴All a/c for information			
	$000		$000
Realisation account	1,500	Partners' accounts allocation of shares and debentures:	
		Shares	900
		Debentures	400
		Cash account	200
	1,500		1,500

(b)

Floors⁴All Pty. Ltd.
Statement of Financial Position
As at 1 April 20X9

	Note	$'000	$'000
Non-current assets			
Goodwill	1		561
Property at valuation			1,000
Fixtures, fittings and equipment at valuation			20
Motor vehicles at valuation			93
			1,674
Current assets			
Inventory		32	
Trade receivables		80	
Short term deposit		88	
			200
Total assets			1,874
Current liabilities			
Trade payables		124	
Bank overdraft		200	
			324
Non-current liabilities			
Bank loan		250	
2% Debentures		400	
			650
Total liabilities			974
Ordinary shares of $1 each			900
Total capital and liabilities			1,874

Note 1

	$'000	$'000	$'000
Purchase consideration			1,500
Fair value of net assets acquired:			
Non-current			
Property	1,000		
Fixtures, fittings and equipment	20		
Motor vehicles	93		
		1,113	
Current			
Inventory	32		
Trade receivables	80		
Short-term deposit	88		
		200	
Non-current liabilities			
Bank loan		(250)	
Current liabilities		(124)	
			(939)
Goodwill			561

22 $Link Provision

This question requires knowledge of IFRS 8 (syllabus section 11.5). IFRS 8 was published in November 2006 and although its effective date was 1 January 2009 early adoption by companies was encouraged.

(a)   IFRS 8 defines an operating segment as a component of the company whose operating results are regularly reviewed by the entity's 'chief operating decision maker' to make decisions about resources to be allocated to the segment and assess its performance. The segment information is therefore based on the way in which the company is actually managed. As $Link Provision's entire scope of operations concerns one type of service 'contract logistical services' it would be inappropriate to produce a segmental report based on its type of business.

The company is actually organised on a geographical basis and therefore it will produce a segment report based on its geographical segments. The UK will comprise one segment (with 68% of revenue). The other four geographical areas are equivalent in terms of revenue and therefore each produce 8% of the company's revenue. None of them therefore meets the criteria (>10%) for being disclosed as an individual segment. Unless there are compelling reasons (ie two or three of the other segments may be aggregated if they have similar economic characteristics which are different to the other segments – eg the company must consider how similar the risks and rewards associated with France/Spain and Germany are compared with Central and Eastern Europe) it is likely the other four segments will comprise a second segment 'Rest of Europe'. However, IFRS 8 allows separate disclosure of each of the segments if management believes that this information would be useful to used of the financial statements.

IFRS 8 applies to entities whose equity or debt securities are publicly traded. The question does not say whether $Link Provision is such an entity but any company voluntarily providing segmental information must do so by complying with IFRS 8.

Segmental information must be based on the information actually provided to management for decision making purposes. This means that amounts (such as profit, total assets and total liabilities) will not necessarily be measured in the same way as the amounts reported in the financial statements.

(b) IFRS 8 adopts a 'managerial' approach rather than the 'risks and rewards' approach adopted by IAS 14. The board should take this into accounts when considering the new internal reporting system. The reportable segments will be those used for internal management purposes.

Also impacting on the structure of the internal reporting system will be:

- Analyses of revenues and certain non-current assets are required in two geographical segments; 1, 'company's country of domicile' (UK) and 2, 'all other foreign countries' (by individual country if material) irrespective of the company's organisation.

- Although Link Provision provides only one type of service, information is required about that service.

- There is a requirement to disclose information about transactions with major customers (10% or more of the entity's revenue)

- The segment information is not required to be prepared in accordance with the company's accounting policies adopted in its financial statements (unlike IAS 14). If the internal reporting system adopted different policies reconciliations would then be necessary in the company's financial statements reconciling the segment information with the accounts.

23 Sky Construction

This question requires an understanding of the requirements of IAS 11 (section 11.4) concerning the identification of costs to be accounted for as construction costs. In this respect it also requires knowledge of IAS 23 *Borrowing costs* (section 11.2).

The first step is to calculate whether the contract will make an overall profit. This is achieved by calculating the costs which are correctly attributable to the contract under IAS 11.

	Note	20X0 $m	20X1 $m	20X2 $m
Labour	i	4.65	13.95	12.40
Materials	ii	6.58	17.20	19.22
Depreciation of plant and equipment	iii	1.10	1.10	1.10
Depreciation of fixtures and fittings	iv	–	–	–
Design	v	4.40		
Hire and transport of equipment	vi	0.35	0.98	0.67
General administration	vii	0.40	0.40	0.40
Borrowing costs	viii	0.45	1.78	2.49
Total costs incurred $89.62		17.93	35.41	36.28
Total profit to be recognised $10.38m	ix			
Percentage stage of completion (%)		20.0	39.5	40.5
Profit to be recognised each year ($m)		2.08	4.10	4.20

Note. The retention of 10% will have an impact on the amount outstanding from the developer and will have no effect on the calculation of revenue.

(i) All labour costs are correctly attributable to the contract.

(ii) Materials must be adjusted by the inventory £300,000 in store at the end of each year.

(iii) Depreciation has been adjusted for the month plant and equipment is lying idle; although logically correct, such an adjustment would depend upon its significance.

(iv)   Not allowed as contract costs unless they can be allocated on a rational basis. There is no evidence of this in the question.

(v)   The schedule shows design costs of $2.20m but the question tells us that all design costs are applicable to the Yucca Island contract and should not therefore have been allocated equally between the two contracts; ie total costs of $2.20m × 2 = $4.40m should be allocated to the Yucca Island contract and in the first year.

(vi)   As in v above, total hire and transport costs are $1.50m × 2 = $3.00m. The question tells us that 2/3 of these are applicable to the Yucca Island contract; ie 20X0 $2m × .26/1.50 = $0.35m, 20X1 $2m × .74/1.50 = $0.98m, 20X2 $2m × .50/1.50 = $0.67m

(vii)   Administration costs can only be included if they can be rationally allocated to the contract or can be recovered from the customer; $1.60m × ¼ = $0.40mpa

(viii) Borrowing costs may be capitalised on the basis that they meet the criteria as set down in IAS 23. The company has obtained draw down facilities totalling $50m but cannot directly attribute any of the amounts borrowed to the Yucca Island contract and so must apply the 'capitalisation rate'; ie the weighted average of the borrowing costs applicable to the borrowings outstanding during each year.

$$\frac{(8\% \times 20) + (9.5\% \times 30)}{50 \qquad\qquad 50} = 8.9\%$$

Interest =	20X0 $5m × 8.9% =	$0.45m
	20X1 $20m × 8.9% =	$1.78m
	20X2 $28m × 8.9% =	$2.49m

(ix)   Calculated as $100.00m – $89.62m. Note the 10% retention has no impact on the amounts shown as revenue.

24 Hackemov

This question requires an understanding of the circumstances by which a non-current asset may be treated as held for sale under IFRS 5 *Non-current assets held for sale and discontinued operations* (syllabus section 11.1) and the extent to which a company may be liable for warranty and personal injury claims under IAS 37 *Provisions, contingent liabilities and contingent assets* (section 11.2).

(i)   For a non-current asset to be 'held-for-sale' it must be available for immediate sale in its present condition. This does not apply to the North Plain shop as its 'present condition' includes a backlog of orders which it must complete before a transfer of ownership can take place.

The shop should be treated like any other item of property, plant and equipment; i.e. it should not be shown separately and should be depreciated in the normal way.

(ii)   Manufacturing defects:

Assuming that these complaints are found to be justified, any returns made within a year of purchase must be at the manufacturer's expense. Hackemov will simply act as an agent between customer and manufacturer with the only financial statement effect being for any fee received as a result of handling the defects.

Hackemov cannot avoid bearing the cost of replacing any shoes returned within the second guarantee year. It must make a provision for these based upon its experience during the first year.

If the complaints are found to be unjustified then no action will be required.

Personal injuries:

Hackemov's lawyers must be consulted and the extent of its liability established. It is likely that if personal injury liability is established then the manufacturer will be liable for all claims. Hackemov would not then need to make a provision. However, the nature of the contract between Hackemov and the manufacturer will have to be examined before any firm decision can be made.

25 Bald Hill

This question requires an understanding of the deferred tax calculations required by IAS 12 *Income taxes* using the liability method.

The first step should be to calculate the timing differences and tax effects:

			For information				
Year ended 31 October	20X1	20X2	20X3	20X4	20X5	20X6	20X7
	$000	$000	$000	$000	$000	$000	$000
Depreciation 1	120	120	120	120	120	120	120
Tax based depreciation 2	240	180	135	101	76	57	51
Timing difference	120	60	15	–19	–44	–63	–69
Tax at 30%	36.0	18.0	4.5	–5.7	–13.2	–18.9	–20.7
Cumulative timing difference	120	180	195	176	132	69	–
Tax at 30%	36.0	54.0	58.5	52.8	39.6	20.7	–

Note. The above figures will be shown as deferred tax liabilities in the statement of financial position

The second step is to calculate the tax payable:

			For information				
Year ended 31 October	20X1	20X2	20X3	20X4	20X5	20X6	20X7
	$000	$000	$000	$000	$000	$000	$000
Profit before tax	1.600	1.600	1.600	1.600	1.600	1.600	1.600
Add depreciation	120	120	120	120	120	120	120
	1,720	1,720	1,720	1,720	1,720	1,720	1,720
Less tax based depreciation	(240)	(180)	(135)	(101)	(76)	(57)	(51)
	1,480	1,540	1,585	1,619	1,644	1,663	1,669
Tax payable @ 30%	444.0	462.0	475.5	485.7	493.2	498.9	500.7

Step three is to show the profit for the year after tax:

			For information				
Year ended 31 October	20X1	20X2	20X3	20X4	20X5	20X6	20X7
	$000	$000	$000	$000	$000	$000	$000
Profit before tax	1,600	1,600	1,600	1,600	1,600	1,600	1,600
Income tax	444.0	462.0	475.5	485.7	493.2	498.9	500.7
Deferred tax	36.0	18.0	4.5	–5.7	–13.2	–18.9	–20.7
	480.0	480.0	480.0	480.0	480.0	480.0	480.0
Profit after tax	1,120	1,120	1,120	1,120	1,120	1,120	1,120

1 Depreciation for financial statements:
$960,000 – $120,000 = $840,000/7 = $120,000

2 Tax based depreciation (using reducing balance):
20X9: $960,000 × 25% = $240,000
20X0: $720,000 × 25% = $180,000
and so on.

26 Pearl Waters

This question requires an understanding of IAS 40 *Investment property* (section 11.2). In particular, which type of properties are/are not covered by its provisions.

Wuhan — As the directors are undecided about the use to be made of the property, IAS40 requires it be dealt with as investment property held for capital appreciation; ie the company can choose to use either initial cost or a fair value model. If the company chooses to use fair values then it must be applied to all investment properties and the fair value increase must be dealt with in profit or loss.

Nanchang — These assets have been purchased with the express intention of resale and should be accounted for under IAS2 Inventories; i.e. at cost plus attributable overheads.

Lhasa — As the property is being constructed on behalf of a third party client it must be accounted for under IAS11 Construction Contracts; ie based upon the stage of completion to date whereby a proportion of overall profit may be recognised if the outcome can be foreseen with reasonable certainty.

Beijing — The property is being developed for use as the company's head office and therefore for administrative purposes. The asset must be dealt with under IAS16 Property, Plant and Equipment; ie at cost or at a revaluation. If revaluation is used the asset must be shown at its fair value less any subsequent depreciation and accumulated impairment losses. Fair value must be reliable and any increase in fair value is taken to revaluation reserve not income.

27 Pumice

(a) The acquisition of an 80% holding in Silverton can be assumed to give Pumice control. Silverton should therefore be treated as a subsidiary from the date of acquisition and its results consolidated from that date.

As Silverton is being treated as a subsidiary, the investment in loan notes is effectively an intra-group loan. This should be cancelled on consolidation, leaving the remaining $1m of Silverton's loan notes as a non-current liability in the consolidated statement of financial position.

The shares in Amok represent a 40% holding, which can be presumed to give Pumice 'significant influence', but not control. Amok should therefore be treated as an associate and its results brought into the consolidated financial statements using the equity method.

(b) PUMICE GROUP
CONSOLIDATED STATEMENT OF FINANCIAL POSITION AT 31 MARCH 20X6

	$'000
Non-current assets	
Property, plant and equipment (20,000 + 8,500 + 1,800 (W3))	30,300
Goodwill (W4)	3,600
Investment in associate (W5)	11,400
Investments – other (W8)	1,400
	46,700
Current assets (15,000 + 8,000 – 1,000 (W2) – 1,500 (intragroup))	20,500
Total assets	67,200
Equity and liabilities	
Equity attributable to owners of the parent	
Share capital (parent)	10,000
Retained earnings (W7)	37,640
	47,640
Non-controlling interest (W6)	2,560
	50,200
Non-current liabilities	
8% loan note	4,000
10% loan note (2,000 – 1,000 (W8))	1,000
Current liabilities (10,000 + 3,500 – 1,500 (intragroup))	12,000
Total equity and liabilities	67,200

Workings

1 Group structure

```
              Pumice
        80%  /      \  40%
    Silverton        Amok
```

2 Unrealised profit

	$'000
Sale of goods to Silverton	6,000
Cost to Pumice	(4,000)
Profit	2,000
50% still in inventory	1,000

DR Retained earnings/CR Inventories

3 Fair value adjustments

	Acquisition date $'000	Movement $'000	Reporting date $'000
Land	400	–	400
Plant	1,600	(200)	1,400
	2,000	(200)	1,800

4 Goodwill

	$'000	$'000
Cost of investment		13,600
Non-controlling interest (20% × 12,000)		2,400
		16,000
Less: fair value of net assets acquired:		
Share capital	3,000	
Pre-acquisition retained earnings (8,000 – 1,000)	7,000	
Fair value adjustments: land	400	
plant	1,600	
		(12,000)
Goodwill		4,000
Impairment to date		(400)
Carrying value		3,600

5 Associate

	$'000
Cost of investment ($6.25 × 1.6m)	10,000
Share of post-acquisition profit (8,000 (note (iii) × 6/12) × 40%)	1,600
	11,600
Less impairment	(200)
Carrying value	11,400

6 Non-controlling interest

	$'000
Silverton – net assets	11,000
Fair value adjustments (W3)	1,800
	12,800
Non-controlling share 20%	2,560

7 Group retained earnings

	Pumice $'000	Silverton $'000	Amok $'000
Per statement of financial position	37,000	8,000	20,000
Additional depreciation (W3)		(200)	
Unrealised profit ((6,000 – 4,000) /2)	(1,000)		
Pre-acquisition retained earnings (W4)	–	(7,000)	(16,000)*
	36,000	800	4,000
Group share: 800 × 80%	640		
4,000 × 40%	1,600		
	38,240		
Impairment: Silverton	(400)		
Amok	(200)		
	37,640		

* (20,000 – (8,000 × 6/12))

8 Investments

	$'000
Pumice – per statement of financial position	26,000
Investment in Silverton	(13,600)
Investment in Amok	(10,000)
Intra-group loan note	(1,000)
Other investments	1,400

28 Toro

This question examines the candidates' ability to apply the principles of IAS 16, IAS 20, IAS 37, IAS 40, IAS 38 and IAS 23 (syllabus section 11.2) to account for a variety of non-current asset transactions.

(i)   Before we can adjust for the revaluation at 31 March 2010 the sale of the office must be dealt with.

(a)   Calculate depreciation from 1 April 2009 to date of sale on 30 June 2009 (3 months)

	Land $'000	Buildings $'000
Valuation	26	56
Depreciation (56/50×3/12)	–	0.28

(b)   Calculate gain on sale

Consideration		100
Carrying value		
Valuation (26 + 56)		
Accumulated depreciation (15 + 0.28)		
		66.72
Gain on sale		33.28

Debit bank	100.00	
Debit acc. Depreciation	15.28	
Credit Office		82.00
Credit Gain on sale		33.28

The revaluation surplus in respect of the office which will be shown in the statement of changes to equity under revaluation reserve may be transferred directly to retained earnings when the surplus is realised (IAS 38 para 87).

(c)   Calculate depreciation charge for year (buildings only).

	Offices $'000
Valuation at 1 April 2009	524
Asset sold	(56)
Carrying Value	468
Useful life	50
Depreciation charge (468/50)	9.36

(d)   Incorporated year end revaluation

$'000	Net carrying value	Valuation 31 March 2010	Gain/ (Loss)
Land			
– valuation(135 – 26)	109	120	11
Buildings			
– valuation(524 – 56)	468.00		
– depreciation (21 + 0.28 – 15.28 + 9.36)	(15.36)		
	452.64	400	(52.64)

The revaluation surplus should be recognised as other comprehensive income and credited to the revaluation (IAS 16 para 39). Any loss on revaluation should be set against any credit balance on the revaluation reserve from a previous revaluation.

	Land $'000	Buildings $'000
Revaluation reserve at 31 March 2007	56	53
Transfer to retained earnings	(8)	(13)
Revaluation gain/(loss)	11	(40)*
Revaluation reserve at 31 March 2010	59	–

*However once the revaluation reserve has been eliminated any remaining loss must be debited to profit or loss ($52.64 – 40 = 12.64).

(ii) The treatment of government grants is covered by IAS 20 *Accounting for government grants and disclosure of government assistance*.

(a) Grant relating to assets.

Toro should continue to transfer the balance on the deferred income account to profit or loss over the remaining useful life of the assets. The assets were purchased 1 April 2006 and had a useful life of 10 years. The balance of $70,000 at 1 April 2009 should be recognised as income over the remaining seven years as long as all conditions attached to the grant are met.

DEBIT Deferred income (statement of financial position) $10,000
CREDIT Government grant (statement of profit or loss and $10,000
  other comprehensive income)

(b) Grant relating to employment.

Toro breached the conditions of the employment related grant in September 2009 when as a result of a redundancy programme employee numbers fell below the agreed level. In the year ended 31 March 2009 Toro appear to have treated the grant correctly by setting up a deferred income account for the total grant in the Statement of Financial Position.

DEBIT   Cash $160,000
CREDIT   Deferred Income $160,000

The grant condition was an agreed level of employee numbers for a period not less than 24 months therefore at 31 March 2009 12 months had passed so 50% of the grant was credited to the statement of profit or loss to match the grant against the related costs. The balance in relation to this grant was $80,000 at the 31 March 2009.

DEBIT   Deferred Income $80,000
CREDIT   Government grant (SOCI) $80,000

It is difficult to determine the accounting treatment necessary in 2010 without fully ascertaining the reaction of the government department to the breach of the condition and the exact amount of repayment required. If full payment of the grant is required this should be dealt with in accordance with IAS 37 *Provisions, contingent assets and contingent liabilities* and a provision set up for the full amount along with the necessary disclosure.

DEBIT   Deferred Income $80,000
DEBIT   Statement of profit or loss and other comprehensive income $80,000
CREDIT   Provision for repayment $160,000

The provision would be eliminated when repayment is made.

DEBIT   Provision for repayment $160,000
CREDIT   Cash $160,000

It may be that the grant would be partially granted on the basis of the time period during which the conditions had been met in this case 18 months (3/4 of $160,000 = $120,000 would be credited to the statement of profit or loss and other comprehensive income over the life of the grant and a provision for the repayment of $40,000 created).

IAS 20 para 32 states that when a grant becomes repayable it should be accounted for as an accounting estimate and not a material error and therefore should not be treated as a prior year adjustment.

(iii) The warehouse was originally intended for Toro's own use in which case the principles of IAS 16 would apply. However since the property has now been rented to a third party the property would be classified as an investment property and the principles of IAS 40 would apply. Initially this would mean that the property would be recognised at cost (para 20). The initial costs of the property, with the exception of the general overheads which are not direct costs, would be capitalised. IAS 23 (revised) states that borrowing costs incurred in the construction of certain assets should be capitalised. Toro should capitalise costs of $140,000. Thereafter IAS 40 allows the choice of either:

(1) The cost model – property is held at cost and depreciated under IAS 16 OR;

(2) Fair value model.

Assuming the fair value model is applied, at 31 March the property would be included at its fair value of $240,000. The gain of $100,000 would be credited to profit or loss in the statement of profit or loss and other comprehensive income.

(iv) IAS 38 (paras 51–67) deals with the accounting of internally generated intangible assets and states that an intangible asset can only be recognised if:

(1) It is probable that future economic benefits to the asset will flow to the entity; and

(2) The cost of the asset can be reliably measured.

With research and development work it is typically difficult to ascertain whether future economic benefit will flow to the business and the standard (paras 54 and 57) states that;

(1) Expenditure on research should be written off to profit or loss and

(2) Expenditure on development should only be capitalised if certain things can be demonstrated – these include technical feasibility, intention and ability to sell/use asset, how future benefit will be generated, availability of resources to complete and the ability to measure expenditure on the asset reliably.

In this case capitalising on the basis of the development team's confidence would appear to be optimistic and in practice more credence would always be given to external evidence of commercial viability. You may argue that Toro's experience and reputation in this field and the fact that they are in the process of applying for a patent should be sufficient evidence to capitalise the 2010 costs incurred after all conditions were met however many companies never recover the cost of their patent application despite their optimism. Also uncertainty over timing of commercial viability of electric car would raise doubts as to whether development costs could be recovered through future sales.

Toro should write off all expenditure in 2010.

29 Pyne

This question examines the candidates' ability to prepare simple consolidated financial statements covering non-controlling interests, intra group trading, goodwill and impairment (syllabus section 11.3). The question also requires an understanding of IAS 24 *Related party disclosures* (syllabus section 11.1).

Note that the solution to part (b) has been amended as a result of the issue of a revised IAS 24 in November 2009.

(a)

CONSOLIDATED STATEMENT OF FINANCIAL POSITION AS AT 30 SEPTEMBER 2009

	$'000
Non current assets	
Property, plant and equipment (10,000 + 4,000 – 24)	13,976.0
Goodwill (W1 + 2)(650 – 150)	500.0
	14,476.0
Current assets	
Inventories (1,800 + 1,200 + 20 – 40)	2,980.0
Trade receivables (1,600 + 600 – 100)	2,100.0
Cash and cash equivalents (200 + 400)	600.0
	5,680.0
Total assets	20,156.0
Equity and liabilities	
Equity shares of £1 each	2,000.0
Share premium	1,200.0
Retained earnings (W9)	10,375.2
Non controlling interest (W8)	1,060.8
Non current liabilities	
10% Debenture (1,000 + 800)	1,800.0
Current liabilities (W3) (2,000 + 1,800 + 20 – 100)	3,720.0
Total equity and liabilities	20,156.0

CONSOLIDATED STATEMENT OF PROFIT OR LOSS FOR THE YEAR ENDED 30 SEPTEMBER 2009

	$'000
Revenue (10,000 + 5,000 – 700) (W4)	14,300
Cost of sales (7,600 + 3,400 – 700 + 40 + 24) (W4, W5, W6)	(10,364)
Gross profit (2,400 + 1,600 – 40 – 24)	3,936
Goodwill impairment	(150)
Other income (240 – 240) (W7)	–
Distribution costs (500 + 100)	(600)
Administration expenses (300 + 180)	(480)
Finance costs (100 + 100)	(200)
Profit before taxation	2,506
Income tax expense (500 + 400)	(900)
Profit for the year	1,606
Profit attributable to:	
Owners of the parent (W9)	1,379.2
Non-controlling interest	226.8
	1,606

Workings ($'000)

1   Goodwill

	$'000	$'000
Consideration transferred		2,400
Non-controlling interest (W8)		750
Net assets acquired as represented by:		
Ordinary share capital	1,200	
Share premium	1,000	
Retained earnings on acquisition	300	
	(2,500)	
Goodwill		650

Goodwill must be capitalised in the consolidated statement of financial position.

2   Impairment of goodwill

Remember goodwill arising on acquisition must be reviewed annually for any loss of value in accordance with IFRS 3. Any impairment must be accounted for in the consolidated financial statements using the following journal entry:

Debit   Group retained earnings   150
Credit Goodwill   150

3   Agree current accounts

Pyne has stock which has not been recorded in its financial statements at the year end. This must be adjusted for:

Debit Inventories   20
Credit Trade payables (Syne)   20

Current accounts will now agree at $100,000 and should be cancelled

4   Intra group trading

Since the consolidated statement of profit or loss should show sales to external customers and purchases from external suppliers it is necessary to adjust for any intra group trading using the following journal entry:

Debit Revenue   700
Credit Cost of sales   700

5   Profit not realised on intra group trading

Similarly the consolidated statement of profit or loss should only show profits earned by the group. This means that any intra group sales still held in inventory at the year end must give rise to an adjustment to remove unrealised profits. Remember since Syne is not a wholly owned subsidiary from the point of view of the non controlling interest the profit has been realised. The following adjustment is required: $(25/125 \times 200,000 = \$40,000)$

Debit Group retained earnings   28
Debit Non controlling interest   12
Credit Group inventory   40

6   Intra group sale of non current asset

As with unrealised profits on inventory arising from intra group trading any profit or loss created by an intra group sale of a non-current asset must also be removed from the consolidated financial statements. In addition we must also adjust for the fact that after the sale any depreciation charge will have been calculated on the basis of the cost to the purchasing company as opposed to the cost to the group. In practice these adjustments are commonly combined. Again since Syne is not a wholly-owned subsidiary from the point of view of the non controlling interest the profit has been realised. The following adjustment is required:

Asset bought 2004	400
5 years' depreciation (400/10 × 5)	(200)
Carrying value	200
Sold for	230
Gain in Syne's records	30
Depreciation in 2009 (230/5)	46
Depreciation based on original cost (400/10)	40
Excess additional depreciation	6
Total provision for unrealised profit (30 − 6)	24

Debit Group retained earnings (24 × 70%)	16.8
Debit Non controlling interest (24 × 30%)	7.2
Credit Group non current asset	24.0

7 Intra group dividend

This is a dividend paid out of post acquisition profits and therefore the amount of $240 paid to Pyne is simply cancelled on consolidation with the amount paid by Syne.

8 Calculate non controlling interest

At acquisition

Synes net assets (W1)	2,500
× NCI 30%	750

At date of year end consolidation

Syne's net assets	3,600
Less unrealised profits (W5)	(40)
Less profit on sale of equipment net of depreciation (W6)	(24)
	3,536
× NCI 30%	1,060.8

9 (i) Profit attributable to owners of parent

Profit for year before dividends received from Syne (1,240 − 240)	1,000
Less: goodwill impairment	(150)
Add: share of Syne's profit (less unrealised profits)	
70% × (820 − 40 − 24)	529.2
	1,379.2

(ii) Non-controlling interests

30% of (820 − 40 − 24)	226.8

(iii) **Consolidated retained earnings**

		$'000	$'000
		Pyne	*Syne*
Retained earnings per question		9,800	1,400
Profit for year		1,240	477*
Retained earnings b/f		8,560	923

*Profit for year	820	
Dividends paid (240 × 100/70)	343	
	$477	

Retained earnings b/f	8,560	923
Less pre acquisition		(300)
		623
Share belonging to Pyne 70% × post acquisition		436
	436	
Retained earnings b/f	8,996	

Retained earnings b/f	8,996.0
Profit for year	1,379.2
Retained earnings c/f	10,375.2

Or alternative retained earnings working:

	Pyne	*Syne*
	$'000	$'000
Retained earnings at reporting date	9,800	1,400
At acquisition date		(300)
URP in inventory		(40)
URP in non-current assets		(24)
		1,036
S × 70%	725.2	
Impairment of goodwill	(150)	
Group retained earnings	1,0375.2	

(b) **Related party transactions.**

Parties are considered to be related if one party has the ability to control the other party or to exercise significant influence or joint control over the other party in making financial and operating decisions. One entity is related to another entity if: (IAS 24.9)

(i) They are members of the same group;

(ii) One is an associate or joint venture of the other;

(iii) Both are joint ventures of the same third party;

(iv) One is a joint venture and the other is an associate of the same third party;

(v) One entity is controlled by someone who also controls, has significant influence over or is key management personnel of the other entity;

(vi) Someone who controls, has significant influence or is key management personnel of one entity has significant influence over the other or is a member of the other's key management personnel.

The following are *not* related: (IAS 24.11)

(i) Two entities simply because they have a director or key manager in common;

(ii) A single supplier with whom an entity transacts a significant volume of business merely by virtue of the resulting economic dependence

In this case Pyne's dealings with Levee could be deemed to be of a related party nature – 16% shareholding, significant trade, seat on board all indicate that Levee can participate in the financial and operating policy decisions of Pyne and that significant influence might exist. If this is the case the financial statements should disclose the nature of the related party relationship, the type and amount of transactions and outstanding balances for each type of transaction. Please note that IAS 24 is mainly concerned with the disclosure of the related party activity. Devere and Vivre are not related companies merely through trade with the Pyne group.

30 Ferrar

This question examines the candidates' ability to calculate financial ratios for a business entity and comment on the commercial significance of the movements in these ratios (syllabus section 11.5). The question also requires the application of IAS 33 *Earnings per share* as it applies to rights issues (syllabus section 11.5).

(a) **Financial ratios**

				2009			*2008*
(i)	Return on total capital (before tax) %	$\dfrac{5,500}{42,000}$	$\times 100 =$	13.1%	$\dfrac{5,000}{25,500}$	$\times 100 =$	19.6%
(ii)	Gross profit %	$\dfrac{10,000}{40,000}$	$\times 100 =$	25%	$\dfrac{9,000}{32,000}$	$\times 100 =$	28%
(iii)	Current ratio	$\dfrac{13,800}{14,800}$		0.93:1	$\dfrac{10,100}{4,300}$		2.3:1
(iv)	Accounts receivable days	$\dfrac{8,300}{40,000}$	$\times 365$	76 days	$\dfrac{6,000}{32,000}$	$\times 365$	68 days
(v)	Inventory days	$\dfrac{5,000}{30,000}$	$\times 365$	61 days	$\dfrac{3,000}{23,000}$	$\times 365$	48 days
(vi)	Accounts payable days	$\dfrac{14,000}{30,000}$	$\times 365$	170 days	$\dfrac{3,800}{23,000}$	$\times 365$	60 days

Return on total capital is typically seen as a measure of managements overall efficiency in generating profits from the capital it has available. In Ferrar's situation ROCE has deteriorated in the year. This will either be the result of the company not generating sufficient sales for the level of capital invested in it and/or of each sale making insufficient profit. On further investigation we can see that the net asset turnover has fallen from $2.06/$1 to $1.81/$1 and that operating profit margins have also fallen from 15.65% to 13.75%.

Gross profit percentage has fallen to 25% from 28% in 2008. Without a detailed breakdown of sales and product costs it is difficult to say why this might have occurred. However given our knowledge of the business it would be reasonable to suggest:

- That increased competition in the lock area of the business would put pressure on selling prices perhaps from overseas suppliers

- There may be problems when entering new product areas of sourcing new suppliers and stream lining processes and

- Now not only selling in the domestic market but also to commercial customers who may be more skilled at negotiating better prices.

Falling gross profit margins are not necessarily a cause for concern as long as sales volume is increasing at a sufficiently high level to compensate for the reduced margin. In Ferrar's case although the gross profit margin has deteriorated by 3% the gross profit has increased by $1 million.

Current ratio has fallen from 2.3 to 0.93. This appears to be a dramatic decrease and could mean that the company has severe liquidity problems which may result in suppliers not being paid on time. Alternatively, this could mean that current assets are being managed more efficiently than they were previously as money tied up in current assets could usually be invested elsewhere to generate increased profits for the business. It is always important to look behind the current ratio to determine whether it is masking potential cashflow problems.

Accounts receivable days have increased from 68 days to 76 days. This figure should always be compared with the credit terms granted to ensure that customers are meeting their obligations. If they are not, Ferrar must make sure that it puts effective collection procedures in place (– follow up as soon as due date has passed, reminders (invoices, statements, letters) phone calls, visit customers, monitor credit limits to make sure they aren't exceeded, re-assess credit limit in light of slow payment and finally take legal action to recover the debt.) If debtors are just slow payers but are not otherwise problematic, Ferrar could consider factoring. If Ferrar has extended the credit period in an attempt to increase sales, management must be careful to monitor the occurrence of bad debts and be aware of the cost of financing additional debtors either by the amount of interest they will pay on increased borrowings or the reduced interest they could earn if money was received earlier.

Inventory days have increased from 48 days to 61 days. This means that more money is tied up in the cost of purchasing and holding inventories. These costs will include such things as interest, property costs, wages insurance and obsolescence all resulting in lower profits.

Legitimate reasons for higher inventory levels are:

- Purchasing before price increase or scarcity;
- Purchasing at low price because of bulk buying or competitor in trouble;
- Stocking up for sale or promotion.

Corrective action is to get rid of excess inventory at the best price you can.

Ensure that purchases are related to sales forecasts and that sales forecast is reviewed on a regular basis.

Accounts payable days have increased from 60 days to 170 days which is extremely worrying and indicates that the business has severe cash flow problems. Unless Ferrar have renegotiated terms with suppliers it is likely that they may be put on a cash on delivery basis and the company's reputation will be damaged impacting on their ability to obtain future borrowing and enter into transactions with third parties.

(b) **Basic earnings per share** (EPS)

Profit attributable to ordinary equity holders

Weighted average no. of ordinary shares outstanding during the period

If there have been no changes in the share capital of the company during the period then the weighted average is just the number of shares in issue throughout the period.

		$'000	2009	$'000	2008
EPS =	Profit before ord.dividend	2,300	= 0.23p	2,800	= 0.35p
	No. of ordinary shares	10,000		8,000	

However Ferrar raised part of the finance needed for its expansion from a 1:4 rights issue on 1 January 2009. A rights issue is made at an exercise price below the market value so there is an element of a bonus issue here. To truly compare like with like the number of shares before the rights issue should be multiplied by a factor adjusting for the element of bonus. The prior years EPS should be restated on the basis of this adjusted number of shares.

Since the rights issue took place on 1 January 2009 EPS for the year ended 31 December 2009 does not need to be adjusted however the EPS for the previous period does.

The number of shares to be used in the EPS calculation should be multiplied by a factor adjusting for the bonus element. The factor is defined as:

$$\frac{\text{Theoretical ex-rights fair value}}{\text{Fair value per share before rights issue}}$$

The theoretical ex-rights fair value is the expected share price after the rights issue and is calculated as follows:

4 shares × $2.75 = $11.00

<u>1</u> share × $ 2.40 = <u>$2.40</u>

<u>5</u>   <u>13.40</u>

Ex rights price $2.68

Thus adjustment factor is $2.75/$2.68 = 1.0261

Applied to number of shares in issue in 2008 = 8,000 × 2.75/2.68 = 8,209

		$'000	2009	$'000	2008
EPS =	Profit before ord. dividend	2,300	= 0.23p	2,800	= 0.34p
	No. of shares	10,000		8,209	

31 Convergence

The question examines the candidates' understanding of off balance sheet financing and the concept of substance over form (syllabus section 11.4). The question also requires an understanding of the general guidance given in the *Conceptual Framework for Financial Reporting (Conceptual framework)* for reporting the substance of transactions (syllabus section 11.2).

Note that the solution to part (b) has been amended as a result of the issue of *the Conceptual Framework* in September 2010.

(a) Off balance sheet finance can be defined as the funding of a company's operations in such a way that under legal requirements and traditional accounting conventions, some or all of the finance may not be shown in its statement of financial position. Some of the more common examples of off balance sheet finance include leasing, consignment inventory, factoring of debtors, business combinations and securitised assets.

Historically the problem with off balance sheet finance was that the financial statements did not give the user a proper view of the state of the company's affairs as not only were liabilities and assets removed from the statement of financial position but there was frequently an impact on reported profits and insufficient disclosure. This lack of transparency and the inability to make meaningful comparisons has led to the development of the substance over form argument. The main argument states that it is the true substance of a transaction that should be recorded in the financial statements not merely the legal form of the transaction.

(b) This principle of substance over form is included as part of the original *Framework for the preparation and presentation of financial statements (Framework)* – now revised to the *Conceptual Framework for Financial Reporting*. The *Conceptual Framework* states that when considering whether an item meets the definition of an asset, liability or equity, attention needs to be given to its underlying substance and economic reality and not merely its legal form. The example provided in the *Conceptual Framework* is that of a finance lease where the substance and economic reality are that the lessee acquires the economic benefits of the use of the leased asset for the major part of its useful life in return for entering into an obligation to pay for that right an amount approximating to the fair value of the asset and the related finance charge. Hence, the finance lease gives rise to items that satisfy the definition of an asset and a liability and are recognised as such in the lessee's statement of financial position.

If no specific rules apply to a transaction the principles of the *Conceptual Framework* should be used and the substance of a transaction recorded in the financial statements. When it is not clear what the substance of the transaction is the *Conceptual Framework* lays down the definition of what constitutes an asset and a liability and what gives rise to their recognition in the financial statements. This should be used in determining the accounting treatment of each transaction.

Several accounting standards now dictate the treatment of certain situations which in the past gave rise to off balance sheet finance. These include IAS 17 which deals with finance leases (the position of operating leases is under review), IAS 24 *Related party disclosures* and IAS 11 *Construction contracts*. The IASB and FASB are currently reviewing the accounting standards relating to off balance sheet activities with a view to bringing them into line with each other as soon as possible.

32 Nemix

This question examines the candidates' ability to apply the requirements of IAS 17 (syllabus section 11.4) to various transactions in the accounts of the lessee.

The objective of IAS 17 (Revised 1997) is to prescribe, for lessees and lessors, the appropriate accounting policies and disclosures to apply in relation to finance and operating leases.

(i) During the year Nemix will have made two payments of $11,000: according to the question these will have been charged in the statement of profit or loss as an expense:

Debit: Lease payments $22,000

Credit: Bank $22,000

However for operating leases, the lease payments should be recognised as an expense in the statement of profit or loss over the term of the lease on a straight-line basis, unless another

systematic basis is more representative of the time pattern of the user's benefit, **(IAS 17.33).**
Given the lease period is for 5 years the lease payments should be allocated as follows:

Total lease payments: $11,000 × 2 = $22,000 × 3 years = $66,000

Lease term: 5 years

Annual charge: $66,000/5 = $13,200 p. a

To correct the accounts, a year end adjustment should be made:

Debit: Prepayments $8,800

Credit: Lease payments $8,800

Nemix must disclose the amount of minimum lease payments at the end of the reporting period under non-cancellable operating leases for:

(1)   the next year; $13,200

(2)   years 2 through 5 combined; $39,600

(3)   beyond five years.   –

(ii)   In the second situation Nemix has entered into a finance lease. The following principles should be applied in the financial statements of Nemix:

(a)   At commencement of the lease term, the finance lease should be recorded as an asset and a liability at the lower of the fair value of the asset and the present value of the minimum lease payments (discounted at the interest rate implicit in the lease, if practicable, or else at the entity's incremental borrowing rate); (IAS 17.20).

Debit: Asset ($150,000 plus professional fees $3,000) $153,000

Credit: Obligation under finance lease $150,000

Credit: Bank $3,000

(b)   The depreciation policy for assets held under finance leases should be consistent with that for owned assets. If there is no reasonable certainty that the lessee will obtain ownership at the end of the lease - the asset should be depreciated over the shorter of the lease term or the life of the asset; (IAS 17.27).

Nemix are going to take up the secondary lease period therefore the asset should be depreciated over the useful life of the asset using the straight line method.

Cost of asset   =   153,000
Less: residual value =   (13,000)
                         140,000/useful life of 10 years
Depreciation charge =   14,000
Debit: Depreciation charge $14,000
Credit: Accumulated depreciation $14,000

(c)   Finance lease payments should be apportioned between the finance charge and the reduction of the outstanding liability (the finance charge to be allocated so as to produce a constant periodic rate of interest on the remaining balance of the liability); (IAS 17.25).

(d)   *Workings*

Date	Liability (start of period)	Payment	Liability (during period)	Interest (16.88%)	Liability (End of period)
1.10.08	150,000	40,000	110,000	18,568	128,568
1.10.09	128,568	40,000	88,568	14,950	103,518
1.10.10	103,518	40,000	63,518	10,722	74,240
1.10.11	74,240	40,000	34,240	5,760*	40,000
1.10.12	40,000	40,000	–		
		200,000		50,000	

*Adjust for rounding of $19 ($34,240 × 16.88% = $5,779)

Disclosure: Lessees – Finance Lease (IAS 17.31):

- Carrying amount of asset;
- Reconciliation between total minimum lease payments and their present value;
- Amounts of minimum lease payments at the reporting date and the present value thereof, for:
- The next year;
- Years 2 through 5 combined;
- Beyond five years.

In the financial statements and supporting notes you would expect to see the following:

STATEMENT OF FINANCIAL POSITION

Non current assets

Plant and equipment

(cost 150,000 + 3000 less 14,000 depreciation) $139,000

Current liabilities

Obligations under finance leases $40,000

Non current liabilities

Obligations under finance leases $88,568

STATEMENT OF PROFIT OR LOSS

Finance charges $18,568

NOTES TO THE ACCOUNTS

	Minimum lease payments	Present value of min. lease payments
Payable		
• The next year;	40,000	40,000
• Years 2 through 5 combined;	120,000	88,568
• Beyond five years;		
Less finance charges	(31,432)	
	128,568	128,568

(iii)   In the sale and leaseback transaction Nemix has entered into a finance lease and therefore has effectively raised finance using the office as security. The asset is effectively still held by Nemix ie the risks and rewards of ownership have not been disposed of. IAS 17 states that any profit on sale should not be recognised in the statement of profit or loss immediately but should be deferred and amortised over the term of the lease.

The entries to reflect this in the financial statements would be as follows:

(1)   Debit   :   Cash $6.1

        Credit :   Buildings $4.6

        Credit :   Deferred income $1.5

        To recognise sale of building

(2)   Debit   :   Assets held under finance leases $6.1

        Credit :   Finance leases obligation $6.1

        To set up finance lease asset and liability

        In years 1–25

(3)   Debit   :   Deferred income $0.06

        Credit :   Statement of profit or loss $0.06

        To release the deferred income over the lease term ($1.5/25)

(4)   Debit   :   Depreciation $0.244

        Credit :   Assets held under finance leases $0.244

        To recognise depreciation on leased asset   ($6.1/25)

(5)   Debit   :   Interest $x

        Debit   :   Finance lease obligation $(300 – X)

        Credit :   Cash $300

        To record rentals paid

Mock exam 1 questions and answers

MODULE D

PROFESSIONAL EXAMINATION 1

PAPER 11 – FINANCIAL ACCOUNTING 2

TUESDAY 21st MAY 2013

TIME ALLOWED – 3 HOURS

Answer ALL questions

You are allowed an additional 15 minutes reading time before the exam begins, during which you should read the question paper and, if you wish, make notes on the question paper. You are **not** allowed to open the exam script booklet and start writing or use your calculator during the reading time.

CREATING WORLD CLASS ACCOUNTANTS

Question 1

You are the chief accountant of Delta, a manufacturing company. Several days ago you emailed a set of draft financial statements to Delta's chief executive. You have just received the following set of amended accounts from the chief executive in response:

Delta
AMENDED DRAFT STATEMENT OF COMPREHENSIVE INCOME
FOR THE YEAR ENDED 30 APRIL 2013

	$'000
Revenue	135,000
Cost of sales	(36,000)
Gross profit	99,000
Distribution costs	(11,000)
Administrative expenses	(13,000)
Investment income	2,100
Finance costs	(4,800)
Profit before tax	72,300
Tax	(15,900)
Profit for the year	56,400
Other comprehensive income	
Gain on revaluation	32,000
Total comprehensive income	88,400

Delta
AMENDED DRAFT STATEMENT OF FINANCIAL POSITION
AS AT 30 APRIL 2013

	$'000
ASSETS	
Non current assets	
Property, plant and equipment	210,000
Investment	60,000
	270,000
Non current assets	
Inventory	2,700
Trade receivables	18,200
Bank	520
	21,420
TOTAL ASSETS	291,420
EQUITY AND LIABILITIES	
Equity	
Ordinary share capital ($1 shares, fully paid)	40,000
Revaluation reserve	60,000
Retained earnings	122,320
	222,320
Non current liabilities	
Loans	50,000

Current liabilities

Trade payables	3,600
Current tax	15,500
	19,100

TOTAL EQUITY AND LIABILITIES	291,420

The amended draft was accompanied by a memo that included the following:

"I have revised the figures in your initial draft to take account of the following:

(i)   You have changed the basis for the calculation of depreciation on the networked IT system that we use for planning and control. This was purchased for $20m on 1 May 2011 and it was decided then that it should be depreciated at a rate of 25% on the reducing balance basis. You revised the asset's expected useful life during the present financial year and have increased the depreciation rate to 40% with effect from 1 May 2012.

      Your change is clearly a voluntary change of accounting policy, as specified by IAS 8, *Accounting Policies, Changes in Accounting Estimates and Errors*. On that basis I have restated the figures to apply your new policy retrospectively.

(ii)   You have treated the new production equipment as having been impaired even though it was purchased in May 2012 and is, therefore, only two years ago and has an estimated remaining useful life of eight years.

      The equipment cost $40m when it was new and I believe that it should continue to be carried at cost less straight line depreciation.

      You have based your calculation on the basis that the equipment's resale value was $23m on 30 April 2013. You feel that the equipment is quickly becoming obsolete and will have to be replaced soon.

      I have reviewed the project appraisal documents submitted to the board when the decision to invest in the equipment was taken and projected cash flows were strong for the whole of the equipment's life. The supplier assured the board at that time that the equipment was "future proof". Using this information I have determined that the net present value of the cash flows from the equipment is $39m. The machine is not impaired.

(iii)   You have misclassified the arrangements that we have put in place with our factoring company. As you know the arrangement is that we submit copies of invoices for sales to our largest and most solvent customers to Speedcash Factors. Speedcash then makes an immediate payment of 80% of the face value of the invoiced amount. We remain responsible for collection of the customer's payment and we use the proceeds to settle our balance due to Speedcash, plus an element of interest. Technically, we do not even have to wait until such time as the payment is received from the customer and so we remain fully in control.

      Our factoring arrangements apply only to selected customer balances that are almost certain to be paid in full. There is, therefore, no risk to us of any problems arising from this arrangement.

      We had factored $5.2m of invoices as at the year end, all of which were current balances. I have eliminated the balances that you had shown in the financial statements with respect to these invoices.

(iv)   You have indicated that you wish to prepare consolidated financial statements for a "Delta Group" of companies. I do not understand the reasoning behind this because we have never prepared consolidated financial statements in the past.

      We have paid the founder of Trent Industries $60m for 10% of the equity share capital of his company. That is hardly a controlling interest. We do have a slightly unusual arrangement because the founder will retain the remaining 90% of Trent's shares, but he has agreed to vote in accordance with our wishes. Furthermore, we have agreed to protect him from any risks associated with his continuing ownership of the company by paying him a salary of $1m per year for life. In return, he will remit any dividends paid by Trent to us. That was the source of our investment income.

In the event of the founder's death, his 90% interest in Trent will be transferred to his family's lawyers, who will continue to vote in accordance with our instructions and will pay the $1m fee into the founder's estate.

There can be no great advantage to us in preparing consolidated accounts. Trent has heavy borrowings and is presently making almost no profit."

Required

(a) Discuss the validity of the chief executive's treatment of matters (i) to (iii) and restate the draft statement of comprehensive income and draft statement of financial position to take account of any disagreements with the treatments adopted.

(Marks will be allocated on the basis of 8 marks per matter) **(24 marks)**

(b) Calculate the return on capital employed (ROCE) and liquidity ratios for Delta, using both the draft financial statements provided above and your restated figures from part (a) above. Comment on the liquidity and profitability of the company under both sets of reported figures. **(8 marks)**

(c) Discuss the chief executive's arguments relating to the treatment of Trent and explain how the figures in Delta's financial statements will differ if the draft financial statements for Delta are compared with those of the Delta Group. **(8 marks)**

(Total = 40 marks)

Question 2

Michael started a business on 1 March 2012, with an investment of $60,000 in cash.

The business made the following payments on 1 March 2012:

	$
Deposit paid on premises	30,000
Purchase of equipment	18,000
Purchase of inventory	12,000
	60,000

The premises cost $110,000. They were purchased with the assistance of an $80,000 mortgage on the property. The loan, together with interest thereon, was to be repaid with half yearly instalments of $7,000, payable on 31 August and 28 February each year. The company will be charged interest of 6% per half year on the outstanding balance.

The following historical cost figures have been prepared for the year ended 28 February 2013:

Michael

HISTORICAL COST INCOME STATEMENT
FOR THE YEAR ENDED 28 FEBRUARY 2013

	$	$
Sales (all cash)		248,000
Opening inventory	12,000	
Purchases	160,000	
Closing inventory	13,334	
Cost of inventory consumed	158,666	
Wages	22,000	
Depreciation - premises	2,200	
Depreciation - equipment	3,600	
Interest on mortgage	9,468	
Total expenses		195,934
Profit for the year		52,066

Michael

HISTORICAL COST STATEMENT OF FINANCIAL POSITION
AS AT 28 FEBRUARY 2013

	$	$
Property plant and equipment		
Premises		107,800
Equipment		14,400
		122,200
Current assets		
Inventory	13,334	
Bank	54,000	
		67,334
		189,534
Equity		
Share capital		60,000
Retained earnings		38,066
		98,066
Non-current liabilities		
Mortgage on premises		75,468
Current liabilities		
Trade payables		16,000
		189,534

A $14,000 dividend was paid on 28 February 2013.

The retail price index was as follows:

At 1 March 2012	200
At 31 August 2012	212
At the date of purchase of closing inventory	223
At 28 February 2013	225
Average for the year ended 28 February 2013	213

Required

(a) Restate Michael's financial statements to a current purchasing power basis, using 28 February 2013 $ as the basis for the statements. **(9 marks)**

(b) Briefly explain why the statements prepared in (a) above may be more useful than the original historical cost financial statements. **(3 marks)**

(Total = 12 marks)

Question 3

Kappa runs a national chain of pizza restaurants. In March 2013 the company received a letter from a law firm representing one of Kappa's largest customers. The letter claims that the customer was severely injured after slipping on a wet patch of floor in one of Kappa's restaurants. The customer is a professional dancer and the fall has led to major loss of earnings, in addition to the pain and suffering caused by the injury.

Kappa's directors obtained the health and safety records from the restaurant where the accident was alleged to have occurred. The restaurant manager had completed a full report on the accident. The restaurant had been busy and a customer had spilled a cup of tea on the restaurant floor. A member of staff had placed bright orange plastic cones on the floor on either side of the spillage and was waiting for a colleague to bring a mop to clean up the mess when a customer stepped past the plastic cones and slipped. The customer did not appear to be injured and refused the manager's offer to call for a taxi to take him to the local hospital's accident and emergency department.

The lawyer claims that the customer slipped because the spillage was not cleared up quickly. Furthermore, the restaurant manager was negligent because the customer was in shock after falling and should not have been permitted to leave the restaurant without receiving proper medical attention. A medical specialist has examined the customer and has reported that the customer's back has suffered a trauma consistent with a slip or a fall and that the customer should rest until fully recovered. The customer's business manager has supplied copies of contracts which show that the customer has been unable to fulfil a number of contractual commitments for which sizeable fees had been agreed.

Kappa has consulted a lawyer who has agreed to represent the company in resolving this claim. Kappa's finance director has asked the lawyer to help decide the appropriate accounting treatment for this claim because the amounts are potentially material for the financial statements for the year ended 30 June 2013. The finance director provided the lawyer with definitions for both provisions and contingent liabilities, but the lawyer has refused to classify the claim as either one or the other.

The lawyers on both sides are confident that the claim will be settled by December 2013.

Required

(a) Explain how Kappa should determine whether the customer's claim should be accounted for as a provision or a contingent liability. **(8 marks)**

(b) Discuss the potential implications for the credibility of Kappa's directors of the fact that the case will be settled several months after the financial statements have been published with disclosures concerning the board's expectations for the outcome. **(4 marks)**

(Total = 12 marks)

Question 4

Two firms of surveyors, Alpha and Beta, are planning to merge their respective partnerships into one entity. The partnership will be effective from 31 May 2013. At that date the draft statements of financial position for the two firms were as follows:

	Alpha $	Beta $
Property, plant and equipment	380,000	700,000
Current assets		
Trade receivables	25,000	50,000
Bank	17,000	23,000
	42,000	73,000
Total assets	442,000	773,000
Capital accounts		
Mr Smith	200,000	
Mrs Jones	200,000	
Mr Green		330,000
Miss Brown		370,000
Current accounts		
Mr Smith	10,000	
Mrs Jones	11,000	
Mr Green		9,000
Miss Brown		12,000
	421,000	721,000
Long term liabilities		
Loan		50,000
Current liabilities		
Trade payables	1,000	2,000
	422,000	773,000

Both partnerships share profits equally.

Each pair of partners has agreed to the following:

A new partnership will be formed, to be named Gamma.

Goodwill in Alpha will be valued at $300,000 and goodwill in Beta at $500,000.

Alpha's property, plant and equipment will be revalued at $440,000 and Beta's at $740,000.

Gamma will settle the balances on all partners' current accounts within six months of the merger.

All four partners will be credited with capital account balances that are equal to those in the adjusted statements of financial position of Alpha and Beta. All four partners will share profits and losses equally.

Required

(a) Prepare the statement of financial position of Gamma as at 31 May 2013. **(8 marks)**

(b) Explain why the figures in the two separate partnership accounts had to be adjusted prior to the creation of Gamma. **(4 marks)**

(Total = 12 marks)

Question 5

Sigma manufactures components for the motor industry. The company held its annual inventory count on 30 April 2013. Members of Sigma's accounts department staff are working through the physical count records to value the inventory. Sales and profits for the year ended 30 April 2013 are likely to be disappointingly low.

Sigma's inventory includes partly completed goods. The following table shows the overhead costs that have been incurred during the year:

	$'000
Fixed costs:	
Factory rent, rates and insurance	3,000
Administration expenses	4,800
Factory security	2,200
Variable costs:	
Factory heat, light and power	6,000
Sales commission and selling costs	2,400
Depreciation of machinery	4,000
Depreciation of delivery vehicles	1,400

Sigma absorbs overheads on the basis of labour hours. A total of 5,000 labour hours have been included in work-in-progress. A total of 140,000 hours were worked by production staff during the year. In a more typical year the production staff work 200,000 hours.

The material content of partly completed goods is $800,000 and the labour cost to date is $500,000.

Sigma's finished goods have already been valued at $6.0m. This figure includes some obsolete items that cost $600,000 to produce, but which are likely to be sold at a scrap value of $100,000. A member of the clerical staff has valued this inventory at its original cost on the basis that the total cost of all finished goods comfortably exceeds the total net realisable value of all materials.

Required

(a) Calculate the value of Sigma's inventories of work-in-progress and finished goods. **(6 marks)**

(b) Explain the logic behind your treatment of overheads in valuing work-in-progress. **(4 marks)**

(c) Explain your logic in the valuation of finished goods. **(2 marks)**

(Total = 12 marks)

Question 6

Tau had 6,000,000 fully-paid $1 ordinary shares in issue on 30 April 2012.

Tau made a rights issue of 1 for 5 at $7.50 per share on 31 July 2012. Tau's share price was $8.60 just before the issue.

The following information has been extracted from Tau's financial statements for the year ended 30 April 2013:

Extract from income statement

	$'000
Operating profit	2,600
Finance charges	(800)
Profit before tax	1,800
Tax	(560)
Profit for year	1,240

Extract from statement of changes in equity

	Ordinary share capital $'000	Share premium $'000	Capital reserve $'000	Retained earnings $'000	Total $'000
Balance as at 1 May 2012	6,000	2,000	1,000	11,000	20,000
Issue of share capital	1,200	7,800			9,000
Options issued			400		400
Profit for year				1,240	1,240
Dividend				(700)	(700)
Balance as at 30 April 2013	7,200	9,800	1,400	11,540	29,940

Tau has an executive share option scheme in force. At the 30 April 2013 there were 2.6m options outstanding at the year end. If all of the options were exercised on 30 April 2013 the company would raise $18.2m. The share price as at 30 April 2013 was $9.30.

Required

(a) Calculate Tau's basic and diluted earnings per share. **(9 marks)**

(b) Explain the logic underlying the diluted earnings per share calculation. **(3 marks)**

(Total = 12 marks)

MODEL ANSWERS

MODULE D

PROFESSIONAL EXAMINATION 1

PAPER 11 – FINANCIAL ACCOUNTING 2

TUESDAY 21st MAY 2013

Question 1

Part (a)(i) draws on section 1 of the syllabus Accounting Theory, part (a)(ii) on section 2 International Accounting Standards, and part (a)(iii) on section 4 Accounting for specialised transactions. Part (b) draws on section 5 of the syllabus Financial Analysis. Part (c) draws on section 3 Proprietorship accounting and entity accounting.

Collectively, the theme running through this question is that the accounting standards prevent the distortion of the financial statements by making it more difficult to justify distorted and aggressive accounting practices.

(a) (i) IAS 8 *Accounting Policies, Changes in Accounting Estimates and Errors* defines the consumption of assets as a change in accounting estimate rather than a change in accounting policy. It would not be appropriate to classify a change in the rate of depreciation as a change in accounting policy and so the changes should not be applied retrospectively because that would have the misleading effect of charging an element of depreciation directly to retained earnings.

The correction should be calculated as follows:

	25% $000	40% $000
Cost	20,000	20,000
Depreciation charge for year ended 30 April 2011	(5,000)	(8,000)
Net book value as at 30 April 2011	15,000	12,000
Depreciation charge for year ended 30 April 2012	(3,750)	(4,800)
Net book value as at 30 April 2012	11,250	7,200
Depreciation charge for year ended 30 April 2013		(2,880)
Net book value as at 30 April 2013		4,320

The correct depreciation charge for the year = 11,250 x 40% = $4,500,000.

The chief executive has input a decrease in book value as at the start of the year and also retained earnings brought forward of $11,250,000 – 7,200,000 = $4,050,000.

The charge for the year has been understated by $4,500,000 – 2,880,000 = $1,620,000.

Both retained earnings and property, plant and equipment must be reduced by 4,050,000 + 1,620,000 = $5,670,000.

(ii) The decision to treat an asset as impaired will always involve significant judgement. The asset's deprival value cannot be determined objectively.

It appears that the accountant has significant doubts about the net present values of future cash flows that are sufficient to suggest that less than $23m will be recovered from this asset. If that is the case then there is no particular need to estimate the net present value more accurately because the asset is clearly impaired and should be written down.

The fact that the asset was valued with greater optimism when its purchase was being considered is not really relevant to its valuation just now.

Depreciation to date in this asset is $40,000,000 /10 × 2 = $8,000,000.

The impairment adjustment is $40,000,000 – 8,000,000 = $32,000,000 - $23,000,000 = $9,000,000.

Reinstating the impairment will increase cost of sales by $9m and will decrease PPE and retained earnings by the same amount.

(iii) This arrangement requires consideration of the principle of substance over form.

There is no specific IFRS on the accounting treatment of factoring arrangements, but FRS 5 offers some guidance on the specifics of factoring. IAS 8 would suggest that it is acceptable to base an accounting policy on another regulator's standard in the absence of an IFRS.

This arrangement appears to leave Delta exposed to all of the risks and rewards of owning the receivable balances. Delta must continue to apply its own credit control processes and procedures in order to maintain its cash flow from customers. In the event of slow payment or default the factor will hold Delta responsible and will continue to charge interest.

The $5.2m will have to be reinstated in the financial statements. That will require an increase in both trade receivables and in the liability due to the factoring company. The cash has been received so no adjustment to that figure is required as it is already in the bank. As the receivables pay Delta will pay the factoring company back.

Tutorial Note: FRS 5 *Reporting the substance of transactions* is a UK financial reporting standard. See Chapter 8 Section 4 on common forms of off-balance sheet finance; this is closely based on the guidance in FRS 5.

Delta

		Adjustment i	Adjustment ii	Adjustment iii	Adjusted total

RESTATED DRAFT STATEMENT OF COMPREHENSIVE INCOME FOR THE YEAR ENDED 30 APRIL 2013

	$'000	$'000	$'000	$'000	$'000
Revenue	135,000				135,000
Cost of sales	(36,000)	(1,620)	(9,000)		(46,620)
Gross profit	99,000				88,380
Distribution costs	(11,000)				(11,000)
Administrative expenses	(13,000)				(13,000)
Investment income	2,100				2,100
Finance costs	(4,800)				(4,800)
Profit before tax	72,300				61,680
Tax	(15,900)				(15,900)
Profit for the year	56,400				45,780
Other comprehensive income					
Gain on revaluation	32,000				32,000
Total comprehensive income	88,400				77,780

Delta

RESTATED DRAFT STATEMENT OF FINANCIAL POSITION AS AT 30 APRIL 2013

	$'000	$'000	$'000	$'000	$'000
ASSETS					
Non current assets					
Property, plant and equipment	210,000	(5,670)	(9,000)		195,330
Investment	60,000				60,000
	270,000				255,330
Non current assets					
Inventory	2,700				2,700
Trade receivables	18,200			5,200	23,400
Bank	520				520
	21,420				26,620
TOTAL ASSETS	291,420				281,950
EQUITY AND LIABILITIES					
Equity					
Ordinary share capital	40,000				40,000
Revaluation reserve	60,000				60,000
Retained earnings	122,320	(5,670)	(9,000)		107,650
	222,320				207,650

Non current liabilities

Loans	50,000		50,000

Current liabilities

Trade payables	3,600	5,200	8,800
Current tax	15,500		15,500
	19,100		24,300

TOTAL EQUITY AND LIABILITIES	291,420	281,950

(b) The ratios according to the chief executive's figures are:

Return on capital employed = (72,300+4,800)/(222,320+50,000) = 28%

Current ratio = 21,420/19,100 = 1.1:1

Ratios before the incorrect chief executives adjustments are:

Return on capital employed = (61,680+4,800)/(207,650+50,000) = 26%

Current ratio = 26,620/24,300 = 1.1:1

The return on capital employed figure is only 2 percentage points higher despite the correction of the chief executive's adjustments. The company will, however, look more profitable because of those adjustments and the 2% improvement may be used to argue that the company's performance has improved slightly.

The basic current ratio is unaffected by the reclassification of the debt factoring. That ignores the fact that current liabilities include a large sum for tax that will not be payable immediately. Under the original figures, current assets = 21,420/3,600 = 6.0 times trade payables. The amended figures show 26,620/8,800 = 3.0 times. Both figures are high, but the company looks far more liquid using the chief executive's figures.

(c) Delta does not own a controlling interest, but it does have control over Trent. The contractual arrangements indicate that Delta will be able to direct the founder to vote in accordance with Delta's wishes. There are arrangements in place to ensure that this is a permanent arrangement, and Delta's control will continue even after the founder's death.

It is clear that the substance of the arrangement is that Delta has paid $60m plus a perpetuity of $1m per annum for control of Trent.

It sounds as if the consolidation of Trent would make Delta's figures look far less attractive. The pre-acquisition reserves would be cancelled on consolidation. That would leave the liabilities that have caused Trent's high gearing. Consolidating Trent will make Delta appear far more risky because of the high gearing. It may also be necessary to calculate the fair value of the consideration at $60m plus the fair value of the $1m perpetuity. That would increase goodwill on consolidation and would require recognition of the related liability in Delta's books.

Question 2

(a)

	Historical cost $	Index	CPP $
Bank	0	225/200	0
Mortgage	(80,000)	225/200	(90,000)
	(80,000)		(90,000)
Revenue	248,000	225/213	261,972
Purchases	(160,000)	225/213	(169,014)
Wages	(22,000)	225/213	(23,239)
Mortgage interest	(4,800)	225/212	(5,094)
	(4,668)	225/225	(4,668)
Dividend	(14,000)	225/225	(14,000)
Expected net monetary assets			(44,044)
Closing net monetary assets			
Bank			54,000
Mortgage			(75,468)
Payables			(16,000)
			(37,468)
Gain on net monetary assets			6,576

The gain on net monetary assets is a balancing figure. We restate the opening net balance and the net inflows to year end purchasing power and compare the result with the actual net monetary assets. The difference represents the impact of the changing value of money on the net monetary assets (which were clearly negative throughout the year because Michael had a gain, implying the erosion of net liabilities thanks to inflation).

The closing position remains a net monetary liability. The company had nothing but a large mortgage to begin with, but that has changed over the year, with a $54,000 bank balance being built up over the year.

Michael

INCOME STATEMENTS
FOR THE YEAR ENDED 28 FEBRUARY 2013

	Historical cost $	Index	CPP $
Sales (all cash)	248,000	225/213	261,972
Opening inventory	(12,000)	225/200	(13,500)
Purchases	(160,000)	225/213	(169,014)
Closing inventory	13,334	225/223	13,454
Cost of inventory consumed	(158,666)		(169,060)
Wages	(22,000)	225/213	(23,239)
Depreciation – premises	(2,200)	225/200	(2,475)
Depreciation – equipment	(3,600)	225/200	(4,050)
Interest	(4,800)	225/212	(5,094)
	(4,668)	225/225	(4,668)
Gain or loss on monetary items			6,576
Total expenses	(195,934)		(202,001)
Profit for the year	52,066		59,961

Michael

HISTORICAL COST STATEMENT OF FINANCIAL POSITION
AS AT 28 FEBRUARY 2013

	$	$	CPP $
Property plant and equipment	107,800	225/200	121,275
Premises	14,400	225/200	16,200
Equipment	122,200		137,475
Current assets			
Inventory	13,334	225/223	13,454
Bank	54,000	225/225	54,000
	67,334		67,454
	189,534		204,929
Equity			
Share capital	60,000	225/200	67,500
Retained earnings	38,066		45,961
	98,066		113,461
Non-current liabilities			
Mortgage on premises	75,468	225/225	75,468
Current liabilities			
Trade payables	16,000	225/225	16,000
	189,534		204,929

Operating profit has changed only very slightly because of the restatements to 28 February 2013 $, but the gain on net monetary assets is added and that has a major impact.

Some of the items in the statement of financial position are stated in monetary terms already, but there are figures, such as property, plant and equipment, that are shown at historical costs. The adjustments are not particularly significant because the costs are relatively recent, but the adjustments will increase with the passage of time.

(b) The CPP figures will enable Michael to tell whether the profits are sufficient to maintain the purchasing power of his net cash investment in the business. Under historical cost accounting his profit is $52,066, but some of those figures will have been distorted by the effects of inflation. In this case the business had a total profit that was significantly higher because of the use of debt. Michael is gaining at the expense of the business' lenders. If the rate of inflation had been higher then there would have been a more significant difference between the operating profits, before allowing for the gain on monetary items.

Question 3

This question draws on section 2 of the syllabus International Accounting Standards. The question asks for a discussion of the difficulties associated with accounting for provisions and contingent liabilities.

(a) This event should be accounted for in accordance with the requirements of IFRS 37 *Provisions, Contingent Liabilities and Contingent Assets*.

The details provided suggest that it would be possible to develop an argument for either treatment. There is some doubt as to the amount that will be payable.

There is a potential obligation as a result of a past event. The directors will classify the event as a provision if it is probable that there will be a payment and that a reliable estimate can be made of the amount payable.

To some extent the directors can decide whether they intend to make a payment. If the directors believe that they will make a payment then the claim satisfies the "probability" criterion and a provision should be made.

It should be possible to form an opinion on the likely amount by referring to precedent. This case is complicated by the fact that the plaintiff is a dancer and so the effects of the injury are even more serious than they would normally be. The estimation of the value of the lost earnings is not, in itself, a complicated accounting exercise and the plaintiff should be asked to provide figures that will substantiate the claim. All of this suggests that the liability can be estimated to at least an order of magnitude.

If these approaches do not yield satisfactory assurances concerning the amounts payable then the event should be classified as a contingent liability. The case is too strong to dismiss it entirely as a remote possibility of a successful claim.

(b) Unfortunately, the directors will be required to publish the financial statements on the basis of their best estimate of the outcome of the case. That means that the shareholders will be able to compare the accounting estimate with the actual outcome of the case. It is unlikely that the directors will be able to predict the outcome with any certainty and so there is almost certain to be a forecasting error in the financial statements. They may be accused of negligence (or worse) if the outcome is worse than anticipated. It will look as if they have deliberately understated the cost of resolving the issue. Alternatively, the shareholders may question the directors' decision to settle for more than the accounting estimate. The board may appear to have settled the claim carelessly and given the plaintiff more than was deserved.

Question 4

The question draws on section 3 of the syllabus Proprietorship Accounting and Entity Accounting. The question asks for the preparation of financial statements following the amalgamation of two partnerships.

(a)

	Alpha $	Adjustments Goodwill $	Adjustments Revaluation $	Beta $	Adjustments Goodwill $	Adjustments Revaluation $	Gamma $
Goodwill		300,000			500,000		800,000
Property, plant and equipment	380,000		60,000	700,000		40,000	1,180,000
							1,980,000
Current assets							
Trade receivables	25,000			50,000			75,000
Bank	17,000			23,000			40,000
	42,000			73,000			115,000
Total assets	422,000			773,000			2,095,000
Capital accounts							
Mr Smith	200,000	150,000	30,000				380,000
Mrs Jones	200,000	150,000	30,000				380,000
Mr Green				330,000	250,000	20,000	600,000
Miss Brown				370,000	250,000	20,000	640,000
							2,000,000
Current accounts							
Mr Smith	10,000						
Mrs Jones	11,000						
Mr Green				9,000			
Miss Brown				12,000			
	421,000			721,000			
Long term liabilities							
Loan							
Current liabilities							
Trade payables	1,000			2,000			3,000
Current accounts							42,000
							45,000
	422,000			773,000			2,095,000

(b) If the accounts were not adjusted then the partners' capital figures would be distorted. Beta is clearly worth more as a business than Alpha and it is only fair that Beta's directors should have that recognised in the form of larger capital accounts.

The revaluation of goodwill ensures that each of the former partnerships is valued accurately and account is taken of the various factors that contribute to the firm's value as a going concern. Similarly, the recognised values of the partnership property, plant and equipment will require some adjustment or the change will benefit some partners at the expense of others. This can be seen in the case of Gamma because Beta's adjustments were significantly larger than Alpha's, so Beta's partners would have suffered a loss on the amalgamation.

Question 5

This question draws on section 5 of the syllabus Accounting for Specialised Transactions. The question deals with the valuation of inventory under IAS 2.

(a)   Work in progress

	$'000
Materials and labour =$800,000 + 500,000	1,300
Production overheads	
Factory rent, rates and insurance	3,000
Factory security	2,200
Factory heat, light and power	6,000
Depreciation of machinery	4,000
Total	15,200
Apportioned 15,200 × 5,000 / 200,000	380
Value = 1,300 + 380 =	1,680

Finished goods

Cost of non-obsolete items = $6,000,000 − 600,000 = $5,400,000

Obsolete items = $100,000

Total = $5,500,000

(b)   IAS 2 *Inventories* requires the company to include all of the costs associated with bringing goods to their present location and condition. That specifically includes the production overheads associated with the manufacture of goods.

Overheads can be apportioned on any valid basis, but it should be done on the basis of normal levels of output. If actual production levels differ then the amount carried forward will be artificially understated or overstated.

(c)   IAS 2 requires inventory to be valued at the lower of cost and net realisable value on an item by item basis usually.

Doing so ensures that any loss on inventory is recognised in the period in which the loss is incurred. Otherwise the loss would not be recognised until the period in which the inventory was sold and thus the loss would be offset against future gains.

Question 6

This question draws on section 5 of the syllabus Financial Analysis. It deals with issues associated with Earnings Per Share.

(a)   The theoretical ex rights price immediately before the rights issue was (($8.60 × 5)+7.50) / 6 = $8.42.

The bonus element equates to 8.60/8.42 = 1.02

There were 6m shares in issue for the period from 1 May to 31 July 2012 = 31 + 30 + 31 = 92 days. If these are grossed up for the effects of the bonus element of the rights issue that equates to 6.12m shares ie 6m × 1.02 = 6.12m.

There were 7.2m shares in issue for the remaining 365 − 92 = 273 days.

The weighted average number of shares in issue throughout the year was (6.12m × 92/365) + (7.2m × 273/365) = 6.93m.

The basic EPS = 1,240,000/6,930,000 = 17.9 cents

The conversion of the share options will have no impact on earnings. The diluted EPS = 1,240,000/(6,930,000+2,600,000) = 13.0 cents

(b)   Diluted EPS is important because the number of shares in issue can easily increase when options, warrants, etc are converted. The shareholders have to be aware of the possibility that their rights to participate in profits may be affected by such instruments.

The dilution effect has to take account of any savings in interest or other effects of the conversion. For example, convertible loan stock will reduce finance charges when the stock holders exercise their rights to convert.

Mock exam 2 questions and answers

MODULE D

PROFESSIONAL EXAMINATION 1

PAPER 11 – FINANCIAL ACCOUNTING 2

TUESDAY 27th NOVEMBER 2012

<u>TIME ALLOWED – 3 HOURS</u>

Answer ALL questions

You are allowed an additional 15 minutes reading time before the exam begins, during which you should read the question paper and, if you wish, make notes on the question paper. You are **not** allowed to open the exam script booklet and start writing or use your calculator during the reading time.

CREATING WORLD CLASS ACCOUNTANTS

Question 1

Cooper publishes a popular fashion magazine. Cooper's draft financial statements for the year ended 31 October 2012 are shown below:

Cooper
DRAFT STATEMENT OF COMPREHENSIVE INCOME
FOR THE YEAR ENDED 31 OCTOBER 2012

	$'000
Revenue	67,000
Cost of sales	(12,000)
Gross profit	55,000
Distribution costs	(8,000)
Administrative expenses	(4,000)
Finance costs	(2,000)
Profit before tax	41,000
Tax	(12,400)
Profit for the year	28,600
Other comprehensive income	
Gain on revaluation	15,000
Total comprehensive income	43,600

Cooper
DRAFT STATEMENT OF FINANCIAL POSITION
AS AT 31 OCTOBER 2012

	$'000
ASSETS	
Non current assets	
Property, plant and equipment	121,000
Intangible assets	15,000
	135,000
Non current assets	
Inventory	200
Trade receivables	9,700
Bank	180
	11,080
TOTAL ASSETS	146,080
EQUITY AND LIABILITIES	
Equity	$'000
Ordinary share capital ($1 shares, fully paid)	10,000
Preference share capital ($1 shares, fully paid)	20,000
Revaluation reserve	15,000
Retained earnings	29,380
	74,380
Non current liabilities	
Loans	50,000

Current liabilities	$000
Trade payables	9,200
Current tax	12,500
	21,700

TOTAL EQUITY AND LIABILITIES	146,080

The convener of Cooper's audit committee is reviewing these draft financial statements and has prepared the following notes concerning Cooper's accounting policies:

(i) Cooper has published a magazine called "Clothesmonth" for many years. The company owns all of the rights associated with this title. These rights were established when Clothesmonth was first published. The magazine title was created by the magazine's editor and the trademark was registered in Cooper's name at minimal cost. During the year ended 31 October 2012, Cooper's biggest rival sold the rights associated with its magazine to a third party for $15.0m. The rival's magazine is far less popular than Clothesmonth and so Cooper's directors view this transaction as indicating the Clothesmonth title is worth far more than $15.0m.

Cooper's directors have revalued the Clothesmonth title as an intangible asset. Previously, the title was not recognised in Cooper's financial statements.

(ii) Cooper issued its preference shares on 1 November 2011. These shares carry a cumulative preference dividend of 8%. The shares will be redeemed in 2027. The directors believe that the fact that the shares will not be redeemed for 15 years suggests that they are to be regarded as virtually permanent finance. In any case, the directors are confident that the company will benefit from the redemption of the shares on that date.

(iii) Cooper changed its main paper supplier during the year ended 31 October 2012. The previous supplier used to supply Cooper on a month by month basis, with paper being delivered in response to Cooper's orders and paid for on 28 days' trade credit. Cooper's new supplier delivers in bulk and so can save on delivery costs and offer Cooper a substantial discount. The supplier aims to deliver approximately six months' worth of paper with each delivery. The terms of trade are that Cooper must store the paper at its own expense. Cooper is also responsible for securing and insuring the paper. On a monthly basis, Cooper informs the supplier of the quantity of paper consumed during the previous month. The supplier invoices Cooper at a price that was fixed when the paper was delivered. The supplier's contract specifies that Cooper can return any unused paper if it wishes, but Cooper would then be responsible for the safe return of the paper and that would be extremely expensive. The contract states that the paper remains the supplier's property until it has been paid for.

The supplier delivered a large quantity of paper in September 2012. None of that delivery has been used so far and none has been invoiced. The total value of the paper is $2.4m. Cooper has not recorded anything in respect of that paper in its bookkeeping records.

(iv) Cooper received a government grant of $400,000 on 1 August 2012. The grant was part of a government initiative to encourage companies to train employees who have recently been released from prison and who would otherwise struggle to find a job. The grant is intended to pay 50% of the cost of employing former prisoners for a period of four years. It is a condition of the grant that if an employee who has been taken on under this scheme leaves the company that a suitable replacement is employed within one month.

Cooper has employed eight former prisoners since 1 August 2012, each of whom will receive an annual salary of $25,000.

The $400,000 grant has been offset against cost of sales for the year ended 31 October 2012.

Required

(a)   Discuss the validity of the directors' treatment of matters (i) to (iv).   **(24 marks)**

(b)   Restate the draft statement of comprehensive income and draft statement of financial position to take account of any disagreements with the treatments adopted.   **(8 marks)**

(c)   Calculate the return on capital employed (ROCE) and gearing ratios for Cooper, using both the draft financial statements provided above and your restated figures from part (a) above. Comment on the results.   **(8 marks)**

(Total 40 marks)

Question 2

IAS18 *Presentation of Financial Statements* requires companies to disclose the following with respect to their significant accounting policies:

(a)   the measurement basis (or bases) used in preparing the financial statements, and

(b)   the other accounting policies used that are relevant to an understanding of the financial statements.

The following extracts have been taken from the financial statements of Delta, a UK company:

Basis of preparation

The consolidated financial statements have been prepared in accordance with International Financial Reporting Standards (IFRS) and IFRS Interpretations Committee (IFRIC) interpretations as endorsed by the European Union, and those parts of the Companies Act 2006 applicable to companies reporting under IFRS.

The financial statements are prepared on the historical cost basis, except where disclosed otherwise.

The accounting policies set out below have been applied consistently to all periods presented in these consolidated financial statements.

Depreciation and amortisation

The Group exercises judgement to determine useful lives and residual values of Intangibles, property, plant and equipment and investment property. The assets are depreciated down to their residual values over their estimated useful lives.

Required

(a)   Discuss the reasons for requiring these disclosures.   **(4 marks)**

(b)   Explain, stating reasons, whether the disclosures provided by Delta meet the objectives that you have discussed in (a) above.   **(4 marks)**

(c)   Discuss what is wrong with the disclosures and what action could be taken against companies which provide such disclosures.   **(4 marks)**

(Total = 12 marks)

BPP
LEARNING MEDIA

Question 3

Alpha purchased 60% of Beta's ordinary shares on 1 November 2009, when Beta's retained earnings were $800,000. Alpha purchased 30% of Epsilon's shares on 1 November 2010, when Epsilon's retained earnings were $600,000.

The statements of financial position of the three companies as at 31 October 2012 were:

	Alpha $'000	Beta $'000	Epsilon $'000
Property, plant and equipment	5,000	4,000	3,000
Investment in Beta	3,400		
Investment in Epsilon	200		
Current assets			
Inventory	600	500	400
Trade receivables	550	480	370
Bank	80	70	60
	1,230	1,050	830
Total assets	9,830	5,050	3,830
Share capital	4,000	1,500	1,400
Retained earnings	2,320	1,130	900
	6,320	2,630	2,300
Loans	3,000	2,000	1,200
Current liabilities			
Trade payables	510	420	330
Total equity and liabilities	9,830	5,050	3,830

At the date of acquisition, Beta owned land that had a book value of $400,000 and a fair value of $700,000. That fair value has not been reflected in Beta's financial statements.

In October 2012, Beta sold goods that had cost $250,000 to Alpha for $400,000. Alpha had not resold any of that inventory by 31 October 2012.

Alpha paid the $400,000 owed because of the above sale on 26 October 2012. That cash had not been received or recorded by Beta before 31 October 2012.

Required

Prepare a consolidated statement of financial position for the Alpha Group. **(12 marks)**

Question 4

Theta is a building company. The directors are presently finalising the financial statements for the year ended 31 October 2012.

Theta completed the construction of an office block in December 2011. The building was built with the intention that Theta would retain it and rent out office space to third parties. Demand for space in this building has been so poor that Theta has decided to put the block on the market for sale.

The office block cost $12m to build, and that is the value at which it is shown in Theta's books. Theta's property manager has advised that the property has a fair value of $8m if sold on the open market, but Theta's directors have put the building up for sale for $9m, arguing that they will find somebody who is willing to pay that even if they have to wait for two or three years in order to do so. Selling costs will amount to 1.5% of the final selling price.

The company is also building an industrial park that will have several small factory units. These were scheduled for completion in 2013, but the directors of Theta decided to stop construction on 1 May 2012 on a temporary basis, with a view to recommencing when the economy strengthens and there is more demand for factory space. Theta has been capitalising the interest on the construction work on this project. Total interest incurred on the funds borrowed to finance the industrial park were $2.6m.

Required

(a) Demonstrate how the office block should be valued in Theta's financial statements. **(6 marks)**

(b) Discuss how the interest incurred on the construction costs of the industrial park should be accounted for. **(6 marks)**

(Total = 12 marks)

Question 5

Lambda is a food manufacturing company that was established several years ago. Lambda has recently been listed on its national stock exchange and so has become subject to the requirements of IFRS 8 *Operating Segments* for the first time.

Lambda's directors are concerned that the publication of segmental information will harm their competitive position. They are particularly concerned that competitors will discover that certain divisions are highly successful and so they may attract competition into that market.

The directors have been discussing the following summary of the results of each operating division for the year ended 31 October 2012:

	Revenue $m	Profit/loss $m	Net assets $m
Fresh foods - excluding seafood	100	10	18
Fresh seafood	40	8	9
Tinned food	150	110	23
Frozen food	160	87	26
	450	215	76

The production director has suggested that there is actually nothing to worry about. They could simply argue that Lambda reports a single segment, namely food manufacturing and so all four of the above potential segments could be combined into one total.

Required

(a)   Discuss whether it would be acceptable to restrict segmental information on the basis that a full
        report would harm Lambda's competitive position.   **(3 marks)**

(b)   Demonstrate the minimum reporting segmental reporting requirements for Lambda.   **(6 marks)**

(c)   Discuss why the directors regard fresh seafood to be their most successful segment.   **(3 marks)**

(Total = 12 marks)

Question 6

Omega's chief accountant is preparing the draft financial statements for the year ended 31 October 2012.
She is calculating the deferred tax balance and has noted the following points:

•   The tax written down value of property, plant and equipment is $10m as at 31 October 2012,
        compared to an accounting net book value of $16m.

•   Her five year forecasts, produced for tax planning purposes, indicates that the tax written down
        value will be $7m by 31 October 2016 and the accounting net book value will be $9m. Planned
        capital investment will increase the tax written down value to $18m by 31 October 2017 and the
        accounting net book value will be $25m.

•   Omega pays tax at a rate of 30%.

IAS 12 Income Taxes requires that deferred tax on these timing differences be calculated using the full
provision basis, but the chief accountant is interested in comparing the results from the full provision
basis with the two alternatives that have been proposed in the past: the nil provision and the partial
provision.

Required

(a)   Calculate the deferred tax balances that Omega would report as at 31 October 2012 using each of
        the full provision, the partial provision and the nil provision bases.   **(6 marks)**

(b)   Compare and contrast the usefulness of the figures produced under each of these three bases.
                                                                                              (6 marks)

(Total 12 marks)

AIA
THE ASSOCIATION
OF INTERNATIONAL
ACCOUNTANTS

MODEL ANSWERS

MODULE D

PROFESSIONAL EXAMINATION 1

PAPER 11 – FINANCIAL ACCOUNTING 2

TUESDAY 27th NOVEMBER 2012

Question 1

Parts (a)(i) and (iv) draw on section 2 of the syllabus International Accounting Standards, parts (a)(ii) and (iii) draw on section 4 Accounting for specialised transactions. Part (a) describes a company whose financial statements have been prepared with scant regard for the accounting standards on four specific topics. In every case, the reported figures are unduly optimistic. Part (b) draws on section 5 of the syllabus Financial Analysis. It asks candidates to compare the original version of a set of draft financial statements with the adjusted set prepared in response to changes made in the course of answering part (a).

Collectively, the theme running through this question is that the accounting standards exist to protect the shareholders from misleading financial reporting.

(a) (i) The value of the magazine title does not meet the recognition criteria laid down by IAS 38 *Intangible Assets*. The costs have been written off as incurred, presumably because Cooper cannot determine those separately.

There is no doubt that the magazine title will generate future economic benefits, but the problem is that there is no realistic basis by which the fair value of the title can be measured. The fact that a single transaction has occurred and has led to details being released into the public domain does not constitute sufficient evidence of a fair value of the asset, particularly as this is not a generic asset that is capable of comparison.

IAS 38 does not permit the revaluation of intangible assets that have not previously been recognised as assets.

(ii) The preference shares are redeemable, albeit in 15 years' time. That makes the shares meet the definition of a liability as laid down by IAS 32, *Financial Instruments: Presentation*. The IAS defines a financial liability as:

a contractual obligation:

(i) to deliver cash or another financial asset to another entity; or

(ii) to exchange financial assets or financial liabilities with another entity under conditions that are potentially unfavourable to the entity.

The preference shares clearly meet this definition and so should be accounted for as liability.

The fact that the dividends are cumulative adds to the argument that there is an obligation to make payment.

The life of this financial instrument has no bearing on the question of whether the definition of a liability applies.

(iii) This is consignment stock. There is no specific definition of that in IFRS, but there is in FRS 5 Reporting the Substance of Transactions. IAS 8 Accounting Policies, Changes in Accounting Estimates and Errors would recognise FRS 5 as a valid source of guidance on the treatment of this transaction.

The fact that Cooper is effectively responsible for the inventory and has no realistic way to return it to the supplier suggests that it has to be accounted for as a purchase.

Clearly, there is no net expense because of this because the paper is still in inventory, but it will affect both current assets and current liabilities.

(iv) The government grant cannot be offset against revenue in the year in which it is received because there are conditions attaching to the grant that must be met. IAS 20 *Accounting for Government Grants and Disclosure of Government Assistance* requires that the portion of the grant that has been earned in the year (8 x $25,000 x 3/12 x 50% = $25,000) be recognised in the income statement as an offset against the wages paid to the employees. The remaining balance should be shown as a provision.

This treatment is necessary because the alternative would be to recognise income immediately, even though the conditions have not been satisfied and the related expenses against which the grant should be matched have not been incurred.

	Adjustment for (i)	Adjustment for (ii)	Adjustment for (iii)	Adjustment for (iv)	Adjusted total

Cooper
DRAFT STATEMENT OF COMPREHENSIVE INCOME
FOR THE YEAR ENDED 31 OCTOBER 2012

	$'000					$'000
Revenue	67,000					67,000
Cost of sales	(12,000)			nil (net)	(375)	(12,375)
Gross profit	55,000					54,625
Distribution costs	(8,000)					(8,000)
Administrative expenses	(4,000)					(4,000)
Finance costs	(2,000)		(1,600)			(3,600)
Profit before tax	41,000					39,025
Tax	(12,400)					(12,400)
Profit for the year	28,600					26,625
Other comprehensive income						
Gain on revaluation	15,000	(15,000)				
Total comprehensive income	43,600					

Cooper
DRAFT STATEMENT OF FINANCIAL POSITION
AS AT 31 OCTOBER 2012

	$'000					$'000
Assets						
Non current assets						
Property, plant and equipment	120,000					120,000
Intangible assets	15,000	(15,000)				0
	135,000					120,000
Non-current assets						
Inventory	1,200			2,400		3,600
Trade receivables	9,700					9,700
Bank	180					180
	11,080					13,480
						133,480
TOTAL ASSETS	146,080					
EQUITY AND LIABILITIES						
Equity						
Ordinary share capital ($1 shares, fully paid)	10,000					10,000
Preference share capital ($1 shares, fully paid)	20,000		(20,000)			0
Revaluation reserve	15,000	(15,000)				0
Retained earnings	29,380			nil (net)	(375)	29,005
	74,380					39,005
Non-current liabilities						
Loans	50,000					50,000
Preference share capital ($1 shares, fully paid)			20,000			20,000
Provision for government grant					375	375
						70,375

	$'000		$'000
Current liabilities			
Trade payables	9,200	2,400	11,600
Current tax	12,500		12,500
	21,700		24,100
TOTAL EQUITY AND LIABILITIES	146,080		133,480

(b)

	Unadjusted figures	Adjusted figures
ROCE	(41,000+2,000)/(74,380+50,000) =35%	(39,025+3,600)/(39,005+70,375) =39%
Gearing	50,000/(74,380+50,000) =40%	70,375/(39,005+70,375) =64%

Paradoxically, the ROCE figure increases because the biggest impact on the income statement is due to the increase in finance charges. Those are added back when calculating return. The overall capital employed figure is actually smaller because we are no longer recognising the revaluation reserve. Thus, Cooper looks very slightly more profitable in terms of ROCE.

The gearing ratio is far less attractive. Moving preference shares to debt and cancelling the revaluation reserve both have the effect of reducing equity and the former also has the effect of increasing debt, so overall gearing rises dramatically.

Thus, the company looks slightly more profitable, but far more risky.

Question 2

This question is drawn from Section 1 of the syllabus Accounting Theory. It deals with the issues associated with disclosing details of accounting policies as required by IAS 1.

(a) There are a number of accounting bases available to companies. In particular, property, plant and equipment can be valued at cost less depreciation or at fair value (possibly adjusted for depreciation). An explicit as to the measurement basis will ensure that readers can make sense of the figures, bearing in mind the basis upon which they have been prepared.

Accounting policies can vary significantly between companies. Having different policies in place may mean that the statements of two companies may not be directly comparable. Details of the policies in place will enable readers of the financial statements to be aware of the differences and to make an attempt to render the figures comparable.

(b) The note about the measurement basis appears to ignore the most important factors, such as whether assets are shown at cost or fair value. It may be possible to learn more from the detailed notes to the financial statements, but there is very little of any value in this note. The fact that the company has complied with relevant accounting standards is somewhat redundant because the company was required to adhere to those anyway.

The note about depreciation has virtually no value whatsoever. We do not know the method by which depreciation is charged (e.g. straight line or reducing balance) and we do not know the period over which assets are depreciated. This means that we cannot tell whether or not the depreciation charge is comparable with a similar business in the same industry. It would, for example, be impossible to restate the depreciation charge or the book value of PPE.

(c) Boilerplate disclosures do not add any value and are of limited use to the reader. Non-specific general disclosures which could apply to any company are unhelpful taking up space in the annual report. The Financial Reporting Review Panel could request clarification and more detail (accounts to be amended). Auditors could also question the disclosures but failing that shareholders should be encouraged to question them at the AGM.

Question 3

This question draws on section 3 of the syllabus Proprietorship Accounting and Entity Accounting. The question asks for the preparation of a simple consolidated statement of financial position.

Alpha Group
CONSOLIDATED STATEMENT OF FINANCIAL POSITION
AS AT 31 OCTOBER 2012

	$'000
Property, plant and equipment	9,300
Investment in associate	290
Goodwill	1,840
Current assets	
Inventory 600 + 500 - 150 =	950
Trade receivables	1,030
Bank	150
	2,130
Total assets	13,560
Share capital	4,000
Retained earnings	2,518
	6,518
Loans	5,000
Non-controlling interest	1,112
	6,112
Current liabilities	
Trade payables	930
Total equity and liabilities	13,560

Workings

Goodwill on acquisition of Beta

Investment in Beta	3,400
Share capital (60%)	(900)
Reserves 60% × 800,000	(480)
Gain on land 60% × 300,000	(180)
Goodwill	1,840

Profit in unsold inventory = 150 (group share 60%)	90
Non-controlling interest share 40%	60

Non-controlling interest in Alpha = (2,630 × 40%) + (300 × 40%) - 60 → 1,112

Property, plant and equipment = 5,000 + 4,000 + 300 → 9,300

Investment in associate = 200 + (30% × (900-600)) → 290

Group retained earnings = 2,320 + (60% × 1,130-800) – 150 × 60% = 90 +
(30% × 900-600) → 2,518

Question 4

Part (a) of this question draws on section 1 of the syllabus Accounting Theory and part (b) draws on section 4 Accounting for Specialised Transactions. The question deals with two aspects of dealing with the cost of property – holding property for sale and capitalising interest.

(a) This is a non-current asset that is held for resale. As such, it should be accounted for in accordance with the requirements of IFRS 5 *Non-current Assets Held for Sale and Discontinued Operations*.

IFRS 5 requires that the property be accounted for on the basis of the lower of its carrying amount and fair value less costs to sell. The carrying value = $12m. The fair value is $8m and the costs to sell = $8m × 1.5% = $120,000.

So, the valuation required by IFRS 5 = $7.88m.

This treatment is a realistic valuation because the company clearly intends to sell the building. That makes its carrying value somewhat irrelevant, particularly given that the building will almost certainly be sold at a loss.

(b) The interest costs must be accounted for in accordance with the requirements of IAS 23 *Borrowing Costs*.

IAS 23 requires that costs be capitalised while the property is under the course of construction. That means that it is possible to capitalise the interest incurred during the six months from 1 November 2011 until the temporary halt in construction on 1 May 2012. That means that Theta can capitalise 6/12 = $1.3m of interest from this project.

The logic underlying IAS 23 is that the interest costs can be capitalised when they relate to the construction of property, but the costs must be directly attributable to the construction process. If construction stops because the property market means that it makes commercial sense to delay completion then that is not part of the construction process and so the interest cannot be capitalised.

Question 5

This question draws on section 5 of the syllabus Financial Analysis. It deals with issues associated with segmental reporting.

(a) Quoted companies must keep their shareholders informed, even if it is costly to do so because of commercial sensitivity. There would be no point in having accounting standards if their requirements can be set aside on the basis that the directors would prefer not to make those disclosures.

The history of segmental reporting has been about change and development in the regulations in order to force companies to publish useful segmental reports. Lambda's directors are not the only ones who would wish to withhold details of operating segments.

(b) The fact that each of the four elements listed in the analysis being studied by management is an operating division suggests that each has its own separate risk characteristics. A divisional structure implies autonomy and an element of each division having its own risk characteristics.

The analysis being studied by management suggests that each of the four elements is studied separately. IFRS 8 *Operating Segments* states that the fact management tracks the performance of each segment means that all must be disclosed in the segmental information.

The fact that seafood is relatively small may have been sufficient justification to merge it with fresh food, but seafood exceeds the 10% threshold in terms of net assets, which would make it a reportable segment.

The remaining segments all look substantial and it may be necessary for Lambda to break the totals down even further if there are reportable segments within, say, frozen food.

(c)   Seafood is the smallest segment, but it generates profit of $8m from net assets of only $9m. It generates a return on capital employed that is far higher than that on fresh foods generally, as return on capital employed is the best measure of profitability then it can be said that seafood is the most profitable segment. However, tinned and frozen are highly profitable in relation to revenue or net assets. If Lambda's competitors are not already aware of the potential in this market then they may be attracted in and will either force up demand (and therefore) the price for purchases or will compete for sales in several areas of Lambda's market.

Question 6

This question draws on section 3 of the syllabus Proprietorship Accounting and Entity Accounting. It asks for calculations and discussion using the different methods available for accounting for deferred tax.

(a)   Full provision – timing difference = $16m – 10m = $6m.

Tax on $6m @ 30% = $1.8m.

Partial provision – timing difference = $6m, but that will diminish to $9m – 7m = $2m within the foreseeable future. Thus, $4m is expected to reverse.

Tax on $4m = $1.2m

Nil provision = nil

(b)   The full provision is relatively objective. The timing difference is a matter of fact and the assumption that the current tax rate will continue means that there is relatively little scope for distortion.

The fact that the liability may not reverse for many years means that the information being provided has limited value. The shareholders know that the differences will reverse eventually, but they do not know when and so the reversal could be within the foreseeable future (which would imply a significant cash outflow in terms of the payment of tax) or not.

The partial provision lacks the objectivity of the full provision basis. Management could alter their forecasts of capital expenditure or whatever in order to manipulate the deferred tax balance.

The resulting figures are potentially more useful because shareholders know that any liability is payable within the foreseeable future. It is not a liability that may remain hanging into the indefinite future.

The nil provision basis contains no information whatsoever in terms of the closing balance. It may have the advantage of linking the tax expense in the income statement to the actual tax assessment, although that may be a very dubious advantage because the tax rules may lead to income being recognised for tax purposes in periods that bear no relation to that in which the income was earned.

Index

BPP
LEARNING MEDIA

NOTES

NOTES

NOTES